Future Drivers of Growth in Rwanda

Future Drivers of Growth in Rwanda

Innovation, Integration, Agglomeration, and Competition

WORLD BANK GROUP

Government of Rwanda

1 2 3 4 23 22 21 20

ISBN (paper): 978-1-4648-1280-4
ISBN (electronic): 978-1-1236-1
DOI: 10.1596/978-1-4648-1280-4

Cover and interior design: Bill Pragluski, Critical Stages, LLC
Cover illustration: © Municipality of Kigali. Used with permission; further permission required for reuse.

Library of Congress Cataloging-in-Publication Data has been requested.

Contents

Boxes

Figures

Maps

Photos

Tables

Foreword

A widely acknowledged record of more than two decades of strong economic growth—including a three-and-half-fold increase in per capita income since 1994—has placed Rwanda among the fastest-growing economies in Africa and the world. Traumatic memories of the 1994 genocide, still prevalent, are gradually fading, as associations begin to take a more positive form—of a nation on the rise, powered by human resilience, a sense of common purpose, and a purposeful government.

Having launched its development with a measure of success, Rwanda is now keen to forge a future of security, prosperity, and modernity. Sustaining high rates of inclusive economic growth is at the heart of these ambitions. Future aspirations in this regard are high, with Vision 2050 aspiring to achieve upper-middle-income status by 2035 and high-income status by 2050. These aspirations translate into average annual growth rates of more than 10 percent.

Motivated by these aspirations, in May 2017, the government of Rwanda and the World Bank Group jointly initiated this study on the future drivers of growth to inform Rwanda's Vision 2050. The report identifies four essential and interdependent drivers: innovation, integration, agglomeration, and competition. These future drivers of growth, in turn, would receive the necessary boost from reforms in six priority areas: (a) human capital development; (b) export dynamism and regional integration; (c) well-managed urbanization; (d) competitive domestic enterprises; (e) agricultural modernization; and (f) capable and accountable public institutions.

The report has already helped to shape the reform agenda in all of the above six priority areas. The study has been conducted at the same time Rwanda was developing its national strategy for transformation (2017–2024) and Rwanda Vision 2050. Both have been informed by recommendations from the study. For example, the report's findings about challenges facing Rwanda in human capital motivated the government to redouble its efforts by fighting malnutrition, launching reforms for improving the quality of education at all levels, and establishing the National Early Childhood Development

Program to coordinate all interventions on early childhood development and fighting malnutrition.

We are delighted by the close partnership forged between the experts from Rwanda and the World Bank Group in preparation of this report. We are convinced that keeping the momentum in implementing the recommendations offered will support Rwanda's development journey and take it closer to the transformed society it aspires to be.

Hafez M. H. Ghanem
Vice President, Africa Region
The World Bank

Dr. Ngirente Edouard
Prime Minister of the Republic of Rwanda

Acknowledgments

Future Drivers of Growth in Rwanda: Innovation, Integration, Agglomeration, and Competition is a joint initiative of the Government of Rwanda and the World Bank Group, emanating from a March 2017 agreement between President Paul Kagame of Rwanda and Jim Yong Kim, President of the World Bank Group.

The report was written by a joint Rwanda-World Bank Group team under the supervision and guidance of Uzziël Ndagijimana (Minister of Finance and Economic Planning), Claver Gatete (Minister of Infrastructure and Former Minister of Finance and Economic Planning), the late Jan Walliser (Former Vice President, Equitable Growth, Finance, and Institutions Practice Group, World Bank Group), Makhtar Diop (Vice President for Infrastructure and Former Vice President for Africa Region, World Bank Group), Hafez M. H. Ghanem (Vice President for Africa Region, World Bank Group), Diarietou Gaye (Director of Strategy and Operations of Africa Region and Former Country Director for Rwanda, World Bank Group), Ceyla Pazarbasioglu-Dutz (Vice President, Equitable Growth, Finance, and Institutions Practice Group, World Bank Group), and Carlos Felipe Jaramillo (Country Director for Rwanda and Former Senior Director, Macroeconomics, Trade and Investment Global Practice, World Bank Group). The National Steering Committee for the National Strategy for Transformation and Rwanda Vision 2050 provided guidance to the team and validated the report.

A joint Rwanda–World Bank Group team was established to prepare the report. Team leaders were Leonard Rugwabiza Minega (Economic Advisor to the Minister of Finance and Economic Planning) and Sandeep Mahajan (Practice Manager, Macroeconomics, Trade and Investment Global Practice, World Bank Group).

Financial support from the Republic of Korea is gratefully acknowledged.

William Maloney (Chief Economist, Equitable Growth, Finance, and Institutions Practice Group, World Bank Group), Richard Newfarmer (Country Director for Uganda and Rwanda, International Growth Centre), and Andrew Nyamvumba (Former Head, Strategy and Policy Unit, Office of the President, Republic of Rwanda) were senior advisers for the report. The report also benefitted from valuable comments from peer reviewers David Dollar (Senior Fellow, John L. Thornton China Center, Brookings Institution), Mona Haddad (Director, International Finance Corporation), Steve Jaffee (Lead Agriculture Economist, World Bank Group), Godfrey Kabera (Director General, National Planning and Research, Ministry of Finance and Economic Planning), Michael Woolcock (Lead Social Scientist, World Bank Group), and Albert Zeufack

(Chief Economist for Africa Region, World Bank Group), as well as the following reviewers who provided comments on the concept note and the decision draft: Emre Alper (Senior Economist, International Monetary Fund), Iftikhar Malik (Senior Social Protection Specialist, World Bank Group), Laura Rawlings (Lead Social Protection Specialist, World Bank Group), Laure Redifer (Deputy Division Chief, International Monetary Fund), and Alun Thomas (Former Resident Representative in Rwanda, International Monetary Fund).

We extend special thanks for the insights and recommendations received from Abebe Adugna (Practice Manager, Macroeconomics, Trade and Investment, World Bank Group), Anstes Agnew (Country Head for Rwanda at Tony Blair Institute for Global Change), Yasser El-Gammal (Country Manager for Rwanda, World Bank Group), Obald Hakizimana (Economist, Ministry of Finance and Economic Planning), Mary Hallward-Driemeier (Senior Economic Adviser, World Bank Group), Emmanuel Hategeka (Deputy Chief Executive Officer, Rwanda Development Board), Thierry Mihigo Kalisa (Senior Economist, Ministry of Finance and Economic Planning), Danny Leipziger (Managing Director of Growth Dialogue and Professor of Practice of International Business, George Washington University), Norman V. Loayza (Lead Economist, World Bank Group), Johan A. Mistiaen (Program Leader, World Bank Group), Geraldine Mukeshimana (Minister for Agriculture and Animal Resources), Ildephonse Musafiri (Head of the Strategy and Policy Unit, Office of the President, Republic of Rwanda), Richard Mushabe (Division Manager of National Planning and Research Division, Ministry of Finance and Economic Planning), Tom O'Brien (Senior Adviser, World Bank Group), Amina Rwakunda (Chief Economist, Ministry of Finance and Economic Planning), Kampeta Pitchette Sayinzoga (Director General, National Industrial Research and Development Agency of Rwanda), Claudine Uwera (State Minister, Ministry of Finance and Economic Planning), and Ariane Zingiro (Planning and Program Specialist, Ministry of Finance and Economic Planning).

The report was edited by William Shaw. Production and publication were managed by Stephen Pazdan and Patricia Katayama of the World Bank Group's Formal Publishing Program.

The report has an overview and six chapters written by individual chapter teams, whose members are presented in alphabetical order by their surnames.

Overview

Lead authors: Sandeep Mahajan (Practice Manager, Macroeconomics, Trade and Investment, World Bank Group) and Leonard Rugwabiza Minega (Economic Advisor to the Minister of Finance and Economic Planning).

Chapter 1: Human Capital and Innovation

Lead authors: David Evans (Lead Economist, World Bank Group) and François Ngoboka (Division Manager, Former Capacity Development and Employment Services Board).

Core team: Rose Baguma (Director General of Education Policy and Planning, Ministry of Education), Dr. Ignace Gatare (Principal, College of Science and Technology, University of Rwanda), Deepika Ramachandran (Consultant), Jee-Peng Tan (Consultant), and Fei Yuan (Consultant).

Chapter 2: Transformation through Trade: Using Exports and Regional Integration to Drive Future Growth

Lead authors: Thomas R. Kigabo (Chief Economist, National Bank of Rwanda), Richard Newfarmer (Country Director, International Growth Centre), and Victor Steenbergen (Former Country Economist, International Growth Centre).

Core team: John H. Arnold (Consultant), Robert Opirah (Director General for Trade and Investment, Ministry of Trade and Industry), and Cordula Rastogi (Senior Economist, World Bank Group).

Chapter 3: Faster Urbanization, Greater Agglomeration

Lead authors: Narae Choi (Urban Specialist, World Bank Group), Edward Kyazze (Manager of Urbanization and Human Settlements Division, Ministry of Infrastructure), Somik V. Lall (Lead Urban Economist, World Bank Group), and Sally Beth Murray (Former Senior Country Economist, International Growth Centre).

The chapter builds on an International Food Policy Research Institute (IFPRI) research paper by Xinshen Diao, Peixun Fang, Josée Randriamamonjy, and James Thurlow and on background notes by David Bridgman (Lead Private Sector Specialist, World Bank Group) and Hoza Thierry Ngoga (Consultant).

Chapter 4: Competitiveness and Enterprise Development for Innovation-Led Growth

Lead authors: Claire Honore Hollweg (Senior Economist, World Bank Group), Aghassi Mkrtchyan (Senior Economist, World Bank Group), Jani Moliis (Former Country Head for Rwanda at Tony Blair Institute for Global Change), and Jean Louis Uwitonze (Former Director General of Planning, Ministry of Trade and Industry).

Core team: Teymour Abdel Aziz (Senior Financial Sector Specialist, World Bank Group), Brice Gakombe (Financial Sector Specialist, World Bank Group), Justin Piers William Hill (Senior Private Sector Specialist, World Bank Group), Louise Kanyonga (Head, Competitiveness and Business Reforms, Rwanda Development Board), Hibret Belete Maemir (Economist, World Bank Group), Gaurav Nayyar (Senior Economist, World Bank Group), Peace Aimée Niyibizi (Economist, World Bank Group), Pierre Sauve (Senior Private Sector Specialist, World Bank Group), and Marcio Jose Vargas da Cruz (Senior Economist, World Bank Group).

The chapter builds on background papers and notes prepared by David Bridgman (Lead Private Sector Specialist, World Bank Group), Joern Huenteler (Energy Specialist, World Bank Group), Maksym Iavorskyi (Operations Analyst, World Bank Group), Danny Leipziger (Managing Director of Growth Dialogue and Professor of Practice of International Business, George Washington University), Hibret Belete Maemir (Economist, World Bank Group), William Peter Mako (Consultant), Hoza Thierry Ngoga (Consultant), Ha Minh Nguyen (Economist, World Bank Group), Yadviga Viktorivna Semikolenova (Senior Energy Economist, World Bank Group), Victor Steenbergen (Former Country Economist, International Growth Centre), Desiree Van Welsum (Consultant), Jan Erik von Uexkull (Senior Economist, World Bank Group), and Ezequiel Zylberberg (Consultant).

Chapter 5: Transitioning Agriculture and Food as an Engine of Growth

Lead authors: Christopher L. Delgado (Consultant) and Dr. Octave Semwaga (Director General of Planning, Ministry of Agriculture and Animal Resources).

Core team: Winston Dawes (Senior Agriculture Economist, World Bank Group), Aparajita Goyal (Senior Economist, World Bank Group), Christopher Jackson (Senior Agriculture Specialist, World Bank Group), and Aimée Marie Ange Mpambara (Agricultural Specialist, World Bank Group).

The chapter builds on an International Food Policy Research Institute (IFPRI) research paper by Xinshen Diao, Peixun Fang, Josée Randriamamonjy, and James Thurlow.

Chapter 6: Capable and Accountable State Institutions

Lead authors: Shyaka Anastase (Former Chief Executive Officer, Rwanda Governance Board), Nicoletta Feruglio (Senior Public Sector Specialist, World Bank Group), and Gael J. R. F. Raballand (Lead Public Sector Specialist, World Bank Group).

Core team: Monica Beuran (Consultant), Deborah Hannah Isser (Lead Governance Specialist, World Bank Group), and Felicién Nsengumukiza (Head, Governance, Research, and Monitoring Department, Rwanda Governance Board).

The chapter builds on background papers by Jonathan Argent (Consultant), Tania Begazo (Senior Economist, World Bank Group), David Bridgman (Lead Private Sector Specialist, World Bank Group), Maksym Iavorskyi (Operations Analyst, World Bank Group), and Hoza Thierry Ngoga (Consultant).

Administration and coordination activities were managed by Lydie Ahodehou (Program Assistant, World Bank Group) and Sylvie Ingabire (Executive Assistant, World Bank Group).

It is with great pleasure that the Government of Rwanda and the World Bank Group introduce the report *Future Drivers of Growth in Rwanda: Innovation, Integration, Agglomeration, and Competition*. We hope that Rwandan citizens and all actors of development in Rwanda will find it useful.

Executive Summary

Rwanda: the land of a thousand hills, untold beauty, a poignant past, and boundless ambition. It has, in a way, become an important fragment of modern consciousness. Traumatic memories of the 1994 genocide against the Tutsi, still prevalent, are fading gradually, as associations begin to take a more positive form: a nation on the rise, powered by human resilience, a sense of common purpose, and a purposeful government. Past successes, combined with a sense of frailty, have fueled bold ambitions for the future. But these are early days, and Rwanda is keen to continue taking meaningful strides toward becoming a more hopeful, secure, modern, and prosperous nation. Strong and inclusive growth sustained over an extended period is at the heart of these ambitions. This report—a joint undertaking by experts from Rwanda and the World Bank—seeks to evaluate the country's possibilities and options in this endeavor.

Introduction

> *After 1994 everything was a priority and our people were completely broken. But we made three fundamental choices that guide us to this day. One—we chose to stay together. Two—we chose to be accountable to ourselves. Three—we chose to think big.*
>
> —His Excellency President Paul Kagame in a speech on the 20th Commemoration of the genocide against the Tutsi (April 7, 2014)

Every country, born of unique circumstances, can claim with good justification to be special. Rwanda's claims are self-evident in both what is manifest and what is being sought. A strong and widely acknowledged record of economic success—including a three-and-a-half-fold increase in per capita income since 1994—places Rwanda among the world's fastest-growing economies, surpassed on the continent only by Ethiopia. Equally striking are its ambitions and approaches. In ambition, it models itself after the East Asian Tigers, seeking a development trajectory to take it from abject poverty to prosperity within a couple of generations. In approach, it has adopted high standards and demands discipline, self-reliance, and hard work of itself—its formula for escaping the vortex of low expectations, corruption, and chaos that it rejected early on.

Having launched its development with a measure of success, Rwanda is now keen to forge a future of security, prosperity, and modernity. Sustaining high rates of inclusive economic growth is at the heart of these ambitions. Future aspirations in this regard have been set extremely high. Recent formulations of Vision 2050 set a target of achieving upper-middle-income status by 2035 and high-income status by 2050. These aspirations translate into average annual growth rates of more than 12 percent (more than 10 percent in per capita terms).

Opportunities and Risks

Bold aspirations require Rwanda to play closely to its strengths and make the most of all available opportunities, while judiciously managing risks. Rwanda's main endowment is its people, whose determination, *agaciro* (dignity), and strong sense of personal and social responsibility should serve it well. How well the country nurtures and deploys this resource will determine its true potential. The country's record of good economic governance, policy coherence, and strong focus on implementation also will prove useful. Major opportunities lie in favorable demographics, an emergent and rapidly urbanizing middle class (in Rwanda and regionally), a fertile (though hilly)[1] agricultural landscape, and untapped regional and global market potential that offers opportunities for economic specialization and scale economies that Rwanda otherwise lacks. Counterbalancing these opportunities are challenges associated with being a small, landlocked economy and risks from regional security and stability, a potential widening of domestic disparities, intensifying population pressures, and global climate change.

Rwanda's population dynamics present a significant domestic challenge and possibly also an opportunity. Rwanda is a youthful nation, with a median age of just 19 years, a result of rapid demographic shifts that are influenced by relatively high but declining fertility rates and sharp reductions in child mortality. But there also are legitimate concerns regarding the pace of rising population density, already the highest in mainland Africa, and the growing population pressures on the country's environment and limited natural resources. Managed well, the population pressures can be contained, and the underlying demographic shifts can be harnessed to achieve significantly higher growth and faster poverty reduction.[2] Policy options include better-targeted family planning measures and continued emphasis on female education, health, and economic empowerment (United Nations Population Fund 2017).

New technologies associated with industry 4.0—robotics, the Internet of Things, three-dimensional printing—will remain disruptive for Rwanda (as for the rest of the world), presenting more risks and opportunities, with Rwanda's net benefits depending on its responses. The immediate gains for Rwanda are from the adoption and diffusion of new technologies and improved production processes, rather than the development of sophisticated research and development capabilities. On the one hand, to the extent that the new technologies are labor saving, they risk narrowing the scope for manufacturing as a pathway to development. On the other hand, the diffusion and adoption of new technologies can help to leapfrog traditional enablers of development. For example, Zipline, which uses unmanned drones to deliver critical medical supplies across Rwanda, has the potential to overcome geographical barriers and increase efficiency in distribution of medical supplies. Modern services, enabled by information and communication technology and sharing the special characteristics (scalability, international tradability, and amenability to technological upgrading) that allowed productivity convergence in manufacturing, are another area of opportunity, with business process outsourcing, banking, and health care as examples.

Future growth has to be powered by trade and regional integration. As a small, landlocked economy, Rwanda does not have the scale economies to sustain high growth on its own. It has to stay alert to major shifts in patterns of global trade and production. For one, the global value chains are maturing and losing momentum since the "unbundling of production" has largely already happened (OECD 2017). At the same time, production is becoming increasingly concentrated in regional or local hubs closer to end markets: the share of intra-African trade for most manufacturing industries rose between 2000 and 2014 (Hallward-Driemeier and Nayyar 2017).

Fortunately for Rwanda, the region around it abounds in (largely untapped) opportunities. Plus, with its landlocked geography as a limiting factor, the ability of Rwandan firms to compete globally depends on the "competitiveness" and "connectedness" of its neighbors. Rwanda is thus likely to seize regional trade opportunities through intraregional trade and participation in regional value chains connected to the global market.

The strongest regional opportunities exist in commodity-based processing and exports and services trade—what some have called "industries without smokestacks" (Newfarmer, Page, and Tarp, forthcoming). Taken together, these activities hold the promise of doing for Rwanda what manufacturing did for East Asia. This promise applies particularly to agribusiness and food processing, the only subsectors in which Rwanda currently has a revealed comparative advantage (Hallward-Driemeier and Nayyar 2017). These subsectors employ unskilled workers, have low intensity of physical capital, and exhibit high returns from the application of basic research and development while, for now, being less exposed to automation. The products (for example, wood products, beverages) typically are traded regionally (rather than internationally) because they are bulky to transport or require proximity to raw materials (for example, food production). Rwanda could look to expand high-value agricultural exports (such as horticulture)—much like Peru has done with specialty agricultural products such as artichokes, asparagus, and avocados, among others—even beyond the region, building on its reputation for having a superior regulatory and policy environment.

The region also offers major opportunities for trade in services, which already provides more than half of Rwanda's export earnings. While tourism has the most immediate potential, Rwanda also could look toward higher-skill services such as business process outsourcing, health care, and higher education. Medical tourism is on the rise in Sub-Saharan Africa, as it is elsewhere (Dihel and Goswami 2016). With its many investments and innovations in the health sector, Rwanda could become a hub for modern medical services for the region. Similarly, in higher education, Rwanda has attracted top-flight university subsidiaries, such as Carnegie Mellon. A recent grant from the Buffett Foundation will enable the country to build a first-class agriculture school. Another logical services export, given Rwanda's location, could be mining services.

The presence of new technologies and business and trade opportunities bodes well, but it is not in itself enough to generate high growth. This issue connects to the broader "productivity paradox," whereby global productivity growth has slowed considerably since 2004 or so, even as new technologies have emerged and diffused at a rapid clip. Frustrated by a similar disconnect (between massive investments in information technology and productivity growth), Robert Solow, a Nobel laureate in economics, famously said in 1987 (36), "You can see the computer age everywhere but in the productivity statistics." The productivity statistics did pick up eventually, but only after a considerable lag in the mid-1990s. The missing link then, as it likely is now, was capabilities—of people, firms, and institutions—that take time to build. That missing link is also Rwanda's main challenge—and the focus of this study—as the country seeks to harness the new wave of technologies and trade patterns for future high growth. Its investments in this regard need to bring the core capabilities continually closer to the ever-moving global frontier.

An Agenda for Reform

Rwanda's aspiration for upper-middle income by 2035 and high income by 2050 calls for stretch targets for future growth rates. Such targets may prove helpful in lifting the nation's vision and infusing a future orientation among the people, while mobilizing citizen support and resources for the needed economic reforms. This has to be supported with periodic and systematic review of goals and targets, with an eye to reassessing their feasibility according to evolving trends and with scope for readjustment if needed.

Any future high-growth strategy will require a multisectoral approach. Relying on manufacturing alone as a pathway for high growth clearly has become trickier than in the past. Services can offer significant scope for productivity gains (IMF 2018), but the service sector alone cannot yet absorb all of the unskilled labor released by agriculture. Moreover, important interdependencies between sectors (most notably between services and manufacturing) prevent any one sector from growing too large without sufficient inputs from others—for example, in China from 2000 to 2014, services inputs into manufacturing accounted for 38 percent of growth in services value added, while manufacturing inputs into services accounted for 30 percent.

The reform agenda is complex and highly demanding: nothing short of an extraordinary effort will suffice. The hard work begins in classrooms. The country needs a massive effort to build human capital—its own education-focused Marshall Plan—if it is to realize its ambitious growth targets. With all of its achievements, Rwanda still lags the average of low-income countries in crucial aspects of human capital—for example, in stunting and primary and lower-secondary school completion. Moreover, the concern is as much about *quality* as it is about *quantity*.[3] An important related issue is high stunting rates in early years—with implications for children's future learning abilities and participation in the knowledge and services-led economy that Rwanda envisages.

The next requirement is higher investment and savings rates. Rwanda already has a relatively high investment rate of about 26 percent of GDP, well in excess of the domestic savings rate of less than 10 percent. But double-digit growth rates would require the investment rate to be significantly higher. Achieving this level of investment would require a sharp increase in investment by the private sector; a multifold rise in the domestic savings rate; and higher foreign direct investment. Nothing short of this will achieve the growth ambitions that Rwanda has.

A higher-order challenge is to boost productivity growth, which also has a bearing on Rwanda's ability to maintain high investment rates. Rwanda's labor productivity (output per worker) and total factor productivity (output generated by a given quantity of labor and capital) are low for its income level. Moreover, the rate of total factor productivity growth has slowed significantly in recent years.

The principal requirements for sustained high productivity growth are scale economies and economic specialization in areas of Rwanda's comparative advantage, with competition and technology diffusion as essential complements. These elements have proved essential for sustaining high growth across the world, but they are even more important for a small, landlocked country like Rwanda. Scale and specialization require Rwanda to make the most of external opportunities and to enhance the benefits of urban agglomeration. But, to succeed in these areas, Rwanda has to have a competitive domestic enterprise sector, both public and private, with a strong potential to do well in competitive environments. Such enterprises themselves have three critical requirements: a strong ecosystem for technological innovation, world-class human capital, and robust institutions of governance. This chain of priorities forms the high-growth strategy for Rwanda.

Rwanda's strategy for high growth thus has four essential and interdependent drivers—innovation, integration, agglomeration, and competition (figure ES.1). These future drivers of growth, in turn, would receive the necessary boost from reforms in six high-priority areas: (1) human capital development; (2) export dynamism and regional integration; (3) well-managed urbanization; (4) competitive domestic enterprises; (5) agricultural modernization; and (6) capable and accountable public institutions. The six reform areas are discussed in more detail in the next section.

Doing well on each of these six necessary reform areas is what separated the

FIGURE ES.1 Future drivers of Rwanda's growth: Innovation, integration, agglomeration, and competition

high-growth East Asian economies from those that achieved rapid growth for a decade or two, only to see it fizzle out. Even more challenging perhaps is to go beyond the necessary to the sufficient conditions. Rwanda sees rapid development not as a choice but as an existential matter and will be pushed to take high-risk strategic bets to gain high returns. These efforts have to be calibrated and managed carefully. Unlike the East Asian economies, Rwanda does not have the luxury of high savings, which gives it far less scope to make costly mistakes. Policy responses first need to address key cross-cutting constraints (such as skills, finance, infrastructure, and business regulation), clarify the future role of state-owned enterprises (SOEs), and then, if deemed necessary, selectively pick areas for direct support that are aligned closely with Rwanda's comparative advantages and focused on export promotion rather than import substitution. Any direct support will have to set clear policy objectives and performance targets for beneficiary firms; be coordinated closely across government entities; and include a rigorous system for monitoring progress and enforcing sanctions as well as incentives for rewarding success and punishing failure—a model that the Republic of Korea closely followed in its early years of development.

Reform Priorities for High Growth

Reform Priority 1: Develop Higher-Order Human Capital

Building an innovation-led economy, as well as getting the most out of greater integration (especially services trade) and agglomeration, will require much higher investments in human capital. Such investments, particularly in the priority areas of reducing stunting and improving basic education, contribute to growth only after considerable time, so moving on them early is essential for Rwanda's growth aspirations.

Building human capital involves a wide array of investments across the life cycle. Allocating more resources and providing better information on outcomes are key, together with making dramatic progress in the following five policy areas:

1. *Reduce stunting.* A big push is needed to improve food security and nutritional practices and to increase access to clean water, good sanitation, and nutritional supplementation. Careful monitoring systems are required to evaluate which policies deliver the greatest gains.
2. *Expand access to basic education.* Achieving universal basic education requires ensuring that children are not turned away for failure to pay incidental fees, which may require increasing the per student benefit paid to schools, and reducing repetition in early grades so that children do not become too old for their grade level. Providing information on the financial returns to schooling has been demonstrated to increase parent and student investment in education, while improving the quality of schooling facilitates both reduced repetition and higher perceived returns.

3. *Improve the quality of education.* Improved teaching practices are necessary to ensure that children in the first three years are literate in Kinyarwanda before transitioning to English. There is good evidence regarding effective programs, including partially scripted lessons, on which Rwanda can draw. Because these improvements take time, transitioning to English later (end of primary) may be valuable. Rwanda could leverage its major investment in technology to provide upper-primary and secondary school teachers with regular opportunities to improve their English and to increase students' learning performance. Recruiting expatriates may help to remedy the immediate shortage of teachers and train a core group of high-quality Rwandan teachers.
4. *Strengthen technical and vocational training.* Collecting and disseminating information on the quality of skills providers and the returns to different skills would improve quality and encourage participation in high-return programs.
5. *Build the tertiary sector and foster innovation.* Increasing access to financing (including private) would expand enrollment. Enrollment in high-return fields could be increased through financing incentives and higher-quality science and engineering instruction in earlier grades. Creating incentives for researchers to develop and to adapt innovations to benefit industries and getting industries to pay for the research are essential to reaping the maximum returns to innovation.

Reform Priority 2: Establish Export Dynamism and Leverage Regional Integration

Although exports have grown rapidly and diversified over the past decade, the sector remains too small and narrow to achieve the country's aspirations for growth. Development of a more robust export sector serving both regional and global economies and a renewed effort to attract foreign direct investment in tradable sectors would boost scale economies and specialization and constitute an important source of competition and innovation.

Meeting Rwanda's export objectives requires a comprehensive trade policy that spans services, industry, and agriculture. Producing high-quality products for the region (especially in manufacturing and agroprocessing) and developing other, less location-dependent sectors (such as horticulture, tourism, professional services, and information and communication technology) for broader markets could do for Rwanda what manufacturing did for East Asia from the 1990s. These products are labor intensive, tradable, and capable of scale economies; and they have high value added per worker. As in traditional manufacturing, technological change can occur quickly and drive rapid productivity growth. There are five major priorities to meet medium-term trade objectives:

1. *Harness the regional blocs as platforms for transformation.* Key priorities are to lower and revise the common external tariff within the East African Community (EAC) to benefit Rwandan producers and consumers better, promote harmonized standards in goods and services, and reduce nontariff barriers. For key sectors such as energy and finance, the regional blocs should develop regional value chains to achieve scale economies. Finally, Rwanda should advocate for stronger regional Economic Communities' secretariats to review and discuss potential violations of common market protocols. The recently agreed African Continental Free Trade Area can also be advantageous, once details are penned and implementation modalities agreed to.
2. *Closely monitor the exchange rate to maintain export competitiveness.* Greater flexibility and close monitoring of exchange rates are necessary to avoid inadvertent episodes of overvaluation, especially in regional markets. It may be important to require the accommodation of import surges or the use of reserve

accumulation to sterilize capital inflows. A first step is to undertake more analytical work on the past relationship between exchange rate policy and export growth, particularly for dynamic export sectors.

3. *Invest in economic diplomacy.* More investment in staff knowledge is needed regarding how to prioritize, prepare for, and undertake external negotiations.
4. *Improve trade connectivity by lowering transport costs.* Building railway lines along the two East African trade corridors holds promise for reducing freight costs but is expensive. Developing Rwanda as a regional logistics hub offers another way to lower transport costs. Lowering regional road tolls, ensuring their uniform application across all EAC vehicles, and applying a standard tax policy for truckers from all countries would lower costs further. An aggressive push for open skies within the EAC would help to improve air connectivity and reduce the costs of air cargo.
5. *Increase service sector productivity.* Backbone services (such as transport, telecommunications, and professional services) need fewer policy barriers to competition for both domestic and foreign firms and improved access to EAC and South African Development Community professionals. Services trade also offers prominent opportunities for direct exports, particularly in tourism, but also in mining services, education, and business services.

Reform Priority 3: Leverage the Urban Dividend

Urbanization, managed well, can be an important driver of growth by generating agglomeration economies that enhance productivity, spur innovation, and foster economic diversification. More than one-quarter of Rwanda's population lives in urban areas, which contributed more than one-third of national structural change and half of national labor productivity growth over the past 15 years. However, urbanization has driven economic growth through the reallocation of labor off-farm, without the accompanying agglomeration economies essential for rapid growth of productivity.

Policy should focus on delivering the fundamental drivers that *link* urbanization to robust economic growth. This approach means focusing on *where* to prioritize urban development, *what* package of policies and investments to include, and *who* needs to be in charge of implementing solutions. On *where*, Kigali is Rwanda's main interface with the world and needs to fulfill its significant economic potential following market demand. This effort would be accompanied by a more calibrated approach toward a complementary (and well-networked) set of secondary cities and small towns. On *what*, reforms to strengthen land markets and urban planning are essential to enhance the efficiency of necessary capital investments in infrastructure, housing, and commercial structures. Finally, on *who*, stronger intergovernmental coordination of economic and spatial planning is needed to avoid coordination failures in urban development. The reform agenda has the following three main elements:

1. *Unleash Kigali's potential.* Kigali's urban fabric is fragmented by small-scale, patchy land development, which undermines the potential to achieve agglomeration economies; and raises costs. Addressing this fragmentation requires integrating labor markets through efficient, affordable, integrated public transport; prioritizing dense central infrastructure (particularly roads) to crowd in dense private investment in firms and houses; and promoting connectivity to global product markets.
2. *Strengthen land markets.* Rwanda may want to consider moving from the quantity-based regulation of land use to price-based allocation. This effort requires strengthening institutions so that they can independently and reliably value and publicly disseminate land values across uses and assign and protect property rights. Credible land valuations would also enable urban areas to fiscalize public investments

in land through land value capture. Moreover, regulations on structures should be used to mitigate negative externalities like environmental degradation.

3. *Foster institutional coordination.* The main priorities are first to unite spatial and economic planning, second to strengthen cross-district and municipal coordination, and finally to boost district capacity for urban planning and land valuation.

Reform Priority 4: Enable the Emergence of Competitive Domestic Enterprises

Strengthening the enabling environment for both private firms and SOEs to achieve efficient market-led outcomes is the cornerstone of improving the four future drivers of growth—innovation, integration, agglomeration, and competition. Competitive firms are essential to reap the benefits of integration and agglomeration and are also at the center of innovation activity. This effort calls for a strong state and a strong private sector, with complementary functions. The following are the main elements of the reform agenda:

1. *Address cross-cutting constraints.* The first imperative is to provide affordable access to finance, probably best achieved through regional (rather than national) banking institutions. Over time, capital markets and nonbank financial institutions need to be developed (again, preferably as part of regional agreements). Efforts to reduce logistics costs are important, as is improved access to—and reduced cost of—broadband connectivity, backed by effective competition in key telecommunications markets. To reduce the cost and increase the reliability of electricity, Rwanda needs to push forward for the establishment of a regional energy pool, build capacity to procure and implement power-purchasing agreements, strengthen demand forecasting, and better integrate system planning and system operations functions in the utility sector.
2. *Improve targeting and monitoring of industrial incentives.* The effectiveness of the government's extensive industrial policy interventions could be improved by shifting from general support to targeting successful enterprises. Crucially, a performance-based approach (focused on firm productivity and exports) should be mainstreamed in all interventions. Industrial incentives also need to be coordinated better across government agencies. Incentives also could do a better job of attracting foreign direct investment in tradable activities. Building and rigorously implementing a credible performance monitoring system are critical for this effort.
3. *Define the future role of SOEs.* An assessment of the level of competition, the competitiveness of SOEs versus private firms, economic development goals, and social considerations could be used to divide key sectors into four groups: (1) sectors in which SOEs will retain a monopoly; (2) sectors in which SOEs will compete with private firms; (3) sectors from which SOEs will withdraw when efforts to build up private sector capacity prove successful; and (4) sectors from which SOEs will withdraw immediately because the private sector is already capable and there is no compelling social rationale for them. Public-private boundaries can shift as the private sector gains strength.
4. *Build an effective national innovation system.* Wide-ranging policies are needed in this regard. On the demand side, a strong competitive environment would encourage firms to seek out the best available knowledge and strengthen managerial capabilities to introduce new processes and technologies, integrate them in the production system, allocate skilled staff to use them, and make them financially viable. Key steps to help firms to meet technical standards would involve a more effective standards board; effective, more easily available, and affordable key services; greater firm awareness of the benefits of following standards; and better

collaboration among firms or between firms and knowledge providers. Stronger coordination, monitoring, and evaluation of funding programs for science, technology, and innovation are also needed. The agenda on the supply side of innovation is discussed under reform priority 1.

5. *Maximize gains from the mining sector.* Recent discoveries of mineral deposits bode well, but they require greater efficiency and attention toward raising fiscal revenues. It is necessary to provide extensive support for artisanal miners, to improve the bargaining position of the miners, and to provide well-targeted extension services. Undertaking detailed geological investigations for promising deposits and developing a consolidated information system are important initial steps. Other measures include improving land management, incorporating social impact assessments, strengthening the capacity of the Rwanda Mining Board, and developing an optimal fiscal regime to capture an efficient and fair share of mineral wealth.

Reform Priority 5: Transition Agriculture and Food to Be an Engine of Growth

The transformation of agriculture from supplying commodities for domestic use to producing higher-value-added goods through regional and global food supply chains requires continued modernization and greater responsiveness to market signals. Agriculture is central to the four drivers of growth, because it is an important source of exports and a key driver of the pace at which rural resources are released for urban agglomeration; the transformation itself will be built on more competition and innovation within the sector.

Achieving higher productivity through private sector–led growth requires using direct public support of the private sector more strategically and strengthening the public sector's role as a regulator, facilitator, and provider of public goods. The following seven priorities are key:

1. *Strengthen research and regulatory institutions.* These institutions should be adapted continually to evolving opportunities and threats. Certifications, a key element of Rwanda's comparative advantage, have to remain credible. The high technical expertise of the Rwanda Agriculture Board will be increasingly important as the frequency and importance of sanitary and phytosanitary issues increase.
2. *Strengthen vertical coordination.* More effective vertical coordination in agriculture requires private sector partners to provide skills, capital, and entrée into international markets. Private sector vertical coordination arrangements and changes in horizontal coordination through producer groups are likely to grow rapidly. Government promotion of more standardized approaches would serve the interests of both farmers and aggregators.
3. *Engage the region more effectively.* Rwanda could engage more effectively and opportunistically with the EAC, the South African Development Community, and the Common Market for Eastern and Southern Africa and bilaterally with the Democratic Republic of Congo on a regional division of labor, both in production based on comparative advantage and in knowledge generation and diffusion. Regional approaches could help to satisfy the demand for food staples; improve certification of food safety, sanitary, and phytosanitary conditions; and adopt transparent science-based standards, product registrations, and certification of agricultural inputs.
4. *Profit from the big-data revolution in innovation.* The benefits of big data can be made more accessible to smallholders. "Smart farming," where just the right amounts of the right inputs are used for each parcel on the basis of information gathered by handheld devices with the right sensors, offers one such opportunity. Big-data approaches such as blockchain technology similarly offer the potential for lowering the costs of small financial

transactions that require secure record keeping and decentralized input, such as land registration and mortgages.

5. *Improve targeting of public investment in infrastructure.* Public spending on agriculture is low, and greater resources are needed for irrigation, especially in the drier eastern regions of the country. However, such investments are high cost (due to Rwanda's hilly landscape) and have to be targeted on high-return products (for example, horticulture exports).
6. *Develop a more robust policy on high-level human capital formation in agriculture.* In particular, a more consistent approach to vertical integration is needed for training managers and technical experts working for aggregators. Companies might be involved in this process by instituting training programs to build up nationally needed skill sets in agribusiness, high-value supply chains, and agricultural technology.
7. *Address land degradation and the impact of climate change.* Although considerable progress has been made in constructing robust "bench" (wide) terraces, much more needs to be done to secure land assets. Proactive promotion of adaptation to climate change is also vital. Fortunately, the soil and water management interventions central to halting land degradation support adaptation through better water retention and improved soil quality. Landscape restoration and conservation require the involvement of local government, producer groups, and national technical expertise and funding.

Reform Priority 6: Develop Capable and Accountable Institutions of Governance

Rapid improvements in governance, including control of corruption, rule of law, regulatory quality, and civil service performance, give Rwanda a competitive edge over its peers. Even so, its ambitious aspirations are bound to test its institutions severely. Building effective institutions is a long-term endeavor where improvements are necessarily incremental.

Considerable progress in restoring trust between the country's leadership and citizens, and more broadly within the society, has been achieved from the low level following the 1994 genocide against the Tutsi. However, further progress is essential to maintaining stability, promoting innovation, and achieving rapid growth.

Key recommendations are organized around the three pillars of state effectiveness and societal trust, all of which are essential for rapid growth:

1. *Build the state's core capabilities on the basis of capacity, meritocracy, coordination, and rule-based authority.* This effort requires empowering local governments and civil servants, which could mean adopting more flexible *imihigo* (performance contracts) with multiyear targets; improving coordination of policies on key cross-cutting issues; expanding the training offered by the Rwanda Management Institute, supported by skills audits and functional reviews to identify key gaps; paying higher compensation to individuals with scarce skills; and developing nonfinancial incentives to attract competencies in the civil service.
2. *Strengthen market economy foundations.* Strengthening corporate governance of SOEs, ensuring that they are not accorded an advantage over private firms, operationalizing the Rwanda Inspectorate and Competition Authority. Creating special courts and fast-track procedures to adjudicate small claims; promoting alternative means of resolving commercial disputes; boosting reliance on technology; increasing training and specialization of justice sector employees, including judges, prosecutors, and investigators; and improving case management techniques would enhance the judiciary's effectiveness in enforcing contracts. The proper enforcement of expropriation procedures, a more efficient land management system, and full enforcement of the law on intellectual property would

strengthen property rights. Further, tighter controls on public investment allocations and prudent fiscal management to build fiscal policy buffers are essential to developing the state's financial capacity.

3. *Strengthen accountability of the state and ensure that policies and programs are aligned with the needs of citizens.* Enhancing the performance of key watchdog agencies, increasing revenue-raising by local governments, streamlining expenditure assignments, and ensuring greater involvement of citizens in local decision making (for example, in setting *imihigo* objectives), coupled with reliance on more qualitative information in monitoring performance, could make local officials more accountable and improve the quality of services.

Notes

1. Ninety percent of cropland is on slopes of 5 percent to 55 percent.
2. There are important gains to be had from a demographic dividend if the decline in the fertility rate, and thus the population growth rate, could be accelerated. A recent United Nations Population Fund report (UNFPA 2017) found that Rwanda could boost its gross domestic product growth 1 percentage point by targeting a lower dependency ratio, which is the number of people who are under and above the working ages of 15–64 for every 100 persons within the working-age population.
3. Eighty-five percent of students at the end of grade 3 were rated "below comprehension" on a recent reading test, and one in six students in grade 3 could not answer a single reading comprehension question.

References

Dihel, N., and A. G. Goswami. 2016. *The Unexplored Potential of Trade in Services in Africa: From Hair Stylists and Teachers to Accountants and Doctors.* Washington, DC: World Bank. https://openknowledge.worldbank.org/handle/10986/24968.

Hallward-Driemeier, M., and G. Nayyar. 2017. *Trouble in the Making: The Future of Manufacturing-Led Development.* Washington, DC: World Bank.

IMF (International Monetary Fund). 2018. *World Economic Outlook: Cyclical Upswing, Structural Change.* Washington, DC: IMF, April.

Newfarmer, R., J. Page, and F. Tarp, eds. Forthcoming. *Industries without Smokestacks: African Industrialization Revisited.* Oxford, U.K.: Oxford University Press.

OECD (Organisation for Economic Co-operation and Development). 2017. "The Future of Global Value Chains: 'Business as Usual' or 'A New Normal'?" Directorate for Science, Technology, and Innovation Policy Note, OECD, Paris.

Solow, Robert. 1987. "We'd Better Watch Out." *New York Times Book Review*, July 12, 36.

UNFPA (United Nations Population Fund). 2017. "Unlocking Rwanda's Potential to Reap the Demographic Dividend." Policy Brief, UNFPA, New York, October.

Abbreviations

AfCFTA	African Continental Free Trade Area
ASEAN	Association of Southeast Asian Nations
ASM	artisanal mining
AVE	ad valorem equivalent
BNR	Banque Nationale du Rwanda (National Bank of Rwanda)
BRD	Banque Rwandaise du Développement (Development Bank of Rwanda)
CET	common external tariff
CGE	computable general equilibrium
CIP	Crop Intensification Program
COMESA	Common Market for Eastern and Southern Africa
CSO	civil society organization
DRC	domestic resource cost
EAC	East African Community
EAPP	East Africa Power Pool
EICV	Integrated Household Living Conditions Survey
FDI	foreign direct investment
GDP	gross domestic product
GHG	greenhouse gas
HACCP	hazard analysis and critical control point
HRDC	Human Resources Development Council
HRDF	Human Resources Development Fund
IBES	Integrated Business Enterprise Survey
ICT	information and communication technology
IECMS	Integrated Electronic Case Management System
IER	Institute of Engineers of Rwanda
IFC	International Finance Corporation
IFRS	International Financial Reporting Standards
IPA	investment promotion agency
ITE	Institute of Technical Education (Singapore)
JADF	Joint Action Development Forum
KIC	Kigali Innovation City
KSEZ	Kigali Special Economic Zone
LUCP	Land Use Consolidation Program

MCC	milk collection center
MDE	million dollar exporter
MICE	meetings, incentives, conferences, and exhibitions
MINAGRI	Ministry of Agriculture and Animal Resources
MINALOC	Ministry of Local Government
MINEAC	Ministry of East African Community
MINECOFIN	Ministry of Finance and Economic Planning
MINICOM	Ministry of Trade and Industry
MINILAF	Ministry of Lands and Forestry
MININFRA	Ministry of Infrastructure, Water and Sanitation
MRA	mutual recognition agreement
MTRC	Mass Transit Railway Corporation
NAEB	National Agricultural Export Development Board
NCIP	Northern Corridor Integrated Projects
NCST	National Commission of Science and Technology
NECDP	National Early Childhood Development Program
NEET	not in education, employment, or training
NGO	nongovernmental organization
NIRDA	National Industrial Research and Development Agency
NIS	national innovation system
NST	National Strategy for Transformation
OAG	Office of the Auditor General
ODA	official development assistance
OECD	Organisation for Economic Co-operation and Development
OLPC	One Laptop per Child
PEIEX	Industrial Extension Project for Exporting
PIM	public investment management
PIRLS	Progress in International Reading Literacy Study
PISA	Programme for International Student Assessment
PPF	production possibility frontier
PPP	public-private partnership/purchasing power parity
PSDS2	Private Sector Development Strategy
PSMB	*Pembangunan Sumber Manusia Berhad* (Registration of Employers and Payment of Levy)
PSTA	Programs for Support to Agriculture
R&D	research and development
RDB	Rwanda Development Board
RDF	Rwanda Defense Forces
RICA	Rwanda Inspectorate and Competition Authority
RMB	Rwanda Mining Board
RMC	Rwanda Media Commission
RMI	Rwanda Management Institute
RPF	Rwandan Patriotic Front
RRA	Rwandan Revenue Authority
RSB	Rwanda Standards Board
RSSB	Rwanda Social Security Board
RURA	Rwanda Utilities Regulatory Authority
SACCO	savings and credit cooperative
SADC	Southern African Development Community
SAM	social accounting matrix

SDF	Skills Development Fund
SI	sensitive items
SMA	Seoul Metropolitan Area
SME	small and medium enterprise
SOE	state-owned enterprise
STEM	science, technology, engineering, and mathematics
TFP	total factor productivity
TFPR	total factor productivity revenue
TIMSS	Trends in Mathematics and Science Study
TVET	technical and vocational education and training
VAT	value added tax
WASH	water supply, sanitation, and hygiene
WGI	Worldwide Governance Indicators

Overview

Future Drivers of Growth in Rwanda

Innovation, Integration, Agglomeration, and Competition

Introduction

Rapid economic growth is Rwanda's overarching development goal—a strategic choice to anchor its long-term vision. Vision 2050 encapsulates this choice with long-term, income-based goals that aim for upper-middle-income status by 2035 and high-income status by 2050. With this vision, Rwanda has aligned itself with the successful East Asian economies that began their development journey with a similar quest for high growth. The prioritization of long-term growth recognizes an important truth—sustained growth does not just happen, especially in a global landscape marked by forces of technology, trade, and tremendous competition. It requires a combination of leadership, social cohesion, and deep investments in core capabilities—of people, firms, and institutions—to harness the opportunities on offer.

The implications of different growth pathways are staggering. At its current pace of growth (4 percent per capita), Rwanda will barely cross the threshold for lower-middle-income status by 2035. At growth of 7 percent per capita, average income would reach US$2,400 (2017 prices). To become an upper-middle-income country by 2035, Rwanda will need to grow at more than 10 percent per capita. In 2035, the economic landscape of Rwanda could resemble that of present-day Bangladesh or, alternatively, surpass that of today's Vietnam or even Georgia and Indonesia. It is not surprising, therefore, that almost 70 percent of Rwandan respondents in a recent survey mentioned high economic growth as their first priority for the country (World Values Survey, Wave 6: 2010–2014; Inglehart et al. 2014).

But economic growth is not only a matter of income. Growth matters for a broad range of other development outcomes, including poverty reduction, as shown globally and in Rwanda's own experience as chronicled in this report.[1] Sustained high growth has another, higher purpose for Rwanda: to escape from its tragic past. The country is keen to put great distance between a bright future and a painful past.

This is not to say that economic growth should be the only area of policy focus.

The challenges of inequality, public service delivery, and environmental sustainability, among others, are just as important for development and need to be looked at in parallel, as is being done in Rwanda.

Rwanda's income ambitions are built on a strong and widely acknowledged record of success. Emerging from the devastation of the 1994 genocide against the Tutsi, which itself followed three decades of economic stagnation, the country has seen its average income rise three-and-a-half-fold. In 1994, only Mozambique was poorer than Rwanda, which today is ahead of 20 countries. This rapid progress was made possible by the second-fastest growth of gross domestic product (GDP) per capita on the continent, sustained over two decades.

Past successes justify bold ambitions but do not guarantee them. The reform agenda for accelerating growth to even higher levels and then sustaining it is complex and highly demanding, as described in this report.

A Strong Start despite Initial Conditions and Emerging Concerns

The genocide against the Tutsi in 1994 left in its wake a shattered and traumatized nation. It was, above all, a human tragedy, with few precedents. More than one million people perished, leaving behind suffering in indescribable forms and on immeasurable scales. About two million Rwandans sought refuge in neighboring countries, and at least one million were internally displaced (Chukwuma 2003). The economic and social costs were enormous. The country's GDP collapsed that year, falling in half from an already low base. Inflation climbed to more than 60 percent. Four out of every five persons were living below the official poverty line. Life expectancy at birth fell to below 30 years, and hunger and food insecurity were widespread, with severe long-term consequences. Of all the countries in the world, only Mozambique had lower per capita income in 1994, and none had lower life expectancy at birth than Rwanda.

Facing these grim conditions, a new Government of National Unity took over in 1994. Its task was made more difficult by the fact that its coffers were running empty, infrastructure (social and physical) had been decimated, trade links were broken, businesses and agricultural assets had collapsed, and institutions of governance needed to be rebuilt. Insecurity and instability loomed large, both internally and from threats within the region, and social trust had fallen to worrying depths.

Even so, relief, recovery, and reconstruction efforts were swift and multipronged. National reconciliation and healing evolved through homegrown initiatives, including the establishment of a National Unity and Reconciliation Commission in 1999 and, eventually, the *Gacaca* courts, modeled after a traditional approach to settling disputes. In December 1994, the Government of National Unity issued and implemented (and subsequently closely followed) a Declaration of Principles that outlined its political, social, and economic agenda for a "New Rwanda." The declaration emphasized social stability, national security, and a commitment to a market economy, backed by a capable state and a strong private sector (World Bank 2007). In the absence of a viable private sector, the state led the economic recovery through large public investments that were financed through external assistance. At the same time, to strengthen the foundations for growth, a series of reforms liberalized the economy,[2] promoted private investment, and sought to privatize some of the state-owned enterprises (SOEs) that dominated industry. A multiphase decentralization program was launched in 2000.

These early efforts proved effective. The poverty rate had declined to 60 percent by the early 2000s, on the back of a solid economic recovery. GDP had recovered to pre-genocide levels by 2000. And, by 2005, per capita income had surpassed pre-genocide peak levels, as had many health and education indicators such as infant and child mortality, life expectancy, and primary school enrollment rates.[3] Government revenues (excluding grants) had picked up to 14 percent of GDP by the mid-2000s (from 4 percent in 1994), which together with the consolidation of expenditures led to higher government and national savings. The task of accommodating and reintegrating the influx of returning refugees had also proceeded well.

With the dual post-genocide objectives of economic recovery and social and political stability largely met, a strong platform was laid for long-term growth and development. This agenda was picked up early under Vision 2020 (adopted in 2000), with far-reaching development targets that were later backed by ambitious reform programs implemented under a series of poverty reduction strategies. Reform efforts were most noteworthy in strengthening business regulations, as reflected in Rwanda's strong standing on the World Bank's Doing Business Indicators, where Rwanda is ranked 29th in the world (figure O.1)—above all other low-income countries and second only to Mauritius on the continent (World Bank 2019). Decentralization was deepened further, aimed at strengthening quality and accountability in service delivery. Large-scale public investments continued to close the infrastructure gaps, particularly in energy, telecommunications, and road transport. Trade integration was also accelerated with Rwanda's accession to the East African Community (EAC) in 2009, which significantly brought down tariffs—from an average of 16.5 to 11 percent.

Economic and social achievements in the post-recovery phase (2006 onward) have continued to be impressive. Growth of GDP per capita has averaged 5 percent a year since 2006, second only to Ethiopia on the continent (figure O.2). GDP growth, for the most part, has been broad based,

FIGURE O.1 Rwanda's global rankings on Ease of Doing Business indicators

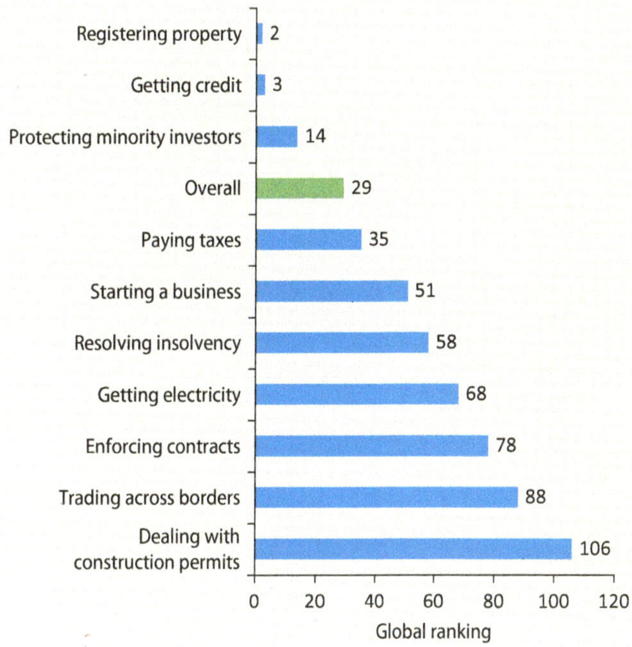

Source: World Bank 2019.

supported by robust performance in each of the major economic sectors. Industry (propelled by construction) and services (driven by information and communication technology [ICT] and trade and transport) each has grown at an annual rate between 9 and 10 percent since 2006, and agriculture (led by crops and livestock) has grown at 5.4 percent.

Broad-based sectoral growth facilitated rapid structural transformation, meaning the movement of labor out of low-productivity agriculture and into industry and services and from farms to cities. Close to two-thirds of GDP growth since 2000 has been on account of structural transformation, with the rest coming from growth within sectors. The percentage of the population in urban areas increased from 16 percent in 2002 to 27 percent in 2015, and the urban population more than doubled (from 1.5 million to 3.5 million). Because the agriculture sector had such low labor productivity at the beginning

FIGURE O.2 Average growth of GDP per capita in Rwanda and select countries, 2006–16

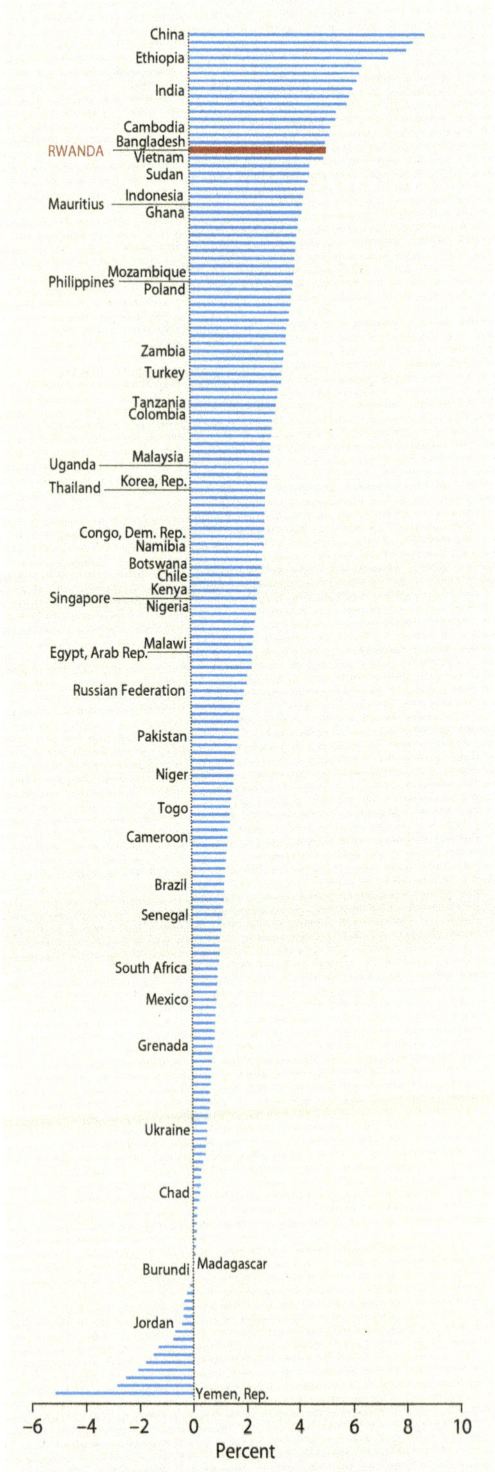

Sources: World Development Indicators data (World Bank, various years); National Institute of Statistics of Rwanda data.

of the process, the transformation brought significant gains. With close to 70 percent of the labor force still in agriculture—the sector even now with the lowest labor productivity (figure O.3)—significant potential remains for realizing continued gains from structural transformation, which is still in its early stages in Rwanda.

Rwanda has also seen impressive improvements in social indicators, including gender equality (table O.1). On many of the health indicators, Rwanda is now closer to the average of lower-middle-income countries, well ahead of its low-income peers. Maternal and child mortality rates have fallen 80–90 percent, and life expectancy at birth has more than doubled (to 69 years) in the past 20 years or so. Basic infrastructure—from roads to telecommunications and energy supply—has improved solidly. A nationwide rollout of health care, including health insurance coverage for more than 80 percent of the population, is also impressive. Rwanda has surpassed several financial inclusion targets, with almost 90 percent of the adult population having some access to financial institutions. Crucially, the institutions of governance have been strengthened significantly, earning the government a reputation for efficiency and probity (Ggombe and Newfarmer 2017).

In some areas, progress has been less satisfactory. Some of the more visible gaps are in educational outcomes. Rwanda's current levels of human capital and its current trajectory of investment in human capital are not consistent with its ambitions. In some areas—for example, stunting and primary and lower-secondary school completion rates—Rwanda lags behind the average of low-income countries (figure O.4). Achieving rapid economic growth and job creation will require a large increase in the quality of human capital.

A second area of policy concern is the low savings rate. The domestic savings rate is less than 10 percent, well short of the investment rate of 26 percent and behind that of many of Rwanda's regional peers (figure O.5). The domestic savings rate, which tends to move with income levels, has remained virtually unchanged since the mid-2000s, despite a 70 percent increase in per capita income (figure O.6).[4] The gap has been made up by external assistance and, increasingly, by inflows of foreign direct investment (FDI). To meet its growth objectives, Rwanda will need to raise its domestic savings rate to at least 30 percent and to attract more FDI in tradable sectors.[5] The high-growth East Asian economies, whose record Rwanda would like to surpass, had savings rates that were at least double Rwanda's at similar income levels. Determining the causes of Rwanda's low savings rate and identifying specific reform options require more in-depth analysis. Further, continued reliance on external assistance, in any case, carries risks. As a share of GDP, this assistance has been declining since 2004, and, as Rwanda approaches middle-income status, it can be expected to continue declining. Even if Rwanda can fill the gap through inflows of private capital, the associated macroeconomic challenges are substantial if the gap continues to be large for an extended period.

FIGURE O.3 Sectoral labor productivity and annual change in share of employment in Rwanda, 2000–16

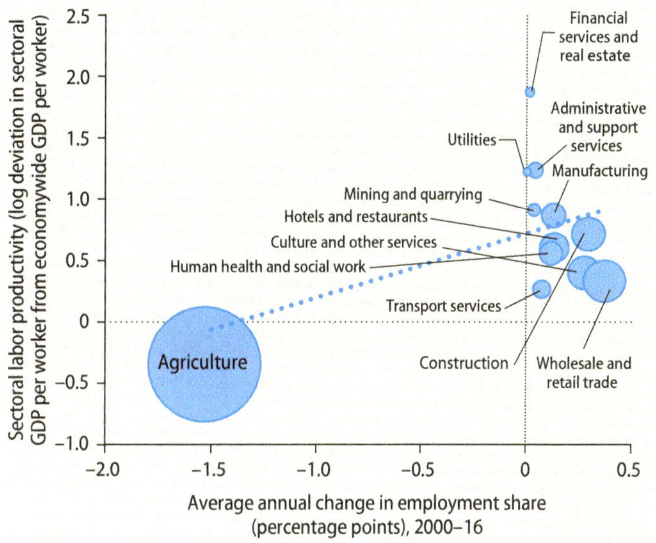

Source: Derived from Diao, Randriamamonjy, and Thurlow 2017.
Note: The bubble sizes indicate the share of total employment in 2016.

A third challenge is low productivity. Despite high GDP growth, Rwanda lags other countries on labor productivity (output per worker) (figure O.7). Rwanda's performance on this measure is explained to a

TABLE O.1 Social and economic indicators in Rwanda compared with low- and middle-income-country averages, 1994 and 2015

Indicator	Rwanda: Initial condition (1994)[a]	Rwanda: Latest (2015)[a]	Low-income-country average (2015)[a]	Low- and middle-income-country average (2015)[a]
% of population below national poverty line	80	< 40 (2014)	n.a.	n.a.
Gini index[b]	0.49 (2000)	0.50 (2014)	n.a.	n.a.
Immunization, measles (% of children ages 12–23 months)	76 (1996)	96	76	80
Improved sanitation facilities (% of population with access)	39	62	28	52
Improved water source (% of population with access)	62	76	66	90
Births attended by skilled health staff (% of total)	27 (2000)	91	49 (2012)	59 (2012)
Maternal mortality ratio (modeled estimate, per 100,000 live births)	1,270	290	496	254
Mortality rate, under-five (per 1,000 live births)	284	41	76	53
Life expectancy at birth, total (years)	31	69	64	70
Secondary school enrollment (%, gross)	9 (1999)	37	n.a.	n.a.
Literacy rate, adult females (% of females ages 15 and above)	49 (1991)	68	49 (2010)	66 (2010)
Literacy rate, adult males (% of males ages 15 and above)	68 (1991)	75	66 (2010)	80 (2010)

Sources: World Development Indicators data (World Bank, various years); National Institute of Statistics of Rwanda data.
Note: n.a. = not applicable.
a. Unless specified otherwise.
b. The Gini index is a measure of income inequality. Zero represents perfect equality, and 1 represents the most extreme inequality.

FIGURE 0.4 Human capital outcomes in Rwanda and other countries, by income level, 2015

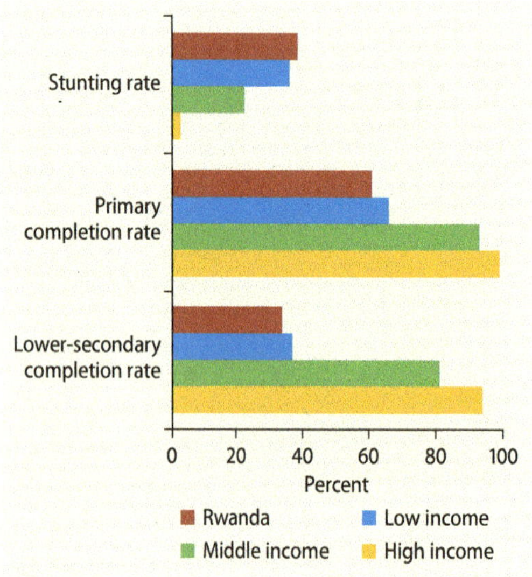

Source: World Development Indicators data (World Bank, various years).

FIGURE 0.6 Rwanda's domestic savings and investment rates, 1995–2015

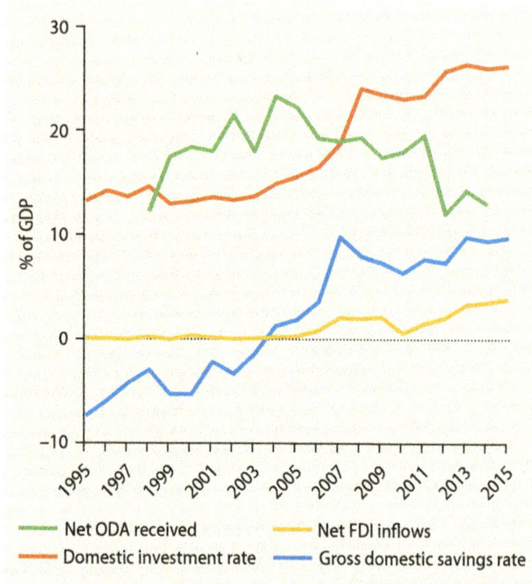

Sources: Calculations based on data from World Development Indicators (World Bank, various years) and National Institute of Statistics of Rwanda data.
Note: FDI = foreign direct investment; ODA = official development assistance.

FIGURE 0.5 Average gross domestic savings rate for Rwanda and regional comparators, 2014–16

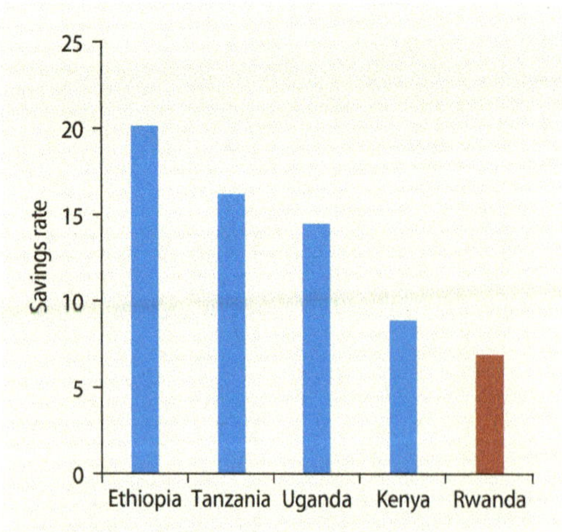

Sources: Calculations based on data from World Development Indicators (World Bank, various years) and National Institute of Statistics of Rwanda data.

FIGURE 0.7 Labor productivity and GDP per capita in Rwanda and other countries

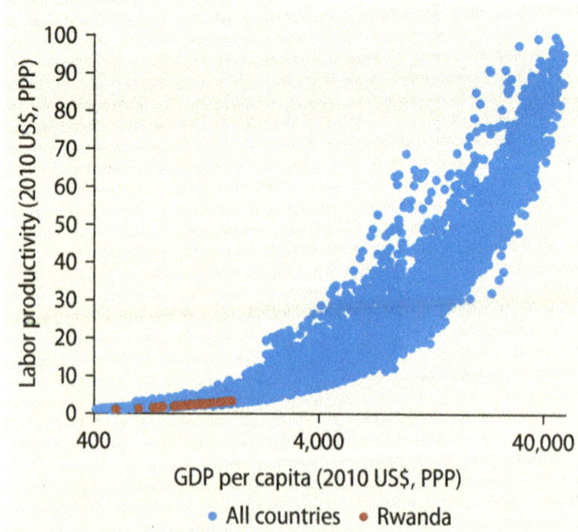

Source: Calculations based on Penn World Tables 9.0 data (Feenstra, Inklaar, and Timmer 2015).
Note: PPP = purchasing power parity.

large extent by weak total factor productivity (TFP) (figure O.8). TFP growth has fallen to just 1 percent since 2008. Although resources have moved broadly from agriculture to other sectors with higher labor productivity, the allocative efficiency within sectors has been suboptimal in Rwanda. Within-sector labor productivity either fell or rose only slightly across most sectors from 2001 to 2016 (figure O.9).

Fourth, the private sector still maintains a relatively limited presence, has shown low capacity for innovation, and lacks the scale economies that are crucial for productivity. In large part, this reflects the historical legacy, whereby the formal private sector was decimated after the genocide. Rwanda has since been successful in streamlining business regulations, as seen, for example, in its high ratings on the Doing Business Indicators. But the work is by no means over. A key issue is that costs faced by businesses are higher in Rwanda than in economies at similar stages of their development. For example, the high-growth East Asian economies had Rwanda's cost levels only *after* they had crossed the upper-middle-income-country threshold (figure O.10).[6] The high costs of energy, finance, and trade logistics have been important contributing factors. Private investors will also look for stronger economic returns, for which a pickup in productivity growth would be essential.

Fifth, in the midst of high growth and rapid structural transformation, the performance of the manufacturing sector has been subpar. Growing at a pace just short of the overall economy, the sector's share of total value added has dropped to just 6 percent—2 percentage points lower than at the turn of the century. Only 4 percent of the labor force is in manufacturing (two-thirds in agro-processing), and even that share has been declining (World Bank 2015b). As a result, Rwanda has fallen behind in generating manufacturing value addition (figure O.11).

Finally, Rwanda's outward orientation has not kept pace with its economic objectives. The ratio of exports to GDP remains low (at about 20 percent) for a small economy seeking high growth. Goods exports have edged up only slightly (from 4.8 percent of GDP in 2005 to 8.4 percent in 2015), and much of the increase was accounted for by

FIGURE O.8 Total factor productivity (TFP) and GDP per capita in Rwanda and other countries

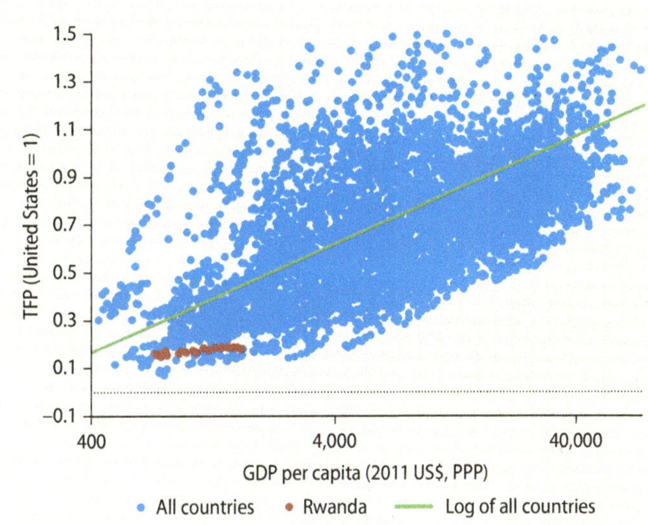

Source: Calculations based on Penn World Tables 9.0 data (Feenstra, Inklaar, and Timmer 2015).
Note: PPP = purchasing power parity.

FIGURE O.9 Average growth of labor productivity in Rwanda, by sector, 2001–16

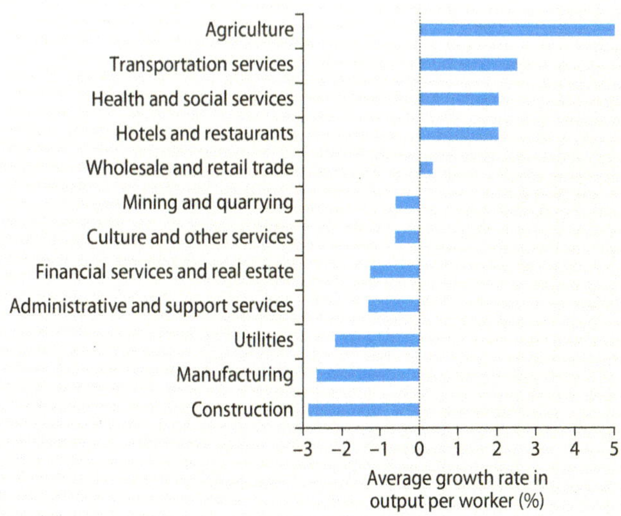

Source: Calculations based on Diao, Randriamamonjy, and Thurlow 2017.

FIGURE O.10 Price levels and GDP per capita in Rwanda and comparator countries and economies, 2011

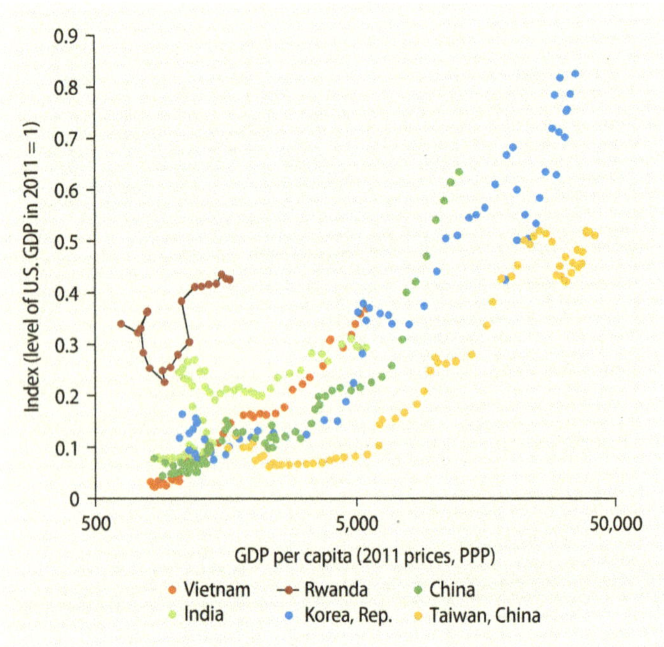

Source: Calculations based on Penn World Tables 9.0 data (Feenstra, Inklaar, and Timmer 2015).
Note: PPP = purchasing power parity.

FIGURE O.11 Manufacturing value added in the East African Community, 2006–16

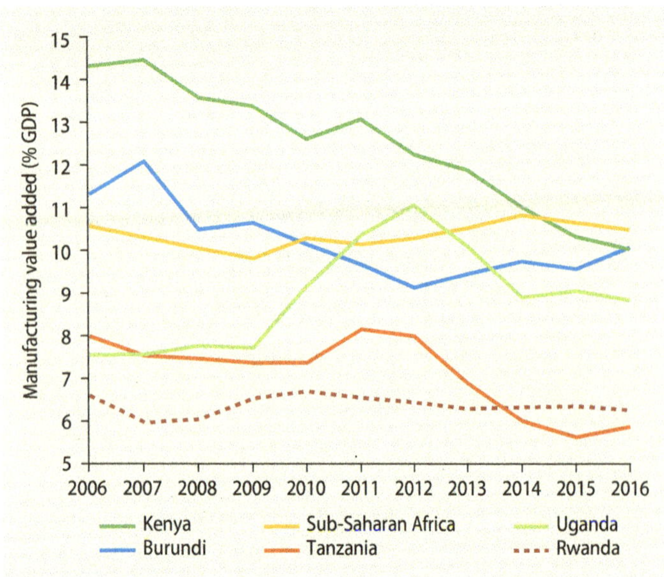

Source: World Development Indicators data (World Bank, various years).

(largely unprocessed) commodities such as coffee, tea, and reexported minerals. Value addition from manufactured exports has not made a major contribution to early-stage growth, even though the export base has become more diversified. Export of services (dominated by tourism) has risen at an uneven pace, with their share of GDP rising sharply from 2002 to 2007 and falling thereafter, finally settling in at about 6 percent. FDI in export-oriented activity also has been relatively low, again despite Rwanda's very strong performance on the Doing Business Indicators and efforts to attract FDI.

Future Aspirations

Building on its strong record, Rwanda's future aspirations are ambitious, as reflected in the country's Vision 2020 and Vision 2050 currently under preparation. These documents, products of extensive national consultations, are being operationalized by a series of economic development and poverty reduction strategies and seven-year government programs. For 2018 to 2024, they are being combined into a single process, the National Strategy for Transformation.

Vision 2020 set the country on an ambitious course. Achieving middle-income status and reducing the poverty rate to 20 percent by 2020 were among its key objectives. The vision identified six pillars to achieve its goals: (1) human resource development and a knowledge-based economy, (2) regional and international economic integration, (3) infrastructure development, (4) a private sector–led economy, (5) productive and market-oriented agriculture, and (6) good governance and a capable state. Gender equality, environmental sustainability, and long-term commitment to science and technology were the cross-cutting themes to support the six pillars.

Vision 2050 aspires to take Rwanda to upper-middle-income-country status by 2035 and high-income status by 2050, with the intention of providing productive economic opportunities and higher-quality living standards to all Rwandan citizens (Government of Rwanda 2017). These aspirations translate into double-digit average annual growth rates (more than 10 percent in per capita terms), requiring Rwanda to grow faster than China or the Republic of Korea at similar stages of their development (figure O.12). If growth falls even slightly short of this, Rwanda's upper-middle-income-country ambitions would be pushed back by at least a decade. The aspirational growth scenario has major underlying requirements, as described in box O.1.

To achieve these ambitions, Vision 2050 adopts four broad priorities, which also underpin the design, policies, and actions of the National Strategy for Transformation:

1. *Higher quality of life and standard of living.* To move beyond meeting basic needs to ensuring a higher standard of living for all people, Rwanda will focus on (1) access to affordable high-quality education and health care; (2) modern housing and settlements with environmentally friendly and climate-resilient surroundings; (3) comprehensive adequate social security and safety nets; (4) universal access to daily amenities; and (5) comprehensive personal security and safety.
2. *Transformation for prosperity (development of high-value and competitive jobs and sectors).* To improve productivity and competitiveness, Rwanda will target diversified tourism, manufacturing driven by competitive local industries, business and financial services, information technology, logistics and aviation, agroprocessing, science and technology innovation, construction, and extractive industries. All of these efforts will be underpinned by high-quality services in public and private sectors.
3. *Development of modern infrastructure and productive livelihoods.* This effort would involve modernization with smart green cities, towns, and rural settlements; well-designed transport facilities and services; and efficient public and private services.

FIGURE O.12 Projected GDP per capita for Rwanda under alternate growth scenarios, 2016–50

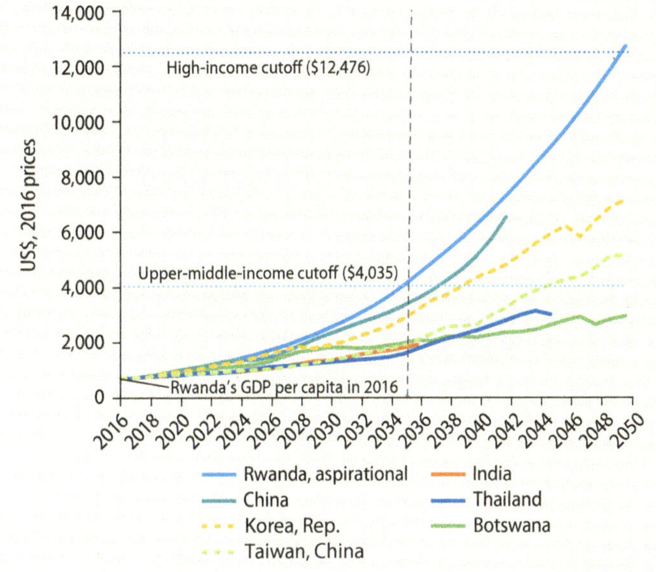

Sources: Calculations based on World Development Indicator data (World Bank, various years); Penn World Tables 9.0 data (Feenstra, Inklaar, and Timmer 2015)
Note: Alternate GDP per capita trajectories if Rwanda were to grow at the pace of other countries from a similar income level as Rwanda in 2016.

4. *Positive contributions to international peace and prosperity.* Rwanda will forge its own place in the world in the context of regional integration, multilateral and bilateral cooperation, freedom from aid dependency, pan-Africanism, and South-South cooperation.

These objectives will be underpinned by strong and sustainable macroeconomic fundamentals, effective institutions, and positive Rwandan values. The values underpinning economic and social progress are self-reliance and self-determination, dignity, unity and Rwandan identity, integrity, equity (including gender and youth), transparency and openness, participation in the global community, good governance and accountability, community participation, local innovation, and national stability.

Centered on the Rwandan people, Vision 2050 considers Rwandans as the country's main resource, reflects the society's core values, recognizes a strong collaborative role

BOX O.1 Major requirements of Rwanda's income aspirations

The aspirational income targets of Vision 2050 require substantial increases in savings and investment, as illustrated in the aspirational high-growth scenario summarized in table BO.1.1. The scenario assumes that gross domestic product (GDP) growth rises to 12.5 percent a year (10.2 percent in per capita terms) by 2022 and stabilizes at that level for the foreseeable future (the slightly lower GDP growth rate in table BO.1.1 reflects slower growth from now until 2022). As a result, GDP per capita rises to just over US$4,000 in 2035 and to more than US$12,000 in 2050, which is the threshold currently used to determine high-income status. The investment rate would have to rise to about 40 percent, in a context of declining foreign assistance. The slack would have to be picked up by increased private investment, because public investment is already at the limits set by financing options. Further, the savings rate would need to increase four- to fivefold (from 8 percent in 2016) in the next two decades to finance these much higher levels of investment.

Total factor productivity growth also would need to accelerate rapidly (tables BO.1.2, BO.1.3, and BO.1.4)—to about 6 percent a year—and to account for two-thirds of future growth. Another crucial requirement is greater human capital, calling for strong improvements in the level and quality of education and worker skills. A much stronger external orientation also would be necessary, with the ratio of exports to GDP more than doubling to well over 40 percent by 2035.

The aspirational high-growth scenario would further require significantly higher labor productivity growth—aggregate and within each of the major sectors. The demands on industry would be especially strong, with labor productivity in the sector having to switch from a declining trend in the past decade to solid 6 percent annual growth in the coming period. Labor productivity growth in agriculture and services also would have to accelerate significantly. Even with strong within-sector improvements, almost 70 percent of the overall growth of labor productivity in the next couple of decades would be generated by structural transformation, reflecting massive movement of labor out of agriculture and into industry (mining, construction, manufacturing, utilities) and services.

The requirements of less ambitious income growth trajectories (by matching, for example, the growth rate of China or the Republic of Korea or the slightly lower growth rate of Botswana, India, or Vietnam at a similar stage) would be slightly less onerous, but not by much. Rwanda would require significantly higher savings and private investment rates and productivity growth.

TABLE BO.1.1 Aspirational high-growth scenario for Rwanda: Demand-side requirements, 2000–35

	Share of GDP (%)			Average annual growth (%)	
Indicator	**2016**	**2025**	**2035**	**2000–16**	**2016–35**
Gross domestic investment	28	39	40	12.9	13.6
Public	12	10	8	n.a.	n.a.
Private	16	29	32	n.a.	n.a.
Domestic consumption	92	77	62	7.3	9.2
Gross domestic savings	8	23	38	n.a.	21.0
External transfers (net)	4	3	2	n.a.	6.9
Gross national savings	12	26	40	n.a.	18.6
Exports of goods and services	17	27	46	12.4	17.7
Imports of goods and services	37	43	48	10.8	13.1
Trade balance	−20	−16	−2	n.a.	n.a.
Current account balance	−16	−13	0	n.a.	n.a.

Sources: Estimates based on World Development Indicators data (World Bank, various years); National Institute of Statistics of Rwanda data.
Note: n.a. = not applicable.

(Box continues next page)

BOX O.1 (continued)

TABLE BO.1.2 Aspirational high-growth scenario for Rwanda: Productivity requirements

Indicator	Average annual growth (%)				
	2000–14	1999–2008	2009–16	2015–35	2017–35
Labor productivity	5.3	—	—	8.1	—
Agriculture	3.1	—	—	5.0	—
Industry	−2.8	—	—	6.1	—
Services	3.2	—	—	6.1	—
Total factor productivity	—	4.3	1.1	—	6.0

Sources: Estimates based on World Development Indicators data (World Bank, various years); National Institute of Statistics of Rwanda data.
Note: — = use of different time periods for labor productivity growth and total factor productivity growth.

TABLE BO.1.3 Aspirational high-growth scenario for Rwanda: Sectoral share of employment, 2000–35

Indicator	Share of total employment (%)			Average annual growth (%)	
	2015	2025	2035	2000–14	2015–35
Total employment	100	100	100	2.5	2.8
Agriculture	66	49	36	0.6	−0.2
Industry	9	16	27	14.6	8.6
Services	24	36	37	9.4	4.8

Source: Estimates based on National Institute of Statistics of Rwanda data.
Note: The assumed decline in average growth in agriculture from 2000–14 to 2015–35, despite higher labor productivity growth in the sector, in part reflects the massive movement of labor to other sectors.

TABLE BO.1.4 Aspirational high-growth scenario for Rwanda: Sectoral share of GDP, 2000–35

Indicator	Share of total GDP (%)			Average annual growth (%)	
	2015	2025	2035	2000–14	2015–35
Total GDP	100	100	100	8.0	10.1
Agriculture	30	16	9	5.4	3.8
Industry	19	27	38	10.0	14.1
Services	51	57	53	9.6	10.1

Source: Estimates based on National Institute of Statistics of Rwanda data.
Note: The assumed decline in average growth in agriculture from 2000–14 to 2015–35, despite higher labor productivity growth in the sector, in part reflects the massive movement of labor to other sectors.

for both the state and the private sector, and signals an outward reach to make up for the small domestic market and to access critical knowledge and ideas. Strong connective infrastructure and a focus on efficient urban development are viewed as being crucial for future growth. The vision further envisages a dynamic knowledge-based economy, with the service sector playing a leading role: Rwanda is envisioned as the innovation, telecommunications, financial, and logistics hub for East Africa.

Rwanda in 2050 will be a vastly altered place—an innovative, knowledge-based, and globally integrated economy with a highly creative population and world-class enterprises. Not only will it be substantially richer, but also its people will be universally endowed with much higher levels of human capital, and its cities, hosting more than 60 percent of the country's population, will be brimming with economic vitality and serving as continental centers of specialized knowledge. High levels of societal trust will be the glue holding the country firmly together. Rwanda also will have comfortably transitioned to becoming an open economy (akin to today's Singapore)—with cross-border trade, connective infrastructure, investment flows, and people-to-people exchanges marking close economic ties across the continent and beyond. Drawing on the vitality of its cities and the highly developed capabilities of its people, Rwanda will transition to becoming a continental hub for higher-end services, having maximized the industrial opportunities along the way. The institutions of governance will evolve into even higher forms of capability and accountability, with the country ranked alongside high-income nations on key measures of governance.

Opportunities and Risks

Global Megatrends

Global megatrends of technological innovations, shifting patterns of production, and changing sources of cross-border investments have major implications for economic activity in Rwanda and elsewhere. Global climate change is another major trend, with significant downside risks for all countries, but especially for those in the low- and middle-income world that are reliant on agriculture and have limited resources to mitigate the impact. Rwanda can shape the net benefits of these forces in its favor with early and decisive action to develop the capabilities of its workers, firms, and public institutions, the right investment decisions, and more effective business regulations.

Technology Megatrends

Global technological and business innovations, powered by the information revolution, are increasingly disrupting the patterns of production and trade across the world, with major implications for low- and middle-income countries. The innovations are affecting *what* is produced, *how* it gets produced, and *where* it is produced—not just for advanced goods but also for more traditional manufactured goods.

New technologies associated with industry 4.0—or the fourth industrial revolution, including industrial automation and advanced robotics, digitalization and integration of Internet-based systems (the Internet of Things), and additive manufacturing (three-dimensional printing)—are part of a larger trend of automation and data exchange in economic activity. For example, consumer goods are increasingly embedded with electronics, software, sensors, and network connectivity to enable these objects to connect and exchange data, which is changing manufacturing. The service sector, traditionally a nontradable sector, is becoming a major part of the global trade story.

Technology and the information revolution are also enabling disruptive innovations in business models. Apple is an early (and highly successful) example, with its disruption of a wide range of industries, including personal computers, music, movies, media, and telecommunications. Other prominent examples include digital platform companies like Airbnb and Uber, which have fundamentally altered the hospitality and taxi industries, respectively. Increased automation is further affecting production locations, enabling, for example, some leading firms, albeit still in small measure, to return labor-intensive manufacturing back to high-income economies and closer to consumers.

Their disruptive nature notwithstanding, technological innovations, for the most part, bring upside opportunities for low- and middle-income countries. There is evidence that more widespread use of scale-neutral digital technologies, such as ICT, allows firms in emerging economies to access wider markets by cutting entry costs and by reducing the impact of distance.[7] For example, scale is expected to matter less with additive manufacturing technologies, such as three-dimensional printing. Combined with the demand for customized, fast-delivered goods, widespread use of digital technologies could lead to geographically dispersed production, potentially helping small economies like Rwanda to overcome some of their scale and locational constraints.[8] ICT in the Internet of Things space, such as big data and cloud computing, can similarly reduce the impact of distance on firms' competitiveness. This, too, is positive news for Rwanda, given its landlocked geography and distance from markets. The Rwandan government aims to capitalize on this emerging trend by continuing to invest in network connectivity and sensor deployment in different applications.

In services, the information revolution has allowed low- and middle-income countries to go beyond traditional export sectors such as tourism and transport to more modern ones such as health care and business. These new export products can be exported electronically (taking distance out of the equation), can achieve scale economies, and are an effective channel for technology diffusion. The spread of productivity-enhancing characteristics in services expands the range of activities available as pathways for development.

Modern technological innovations also pose major threats. To the extent that they are labor efficient and skills intensive, the concern is that they will narrow the paths for low- and middle-income countries to benefit from manufacturing. Some observers have raised the specter of premature deindustrialization (Rodrik 2015). The implication is not just that machines will displace unskilled labor, but also that production will be retained in higher-income economies. In addition to reshoring of manufacturing activity from low- and middle-income countries back to high-income countries, there is also a concern that the expected migration of labor-intensive activities from China to poorer economies with lower labor costs might not happen or might happen only in select locations that form part of China's regional value chains. Technological innovations also threaten to exacerbate inequality, both within and across countries, as countries in a position to leverage technology gain higher incomes.

Consequently, cheap labor as a source of competitive advantage is increasingly giving way to a more demanding ecosystem. It is still not a zero-one choice for global producers, which remain open to producing in both high-income and low- and middle-income countries. But their requirements are getting more stringent with regard to infrastructure, available skills, logistics, other backbone services, regulations, supplier base, and intellectual property rights. There is also growing demand for low- and middle-income-country firms to adopt new technologies to remain competitive, but to do so they need to have greater capacity to use the new technologies, raising the bar further in terms of the mentioned prerequisites.

An early mover in some areas, Rwanda may be well placed to take advantage of these trends. The cell phone revolution, for example, has lessened the need for landline connectivity, reducing the potential cost of investing in such legacy technologies.[9] Similarly, drones can potentially reduce the need for air transport–related infrastructure. The much-cited example of Zipline, which uses unmanned drones to make 50–150 daily deliveries of critical medical supplies to various locations across Rwanda, is perhaps just the beginning. Furthermore, commercial drone services could transport items other than emergency supplies.[10] The impact is already being felt in agriculture. e-Soko—an electronic platform that gives farmers, consumers, and traders up-to-date market price information by short message service—is widely used in Rwanda, enabling farmers to market their agricultural produce better and to get premium prices.

ICT-enabled modern services could enable Rwanda to leapfrog—at least in part—the stage of manufacturing-led development in the conventional process of structural change. Business process outsourcing services, for example, can be developed without a manufacturing core, with the potential to become a major export area. To derive the most benefits, Rwanda will have to build its human capital rapidly, enable the emergence of vibrant and competitive domestic enterprises, and invest further in building resilient market institutions.

BOX O.2 The importance of regional value chains for growth and outward orientation in East Asia

Light manufacturing has long been seen as a catalyst for economic development. It is labor intensive, is capital parsimonious, and offers viable development pathways for low- and middle-income countries. Various economies in East Asia, including the Republic of Korea and Taiwan, China, began their engagement with buyer-driven value chains in apparel and footwear, among others, by importing intermediate goods and assembling them into final products, often in export-processing zones. Over time, firms in these countries were able to upgrade into full package production. Some were eventually able to develop and commercialize brands of their own (Gereffi 1999; Gereffi and Memedovic 2003). In the process, they offshored lower-value-adding activities to other countries in the region, which eventually upgraded into higher-value-adding functions themselves, sending their previously held competencies elsewhere (Akamatsu 1962). The shift of manufacturing activity from coastal China to Vietnam is the latest step in this "flying geese" pattern of industrial development.

FIGURE O.13 Measures of global vertical integration in Rwanda, 1995–2014

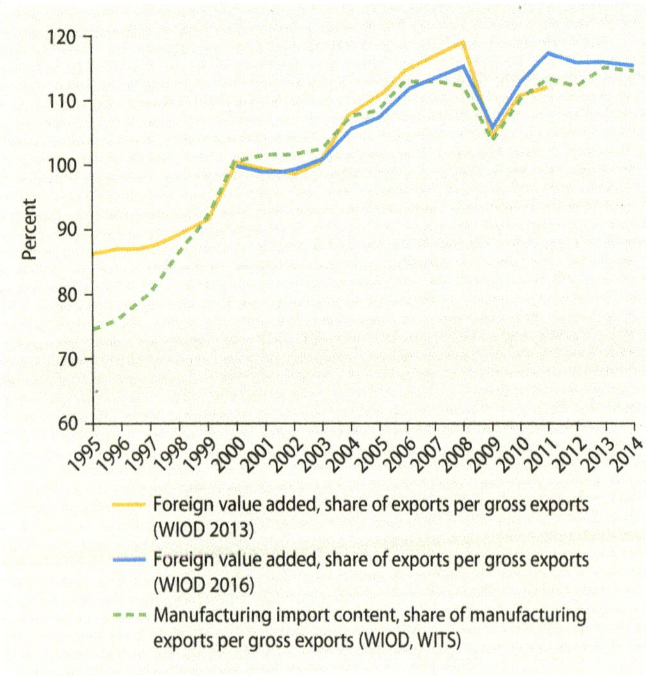

Source: Hallward-Driemeier and Nayyar 2017.
Note: WIOD = World Input-Output Database; WITS = World Integrated Trade Solution.

Regional Value Chains

Fragmentation of production into global value chains has created a critical opportunity for countries to develop through export-led manufacturing. In East Asia, for example, several countries have leveraged these opportunities to achieve export-led rapid development (box O.2). These trends have brought tremendous benefits to participating countries, seen in their growing heft in the world economy: the share of low- and middle-income G-20 countries[11] in world GDP rose from 11 percent in 1990 to 28 percent in 2016. China's share alone increased from less than 2 percent to 15 percent, as its share of global manufacturing rose from less than 5 percent in 1990 to 10 percent in 2016.

The world economy is now experiencing structural shifts that could dramatically change the outlook for global value chains in the coming years (OECD 2017). On the one hand, global value chains are maturing and losing momentum because the "unbundling of production" has largely already happened, as seen in the flattening of the share of foreign value added in gross exports of goods and services since the onset of the 2008 global financial crisis (figure O.13). On the other hand, new forces are reorienting production within global value chains. Production costs have risen significantly in some low- and middle-income economies, eroding their competitiveness in labor-intensive manufacturing activities and driving the transition from labor- to capital-intensive industries.[12] Digitalization of production is also shaping global value chains by reorienting global production and trade closer to demand.[13]

Production is becoming increasingly concentrated in regional and local hubs closer to end markets. This concentration has implications for manufacturing-led growth in Africa, where cross-border production networks have yet to materialize because of weak regional integration. Enormous opportunities for cross-border trade in food products, basic manufactured goods, and services therefore remain unexploited because of high transport costs, nontariff barriers, and regulatory constraints (Brenton and Isik 2012). Enhanced regional integration is important to derive the benefits on offer. The continent also will need to keep a close eye on the rapid technological innovations and changing sources of FDI (discussed next).

The growing regionalization-in-production trend can work in Rwanda's favor. The region around it abounds in (largely untapped) opportunities (box O.3). Moreover, the ability of Rwandan firms to compete globally depends on the "competitiveness" and "connectedness" of its neighbors. Rwanda is therefore likely to seize regional trade opportunities through intra-regional trade and participation in regional value chains connected to the global market.

The strongest regional opportunities for Rwanda exist in commodity-based processing and exports and services trade. These opportunities apply in particular to agribusiness and food processing, subsectors in which Rwanda currently has a revealed comparative advantage (Hallward-Driemeier and Nayyar 2017). These activities employ unskilled workers and have relatively low intensity of physical capital and research and development. The products typically are traded regionally (rather than internationally) because they are bulky to transport (for example, wood products, beverages) or require proximity to raw materials (for example, food production). The region also offers major opportunities for trade in services, which already forms more than half of Rwanda's export earnings. There is significant potential to boost services exports further, while benefitting from the greater competition, lower prices, and improved quality that come with services imports.

Changing Sources of Outward FDI

The sources of FDI are changing, a trend that is likely to continue (figure O.14). In response to higher labor costs, labor-intensive manufacturing is moving out of China, and with it new opportunities are emerging for other low- and middle-income countries.

BOX O.3 Opportunities in the region around Rwanda

The regional economic blocks around Rwanda abound in opportunities for trade, investment, and transfer of ideas. They also offer scale economies and specialization in production, which would be hard for Rwanda to achieve by relying solely on its own small, landlocked economy.

The most significant regional opportunity arises from Rwanda's membership in the East African Community (EAC), an ambitious platform for economic, political, social, technological, and security cooperation for six Great Lakes countries: Burundi, Kenya, Rwanda, South Sudan, Tanzania, and Uganda. The combined population of the EAC is 170 million (about 15 times that of Rwanda), and its combined gross domestic product (GDP) in 2016 was US$163 billion (about 18 times larger than that of Rwanda). Revived as a free trade area in 2000 (following dissolution of a previous arrangement in 1977) and upgraded to a customs union in 2005, the community aims to create a common currency and aspires to establish itself as a full political federation. EAC members have duty-free preferential access to the United States through the African Growth and Opportunity Act and to the European Union through Everything But Arms.

The EAC Customs Union entails three key aspects: duty-free trade within the EAC; common external tariffs (CETs) on imports from a third country;[a] and common customs procedures. The securities exchanges of four countries (minus Burundi, which does not have one) are members of the East African Securities Exchanges Association. Other areas of

(Box continues next page)

BOX O.3 (continued)

cooperation include a regional power pool, transport links, and trade facilitation. EAC-wide competition policy and law are in place.

Despite this good progress, several impediments prevent more meaningful economic integration. First, free trade is hampered by a long list of duty exemptions and significant nontariff barriers. Second, lack of policy harmonization holds back cross-border infrastructure development (Dihel, Fernandes, and Mattoo 2012). Third, although member countries have committed themselves to developing harmonized and complementary trade and transport policies, these commitments generally remain on paper only.[b] Fourth, the region is still some way from enabling free cross-border mobility of labor and capital. Issues such as permanent residency and the right of access to, and use of, land remain subject to national policies rather than being part of the common market protocol. Fifth, EAC member states still have to harmonize customs procedures in practice. Moreover, customs revenues are not pooled.[c] Finally, regional institutions are weak, and enforcement mechanisms are especially so.

Further opportunities lie in the Common Market for Eastern and Southern Africa (COMESA) and the expected opening of the African Continental Free Trade Area (AfCFTA). COMESA, a free trade area with Rwanda as one of its members, has 40 times Rwanda's population and 80 times its GDP. The AfCFTA, an even bigger opportunity, is a pan-African push to promote and harmonize trade liberalization across the continent's subregions. Once operational, it will be one of the world's largest free trade areas, potentially involving 55 nations (only 44 have signed the agreement thus far) with a combined population of more than 1.2 billion and GDP of more than US$2 trillion (UNCTAD 2018). The United Nations Economic Commission for Africa estimates that intra-African trade could increase more than 50 percent under the AfCFTA if import duties were eliminated, and more than 100 percent if nontariff barriers were also reduced (UNECA 2018).

Finally, there is significant untapped market potential to the west in the Democratic Republic of Congo. While conflict in the Democratic Republic of Congo limited trade prior to 2007, exports have increased considerably in the last decade. By 2016, Rwanda exported more goods to the Democratic Republic of Congo than to the EAC. The main exports include livestock and crops, but there also is significant (informal) cross-border trade in services such as finance, transportation, and wholesale trading.

a. Currently, there are three CET rates: 0 percent for raw materials, 10 percent for intermediate goods, and 25 percent for finished goods.
b. For example, regulations on vehicle dimensions, axle-load limits, road transit charges, and highway codes have yet to be harmonized. Even common definitions of road classes and route numbers are missing. Similarly, rail connectivity is impeded by minimal integration of national technical standards, such as those for building and maintaining railway facilities. Shipping on inland waterways and lakes would benefit from common regulations on ship registration as well as safety standards, including those on periodic ship surveys, staffing requirements, and aids to navigation and radio communication (World Bank 2015a).
c. Customs operations, including revenue collection, are managed by national authorities, creating delays and increasing transaction costs.

FDI outflows from East Asia rose 7 percent in 2016 to US$363 billion, mainly because of new outflows from China. On the back of surging cross-border mergers and acquisitions by Chinese firms, China has become the second-largest Asian investor, after Japan (UNCTAD 2017).

Investment abroad by Chinese firms targets a wide range of manufacturing and services industries,[14] with increasing attention to Africa as a destination. African countries still account for a small share of net global FDI inflows (2.4 percent in 2015), but the continent's share has almost tripled since 2000, as has the stock of Chinese FDI in the continent. In 2015, 4 of the top 10 FDI investors in Africa were Asian economies, led by China.[15] Notably, greenfield FDI into Africa is coming largely from low- and middle-income economies, whose companies are also participating through mergers and acquisitions and purchases of assets held by high-income-country multinationals. In 2016, almost 80 percent (US$73.6 billion of US$94.1 billion) of announced greenfield FDI projects in Africa were from low- and middle-income countries, nearly half of it (US$36.1 billion) from China alone

(UNCTAD 2017). However, these projects are mostly in real estate, natural gas, infrastructure, renewable energy, chemicals, and automotive; FDI in manufacturing is still relatively rare in Africa.

The top FDI investors in Rwanda are already low- and middle-income nations. Faced with declining foreign assistance, Rwanda surely needs more FDI to address its massive investment needs. However, it also needs to make sure that FDI is targeted increasingly to the tradable sector to support the massive export drive needed for high growth. The regional trade agreements are likely to enhance Rwanda's (and the rest of the continent's) attractiveness to FDI, as they promote a unified market structure and integrated production networks.

Global Climate Change

Climate change is potentially the most consequential global issue. Greenhouse gas emissions are on path to cause a 3.5°C to 4.0°C warmer planet by the end of the century. Climatic conditions, heat, and other weather extremes considered highly unusual or unprecedented today could become the new normal. The impact of global climate change is already being felt, with the number of category 4 and 5 storms having risen sharply over the past 35 years. The Arctic Ocean's ice has shrunk to its lowest area on record, and global sea levels have risen about 10–20 centimeters in the past century, increasing the risk of storm surges and fluctuations in precipitation (World Bank 2016).

The threat to Rwanda's economy from climate change is already being felt. The average temperature in Rwanda has increased at a higher rate than the global average. Its rainfall patterns are becoming more irregular and unpredictable, with shorter rainy seasons, which has had a major impact on food production. Rwandan agriculture is mostly rainfed (less than 10 percent of cultivable land is irrigated), which is why crop production is highly vulnerable to climate- and weather-related risks. These risks are compounded by high levels of soil erosion and periodic floods and landslides.

FIGURE 0.14 Share of global net outflows of foreign direct investment, by region, 1994–2016

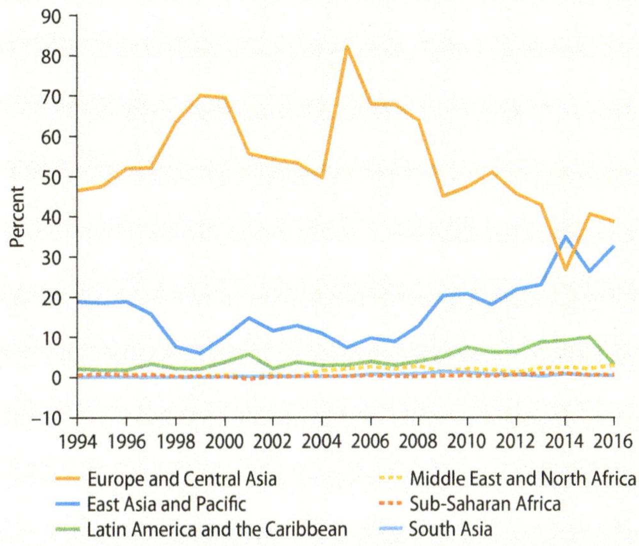

Source: World Development Indicators data (World Bank, various years).
Note: Net outflows of investment from the reporting economy to the rest of the world.

Medium-term climate projections for Rwanda indicate further increases in temperature—between 1°C and 2.5°C—by the middle of this century. Rainfall projections, though less certain, suggest increased year-to-year variability in rainfall. The agriculture and livestock sectors will likely be affected. Rwanda will need to plan for these vulnerabilities and seek to manage them with climate adaptation policies and investments.

Domestic Opportunities and Challenges

Population Dynamics and the Promise of a Demographic Dividend

Rwanda's population has grown about 2.5 percent a year since 1960, a pace that has been sustained since 2000. This is a brisk but not exceptional pace in comparison with the rest of the low- and middle-income world: 54 nations have seen a faster increase in population since 1960 (44 since 2000). As a result of demographic shifts, influenced by relatively high but declining fertility rates and sharp reductions in child mortality, today's Rwanda is a youthful nation, with a median age of just 19 years: 40 percent of the population is under the age of 15, and almost 70 percent is under the age of 30 (UNFPA 2017).

Rwanda has the potential to harness its demographic dividend. Yet risks associated with population increase are heightened by Rwanda's high population density (the highest in mainland Africa) and rising pressures on its limited natural resources and the environment. In addition, the fertility rate, one of the main drivers of population growth, has declined only gradually on average—from an average of 5.6 births per woman in 2000 to 4.2 births per woman in 2015, including a brief rise and fall during that period. At the current pace, Rwanda's population, 11 million in 2016, is projected at least to double by 2050, which would more than double the density of population to close to 1,000 people per square kilometer of land area.

Important gains from a demographic dividend are possible if the decline in the fertility rate—and thus in the population growth rate—could be accelerated. Rwanda could boost its GDP growth 1 percentage point by targeting a lower dependency ratio—the number of people who are under and above the working ages of 15–64 years for every 100 persons of working age—in parallel with improved schooling (UNFPA 2017).[16] Rwanda's dependency ratio is relatively high at 75 percent. The United Nations Population Fund estimates that the dependency ratio could fall to anywhere between 53 and 64 percent by 2050, depending on the pace of the decline in fertility. High-growth countries in East Asia bottomed out at dependency ratios of about 40 percent, so perhaps there is scope to accelerate Rwanda's progress. Policy options include better-targeted family planning measures and continued emphasis on female education, health, and economic empowerment (UNFPA 2017).

Emerging Middle Class

High growth sustained over an extended period can profoundly affect the income characteristics of the population. If GDP growth remains high, Rwanda can expect a rapid decline in the poverty rate and a concomitant rise in the share of its middle-class population. With 7.5 percent growth of GDP per capita and with income distribution assumed to remain unchanged, Rwanda would virtually eliminate extreme poverty (those spending less than US$1.90 purchasing power parity a day) somewhere between 2035 and 2040 and more than halve the share of the moderate poor (those spending between US$1.90 and US$3.20 purchasing power parity a day) from the 21 percent rate observed in 2014 (figure O.15). At the same time, more than 70 percent of its population would be middle class or higher (persons categorized as emerging consumers and global middle class). Even if per capita growth comes in at about 5.5 percent a year (still quite high by global standards), half of Rwanda's population would be middle class by 2040.

These projected shifts are likely to be replicated at the regional level and will have profound implications for the population's purchasing power, preferences, aspirations, and expectations of government. The thrust of Rwanda's growth strategy would still need to be oriented outward, producing tradable goods and services to meet regional and global demand rather than internal demand. This orientation is the only way for Rwanda to overcome the constraints of being a small economy and reach the scale economies and specialization necessary for high growth. But rising consumer incomes will generate strong demand for nontradable products, which will create an important secondary opportunity for local businesses.

Strong Potential for Structural Transformation

With close to 70 percent of the labor force still in agriculture, which has much lower labor productivity than the major subsectors within industry and services (figure O.16), a significant potential remains for realizing further gains from structural transformation—the process by which labor and other resources shift from one economic sector to another. By this report's estimate, more than

FIGURE O.15 Growth scenarios for Rwanda and share of the population, by consumption category, by 2040

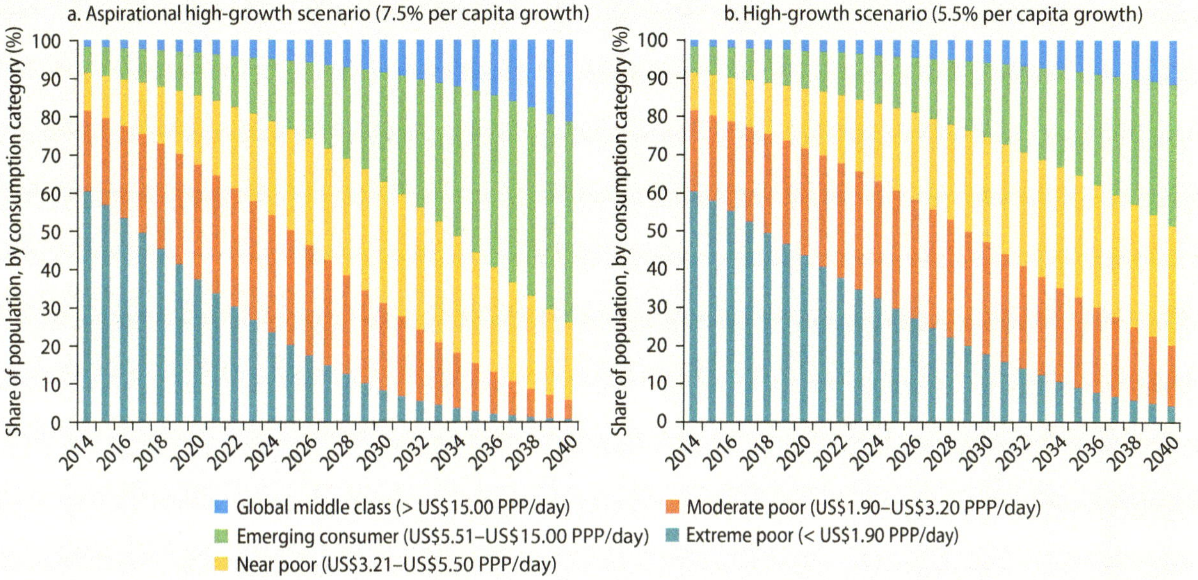

Source: Calculations based on National Institute of Statistics of Rwanda data.
Note: PPP = purchasing power parity.

70 percent of Rwanda's GDP growth in the next two decades is likely to be accounted for by structural transformation, even under a high-growth scenario. But gains from structural transformation cannot be taken for granted. Only strong labor productivity growth within sectors can assure continued gains from structural transformation. For that assurance, policies to boost competitiveness within sectors, as discussed in this report, and well-functioning factor markets (for land, labor, and capital) are essential.

Main Elements of Rwanda's Growth Strategy

As noted, aspirations have been set extremely high, targeting an upper-middle-income Rwanda by 2035 and a high-income economy by 2050. These aspirations translate into double-digit average annual growth rates (more than 10 percent in per capita terms)—targets that will require Rwanda to grow faster than any country (China and Korea included) has in the past. The requirements—regarding future investment and savings rates, human capital development, export orientation, technological innovation, and other forms of productivity improvements—are demanding.

FIGURE O.16 Labor productivity gaps in Rwanda, by sector, 2014

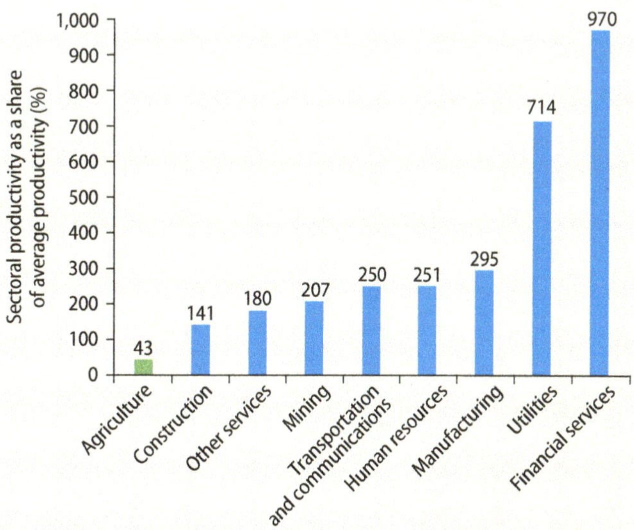

Sources: Estimates based on World Development Indicators data (World Bank, various years); National Institute of Statistics of Rwanda data.

Essential ingredients for success are strong leadership, social cohesion, and deep investments in core capabilities—of people, firms, and institutions—to harness the global and technology-related opportunities that are on offer.

The reform agenda is complex and highly demanding: nothing short of an extraordinary effort will suffice, given the level of Rwanda's ambition. The hard work begins in classrooms. The country needs a massive effort focusing on human capital development—its own education-focused Marshall Plan—if it is to achieve its income ambitions. With all of its achievements, Rwanda still lags the average of low-income countries in crucial aspects of human capital—for example, in stunting and in primary and lower-secondary school completion. An important related issue is the high stunting in early years, with implications for children's future learning abilities and participation in the knowledge and services-led economy that Rwanda envisages.

The next requirement is to achieve higher investment rates. Rwanda already has a relatively high investment rate of about 26 percent. But double-digit growth rates would require investment to be significantly higher still—at least 35–40 percent—in an environment of declining external assistance. Achieving this level of investment will require a sharp increase in investment by the private sector, because public investment is already at the limit set by the available financing options; a more than fourfold rise in the domestic savings rate; and even higher FDI.

A higher-order challenge is to boost productivity growth, which also has a bearing on Rwanda's ability to raise the investment and savings rates. High productivity growth, in turn, will require scale economies and economic specialization in areas of Rwanda's comparative advantage, with competition and technology diffusion as essential complements. Scale economies and economic specialization have proved essential for sustained high growth across the world (Commission on Growth and Development 2008), but it is even more important for a small, landlocked country like Rwanda.

For scale and specialization, Rwanda will need to make the most of external opportunities and enhance the benefits of urban agglomeration. To succeed in these areas, Rwanda needs to have a competitive domestic enterprise sector, both public and private, with a strong potential to do well in competitive environments. Such enterprises themselves have three critical requirements: a strong ecosystem for technological innovation, world-class human capital, and robust institutions of governance. This chain of priorities forms Rwanda's high-growth strategy.

Rwanda's strategy for high growth thus has four essential and interdependent drivers—innovation, integration, agglomeration, and competition (figure O.17). These future drivers of growth, in turn, would receive the necessary boost from reforms in six high-priority areas: (1) human capital development; (2) export dynamism and regional integration; (3) well-managed urbanization; (4) competitive domestic enterprises; (5) agricultural modernization; and (6) capable and accountable public institutions. The six reform areas are discussed in more detail in the report.

FIGURE O.17 Future drivers of Rwanda's growth: Innovation, integration, agglomeration, and competition

Doing well on each of these six necessary reform areas is what separated the high-growth East Asian economies from countries that achieved rapid growth for a decade or two, only to see it fizzle out (box O.4). The more challenging part is to go beyond the necessary to the sufficient conditions. Rwanda will be pushed to take high-risk strategic bets to gain high returns. These efforts must be calibrated and

BOX O.4 An international comparison of Rwanda's long-term growth trajectory

Only a handful of economies in East Asia have achieved an income trajectory even approaching the one Rwanda aspires to achieve. A comparison with those economies, therefore, can shed useful light on the fundamental areas that need to be at the center of Rwanda's policy focus.

Rwanda's long-term growth trajectory stacks up well against the early growth records of global economies that sustained rapid growth over several decades. Figure BO.4.1 compares Rwanda against two Asian Tiger economies plus Brazil, China, Morocco, and Thailand. The figure is striking on two counts. First, the long-term acceleration of growth in each of these economies started at similar per capita income levels—between US$1,000 and US$1,600 (in 2010 U.S. dollar purchasing power parity). Second, by 2016, Rwanda (roughly a decade into its postrecovery growth acceleration) had kept pace with comparators (including China) at a similar stage.

What happens from here on seems critical on the basis of international comparisons. About a decade into their respective growth accelerations—Rwanda's current stage—successful economies such as China, the Republic of Korea, and Taiwan, China, started to pull ahead of the rest. They were able in years 10–50 either to maintain or to surpass their growth records of the first 10 years. However, economies such as Brazil, Morocco, and Thailand saw their growth plunge early in the latter period. The challenge for Rwanda is to follow the trajectory of the former group and to avoid that of the latter group. Doing so will mean raising its growth of gross domestic product per capita to the 7–8 percent range. However, if recent-year growth rates of about 4 percent per capita continue, then even after three decades or so, Rwanda could not expect to get past where Brazil or Thailand is today.

Rwanda therefore is at a seemingly important juncture. Decisions in the next 5–10 years will matter for meeting its long-term aspirations. In this critical period, the successful economies focused on a core set of fundamentals. Common elements included high rates of savings and investment; strong agricultural productivity; early and sustained emphasis on human capital; strong outward orientation; robust urban agglomeration; a competitive domestic enterprise sector; and strong, stable, and adaptable institutions of governance. Those conditions are necessary for Rwanda to achieve its long-term growth aspirations.

FIGURE BO.4.1 GDP per capita in Rwanda and select countries and economies

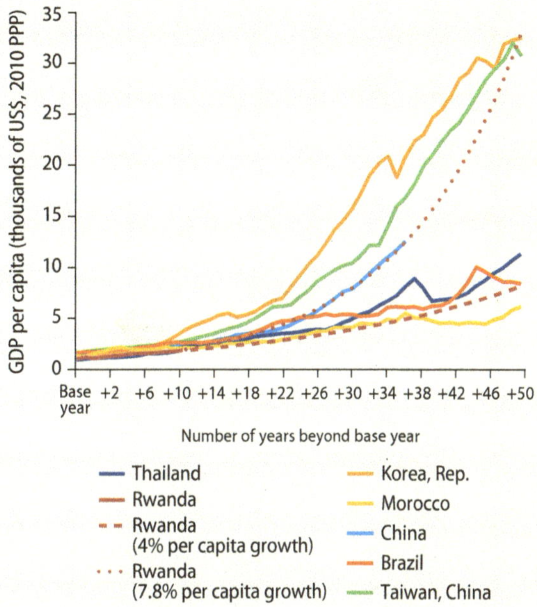

Sources: Calculations based on Penn World Tables 9.0 data (Feenstra, Inklaar, and Timmer 2015); National Institute of Statistics of Rwanda data.
Note: The base year is the year prior to the one in which long-term growth began to accelerate in each economy. It is 1951 for Taiwan, China, and Brazil; 1958 for Thailand; 1959 for Morocco; 1962 for the Republic of Korea; 1977 for China; and 2005 for Rwanda. The base year for Rwanda is 2005 because that is when GDP per capita recovered to the pre-genocide peak levels. PPP = purchasing power parity.

managed carefully. Policy responses need first to address key cross-cutting constraints (such as skills, finance, infrastructure, and business regulation), clarify the future role of SOEs, and then selectively target areas for direct support that are closely aligned with Rwanda's comparative advantages. Any such direct support will have to set clear policy objectives and performance targets for beneficiary firms, be coordinated closely across government entities, and include a rigorous system to monitor progress, enforce sanctions, and provide incentives to reward success and punish failure—a model that Korea followed closely in its early years of development.

Any future growth strategy is unlikely to succeed if it leads to further widening of income disparities or does not provide equality of opportunity for all citizens. Growth accelerations can widen inequalities in the initial stages as returns on skill levels rise and urban agglomeration leads to spatial concentration of economic activity. Rwanda will need to be keenly mindful of its future trends. Building a strong system of social protection to provide basic safety nets to the most vulnerable and expanding access to quality public services (education, health care, and basic infrastructure such as sanitation, potable water, electricity, and road and telecommunications connectivity, for example) to give everyone a fair chance to enjoy the fruits of growth will be important efforts in this regard. A stronger emphasis on educating girls and empowering women can be especially fruitful in breaking the initial cycle of poverty and expanding the country's base of human capital.

The growth strategy also will have to protect the environment: economic growth, however fast-paced it may be, at the cost of the environment is not sustainable. Low- and middle-income countries often make the mistake of neglecting these aspects in the early stages of development, only to find the cost of reversing them later to be much higher—both financially and in terms of lost growth potential. It is not necessary to adopt high-income-country environmental standards from the beginning. But it is necessary to put a price on water and air pollution from early on, to protect the quality of natural resources (air, land, water), to build climate resilience into economic planning and infrastructure investments, and to meet international commitments on cutting greenhouse gas emissions.

The high-growth strategy thus enunciated, with emphasis on economic specialization, scale economies, and trade, leaves open the question of food security at the national level. Rwanda will need to work closely with its regional partners to ensure an uninterrupted flow of food staples—for example, through the provision of financial guarantees under a regional process. If the country decides to maintain self-sufficiency in any particular staple, then it should do so after a careful analysis of the full economic implications of such a move. For example, Japan and Korea still produce their own rice and beef, but at significant economic costs, which they fully recognize and willingly accept.

Finally, the reform agenda and investment programs underlying the high growth strategy will be financially and institutionally demanding. Given the limited fiscal space available and expected continued decline of external concessional financing, future interventions will require far greater involvement of the private sector, together with efforts to enhance access to domestic and external capital markets and to strengthen the planning and implementation capabilities of the government. The latter involves better prioritization and greater efficiency of public spending, increased flow of government revenues, and stronger and more transparent public financial management systems. Strong emphasis on macroeconomic and social stability will remain essential to these efforts, even as Rwanda navigates a more uncertain global economic and political landscape.

Six Reform Areas of Importance for Rwanda

This section discusses in more detail the six reform areas of importance for Rwanda.

Human Capital and Innovation

Introduction

Rwanda's aspirations to reach upper-middle-income status by 2035 require dramatic improvements in human capital. Economies that have grown rapidly over an extended period have made substantial investments in the education and health of their citizens. Human capital includes the knowledge and skills of the population, and it results from investments in education and health. Ultimately, human capital investment and economic growth form a virtuous cycle: greater human development increases economic growth, and greater economic growth finances further human development. Cross-country analysis demonstrates that countries that invest in human capital early in the cycle enjoy the benefits of this virtuous cycle, whereas countries that experience high initial economic growth without investing in human capital almost always fall into a vicious cycle of low human capital followed by a slowdown of economic growth (Ranis, Stewart, and Ramirez 2000).

A broad set of policies is needed to support human capital formation. Building human capital entails a wide array of interventions across the life cycle, starting with investments in early childhood, including prenatal and early child nutrition and cognitive stimulation, and continuing with high-quality basic education, higher education opportunities, and skills that individuals gain as adults, both through on-the-job training and through adult education. Interventions also include health investments beyond early child nutrition, from vaccinations for children to preventive and curative health care for children and adults. Finally, a strong economy invests in innovation to continue creating new opportunities.

Recognizing the country's strong future ambitions, progress on human capital needs to be dramatic and swift. Under the current rate of improvement, Rwanda will still have low-income-country rates of human capital in 2035, which is insufficient given the country's ambitious aspirations. Moreover, investments in human capital, particularly efforts to reduce stunting and improve basic education, contribute to growth only after considerable time (the beneficiaries have to grow up). Only a small fraction of the population enters the labor force each year, so even dramatic improvements in education will adjust the skills of the overall workforce only slowly. The sooner Rwanda increases its human capital investments, the sooner it will be on track to achieve more rapid growth.

Challenges and Opportunities

Human capital efforts are urgent for Rwanda on a wide range of interventions, including prevention of stunting, improvement of access to and quality of basic education, increase in enrollment in higher education, and building of innovation capacity.

Despite the launch of several successful initiatives, stunting still represents a major challenge in Rwanda. At last measure, 36.5 percent of children suffered from stunting. Furthermore, the elasticity of stunting with respect to economic growth in Rwanda is less than half the elasticity in the rest of the world, so future economic growth cannot be counted on to eliminate it. Stunting has significant short- and long-term impacts on Rwanda's human capital and—ultimately—on economic growth. Adults who were stunted in childhood have poorer health and shorter height, are at risk of suffering noncommunicable diseases, and have lower cognitive ability and fewer socioemotional skills. These effects translate into reduced productivity, lower wages, and slower economic growth. By one estimate, the per capita income of today's workforce would be 10 percent higher if adult Rwandans had not been stunted as children. These impacts spill over to the next generation, with stunted women more likely to have babies who are underweight and who have cognitive challenges (Galasso et al. 2016).

Rwanda faces the same two challenges in basic education as many other countries: access and quality. Virtually all children in Rwanda begin primary school, but only about two-thirds of them complete it. One reason is out-of-pocket costs. Another is high opportunity costs, which are accounted for in part by high repetition rates in the early grades. Nearly one-quarter of first-grade students are made to repeat that grade (USAID 2017). Repetition—along with other factors, such as limited early childhood education coverage and late school starters—results in a large "bulge" of students in P1 (first grade) (figure O.18), lowering the likelihood of primary school completion and making improvements in quality difficult.

The concern about the *quality* of education is just as serious as the concern about access. If students are failing to learn, then economic growth will not follow from investments in education. Yet 85 percent of Rwandan students at the end of grade 3 were rated "below comprehension" on a recent reading test, and one in six students in grade 3 could not answer a single reading comprehension question (EDC 2017). In addition, youth who are approaching the job market also need better opportunities for skills training to help them to transition to employment.

FIGURE O.18 Early-grade "bulge index" in Rwanda and select countries

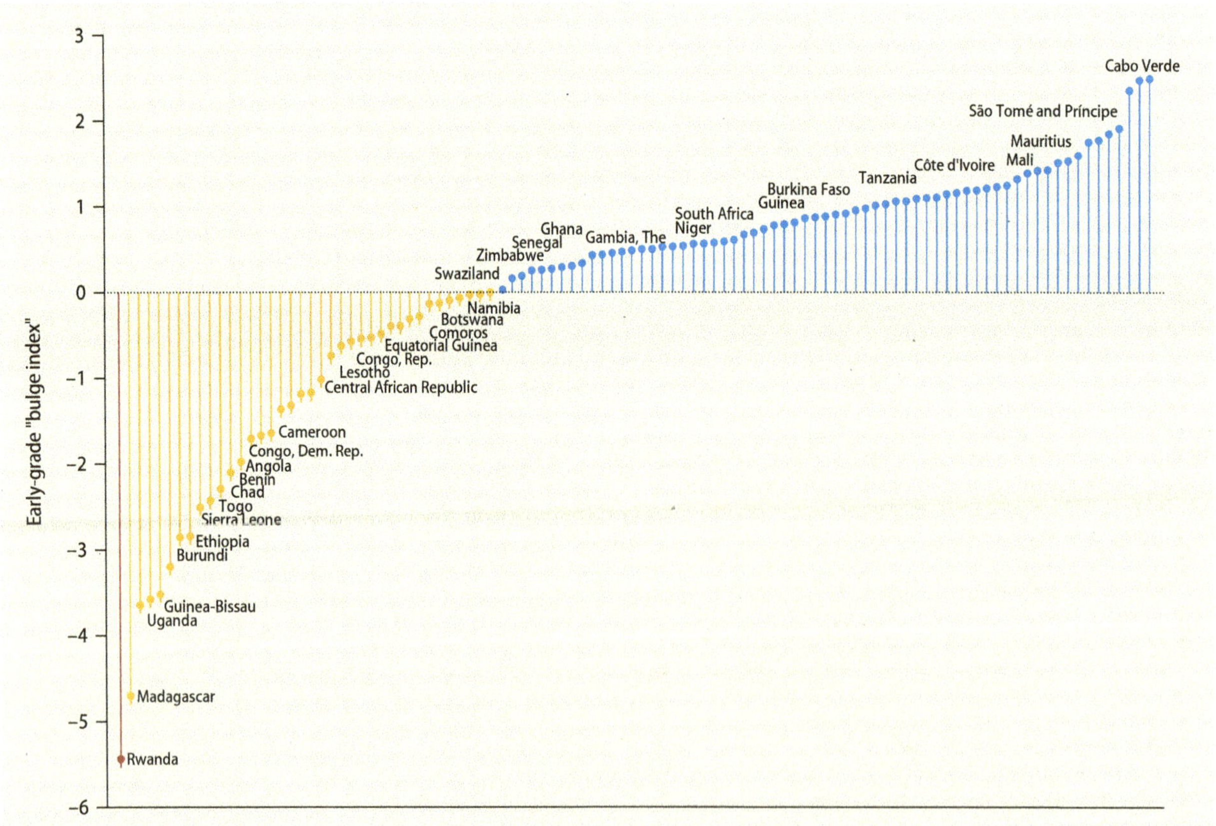

Source: Bashir et al. 2018.

Note: Low values in Rwanda reflect high enrollment in P1 (first grade) relative to the age group, low progression to P2 (second grade) (that is, many repeaters), and low preprimary coverage.

Rwandan teachers attend and put forth significant effort, yet this effort is undermined by skills and pedagogy. Crucially, many teachers have limited command of the language of instruction: a recent assessment found that less than half of teachers are at the "intermediate level" in English. A lack of proficiency in the language of instruction inevitably affects student performance not only in English reading, writing, and speaking ability but also in all other subjects that are taught in English, including math, science, and social studies. The government has invested extensively in teacher language training, but more intensive efforts are needed to bring teachers the rest of the way to fluency in the language of instruction.

Currently, relatively few Rwandans complete tertiary education, although enrollment rates are rising rapidly. The latest numbers (2015) suggest that just 8 percent of tertiary-age youth are enrolled in tertiary education, well below the level in middle-income countries. Furthermore, even with rising tertiary enrollments—and those enrollments have doubled in the last 10 years—shifting the proportion of the population with tertiary education in the workforce takes significant time, because only a small proportion of the workforce changes with each graduating cohort (figure O.19). Moreover, relatively few graduates are specializing in key job creation fields, such as science and engineering. Just 6 percent of university students in Rwanda are enrolled in engineering, manufacturing, and construction; and only 9 percent are studying sciences. If Rwanda intends to grow its manufacturing and technology sectors, then the number of students in sciences and engineering clearly also needs to grow. Even though historically Rwanda has invested more in higher education than other countries in the region, public financing of higher education has declined recently, even as demand for higher education continues to grow. Financing for innovation in Rwanda also remains very low, most recently estimated at 0.4 percent of GDP (Lemarchand and Tash 2015), which is a tenth of the share in countries like Korea and Singapore.

FIGURE O.19 Projected share of Rwanda's workforce with tertiary education under two growth scenarios, 2010–50

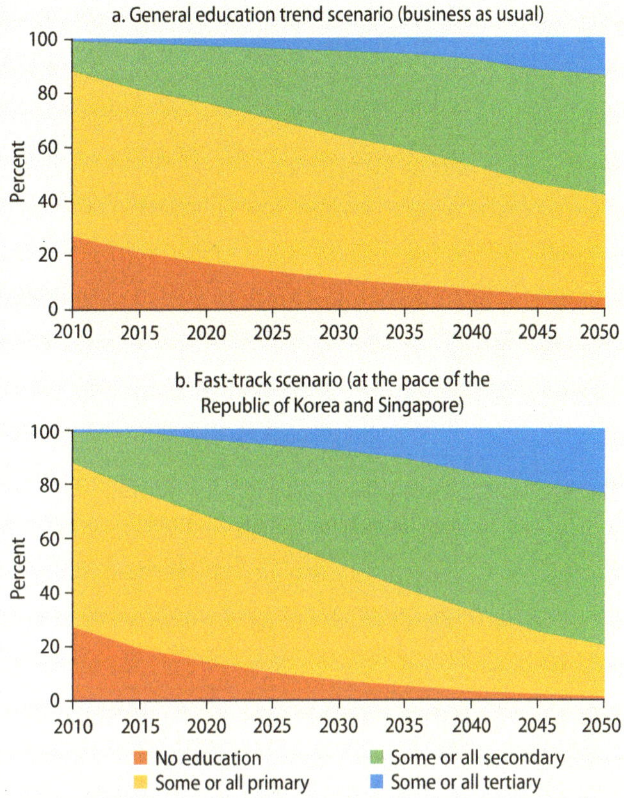

Source: Construction based on data from Lutz, Butz, and KC 2014.
Note: Panel a is based on the current rate of growth of enrollment in Rwanda. Panel b is based on the rate of growth of enrollment in the Republic of Korea and Singapore.

Recommendations

Rwanda faces an array of needs with regard to human capital investment and needs to expand investment at all levels of human capital formation. Each human capital investment builds on previous ones. Therefore, investments yielding returns that are realized more quickly need to be balanced with investments in younger generations. For example, the returns from investments in tertiary education and skills training are realized most immediately. However, their continued expansion is dependent on an increased flow of well-educated individuals from earlier levels, and their returns are complemented by a population with broad literacy and numeracy.

Government should consider two principles in setting investment priorities to maximize the impact on growth. First, it is necessary to identify the "binding constraints": Which problems are so severe that, unless they are solved first, no amount of money or time spent solving the less severe problems will help? Second, it is necessary to identify the investment required in activities that yield economic growth both now and later. Complementary investments, such as safety nets, can help households to make investments that will contribute to inclusive growth.

A holistic approach is needed, with special emphasis on the following areas.

Drastically Lower the High Rates of Stunting. Reducing Rwanda's stunting rate requires multiple coordinated interventions, and incentives are key. Currently, many programs to address these incentives in Rwanda suffer from limited coverage and inconsistent financing from a patchwork of donors. A big push is needed to improve food security and nutritional practices and to increase access to clean water and good sanitation. Careful monitoring systems are required to evaluate which policies deliver the greatest gains. The good news is that high rates of stunting are not inevitable. Many countries (including Peru and Senegal) have made dramatic gains, with political will, civil society cooperation, media campaigns, robust monitoring, adequate resources, and a multipronged approach seen as key to their success.

Expand Access to Basic Education. In Rwanda, expanding access first means reducing costs and improving perceived benefits. Countries that have achieved widespread basic literacy have offered free primary education. Achieving universal primary education requires ensuring that children are not turned away for failure to pay incidental fees, which may require increasing the per student benefit paid to schools and reducing repetition in early grades so that children do not become too old for their grade. It is also important to provide information on the financial returns to schooling because such information has been demonstrated to increase parent and student investment in education and to improve the quality of education.

Improve the Quality of Education. Improving the quality of teachers is essential. Teachers in Rwanda generally attend school and teach, which is itself a great challenge in many countries. But primary school teachers need to be trained in improved pedagogies so that children in the first three years get a firm grasp on literacy before transitioning to English. There is good evidence on effective programs to teach literacy in the early years, including partially scripted lessons and ongoing coaching of teachers. Because these improvements take time, transitioning to English later (for example, at the end of primary) may also be valuable. Many teachers in the upper grades of primary and in secondary have a limited grasp of the language of instruction: a recent assessment showed that only 43 percent of teachers have the "intermediate level" in English. Rwanda could consider leveraging its major investment in laptops in schools to provide teachers with regular opportunities to improve their English. Technology could also be applied to increase students' learning performance.[17] Rwanda also could consider recruiting English-speaking expatriates to remedy the immediate shortage of teachers and, for the longer run, to train a core group of high-quality Rwandan teachers.

Strengthen the Provision of Technical and Vocational Training. Collection and dissemination of information on the quality of skills providers and the returns to different skills would encourage youth to participate in sectors with high returns and help to improve the quality of skills training programs. Many high-growth countries, including Korea, Malaysia, and Singapore, used an activist approach to skills development by setting a strategic direction, tone, and culture for efforts to improve workforce skills; creating an organizational infrastructure with the appropriate governance design; and fostering efficient and effective management of service delivery by providers.

Develop a Quality Tertiary Education System Focused on High-Return Activities. Rwanda has taken dramatic steps to improve the quality of tertiary education in recent years, consolidating public universities into the University of Rwanda for better governance. Increasing access to financing, including loosening restrictions on private financing, would help to expand enrollment. Rwanda also needs to focus its tertiary education system on key areas of investment: more science and engineering. Strategies used in high-income countries to encourage university students to enter high-return fields—including financing incentives (as in Argentina and Australia) and improving the quality of science and engineering instruction in earlier grades (as in Norway and Poland)—could be considered.

Foster Innovation. The tertiary education sector is an ideal space to foster innovation in Rwanda. Publications and patents in Rwanda have been rising, although from a very low base. Likewise, Rwanda has invested in a range of graduate and postgraduate centers for technical training, including Carnegie Mellon University and the various centers of excellence. Creating incentives for researchers to develop and adapt innovations that benefit industries in Rwanda can help Rwanda to reap the maximum returns to local innovation. A practical way to do this follows the model common in high-income countries, where private firms finance university research to solve production challenges. Given the nascent private sector, the government will have to continue to play a supporting role.

Allocate More Resources to Human Capital Development. The amount that successful countries spend on health and education varies, and financing is far from the only factor in successful human capital investment. Governance of the sectors arguably matters far more and is a strength in Rwanda. It is impossible to imagine achieving universal primary education and a significant increase in secondary education without expanding the amount of resources devoted to education over time.

Provide Better Information on Outcomes. Rwanda is an innovator in holding service providers accountable, with performance contracts for educators and health workers, along with innovations in performance-based pay (Basinga et al. 2011; Zeitlin et al. 2017). In many countries, service provision has improved because of the effective involvement of parents, pointing to the importance of dissemination of information on learning outcomes and other elements of school performance. More regular measurement of learning outcomes and stunting reduction would allow the government to evaluate the effectiveness of different interventions and to accelerate progress on both aims.

Transformation through Trade: Using Exports and Regional Integration to Drive Future Growth

Introduction

To achieve its aspiration of becoming a high-income country by 2050, Rwanda needs to accelerate the growth of trade. Inflows of development assistance have financed a large share of investment and powered GDP growth in the past two decades, but they are likely to attenuate in the coming two decades as Rwanda progresses toward middle-income status. Trade will become an increasingly important driver of growth. Exports will provide foreign exchange to purchase much-needed investment in equipment, high-technology goods, intermediate components, and product varieties and will foster productivity by allowing firms to exploit increasingly large economies of scale. Increased import capacity will facilitate access to high-technology goods and foster competition that drives productivity. Trade expansion also implies the need to attract FDI, because multinational companies bring in managerial, technical, and design skills while their networks facilitate access to new export markets (Freund and Moran 2017).

FIGURE O.20 Exports as a share of GDP and log GDP per capita in Rwanda, 2000–16

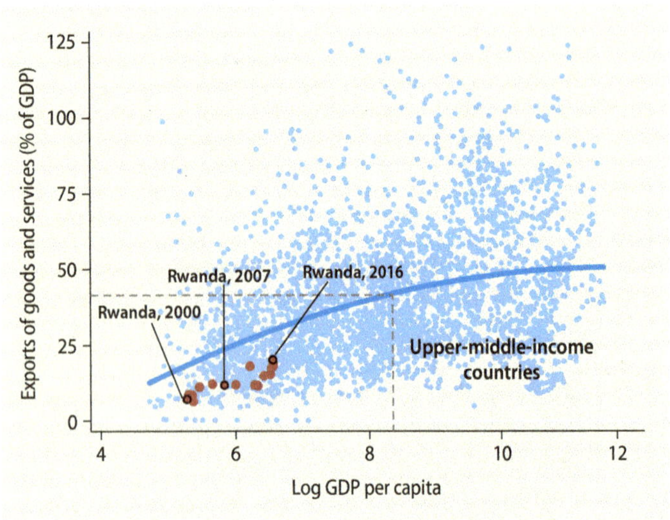

Source: Calculations based on Comtrade data (United Nations, various years).

Trade expansion is central to creating new, higher-productivity jobs that facilitate growth through structural transformation. Moving labor from low-productivity jobs mainly in agriculture to higher-productivity jobs in a range of mostly urban activities is imperative for growth. East Asia made this transition to high growth by relying on labor-intensive manufacturing for export. Rwanda, as with much of Africa, requires not only labor-intensive manufacturing but also agribusiness, horticulture, and selected services—what some have called "industries without smokestacks" (Newfarmer, Page, and Tarp, forthcoming). These activities, taken together, hold the promise of doing for Rwanda what manufacturing did for East Asia in the 1990s. They are labor intensive and tradable, and they have high value added per worker. As in traditional manufacturing, technological change is rapid and can spawn rapid productivity growth. In a world of recent technological revolutions in ICT, manufacturing techniques, and global value chains, Rwanda has an opportunity to leverage greater integration into regional and global markets and to propel structural transformation and growth (Hallward-Driemeier and Nayyar 2017).

Challenges and Opportunities

On the basis of a comparison with countries experiencing high rates of economic growth, Rwanda's exports as a share of GDP have to increase significantly for Rwanda to achieve its income objectives for 2050. A review of global experience shows a large spread of exports-to-GDP ratios as countries achieve upper-middle-income status, but that ratio tends to be upward of 40 percent (figure O.20). Since 2000, Rwanda has consistently increased its share of exports in national income, but the share is still far below the average for upper-middle-income countries. Rwanda needs to have double-digit year-on-year export growth every year up to 2035 if it is to cross the 40 percent threshold. Meeting such a target is difficult but not impossible, given that the share of exports in national income is still low relative to that of other countries with comparable levels of per capita income. Therefore, significant export opportunities are available to Rwanda, and exports still have ample room to grow.

Rwanda has begun laying the foundations for an export push. Over the last decade, exports have grown about 20 percent annually, and the export portfolio has become more diversified, with the share of coffee, tea, and minerals falling from 41 percent in 2005 to 25 percent in 2015. New activities, particularly services exports, have surged in importance. Tourism alone now accounts for 23 percent of export earnings, and services account for about half. New exports of goods are also becoming important, especially exports to regional markets. In 2014, the EAC accounted for 41 percent of manufacturing exports, 66 percent of leather goods, and 53 percent of horticultural products sold abroad. Non-EAC neighboring markets have also become important. Exports to the Democratic Republic of Congo have increased considerably in the last decade: by 2016, Rwanda exported more goods to the Democratic Republic of Congo than to the EAC.[18] Rwanda has also attracted more FDI of late, which is contributing to export performance.

That said, Rwanda still exports below the average of other countries at its per capita income. Whereas exports in agro-processing have been dynamic, exports in other manufacturing areas have been disappointing, declining from 8 percent of total exports (2012–14) to 5 percent in 2016. This decline is largely due to reductions in some of the higher-skill export products such as machinery, mechanical appliances, and electrical equipment. Further, Rwanda's exports remain concentrated in a small number of firms. Over 2009–16, the top 1 percent of exporters accounted for more than 40 percent of the total value of exports (while the top 5 percent accounted for 80 percent). Exporter survival rates are also low. Export performance continues to suffer from low labor productivity in key backbone services such as transport and ICT and low levels of private investment in tradable sectors.

An important challenge is that the benefits to trade from regional integration in the EAC have been limited so far. By removing internal tariff and nontariff barriers, regional integration is expected to result in trade creation. Yet a comparison of intra-regional imports as a share of GDP before and after joining the EAC shows that this effect has been limited (figure O.21). After a small increase in the first five years, the EAC's intra-bloc imports of goods as a share of GDP fell to a level below initial integration 10 years after membership. In contrast, other regional bodies experienced a considerable increase in intra-bloc trade. After 10 years of regional integration, the Southern African Development Community (SADC) saw a tripling of intra-bloc imports, while the Association of Southeast Asian Nations doubled intra-bloc imports to almost 16 percent of GDP.

Trade connectivity and high transport costs pose a constraint for Rwanda. The single most important determinant of long-run trade growth, in fact, is the cost of

FIGURE O.21 Intra-bloc goods imports as a share of GDP before and after joining the bloc

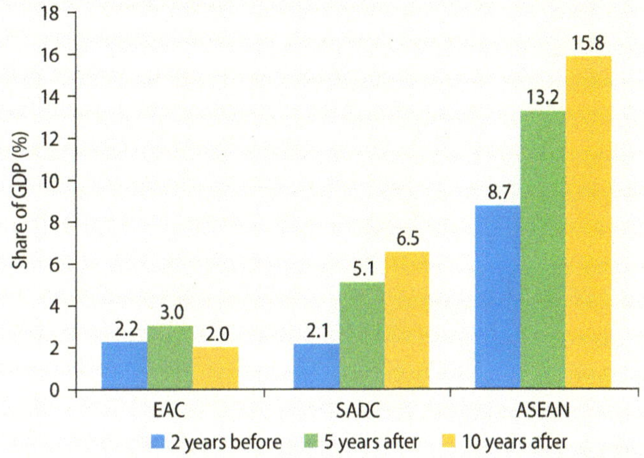

Source: Shepherd, de Melo, and Sen 2017.
Note: EAC = East African Community; SADC = Southern African Development Community; ASEAN = Association of Southeast Asian Nations.

getting goods to market and getting inputs to local producers. Rwanda is a landlocked country, which means that transport costs typically add some 50 percent to the cost of exporting products and importing inputs. Because more than 90 percent of goods exports are transported by truck, Rwanda relies heavily on the land transport corridors of other countries for access to the sea. Almost all of its trade in global markets goes through two East African trade corridors: the Northern Corridor (Mombasa) and the Central Corridor (Dar es Salaam). The lack of facilitation at the border, fragmentation of the supply chain, and limited access to affordable air cargo opportunities also contribute to the high cost of trading.

Recommendations

Meeting Rwanda's export objectives requires a comprehensive trade policy that spans services, industry, and agriculture. Analysis from this report suggests that no one sector can drive the necessary export and employment growth on its own. Rwanda should look to produce high-quality products for the region (especially in agribusiness and food processing) and to develop other sectors that are similarly tradable and productive, but less dependent on location (such as horticulture, tourism, professional services, and ICT). The government thus has to build further on the service sector (the largest current source of exports), strongly accelerate industrial growth, and expand into other high-value agricultural exports (such as horticulture).

Six major policy priorities should figure prominently in a comprehensive reform program that uses trade to accelerate and sustain growth.

Harness the Regional Blocs as Platforms for Transformation. The region offers a crucial learning ground for exporting higher-quality products, especially in manufacturing and agroprocessing. Entering regional supply chains can help to prepare Rwandan firms to enter the global market. The region can also be used to stimulate within-sector productivity growth and to develop other tradable sectors such as tourism, transport, and professional services through greater regional scale economies and greater competition from leading firms. A key focus should be on revising and lowering the common external tariff within the EAC to benefit Rwandan producers and exporters that use imported inputs and poor consumers who disproportionately consume heavily taxed imports. The integrated market can also be extended by promoting harmonized standards in goods and services and by reducing nontariff barriers. For key sectors such as energy and finance, the EAC should develop regional supply chains that can result in economies of scale. *Intra-industry regional trade* competition can force firms to larger scale and drive out less productive firms. Finally, Rwanda could advocate for a stronger EAC secretariat that can review and discuss potential violations of common market protocols. The recently agreed African Continental Free Trade Area, a pan-African initiative to liberalize continental trade, can also be advantageous, once details are penned and implementation modalities agreed to.

Monitor the Exchange Rate Closely to Maintain Export Competitiveness. Export drives in other countries have been sustained by maintaining a competitive real exchange rate over a long period. Similar benefits may be on offer for Rwanda, but greater flexibility and close monitoring of exchange rates are needed to ensure that the real exchange rate remains in line with fundamentals and that episodes of overvaluation are avoided, especially in regional markets where manufactured goods and new products predominate. A first step is to undertake more analytical work on the link between exchange rates and export growth,[19] particularly as it affects potentially dynamic export sectors. Because imports consume capital inflows for foreign exchange payments, it is advisable for the government to focus on export growth rather than on the trade deficit as a macroeconomic objective.

Invest in Economic Diplomacy. The complex issues under consideration in trade negotiations require more investment in staff knowledge and expertise to usefully engage in and undertake negotiations, especially in highly specialized sectors.

Improve Trade Connectivity by Lowering Transport Costs. Intensive collaboration along Rwanda's two trade corridors has already lowered costs and increased exports, but costs can decline even more. Lowering regional road tolls and ensuring their uniform application across all EAC vehicles is one avenue. Reviewing tax policy to ensure that truckers from all countries compete on a level playing field is another. Developing Rwanda as a regional logistics hub by attracting pioneer foreign firms in logistics would further lower transport costs and strengthen nascent services exports. RwandAir has provided the basis for expanding air connectivity, and its efforts have reduced the cost of air cargo. More can be done here, in part by aggressively pursuing open skies arrangements within the EAC and SADC. Rail connectivity also could become important eventually; a long-standing ambition to build a railway along the two trade corridors continues to hold promise for reducing freight costs.

Increase Service Sector Productivity. Lower policy barriers to services competition and stronger services trade within the region would enhance competitiveness across the EAC. Rwanda should look to broaden value added tax exemptions on services exports by aligning itself with leading African countries such as Mauritius and South Africa. Rwanda would benefit from elevating tourism promotion in a separate, high-visibility strategy that seeks to expand leisure tourism beyond gorillas and to convince tourists to spend more time in Rwanda. In the decades ahead, Rwanda is strategically positioned to take advantage of exports in mining, education, and business services. Realizing these opportunities requires seeking out foreign firms and facilitating near-term services trade for EAC and SADC professionals, which can be strengthened by extending mutual recognition agreements beyond architecture, accounting, and engineering to include, for example, legal, finance, and consulting services. Abolishing limits in work-permit regimes for all eligible professionals is also critical and would help to facilitate services trade for short-term assignments. However, stimulating services exports requires considerable investment in addressing Rwanda's skills deficit.

Attract Private (Foreign and Domestic) Investment into Tradable Sectors. More private investment is needed in tradable sectors. Building on its investor promotion activities, the government could track firm performance and tailor specific incentives to priority sectors. To improve Rwanda's export competitiveness and compensate for relatively high transport costs, the government could offer additional, integrated assistance across ministries (for example, by linking the Rwanda Development Board's investment promotion with the Rwanda Revenue Authority's ability to exempt import tariffs and the Rwanda Standards Board's support for standards upgrading and certification). The solid results in the special economic zone offer a model that could be extended to the whole productive sector. Upgrading the product quality of domestic firms through a designated supplier development program would offer great potential by enabling domestic firms to supply large international firms, which could facilitate integration within global value chains. Such a program also would provide an opportunity for strengthening regional manufacturing exports.

Faster Urbanization, Greater Agglomeration

Introduction

Few countries have attained upper-middle-income status without substantial urbanization. Urbanization is the spatial corollary of structural transformation that involves the movement of workers from less to more productive sectors—typically from farming to off-farm sectors in the early stages of development. Urbanization has the potential to generate enormous benefits by increasing economic density, which, when managed well, facilitates the transmission of knowledge and ideas, increases economies of scale and opportunities for specialization, and improves firms' access to both critical services and a large pool of labor with a wide variety of skills. Cities are also instrumental in matching skilled people with jobs that value those skills. The presence of these *agglomeration economies* means that the more workers and firms are added to an urban location, the higher their individual productivity becomes. International evidence suggests that a 1 percentage point increase in the urban population is associated with a 3–8 percent increase in a country's per capita income.

The close association between urbanization and economic development is seen most vividly in the high-growth economies of East Asia. These economies have had intense spatial concentration of economic activity, typically in locations well connected to domestic and external markets.

Consider the "flat" development trajectories of China, Korea, Thailand, and Vietnam in figure O.22, panel a. The flat slopes reflect the fact that their urbanization has been accompanied by sharp increases in per capita income. However, in an unsupportive policy environment, urbanization can just as easily be disconnected from economic transformation; many countries in Sub-Saharan Africa have urbanized even more rapidly than their East Asian counterparts, but with minimal or negative growth of GDP per capita (figure O.22, panel b).

Rwanda is on a path to rapid urbanization and needs to manage the process well to harness the urban agglomeration economies that are essential for future high growth. The country's urban population has more than doubled since 2002, and Kigali has been one of the fastest-growing African cities. This report's analysis shows that urbanization has accounted for 37 percent of national structural change in Rwanda, and urban areas have accounted for 48 percent of national labor productivity growth over the past 15 years. However, urban areas in Rwanda—and Kigali in particular—have not generated the kind of productivity gains and agglomeration economies that rapidly growing cities in successful East Asian economies have achieved. The pace of rural-to-urban migration also has been relatively muted,[20] which has limited the potential benefits of urbanization.

Institutional, regulatory, and infrastructural reforms are needed along three dimensions—spatial, sectoral, and institutional—and should be supported by even faster rural-urban migration and deeper economic specialization. The nature of agglomeration economies, however, differs by the function of different urban settlements. Rwanda's small towns, secondary cities, and Kigali should perform complementary functions, differentiated by the type of scale and agglomeration economy they can deliver.

FIGURE O.22 Changes in urbanization and income in East Asia and Pacific and in Sub-Saharan Africa, 1985–2010

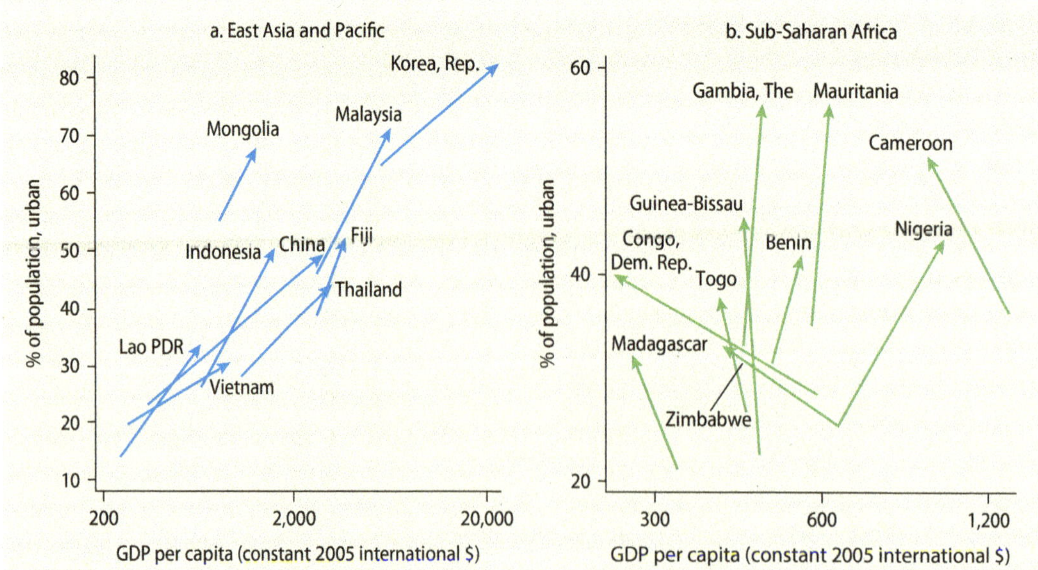

Sources: Based on World Development Indicators data (World Bank, various years); *Economist* 2012.
Note: Bottom of arrow = 1985; top of arrow = 2010.

Challenges and Opportunities

To achieve the rapid economic growth targeted until 2050, Rwanda needs to have an efficient portfolio of urban locations. With its relatively small population, Rwanda requires one especially strong urban economic powerhouse—of the sort that Seoul was for Korea or Tokyo for Japan. Kigali has that potential. To fulfill its urbanization potential, Rwanda also needs to have a portfolio of complementary secondary cities and small towns.

However, although Kigali has seen rapid urbanization and strong urban infrastructure investments, its urban fabric remains fragmented by small-scale, patchy land development. Kigali needs to operate more like an effective, integrated labor and product market, which would increase its potential for realizing agglomeration economies and reduce the costs of private inputs and public infrastructure. As regards the secondary cities and small towns, Rwanda should be ready to support the emerging economic activities in those locations. There is great uncertainty concerning what kinds of economic activities will settle in which locations. All urban locations are showing similar trends, manifested in fragmented spatial development, poor transport connectivity, and weak fiscal handles.

Urban fragmentation in Rwanda is driven by institutional and infrastructural constraints. Inefficiencies in land use management are exacerbated by the ineffective implementation of master plans and urban design documents with targets for densities, building structures, and land uses that do not match current market demand. Rwanda essentially has been managing cities by regulating the type and intensity of private development by location—epitomized by the zoning of structural characteristics and building uses. Such mismatches, not uncommon in low- and middle-income countries, are particularly serious in Rwanda, because master plans are updated only irregularly. A lack of local planning capacity and inconsistent application of regulations exacerbate the problem.

Rural and urban connectivity is another key challenge. A third of Rwanda's poor live within 20 kilometers of a secondary city, yet the locational advantages are undetectable more than 5 kilometers from the city center. Half of the rural population lacks access to a road network in good condition within a 2-kilometer walking distance. Better rural-urban transport links around secondary cities would improve both their access to inputs and their impact on surrounding areas. Stronger rural-urban transport links also would enhance the benefits of growing urbanization along Rwanda's major transport routes, most notably along the Rubavu-Nyabihu-Musanze corridor, but also along corridors running south from Kigali to Burundi and the newly developed Kivu shoreline.

Outside of Kigali, own-source revenue mobilization is low—estimated at 10 percent of district budgets in 2013–14. Districts rely on central revenues and do not capture many of the gains from their investments. This reliance reduces both district resources for investment and the incentives to identify and prioritize investments where they are most likely to unlock growth.

Recommendations

Kigali has a crucial role to play in Rwanda's future development, because "urbanization" economies—especially those involving knowledge spillovers—are generated mainly by large cities. Market forces—reflected by the location decisions of people and businesses—have chosen Kigali. Durable investments in infrastructure, housing, and other amenities are needed to ensure that the city is productive and livable. However, Rwanda's small towns, secondary cities, and Kigali should be performing complementary functions, each differentiated by the type of scale and agglomeration economy they can deliver. These complementary urban locations do not have to be huge to generate agglomeration benefits. The size of settlements matters less than their function: with reasonable transport costs, towns can be large enough to facilitate internal scale economies. Medium-size cities are often large enough for "localization" economies that come from thick input markets. The implication is that policy makers should focus on the functions of different types of cities and support agglomeration though economic density.

As a general principle, policy makers should look to deliver a basic standard of services to all people, while letting markets pick the pace and form of private sector development by location. This principle is exemplified by Korea, which allowed the dense concentration of economic activity in Seoul, while delivering basic services like education, health care, and clean water evenly across the population. Investments in human capital are especially "safe" bets, because human capital is a portable asset that can have powerful effects on people's welfare and mobility.

Getting on the path to faster urbanization and greater agglomeration will involve *reshaping regulatory policy*, *prioritizing investments*, and *strengthening institutions* along three dimensions: spatial, sectoral, and institutional. On spatial reforms, a more bullish view is needed to unleash the economic potential of Kigali, which market forces have chosen as the main center of production and commerce. On sectoral reforms to enhance the efficiency of capital investment in infrastructure, housing, and commercial structures, there is an urgent need to strengthen land markets. On institutional reforms, stronger intergovernmental coordination of economic and spatial planning processes is needed.

Reshape Regulatory Policy. The main priority is to strengthen land markets so that private developers have the appropriate incentives to increase density. Rwanda should explore moving from the quantity-based regulation of land use, epitomized by highly prescriptive zoning requirements for structures, to price-based allocation. Land prices, which reflect the demand for and scarcity of locations, should become the basis for allocating private investments across space and for allowing structures to serve the evolving economy. Regulations on structures should be used to mitigate *negative externalities* like environmental degradation and structural safety.

Prioritize Investments. Another priority is to provide efficient, affordable, and integrated public transport and to boost investment in roads. Public transit routes to Kigali's center are congested and likely to become more so. To limit sprawl, excellent central public transport should be combined with quality public transport to a small number of strategic peripheral locations. Grids should be provided (in Kigali and in secondary cities) to ensure that rapid peripheral development takes place in a planned way. Greater investment in roads also is necessary to improve the integration of Rwanda's cities with the countryside and with neighboring countries and to strengthen connections between urban centers.

Kigali's growth needs to be accompanied by a more calibrated approach toward developing a complementary set of secondary cities and small towns. Potential investments in other settlements should be divided into those that can be made at low risk before market demand has emerged versus those that are better suited after it has emerged. Here, choices need to be made between investments in place-specific durable assets (such as infrastructure, industrial complexes, and housing) and people-focused portable assets (such as health, education, and water and sanitation). International experience shows that such investments should center on increasing external connectivity. Stronger connectivity, however, does not guarantee the greater development of secondary cities and other towns versus Kigali. Connectivity and specialization may well entail greater concentration of activities in Kigali.

The government has pursued a policy of grouped villages (*imidugudu*). The program provides rural-urban links by preparing future urban dwellers for urban life while they are in rural areas, and aims to preserve agricultural land. Improvement in the planning and establishment of settlements is needed to ensure that they serve the intended purpose while minimizing huge infrastructure costs and potential future financial losses. Prioritization of rural-urban connectivity and better anticipation of migration to larger urban areas are needed to address underlying concerns. This effort can be complemented with "off-grid" rural infrastructure (for example, maintenance of rural roads and bridges) that delivers key services while placing smaller "bets" on the long-run vocation of the location.

Strengthen Institutions. Faster urbanization and greater agglomeration require stronger institutions. Urban planning capabilities at the city and district levels need to be considerably stronger. Plans should respond to markets and community needs, while safeguarding against capture by special interests through strong public oversight and engagement. Further, broad institutional and governance reforms such as clarification of land and property rights set the foundations for urbanization and urban development.

Rationalization of planning activities is needed to foster institutional coordination. To accomplish this, economic planners should start to think spatially, and spatial planners should become more aligned with economic planning and goals.

Further, economically connected districts have to be encouraged and required to coordinate land use plans, transport and service provision, major infrastructure like special economic zones, tourism infrastructure, and so on to exploit complementarities.

Finally, stronger institutions are needed to value land, to disseminate land values publicly across uses, and to assign and protect property rights. Rwanda has a strong basis for efficient and transparent valuation, with centralized and digitized landownership and transaction records, a professional valuation body, and credible institutions for oversight. Credible land valuation would enable urban areas to fiscalize public investments in land through land value capture.

Competitiveness and Enterprise Development for Innovation-Led Growth

Introduction

Emergence of a vibrant, competitive, and innovation-driven enterprise sector—both private and public firms—that responds with agility to emerging domestic, regional, and global opportunities is essential for future growth. As Rwanda's economy develops and matures, the need for the private sector to play a leading role in achieving the rapid growth required to reach Rwanda's ambitious income aspirations only increases. Private enterprises create jobs and generate income, drive economic transformation, compete in global export markets, and, ultimately, drive aggregate productivity growth and innovation. Moreover, the private sector has to provide much of the huge investment needed to support future growth ambitions.

Rwanda needs to strengthen the competitiveness of the private sector as it undertakes necessary infrastructural investments. To support the development of viable enterprises, the government has continued the strong track record of reforms initiated after the genocide against the Tutsi, as evidenced, for example, in Rwanda's rapidly improved ranking in the Ease of Doing Business Index, which now need to be followed through with the reform measures described below.

The state has an equally important, but complementary, role to play in correcting market failures and defining its role in private investment—by implementing well-targeted public investments, strengthening bureaucratic capacity, withdrawing gradually from productive activity while enhancing its regulatory and facilitation functions, and developing capable and accountable market institutions. Public investments will remain important for several years to come, given the vast infrastructural and social needs of the country; that said, with growing financing needs under the National Strategy for Transformation and tightening limits on public borrowing, the relative share of public investment will decline over time as the private sector share increases. SOEs will also remain crucial for several years to come, because the private sector needs time to build.

The reform agenda to boost the competitiveness and innovativeness of the enterprise

FIGURE O.23 Share of firms in Rwanda, by firm size, 2011 and 2014

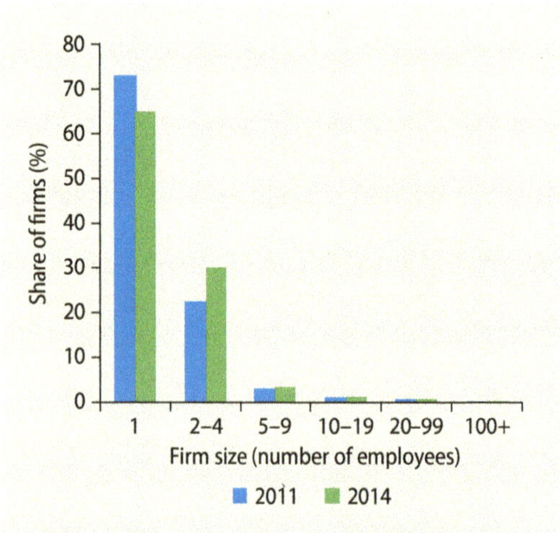

Sources: Calculations based on 2011 and 2014 Rwanda Census of Business Establishments data (NISR 2011, 2015).

sector is comprehensive and demanding, reflecting Rwanda's strong ambitions for future growth.

Challenges and Opportunities

The enterprise sector in Rwanda, in its current form, remains relatively small, young, and concentrated in the nontradable sector. Private sector firms are small (figure O.23); they lack the scale economies critical for competitiveness and have limited export presence. Moreover, as in other low-income countries, informality is prevalent.

The limited presence of formal enterprises reflects high cross-cutting costs, lower productivity than what is needed to sustain rapid economic growth, and low capacity for innovation.

Price levels and thus input costs are high in Rwanda, which constrains the competitiveness of its enterprises. Low- and middle-income economies tend to have lower price levels than high-income economies because of the lower costs of nontradable goods and services (the prices of tradable goods tend to be similar across all countries). This divergence in prices tends to close as countries' income levels rise. Rwanda's relative prices have followed such patterns, but at more elevated levels compared with other economies at similar stages of development. The contrast is especially stark when compared with the relative price trajectories of the Asian high-growth economies whose long-term performance Rwanda aspires to surpass. It was only when these economies reached income per capita of more than US$5,000 (2010 U.S. dollars, purchasing power parity) that the ratio of their price levels to those of the United States exceeded Rwanda's current ratio.

Low returns (real and perceived) also contribute to the slow uptake in private sector activity. Rwanda's labor productivity (output per worker) is low by international standards, explained by negative or weak growth in within-sector labor productivity across most sectors. Moreover, Rwanda's TFP levels (output generated by a given quantity of labor and capital) are low for its income, and the rate of TFP growth has slowed significantly in recent years, further widening the gap with other countries.

What explains Rwanda's weak TFP performance? A country's TFP has two key determinants. The first is the allocative efficiency of its resources (land, labor, capital)—that is, the extent to which these public and private resources get channeled to their most productive use. The second is the pace of technological innovation in the economy—that is, the pace at which the frontiers of technology and good business practices expand. The significance of technological innovation will gather pace as the Rwandan economy moves toward middle-income status and beyond, becoming an increasingly pressing subject of reform for future growth.

Resource misallocation refers to inefficient enterprises commanding more resources (land, labor, capital) than warranted by their productivity levels. Analysis of Rwanda's manufacturing sector suggests that TFP in Rwanda's manufacturing sector could be doubled if resource misallocations were reduced drastically (figure O.24). The scope for improving productivity through this channel is likely even larger in other sectors.[21]

Some of the underlying causes for misallocation are straightforward, rooted in

FIGURE O.24 Resource misallocation in formal manufacturing in Rwanda and select countries

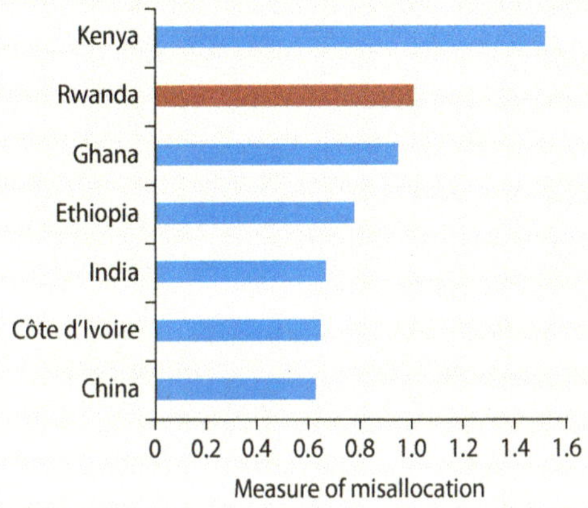

Source: Calculations based on NISR 2017.
Note: Resource misallocation is measured by the dispersion of marginal products of inputs across firms. Large dispersions suggest that frictions in input and output markets prevent the movement of productive resources across firms and that inefficient firms command more resources than warranted by their productivity.

the way in which both the state and markets allocate resources. Decisions on public investment—accounting for more than half of total investment in the economy—need to be guided by clear analysis of economic returns. Rwanda has made good progress in this regard, for example, in developing a robust public investment management system. Moreover, the government's focus in its industrial policy needs to shift toward differentiating firms and sectors by performance (past or potential).

Rwanda is in the early stages of building its innovation capacity, which is the ability to introduce new products, processes, ideas, technologies, and solutions. It needs to continue strengthening these capabilities for productivity-led growth to meet its long-term income ambitions. Although structural transformation and improved allocation of resources can stimulate labor productivity growth for another decade or so, sustaining it over a longer period will only be possible through the diffusion of innovation and technology.

Innovation capacity of Rwandan firms has been on an upward trend, but several challenges need to be addressed for Rwanda to be strongly positioned on innovation capacity. Currently, private enterprises do not serve as strong demanders of innovation. On top of that, managerial capabilities remain low, which undermines firms' capacity and incentives for upgrading technology and operating practices. Innovation is also hampered by the scarcity of links with foreign firms and export markets and by limited FDI in tradable sectors. The supply side of Rwanda's innovation system is only starting to emerge.

Recommendations

Rwanda's demanding reform agenda to boost the competitiveness and innovativeness of the enterprise sector reflects the government's great ambitions for growth. Key areas include the following.

Reduce Business Costs by Tackling Cross-Cutting Constraints. Rwanda has made substantial reforms to improve the business environment and support firms. The first imperative is to continue to improve affordable access to finance. Over time, capital markets and nonbank financial institutions need to be developed. There also is considerable potential for tapping into foreign sources of funding, which would require actions at the regional level to harmonize regulations and reduce barriers to services trade and investment. Next, to reduce the cost and increase the reliability of electricity, Rwanda needs to forecast and manage domestic supply and demand of energy, build capacity to procure and implement power-purchasing agreements, and better integrate system planning and system operations functions in the utility. Efforts to reduce logistics and broadband costs are also important for the competitiveness of enterprises in Rwanda.

Improve Effectiveness of the Government's Tax Incentives and Other Industrial Policy Interventions. Rwanda has already established some of the key preconditions for an effective industrial policy. However, incentives need to be linked more clearly to the productivity and export performance of beneficiary firms. Direct support should be focused on maximizing foreign exchange earnings (or savings) and targeted to strategic sectors well placed to generate exports, economic growth, and job creation. Crucially, a strongly monitored performance-based approach (focused on firm productivity and exports) should be mainstreamed in all interventions. Rwanda's industrial incentives need to be better coordinated across government agencies. Incentives also could do a better job of attracting FDI in tradable activities.

Define the Future Role of SOEs and Further Strengthen Their Corporate Governance. SOEs played an important role in the early stages of Rwanda's economic development and will continue to do so in the medium term. On the basis of sectoral assessment of the level of competition, competitiveness of SOEs versus private firms, economic development goals, and social considerations, a useful starting point would be to divide key sectors into four groups: (1) sectors in which SOEs will retain a monopoly; (2) sectors in which SOEs will compete with private firms; (3) sectors from which SOEs will withdraw when efforts to build up private sector capacity prove successful; and (4) sectors from which SOEs will withdraw immediately because the private sector is already capable and there is no compelling social rationale for them. Public-private boundaries can shift as the private sector gains strength. Strong government support will still be needed, but its role will increasingly be to facilitate private investment and build strong market institutions that signal priority sectors. Enterprise development in Rwanda must somehow resolve the sometimes-conflicting goals of alleviating market failures and encouraging private sector development. The reluctance of private investors to invest enough in public goods such as infrastructure is one market failure. Another may be low investment capacity among Rwanda's private sector.

Build an Effective National Innovation System. On the demand side, a strong competitive environment would encourage firms to seek out the best available knowledge and strengthen managerial capabilities to introduce new processes and technologies, integrate them in the production system, allocate skilled staff to use them, and make them financially viable. Improvements in management practices can be achieved through various training and coaching services, improvements in graduate-level management courses, and efforts to encourage increased interaction between multinational firms and local suppliers. Stronger coordination, monitoring, and evaluation of funding programs for science, technology, and innovation are also needed. The agenda on the supply side of innovation is discussed in chapter 1.

Transitioning Agriculture and Food to Be a Longer-Term Engine of Growth

Introduction

Agriculture has been a major source of national income and growth for Rwanda. It accounts for close to 70 percent of employment, more than 30 percent of GDP, and more than 50 percent of exports of goods. Agricultural value added has risen more than 5 percent a year over the past 15 years, which is a high rate of growth by global standards; and productivity in the sector has increased strongly. Further, growth in agriculture has likely stimulated growth in other sectors through backward links (for example, by encouraging input industries such as fertilizers) and forward links (for example, by increasing food processing). Widespread growth in the purchasing power of farm households in remote areas has also helped to mobilize unemployed local resources by increasing demand for local goods and services.

Considerable government effort has been devoted to developing the sector, especially after the food price shocks of 2007–08. Major government efforts have included development of new irrigated land, large-scale land consolidation, and land registration. The development of cooperatives has been a major component of state-led collective action, although there is scope for much more. Promotion of the use of fertilizers and improved seeds and effective interventions in livestock production have also contributed to growth in agriculture.

With this strong start, the main question now is how long and to what extent agriculture will remain an engine of growth in the Rwandan economy. Does Rwanda's highly ambitious economic future continue to have agriculture at its core, or will the sector be useful mostly to launch high long-term growth and then gradually take a back seat? This report contends that the agriculture sector will remain a major source of comparative advantage for Rwanda, even as the country climbs the income ladder over the coming decades.

Challenges and Opportunities

Periods of rapid growth in the past have largely reflected either the expansion of agricultural land or the increased use of inputs (figure O.25). However, there is diminishing marginal scope for further expansion of cultivated land. There is significant potential for continuing to improve farmer skills, extend irrigated area, stabilize and expand terraces, boost the use of more adapted fertilizers, and increase farmers' use of better seeds. Programs targeting these improvements could boost agricultural growth over the next decade or so. Maintaining rapid growth over a longer period, however, requires greater emphasis on TFP growth through more efficient allocation of resources and greater reliance on technological innovation.

For stronger productivity growth, the sector has to continue to modernize, become more responsive to market signals, and integrate more effectively with regional and global markets. Its contribution needs to shift from supplying commodities primarily for domestic use to producing higher-value-added goods as an integral part of food supply chains linked to regional and international markets. This effort requires an institutional, infrastructural, and policy environment led by the market, with a commensurate gradual shift in the public role to facilitating the fair implementation of those private sector decisions. Like any rapidly growing economy, Rwanda needs to evaluate shifting patterns of demand in regional and global markets, discover its core advantages, and then assess how they can best be deployed to specialize in food and other agricultural products that will maximize income gains.

Rapid increases in productivity also require more mechanization, higher use of inorganic fertilizer and improved seeds, and improved access to financing. Despite substantial progress in land consolidation, most of Rwandan agriculture is carried out under conditions of abundant labor on small plots, mostly on hillsides. The use of labor-saving machinery, such as tractors and combine harvesters, is confined to a few small niches. However, mechanical solutions are needed to expand bench terraces and extend irrigation at lower costs per unit, in both cases involving whole communities. Mechanical solutions also are needed for postharvest functions such as transport, processing,

FIGURE O.25 Decomposition of sources of agricultural growth in Rwanda, 1961–2014

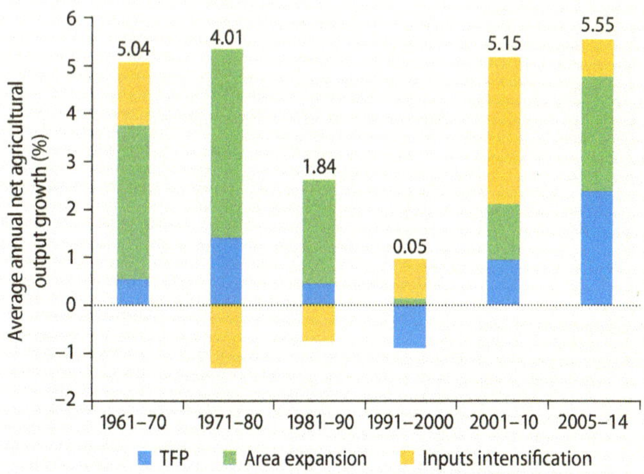

Source: Compiled from U.S. Department of Agriculture 2017 data.
Notes: The three sources of growth listed sum to output growth in the period in question. Output growth may be different than column height because of negative contributions to growth in the period in question. Growth not explained by area expansion or increased use per hectare of inputs (including labor) is attributed to total factor productivity (TFP). TFP is a combination of increased allocative and technical efficiency and technological change. Because the numerator of TFP (output growth) is highly affected by weather outcomes in any given year, it makes sense to consider TFP outcomes over at least a 10-year period that includes both good and less good weather. This explains the strategy for handling differences between the early and later parts of the period 2001–14.

and packaging. The declining use of inorganic fertilizer also needs to be reversed, by continuing to expand the coverage of locations and to improve the formulation of fertilizers. The government is already modernizing its seeds regulations and is also taking steps to legalize agricultural genetically modified organisms. Finally, limited agricultural finance remains a major constraint: the use of formal financial services in the agriculture sector is quite low.

Environmental concerns arising from global climate change and land degradation are a particular challenge that needs to be managed proactively for improving agricultural prospects in Rwanda. Rwanda has experienced a 1.4°C mean temperature increase since 1970 and is on track to experience another 1°C to 2.5°C increase over the next three decades. Higher temperatures have led to the spread of pests and diseases, impairing the health of livestock and humans, lowering crop yields, harming food security, and decreasing export earnings. Rainfall patterns, already highly variable in Rwanda, have become even more variable, with projections of a 20 percent increase in variability by the 2050s. In the east and parts of the south, this limits the availability of water and feed for livestock and increases the vulnerability to diseases. At the same time, heavier rains, particularly in the north and west of the country, increased floods and landslides, resulting in crop losses, health risks, and damage to infrastructure. Moreover, the combination of rain-fed, small-scale agriculture, high rainfall levels, and steep hillsides (where most of Rwanda's agriculture is practiced) leads to very high rates of soil erosion.

Rwanda can harness its comparative advantage in high-value crops and livestock products benefitting from a hillside environment combined with extensive biomass, intensive inputs of skilled labor, the ability to brand credibly (as in organic or Fair Trade), and the ability to support higher transport costs to final markets. Potential products include branded mountain cheeses, essential oils, potato chips, baby food, certified organic fruits and vegetables including jams and frozen dinners, packaged perishable animal products, cut flowers, and gourmet teas and coffees of specific geographic origins. Even under current conditions, Rwanda's comparative advantage in these items relative to its neighbors is strong by conventional measures.

Recommendations

In the medium term, Rwanda will have an agriculture sector that is increasing in productivity and adapting to the future. State-led efforts to increase agricultural productivity and maximize the sector's potential in Rwanda remain relevant in the medium term. These efforts involve extending the approach to consolidation of production decisions and intensification of staple food crops. Public support should continue to improve the efficiency of small farms that are still not using fertilizer in appreciable amounts, lack access to adequate agricultural water, are situated on unprotected hillside slopes, or use inferior seeds, so that such farms can achieve the technical efficiency of Rwanda's better farmers.

Higher agricultural growth in the longer run can only be achieved by reaping the benefits of scale economies and specialization through trade and the production of higher-value-added goods. Such efforts require a rapid response to market signals, ready access to investment resources, technical expertise, and ability to organize production and provide appropriate incentives for workers, led by the private sector. The state needs to continue playing a leading role as umpire, generator of public knowledge, provider of public goods such as infrastructure and basic research, and responder to other market failures. Targeted high-return initiatives should receive public financial support, accompanied by a rigorous evaluation to determine whether adequate returns are being achieved.

Public sector activities in agriculture will increasingly be targeted more effectively to providing key public goods in seven key areas.

Adapt Rwanda's Research and Regulatory Institutions to Evolving Opportunities and

Threats. A key element of Rwanda's comparative advantage is the credibility of its certifications, including ISO 22000 certification for food safety and Fair Trade standards under the Rwanda Standards Board. Organic certification also may become advantageous. The high technical expertise of the Rwanda Agriculture Board will be increasingly important as improving standards and Rwanda's efforts to expand exports increase the frequency and importance of sanitary and phytosanitary issues. Rwanda's reputation for probity and accountability is one of its most precious assets and is especially important in agriculture, where quality and food safety issues are dominant concerns of consumers.

Improve the Effectiveness of Policies on Vertical Coordination. Improved policies can be achieved by expanding participation in cooperatives and encouraging private sector aggregators. More effective vertical coordination in agriculture would be where private sector partners provide skills, capital, and entrée into international markets and where farmers acquire higher incomes and new resources. Government can improve general operating conditions for aggregators and develop a knowledge platform regarding which forms of industrial organization work best for addressing specific industrial organization problems. The platform could provide reliable data on vertical coordination, finance, prices, costs, and weather; this information is critical to reducing uncertainties and lowering risks for private investors and should encourage competition.

Engage with Neighboring Countries on a Regional Division of Labor. A regional division of labor would include both production based on comparative advantage and knowledge generation and diffusion. Rwanda has a major stake in increasing the importation of raw materials such as cereals for its food-processing and animal protein industries, while increasing its exports of processed foods and high-value calories, for example, from milk and meat products. Ways should be explored to guarantee the integrity of food security. Regional integration also should be pursued through continuing efforts to adopt science-based standards, product registrations, and certification of agricultural inputs.

Profit from the Big-Data Revolution in Innovation, and Make the Benefits of Big Data Accessible at Reasonable Cost to Smallholders. This effort is critical both to increasing innovation and private sector investment and to dealing with the smallest farms and most densely settled rural areas in Africa. "Smart farming," where just the right amounts of the right inputs are used for each parcel in response to information gathered by handheld devices with the right sensors, offers one such opportunity. Big-data approaches such as blockchain technology could offer the potential for lowering the costs of small financial transactions that require secure record keeping and decentralized input, such as land registration and mortgages.

Link Public Investments in Infrastructure More Effectively to Agricultural Development and Higher-Value-Added Products. Irrigation is clearly a constraint, especially in marshlands and in the drier eastern regions of the country. High-value export crops (such as horticulture for export) would likely cover the cost levels much more easily if cost-effective supply chains were in place that could realize international prices.

Further Develop High-Level Human Capital Formation in Agriculture. In particular, to achieve vertical integration, a more consistent approach is needed to training managers and technical experts working for aggregators. Companies could be involved in this effort through training programs to build up nationally needed skill sets in agribusiness, high-value supply chains, and agricultural technology. The best multinational companies have a track record of making these investments and provide examples of how investments in human capital can be done to mutual advantage.

Address Land Degradation and Global Climate Change More Comprehensively. Although considerable progress has been made in constructing robust "bench" (wide) terraces, much more needs to be done to secure Rwanda's land asset. Fortunately, the soil and water management interventions central to halting land degradation also would increase the ability of farmers to adapt to climate change through better water retention and improved soil quality. Landscape restoration and conservation are a community-level activity, not an individual one. Local government, producer groups, and national technical expertise and funding all have a role to play in implementation. The development and use of climate-smart and big-data agricultural technologies can further help farmers to cope with the challenges of climate change.

Capable and Accountable Institutions

Introduction

Emerging from very difficult initial conditions after the 1994 genocide against the Tutsi, Rwanda's leadership faced an enormous challenge not only of rebuilding a devastated economy but also, more broadly, of constructing a national identity and renewed sense of national purpose. Reestablishing peace and social stability and building the decimated social capital of trust were viewed as the underlying sociopolitical challenges of governance (see Jones and Murray 2018). The government's response was decisive in several forms, establishing security and seeking to channel social energies toward the national purpose of raising incomes, improving opportunities, and providing health and education to all citizens.

Along the way, the government created new homegrown solutions and programs to create an integrated Rwandan community, including revitalizing the community work program to bring people together around a common community purpose ("*Umuganda*") once a month; reestablished the traditional community courts (*Gacaca*) and created mediation committees (*abunzi*) to achieve reconciliation and mete out justice; sought to hold all government officials accountable for performance through the system of performance contracts (*imihigo*); established the Joint Action Development Forum, a participatory planning mechanism to improve the alignment of citizens' and districts' priorities; and created an annual forum for national dialogue (*Umushyikirano*) to allow all citizens to have direct access to the most senior leadership in government.

These efforts have proved effective, well reflected in Rwanda's international rankings, with particularly strong performance on indicators of government effectiveness, control of corruption, rule of law, and regulatory quality (figure O.26). Reflecting the government's high-profile anticorruption efforts, Rwanda was ranked 48 (out of 180 countries) for control of corruption on Transparency International's Corruption Perceptions Index in 2018, marking a vast improvement over its 2006 ranking of 121.

Challenges and Opportunities

Rwanda's strong overall governance has been a driving force behind its rapid growth and

FIGURE O.26 Benchmarking of Rwanda along the various dimensions of governance

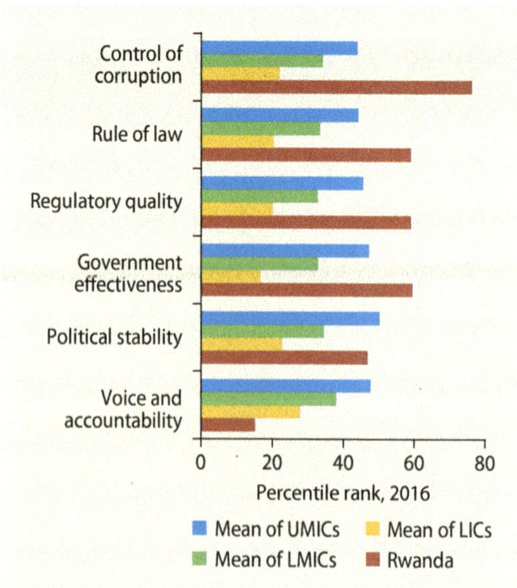

Source: 2016 Worldwide Governance Indicators from Kaufmann, Kraay, and Mastruzzi 2010.
Note: LIC = low-income country; LMIC = lower-middle-income country; UMIC = upper-middle-income country.

provides a key comparative advantage over most peers in the region. But the requirements of a middle-income Rwanda will be different—more demanding—than those that sufficed in the low-income period. Building effective institutions is a long-term endeavor. The improvements are necessarily incremental, building on global and local lessons and factoring in the specific context of the country.

To strengthen institutional effectiveness requires greater social capital of trust—between citizens, between civil society and government, and even within national political leadership. In Rwanda, interpersonal trust was understandably very low in the immediate aftermath of the genocide against the Tutsi. Impressive progress has been made since then on achieving reconciliation, promoting economic and social development, and strengthening the structures of governance. But more work is needed in this regard, given the strong positive relationship between trust and long-term development.

Key challenges also relate to limited innovation for public civil servants and local governments. *Imihigo* has made a strong contribution to instilling a culture of results. Building a more complex, richer society requires an approach where civil servants, local officials, and civil society can serve as a source of innovation. It also requires the government to obtain and act on feedback from citizens. Essentially, public institutions need to become more innovative, better coordinated, and more adaptive.

To achieve continued, rapid growth, an effective market-based economic system is needed to encourage private sector development, matched by financial resources of the state. Despite Rwanda's impressive improvements in governance, private sector investment and the entry of new firms remain low, reflecting gaps in market institutions. Creating special courts and fast-track procedures to adjudicate small claims; further promoting alternative means of resolving commercial disputes (such as arbitration, mediation, and conciliation); boosting reliance on technology; increasing training and specialization of justice sector employees, including judges, prosecutors, and investigators; and improving case management techniques would enhance the judiciary's effectiveness in enforcing contracts. Further improvements in the efficiency of the land management system and provision of more resources to implement the law on intellectual property would strengthen property rights. Reviewing the performance of fiscal incentives with a view to reducing expansion in Rwanda's tax expenditures, increasing local government revenue collection, ensuring that the state captures an appropriate share of the expected rise in mineral revenues, and taking further steps to raise Rwanda's strong public financial management to international standards would strengthen the state's financial capacity.

A final set of governance challenges has to do with accountability mechanisms between the government and citizens. Rwanda has in place homegrown initiatives, which aid in creating demand for accountability by citizens through making them shareholders of development.

Recommendations

Strong growth over the next decades will depend on specific institutional requirements, including a market system that encourages entrepreneurs to take more risks in search of higher rewards by protecting private property and minimizing policy uncertainty.

Strong growth also requires enhancing state effectiveness through three core institutional pillars: (1) enabling innovative, coordinated, capable bureaucracy and local governments; (2) using efficient market signals to enable strong cooperation between the state and the business sector and maintaining fiscal prudence; and (3) strengthening public administration accountability. All three components are essential for an effective state (figure O.27), which, in turn, is necessary for sustained high growth.

Pillar 1: Enable Innovative, Coordinated, Capable Bureaucracy and Local Governments. To achieve strong growth

FIGURE O.27 A framework for assessing effectiveness of state institutions in Rwanda

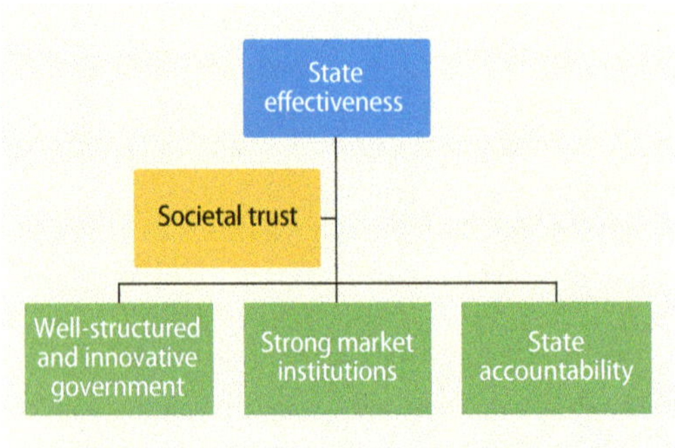

over the next decades, well-structured, capable, and empowered civil service and local governments are needed, with the resources and other incentives to be innovative (even entrepreneurial). Such innovation entails the incentives and resources to inform decision makers and challenge them with evidence and analysis when needed; to share information and coordinate actions within and outside the administration; and to take informed risks, experiment, scale up successes, and learn from failures. Creating such institutions will strengthen capacity and coordination within the government and make progress on decentralization to encourage local initiative and eliminate overlaps in responsibilities.

Modifying the *imihigo* to adopt multiyear targets with annual benchmarks (rather than focusing only on short-term goals), making greater use of qualitative surveys, and placing a stronger focus on outcomes rather than processes could enhance innovation. Increasing the importance of the joint *imihigo* and a strong delivery unit to coordinate policies on key cross-cutting issues would improve interagency coordination. Further increases in training by the Rwanda Management Institute should be supported by skills audits and functional reviews to identify the missing skills in the public sector. Regular compensation reviews, higher compensation for individuals with scarce skills, and the development of nonfinancial incentives could become increasingly important to retain and attract highly skilled staff as competition for scarce skills increases from private companies.

Pillar 2: Strengthen Market Institutions and Fiscal Prudence. The evidence is compelling that functioning markets require well-defined rules of the game, enforced transparently and predictably. Advanced economies (almost as a rule) have a system of highly evolved economic institutions that convey prices, define property rights, enforce contracts and competition policies, and close informational gaps between buyers and sellers (Commission on Growth and Development 2008). As part of its long-term development, Rwanda has to develop these key market institutions (for competition, contract enforcement, and property rights), backed by strong financial capacity of the state.

Establishing the Rwanda Inspectorate and Competition Authority and extending its mandate to monitor the impact of SOEs on competition, promoting the principle of competitive neutrality to ensure equal treatment of all investors, and removing regulatory barriers to entry and rivalry in input sectors would improve the competition framework. Creating special courts and fast-track procedures to adjudicate small claims, promoting alternative means of resolving commercial disputes (such as arbitration, mediation, and conciliation); boosting reliance on technology; increasing training and specialization of judges, and improving case management techniques would enhance the effectiveness of the judiciary system for contract enforcement. Further improvements in the efficiency of the land management system, better public information on market values of all categories of land, and provision of more resources to implement the 2008 law on intellectual property would strengthen property rights. Increasing local government revenue collection, ensuring that the state captures an appropriate share of the expected rise in mineral revenues, and taking further steps to strengthen Rwanda's public financial management will be crucial. A better balance has to be found between public investments that are expected to generate high returns over the long term versus investments in areas with potentially high short-term returns based on market signals of scarcity.

Pillar 3: Enhance the State's Accountability to Citizens. For institutions to remain legitimate, the state has to be "citizen-centered," supported by an effective feedback loop between civil society and local governments and service providers. The capacity and motivation of citizens to participate with state actors in assessing service delivery and finding solutions are critical for Rwanda's emergence as a strong, successful middle-income economy.

Reform measures can seek to strengthen checks and balances further to improve accountability over the executive, local officials, and service providers. Strengthening key watchdog agencies (the Public Accounts Committee, the Office of the Auditor General, the Office of the Ombudsman, and the Rwanda Governance Board) could improve government accountability. Greater involvement of citizens in local decision making (for example, in setting *imihigo* objectives) and reliance on more qualitative information in monitoring performance would strengthen support for local government and improve the quality of services.

Notes

1. Worldwide, almost 80 percent of income growth of the poor is due to increases in countries' income levels (Dollar and Kraay 2016). Rwanda, too, has witnessed the close association between growth and general improvements in welfare along several dimensions of welfare in the past two decades, as chronicled in this report.
2. Key liberalization measures included (1) elimination of most price controls; (2) liberalization of exchange rates in 1995; (3) lowering of tariff rates from 35 to 18 percent; (4) liberalization of the monetary and financial sectors, including adoption of new currency exchange regulations, creation of private commercial banks, and privatization of state-owned banks; (5) liberalization of current account operations (imports, exports, services); (6) elimination or easing of certain restrictions on capital flows, including the transfer of capital and revenues related to foreign direct investment and the free withdrawal from foreign exchange accounts in commercial banks (Ggombe and Newfarmer 2017).
3. This report considers the period 1995–2005 as the recovery period and the subsequent phase as the postrecovery period.
4. This stagnation mostly reflects a decline in private savings, as government savings increased. The savings-investment gap has been made up by external assistance and, increasingly, by FDI inflows.
5. Although future investment does not have to be financed through domestic savings if the country has ready access to external financing, running large external imbalances over long periods has proved unsustainable for countries.
6. Rwanda's high costs stem from the small market size, long distance to external markets (by virtue of being landlocked), shallow and costly credit markets, high cost of energy generation, and scarcity of land that increases the rent on it.
7. For example, Lendle and Olarreaga (2017) find that the impact of distance on cross-border trade flows—across 61 countries and 40 product categories—is about 65 percent smaller for eBay transactions relative to total international trade. More generally, Osnago and Tan (2016) find that a 10 percent increase in an exporter's rate of Internet adoption leads to a 1.9 percent increase in bilateral exports.
8. Initial signs are encouraging. FabLab, an innovation hub at the government-backed ICT park, has started to work with three-dimensional printers (BBC 2016).
9. Rwanda's priorities in this regard are already well reflected, for instance, in the soon-to-roll-out 4G LTE broadband network—a wireless broadband technology designed to support roaming Internet access via cell phones and handheld devices.
10. Three drone ports, which will allow the drone network to send supplies to 44 percent of the country, are expected to be completed by 2020.
11. These countries are Argentina, Brazil, China, India, Indonesia, Korea, Mexico, the Russian Federation, Saudi Arabia, South Africa, and Turkey. Korea is counted in this group because it was not yet a high-income country in 1990, the base year for the comparison.
12. For example, Chinese domestic companies have captured larger market shares and moved

up the value chain in highly competitive manufacturing industries, such as high-end chemicals, electronics (in particular, information technology), automotive, and aircraft.

13. Robotics, automation, computerized manufacturing, and artificial intelligence could reduce the advantages of production in low-labor-cost emerging economies, discouraging offshoring from and favoring reshoring to these countries.
14. Purchases of real estate properties by Chinese individuals in high-income countries also contributed to the boom in FDI outflows. Outflows from Korea have also increased, driven by rising greenfield investments.
15. In 2015, the top 10 investors (by FDI stock) in Africa were the United States, United Kingdom, France, China, South Africa, Italy, India, Singapore, Switzerland, and Malaysia.
16. High dependency imposes costs at the household and national levels, in the form of education, health care, social protection, and other essential needs of children and the elderly. When dependency ratios are low, under conducive conditions, lower costs should support higher growth through higher savings and investments, including in building human capital of children.
17. For example, Mindspark, an interactive computer-assisted learning software, increased math scores by 0.59 standard deviation and language scores by 0.36 standard deviation for a group of Indian students in 90 days (Muralidharan, Singh, and Ganimian 2017). Similarly, the Adaptive Mathematics Platform that has been used by half of students in grades 3–6 in Uruguay improved math scores by 0.2 standard deviation, equivalent to half a semester of schooling (Perera and Aboal 2017).
18. The main exports to the Democratic Republic of Congo include livestock and crops, but the Democratic Republic of Congo also provides an important source of (informal) cross-border trade in services such as finance, transportation, and wholesale trading (Lalui 2016).
19. Nguyen (2017) shows that a competitive exchange rate is likely to boost Rwanda's growth by boosting its exports and manufacturing production but also cautions that the costs and institutional requirements of maintaining an undervalued exchange rate have to be considered before embarking on any such policy.
20. Only 14 percent of Rwanda's urban population were recent migrants from rural areas in 2014, while only 20 percent of recent internal migrants moved from rural to urban areas (NISR 2015).
21. Efficiency of resource allocation across sectors can be just as important as allocation within sectors. However, the available data do not permit a comparison of the magnitude of misallocation of resources across sectors in Rwanda and in other countries.

References

Akamatsu, K. 1962. "A Historical Pattern of Economic Growth in Developing Countries." *Journal of Developing Economies* 1 (s1): 3–25.

Bashir, S., M. Lockheed, E. Ninan, and J.- P. Tan. 2018. *Facing Forward: Schooling for Learning in Sub-Saharan Africa*. Washington, DC: World Bank.

Basinga, P., P. J. Gertler, A. Binagwaho, A. L. B. Soucat, J. Sturdy, and M. J. C. Vermeersch. 2011. "Effect on Maternal and Child Health Services in Rwanda of Payment to Primary Health-Care Providers for Performance: An Impact Evaluation." *Lancet* 377 (9775): 1421–28.

BBC (British Broadcasting Corporation). 2016. "Rwanda's Technology Revolution Helps Country Forge New Path after Genocide." BBC, May13. http://www.bbc.com/news/world-africa-36285889#.

Brenton, P., and G. Isik. 2012. *De-Fragmenting Africa: Deepening Regional Trade Integration in Goods and Services*. Washington, DC: World Bank.

Chukwuma, O. 2003. "Rwanda—The Search for Post-Conflict Socio-Economic Change, 1995–2001." Africa Region Working Paper 59, World Bank, Washington, DC. http://documents.worldbank.org/curated/en/643271468759893135/Rwanda-the-search-for-post-conflict-socio-economic-change-1995-2001.

Commission on Growth and Development. 2008. *The Growth Report: Strategies for Sustained Growth and Inclusive Development*. Washington, DC: World Bank.

Diao, X., J. Randriamamonjy, and J. Thurlow. 2017. "Urbanization and the Future of Economic Development in Rwanda." International Food Policy Research Institute, Washington, DC. Background paper for *Future*

Drivers of Growth in Rwanda, World Bank, Washington, DC.

Dihel, N., A. M. Fernandes, and A. Mattoo. 2012. "Developing Professional Services in Africa through Regional Integration." In *De-Fragmenting Africa: Deepening Regional Trade Integration in Goods and Services*, edited by P. Brenton and G. Isik. Washington, DC: World Bank.

Dollar, D., and T. Kraay. 2016. "Growth Is Still Good for the Poor." *European Economic Review* 81 (January): 68–85.

Economist. 2012. "Daily Graph: The Urbanisation Trap." *Economist* (online), October 2.

EDC (Education Development Center). 2017. *Literacy, Language, and Learning Initiative (L3): National Fluency and Mathematics Assessment of Rwandan Schools*. Report for the U.S. Agency for International Development. Waltham, MA: EDC.

Feenstra, R. C., R. Inklaar, and M. P. Timmer. 2015. "The Next Generation of the Penn World Table." *American Economic Review* 105 (10): 3150–82. www.ggdc.net/pwt.

Freund, C., and T. Moran. 2017. "Multinational Investors as Export Superstars: How Emerging Market Governments Can Reshape Comparative Advantage." Working Paper 17-1, Peterson Institute for International Economics, Washington, DC.

Galasso, E., A. Wagstaff, S. Naudeau, and M. Shekar. 2016. "The Economic Costs of Stunting and How to Reduce Them." Policy Research Note, World Bank, Washington, DC.

Gereffi, G. 1999. "International Trade and Industrial Upgrading in the Apparel Commodity Chain." *Journal of International Economics* 48 (1): 37–70.

Gereffi, G., and O. Memedovic. 2003. "The Global Apparel Value Chain: What Prospects for Upgrading by Developing Countries?" United Nations Industrial Development, New York. https://ssrn.com/abstract=413820.

Ggombe, K., and R. Newfarmer. 2017. "Rwanda: From Devastation to Services—First Transformation." WIDER Working Paper 2017/84, United Nations University World Institute for Development Economics Research, Helsinki.

Government of Rwanda. 2017. "7 Years Government Programme: National Strategy for Transformation (NST1): 2017–24." Draft. Government of Rwanda, Kigali.

Hallward-Driemeier, M., and G. Nayyar. 2017. *Trouble in the Making: The Future of Manufacturing-Led Development*. Washington, DC: World Bank.

Inglehart, R., C. Haerpfer, A. Moreno, C. Welzel, K. Kizilova, J. Diez-Medrano, M. Lagos, P. Norris, E. Ponarin, and B. Puranen, eds. 2014. *World Values Survey: Round Six—Country-Pooled Datafile 2010–2014*. Madrid: JD Systems Institute. http://www.worldvaluessurvey.org/WVSDocumentationWV6.jsp.

Jones, W., and S. Murray. 2018. "Consolidating Peace and Legitimacy in Rwanda." Country Study, London School of Economics, Oxford Commission on Fragility, Growth, and Development, London.

Kaufmann, D., A. Kraay, and M. Mastruzzi. 2010. *The Worldwide Governance Indicators: Methodology and Analytical Issues*. Washington, DC: Brookings Institution Press.

Lalui, A. 2016. "Analysis of Cross-Border Trade in Services: Issues and Trends with a Focus on Rwanda and DRC." TradeMark East Africa, Kigali.

Lemarchand, G. A., and A. Tash, eds. 2015. *Mapping Research and Innovation in the Republic of Rwanda*. GO-SPIN Country Profiles in Science, Technology, and Innovation Policy, vol. 4. Paris: United Nations Educational, Scientific, and Cultural Organization (UNESCO).

Lendle, A., and M. Olarreaga. 2017. "Can Online Markets Make Trade More Inclusive?" ADBI Working Paper 742, Asian Development Bank Institute, Tokyo.

Lutz, W., W. P. Butz, and S. KC. 2014. *World Population and Human Capital in the Twenty-First Century*. Oxford, U.K.: Oxford University Press.

Muralidharan, K., A. Singh, and A. J. Ganimian. 2017. "Disrupting Education? Experimental Evidence on Technology-Aided Instruction in India." NBER Working Paper 22923, National Bureau of Economic Research, Cambridge, MA.

Newfarmer, R., J. Page, and F. Tarp, eds. Forthcoming. *Industries without Smokestacks: African Industrialization Revisited*. Oxford, U.K.: Oxford University Press.

Nguyen, H. 2017. "Real Exchange Rate Misalignment and Its Relationship to Output Growth in Rwanda." Background paper for *Future Drivers of Growth in Rwanda,* World Bank, Washington, DC.

NISR (National Institute of Statistics of Rwanda). 2011. *Establishment Census 2011*. Kigali: NISR, September.

———. 2015. *Rwanda Poverty Profile Report 2013–2014: Results of Integrated Living Conditions Survey (EICV)*. Kigali: Government of Rwanda. September.

———. 2017. "Seasonal Agricultural Surveys—Season A (May) and Season B (September)." NISR, Kigali.

OECD (Organisation for Economic Co-operation and Development). 2017. "The Future of Global Value Chains: 'Business as Usual' or 'A New Normal'?" Directorate for Science, Technology, and Innovation Policy Note, OECD, Paris.

Osnago, A., and S. W. Tan. 2016. "Disaggregating the Impact of the Internet on International Trade." Policy Research Working Paper 7785, World Bank, Washington, DC. https://openknowledge.worldbank.org/handle/10986/24866.

Perera, M., and D. Aboal. 2017. "Evaluación del impacto de la plataforma adaptativa de matemática en los resultados de los aprendizajes." Centro de Investigaciones Económicas, Montevideo.

Ranis, G., F. Stewart, and A. Ramirez. 2000. "Economic Growth and Human Development." *World Development* 28 (2): 197–219.

Rodrik, D. 2015. "Premature Deindustrialization." NBER Working Paper 20935, National Bureau of Economic Research, Cambridge, MA.

Shepherd, B., J. de Melo, and R. Sen. 2017. "Reform of the EAC Common External Tariff: Evidence from Trade Costs." IGC Policy Paper, International Growth Centre, Kampala.

UNCTAD (United Nations Conference on Trade and Development). 2017. *Science, Technology, and Innovation Policy Review*. Geneva: UNCTAD.

———. 2018. "The Task Ahead Is Great Say African Leaders as Continent-wide Free Trade Deal Is Signed." UNCTAD (news), March 21. http://unctad.org/en/pages/newsdetails.aspx?OriginalVersionID=1695.

UNECA (United Nations Economic Commission for Africa). 2018. "Signing AfCFTA Giant Stride Forward for the Development of Africa: ECA's Vera Songwe." UNECA (news), March 21. https://www.uneca.org/stories/signing-afcfta-giant-stride-forward-development-africa-eca%E2%80%99s-vera-songwe.

UNFPA (United Nations Population Fund). 2017. "Unlocking Rwanda's Potential to Reap the Demographic Dividend." Policy Brief, UNFPA, New York, October.

United Nations. Various years. Comtrade database. New York: United Nations.

USAID (U.S. Agency for International Development). 2017. *Literacy, Language, and Learning Initiative: National Fluency and Mathematics Assessment of Rwandan Schools*. Washington, DC: USAID.

U.S. Department of Agriculture. 2017. International Agricultural Productivity database. Washington, DC: Economic Research Service. https://www.ers.usda.gov/data-products/international-agricultural-productivity/.

World Bank. 2007. *Rwanda: Toward Sustained Growth and Competitiveness*. 2 vols. Washington, DC: World Bank. https://openknowledge.worldbank.org/handle/10986/7700.

———. 2015a. "Building a Reform Consensus for Integrated Corridor Development in the East African Community." World Bank, Washington, DC.

———. 2015b. *Rwanda: Employment and Jobs Study*. Washington, DC: World Bank.

———. 2016. *Vietnam 2035: Toward Prosperity, Creativity, Equity, and Democracy*. Washington, DC: World Bank.

———. 2019. *Doing Business 2019: Training for Reform*. Washington, DC: World Bank.

———. Various years. World Development Indicators database. Washington, DC: World Bank. https://data.worldbank.org/data-catalog/world-development-indicators.

Zeitlin, A., C. Leaver, O. Ozier, and P. Serneels. 2017. "Recruitment, Motivation, and Retention Effects of Teacher Performance Pay." Project Report S-38408-RWA-1, International Growth Centre, London School of Economics, London.

1

Human Capital and Innovation

Introduction

The government's aspirations to reach upper-middle-income status by 2035 will require dramatic improvements in both the amount and the quality of human capital. Economies that have grown rapidly over an extended period have made substantial investments in the health and education of their citizens. These efforts are urgent: Rwanda's investment in human capital lags behind the average of low-income countries—for example, in stunting and in primary and lower-secondary school completion (figure 1.1). Moreover, investments in human capital contribute to growth only after beneficiaries have grown up. Only a small fraction of the population enters the labor force each year, so even dramatic improvements in education will improve the skills of the overall workforce only slowly. Under the current rate of improvement, Rwanda will still have low-income-country rates of human capital in 2035. The sooner Rwanda increases its human capital investments, the sooner it will be on a track to achieve more rapid growth.

Rwanda also has to improve the quality of human capital: 85 percent of Rwandan students at the end of grade 3 were rated "below comprehension" on a recent reading test, and one in six students in grade 3 could not answer a single reading comprehension question (EDC 2017). Holding the amount of knowledge constant, there is no clear link between education and growth: if students are failing to learn, then investments in education will not stimulate economic growth.

Human capital investments begin in early childhood, including prenatal and early child nutrition and cognitive stimulation; they continue with high-quality basic education, higher education opportunities, and on-the-job training and adult education. They also include investments in health, including early child nutrition but also vaccinations for children and preventative and curative health care for children and adults. Finally, a strong economy invests in innovation to create new opportunities. To achieve long-term, rapid growth, dramatic progress is needed in a wide range of policies supporting human capital formation.

Government can invest in a range of interventions to address stunting, including investments to improve food security, access to clean water and good sanitation, access to nutritional supplementation, and awareness of good nutritional practice. The National Early Childhood Development Program (NECDP) has been established to

FIGURE 1.1 Human capital outcomes in Rwanda and other countries, by income level, 2015

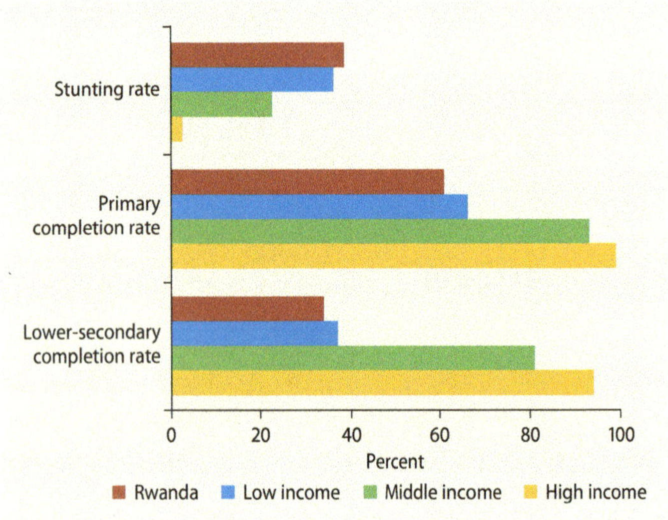

Source: World Development Indicators data (World Bank, various years).

address issues of coordination and inconsistent financing. Rwanda will need a big push across areas, with careful monitoring to evaluate which policies deliver the greatest gains.

Expanding access to basic education means reducing the costs for families. Countries that have achieved widespread basic literacy have offered free primary education. Although Rwanda provides primary education without charge, families are often obliged to pay incidental fees. Achieving universal primary education will require ensuring that children are not turned away for failure to pay incidental fees and providing families with information so that they understand the financial returns to schooling.

Improving the quality of education in Rwanda means improving the quality of teachers. Rwanda's teachers generally attend school and teach, but teachers need better training so that children in the first three years get a firm grasp on literacy before transitioning to English. Because these improvements take time, transitioning to English later (for example, at the end of primary) may also be valuable, so that children do not transition to a new language until they have mastered basic skills in the first language. Many teachers in the upper grades of primary and in secondary have a limited grasp of the language of instruction: at last measure, only 43 percent of teachers were assessed at the "intermediate level" in English. Although a great improvement over a decade ago, this level of competency falls far short of what is needed for effective teaching. Rwanda may wish to leverage its major investment in laptops in schools to provide teachers with regular opportunities to improve their English.

Technical and vocational training is hard to get right, so Rwanda needs to ensure quality and encourage youths to participate in high-return programs. Many high-growth countries (the Republic of Korea, Malaysia, and Singapore) have supported skills development by setting a strategic direction, tone, and culture for efforts to improve workforce skills, creating an organizational infrastructure with appropriate governance, and fostering efficient and effective management of service delivery by providers. Collection and dissemination of information on the quality of skills providers and the returns to different skills would encourage youth to participate in high-return sectors and help to improve the quality of skills training programs.

Rwanda is building its tertiary sector, but more focus is needed on high-return activities. University enrollment has doubled from a decade ago, and Rwanda has taken dramatic steps to improve the quality of tertiary education, consolidating public universities into the University of Rwanda for better governance. Increasing access to financing, including loosening restrictions on private financing, would help to expand enrollment. At the same time, it is important to encourage university students to enter high-return fields; high-income countries do so by offering financing incentives (as in Argentina and Australia) and by improving the quality of science and engineering instruction in earlier grades (as in Norway and Poland).

The tertiary sector is an ideal space to foster innovation. Publications and patents in Rwanda have been rising, and Rwanda has invested in a range of graduate and postgraduate centers for technical training. Creating incentives to develop and adapt innovations that benefit industries in Rwanda can help to reap the maximum returns to local innovation. In high-income countries, private firms finance university research to solve production challenges. In Rwanda, given the small private sector, government may need to continue to play a supporting role.

It will be impossible to expand human capital dramatically without spending more. Each human capital investment builds on previous investments. The returns from investments in tertiary education and skills training are realized almost immediately. However, for returns to expand, Rwanda needs to increase the flow of well-educated individuals from earlier levels and, ultimately, to produce a population with broad literacy and numeracy.

Better information can improve the quality of human capital investments. Rwanda is an innovator in holding service providers accountable, with performance contracts for educators and health workers, along with innovations in performance-based pay (Basinga et al. 2011; Zeitlin et al. 2017). In many countries, service provision has improved because of the effective involvement of parents, pointing to the importance of dissemination of information on learning outcomes and other elements of school performance.

This chapter analyzes each element of human capital in turn—health (with a focus on stunting and fertility), basic education, skills training, and tertiary education—with an analysis of the current state, key challenges, and potential investments to help Rwanda to meet its ambitions. This discussion is informed by lessons from the experiences of countries that have achieved rapid gains across these areas and begins by proposing a framework for thinking about human capital investments in Rwanda.

Why Is Human Capital Important for Growth?

Investments in human capital have been linked closely to growth. A decade ago, a high-level commission identified 13 economies that had grown at an average rate of 7 percent a year or more for 25 years or longer since 1950. They concluded, "Every country that sustained high growth for long periods put substantial effort into schooling its citizens and deepening its human capital" (Commission on Growth and Development 2008). Human capital includes the knowledge and skills of the population and results from investments in education and health. Ultimately, human capital investment and economic growth form a virtuous cycle: greater human development increases economic growth, and greater economic growth finances further human development. Cross-country analysis demonstrates that countries that invest in human capital early in the cycle enjoy the benefits of this virtuous cycle, whereas countries that experience high initial economic growth without investing in human capital virtually always fall into a vicious cycle of low human capital followed by a slowdown of economic growth (Ranis, Stewart, and Ramirez 2000).

Human capital is essential because it influences growth directly and increases total factor productivity. In the long-run history of global economic growth, education leads to greater technological development, and technology tends to complement skills, thus raising the returns to education (Commission on Growth and Development 2008). Current cross-country estimates of the drivers of economic growth demonstrate that human capital leads to higher total factor productivity, which in turn boosts economic growth (Ranis, Stewart, and Ramirez 2000). Regardless of what other natural resources Rwanda may identify, human capital investments are crucial to a sustained, high economic growth strategy.

To achieve growth via services or manufacturing or innovation, Rwanda needs human capital investments. Economic growth through services comes not from low-skill services, such as petty trading, but from services that are higher on the supply chain, such as processing goods for sale in the market. To organize and support such an industry at scale requires workers with skill. Economic growth through manufacturing can employ low-skill workers, certainly, but a sizable cohort of high-skill managers and technicians is essential. Higher-skill workers are capable of carrying out higher-skill tasks, which add greater economic value. Economic growth through innovation requires a significant cohort of workers with strong training in their field, usually with tertiary or postgraduate education. For a highly skilled cohort of tertiary graduates, Rwanda needs to have a broad base of secondary school graduates with good skills.

Korea offers an example of the link between human capital and high, sustained economic growth. When Korea was at the same level of per capita income as Rwanda today, in 1967, it had much higher rates of skill in the workforce than Rwanda (figure 1.2). For example, whereas about 59 percent of Rwanda's population has at least a primary education, 70 percent of Korea's population was at that level. A decade into its high growth, 85 percent of Korea's working-age population had at least a primary education and 4 percent had completed tertiary. Current projections for Rwanda 10 years from now are 72 percent with at least primary and just 1.2 percent with completed tertiary. Furthermore, Korea experienced growth in an era when average human capital was much lower globally, so the returns to even low levels of human capital were higher. In recent years, human capital investments have expanded globally, which means that higher and better investments will be needed to sustain high rates of economic growth.

FIGURE 1.2 Rates of human capital in Rwanda and the Republic of Korea at similar income levels

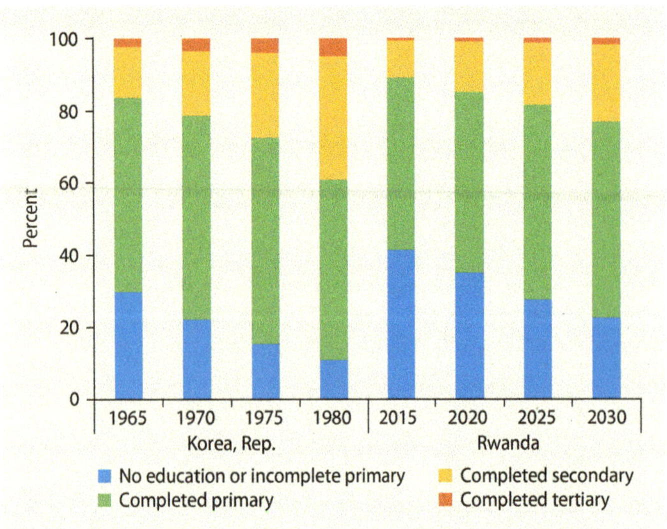

Sources: Data from Barro and Lee 2015; Lee and Lee 2016.
Note: In 1967, the Republic of Korea was at a similar level of per capita income as Rwanda today.

A Framework for Thinking about Human Capital

Investments in human capital have a strong link to economic growth. Investments in human capital continue throughout the life cycle and include investments in early childhood development, basic education, higher education, skills formation as adults, health services, and innovation (figure 1.3). All of these investments are tied to growth over the long term. For example, Rwanda had a stunting rate of 36.5 percent at last measure, and economic estimates suggest that per capita income for today's workforce is 10 percent lower than it would be if no one in the workforce had been stunted as a child (Galasso et al. 2016; World Food Programme 2016). The quality of learning has a clear, positive association with economic growth, much more so than the enrollment rate (Hanushek et al. 2008). While the relationship between higher education and economic growth depends on the quality of higher education, "One does not get electrical engineers and computer scientists without investing in higher education," as Hanushek (2016) puts it. On-the-job training likewise shows clear economic returns (Saraf 2017). Health services are essential to a productive workforce, and innovation is key to job creation.

Rwanda—along with other countries—faces an array of needs with regard to human capital investment. Investments tend to favor

FIGURE 1.3 The array of human capital investments

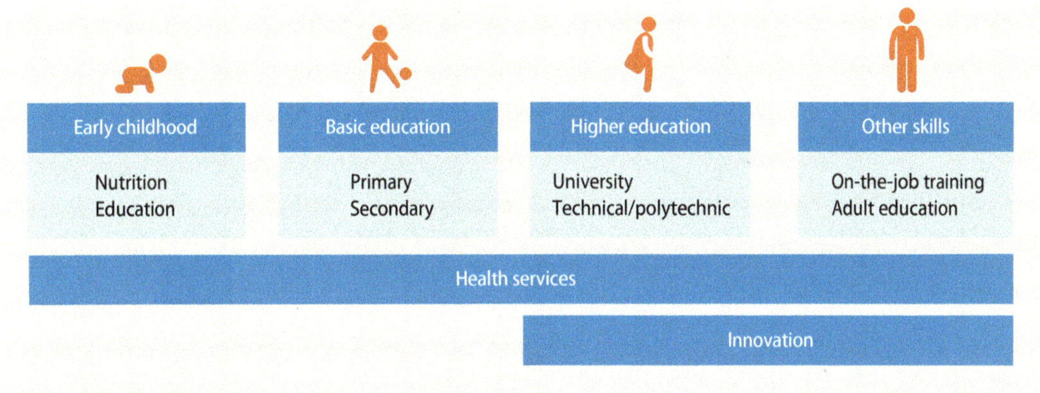

today's needs (persons in the workforce or about to enter it) or tomorrow's needs (persons early in their education). Investments in favor of today's needs—such as investments in vocational training, innovation, and higher education—tend to deliver the quickest returns because the beneficiaries are about to enter the workforce. Investments in favor of tomorrow's needs—reducing stunting, improving early child development, and increasing the quality of primary education—tend to deliver the highest returns because early investments increase the productivity of later investments (Carneiro and Heckman 2003; figure 1.4). Children with good nutrition in the early years go on to learn more effectively throughout their school career, and children who master reading in the early grades are most equipped to learn professional or technical skills later. Of course, Rwanda will continue to invest in each stage. But investments yielding returns that are realized more quickly need to be balanced with investments in younger generations; otherwise, higher education will forever be playing catch-up.

Government should consider two principles in setting investment priorities to maximize the impact on growth. First, it is necessary to identify the "binding constraints." Which problems are so severe that, unless they are solved first, no amount of money or time spent solving the less severe problems will help (van der Berg et al. 2016)?

FIGURE 1.4 The trade-off between lower returns now and higher returns later

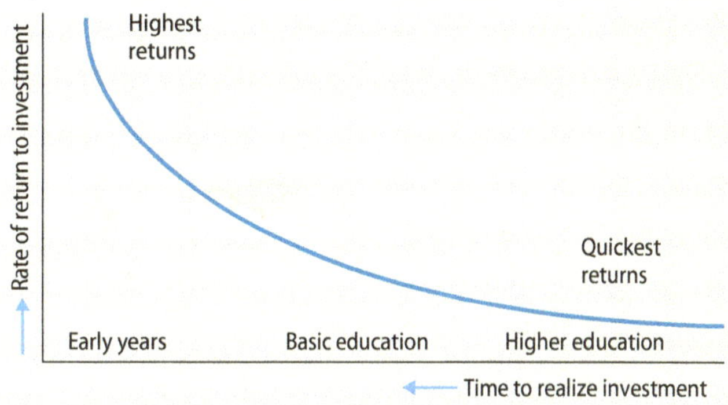

Second, it is necessary to identify the investment that will be required in activities that yield economic growth both now and later. Considering these two criteria together, Rwanda will continue to make investments in both the early and the later years (for economic growth both now and sustained over time) and to identify the binding constraints in each of those areas. Complementary investments, such as safety nets, can help households to make investments that will contribute to inclusive growth (box 1.1).

Stunting

Current Status

Despite the launch of several successful initiatives, representing strong political will

BOX 1.1 What is the role of social safety nets for economic growth?

Rwanda has invested heavily in social safety nets, through the Vision 2020 *Umurenge* Program and others. Social safety nets play two potential roles in sustained economic growth. First, they increase the inclusivity of growth. Not all economic growth is equally effective at reducing poverty. Indeed, economic growth has reduced poverty less in Sub-Saharan Africa than in other regions (Chuhan-Pole et al. 2013). They also protect the most vulnerable households from extreme poverty and give them opportunities to make productive investments. Cash transfers in Brazil and Mexico dramatically reduced inequality, improving the quality of life for the poorest households (Soares, Ribas, and Osório 2007). Across Africa, households receiving transfers have invested in productive assets such as livestock (Ralston, Andrews, and Hsiao 2017).

Second, social safety nets have the potential to increase the rate of economic growth. In Zambia, households that had received three years of transfers were spending 67 percent more than the size of the transfer. This suggests a multiplier effect. Households are able to convert every dollar received in transfers into much more than a dollar's worth of income through both agricultural production and off-farm activity (Handa et al. 2018). Furthermore, safety nets may contribute to growth by increasing human capital investments and helping households to manage risk (Alderman and Yemtsov 2013).

and civil society cooperation, stunting still represents a major challenge in Rwanda.[1] At last measure, 36.5 percent of children suffered from stunting. Although this is a major improvement since 2005, when half of all children were stunted, it exceeds global and regional rates of stunting. The global rate is 22.9 percent, while East Asia and Pacific, Latin America and the Caribbean, and Sub-Saharan Africa have achieved lower levels of stunting (figure 1.5). Rates are also higher in Rwanda than in many countries with similar levels of income (figure 1.6). Senegal has achieved significantly lower levels of stunting—18.7 percent—because of major programs to tackle child undernutrition. Furthermore, the elasticity of stunting with respect to economic growth in Rwanda and elsewhere in Africa is less than half that in the rest of the world, so future economic growth cannot be counted on to eliminate stunting. Although Rwanda has made impressive progress on acute malnutrition—wasting—chronic malnutrition, represented by stunting, has been slower to improve, and stunting shows strong links with household poverty and national economic growth.

The average level of stunting masks variations related to socioeconomic and geographic characteristics across Rwanda. The poorest 20 percent of the population has a stunting rate of 49 percent, whereas the richest 20 percent has a rate of 21 percent (figure 1.7). Between 2000 and 2015, stunting rates for children in richer households declined 3.2 percent a year, whereas rates

FIGURE 1.5 Stunting rate in Rwanda versus the world, 1995–2015

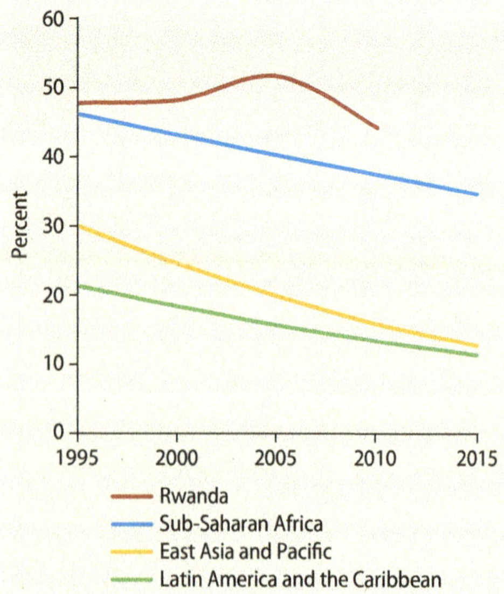

Source: World Development Indicators 2017 data (World Bank, various years).

FIGURE 1.6 Prevalence of stunting and GDP per capita, 2017

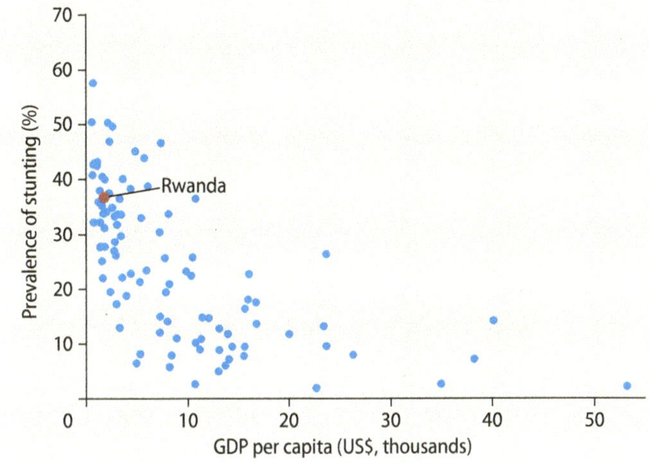

Source: World Development Indicators 2017 data (World Bank, various years).

FIGURE 1.7 Prevalence of stunting in Rwanda, by wealth quintile, 2000–15

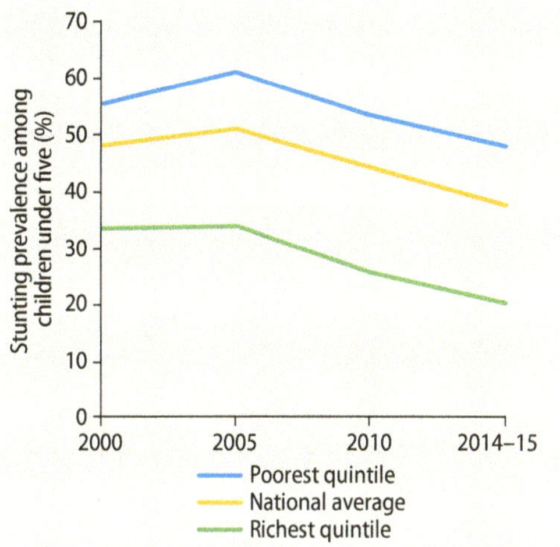

Source: Eozenou and Shekar 2017.

for children in poorer households declined only 1 percent a year (Eozenou and Shekar 2017). The western districts of Rwanda have a higher concentration of stunting (map 1.1), and stunting levels are much higher among rural residents (40.6 percent) than among urban residents (24 percent).[2] Among children under five, boys have a higher rate of stunting (41 percent) than girls (33 percent). Children whose mothers have attained secondary education or higher have stunting levels of 20 percent, compared with 47 percent for children whose mothers have no education. Households struggle to satisfy the nutritional needs of their children as family size increases. Among poorer populations, there is a positive relationship between stunting rates and increasing birth order—approximately 40 percent of children in the first two birth orders are stunted, and this rises to 47 percent of children in the third and 50 percent of those in the fourth birth order. Poorly nourished mothers have children with higher levels of stunting than well-nourished mothers.

This stunting has significant short- and long-term impacts on human capital and—ultimately—on economic growth. Adults who were stunted in childhood have poorer

MAP 1.1 Prevalence of stunting in Rwanda, by district, 2014–15

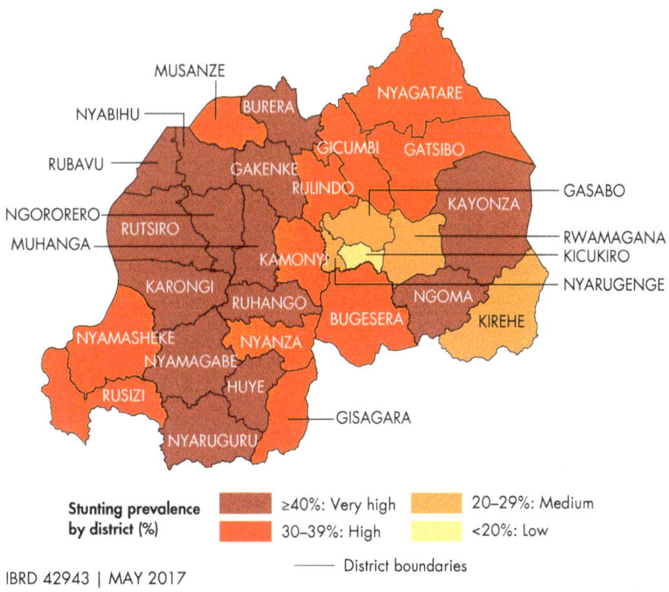

Source: Eozenou and Shekar 2017.

health and shorter height, are at risk of suffering noncommunicable diseases like hypertension, and have lower cognitive ability and fewer socioemotional skills. This relationship translates into reduced productivity and lower wages, which ultimately affects economic growth. By one estimate, the per capita income for today's workforce could be 10 percent higher in Rwanda if the adults had not been stunted as children (Galasso et al. 2016). By another estimate, stunting currently leads to a loss of US$820 million—11.5 percent of Rwanda's gross domestic product (USAID 2014). These impacts spill over to the next generation, with stunted women more likely to have babies who are underweight and who have cognitive challenges (Galasso et al. 2016).

Proximate Causes

Lack of diversity in food intake and inadequate frequency of meals before the age of two increase the incidence of malnutrition and stunting. Inadequate diets are a result of limited knowledge about feeding practices and food insecurity. Approximately 40 percent of households in Rwanda are food insecure. These households typically are rural, depend on low-income agriculture, and have few adult household members. They often have high micronutrient deficiencies: "45% of food insecure households had not consumed any protein-rich food in the week prior to the Comprehensive Food Security and Vulnerability Analysis Survey" (Hjelm 2016). As a result, only 20 percent of Rwandan children consume iron-rich food and only 18 percent of children between 6 and 24 months meet the requirements for a minimum acceptable diet (Hjelm 2016). Within these early months, the first 1,000 days are particularly crucial, with longer-term impacts (Shekar et al. 2016).

There is a high incidence of deficient WASH (water supply, sanitation, and hygiene) practices and poor environmental health, which influences stunting levels. Although access to improved water and sanitation facilities has increased significantly since 2005, children from poor and vulnerable households do not have sufficient coverage. According to the 2014/15 Demographic and Health Survey, more than 91 percent of rural households do not have a handwashing station and approximately 60 percent of rural households drink untreated water (NISR, various years). Only one-third of two-year-olds have access to both improved water sources and sanitation facilities (Eozenou and Shekar 2017). The lack of access to WASH facilities induces diarrheal diseases, inhibits children's ability to absorb nutrients, and leads to malnourishment and stunting.

Despite improvements over the past 15 years, care practices for mothers and children remain inadequate. The first 1,000 days of a child's life are a critical period of intervention: inadequate care during this period leads to irreversible damage. Rwanda has made great strides in increasing exclusive breastfeeding rates until the six-month mark; in 2015, 80 percent of children were breastfed (USAID 2014). However, suboptimal complementary feeding practices between 6 and 24 months of age hinder early childhood development—between 6 and 9 months of age, one in three infants is not fed the recommended mix of breast milk and solid food (USAID 2014). With respect to care practices for mothers, only 42 percent of women receive the recommended four antenatal visits (World Bank 2017a). Other care practices, including facility delivery and postnatal care, also have increased, but coverage in rural Rwanda remains low.

Across individual interventions (adequate access to food, care, and WASH practices), improved care practices (specifically antenatal visits and facility delivery) are most significant in explaining changes in stunting. An intervention that addresses only care practices reduces the probability of being stunted by 8 percent. Given that stunting is a result of multiple interrelated factors, these interventions are most effective when combined. For example, interventions that improve both environmental health and care practices reduce the probability of stunting by 12.5 percent.

Investments for Transformation

High rates of stunting are not inevitable, and many countries have made dramatic gains over time. Many countries that already had stunting rates below 50 percent have achieved significant reductions in stunting (figure 1.8), including Peru, Senegal, and others. If Rwanda were to reduce stunting in the coming years at the same rates as quick-reducers have done, stunting could be significantly lower in coming years (figure 1.9). Peru reduced its stunting by 50 percent over the course of 10 years through a program endorsed publicly by high-level political officials, including micronutrient supplements (which Rwanda already includes in its program), a massive media campaign, a careful monitoring system, and a performance-based incentive program. Senegal likewise made impressive gains in a short time period, despite weak economic growth, through high-level political commitment, nutrition financing, and a multisectoral strategy.

How did Peru reduce its stunting rates? Peru's strategy for reducing stunting had four key components:

1. *Performance-based incentive program.* The Ministry of Economy and Finance coordinated efforts by providing a monetary incentive through its results-based budgeting program. Every agency's budget was dependent on improving stunting-related indicators, such as the number of child-growth checkups and nutrition counseling sessions.
2. *Media campaigns.* Across Peru, there was a drive to deepen parents' understanding of malnutrition through various outlets, including radio and television. The dissemination of information made the problem more visible, which increased the demand for health and nutrition services among vulnerable populations.
3. *Monitoring systems.* The government implemented regular data collection and monitoring systems in order to focus on results and to ensure accountability.
4. *Multisectoral effort.* The government integrated nutrition into social protection policies. The supply of health and nutritional services was tied to *Juntos*, a nationwide conditional cash transfer program.

FIGURE 1.8 Reduction in stunting in countries with less than 50 percent stunting

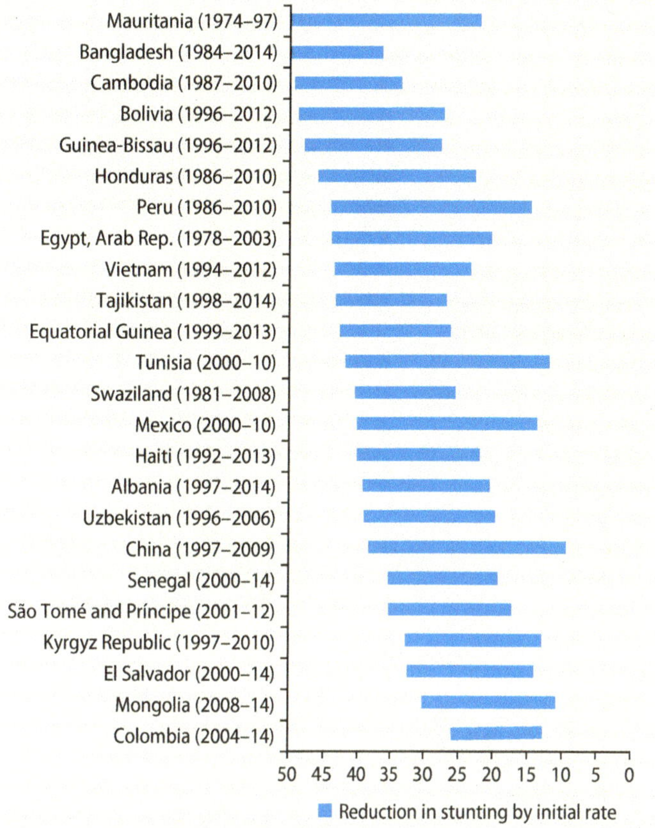

Source: Based on data from World Development Indicators (World Bank, various years).
Note: The time period next to the country name indicates the period over which the stunting reduction was calculated. The bars indicate the level of stunting at the beginning (left) and end (right) of the period.

How did Senegal reduce stunting rates?

- *Nutrition financing.* The government tied financing to nutrition-based outcomes to improve the demand for and supply of health and nutrition services.
- *Community-based multisectoral strategy.* The Prime Minister's Office coordinated efforts between local governments and civil society organizations to deliver health and nutrition services, such as health education and breastfeeding promotion, to communities.

Reducing Rwanda's stunting rate will require multiple interventions, but incentives are key. Stunting results from poor child

FIGURE 1.9 Projected reduction in stunting in Rwanda, 2000–35

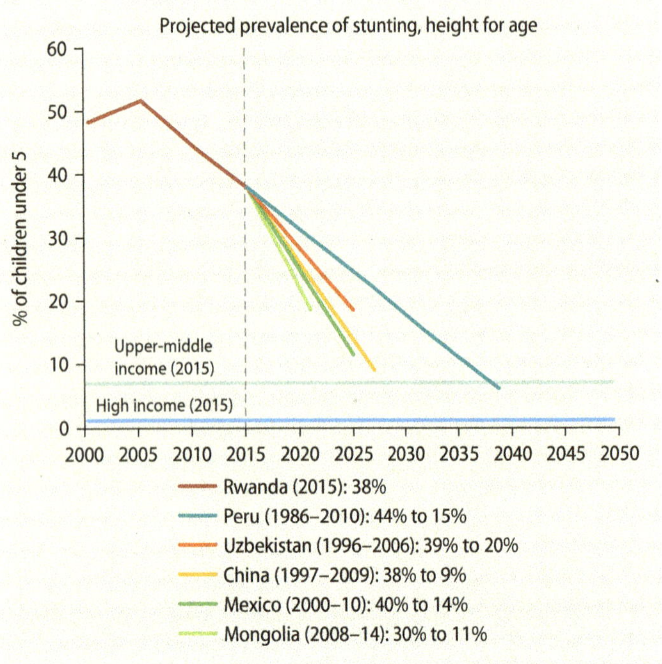

Source: Based on data from World Development Indicators (World Bank, various years).
Note: Projections are based on actual rates of stunting reduction in other countries. The legend shows the period over which the reduction in stunting was calculated, as well as the level of stunting at the beginning and end of the period. All comparator countries began their period of rapid reduction at a level comparable to that of Rwanda.

nutrition, but solving it requires a range of investments: food security, access to clean water and good sanitation, access to micronutrient supplementation, and awareness of good nutritional practices. Many programs to address these issues are in place, and the NECDP has been established to address issues of coordination and inconsistent financing. To reap the gains in long-term growth from having well nourished children, Rwanda will need to make a big push across areas and to monitor carefully which policies deliver the greatest gains, Without regular measurement, it is impossible to gauge progress. One key factor in Kirehe District, which reduced stunting in the youngest children to 7 percent in 2015, was incorporating nutrition indicators in performance contracts at all levels, including the household (World Bank 2017a).

Rwanda already has a strategy for reducing stunting, but greater effort is required. The Economic and Poverty Reduction Strategy for 2013–18 and the National Strategy for Transformation (NST) 2017–2024 prioritized nutrition, food security, and early childhood development. There are district plans to eliminate malnutrition for all 30 districts, including several initiatives at the local and central levels. Monitoring and evaluation systems measure progress on nutrition-specific performance indicators. These monitoring systems include baseline and endline surveys to understand important nutrition behaviors, practices, and coverage levels and to assess the quality of service delivery. In addition, information systems are used to monitor the health of vulnerable women and children. However, key barriers are hindering the impact of these initiatives. Despite the development of an overarching national strategy, a lack of consistency in communicating messages around childhood stunting has led to inefficiencies. Often, stunting prevention is not a priority in donor-funded activities and is not aligned with WASH intervention strategies. Hence a key action is to fast-track implementation of the National Social and Behavior Change Communication Strategy for Integrated Early Childhood Development, Nutrition, and WASH (2018–2024).

More human and financial resources should be devoted to preventing stunting. Several existing interventions, such as antenatal care, micronutrient supplementation for pregnant women, malaria treatment in pregnancy, zinc supplementation, and the public provision of complementary food, could be scaled up across Rwanda in order to improve coverage. Sustainability and accountability mechanisms are key aspects of effectively scaling up an intervention. Service delivery should build the capacity of local governments and civil society. Nutrition-specific indicators tied to performance contracts at all levels of implementation can serve as an effective accountability mechanism.

Finally, interventions should target the first 1,000 days of a child's life. Because the first 1,000 days are crucial in determining a child's developmental trajectory, interventions should target the demand for and supply of services during this critical period. Specifically, interventions should target complementary feeding practices between 6 and 24 months of age. Food fortification and the promotion of diversified, nutrient-rich food for both mothers and children drastically reduce the incidence of stunting.

Fertility

Current Status

Between 2005 and 2010, Rwanda achieved one of the fastest reductions in fertility rates—a drop from 6.1 births per woman to 4.6—in Sub-Saharan Africa.[3] This notable decline was a result of several population reforms, particularly the new National Population Policy of 2003, which addressed high fertility and mortality rates as well as maternal and early childhood morbidity. The provision of family planning services is likely to have had the most significant impact on lowering fertility rates, primarily by increasing the use of contraceptives among married women, from 17 percent in 2005 to 52 percent in 2010 (Westoff 2013). In addition, influential mass media campaigns by the government increased contraceptive use and decreased family sizes. A substantial downward trend in under-five child mortality, from 196 per 1,000 births in 2000 to 38.5 in 2015, may have influenced fertility as parents saw a rise in their children's survival rates.[4] These reforms, coupled with an improving socioeconomic environment, led to changes in reproductive behavior and a subsequent decline in birth rates.

However, fertility rates are now declining slowly, similar to pre-2005 levels. Between 2010 and 2015, fertility rates fell from 4.6 to 4.2 births per woman. Rwanda needs to accelerate this decline in order to decrease the pressures of a high youth dependency ratio on the country. As of 2015, 40 percent of the population was under the age of 15, limiting the ability to save and invest for the future (UNFPA 2017). Achieving a steep decline in birth rates will allow for a favorable demographic transition, with more working-age adults and less youth dependency. Concurrent investments in economic and social spheres are crucial, because a large working-age population with no access to employment could become a source of social risk.

Investments for Transformation

Several policy options are available for accelerating a decline in fertility rates.

- *Improve adoption of, access to, and effectiveness of family planning programs.* This could include increasing the use of contraceptives among underserved populations (teenagers and women in rural areas), scaling up community-based distribution of family planning services, and retraining health care providers on permanent methods of contraception (intrauterine devices, implants, and sterilization). Examples include Bangladesh, India, and Sri Lanka, where female and male sterilization was incentivized to increase the adoption of family planning services in the 1970s (Silva de Tiloka 2017).
- *Education programs.* The Comprehensive Sexuality Education Program could be implemented in schools, and students could be given improved access to youth-friendly facilities that specialize in sexual and reproductive health services. Effective education campaigns that reduce teenage pregnancies and early marriage could be scaled up. Rwanda could continue its efforts to encourage small family norms. Brazil took a unique approach to educating its citizens about reproductive health and family planning by including relevant messages in soap operas (Silva de Tiloka 2017).
- *Address neonatal mortality rates (death in the first month of life).* Health care facilities could be better equipped to address postpartum health complications. In addition, women could have greater access to antenatal, postnatal, and

delivery care. In order to address high neonatal mortality rates in Vietnam, all children under the age of six from poor households were eligible for free health care through the Health Care Fund for the Poor (WHO, World Bank, and Ministry of Health, Vietnam 2015).

An accelerated decline in fertility can positively affect economic growth if Rwanda harnesses the demographic dividend. As the working-age population grows and youth dependency ratios fall, incomes rise. The decline in youth dependency ratios can increase investments in the health and education of every child, creating a more productive workforce in the future. Evidence shows that lower fertility can improve labor force participation rates and education levels, particularly for women. It can also affect national savings rates and investment (Karra, Canning, and Wilde 2017). In order to harness the benefits of this favorable age structure, Rwanda will simultaneously have to develop a healthy and skilled workforce, create quality jobs in sectors other than agriculture, and strengthen governance systems by improving efficiency and accountability.

Basic Education

Current Status

Rwanda faces the same two challenges as many other countries: access and quality of education. Rwanda has made great strides in ensuring access to education. Net primary school enrollment—the proportion of children of primary school age who are actually in primary school—exceeds 95 percent. Secondary school enrollment, although much lower, has also been rising. Gross secondary enrollment—the number of children in secondary school divided by the number of children of secondary school age—is 37 percent, more than three times as high as it was in 2000. This is great progress. Net secondary enrollment—the number of children of secondary school age in secondary school divided by the number of children of secondary school age—is slightly lower, at about 27 percent, because it does not capture overage students due to grade repetition in earlier years.

Although access has improved over time, Rwanda still lags behind the average of countries of similar income. One measure of access is the primary or secondary completion rate. This measures not only whether youths are enrolling in school but also whether they are completing levels of schooling. Currently, Rwanda's primary completion rate is about 61 percent, as opposed to about 66 percent in low-income countries as a whole. Likewise, completion rates for lower-secondary school are at 34 percent in Rwanda versus 37 percent in low-income countries as a whole.

Rwanda will not achieve upper-middle-income status without a dramatic increase in school completion. Even the bottom 25th percentile of upper-middle-income countries have primary completion rates of 94 percent, about 50 percent higher than Rwanda's current rate. The median primary completion rate in upper-middle-income countries is nearly 100 percent (figure 1.10). Likewise, the median lower-secondary completion rate for upper-middle-income countries is 87 percent, more than 2.5 times Rwanda's current rate. The disparity is even greater for upper-secondary completion. Expanding basic education, together with ensuring quality, is essential for Rwanda's sustained growth.

Even among students in school, the quality of education in Rwanda needs to be raised. The first recommendation coming out of the 2017 Joint Review of the Education Sector was to emphasize "quality of education at all levels, particularly in lower grades for Kinyarwanda, English, and mathematics" (Ministry of Education, Rwanda 2017). Why so? Recent measures indicate that students in P1 (first grade) can read 7.7 words per minute in Kinyarwanda, and students in P2 can read 25 words per minute. Although the number of words that children need to be able to read in order to understand what they are reading—a reasonable definition of literacy—varies from language to language, this level is well below literacy in any measured language. In P1, 60 percent of students could not answer a single reading comprehension question, and more than 85 percent were graded as reading "below comprehension," meaning that they could not answer four out of five comprehension questions correctly.[5] At the end of P3 (third grade), the final year of instruction in Kinyarwanda, the percentage of students scoring zero on the comprehension test is better: just 17 percent or one in six students. However, 85 percent were still reading "below comprehension," and 50 percent were still reading between 1 and 32 words per minute. In P4 (fourth grade), the official language of instruction switches to English. At the end of P4, reading comprehension in Kinyarwanda (which is still taught as a school subject) rises to 40 percent—still well under half—but nearly 50 percent of learners cannot answer a single comprehension question in English, the language of instruction for all of their subjects over the course of the year.[6]

FIGURE 1.10 School completion rates in primary and secondary school in Rwanda compared with countries at different levels of income, 2017

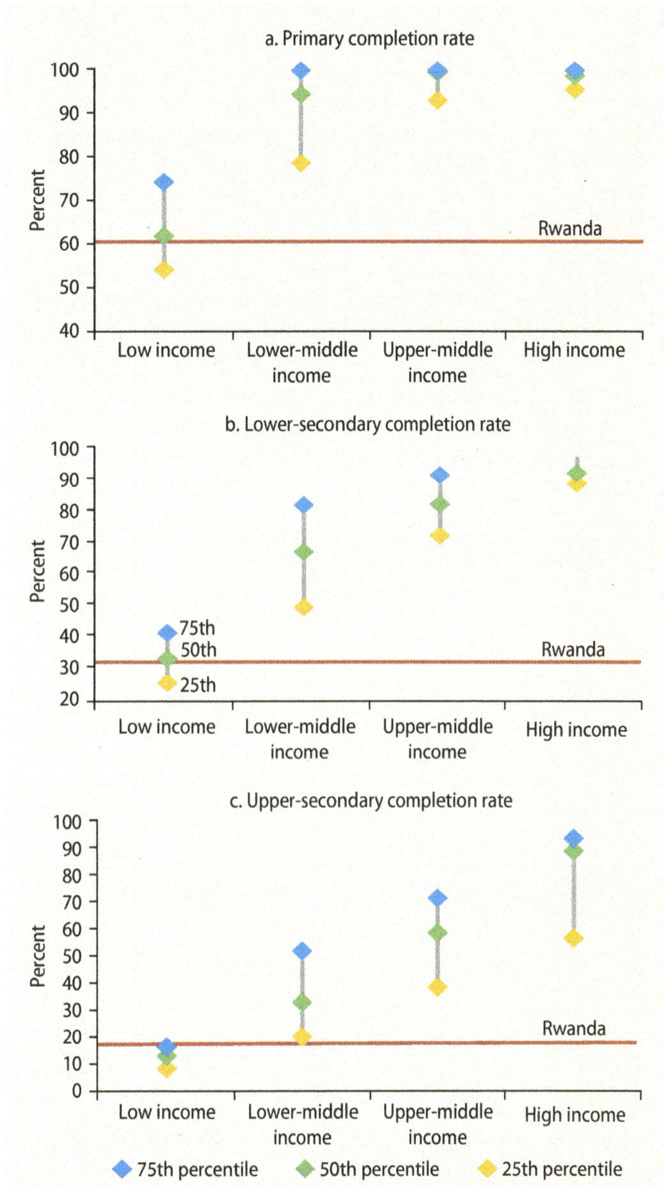

Source: Based on World Development Indicators 2017 data (World Bank, various years).

Proximate Causes

Virtually all children in Rwanda begin primary school, but fewer than two-thirds of them complete it. Some of the reasons include out-of-pocket costs and paying for uniforms and some materials. The elimination of all school fees is key to increasing school participation and advancement. This elimination comes at a cost, but in its absence, universal primary completion will remain elusive, and the poorest children will remain those least likely to complete.

Children also face opportunity costs: by attending school, they sacrifice whatever else they might be doing with their time. Part of the failure to advance in school can come from mistaken perceptions about the returns to schooling. In the Dominican Republic and Madagascar (although not in rural China), communicating accurate data on the future wages of students who complete various levels of schooling significantly increased school participation (Jensen 2010; Loyalka et al. 2013; Nguyen 2008). In Mexico, a similar program even increased student test scores (Avitabile and de Hoyos 2015). Parents with limited access to data on wages may be poorly situated to evaluate the returns to schooling, in which case they may underestimate the benefits relative to the costs. Rwandan data from 2010 suggest that, for wage employment, the return to an additional year of schooling is equal to 22 percent in Rwanda; in fact, Rwanda has the highest measured returns to education of any country in the world (Montenegro and Patrinos 2014). Likewise, Rwandans with more education, regardless of whether or not they have wage work, have more assets.[7]

High repetition rates in the early grades increase the opportunity cost of completing primary and secondary education. In a recent study, 14 percent of learners in P1–P4 were repeaters. In P1, that share was 23 percent, so nearly one-quarter of first-grade students were repeating (USAID 2017). This—along with other factors, such as limited early childhood education coverage and late school starters—results in a large "bulge" of students in P1, lowering the likelihood of primary school completion and making improvements in quality difficult (figure 1.11). The bulge results in exceptionally large class sizes: classes in P1–P3 have more than 50 pupils each, with 64 pupils in P1 classes. One estimate suggests that eliminating the bulge in P1 would "save about 5 percent of the primary education budget," which would allow for more investments in other parts of the system (Crouch and Merseth 2017). Although children in P1 may not have much economic value to the household, as children grow older without progressing or completing primary school, their economic value from participating in childcare or agricultural activities increases.

The quality of instruction in these first years of school has major implications for all future educational investments. If students do not learn to read in the first few

FIGURE 1.11 Early-grade "bulge index" in Rwanda and select countries

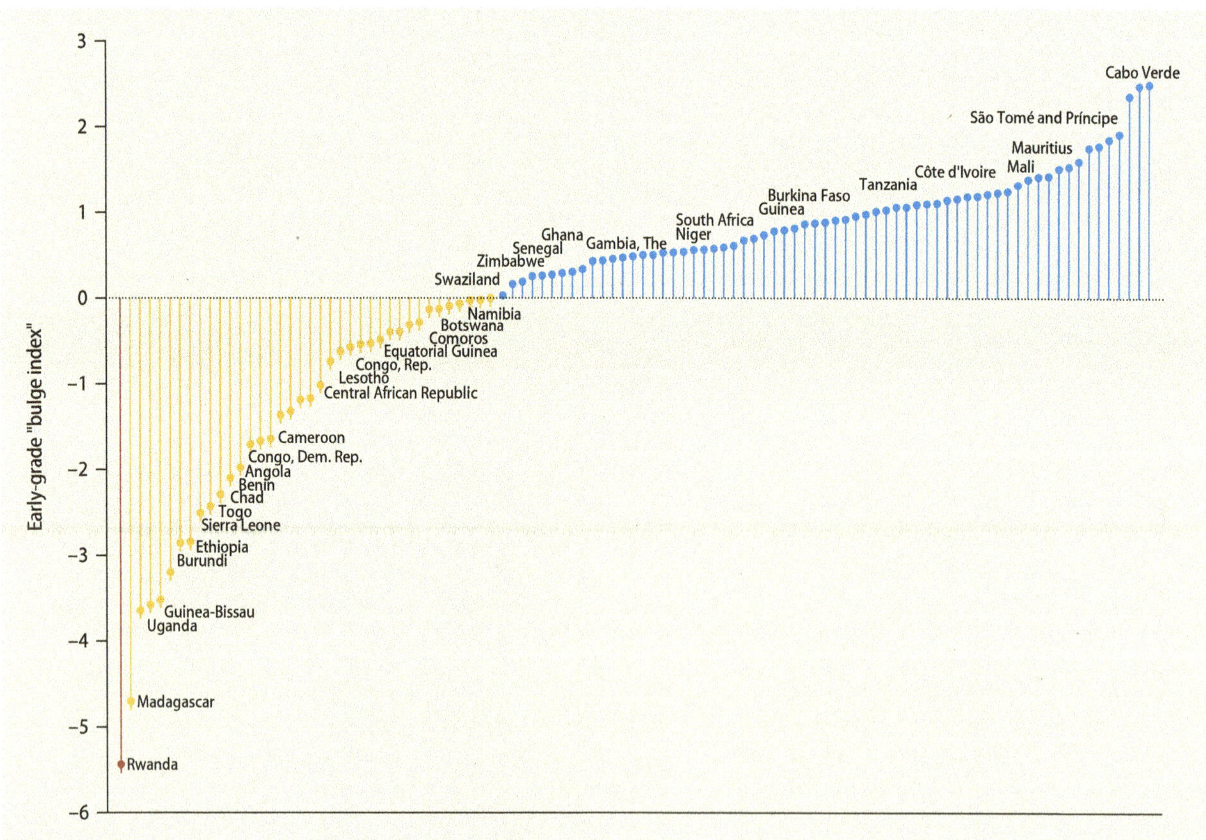

Source: Bashir et al. 2018.
Note: Low values in Rwanda reflect high enrollment in P1 (first grade) relative to the age group, low progression to P2 (second grade) (that is, many repeaters), and low preprimary coverage.

years of school, they cannot effectively learn mathematics or science or social science. Furthermore, the use of mother-tongue instruction in the first three years of primary school heightens the importance of making sure that children master reading in the early years of primary school. Students who are taught in their mother tongue in the early years learn to read faster than those who are taught in an unfamiliar language. Learning to read becomes more difficult for children who enter school after the language of instruction has transitioned to English, which is one reason research has suggested that a later transition to English would allow students to first master literacy in a familiar language (Bashir et al. 2018).

Some have argued that eliminating automatic promotion will improve quality. However, repetition is exactly what drives the bulge in early grades. Rather than repealing a policy of automatic promotion, the solution is to improve the quality of instruction so that pupils meet quality standards and advance appropriately.

Once in school, why do children fail to learn? Not all schooling is created equal. Across school systems, students learn dramatically different amounts of knowledge. For example, a recent study compared the average years of schooling and level of knowledge of young adults (figure 1.12). (Unfortunately, because Rwanda has not participated in international exams, it is not included in this analysis.) Young adults between the ages of 25 and 29 in Singapore, for example, have completed nearly 15 years of schooling. A young adult of the same age in the United States would have completed a similar number of years of schooling but would have the cognitive ability of a Singaporean young adult who had completed less than 12 years of schooling. In other words, the quantity of education is similar across the two countries, but the quality of education differs dramatically. In South Africa, young adults have

FIGURE 1.12 Gap between actual and learning-adjusted years of schooling in select countries and economies

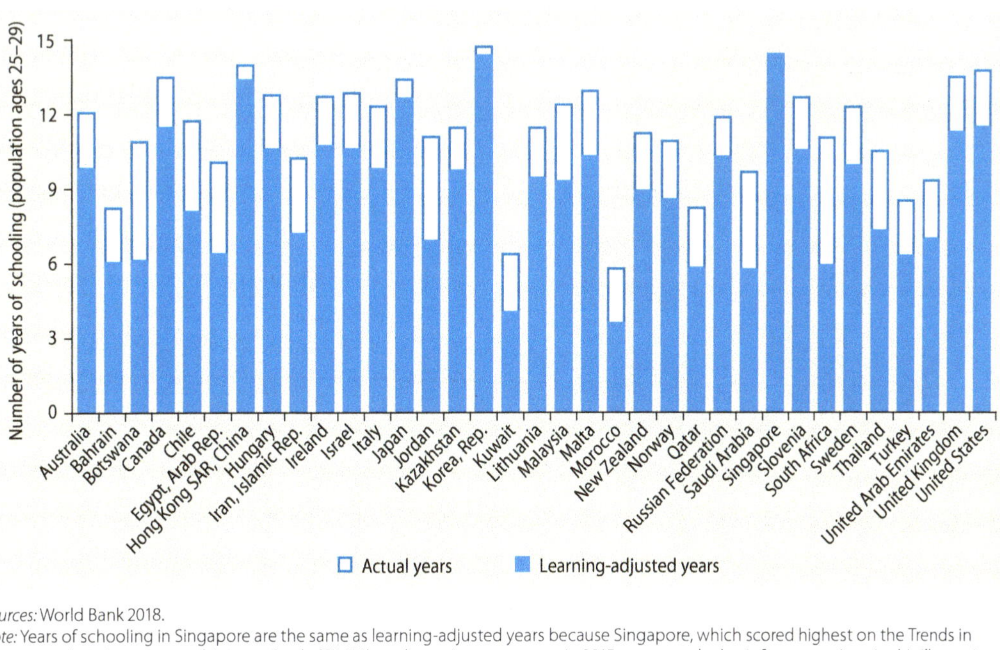

Sources: World Bank 2018.
Note: Years of schooling in Singapore are the same as learning-adjusted years because Singapore, which scored highest on the Trends in International Mathematics and Science Study (TIMSS) mathematics assessment in 2015, serves as the basis for comparison in this illustration. For the purposes of this illustration, data for years of education in the United Kingdom are adjusted using the TIMSS score for England. Note that for all countries and economies, the size of the adjustment will reflect the scale of the metric used to make it.

completed roughly 11 years of schooling, but their level of knowledge is equivalent to just 6 years of Singaporean education (World Bank 2018). Furthermore, economic growth analysis demonstrates that what matters for economic growth is not the years of schooling completed, but rather the amount of learning (Hanushek and Woessmann 2012).

The World Bank's *World Development Report 2018* on education highlights the proximate determinants of learning (World Bank 2018). These determinants include having prepared and motivated learners (or students), skilled and motivated teachers, school inputs (such as infrastructure and materials, including technology) that complement the interactions between teachers and learners, and effective school management (figure 1.13). A significant element of having prepared, motivated learners is ensuring nutrition at early ages and eliminating stunting, as discussed earlier. After the students themselves, teachers are central to the learning experience. A recent, comprehensive review of interventions intended to improve learning outcomes found the highest, most consistently large effects for interventions that sought to improve the quality of teaching, much more than efforts to improve school infrastructure, materials, or management (Snilstveit et al. 2016). Likewise, studies from countries as diverse as Ecuador and Pakistan have demonstrated that the difference between a highly effective teacher and a less effective teacher tends to equal at least the amount of learning that students normally gain over the course of a regular school year and sometimes much more (Popova et al. 2017).

FIGURE 1.13 Key proximate determinants of learning

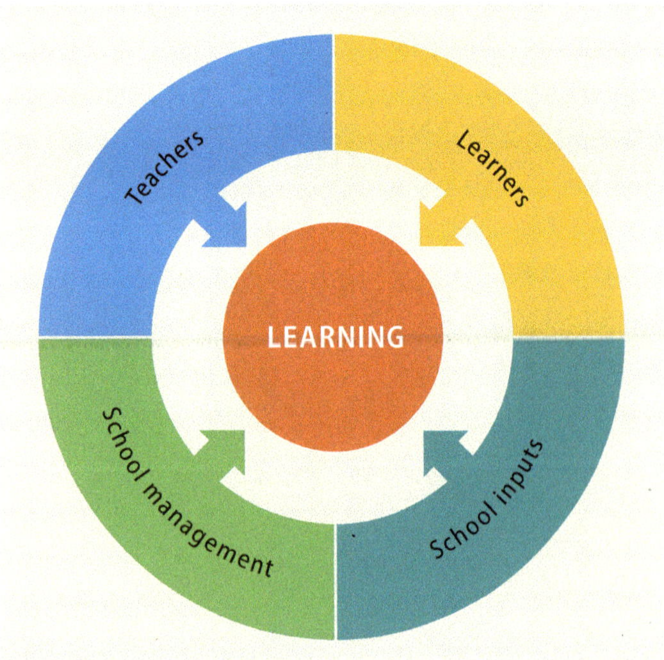

Source: World Bank 2018.

The World Bank's regional study of basic education, *Facing Forward: Schooling with Learning in Africa,* identifies Rwanda-specific priorities for policy makers to consider (Bashir et al. 2018). Rwanda has invested heavily in basic education, prepared good policies and plans—often informed by evidence and experience from other countries—and aligned donor financing accordingly. Yet lagging completion rates and poor learning outcomes suggest that, although the country's overarching policies as presented in sector strategies and plans are generally sound, more attention needs to be focused on bridging the gap between policy and implementation (box 1.2). A focus on implementation means paying more attention to schools and to teachers and administrators, the main personnel involved in the delivery of education services. Systematic reinforcement and oversight of these frontline agents and the provision of adequate learning conditions in schools are thus critical. Rwanda can learn from other countries in this regard as well as from its own experience with policy implementation.

Rwandan teachers seem to put forth relatively high effort. Systematic data on teacher absenteeism and punctuality are not available, but certain statistics suggest that Rwanda is ahead of other countries in the region in this regard. In a survey from 2008, teacher absenteeism was reported at under 10 percent in government and

BOX 1.2 Confronting a learning crisis in basic education: Key areas for action

Rwanda is not alone among African countries in confronting a learning crisis in basic education. Bashir et al. (2018) identify four top areas for action by countries—like Rwanda—that share this challenge: (1) completing the unfinished agenda of universalizing basic education with quality; (2) ensuring effective management and support of teachers; (3) increasing financing of education and focusing spending and budget processes on improving quality; and (4) closing the institutional capacity gap.

government-subsidized primary schools and under 14 percent in secondary schools (Bennell and Ntagaramba 2008).[8] More than 90 percent of respondents say that teachers come to school on time. By contrast, recent surveys across seven African countries found average teacher absenteeism rates of 23 percent, reaching as high as 45 percent in Mozambique (Bold et al. 2017). In those same countries, teacher absenteeism from class was even higher: on average, teachers were not in class teaching during 44 percent of class time, reaching as high as 57 percent in Uganda. Although comparable numbers are not available for Rwanda, the fact that tardiness is not regarded as a broad challenge suggests that teacher effort in class may be higher. This relatively high effort means that, rather than needing to solve a wide array of challenges regarding teacher effort, as many countries must, Rwanda can focus on improving teacher skills.

Teachers do not have the skills they need. Many teachers have limited command of the language of instruction. In one recent assessment (in 2014), only 43 percent of teachers were assessed at the "intermediate level" in English (Upper Quartile and Institute of Policy Analysis and Research Rwanda 2015). A lack of proficiency in the language of instruction will inevitably affect student performance not only in English reading, writing, and speaking ability but also in all other subjects that are taught in English, including math, science, and social studies. With the shift of language of instruction from French to English in 2008, the government of Rwanda has invested extensively in teacher language training, with initial intensive efforts and subsequently a shift to more in-school mentoring. No doubt these efforts are largely responsible for the fact that many teachers have reached an intermediate level. However, continued intensive efforts will be necessary to bring teachers the rest of the way to fluency in the language of instruction.

Is teacher pay a binding constraint? Teacher pay in Rwanda falls in varying places across the spectrum of low-income African countries (figure 1.14). Evidence from Indonesia suggests that average teacher salaries do not have a major impact on day-to-day teacher effort (De Ree et al. 2018). However, low salaries may have an impact on the quality of individuals who apply to become teachers, and major inequality between primary and secondary teachers can create strange incentives, such as encouraging all of the more qualified candidates to become secondary school teachers. Recent moves to incorporate bonuses based on performance may be useful, although current teacher performance contracts (*imihigo*) are not well defined with regard to learning outcomes.

Investments for Transformation

Improving basic education is fundamental to achieving sustained economic growth, and large gains for new cohorts are possible. President Paul Kagame recently highlighted the need for a "revolution" in the quality of Rwandan education "at all levels"

FIGURE 1.14 Lag in teacher salaries in Rwanda, by primary and secondary levels

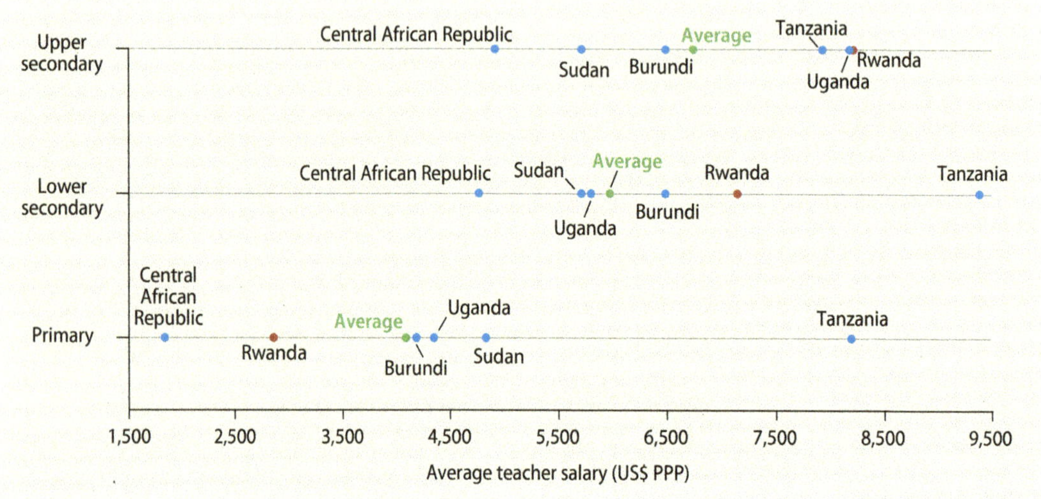

Source: Ministry of Education and Sports, Uganda 2014.
Note: PPP = purchasing power parity.

(Tashobya 2017). Korea and Singapore prioritized investments in basic education as the foundation of long-term economic growth. In Korea, "Considerable capital accumulation and investment in primary education during [the 1950s] allowed a gradual shift up the value-added chain toward more sophisticated commodities." Korea staged its educational investments: "The focus of the government's educational plan has moved from primary to secondary education and finally to the tertiary level, according to the nation's economic advancement" (Pillay 2010). Likewise, in the 1960s, Singapore expanded education; but, in the late 1970s and 1980s, it made major investments in quality, permitting a shift into a broad-based knowledge economy (Rodríguez, Dahlman, and Salmi 2008). If Rwanda desires long-term growth, then quality education in the early school years is crucial. Furthermore, many countries have shown that large gains in primary school completion are possible (figure 1.15).

The way to expand access is to reduce costs and improve perceived benefits. Countries that have achieved widespread basic literacy have offered free primary education. Achieving universal access to basic education will require resources, but it can pay off, as was the experience in the Republic of Korea (box 1.3). The budgetary implications can be reduced, if necessary, by targeting this policy to areas with the lowest completion rates.

It is impossible to know whether performance is improving without regularly measuring it. Regularly assessing students and then sharing that information can play a transformative role. First, having more information about school performance can create incentives for all participants in the education system to focus on learning. If citizens have access to regular data on student learning outcomes, they are more likely to demand improved learning outcomes from schools. In many communities, parents themselves have limited literacy, so if they do not receive credible information, they may find it difficult to evaluate the quality of education. In Brazil, the government sets targets that combine student passing rates with student test scores. Each year, school and state performance on these targets is widely publicized, and communities hold their local government accountable. Second, regular

FIGURE 1.15 Current and projected primary and lower-secondary completion in Rwanda, 2000–35

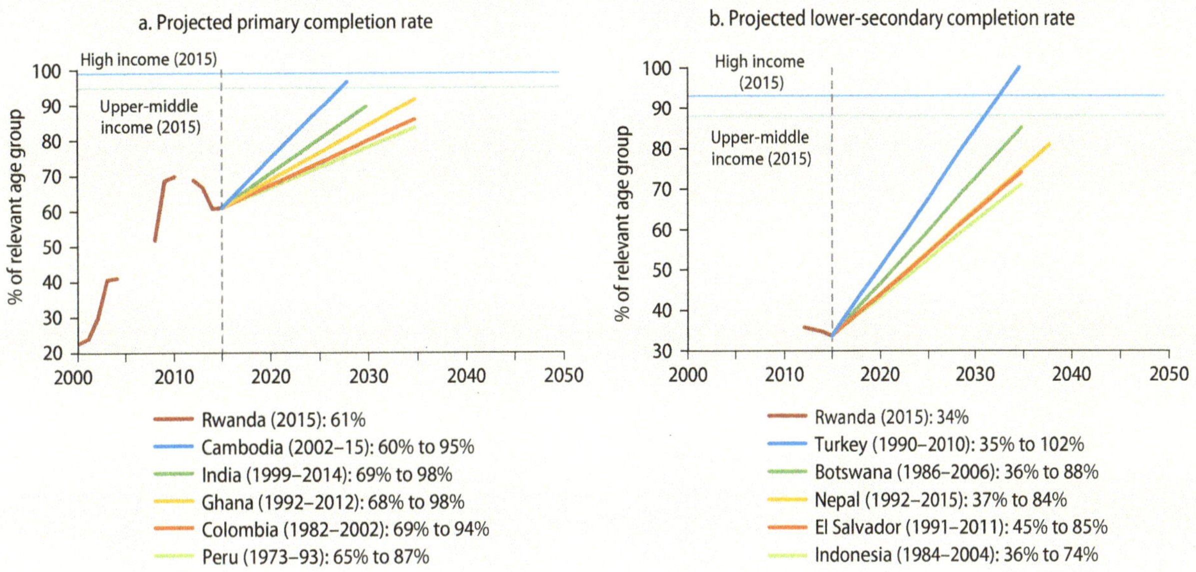

Source: Based on World Development Indicators 2017 data (World Bank, various years).
Note: Projections are based on the rate of increase in other countries. The legend shows the period over which the primary or lower-secondary completion expansion was calculated, as well as the level of primary or lower-secondary completion at the beginning and end of the period. All comparator countries began their period of rapid expansion at a level comparable to that of Rwanda.

BOX 1.3 Increasing access to education and training in the Republic of Korea

Since the 1950s in Korea, gross enrollment rates have risen rapidly across elementary, secondary, and tertiary schools. Elementary school enrollment rates have been high (approximately 100 percent) since the early 1950s. In 2010, approximately 80 percent of the workforce had a high school or college degree. Since 2006, 15-year-old students in Korea have performed consistently better than the Organisation for Economic Co-operation and Development average in mathematics, science, and reading. Their learning outcomes are comparable with levels in Finland; Hong Kong SAR, China; and Japan.

How has Korea achieved high gross enrollment rates?

- *Ensuring access to education.* The Korean government enforced a Six-Year Compulsory Education Expansion Plan from 1954 to 1959 and allocated 80 percent of its education budget toward ensuring compulsory education for students in elementary school.
- *Engaging the private sector.* The private sector played an active role in secondary and higher education by setting up educational institutions and donating resources, allowing the government to focus on strengthening elementary education.
- *Providing effective financing.* Under the Educational Grant Act, the government linked a percentage of the internal tax revenue to the education budget and channeled these resources toward elementary and secondary schooling. As of 2010, 20.27 percent of the internal taxes went to the education budget. The government's investment in education, as a percentage of GDP, has remained above 4 percent since 2005.
- *Providing vocational training.* The government addressed the skills gap in the workforce by investing in vocational education. The country made a concerted effort to build respect for technical professionals. In 1973, it implemented the Specialization Initiatives for Technical High

(Box continues next page)

BOX 1.3 (continued)

Schools, which specialize in one of four themes: mechanical, experimental, specialized, and generalized. The government provided scholarships and stipends to encourage enrollment in these schools. Currently, under the Vocational Training Special Measures Act, private companies must provide mandatory training for their employees. The precursor to this act were government subsidies to companies for employee training.

- *Addressing brain drain.* The government built research institutions to address the problem of brain drain and to foster talent within Korea. For example, American professors served as consultants and resided in Korea, in order to help to transform Seoul National University into a renowned institution.

Source: Hong and Lee 2016.

information on performance can help schools themselves to improve learning performance and the effectiveness of interventions. In Mexico, providing information on school performance to both schools and communities helped head teachers and class teachers to understand whether innovations in the education system were having the desired effect. Regular information on learning helped a scholarship program in Cambodia to reach—over time—the most vulnerable students.

Upgrading the skills of primary teachers is one crucial step (Bashir et al. 2018). From the more than 100 recent studies on improving learning in high-, middle-, and low-income countries, one key finding is that certain types of teacher training can have a strong impact on the quality of education (Evans and Popova 2016). But this teacher training is not about general teacher training, which commonly takes place in one-day or one-week seminars. Rather, teacher training tends to be effective when it is sustained over time and reaches the teacher at her or his level of need. Good teacher development has significant contact hours and focuses on concrete tasks, including mentoring for beginners and peer learning (Popova, Evans, and Arancibia 2016). In countries like Singapore, high-quality teachers are part of the recipe for success in quality education (box 1.4).

A key example of high-quality teacher training is ongoing coaching rather than one-time training opportunities. "Teacher coaching has emerged as a promising alternative to traditional models of professional development" (Kraft, Blazar, and Hogan 2017). These programs have been implemented in high-income countries like the United States to good effect, with large impacts on the quality of instruction and sizable impacts on student achievement. In Singapore, one of the pillars of high school performance is sustained teacher professional development (box 1.4). More recently, these coaching approaches have been implemented successfully in South Africa, with large impacts on student learning, more than double the size associated with more traditional teacher professional development (Cilliers and Taylor 2017). In Kenya, the government used existing school inspectors for this purpose (Gove, Poole, and Pipe 2017). The way to improve teachers' classroom practice is through improved supervision in their schools. Another way is through improved training of school principals. In the United States, a recent intervention trained school principals to observe and provide constructive feedback to teachers, resulting in improved student learning (Fryer 2017).

It may be tempting to think that Rwanda can import high-quality teachers from

BOX 1.4 Achieving world-class education in Singapore

According to the *Global Competitiveness Report, 2007–08*, Singapore ranks first when it comes to quality education (World Economic Forum 2008). The country has consistently performed well in tests that evaluate education systems around the world such as the Trends in Mathematics and Science Study (TIMSS), the Progress in International Reading Literacy Study (PIRLS), and the Programme for International Student Assessment (PISA). Since 1997, through its vision of "Thinking Schools, Learning Nation," Singapore has designed its education system to prepare students for the opportunities of the 21st century.

How has Singapore improved its quality of education?

- *Teacher recruitment, development, and retention.* Teaching is a highly respected profession in Singapore—only the top third of high school graduates are recruited as teachers. Singapore promotes teacher retention through a variety of monetary incentives—for example, a generous bonus scheme based on an appraisal system increases salaries over the course of a teacher's career. There is also a strong focus on professional development among teachers. In addition to making 100 hours of professional development available to every teacher, the government reimburses teachers up to a certain amount to improve their skills and knowledge. This reimbursement allows teachers to join courses, subscribe to magazines, or purchase software, among other things.
- *Collaborative system.* Key stakeholders in the education system—policy implementers, researchers, and educators—work closely together. The National Institute of Education, which conducts research and teacher training, works closely with the Ministry of Education. Officials from the ministry also meet regularly with school principals in order to ensure that their policies are rooted in context.
- *Links to economic development.* As a nation without natural resources, Singapore consistently focuses on leveraging its human capital. Over the last 40 years, it developed an education system that adapted to the changing needs of its economy. Currently, the focus is on innovation, creativity, and research to contribute to the global knowledge economy. In 2004, "Teach Less, Learn More" was introduced to shift students from rote learning toward learning through experimentation and discovery, connecting topics to real life and character building. Singapore also has a unique system for identifying labor force needs and projecting future demand. These skills are then developed in students through higher and postsecondary education.
- *Priority given to mathematics, science, and technical skills.* Mathematics and science are core subjects at the primary and secondary levels, often taught by specialist teachers. Although children are taught far less material than students in other countries, teachers cover these subjects in greater depth. The "Model Method," which involves visual aids to teach mathematics, is used across schools in Singapore.

Sources: Lee et al. 2008; NCEE n.d.; OECD 2010.

outside, but surrounding countries also struggle with quality teaching, and their teachers are unlikely to speak Kinyarwanda. The answer lies within Rwanda's own teachers, but they need to receive a different kind of support than they are used to receiving. This support also involves providing better management to teachers, as education policy makers have done in Shanghai (box 1.5). Rwanda may be able to adapt existing social structures, such as the monthly day of service—called *umuganda*—to encourage well-educated members of society such as university students and members of the business community to contribute to the quality of schools.

Recruiting expatriates can help to remedy the shortage of teachers, especially of teachers who are proficient in English. The current ratio of pupils to teacher in primary schools in Rwanda is 58, among the highest in the world; the ratio of pupils to teacher proficient in English would be much higher. Countries like Botswana and Oman carried out overseas recruitment in the 1970s and 1980s to close the teacher gap created

BOX 1.5 Lessons from China: Teacher management in Shanghai

In 2009 and again in 2012, when Shanghai's 15-year-olds topped the scores on the global PISA tests, the world wondered how this feat could have been achieved in an education system that only three decades earlier had been left in shambles by China's Cultural Revolution (1966–76), a decade when teachers were sent to the countryside to perform manual labor.

Veteran foreign observers and Chinese educators consider Shanghai's method for teacher management to be one of the system's most valuable and unique assets, one that enabled the city to achieve its remarkable results (Tucker 2014). The method has little to do with the workshop model of professional development for teachers and everything to do with enabling effective teaching and rewarding continuous, disciplined improvement of teacher performance. Three ingredients stand out: systemwide structural reforms, active experimentation in schools, and purposeful management of teachers' work.

In the 1990s, when the focus shifted from expanding access to improving quality, Shanghai piloted a new national curriculum, began encouraging more active kinds of pedagogy, and abolished primary school examinations—the latter to encourage schools to focus on deeper learning rather than on teaching to the test. The city also moved to narrow the gap between top-performing "key" schools and those at the bottom that served large numbers of children from poor households, including migrant families from rural areas. It experimented with many approaches: pairing high-performing schools with struggling ones to bring up the quality of leadership and teachers in the latter; asking principals from high-performing schools to manage more than one school; forming clusters of schools to share resources; and giving a high-performing school an "empowered management" contract, with funding attached, to improve a lower-performing school, in which the principals and teachers involved would spend time in each other's school to work on improving management and instruction.

Teachers handle relatively large classes, but they are equipped to teach well through a system of continuing professional development. Mentor teachers gather weekly with teachers from the same subject or grade level to discuss some aspect of instruction that needs improvement. Classroom observation occurs frequently: teachers observing each other, trainee teachers observing master teachers, and teachers visiting from other schools circulating among classrooms. The public nature of teaching practice exerts a subtle influence on teachers who perform less well, putting social pressure on them to improve and allowing them to see how other teachers get better results.

The system incentivizes all teachers to progress up the career ladder, which requires honing not just one's own teaching skills but also getting involved in the professional development of colleagues and improving the overall instructional quality of the school. As teachers move up the career ladder they may lead action research projects, often in collaboration with others. For this research, they focus on an education issue of interest, evaluate the literature, experiment with different approaches in the school, and report on the results. Teachers who wish to reach the top of 13 levels (master teacher level) are expected to spend time teaching in a lower-income area. Being recognized as a master teacher confers great honor on the small percentage of teachers who qualify; such teachers not only work in their own school but also share their expertise with other schools as well.

by rapid educational expansion (Al Maskari et al. 2015; Kesamang et al. 2012). Rwanda might consider hiring more teachers from neighboring English-speaking countries, given the limited capacity of Rwanda's teacher training institutions and the acute demand for teachers in the system.[9] However, dependency on expatriate teachers may lead to high turnover rates, which would impair the quality of education. Also essential would be recruiting expatriate teachers from countries that have a curriculum consistent with Rwanda's.

Expert teachers from abroad can be used to train a core group of high-quality teachers. During Korea's development era (1954–61), the country retrained its medical faculty at U.S. universities, leading to improved teaching methods and a new organizational culture in Korean medical education (Lee and Taejong 2015). Indeed, Rwanda has some history of this approach, requesting teachers from Kenya to provide in-service training to Rwandan teachers in 2011 and establishing agreements with Ugandan teachers in 2009 to provide English instruction (Ochs and Yonemura 2013). Short-term teacher trainings tend to have little impact, so an effort along these lines would need to bring teachers from high-quality education systems for sufficient time to change practice among Rwandan teachers.

Technology can be applied to increase students' learning performance. Mindspark, an interactive computer-assisted learning software, increased math scores by 0.59 standard deviation and language scores by 0.36 standard deviation for a group of Indian students in 90 days (Muralidharan, Singh, and Ganimian 2017). Students signed up to take six 90-minute sessions after school per week; actual attendance was about 58 percent. The software provides students with extensive, high-quality learning materials as well as individualized activities based on each student's learning progress, which is difficult to achieve in a classroom with high heterogeneity in student performance. More promising, a similar intervention implemented at scale has also shown positive impact on learning. The Adaptive Mathematics Platform that has been used by half of students in grades 3–6 in Uruguay improved math scores by 0.2 standard deviation, equivalent to half a semester of schooling (Perera and Aboal 2017). The online platform is accessible at no cost through the laptops distributed to all students in Uruguayan public schools as part of a national education program, Plan Ceibal. On average, 68 percent of students completed at least one exercise on the platform during the three-year evaluation period.

However, to be effective, technology has to be about much more than installing computers and software. Most technological interventions are expensive and challenging to implement, especially in areas with limited technical and human capacity. Indeed, the Ministry of Education encountered similar difficulties when implementing the One Laptop per Child program and building "smart classrooms" in primary and secondary schools in Rwanda (Ministry of Education, Rwanda 2016). Moreover, technology delivers learning gains only when it affects pedagogical practices. For example, the One Laptop per Child program alone could not have been effective without being accompanied by adaptive learning software (Perera and Aboal 2017).

Rwanda has made major investments in education technology, deploying laptops to many schools across the country. As of 2013/14, there were nearly 270,000 laptops in primary schools across Rwanda, although few schools (less than 1 in 10) had Internet access (Lemarchand and Tash 2015). The number of users per computer is 13 in primary schools and 27 in secondary schools (NISR 2016). Before investing further in information and communication technology infrastructure and related interventions, it is crucial to focus on technologies that are compatible and potentially yield the largest returns to the existing education system. For example, although coaching provided under the School-Based Mentoring Program has significantly improved teachers' English skills, the program has had difficulty recruiting and deploying mentors in every school across Rwanda (REB 2016). In other countries, technology has provided innovative solutions to improve adults' language skills (box 1.6). Regular practice with high-quality language-learning software has the potential to improve teacher skills more than occasional practice with an in-school mentor alone. Linking high English proficiency with job certification and remuneration can increase the incentives to practice and improve.

BOX 1.6 Technology for improving teachers' English skills

Technology has been an effective way to improve adult ability in a new language in other countries. The LaGuardia Community College in New York City used a Blackboard website and podcasts to help adult immigrants with basic English proficiency to develop language skills that are expected in the lodging industry. The curriculum was designed specifically for the hospitality industry, and podcast lessons were tailored to the needs of individual students. Students in the program made substantial gains in both English and computer skills (Warschauer and Liaw 2010). Another program, OneAmerica in Washington State, piloted an English teaching program using a combination of technology and classroom instruction. Adult students took self-paced English courses using LiveMocha software through computer or mobile devices and participated in English discussion with volunteers over Skype. Learning outcomes were comparable to those in community college classes, but at a faster pace (Wilson 2014).

Technological innovations hold promise to enhance teachers' language skills in a shorter time than traditional approaches. First, learning software can reach teachers in rural and remote areas through computer or mobile devices when a school mentor is not available. Second, adaptive learning software enables teachers to learn at their own level and pace, better addressing the needs of a teaching force with various levels of English proficiency. Third, language-learning software can combine with pedagogical training as part of teacher professional development. Current school mentors can travel across schools and provide on-site support following the most effective practices (Evans and Popova 2016).

Skills Training

Current Status

In order to reap more immediate economic returns from human capital investment, youth who are approaching the job market need better training to help them to transition. Census projections suggest that the population of working-age Rwandans will increase by roughly 240,000 per year between 2016 and 2025 (World Bank 2017c). At the same time, business people rated "inadequately educated workforce" as the second largest constraint to doing business in Rwanda, after "access to financing" (World Economic Forum 2017). Audits from across sectors (agriculture, energy, manufacturing, mining, urbanization, and meetings, incentives, conferences, and exhibitions) have indicated the need for major skills upgrading.[10] The 2017 Labor Force Survey puts the share of youth who are not in education, employment, or training (NEET) at 25 percent among the population 16–19 years old, 35 percent among the population 20–24 years old, and 40 percent among the population 25–30 years old (NISR 2017).

Increasing numbers of youth are enrolling in technical and vocational education and training (TVET), up nearly 40 percent between 2011 and 2015. Relative to the rest of the region, Rwanda has high TVET enrollment (figure 1.16). As more students complete primary and lower-secondary school, these numbers will likely continue to rise. This population has the potential to meet significant needs for technicians as well as for professional graduates who come from traditional higher education.

Proximate Causes

Rwanda is already innovating in its vocational training system. The five-year plan (2013–18) for priority skills development highlighted seven fields of special focus—infrastructure (including energy), agriculture, natural resources, investment, trade and industry, information and communication technology, and health and education—and set targets based on needs assessments

FIGURE 1.16 Enrollment in secondary TVET, by region and within Africa, circa 2000 and 2014

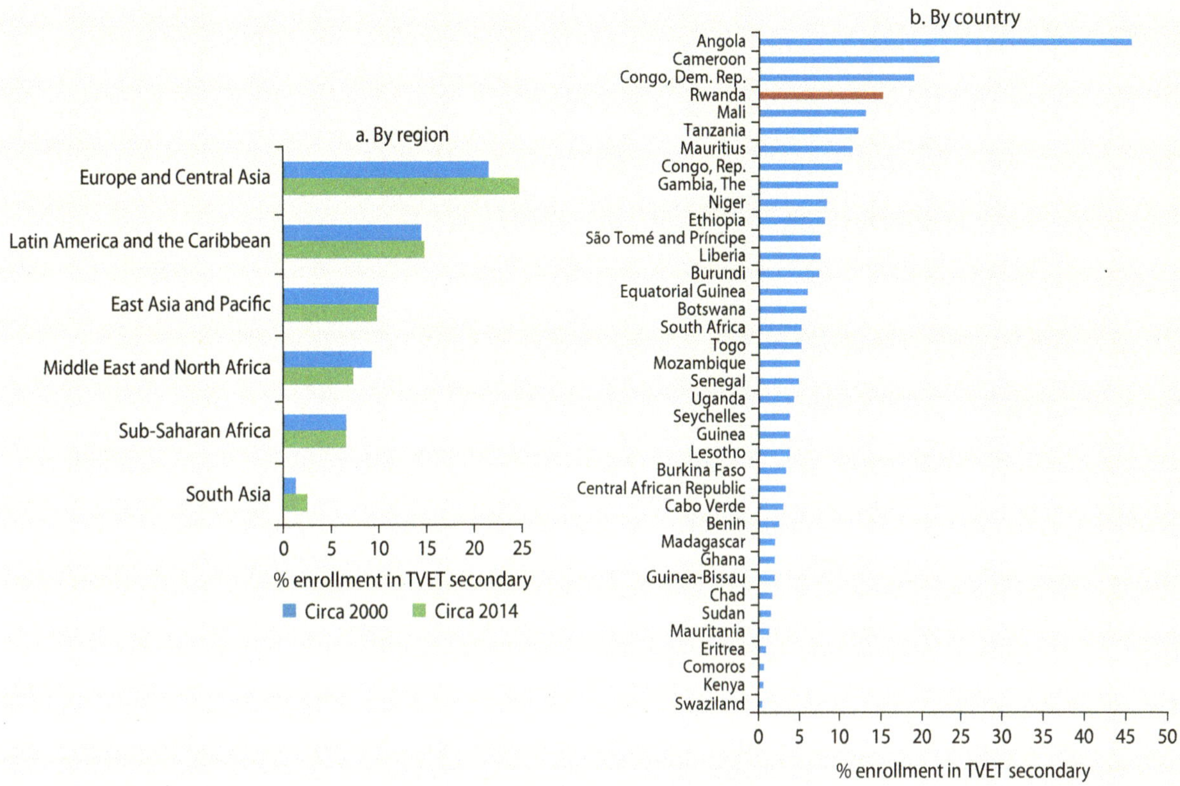

Source: Calculations based on data from United Nations Educational, Scientific, and Cultural Organization, Institute for Statistics (Arias, Santos, and Evans 2018).
Note: On panel b, Angola = 45.2. TVET = technical and vocational education and training.

in each area. A midterm review of the plan revealed that many Rwandans are gaining training and skills, although not necessarily in the priority subfields: In 2016, Rwanda formed the Capacity Development and Employment Services Board to bring skills development and employment creation together under the Ministry of Public Service and Labor (World Bank 2017c).

Technical and vocational training tends to have highly variable returns. Training programs in some fields bring high returns, whereas others provide little benefit above simply obtaining work in the field. In the United States, technical education in health delivers returns more than twice as high as returns in all other fields (Stevens, Kurlaender, and Grosz 2015). For women in Kenya, income for those who had vocational training in hairdressing was more than six times higher than for those who had training in tailoring (Hicks et al. 2015). Getting individuals into high-quality programs with high returns is key.

Two key issues stand out in Rwanda's skills development. On the one hand, the unskilled nature of the bulk of the labor force requires further increases in agricultural productivity and job creation in industries related to agriculture (for example, agribusiness and agroindustry) to improve employment outcomes for the most vulnerable group of workers. On the other hand, the rapid expansion of education means that new labor force entrants will be increasingly educated, which requires the creation of more skilled and semiskilled jobs, preferably through the entrance of larger formal firms. Expansion of economic activity in the secondary cities will be important in this regard, as will be the ongoing efforts to expand access to electricity and improve the domestic and external connectivity of the economy.

Investments for Transformation

What can Rwanda learn from international examples in skills training? Building workforce skills for employment and economic growth is the aspiration of most low- and middle-income countries. The task poses many difficulties for which solutions often involve government action to varying degrees of intensity. In high-income economies, the government's role is often muted or focused on areas of specific needs (for example, apprenticeships in the United States in recent years and training for mid-level jobs through community colleges rather than through four-year colleges). In low-income economies or developmental states that are driven by aspirations for rapid economic transformation, the government's role tends to be more active and broader in scope, if only because the institutions for skills provision are nascent or poorly developed and information gaps impede the smooth functioning of the market for skills. But effective skills training builds on a foundation of basic skills, which is why Singapore's excellent training system builds on a strong foundation of basic education (box 1.7).

The development experience of economies such as Chile, Ireland, Korea, Malaysia, Singapore, and Taiwan, China, exemplify this activist role of government in facilitating the building of skills for employment and growth. Although their approaches respond to country-specific conditions and therefore vary in design, these countries all had to solve challenges in at least three areas to build a system capable of achieving sustainable delivery of quality services: strategy, organization, and implementation. Three lessons stem from the experiences of these countries. First, they set a strategic direction, tone, and culture for efforts to improve workforce skills. Second, they created an organizational infrastructure with the appropriate governance design. Third, they fostered efficient and effective management of service delivery at the level of providers.

Five principles emerge from the analysis of international skills programs (Roseth and Valerio 2016):

1. *Align resources to the strategy.* Ensure that there is political and technical will as well as funding to back up the national workforce development strategy.
2. *Bring employers into the process.* Engage employers not just for providing internships and apprenticeships but also for contributing to policy making and providing training. This engagement requires clear mechanisms and incentives. Malaysia has had success engaging firms in the vocational training space, largely through legislation (box 1.8).
3. *Improve the standing of TVET.* TVET is often seen as the last choice of students who do not succeed in university. Improving the quality of systems and demonstrating the returns to students who are well suited to technical training can improve the attractiveness of these programs. Korea, Singapore, and Taiwan, China, all sought to make technical and vocational training a more attractive option for students (box 1.9).
4. *Focus on what matters.* If the objective is job placement, then programs should be measured on job placement. If the objective is competency, then programs should be measured on an objective set of competencies. Performance information, made publicly available, will let students, their families, and employers make optimal choices.
5. *Gather and use data.* Without systematic data collection, many of these practices are impossible.

Getting more people into priority programs requires information. Information can be a powerful tool to help individuals to access high-return programs. Campaigns that share information on the returns to

BOX 1.7 A strong foundation in basic education for transforming TVET in Singapore

In 2007, Singapore's Institute of Technical Education (ITE) beat more than 100 competitors from 30 countries to win the inaugural Global Award in Transforming Government given by the Ash Institute for Democratic Governance and Innovation at Harvard University's John F. Kennedy School of Government (Law 2015). The award brought attention to one of the world's most successful approaches to providing technical education. Instead of being a last-resort option for low academic achievers, by 2007 ITE was enrolling 25 percent of each cohort of tenth-grade completers. For those with the lowest academic results, ITE used new pedagogies particularly suited for experiential learners, equipping them for success in the labor market and, for some "late bloomers," for further education. This single shift in perspective combined with a massive restructuring of the system to make Singapore a global leader in technical and vocational education and training (TVET).

Few are aware, however, of the critical importance of a firm foundation in basic education for ITE's success. A landmark review of the school system, including vocational training, revealed deep problems among the lowest academic achievers, those exiting the system with just eight years of primary schooling (Government of Singapore 1991). Some 85 percent of each cohort of these students took up TVET, but as many as 60 percent could not complete the lowest-level courses for semiskilled workers, the main reason being their weak academic preparation in mathematics and English (Varaprasad 2016). Moreover, 75 percent of those who did graduate were not getting jobs in their area of training. The poor results came to be recognized as a serious impediment to the country's transition to its next phase of industrial development in the early 1990s.

The 12-member Review Committee recommended two remedies: (1) provide all children with at least 10 years of general schooling before they advance to the next level of education or training and (2) reposition TVET as part of the postsecondary system (Government of Singapore 1991). The second recommendation led to ITE's creation in 1992; the first contained details on giving all students a firm grounding in English, mathematics, and proficiency in the mother tongue. All primary pupils in the first four grades would follow the same curriculum, with the following time allocation: 33 percent for English, 27 percent for the mother tongue, and 20 percent for mathematics. At the end of fourth grade, pupils would separate into classes of English, mathematics, science, and mother tongue of varying difficulty, with the most academically and linguistically able pupils learning English and the mother tongue at a first-language level (10 percent); the majority learning English language as a first language and the mother tongue as a second language (70–75 percent); and weaker pupils learning English as a first language and the mother tongue at oral proficiency (15–20 percent). For the last group, the reduced stress on mother tongue freed up time to concentrate on English and mathematics. Secondary education would last four to five years, with students following either an academically or a technically biased course. The latter course would cater to the 15–20 percent least academically inclined students for whom English, mathematics, and computer applications would be compulsory; strengthening their proficiency in English and mathematics would continue to be emphasized. For students in the academically biased course, some of whom may follow the TVET after completing their course, compulsory subjects would include English, mathematics, and the mother tongue.

The committee's two recommendations presented very significant challenges. Their successful implementation created a strong foundation for TVET and set the stage for changing the face of TVET, in the process producing what Varaprasad (2016) describes as "a modern miracle of transformation."

education have been successful at improving learning in Mexico and reducing dropouts in the Dominican Republic and Madagascar (World Bank 2018). Recent campaigns have sought to inform youth of the returns to different sectors. A program in Kenya that distributed a simple flyer presenting the returns across different vocational training programs had a sizable but short-term impact—it was effective at getting youth into higher-return programs, but not necessarily at getting them to complete them (Hicks

BOX 1.8 Partnering with firms to invest in workforce skills in Malaysia

Malaysia's levy-based system has evolved over the past 30 years and now offers the government a powerful tool for collaborating with employers on the skills agenda. The Eleventh Malaysia Plan (2016–20) envisions using the system to raise the share of Malaysians in skilled jobs, from 28 percent in 2015 to 35 percent by 2020.

The first piece of legislation, an act of Parliament enacted in 1993, created the levy system to replace an ineffective tax incentive scheme in force since 1987. It established the Human Resources Development Fund (HRDF) to hold funds comprising periodic government grants and monthly levies paid by firms into firm-specific accounts. It also created the Human Resource Development Council (HRDC) and a secretariat to administer levy collection and grant disbursements for approved training programs. In 2001, a new act replaced the HRDC with the *Pembangunan Sumber Manusia Berhad* (PSMB)—Registration of Employers and Payment of Levy—an agency under the Ministry of Human Resources. Structured as a corporation, PSMB is governed by representatives of businesses and government entities and is always chaired by a business leader—practices already in place under the HRDC.

In 1993, the system required only manufacturing firms with 50 or more employees to pay a levy; just three years later, it also required smaller manufacturing firms with 10 more employees to do so, along with some firms in services. By 2017, its coverage had spread to 63 subsectors in three industries: services, manufacturing, and mining and quarrying, with nearly 18,000 firms registered. As of April 2017, firms with 10 or more workers were required to pay a levy of 1 percent of payroll, while those with 5–9 workers were required to pay a levy of 0.5 percent. The current plan envisions registering all firms.

Firms could make claims for allowable training expenses, up to the limit of their firm-specific levy contributions. In 2016, the PSMB collected a significant amount in grants to fund nearly 90,000 training places through various schemes, the most popular being training planned by firms themselves. The establishment of the National Human Resources Center in 2011 intensified support for small and medium enterprises to invest in skills. The creation of the HRDF Pool Fund in 2016—financed by a 30 percent claim on levies held in firm-specific accounts and government budget allocations—sought to increase the focus on skills for priority economic sectors authenticated by internationally recognized credentials, not just certificates of attendance at training courses. Evaluations suggest that HRDF grants have helped to raise firm and worker productivity.

Malaysia's levy-based system complements parallel efforts to provide effective training. Legislation in a separate act in 1993 created the National Occupational Skills Standards system—supervised by the National Vocational Training Council—to align skills certification with standards established by industry, particularly those defined by levy-paying firms. Legislation in subsequent years created various accreditation bodies for public and private providers of education and training, culminating in the 2007 creation of the Malaysian Qualification Agency, to bring standards for provision and certification within a single framework. Under the Eleventh Malaysia Plan, further efforts to enhance the coherence and responsiveness of provision to emerging needs include (1) establishing the National Skills Development Council to consolidate TVET and academic programs under a single governing body and (2) creating industry skills councils and critical skills committees to inform the council's work.

Sources: Gobilee 2016; PSMB n.d., 2016; World Bank 2013; Yaacob 2016.

et al. 2015). As in basic education, regular monitoring and publication of information can be crucial to increase the returns of skills programs.

Mentors also play a key role in skills development. When young women in Ethiopia and Uganda were asked why they had entered high-return fields, they credited the influence of a role model (Buehren and Van Salisbury 2017; Campos et al. 2015). A program that gives youth the chance to interact with a role model in target, high-return fields may have a significant impact on moving youth into strategic sectors.

BOX 1.9 Developing skills for economic growth and transformation in the "Asian Tiger" economies

Five to six decades ago, the Republic of Korea, Singapore, and Taiwan, China—the original Asian Tiger economies—faced existential threats, rampant joblessness and poverty, and overwhelming odds in their pursuit of industrialization. Yet, in the space of a generation, all three have lifted living standards to levels that took high-income countries three or more generations to reach. Proactive policies in education and training were a critical enabler. What approaches did the three economies share? Are they still relevant today?

The Asian Tigers each followed their own path to develop their economies. Singapore opted to attract multinational corporations to spearhead its drive up the value chain; Korea developed its own national conglomerates (the *chaebols*) modeled after Japanese counterparts; and Taiwan, China, relied on indigenous small and medium family-owned businesses and on some state-owned enterprises (subsequently privatized), which adopted, where appropriate, leading-edge technology (Ashton et al. 2002). These economies shared three features in their approaches to education and training: (1) mechanisms to link decisions about the output of graduates to priority skills needed by the new industries; (2) regulation of access to the various types of education and training; and (3) continuous upskilling of the workforce aligned to employer demand. Mistakes were made and corrected, in the process building domestic capacity to sustain reforms over decades and achieving tangible economic transformation.

They all aligned education and training to the evolving needs of their new industries. All three Asian Tigers created what might be described as "super-ministries" as the institutional mechanism for this purpose. These entities had the power, over many decades, to steer, coordinate, and, if necessary, override the priorities of other ministries and interest groups, including parents, so as to keep the needs of the economy paramount. In Singapore, it was the Ministry of Trade and Industry; in Korea, the Economic Planning Board; and in Taiwan, China, the Council for Economic Planning and Development. These high-level entities set overall economic strategy, oversaw the distillation of its implications for education and training, and formalized the setting and enforcement of relevant targets through additional structures. In Singapore, this was accomplished through the Economic Development Board and the Council for Professional and Technical Education; in Korea, through Presidential Commissions on Education Reform and other advisory bodies; and in Taiwan, China, through the Council for Economic Planning and Development's Manpower Development Commission and the National Youth Commission (Ashton et al. 2002).

They all affirmed the value of technical and vocational education and training (TVET). While emphasizing a solid foundation in basic education, all three economies used their limited resources at the postsecondary level, especially in the early decades, to expand TVET rather than academic higher education. The employment of TVET graduates was a key metric used to reflect the value of TVET. In Singapore, substantial investments, beginning in the early 1990s, created the Institute of Technical Education as an explicit part of the postsecondary system (no longer part of general education) that today enrolls 25 percent of tenth-grade completers (Law 2015). Singapore's Economic Development Board also partnered with foreign firms to establish numerous stand-alone training institutes, which, after 20 years, were consolidated in 1993 to create a new polytechnic, mainstreaming best practices in industry-relevant training (Tan and Nam 2012). In Korea, as the *chaebols* were being established and demand for semiskilled labor was rising, the government expanded vocational secondary programs, which at the peak in 1973 graduated 60 percent of all high school graduates (Lee and Hong 2014). Parental pressure proved too powerful to sustain these high shares, however (Yoon and Lee 2009). In Taiwan, China, heavy government investment boosted TVET students' share in secondary schools from 40 percent in 1960 to 72 percent by 1990. In line with its development strategy, in 1970 the government created the National Taiwan Institute of Technology, which was authorized to offer degree-level training; it also set and achieved high targets for enrollment in science and engineering in tertiary education (for example, in 1984 these fields enrolled 48 percent of undergraduates) (Ashton et al. 2002).

(Box continues next page)

BOX 1.9 (continued)

They all offered and funded continuous upskilling of workers. In the 1980s, Singapore's National Productivity Board sponsored modular training to equip workers for jobs higher up the value chain in the country's target industries (for example, pharmaceuticals, petrochemicals, and electronics). Of the 170,000 participants during 1983–86, 75 percent were in the Basic Education for Skills Training course, which was designed explicitly for workers with an incomplete primary education to improve their English and mathematics skills (Law 2015). For employers, Singapore previously relied on wage policies (found ineffective and thus dropped) and levies to stimulate employers' investment in worker training. In 2001 the Life Long Learning Endowment Fund, seeded by a large allocation from the government's budget surpluses, replaced the levy scheme. Interest income from the endowment now funds incentives for both workers and firms to invest in workforce skills. Such spending also creates a countercyclical macroeconomic dynamic, protecting jobs and increasing training during an economic downturn, as it did during the 2008–09 global financial crisis. Korea's levy scheme was initially successful—for about a decade—and was later replaced by the Employment and Insurance Scheme. Firms use their claims to subsidize approved in-house reskilling and retraining (Yoon and Lee 2009). In recent years, a tripartite arrangement (called BRIDGE) involving the *chaebols*, universities, and small and medium enterprises has emerged to ensure that skills upgrading remains solidly focused on equipping workers to improve their productivity (Tan and Nam 2012). Finally, in Taiwan, China, the levy scheme met with limited success partly because of the predominance of small and medium enterprises. Budget allocations thus remain a major source of funding for upskilling the workforce. In all three countries, employers are involved in training their workers, by practicing or hosting workplace learning, providing inputs for curriculum design, or contributing faculty for course delivery.

Rwanda is already learning from the Asian Tiger economies. The political leadership is strongly committed to investing in workforce skills across the full spectrum of the education and training system. The country faces different conditions, however. The headwinds of today's integrated global economy are possibly stronger, and the workforce needs rising levels of general education to harness technology's full promise. The Asian economies were relentless in building systemic capacity to manage their education and training systems, treating skills for transformation as teamwork across multiple entities, working collaboratively and pragmatically to overcome implementation difficulties, relying on market forces to shape incentives, but also not shying away from government action, and using simple performance metrics to correct mistakes, test new ideas, and check for progress. A similar mind-set will help Rwanda to overcome its own enormous challenges of system construction in the coming years.

Sources: Almeida, Behrman, and Robalino 2012a, 2012b; Ashton et al. 2002; Green et al. 1999; Law 2015; O'Hare 2008; Rodrik 1995; Sung 2006; Tan and Nam 2012; Tan et al. 2016; Yoon and Lee 2009.

For the significant portion of the population who will continue creating their own jobs, capital-centric programs may be more effective and cheaper to implement than simple training programs. Many Rwandans remain self-employed, often in the informal sector. To allow their enterprises to grow, one approach is to seek to increase their human capital (through training) or their physical capital (through cash transfers, in-kind capital, or subsidized credit). Skills training for self-employed workers tends to be very expensive, and the impacts on wages are often low or nonexistent. At the same time, programs that provide physical capital—whether livestock in India or cash grants in Ghana or Uganda targeted toward growing businesses—have had strong positive impacts (Blattman and Ralston 2015). Some of these programs combine skills training with cash grants. Physical capital may be more of a constraint to entrepreneurs than human capital, or physical capital may allow them to multiply whatever gains they receive from skills training. Regardless, providing physical capital for youth to enable them to become entrepreneurs is a bold, promising approach supported by increasing evidence.

Tertiary Education and Innovation

Current Status

Higher education is important to Rwandan economic growth. Higher education can lead to economic growth through both private and public channels, with higher individual incomes and job creation as well as investments in research and development (figure 1.17). Recent empirical analysis shows that investment in education has a significant impact on growth (Bloom et al. 2014).

Rwanda has low, but rapidly rising enrollments in tertiary education. The latest numbers—for 2015—suggest that just 8 percent of tertiary-age youth are enrolled in tertiary education, well below the level in today's upper-middle-income countries. Furthermore, even with rising tertiary enrollments—and those enrollments have doubled in the last 10 years—shifting the proportion of the population with tertiary education in the workforce takes significant time, because only a small proportion of the workforce changes with each graduating cohort (figure 1.18). However, with rapid expansion of new cohorts, significant improvements are possible in the coming years.

There is historical precedent for a rapid rise in tertiary graduates. Countries such as Korea and Turkey achieved dramatic increases in tertiary education. If Rwanda were to grow its tertiary enrollment at the same rate as these countries did in their fastest periods, it could reach a high rate of tertiary enrollment (figure 1.19). Furthermore, universal tertiary enrollment is not the objective. Whereas tertiary enrollment is very high in some high-income countries (93 percent in Korea and 86 percent in the United States), other high-income countries have much lower rates, with just 57 percent enrollment in the United Kingdom and 74 percent in high-income countries as a whole. In middle-income countries, the average higher education enrollment rate is just 47 percent.

One key role of the tertiary sector is generating and adapting innovations for use in

FIGURE 1.17 Conceptual framework outlining the links between higher education and economic growth

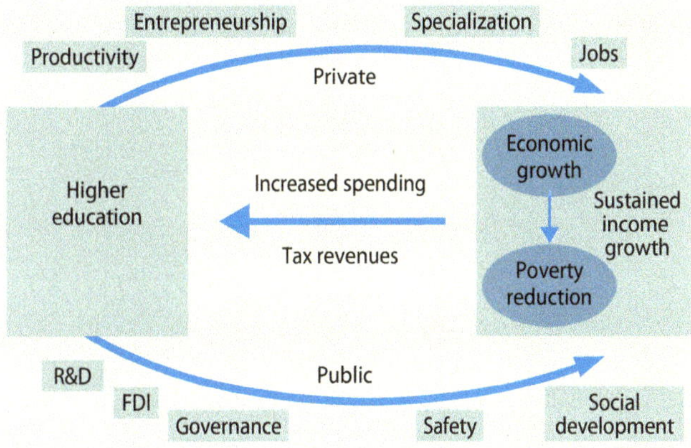

Source: Bloom et al. 2014.
Note: FDI = foreign direct investment; R&D = research and development.

FIGURE 1.18 Projected share of Rwanda's workforce with tertiary education under two growth scenarios, 2010–50

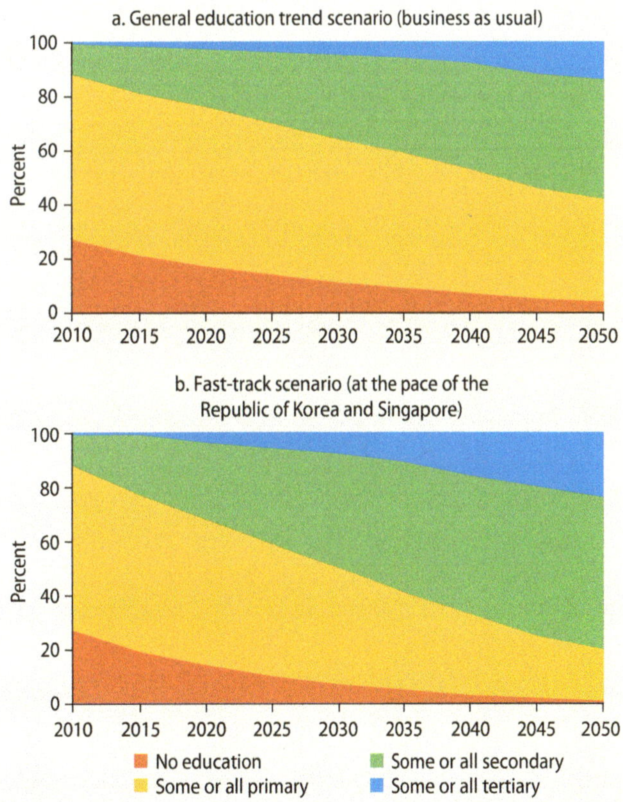

Source: Construction based on data from Lutz, Butz, and KC 2014.
Note: Panel a is based on the current rate of growth of enrollment in Rwanda. Panel b is based on the rate of growth of enrollment in the Republic of Korea and Singapore.

FIGURE 1.19 Current and projected tertiary enrollment in Rwanda, 2000–35

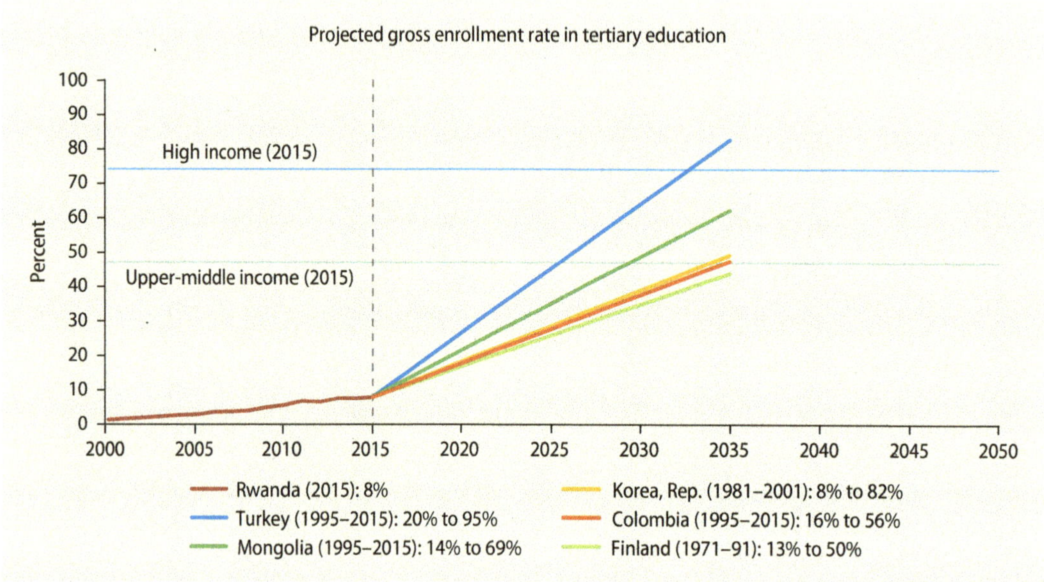

Source: Based on data from World Development Indicators (World Bank, various years).
Note: The projected enrollment rate in Rwanda is drawn from the rate of growth in enrollment of other countries. The legend shows the period over which the tertiary enrollment expansion was calculated as well as the level of tertiary enrollment at the beginning and end of the period. All comparator countries began their period of rapid expansion at a level comparable with that of Rwanda.

FIGURE 1.20 Number of Rwandan scientific publications available on the Web of Science, 1970–2015

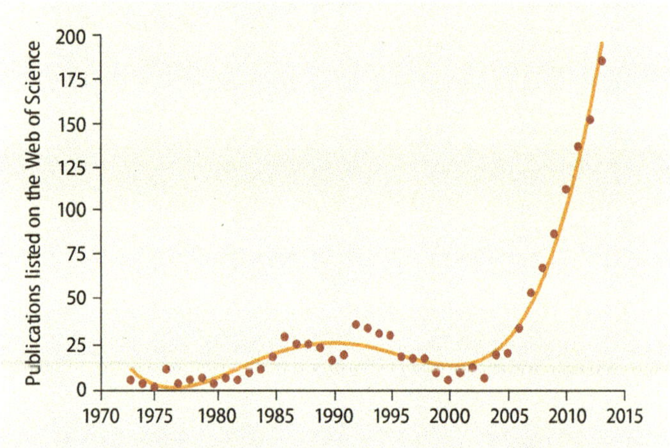

Source: Lemarchand and Tash 2015.

Rwandan industry. Rwanda is making progress in that area. In scientific publications, Rwanda most recently ranked 25 out of 53 countries in the African region and 125 in the world. The number of scientific publications per year has grown dramatically, as shown in figure 1.20. The number of patent applications has been quite low, with some indication of a recent increase (Lemarchand and Tash 2015).

Rwanda is taking action to foster innovation. Over the last decade, the government has taken steps to increase innovation capacity. One of these steps was to establish the research-focused University of Rwanda, formerly 10 other public universities. There are a total of 29 institutes of higher learning across the country. Another step was to establish various institutes that house research and innovation activities, including the National Industrial Research and Development Agency, the Rwanda Agriculture Board, the Rwanda Biomedical Center, Carnegie Mellon University-Africa, the African Institute for Mathematical Sciences, and kLab, an open space for information technology entrepreneurs to collaborate. In addition, the government has entered strategic partnerships to establish a range of "centers of excellence" in fields as diverse as mathematics, biomedical engineering, data science, and innovative mathematical pedagogy.[11] In its most recent

National Science, Technology, Innovation, and Research Policy, Rwanda seeks to establish a clear set of goals to strengthen innovation and to integrate science and technology at every level of the education system.

Nearly a century of economic theory suggests that a country like Rwanda can reap high returns from adoption and adaptation in innovation, which partnerships with higher education can help to develop. The economist Joseph Schumpeter coined the term "creative destruction" 75 years ago, referring to a process of "industrial mutation," in which new processes push out (or "destroy") the old ones (Cox and Alm 2008). Innovation drives that process: it underlies economic growth and is a crucial element of "how countries achieve prosperity" (Cicera and Maloney 2017). Countries that are farther from the development frontier—low- and middle-income countries—have a unique opportunity to benefit from innovation. Firms in Bolivia and Burundi—and Rwanda—should be able to take advantage of innovation in Singapore and Sweden and to experience extraordinary growth while investing far less, adapting innovations rather than coming up with them (Cicera and Maloney 2017).

But expanding tertiary education—and improving the capacity to innovate therein—depends crucially on expanding primary and secondary education. With upper-secondary completion at only 18 percent and lower-secondary completion at only one-third, the university can draw on only a limited number of graduates, even fewer if the university selects only those most prepared for a traditional tertiary education as opposed to technical or vocational training. As figure 1.21 shows, almost every country with higher than 20 percent tertiary enrollment has at least 60 percent of its youth graduating from lower-secondary school. Likewise, expansions in tertiary education require expansions in upper-secondary education, at least to a degree.

Proximate Causes

Relatively few graduates are specializing in key job-creation fields, such as science and engineering. According to last years' statistical yearbook (NISR 2017), nearly half of university students in Rwanda were studying social science, business, and law (table 1.1). The next biggest group was studying education. Just 6 percent were studying engineering,

FIGURE 1.21 Tertiary enrollment rate as a function of secondary completion rates

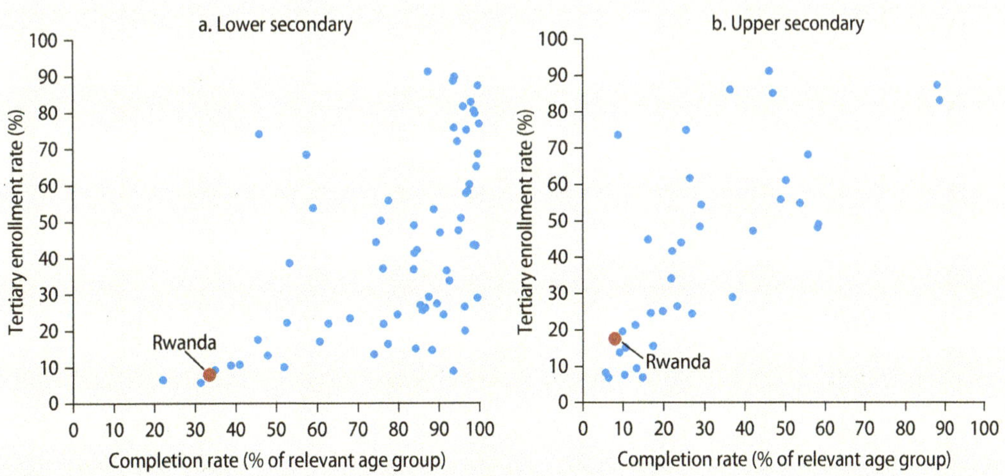

Sources: Based on data from World Development Indicators (World Bank, various years) and from United Nations Educational, Scientific, and Cultural Organization, Institute for Statistics.
Note: Data, which were accessed in 2017, are for the most recent year for the country.

manufacturing, and construction, and 9 percent were studying sciences. This chapter has discussed the importance of improving the quality of education in Rwanda, so having tertiary students in education may be worthwhile. But if Rwanda intends to grow its manufacturing and technology sectors, then the number of students in science and engineering clearly will need to grow.

Historically, Rwanda has invested more in higher education than other countries in the region. In 2000, it spent a larger proportion of its education budget on higher education than almost any other country in the region (figure 1.22). Indeed, in recent years, public financing of higher education has declined, even while the demand for tertiary education continues to grow (University of Rwanda 2016). At the same time, financing for innovation in Rwanda remains very low, most recently estimated at 0.4 percent of gross domestic product (Lemarchand and Tash 2015). In countries like Korea and Singapore, that share is closer to 4 percent.

TABLE 1.1 Distribution of tertiary students in Rwanda, by field of study

Field	% of students
Education	14
Humanities and arts	3
Social science, business, and law	45
Sciences	9
Engineering, manufacturing, and construction	6
Agriculture	5
Health and welfare	9
Service	10

Source: NISR 2017.

Investments for Transformation

Rwanda is already making dramatic reforms to its tertiary education system, both refocusing its public resources on science and engineering training and seeking to improve quality. In 2017, the government suspended some courses in 10 universities because they failed to meet various quality standards. In 2013, those public universities were converted into the single University of Rwanda in order to improve quality and efficiency.

Rwanda needs to focus its tertiary education system on key areas of investment: more science and engineering. The centers of excellence and Carnegie Mellon

FIGURE 1.22 Spending on tertiary education in Rwanda versus other countries, circa 2000 and 2015

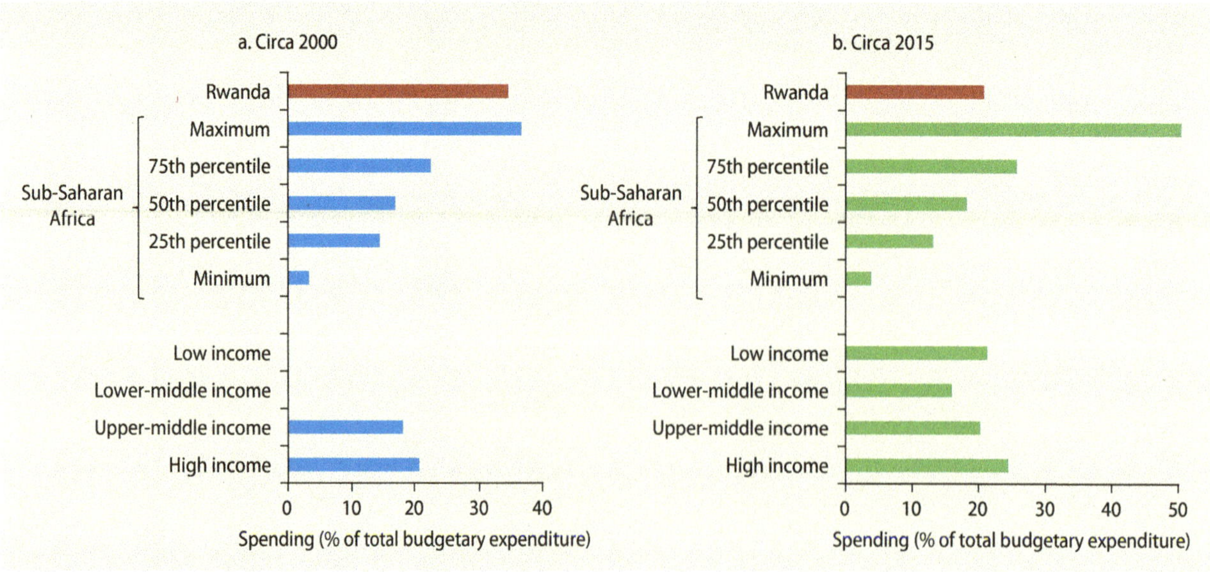

Source: Based on World Development Indicators data (World Bank, various years).

BOX 1.10 Achieving high-quality tertiary education in the Republic of Korea

Over the past 60 years, Korea has prioritized expanding access to education; as a consequence, its tertiary system has grown rapidly. In order to meet the increasing demand for education, the Korean government encouraged philanthropists to establish private universities. These reforms resulted in one of the highest gross enrollment rates in the world. In 2015, Korea had a gross enrollment rate of 93 percent at the tertiary level, which far exceeded the world average of 36 percent.

Korea also implemented several reforms to address its quality of tertiary education. Two-year teacher training programs were extended to four years in order to improve teacher practices and knowledge. Reforms included the expansion and modernization of university libraries and research systems. Resources were funneled toward collaborating with foreign scholars, publishing in leading international journals, and modernizing equipment. Korea also lowered student-teacher ratios to 15 in order to improve the learning experience.

Sources: Jones 2013; Kim 2008.

University-Africa, which offers master's degrees in engineering and information technology, are good starts. This means shifting students into strategic areas in the University of Rwanda as well. The extreme strategy for this shift is exemplified by Japan. In 2015, Japan's Ministry of Education ordered top universities to reduce their humanities and social science programs dramatically. Of 60 national universities, 26 will either close or reduce these faculties and the relevant student admissions (Grove 2015). Notably, Japan's top two universities—the two that are among the world's top 100 universities, University of Tokyo and University of Kyoto—are not making adjustments, so Japan will retain key programs in these areas. But it will shift students into strategic growth areas of study. Another, less draconian, option includes providing financial incentives for students, such as offering scholarships focused on science, technology, engineering, and mathematics (STEM), as Argentina, Australia, and Denmark have done (OECD 2012). The University of Rwanda is already focusing scholarships on STEM. But a third key element of this strategy involves improving the quality of STEM instruction in basic education, so that more students are ready to study it in higher education, as Australia, Norway, and Poland each has done in different ways. This option recalls again that effective tertiary reform relies on effective reform of basic education.

Encouraging innovation is part of transforming Rwanda's universities. In Korea, encouraging researchers to publish innovative research was a key part of the strategy for developing world-class tertiary education (box 1.10). The University of Rwanda currently has incentives in place for publication, providing researchers who publish with additional resources for research. To maximize the productivity of this research, Rwanda will want to encourage researchers to adapt existing innovations to the Rwandan context, thereby reaping the highest gains at the lowest cost.

Financing

These interventions require funding, but Rwanda is currently underspending on education (figure 1.23). Although infrastructure needs (such as roads) often seem more pressing, data from spending in 83 countries suggest that reallocating resources from infrastructure spending to social spending (that is, from roads to schools) can promote growth (Acosta-Ormaechea and Morozumi 2017). Other analysis suggests that investments in schools are more likely to drive growth than many infrastructure investments (Bose, Haque, and Osborn 2007). In the short run, infrastructure may deliver

FIGURE 1.23 **Current spending on education and health in Rwanda relative to other countries in the world**

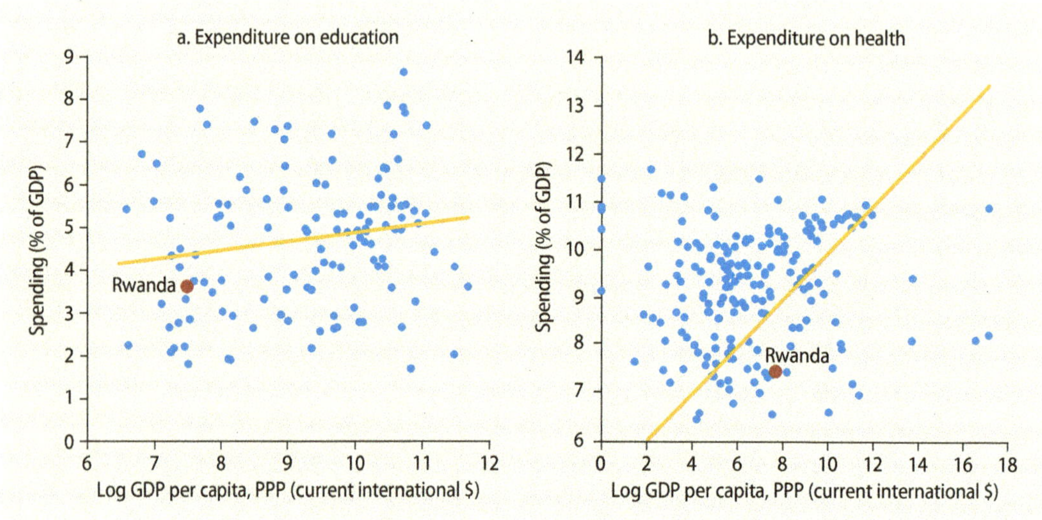

Source: Based on World Development Indicators 2017 data (World Bank, various years).
Note: PPP = purchasing power parity.

quick gains (Atolia et al. 2017), but for sustained growth, economies need to invest in broad-based literacy. Regardless, major investments in human capital are an essential part of Rwanda's growth strategy.

Notes

1. Stunting refers to children who are dramatically shorter than they should be. Specifically, it refers to children who are 2 standard deviations shorter than the median height for that age in a reference population.
2. All statistics in this paragraph are drawn from World Bank (2017b).
3. The fertility rate decline is based on Rwanda's Demographic and Health Surveys from 2005 and 2010 (NISR, various years). This sharp decline varies from the change presented by the World Development Indicators (4.52 total births per woman in 2005 to 3.92 in 2010), which uses five-year period, interpolated data from the United Nations Population Division's World Population Prospects annual data series (UN Population Division, various years).
4. Data for 2015 are from the World Development Indicators (World Bank, various years).
5. One benchmark is that learners should be reading 45–60 words per minute by the end of second grade (Abadzi 2008). The rate will not be the same for Kinyarwanda, but it is unlikely to be significantly lower.
6. All statistics in this paragraph are drawn from EDC (2017).
7. Based on analysis of the 2015 Demographic and Health Survey for Rwanda (NISR, various years).
8. At least two studies report that significant proportions of schools are concerned with absenteeism, but they do not indicate whether the absolute level of absenteeism is high or low (Bennell and Ntagaramba 2008; Valentine and Ongus 2017).
9. Rwanda has been hiring more teachers to respond to the increased number of students; however, the pupil-teacher ratio in primary schools remains high. The average pupil-teacher ratio in primary schools was 41 for low-income countries in 2015 (World Bank, various years). To reach that average, even assuming no growth in the number of new students, Rwanda needs to hire more than 20,000 additional teachers (based on NISR 2016). Currently, the system hires about 2,500 to 3,000 teachers per year, which is close to the training capacity of its teacher training institutions.
10. Owen and Associates Limited (2017). Similar reports exist for the other sectors listed.
11. Data in this paragraph come from Republic of Rwanda (2016).

References

Abadzi, H. 2008. "Efficient Learning for the Poor: New Insights into Literacy Acquisition for Children." *International Review of Education* 54 (5-6): 581–604.

Acosta-Ormaechea, S., and A. Morozumi. 2017. "Public Spending Reallocations and Economic Growth across Different Income Levels." *Economic Inquiry* 55 (1): 98–114.

Alderman, H., and R. Yemtsov. 2013. "How Can Safety Nets Contribute to Economic Growth?" Policy Research Working Paper 6437, World Bank, Washington, DC.

Al Maskari, Z. F. Al Mawali, A. Al Harthi, and A. Al Rasbi. 2015. "Oman." In *TIMSS 2015 Encyclopedia: Educational Policy and Curriculum in Mathematics and Science*, edited by I. V. S. Mullis, M. O. Martin, S. Goh, and K. Cotter. Boston, MA: TIMSS and PIRLS International Study Center, Boston College.

Almeida, R., J. Behrman, and D. Robalino. 2012a. "Overview." In *The Right Skills for the Job? Rethinking Effective Training Policies for Workers*, edited by R. Almeida, J. Behrman, and D. Robalino. Washington, DC: World Bank, Social Protection, Human Development Network.

———, eds. 2012b. *The Right Skills for the Job? Rethinking Effective Training Policies for Workers*. Washington, DC: World Bank, Social Protection, Human Development Network.

Arias, O., I. Santos, and D. K. Evans. 2018. *The Skills Balancing Act in Sub-Saharan Africa*. Washington, DC: World Bank.

Ashton, D., F. Green, J. Sung, and D. James. 2002. "The Evolution of Education and Training Strategies in Singapore, Taiwan, and S. Korea: A Development Model of Skill Formation." *Journal of Education and Work* 15 (1): 5–30.

Atolia, M., B. G. Li, R. Marto, and G. Melina. 2017. "Investing in Public Infrastructure: Roads versus Schools." *Vox*, August 9.

Avitabile, C., and R. de Hoyos. 2015. "The Heterogeneous Effect of Information on Student Performance: Evidence from a Randomized Control Trial in Mexico." Policy Research Working Paper 7422, World Bank, Washington, DC.

Barro, R., and J.-W. Lee. 2015. *Education Matters: Global Schooling Gains from the 19th to the 21st Century*. Oxford: Oxford University Press.

Bashir, S., M. Lockheed, E. Ninan, and J.- P. Tan. 2018. *Facing Forward: Schooling for Learning in Sub-Saharan Africa*. Washington, DC: World Bank.

Basinga, P., P. J. Gertler, A. Binagwaho, A. L. B. Soucat, J. Sturdy, and M. J. C. Vermeersch. 2011. "Effect on Maternal and Child Health Services in Rwanda of Payment to Primary Health-Care Providers for Performance: An Impact Evaluation." *The Lancet* 377 (9775): 1421–28.

Bennell, P., and J. Ntagaramba. 2008. "Teacher Motivation and Incentives in Rwanda: A Situational Analysis and Recommended Priority Actions." Rwanda Education NGO Cooperation Platform, Kigali.

Blattman, C., and L. Ralston. 2015. "Generating Employment in Poor and Fragile States: Evidence from Labor Market and Entrepreneurship Programs." Working Paper, University of Chicago; World Bank, Washington, DC.

Bloom, D. E., D. Canning, K. Chan, and D. L. Luca. 2014. "Higher Education and Economic Growth in Africa." *International Journal of African Higher Education* 1 (1): 22–57. https://doi.org/10.6017/ijahe.v1i1.5643.

Bold, T., D. Filmer, G. Martin, E. Molina, B. Stacy, C. Rockmore, J. Svensson, and W. Wane. 2017. "Enrollment without Learning: Teacher Effort, Knowledge, and Skill in Primary Schools in Africa." *Journal of Economic Perspectives* 31 (4): 185–204.

Bose, N., M. E. Haque, and D. R. Osborn. 2007. "Public Expenditure and Economic Growth: A Disaggregated Analysis for Developing Countries." *The Manchester School* 75 (5): 533–56.

Buehren, N., and T. Van Salisbury. 2017. "Female Enrollment in Male-Dominated Vocational Training Courses: Preferences and Prospects." Africa Gender Policy Brief, World Bank, Washington, DC.

Campos, F., M. Goldstein, L. McGorman, A. M. Munoz Boudet, and O. Pimhidzai. 2015. "Breaking the Metal Ceiling: Female Entrepreneurs Who Succeed in Male-Dominated Sectors." Policy Research Working Paper 7503, World Bank, Washington, DC.

Carneiro, P., and J. J. Heckman. 2003. "Human Capital Policy." In *Inequality in America: What Role for Human Capital Policies?* by J. J. Heckman and A. Krueger. Cambridge, MA: MIT Press.

Chuhan-Pole, P., L. Christiaensen, A. Dennis, G. Kambou, M. Angwafo, M. Buitano, V. Korman, C. Galinda Pardo, and A. Sanoh. 2013. *Africa's Pulse: October 2014.* Washington, DC: World Bank, Office of the Chief Economist, Africa Region.

Cicera, X., and W. F. Maloney. 2017. *The Innovation Paradox: Developing-Country Capabilities and the Unrealized Promise of Technological Catch-up.* Washington, DC: World Bank.

Cilliers, J., and S. Taylor. 2017. "Monitoring Teachers and Changing Teaching Practice: Evidence from a Field Experiment." Georgetown University, Washington, DC.

Commission on Growth and Development. 2008. *The Growth Report: Strategies for Sustained Growth and Inclusive Development.* Washington, DC: World Bank.

Cox, W. M., and R. Alm. 2008. "Creative Destruction." In *The Concise Encyclopedia of Economics*, 2d ed., edited by D. R. Henderson. Indianapolis, IN: Liberty Fund.

Crouch, L., and K. A. Merseth. 2017. "Stumbling at the First Step: Efficiency Implications of Poor Performance in the Foundational First Five Years." *Prospects* 47 (3): 175–96.

De Ree, J., K. Muralidharan, M. Pradhan, and H. Rogers. 2018. "Double for Nothing? Experimental Evidence on an Unconditional Teacher Salary Increase in Indonesia." *Quarterly Journal of Economics* 133 (2): 993–1039.

EDC (Education Development Center). 2017. *Literacy, Language, and Learning Initiative (L3): National Fluency and Mathematics Assessment of Rwandan Schools.* Report for U.S. Agency for International Development. Waltam, MA: EDC.

Eozenou, P. H.-V., and M. Shekar. 2017. *Stunting Reduction in Sub-Saharan Africa.* Washington, DC: World Bank. http://documents.worldbank.org/curated/en/126621505397202676/Stunting-reduction-in-Sub-Saharan-Africa.

Evans, D. K., and A. Popova. 2016. "What Really Works to Improve Learning in Developing Countries? An Analysis of Divergent Findings in Systematic Reviews." *The World Bank Research Observer* 31 (2): 242–70.

Fryer, R. 2017. "Management and Student Achievement: Evidence from a Randomized Field Experiment." Working Paper, Harvard University, Cambridge, MA.

Galasso, E., A. Wagstaff, S. Naudeau, and M. Shekar. 2016. "The Economic Costs of Stunting and How to Reduce Them." Policy Research Note, World Bank, Washington, DC.

Gobilee, R. A. 2016. "The Role of Training Levies in Financing the Expansion of Technical and Vocational Education and Training (TVET) in South East Asia: The Experience of Malaysia through the Human Resource Development Fund (HRDF)." PowerPoint slides, Planning, Strategy, and Development Division, HRDF, Kuala Lumpur.

Gove, A., M. K. Poole, and B. Pipe. 2017. "Designing for Scale: Reflections on Rolling Out Reading Improvement in Kenya and Liberia." *New Directions for Child and Adolescent Development* 155 (Spring): 77–95.

Government of Rwanda. 2016. "Mid-Term Review Report of the Five-Year Priority Skills Development Programme." Government of Rwanda, Kigali.

Government of Singapore. 1991. "Improving Primary School Education." Report of the Review Committee, Government of Singapore.

Green, F., D. Ashton, D. James, and J. Sung. 1999. "The Role of the State in Skill Formation: Evidence from the Republic of Korea, Singapore, and Taiwan." *Oxford Review of Economic Policy* 15 (1): 82–96.

Grove, J. 2015. "Social Sciences and Humanities Faculties 'to Close' in Japan after Ministerial Intervention." *Times of Higher Education*, September 14.

Handa, S., L. Natali, D. Seidenfeld, G. Tembo, and B. Davis. 2018. "Can Unconditional Cash Transfers Raise Long-Term Living Standards? Evidence from Zambia." *Journal of Development Economics* 133 (July): 42–65.

Hanushek, E. A. 2016. "Will More Higher Education Improve Economic Growth?" *Oxford Review of Economic Policy* 32 (4): 538–52.

Hanushek, E. A., D. T. Jamison, E. A. Jamison, and L. Woessmann. 2008. "Education and Economic Growth." *Education Next* 8 (2): n.p.

Hanushek, E., and L. Woessmann. 2012. "Do Better Schools Lead to More Growth? Cognitive Skills, Economic Outcomes, and Causation." *Journal of Economic Growth* 17 (4): 267–321.

Hicks, J. H. H., M. Kremer, I. Mbiti, and E. Miguel. 2015. *Vocational Education in Kenya: A Randomized Evaluation; 3ie Grantee Final Report.* New Delhi: International Initiative for Impact Evaluation (3ie).

Hjelm, L. 2016. "Comprehensive Food Security and Vulnerability Analysis." World Food Programme, Rome.

Hong, S.-C., and J.-H. Lee. 2016. "Accumulating Human Capital for Sustainable Development in Korea." Korea Development Institute, Seoul.

Jensen, R. 2010. "The (Perceived) Returns to Education and the Demand for Schooling." *Quarterly Journal of Economics* 125 (2): 515–48.

Jones, S. R. 2013. "Education Reform in Korea." OECD Economics Department Working Paper 1067, OECD Publishing, Paris.

Karra, M., D. Canning, and J. Wilde. 2017. "The Effect of Fertility Decline on Economic Growth in Africa: A Macrosimulation Model." *Population and Development Review* 43 (51): 237–63.

Kesamang, M., C. Mudongo, O. Keatimilwe, and T. Bolaane. 2012. "Botswana." In *TIMSS 2011 Encyclopedia: Educational Policy and Curriculum in Mathematics and Science*, edited by I. V. S. Mullis, M. O. Martin, C. A. Minnich, G. M. Stanco, A. Arora, V. A. S. Centurino, and C. E. Castle, 177–90. Boston, MA: TIMSS and PIRLS International Study Center, Boston College.

Kim, Y.-C. 2008. "Understanding Korean Educational Policy: Universalization of Tertiary Education." Korea Education Policy Research Institute, Seoul.

Kraft, M. A., D. Blazar, and D. Hogan. 2017. "The Effect of Teacher Coaching on Instruction and Achievement: A Meta-Analysis of the Causal Evidence." Harvard University, Cambridge, MA.

Law, S. S. 2015. *A Breakthrough in Vocational and Technical Education: The Singapore Story*. Singapore: World Scientific Publishing.

Lee, J.-H., and S. C. Hong. 2014. *The Development of Vocational High Schools in Korea during the Industrialization Period*. Seoul: Ministry of Strategy and Finance.

Lee, J.-W., and H. Lee. 2016. "Human Capital in the Long Run." *Journal of Development Economics* 122 (C): 147–69.

Lee, K. W., and K. Taejong. 2015. "Real-Time Impact Evaluation of a Capacity-Building Health Project in Lao PDR." *KDI Journal of Economic Policy*, November 30.

Lee, S. K., C. B. Goh, B. Fredriksen, and J.-P. Tan. 2008. *Toward a Better Future: Education and Training for Economic Development in Singapore since 1965*. Development Practice in Education Series. Washington, DC: World Bank.

Lemarchand, G. A., and A. Tash, eds. 2015. *Mapping Research and Innovation in the Republic of Rwanda*. GO-SPIN Country Profiles in Science, Technology, and Innovation Policy, vol. 4. Paris: United Nations Educational, Scientific, and Cultural Organization (UNESCO).

Loyalka, P., C. Liu, Y. Song, H. Yi, X. Huang, J. Wei, L. Zhang, Y. Shi, J. Chu, and S. Rozelle. 2013. "Can Information and Counseling Help Students from Poor Rural Areas Go to High School? Evidence from China." *Journal of Comparative Economics* 41 (4): 1012–25.

Lutz, W., W. P. Butz, and S. KC. 2014. *World Population and Human Capital in the Twenty-First Century*. Oxford, U.K.: Oxford University Press.

Ministry of Education, Rwanda. 2016. "ICT in Education Policy." Ministry of Education, Kigali.

———. 2017. *2017/18 Forward-Looking Joint Review of the Education Sector Summary Report*. Kigali: Ministry of Education, June.

Ministry of Education and Sports, Uganda. 2014. "Teacher Issues in Uganda: A Shared Vision for an Effective Teachers Policy." UNESCO, International Institute for Educational Planning (IIEP), Pôle de Dakar, Paris.

Montenegro, C. E., and H. A. Patrinos. 2014. "Comparable Estimates of Returns to Schooling around the World." Policy Research Working Paper 7020, World Bank, Washington, DC.

Muralidharan, K., A. Singh, and A. J. Ganimian. 2017. "Disrupting Education? Experimental Evidence on Technology-Aided Instruction in India." NBER Working Paper 22923, National Bureau of Economic Research, Cambridge, MA.

NCEE (National Center on Education and the Economy). n.d. "Singapore: Teacher and Principal Quality." NCEE, Washington, DC.

Nguyen, T. 2008. "Information, Role Models, and Perceived Returns to Education: Experimental Evidence from Madagascar." Working Paper, Abdul Latif Jameel Poverty Action Lab, Cambridge, MA.

NISR (National Institute of Statistics of Rwanda). 2016. *Statistical Yearbook 2016*. Kigali: Government of Rwanda.

———. 2017. *Labor Force Survey 2017*. Kigali: Government of Rwanda.

———. Various years. *Rwanda: Demographic and Health Survey*. Kigali: Government of Rwanda.

Ochs, K., and A. Yonemura. 2013. "Managing Teacher Migration: Implications for Policy and Practice in Africa." Commonwealth Education Partnerships 2012/2013 (online). http://www.cedol.org/wp-content/uploads/2013/09/Managing-teacher-migration-Ochs-and-Yonemura.pdf.

OECD (Organisation for Economic Co-operation and Development). 2010. "Singapore: Rapid Improvement Followed by Strong Performance." In *Strong Performers and Successful Reformers in Education: Lessons from PISA for the United States*, ch. 7. Paris: OECD.

———. 2012. *Science, Technology, and Industry Outlook 2012*. Paris: OECD.

O'Hare, D. 2008. "Education in Ireland: Evolution of Economic and Education Policies since the Early 1990s." In *An African Exploration of the East Asian Education Experience*, edited by B. Fredriksen and J.-P. Tan. Development Practice in Education Series. Washington, DC: World Bank.

Owen and Associates Limited. 2017. "Skills Audit in Agriculture Sector in Rwanda 2017." Report submitted to Capacity Development and Employment Services Board (CESB), Kigali, May.

Perera, M., and D. Aboal. 2017. "Evaluación del impacto de la plataforma adaptativa de matemática en los resultados de los aprendizajes." Centro de Investigaciones Económicas, Montevideo.

Pillay, P. 2010. *Linking Higher Education and Economic Development: Implications for Africa from Three Successful Systems*. Cape Town: Centre for Higher Education Transformation (CHET).

Popova, A., D. K. Evans, and V. Arancibia. 2016. "Training Teachers on the Job: What Works and How to Measure It." Policy Research Working Paper 7834, World Bank, Washington, DC.

Popova, A., D. K. Evans, M. Breeding, and V. Arancibia. 2017. "The Global Landscape of In-Service Teacher Professional Development Programs: The Gap between Evidence and Practice." World Bank, Washington, DC.

PSMB (*Pembangunan Sumber Manusia Berhad*). n.d. "Human Resources Development Fund Malaysia: Moving Forward." Ministry of Human Resources, Kuala Lumpur.

———. 2016. *Annual Report: "Think Different."* Kuala Lumpur: Human Resource Development Fund (HRDF). https://www.hrdf.com.my.

Ralston, L., C. Andrews, and A. Hsiao. 2017. "The Impacts of Safety Nets in Africa: What Are We Learning?" Policy Research Working Paper 8255, World Bank, Washington, DC.

Ranis, G., F. Stewart, and A. Ramirez. 2000. "Economic Growth and Human Development." *World Development* 28 (2): 197–219.

REB (Rwanda Education Board). 2016. "School-Based Mentor Program Framework, 2017–2022." REB, Kigali, July 12. http://www.reb.rw/fileadmin/default/templates/2017_doc/SBMP/SBMP_Framework.pdf.

Republic of Rwanda. 2016. "National Science, Technology, Innovation, and Research Policy." Draft, Republic of Rwanda, Kigali, July.

Rodríguez, A., C. Dahlman, and J. Salmi. 2008. *Knowledge and Innovation for Competitiveness in Brazil*. Washington, DC: World Bank.

Rodrik, D. 1995. "Getting Interventions Right: How South Korea and Taiwan Grew Rich." *Economic Policy* 20 (4): 55–107.

Roseth, V., and A. Valerio. 2016. "Improve Workforce Development Systems in 5 (Not So Simple) Steps." World Bank, Washington, DC.

Saraf, P. 2017. "On-the-Job Training: Returns, Barriers to Provision, and Policy Implications." Policy Research Working Paper 8090, World Bank, Washington, DC.

Shekar, M., J. Kakietek, J. D. Eberwein, and D. Walters. 2016. "An Investment Framework for Nutrition: Reaching the Global Targets for Stunting, Anemia, Breastfeeding, and Wasting." World Bank, Washington, DC.

Silva de Tiloka, T. S. 2017. "Population Control Policies and Fertility Convergence." *Journal of Economic Perspectives* 31 (4): 205–28.

Snilstveit, B., J. Stevenson, R. Menon, D. Phillips, E. Gallagher, M. Geleen, H. Jobse, T. Schmidt, and E. Jimenez. 2016. *The Impact of Education Programmes on Learning and School Participation in Low- and Middle-Income Countries: A Systematic Review Summary Report*. 3ie Systematic Review Summary 7. London: International Initiative for Impact Evaluation (3ie).

Soares, F. V., R. P. Ribas, and R. G. Osório. 2007. "Evaluating the Impact of Brazil's Bolsa Família: Cash Transfer Programmes in Comparative Perspective." IPC Evaluation Note 1, United Nations Development Programme, International Poverty Centre, Brasilia.

Stevens, A. H., M. Kurlaender, and M. Grosz. 2015. "Career Technical Education and Labor

Market Outcomes: Evidence from California Community Colleges." NBER Working Paper 21137, National Bureau of Economic Research, Cambridge, MA.

Sung, J. 2006. *Explaining the Economic Success of Singapore: The Developmental Worker as the Missing Link*. Cheltenham: Edward Elgar.

Tan, J.-P., K. H. Lee, R. Flynn, V. Roseth, and Y.-J. J. Nam. 2016. *Workforce Development in Emerging Economies: Comparative Perspectives on Institutions, Praxis, and Policies*. Directions in Development Series: Human Development. Washington, DC: World Bank.

Tan, J.-P., and Y.-J. J. Nam. 2012. "Pre-Employment Technical and Vocational Education and Training: Fostering Relevance, Effectiveness, and Efficiency." In *The Right Skills for the Job? Rethinking Effective Training Policies for Workers*, edited by R. Almeida, J. Behrman, and D. Robalino, 67–103. Washington, DC: World Bank, Social Protection, Human Development Network.

Tashobya, A. 2017. "Quality Education Must Be Our Priority—Kagame." *New Times*, December 19.

Tucker, M. ed. 2014. *Chinese Lessons: Shanghai's Rise to the Top of the PISA League Tables*. Washington, DC: National Center on Education and the Economy, Center on International Education Benchmarking.

UNFPA (United Nations Population Fund). 2017. "Unlocking Rwanda's Potential to Reap the Demographic Dividend." Policy Brief, UNFPA, New York, October.

UN Population Division. Various years. *World Population Prospects*. New York: United Nations. https://esa.un.org/unpd/wpp/.

University of Rwanda. 2016. "Resource Mobilisation Strategy and Implementation Plan." Directorate of Resource Mobilisation and Investment, University of Rwanda, November.

Upper Quartile and Institute of Policy Analysis and Research Rwanda. 2015. *Final Evaluation Report: Evaluation of Results-Based Aid in Rwandan Education*. Edinburgh: Upper Quartile.

USAID (U.S. Agency for International Development). 2014. "Rwanda Nutrition Profile." USAID, Washington, DC.

———. 2017. *Literacy, Language, and Learning Initiative: National Fluency and Mathematics Assessment of Rwandan Schools*. Washington, DC: USAID.

Valentine, J., and R. W. Ongus. 2017. "Extrinsic Motivation and Its Effects on the Productivity of Teachers of English Language Subject in Primary Schools in Gasabo District of Kigali City, Rwanda." Paper prepared for the "English Language in Education and Research" conference, Mount Kenya University, Kigali, March 7–8.

van der Berg, S., N. Spaull, G. Wills, M. Gustafsson, and J. Kotzé. 2016. *Identifying Binding Constraints in Education: Synthesis Report for the Programme to Support Pro-Poor Policy Development*. University of Stellenbosch, Department of Economics, May 24. http://resep.sun.ac.za/wp-content/uploads/2016/05/PSPPD_BICiE-email.pdf.

Varaprasad, N. 2016. *50 Years of Technical Education in Singapore: How to Build a World Class TVET System*. Singapore: World Scientific Publishing.

Warschauer, M., and M.-L. Liaw. 2010. "Emerging Technologies in Adult Literacy and Language Education." National Institute for Literacy, Emerging Technologies in Adult Literacy and Language Education, Washington, DC, June.

Westoff, C. F. 2013. "The Recent Fertility Transition in Rwanda." *Population and Development Review* 38 (s1): 169–78.

WHO (World Health Organization), World Bank, and Ministry of Health, Vietnam. 2015. *Success Factors for Women's and Children's Health: Viet Nam*. Geneva: WHO.

Wilson, J. 2014. "Investing in English Skills: The Limited English Proficient Workforce in U.S. Metropolitan Areas." Metropolitan Policy Program, Brookings Institution, Washington, DC. https://www.brookings.edu/wp-content/uploads/2014/09/metro_20140924_investing_in_english_skils_report.pdf.

World Bank. 2013. "Malaysia Workforce Development, Country Report, Systems Approach for Better Education Results." Education Global Practice, World Bank, Washington, DC. www.worldbank.org/education/saber.

———. 2017a. "Project Appraisal Document: Stunting Prevention and Reduction Project, Rwanda." World Bank, Washington, DC.

———. 2017b. "Rwanda Nutrition Situation Analysis and Policy Options." World Bank Group, Washington, DC.

———. 2017c. "Rwanda Priority Skills for Growth (PSG) Program-for-Results." Program Appraisal Document Report 116204-RW, World Bank, Washington, DC.

———. 2018. *World Development Report 2018: Learning to Realize Education's Promise.* Washington, DC: World Bank.

———. Various years. World Development Indicators database. Washington, DC: World Bank. http://databank.worldbank.org/data/home.aspx.

World Economic Forum. 2008. *Global Competitiveness Report, 2007–08.* Geneva: World Economic Forum.

———. 2017. "Rwanda 52nd." In *Global Competitiveness Index, 2016–2017* (online edition). Geneva: World Economic Forum. http://reports.weforum.org/pdf/gci-2016-2017/WEF_GCI_2016_2017_Profile_RWA.pdf.

World Food Programme. 2016. "Report Finds Malnutrition Rates in Rwanda Have Improved, but More Work Is Still Needed." World Food Programme News, April 5.

Yaacob, M. 2016. "Private Sector Engagement in TVET—Malaysia's Experience." Presentation at the "8th Annual Expert Meeting of the Initiative on Employment and Skills Strategies in Southeast Asia (ESSSA)," Ministry of Department of Skills Development, Philippines and Ministry of Human Resources, Malaysia, Cebu City, October 11–12.

Yoon, J. H., and B.-H. Lee. 2009. "The Transformation of the Government-Led Vocational Training System in Korea." In *Vocational Training. International Perspectives,* edited by G. Bosch and J. Charest, 163–86. London: Routledge.

Zeitlin, A., C. Leaver, O. Ozier, and P. Serneels. 2017. "Recruitment, Motivation, and Retention Effects of Teacher Performance Pay." S-38408-RWA-1, International Growth Centre, London.

2

Transformation through Trade: Using Exports and Regional Integration to Drive Future Growth

Introduction

To achieve its aspiration of becoming a high-income country by 2050, Rwanda will have to accelerate the growth of trade. Inflows of development assistance have financed a large share of investment and powered gross domestic product (GDP) growth in the past two decades, but they are likely to attenuate in the coming two decades as Rwanda progresses toward middle-income status. Trade will become an increasingly important driver of growth. Exports will provide foreign exchange to purchase much-needed investment in equipment, high-technology goods, intermediate components, and product varieties and will foster productivity by allowing firms to exploit increasingly large economies of scale. Increased import capacity will facilitate access to high-technology goods and foster competition that drives productivity. Trade expansion also implies the need to attract foreign direct investment (FDI), since multinational companies bring in managerial, technical, and design skills at the same time that their networks facilitate access to new export markets (Freund and Moran 2017).

Trade expansion is central to creating new, higher-productivity jobs that facilitate growth through structural transformation. Moving labor from low-productivity jobs, mainly in agriculture, to higher-productivity jobs in a range of mostly urban activities is imperative for growth. East Asia made this transition to high growth by relying on labor-intensive manufacturing for export. Rwanda, as with much of Africa, will require not only labor-intensive manufacturing but also agribusiness, horticulture, and selected services—what some have called "industries without smokestacks" (Newfarmer, Page, and Tarp, forthcoming). These activities, taken together, hold the promise of doing for Rwanda what manufacturing did for East Asia in the 1990s. They are labor intensive and tradable, and they have high value added per worker. As in traditional manufacturing, technological change is rapid and can spawn rapid productivity growth; some exhibit scale and agglomeration economies (Ebling and Janz 1999; Ghani and Kharas 2010). In a world of recent technological revolutions in information and communication technology (ICT), manufacturing techniques, and global value chains (Hallward-Driemeier and Nayyar 2017), Rwanda has an opportunity to leverage greater integration into regional and global markets and to propel structural transformation and growth (Nayyar 2017).

On the basis of a comparison with countries experiencing rates of economic growth similar to those required for Rwanda to achieve upper-middle-income status by 2035, exports as a share of GDP will have to increase significantly. Rwanda will need double-digit year-on-year export growth for every year up to 2035. Meeting such a target will be difficult but not impossible. Efforts begin with recognition that the share of exports in national income is still low relative to that of other countries with comparable per capita income levels; it is low even when compared with that of other landlocked countries. Rwanda cannot achieve its growth aspirations without a major export push.

Meeting Rwanda's export objectives requires a comprehensive trade policy that spans services, industry, and agriculture. Whereas other fast-growing countries (notably in East Asia) relied primarily on export-oriented manufacturing to drive up productivity and absorb low-skill workers, Rwanda still faces significant barriers to becoming globally competitive in manufacturing because of its remote location and detachment from global supply chains. Analysis from this chapter suggests that no one sector will be able to drive the necessary export and employment growth on its own. Rwanda will instead have to produce high-quality products for the region (especially in manufacturing and agroprocessing) and to develop other sectors that are similarly tradable and productive, but less dependent on location (such as tourism, professional services, and ICT). The government of Rwanda will thus have to build further on the service sector (the largest current source of exports), strongly accelerate industrial growth, and expand into other high-value agricultural export goods (such as horticulture).

Regional integration offers a key opportunity to stimulate transformation. Trading with neighboring countries, particularly the East African Community (EAC) and the Democratic Republic of Congo, offers significant opportunities for Rwanda. Although the current volume of direct trade is still limited because of comparable production capabilities, trading with the region can serve as a vital training ground for learning to export and produce higher-quality goods. It also can stimulate productivity in priority sectors (notably services) through competitive pressures and takeovers from leading firms in the region.

To assist the government in meeting its medium-term trade objectives, this chapter highlights five major priorities, together with a subset of policy options, that should figure prominently in a comprehensive program using trade to accelerate and sustain growth:

1. *Harness the EAC and SADC as a platform for transformation by aligning regional incentives, harmonizing standards, and exploiting economies of scale.* Accomplishing this will require assertive negotiations to reform the common external tariff (CET) and the disadvantages it imposes on Rwandan producers and consumers, to remove nontariff barriers that restrict Rwanda's exports, and to harmonize competing tax incentives that erode the tax base while providing minimal economic benefit. Maintaining a competitive value for the Rwandan franc, especially relative to neighboring currencies, is critical to export competitiveness.
2. *Improve trade connectivity by lowering transport costs within and across the region.* Recent progress in lowering transport costs that put Rwanda at a significant disadvantage relative to competitors in the region has already stimulated exports, but more can be done to reduce delays at borders and in transit and to form a logistics hub in Kigali. No less important is aggressive pursuit of open skies agreements that would pave the way for RwandAir to expand into new markets.
3. *Increase service sector productivity, both as a critical input to other priority sectors and as a source of exports.* Rwanda already is a services-exporting economy—some 50 percent of foreign exchange earnings are from tourism and other services exports. Accelerating their development requires promoting regional competition

by reducing obstacles to investments in services, harmonizing regulations and tax policies that otherwise hamper regional competition, and seizing opportunities to develop new services exports. Permitting easy access to imported skills through liberalization of professional services can remedy near-term skills deficits and promote skills upgrading and learning for Rwandans.

4. *Stimulate foreign and domestic investment into tradable sectors by using selective time-bound and performance-driven incentives.* High priorities include mapping tax incentives to ensure that they conform to overall development objectives and then monitoring performance of beneficiaries to ensure that commitments are fulfilled. They also include targeting investment promotion efforts more effectively and improving investor aftercare once foreign companies set up in Rwanda.
5. *Accelerate industrialization through diversification, value addition, and quality upgrading.* Ongoing efforts to add value to coffee production could be complemented through more aggressive efforts in mining (see chapter 4 of this report). A supplier development program could increase local value added by linking large exporters to local sources.

With the adoption of these five priorities, the government will be in a very strong position to raise exports and use trade to create productive jobs and foster the structural transformation necessary to drive growth.

Setting the Stage: Policy, Performance, and Challenges

Recent Developments in Trade Policy

Rwanda has progressively improved its policy framework governing trade. Since 2000, the government has adopted a wide range of reforms to stimulate export growth. These reforms include joining the EAC and COMESA, making significant improvements in the investment climate, and establishing an integrated set of strategies to address both general and sector-specific challenges.

Joining the EAC helped to bring down tariffs, while also spurring substantial reductions in transport costs and time spent at border crossings. The accession into the EAC's CET reduced average tariff rates from 16.5 to 11 percent, which strongly benefitted intraregional trade, especially with Tanzania and Uganda.[1] Regional integration also enabled greater cooperation on trade facilitation along East Africa's two trade corridors: the Northern Corridor (Mombasa) and the Central Corridor (Dar es Salaam), which has significantly reduced the overall cost and time to move goods to port (see priority 2).

The investment climate has improved considerably, largely through establishment of the Rwanda Development Board (RDB). The government has focused extensively on improving and streamlining the country's business environment. The extent of this progress is notable, as is evident in the World Bank's Doing Business rankings, where Rwanda moved from 158 in the world in 2007 to 29 in 2019 (figure 2.1), considerably higher than the regional average (table 2.1).

FIGURE 2.1 Rwanda's Ease of Doing Business Ranking, 2007–19

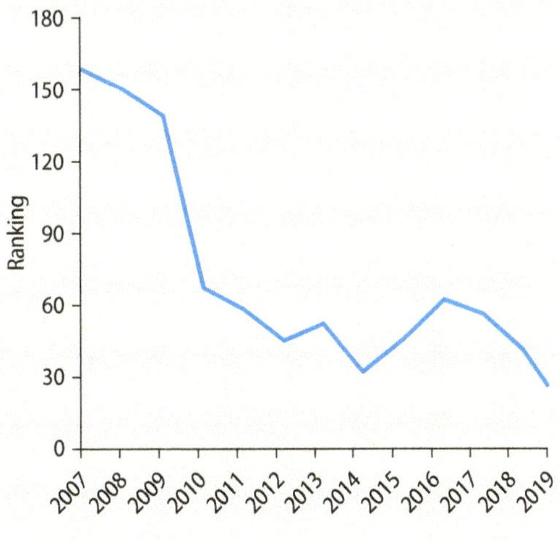

Source: Doing Business database (World Bank, various years).
Note: Out of 190 countries.

TABLE 2.1 Ease of Doing Business 2019 ranking for Rwanda and average for the East African Community

Indicator	Rwanda	EAC average
Ease of doing business rank	*29*	*119*
Starting a business	51	116
Dealing with construction permits	106	143
Getting electricity	68	129
Registering property	2	112
Getting credit	3	83
Protecting minority investors	14	96
Paying taxes	35	97
Trading across borders	88	142
Enforcing contracts	78	91
Resolving insolvency	58	110

Source: Doing Business (World Bank, 2019).
Note: Out of 190 countries. Data cover the period June 2, 2017–May 1, 2018. EAC = East African Community.

Improvements have been particularly evident since establishment of the RDB. Registration and aftercare have improved significantly, company registration can now be completed within a few hours, and all permits and documents can be obtained at RDB's one-stop shop. Investment promotion activities have also become more plentiful and targeted to priority sectors, while private sector concerns are better addressed across the wider government. As a result, Rwanda now ranks second in investment climate in Sub-Saharan Africa, after Mauritius.

The government has adopted a broad trade policy framework of general and sector-specific strategies that directs attention to high-priority areas. Recent years have seen the development of a large set of policy documents, offering both general and sector-specific plans. These policies tend to align closely with regard to both recommended policy instruments and priority sectors. Through extensive private sector consultations, some of these sectoral policies have been particularly effective (illustrated later in box 2.1 for coffee exports). The integrated nature of this policy environment also means that it is increasingly providing guidance for various ministries (see, for example, box 2.4 on the cross-governmental strategy for textiles, apparel, and leather).

Recent Export Performance

Rwanda's policy framework has enabled it to diversify exports while raising the value of traditional commodity exports. Rwanda succeeded in growing its exports by about 20 percent annually from 2000 to 2014, albeit from a low base. By 2016, total exports of all goods and services reached 20.1 percent of GDP. A comparison between 2005 and 2016 (table 2.2) shows that the country's exports have become less dependent on the three traditional exports: tea, coffee, and minerals. Although the share of these traditional exports dropped from 41 to 25 percent, their overall value rose from US$126 million to US$415 million.

Trade policy that focuses on adding value has limited the impact of international commodity price fluctuations on exports. This connection is exemplified by the government's coffee strategy. Through active engagement, the average farm gate price of coffee cherries grew from FRW 50 per kilogram in 2002 to FRW 250 per kilogram in 2015 (box 2.1). These efforts also helped to offset drops in international prices, which fell between 2011 and 2015 and only recently stabilized. By continuing to raise value added, Rwanda is laying a foundation for resurgent earnings once commodity prices rebound.

Rwanda is rapidly becoming a service-exporting economy. Today, half of Rwanda's total export earnings come from services (table 2.2). In 2016, for example, tourism constituted 23 percent of exports, while transport, ICT, construction, and finance jointly accounted for another 11 percent. This does not count services associated with the large volume of reexports. For services to become a driver of growth in the future requires high-level attention to efficiency (a point to which the chapter returns below).

Rwanda's (nonmineral) industrial sector has also started exporting, particularly for agroprocessing. Since 2005, light manufacturing has remained roughly constant in export share (7 percent), but export value has increased from US$23

TABLE 2.2 Rwandan exports, by sector, 2005 and 2016

Sector and subsector	2005 US$ (millions)	2005 Share (%)	2016 US$ (millions)	2016 Share (%)
Services				
Tourism	49	16	390	23
Government goods and services	38	12	254	15
Transport	33	11	91	5
Information and communication technology	0	0	41	2
Construction	0	0	37	2
Financial services	0	0	28	2
Maintenance and repairs	0	0	7	0
Total services	120	39	848	50
Industry				
Minerals	65	21	282	17
Light manufacturing	23	7	94	6
Agroprocessing	1	0	72	4
Total industry	88	28	447	27
Agriculture				
Coffee and tea	61	20	133	8
Other agriculture	0	0	32	2
Horticulture	1	0	9	1
Total agriculture	62	20	174	10
Reexports	41	13	216	13
Total	311	100	1,685	100

Source: Calculations based on Comtrade data (United Nations, various years).

BOX 2.1 Transformation of the coffee sector

In the late 1990s, Rwanda's government closely controlled the coffee sector, dictating a single coffee price for the entire season and providing no incentive for farmers to upgrade to higher-value coffee processing. With little investments, the existing stock of coffee trees aged, soil fertility declined, and crops were weakened by insects and fungal diseases. By 2000, coffee production had declined in volume, and 90 percent of Rwanda's crop was classified as low-quality, "ordinary" coffee.

To break out of this "low-quantity, low-quality" trap, the National Coffee Strategy was adopted in 2002. The strategy fundamentally restructured the coffee sector by drastically increasing the share of high-quality ("fully washed") coffee from 1 percent in 2002 to 60 percent in 2006. Shifting the pricing of beans from volume to quality incentivized farmers to raise the value of their coffee (processing it in a washing station). The sector was also liberalized to attract new washing stations and farmer associations.

The effect of these policies was dramatic. The number of washing stations increased from 2 in 2002 to 245 in 2015. This expansion increased exports of fully washed coffee from less than 1 percent in 2002 to 21 percent in 2010 and up to 50 percent in 2015. The rise in quality increased the average farm gate price of coffee cherries from about FRW 50 per kilogram in 2002, to FRW 200 per kilogram in 2010, and to FRW 250 per kilogram in 2015 (figure B2.1.1). This focus on value addition was the main reason why coffee exports rose from US$14.6 million in 2002 to more than US$62 million in 2015.

(Box continues next page)

BOX 2.1 (continued)

FIGURE B2.1.1 Number of coffee-washing stations and average price of coffee cherries in Rwanda, 2002–15

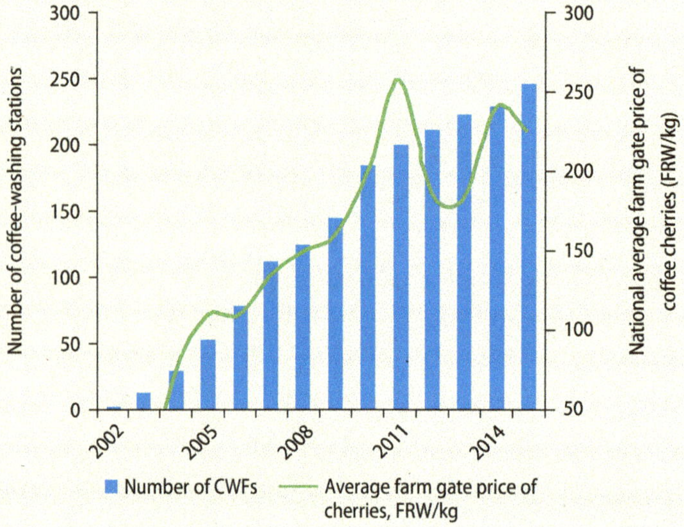

Note: CWF = coffee-washing station; FRW/kg = Rwanda francs per kilogram.

Source: Morjaria and Steenbergen 2017.

FIGURE 2.2 Value of Rwandan exports, by destination, 2001–16

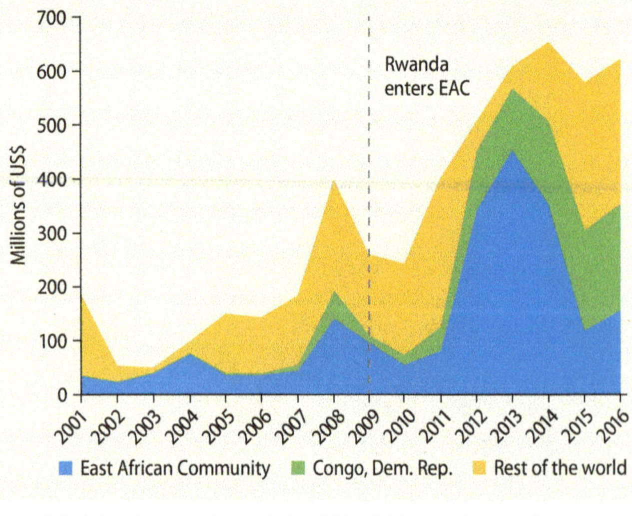

Source: Calculations based on Comtrade data (United Nations, various years).
Note: EAC = East African Community.

million to US$94 million (table 2.2). This reflects a rise in exports for some new industries, including apparel and leather products, mechanical appliances, and beverages. Rwanda has also started exporting agroprocessing goods, where key new sectors such as grain milling and processed animal products now account for 4 percent of overall exports.

Regional markets have expanded considerably. After joining the EAC customs union in 2009, Rwanda experienced a considerable rise in intraregional exports of goods (figure 2.2). Better access to the ports of Mombasa and Dar es Salaam also contributed to large increases in exports. Intra-EAC trade offers a particularly important market for nontraditional exports. In 2014, the EAC accounted for 41 percent of manufacturing goods, 66 percent of leather goods, and 53 percent of horticultural products sold abroad (MINICOM 2015). Non-EAC neighboring markets have also become important. Although conflict in the Democratic Republic of Congo limited trade prior to 2007, exports have grown considerably in the last decade. By 2016, Rwanda exported more goods to the Democratic Republic of Congo than to the EAC (figure 2.3). The main exports to the Democratic Republic of Congo include livestock and crops, but cross-border (informal) trade in services such as finance, transportation, and wholesale trading is also significant (Lalui 2016).

Remaining Challenges

Export-oriented industrialization is growing slowly given Rwanda's growth aspirations. The share of Rwanda's goods and services exports coming from nonmineral industrial products has fluctuated in recent years, moving up from 5 percent in 2006 to 11 percent in 2012 and down again to 9 percent in 2016 (figure 2.4). Whereas agroprocessing exports have been dynamic (rising from almost nothing in 2006 to 4 percent of all exports in 2016), export performance in other manufacturing areas has been disappointing. These exports recently declined from 8 percent of total exports (2012–14) to 5 percent in 2016.

Direct export opportunities within the EAC are constrained by comparable production capabilities. Although further regional integration brings considerable trade benefits, these countries all produce similar goods, as illustrated in figure 2.5, which ranks each country's revealed comparative advantage in 2013 and displays Rwanda's top six products. All EAC countries have vegetables as either first- or second-ranked revealed comparative advantage, all have food products in their top six products, and all besides Tanzania specialize in hides and skin products (such as leather). This duplication limits the potential of direct intraregional trade. Trade opportunities can be created for Rwanda by embracing such similarities (developing regional scale economies) and by pushing for greater specialization (particularly with regard to product quality).

Export-oriented industrialization is growing slowly, while direct export opportunities within the EAC are constrained by

FIGURE 2.3 Exports of Rwandan goods, by destination, 2016

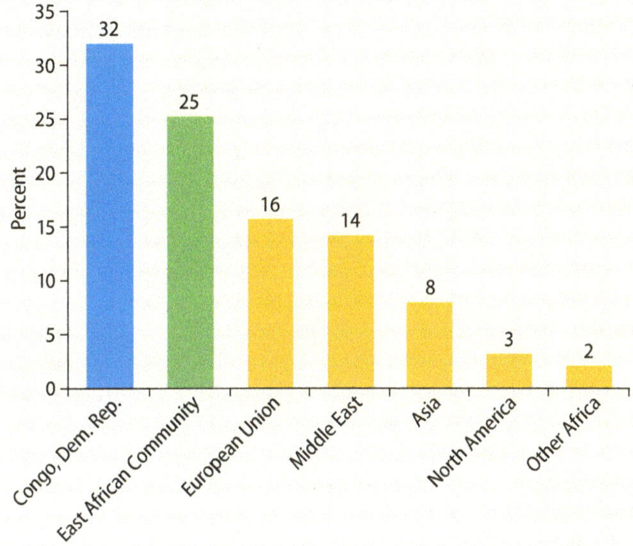

Source: Calculations based on Comtrade data (United Nations, various years).

FIGURE 2.4 Agroprocessing and other manufacturing as a share of total exports in Rwanda, 2005–16

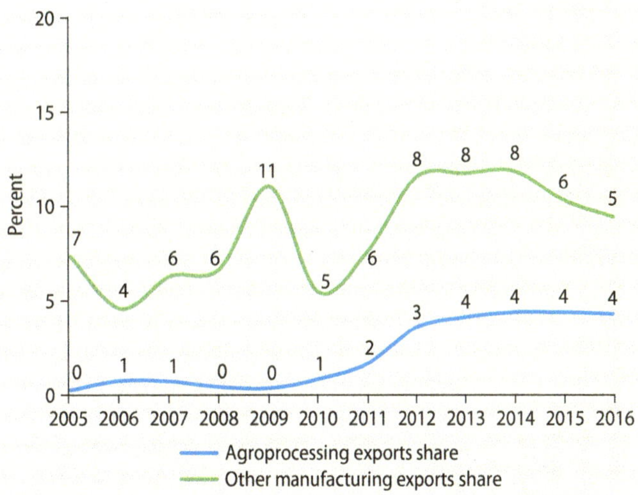

Source: Calculations based on Comtrade data (United Nations, various years).

FIGURE 2.5 **Ranking of revealed comparative advantage for East African Community countries, 2013**

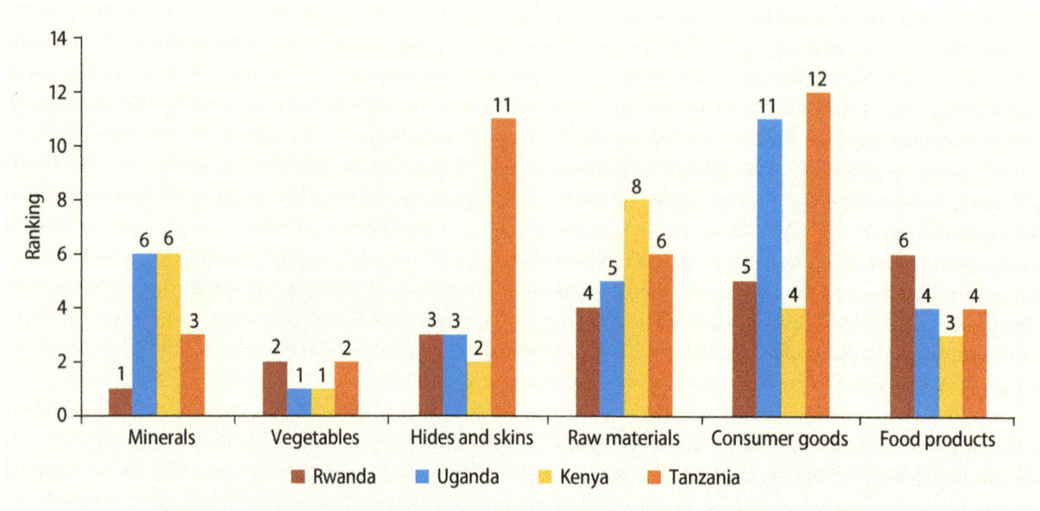

Source: Calculations based on World Integrated Trade Solution data (WTO 2018).

comparable production capacity. Commodity exports have grown considerably, but growth has been undermined by recent global prices. The export sector is dominated by a small number of firms, low productivity plagues sectors where many people work, and more private investment is needed in tradable sectors like tourism and manufacturing. Rwanda, despite recent export growth, still faces large structural challenges.

International commodity prices have undermined export performance, but also increased the pace of diversification. The Rwandan export sector historically has been concentrated in a few commodities, including coffee, tea, and minerals. This concentration was beneficial when international prices were high and rising, as was the case up to 2011. However, since 2011, export volumes have continued to rise at a steady pace, but commodity prices have stagnated or fallen, particularly for minerals (figure 2.6). Mineral goods are still exported mainly without processing, which has made Rwanda particularly vulnerable to price drops. This vulnerability was due to the global slowdown in demand from China as well as restrictive legislation passed in the United States that pushed Rwanda out of some higher-profit markets. It placed additional pressure on the development of nontraditional exports to improve the trade balance, and these products have grown rapidly in recent years. The share of traditional commodities fell from about 40 percent of all exports (including services) in 2005 to only 25 percent by 2016.

Over the period 2009–16, the top 5 percent of exporters in Rwanda accounted for more than 80 percent of the total value of Rwandan exports, and the top 1 percent of exporters accounted for more than 40 percent of total export value (figure 2.7). Although such a highly skewed distribution is not unusual for countries at similar income levels, it has remained relatively constant over the last decade. On average, these Rwandan firms export only two products to 1.5 destinations. Similarly, about 59 percent of all exporting firms in 2016 sold only a single product to a single destination (accounting for about one-third of total export value). Rwanda's export sector is much less diversified than those of its regional peers, with exporting firms in Uganda (3.6 products), Tanzania (4.2 products), and Kenya (7.2 products) all exporting considerably more products on average (World Bank 2017). Concentration of the type and destination of products may also be contributing to Rwanda's low rate of export firm survival (Jaud and Freund 2015).

Rwanda's exporter survival rates are low. Only 30 percent of new exporters in Rwanda are expected to be exporting products in the following year. This is comparable to the level in Tanzania (31 percent), but lower than in Kenya (34 percent), Uganda (36 percent), and especially Ethiopia (51 percent). Many Rwandan exporters are small traders moving goods across the border with neighboring countries, particularly Democratic Republic of Congo, rather than producing goods themselves. Larger exporters have a much higher survival rate. Moreover, firm survival is also higher when a larger number of firms export the same product. Other, cross-firm export synergies may further explain this dynamic (World Bank 2017).

The diversification of export goods has been driven by the sale of Rwanda's current products in more national markets. Decomposing export growth over the period 2008–13 shows that expanding the sale of existing products into new national markets accounted for fully 61 percent of export growth (table 2.3). Selling existing products to markets where Rwanda had a presence prior to 2008 accounted for some 20 percent of export growth in this period. However, only 19 percent of export growth was due to the introduction of new products, mainly in markets where Rwanda had a presence—notably regional markets. This underscores the importance of regional markets as a platform for learning to export.

Although labor productivity has improved, it has been particularly limited in the service sector. Average output per worker in Rwanda increased by about 6 percentage points between 2005 and 2014. About two-thirds of this increase came from shifts in labor from low- to high-productivity areas, while the other one-third came from increases in within-sector productivity. Sectors with the highest growth in labor productivity

FIGURE 2.6 Value and volume index of Rwandan commodity exports, 2000–15

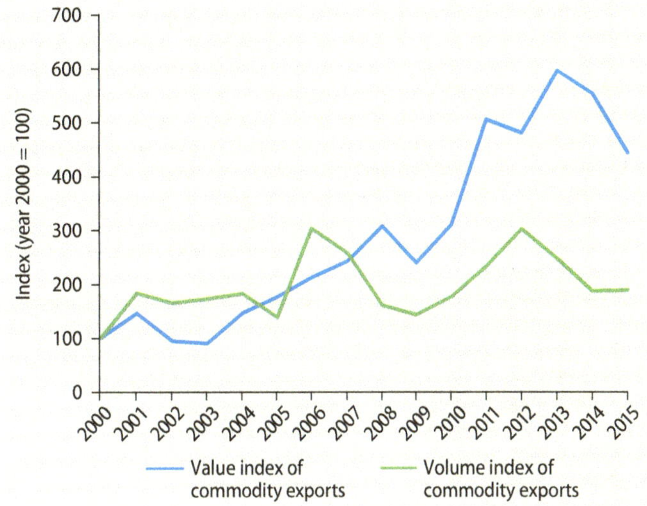

Source: Calculations based on Comtrade data (United Nations, various years).

FIGURE 2.7 Share of export value in Rwanda, 2009–16

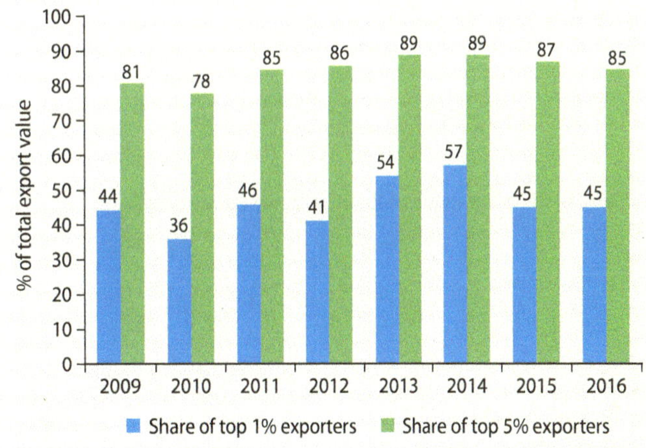

Source: Adjusted from World Bank 2017.

TABLE 2.3 Decomposition of merchandise export growth, 2008–13

	Products	
Market	**Existing**	**New**
Existing	20	19
New	61	<1

Source: MINICOM 2015.

include finance and agriculture (figure 2.8). Yet, productivity declined in service sectors such as hotels and restaurants, construction, and utilities. Other sectors like transport and ICT improved, but still have relatively low productivity compared with the region (World Bank 2017).

FIGURE 2.8 Labor productivity in Rwanda, 2005 and 2014

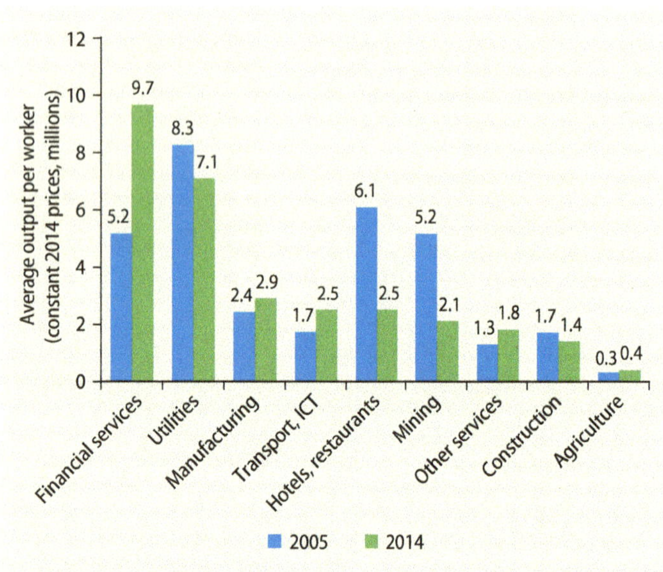

Source: Adjusted from World Bank 2017.
Note: ICT = information and communication technology.

FIGURE 2.9 Rwanda's financing stock, by sector, 2006–15

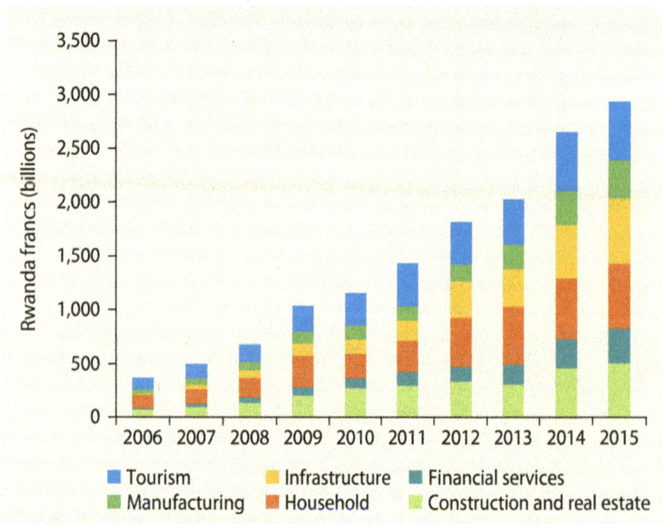

Source: Calabrese, Papadavid, and Tyson 2017.

Low productivity in services undermines a vital input for exporters. Services play an important role as intermediate inputs for other sectors in the economy. Firms need a variety of backbone services (such as logistics, finance, and telecommunications), and these needs are often more pronounced for higher-quality exporting firms. For that reason, Hoekman and Shepherd (2015) found that a 10 percent improvement in services productivity increases merchandise exports of EAC countries by almost 0.5 percent. This low productivity is driven in part by a policy environment that restricts trade in services. If the EAC were to lower the restrictions on trade in services to the level in Ghana (the African country with the lowest trade barriers for services, with an index of 18), exports of EAC countries could increase substantially: by 13 percent for Rwanda and some 20 percent for Kenya, Tanzania, and Uganda (Hoekman and Shepherd 2015).

More private investment is needed in the tradable sectors. Private finance has experienced strong growth over the last decade, with private credit nearly tripling between 2000 (10 percent of GDP) and 2016 (28 percent of GDP). However, most of this private finance has gone to sectors with little to no trade, such as construction and real estate, and to households (microfinance). By contrast, in 2015 only 12 percent of the stock of private finance was in manufacturing and 18 percent was in tourism (figure 2.9). Given the broader aspirations of the government for private-led transformation, more needs to be done to attract additional FDI and domestic private capital into tradable sectors. This issue is discussed further later in the chapter.

Envisioning the Future

To meet its aspirations to become an upper-middle-income economy by 2035, Rwanda will have to accelerate export growth significantly. On the basis of a comparison of Rwanda with countries experiencing similar rates of economic growth, exports as a share of GDP will have to rise considerably for Rwanda to meet upper-middle-income-country status. Compared with upper-middle-income countries (figure 2.10), the spread of exports-to-GDP ratios is large, but ratios tend to be upward of 40 percent. Since 2000, Rwanda has consistently increased its share of exports in national income, but the share is still far below the average for upper-middle-income countries. Therefore, significant export opportunities are available to Rwanda, and exports still have ample room to grow.

To meet these objectives, Rwanda will have to achieve double-digit rates of year-on-year export growth up to 2035. Although not impossible and in line with the growth rates achieved between 2005 and 2016, such growth implies sustaining consistently high export growth for nearly two decades. Historically, only a few countries have achieved this feat.

In developing an export-oriented growth strategy, Rwanda will have to make strategic decisions regarding which sectors have the greatest potential and merit additional investment. These decisions include considering not only the type of explicit incentives provided to sectors but also the wider support structure, including the regulations, skills training, and investment priorities that the government of Rwanda will have to set out in the medium term. The focus here is not to highlight specific products or types of firms to support but rather to identify the activities that are likely to contribute to growth and job creation as part of Rwanda's development strategy.

Although significant opportunities exist for increasing agricultural exports (as noted in chapter 5), transforming manufacturing and services will be even more critical in the medium term. Countries specializing in agriculture are often more vulnerable to price volatility in international markets. Agriculture also tends to have lower average labor productivity than other sectors, whereas productivity improvements are often closely linked with labor-saving technologies (limiting the potential for long-term growth of labor productivity). In addition, as per capita income rises around the world, the share of agricultural products in total expenditure will decline, whereas global consumption of other products (manufactured products, services) will rise (Szirmai 2012). This section focuses mainly on manufacturing and services for exploring medium-term export opportunities.

FIGURE 2.10 Exports as a share of GDP and log GDP per capita in Rwanda, 2000–16

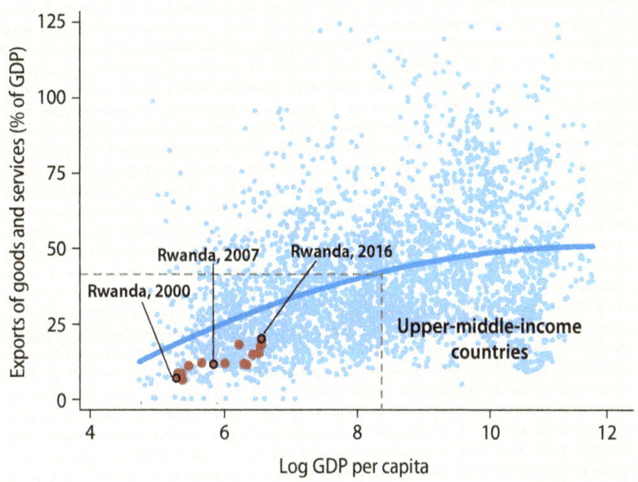

Source: Calculations based on Comtrade data (United Nations, various years).

The Potential of Manufacturing Exports

Most countries that recently achieved high growth did so through export-oriented manufacturing. In East Asian countries, export-oriented manufacturing played a critical role in boosting productivity growth (Newman et al. 2016). It did so in part by being export oriented, which strongly helped to increase the within-sector productivity of manufacturing firms. Having to compete in the international arena meant that firms had to accelerate their learning process to remain competitive: firms that did not adjust went under, freeing up labor and resources for other companies. Greater interaction with other international actors also helped to absorb foreign technology, while larger market size allowed firms to exploit economies of scale, further improving labor productivity

(Herrendorf, Rogerson, and Valentinyi 2013). Manufacturing also stimulated across-sector productivity improvements by absorbing high levels of labor from low-productivity agriculture into higher-productivity modern industries (structural transformation). This was made possible because manufacturing was labor intensive (with manageable investments in physical capital), while offering significant opportunities for low-skill workers, who could easily transition from agriculture into factory employment without much skills training (World Bank 1993). Recent evidence thus suggests that high productivity growth in the manufacturing sector explains about 50 percent of the catch-up in relative aggregate productivity across countries (Duarte and Restuccia 2010).

Four components historically made manufacturing a major driver of development (Hallward-Driemeier and Nayyar 2017):

1. *Tradedness.* Manufacturing's export orientation helped to improve the potential size of the sector, while also stimulating within-sector productivity (for example, through competition, technology absorption, and scale economies).
2. *Labor productivity.* The sector offered opportunities for relatively high and growing output per worker over time.
3. *Scope to employ unskilled workers.* The sector's ability to absorb a large number of low-skill workers, at substantial productivity premiums, helped to promote structural transformation.
4. *Capital and research and development (R&D) intensity.* Modest requirements for initial physical capital and R&D meant that manufacturing had relatively low barriers to entry. A gradual increase in capital requirements, in line with more advanced production of manufactured goods, helped to increase labor productivity over time.

Yet not all manufacturing sectors exhibit all of these components. By combining an international data set[2] with firm-level data from World Bank Enterprise Surveys for six countries,[3] Hallward-Driemeier and Nayyar (2017) identified indicators for each of the four pro-development characteristics and then classified sectors as "high," "medium," or "low" in each category. To relate these to Rwanda's current resource endowments, table 2.4 color-codes them for their potential contribution to growth in Rwandan exports and development (green as greatest potential, blue as medium potential, and orange as current potential).

The manufacturing sectors can be separated into different clusters (Hallward-Driemeier and Nayyar 2017), each with different potential for Rwanda's long-term growth.

Commodity-based regional processing sectors are the most immediate manufacturing priority for Rwanda. These sectors are linked closely with the use of agricultural raw materials (for example, food processing) and so can stimulate backward links with other sectors (for example, agriculture). Their potential is derived from their high scope to employ unskilled workers and relatively low intensity of physical capital and R&D. These goods typically are traded regionally (rather than internationally) because they are bulky to transport (for example, wood products, beverages) or they require proximity to raw materials (for example, food products). These sectors likely have the greatest long-term potential for Rwanda and are the only subsector in which it has a revealed comparative advantage (Hallward-Driemeier and Nayyar 2017). Their prospects depend in part on an integrated and competitive regional market (see priority 1) and a focus on quality upgrading for Rwanda's producers (see priority 5).

Low-skill labor-intensive tradables have strong pro-development characteristics, but it will take time for Rwanda to attain a competitive edge in these areas. Sectors such as textiles, garments, and leather are the only type of manufacturing that combines a high degree of international trade with a high share of low-skill employment (Hallward-Driemeier and Nayyar 2017). For this reason, these sectors are often the highest priorities for low- and middle-income countries seeking to stimulate structural transformation.

TABLE 2.4 Manufacturing subsectors, grouped by pro-development characteristics

Manufacturing sector	Tradedness	Labor productivity	Scope to employ unskilled workers	Capital and R&D intensity
Commodity-based regional processing				
Food, beverages, and tobacco products	Medium (mainly regional)	Medium	Medium	Low
Wood and wood products			High	
Other nonmetallic mineral products				
Fabricated metal				
Paper and paper products; printing and publishing			Medium	
Rubber and plastics products				
Basic metals				
Low-skill labor-intensive tradables				
Textiles, wearing apparel, and leather products	High	Medium	High	Low
Furniture; manufacturing n.e.c. (not specified)				
Capital-intensive processing				
Coke and refined petroleum products	Medium (mainly regional)	High	Low	High
Chemicals and chemical products				
Medium-skill global innovators				
Machinery and equipment n.e.c. (not specified)	High	Medium	Medium	High
Transport equipment				
Electrical machinery and equipment		High		
High-skill global innovators				
Computer, electronics, and optical equipment	High	High	Low	High
Pharmaceutical products				

Source: Based on Hallward-Driemeier and Nayyar 2017.
Note: R&D = research and development. Color-coding is as follows: green = greatest potential, blue = medium potential, and orange = current potential.

However, because of their global export orientation, efficiency-seeking investors mainly select a location on the basis of the lowest possible input, production, and transport costs (rather than proximity to markets or natural resources) (Andersen, Kett, and von Uexkull 2017). So far, this tendency has limited the potential of these sectors in Rwanda. Its landlocked location results in high trade costs. Even though Rwanda appears to have a cost advantage within the EAC, its labor costs are high compared with those of global leaders such as Bangladesh and, increasingly, Ethiopia (table 2.5). Rwanda can only offset these disadvantages in the short term through higher productivity. In the medium term, lower transport costs, programs to improve worker productivity, and access to growing neighboring markets could open the door for more efficiency-seeking investment.

TABLE 2.5 Labor costs in manufacturing in select countries

Country	Years covered	Labor cost per worker in manufacturing (US$ 2010)
Bangladesh	2007–13	835
Ethiopia	2011–15	909
Rwanda	2011–15	1,505
Tanzania	2006–13	1,777
Kenya	2007–13	2,118

Sources: Gelb et al. 2017. For Rwanda, calculations based on Rwanda Revenue Authority pay-as-you-earn tax data.

The opportunities from other manufacturing sectors are less straightforward, held back by higher skill, capital, and R&D requirements. Mineral processing reflects one opportunity for exporting to the global market. However, as shown in table 2.6, this sector will require considerable initial capital investment and tends to employ relatively few (low-skill) workers. Key for structural

TABLE 2.6 Service subsectors in Rwanda, grouped by pro-development characteristics

Service subsector	Tradedness	Labor productivity	Scope to employ unskilled workers	Capital and R&D intensity
Low-skill services				
Construction	Low	Low	High	Low
Hotels and restaurants				
Wholesale and retail	Medium (regional)	Medium		Medium
Transport services				
Tourism	High			
High-skill services				
Professional	Medium	High	Low	Medium
Financial				High
Information and telecommunication technology				

Source: Based on Hallward-Driemeier and Nayyar 2017.
Note: Color-coding is as follows: green = greatest potential, blue = medium potential, and orange = current potential.

transformation in the medium term will be the extent to which the mineral sector creates positive spillovers into other manufacturing industries.[4] Opportunities in other sectors are more remote, depending on sizable capital investment (for example, automation and robotics for transport manufacturing) or on cutting-edge R&D (for example, for computer equipment). Entry into these sectors is likely to be shaped by unforeseen advances in production technology interacting with the pace of skills development in Rwanda.

In several of these activities, intraregional trade can play a pivotal role. Over time, regional trade offers two avenues for growth. The first is participation in regional value chains, often connected to global markets. Coffee is one example: Rwanda exports coffee cherries to roasters in the global markets. Similarly, Rwanda already is part of regional value chains linking manufacturing centers in Kenya and Tanzania with Burundi and the Democratic Republic of Congo. The second avenue is through intraindustry trade in manufactures, including, for example, differentiated consumer products. This avenue relies on unfettered access to the relatively large EAC market and on the development of firms that can operate productively at scale. Competition will drive the allocation of production across the region and national specializations, while consumer desires for variety will drive an increasingly diverse availability of product lines on store shelves. Much as it has in the case of the European integration, this process of country specialization in production and diversification in consumption can drive productivity gains throughout the region.

The Potential of Services Exports

Services are increasingly embedded in other products (industry and agriculture) and constitute a growing share of value added in production processes. Many services are "embodied" in both manufacturing and agricultural production, either as inputs (for example, design, marketing, or distribution) or as enablers for trade to take place (such as logistics services or e-commerce platforms). For that reason, more than one-third of the global value of gross manufactures exports comes from the value added of embodied services, which has risen considerably in recent decades (Baines, Lightfoot, and Smart 2011; Bamber et al. 2017). Services play a similarly important role in manufacturing in the EAC (Hoekman and Shepherd 2015).

The increased "servicification" of manufacturing reflects the growing interdependence of the two sectors and may limit the extent to which either sector can grow independently of the other. Rather than prioritizing either the manufacturing or the service sector over the other, recent examples suggest that they may be interdependent. For example, in China from 2000 to 2014, services input into manufacturing accounted for 38 percent of annual growth in services value added, while manufacturing input into services accounted for 30 percent. Stimulating service sector productivity is thus a critical short-term priority that will assist in driving labor productivity and export growth in other sectors (see priority 3).

Selected services also share the pro-development characteristics traditionally associated with the manufacturing sector and should be given similar high priority. The analysis of pro-development characteristics can also be extended to the service sector (table 2.6). This reflects the increased tradability of services that has been made possible in recent decades. Because of the revolution in ICT, rapidly declining telecommunication costs, and expansion of broadband Internet services, many services that originally required a direct interaction between customer and producer are now "unbundled" and can be delivered at a distance—within and across borders. This offers another important channel of growth for low- and middle-income economies (Loungani and Mishra 2014). McMillan, Rodrik, and Sepulveda (2017) found that during the 2000s the majority of growth-enhancing structural change in Sub-Saharan African was derived from the shift of labor from agriculture into services. However, there are important differences to consider across service sectors, particularly in their degree of tradedness and their scope to employ unskilled workers.

The biggest immediate opportunities for services trade lie with tourism. Table 2.6 illustrates why tourism growth has been so important for Rwanda in recent years—it is the clearest example of a service sector that is highly tradable but also offers significant scope to employ unskilled workers in higher-productivity activities. The country has already launched new efforts to accelerate tourism growth with substantial investments in the Kigali Convention Center, RwandAir, and tourism assets, such as Akagera and Nyungwe National Parks. These laudable efforts warrant even more attention. However, tourism alone will not be enough to meet the export targets. Even under optimistic growth assumptions, tourism can create only a portion of the higher-productivity jobs needed; additional efforts are required to expand services exports other than tourism services as well.

Opportunities for other low-skill services are more limited, but they exist in retail and transport services. The degree of tradedness is critical for low-skill sectors, which often provide relatively little productivity growth, as illustrated by Baumol's (1967) "cost disease."[5] To improve their labor productivity requires capital accumulation, innovation, or economies of scale, all of which are highly related to ability to trade. For that reason, some export opportunities could be derived from wholesale and retail trade (especially cross-border trade with the Democratic Republic of Congo) and from transport services (particularly within the EAC), but other low-skill service sectors offer a less direct priority for an export-oriented medium-term strategy.

Developing a high-skill service sector will be difficult, but it is critical to Rwanda's long-term growth. Many of the "critical services inputs" for manufacturing fall under high-skill service sectors (professional services, finance, and ICT); globally they also constitute a large share of all services exports. Such services are also particularly critical for Rwanda, because they are less constrained by the tyranny of a landlocked geography. Rwanda's superior regulatory and policy environment may facilitate the development of new goods and services exports, such as exporting standards for certification and certification-based products, such as fertilizers, seeds, and pharmaceuticals. Similarly, if Rwanda is able to continue its development of higher education, particularly in specialties close to Rwanda's natural comparative advantages, these specialties too could become an eventual services export. Already Rwanda has attracted top-flight university subsidiaries, such as Carnegie-Mellon. A recent grant from the Buffet Foundation will allow it to build a first-class agriculture school. Another logical services export, given its location, could be mining services. To develop mining services will require investment from foreign companies.

Overall Priorities for Export Promotion

Achieving Rwanda's export objectives will require a multisectoral approach to stimulate services trade, manufacturing, and agricultural exports. No single industry can provide the necessary export growth on its own. Similarly, important interdependencies between sectors (most notably in services and manufacturing) will prevent any sector from growing too large without sufficient inputs from others. For that reason, the most likely scenario for high growth relates to a situation where services, industry, and agriculture all experience high year-on-year export growth up to 2035 (figure 2.11).

FIGURE 2.11 Cumulative exports as a share of GDP in Rwanda, 2005–16, and potential trajectory to upper-middle-income status by 2035

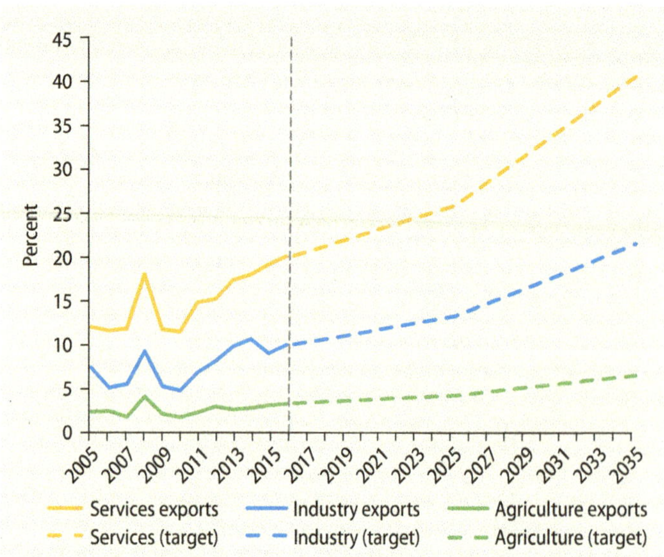

Source: Calculations based on Comtrade data (United Nations, various years).

The region may also be a springboard to future growth, particularly for fostering the development of new services and product exports. Already, the great bulk of nontraditional goods exports is sold either to the Democratic Republic of Congo or to neighboring countries in the EAC. Transport costs to reach global markets, though still high, are falling. With a collective GDP some 25 times the size of the Rwandan economy, the region (EAC plus the Democratic Republic of Congo) offers the potential for substantial long-term growth of both services exports (for example, logistics management) and products exports. Increasingly, new products are likely to be associated with regional value chains and exploitation of economies of scale in sectors such as agroprocessing.

Achieving Rwanda's ambitious growth targets will require a governmentwide push. Policies determining export growth extend far beyond the Ministry of Trade and Industry and the RDB to include several other ministries. For example, the policies of the Ministry of Infrastructure affect road infrastructure and the cost of electricity, vital for manufacturing exports. The Ministry of Environment will oversee policies toward the parks, vital to tourism. The Ministry of Finance and Economic Planning oversees tax policy and tax incentives affecting the decisions of private companies, including FDI. Moreover, Rwanda's success in exports is contingent on its negotiations with regional and foreign partners. The need for concerted efforts of the entire economic cabinet becomes clear when considering the following policy priorities for developing exports.

Five policy clusters are high priority. The next sections elaborate on the rationale for each priority and offer policy recommendations to assist the government in achieving its medium-term objectives:

1. Harness the EAC as platform for transformation, by aligning regional incentives, harmonizing standards, and exploiting economies of scale.

2. Improve trade connectivity by lowering transport costs within and across the region.
3. Increase service sector productivity, both as a critical input to other priority sectors and as a source of exports, capitalizing on regional competition and opportunities.
4. Stimulate foreign and domestic investment into tradable sectors by using selective and performance-driven incentives.
5. Accelerate industrialization through diversification, value addition, and quality upgrading.

Priority 1: Harness the EAC as a Platform for Transformation

The benefits to trade from regional integration in the EAC have been limited so far, especially compared with other regional bodies. By removing internal tariff and nontariff barriers, regional integration is expected to result in trade creation. Yet a comparison of intraregional imports as a share of GDP before and after joining the EAC (figure 2.12) shows that this effect has been limited for the EAC. After a small increase in the first five years, the EAC's intra-bloc imports of goods as share of GDP fell to a level below initial integration 10 years after membership.[6] In contrast, other regional bodies experienced a considerable increase in intra-bloc trade. After 10 years of regional integration, the SADC saw a tripling of intra-bloc imports, while the Association of Southeast Asian Nations doubled intra-bloc imports to almost 16 percent of GDP. The overall trade effect of EAC membership has therefore been somewhat disappointing (Shepherd, de Melo, and Sen 2017).

Rwanda has been using the EAC mainly as a destination for conventional exports, limiting its potential benefits. When Rwanda joined the EAC in 2009, the main impact on trade was from the elimination of tariffs from some countries and the adoption of a CET. Although the EAC has had some trade-generating effects (figure 2.2), the overall impact on developing Rwanda's export sector

FIGURE 2.12 Intra-bloc goods imports as a share of GDP before and after joining the bloc

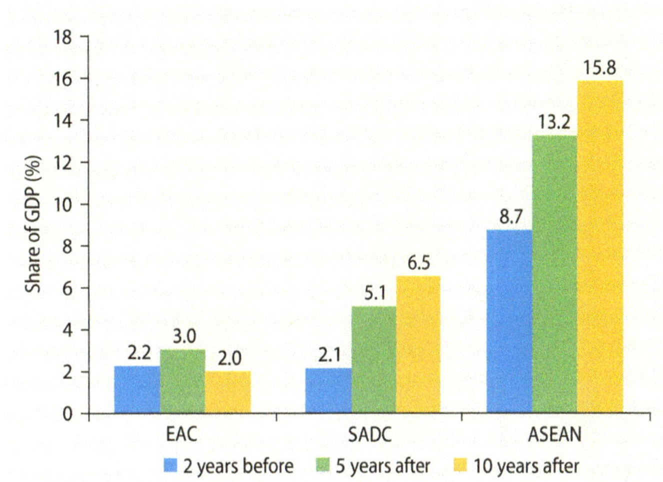

Source: Shepherd, de Melo, and Sen 2017.
Note: EAC = East African Community; SADC = Southern African Development Community; ASEAN = Association of Southeast Asian Nations.

has been limited partly because of comparable production capabilities across EAC partner states (figure 2.5), which has restricted the potential of intraregional trade.

Rwanda can use the EAC as a platform for transformation both by specializing production (particularly in terms of quality) and by embracing comparable production capabilities (regional scale economies). The EAC offers a crucial learning ground for exporting higher-quality products, especially in manufacturing and agroprocessing. Entering regional supply chains can help to prepare Rwandan firms to enter the global market. The EAC can also be used to stimulate within-sector productivity growth and develop other tradable sectors such as tourism, transport, and professional services through greater regional scale economies and greater competition from leading firms.

The EAC offers important untapped opportunities for learning to export. The EAC is an important market for Rwanda's nontraditional exports, especially in higher-skill production. In 2014, for example, it accounted for 41 percent of manufacturing exports, 66 percent of leather goods, and

53 percent of horticultural products sold abroad (MINICOM 2015). However, few Rwandan firms make use of these opportunities. Spray and Wolf (2016) found that Rwanda's sectors have widely varying participation rates in the external sector (table 2.7). The mining sector is best integrated into global supply chains, with 21 percent of firms exporting, mostly to Organisation for Economic Co-operation and Development (OECD) countries. Manufacturing shows the reverse, with 15 percent of firms exporting, primarily to EAC countries. Agriculture and agroprocessing as well as services[7] have lower export rates, spread between the EAC and OECD countries.

Comparisons with Uganda suggest that Rwanda can significantly increase participation in the export sector. Export participation in Uganda lies at about 20 percent for both manufacturing and agroprocessing firms, which is higher than in Rwanda (Spray and Wolf 2016). Crucially for manufacturing, this participation rate was achieved by first increasing exports to the EAC, which then slowly increased exports to the OECD.

Expanding the share of exporting firms will help to increase labor productivity. Exporting firms face greater competition from other international firms and interact with more demanding customers that require higher quality. For that reason, they also tend to have higher average labor productivity than firms operating only in the domestic sectors (Melitz 2003; Tybout, de Melo, and Corbo 2015). Spray (2017a) found that, when a Rwandan firm becomes an exporter,[8] its average output increases 41 percent and output per worker increases 17 percent. This also results in critical spillover for a firm's domestic suppliers, which are found to increase their output and their output per worker by 4 percent simply by being connected to a new exporter. Increasing the share of exporters and improving supplier connectivity are important mechanisms to increase a sector's average labor productivity.

Better access to imports will further assist firm exports and productivity. Imports are typically of higher quality than is available domestically and offer a wider variety of inputs. Faced with high international quality requirements, exporting firms tend to rely more strongly on imported inputs. This is particularly pronounced in Rwanda, where more than 85 percent of all imports flow to exporting firms (figure 2.13). Improving access to imports (through trade facilitation and tariff exemptions) was an important channel through which the Kigali Special Economic Zone (KSEZ) helped firms to improve their average productivity (Steenbergen and Javorcik 2017). This, in turn, helped nascent firms in priority sectors

TABLE 2.7 Rwanda's labor productivity and participation in the external sector, 2015
% unless otherwise noted

Sector	Output per worker (US$)	Exporters			Supplying exporters
		Total	To EAC	To OECD	
Agriculture and agroprocessing	8,166	12	6	8	2
Manufacturing	5,729	15	10	2	14
Mining	16,080	21	2	13	7
Services	9,855	5	2	1	9

Source: Spray and Wolf 2016.
Note: EAC = East African Community; OECD = Organisation for Economic Co-operation and Development.

FIGURE 2.13 Total imports of exporting versus nonexporting firms in Rwanda, 2008–14

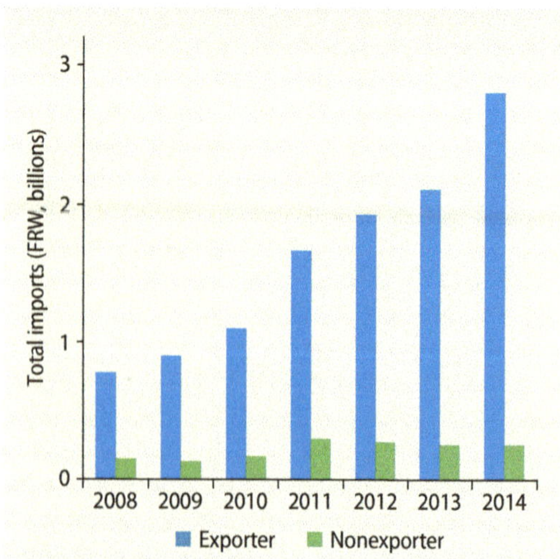

Source: Spray 2017a.
Note: FRW = Rwanda francs.

(such as light manufacturing and agroprocessing) to expand their sales, increase their value added, and increase their overall employment. Ensuring access to cheap imports within and outside the region will thus be critical to strengthen the export sector and improve labor productivity further.

To become a platform for Rwanda's transformation, the EAC needs to move toward an enabling environment that better serves Rwanda. Better aligning regional incentives to Rwanda's productive sector will be an important first step to improving its overall competitiveness, most notably by adapting the CET and by considering the use of a competitive exchange rate. Extending the integrated market through harmonized standards in goods and services is another priority. Effectively exploiting regional economies of scale is also key, which can be done by adopting and extending proactive regional initiatives.

Reform the CET to Benefit Rwanda's Producers

Lowering tariffs will help to increase the productivity of exporting firms. Tariffs are a key factor influencing the price of inputs for exporters, with two-thirds of Rwanda's imports bought by exporting firms (Spray 2017a). Lowering tariffs should be Rwanda's main objective in the upcoming EAC negotiations to reform the CET. Some interest groups are advocating increasing the number of bands from three to five (see Kenya Association of Manufacturers 2017), with the likely consequence that Rwandan producers and consumers will have to pay higher prices and off-setting job creation will be minimal (Frazer 2017). Others have advocated ending derogations that have permitted some importers in some countries to have access to inputs at international prices. The outcome of these discussions will be important for Rwanda because tariffs are a powerful force affecting the competitiveness of the economy and prices people have to pay for products.

Rwanda, along with Burundi and Uganda, operates at a significant cost disadvantage relative to Kenya and Tanzania. In addition to the direct tariffs that their producers and consumers must pay, importing firms in these countries face implicit "extra tariffs" related to the high costs of inland transport. Argent (2014) shows that, accounting for Rwanda's inland transport costs of US$3,000 per container, a kilo of rice faces an ad valorem equivalent (AVE) rate of natural protection of 53 percent, whereas cement faces an AVE rate of natural protection from outside of the EAC of 136 percent. Similarly, because of their higher weight-to-value ratio, natural protection is significantly higher on raw and intermediate inputs (AVE estimated at 37 percent on average) than on consumption goods (22 percent) or capital goods (2 percent) (Argent 2014). A large portion of the tariff protection offered by the CET in effect taxes both inputs into Rwandan industry and Rwandan consumers to create jobs in the coastal countries.

Since its inception, the CET has held a three-band tariff structure (0 percent for raw materials, 10 percent for semifinished products, and 25 percent for finished products), but in practice there are significant deviations and challenges to implementing the CET. The most important is the sensitive items (SI) list, a set of exceptions to the three-band rule for goods that are considered to have high potential for import substitution and thus enjoy extreme levels of tariff protection (rates between 30 and 100 percent). However, few Rwandan firms benefit from the SI list, and Rwanda is a net importer of almost all of the items on it. In 2013, for example, Rwanda only exported US$1.2 million of SI list goods to the EAC but imported US$148 million from EAC partner countries, more than 122 times the amount of SI list exports (Argent 2014). Although some Rwandan firms produce SI list products (for example, sugar, maize flour, wheat flour, rice, and cement), most of these products are exported to the Democratic Republic of Congo. At the same time, the SI list may be hurting export competitiveness, because high input tariffs can impair firm productivity (Amiti and Konings 2007; Frazer 2016b).

The SI list is particularly damaging to the poor. Many of these items are food staples, and the increased prices from high tariffs disproportionately affect poor households. Frazer (2012) estimated that the SI list lowered the average poor person's income by 3.8 percent (two weeks' worth of wages).

To shield itself from the damaging impact of the SI list, Rwanda has made extensive use of "stays of application" (deviations from the EAC-agreed tariffs). Rwanda has targeted goods that are either important consumer goods (for example, sugar and rice) or manufacturing inputs. However, this pragmatic solution has resulted in inconsistencies in EAC tariffs and attracted criticism from neighboring countries (Argent 2014). The system is also biased against small and medium enterprises (SMEs) because only large firms can readily circumvent customs payments for the CET. For that reason, Rwanda should push for formal rules to phase out the SI list and cap tariff rates at 25 percent (Frazer 2017).

Another challenge lies in the misclassification of tariffs. Goods used as raw or intermediate inputs in the manufacturing sector (which should have a tariff of either 0 or 10 percent) continue to be applied high tariffs of 25 percent. Analysis by Frazer (2017) comparing the CET rate with the sectoral breakdown of imports suggests that Rwanda has about 200 product lines, imported primarily by the manufacturing sector, that are charged tariff rates of 25 percent or higher. All such lines may require reclassification. Goods should be allocated to tariff lines on the basis of their main use. Monitoring this allocation for all countries and adopting a common list at the EAC level would constitute an important step toward improved transparency and consistency.[9]

Monitor Maintenance of a Competitive Real Exchange Rate, Especially with Respect to Other EAC Countries

Arguably the most important price in the economy is the real exchange rate. Freund and Pierola (2012) found that sustained surges in exports—that is, significant increases in the growth of exports over a seven-year period or longer—occurred in 97 episodes over the period 1980–2006. Surges were more likely to occur in open economies and typically were preceded by a currency depreciation of 20 percent or more, which was subsequently maintained with low volatility. Tradables suffer disproportionately from government or market failures that keep poor countries from converging toward countries with higher incomes (Rodrik 2008). The effect of the real exchange rate is even stronger for exports of services than for exports of goods; it is especially strong for exports of modern services (Eichengreen and Gupta 2012). As low- and middle-income countries shift from exporting primarily commodities and merchandise to exporting traditional and modern services in the course of their development, appropriate policies toward the real exchange rate become even more important.

Targeting the real exchange rate is difficult in Rwanda, in part because it is a small economy, inflation is often volatile and imported through food prices, and capital inflows can be large relative to exports. Moreover, Rwanda does not have the financial instruments of conventional sterilization. Finally, discussion of exchange rates raises important concerns about managing inflation. Because imports consume foreign capital inflows that might otherwise contribute to an appreciation of the Rwandan franc, the government would be well advised to focus on export growth rather than on the trade deficit as a macroeconomic objective.

Because of its centrality to export growth, continual monitoring of exchange rates, especially relative to neighbors, is vital. Further study is recommended of the growth in nontraditional exports in response to the movement of the value of the Rwanda franc against other currencies, as well as of setting up a monitoring mechanism to ensure that central bank policy is adequately informed of the implications for export growth. This mechanism is especially important for currency movements within the EAC because the region is the destination for a large portion of

Rwanda's manufacturing and nontraditional exports. Because the government aspires to set up a monetary union with a common currency, this issue is all the more important over the long run.

Because establishing a monetary union requires convergence in trade and macroeconomic policies among all members, the government should focus on fully realizing the goals of the common market as a near-term priority and work toward the convergence of macroeconomic policies. Monetary unions entail surrendering monetary and exchange rate policies to a central authority and require policies, particularly fiscal policies, to be sustainable over the medium run. The experience of the European Union, particularly Greece, has illuminated the problems associated with inconsistent fiscal policies and subsequent adjustments. These problems are heightened in the presence of possible asymmetric shocks often associated with volatile commodity prices.

With the new discoveries of oil in some EAC countries, the possibilities of external shocks that affect countries differently are elevated. That said, deepening collaboration within the EAC on elements of trade and improving macroeconomic coordination, particularly in monetary and exchange rate policies, can pay dividends even if a monetary union is not established. Deepening collaboration on reducing restrictions on trade in goods and services—by facilitating trade, reducing nontariff barriers, and adopting common regulations and standards—would promote regional integration and contribute to regional price stability. If greater communication among monetary authorities were to facilitate common monetary decision rules (for example, on inflation targeting) and these efforts were to reduce price-level volatility within the EAC, trade would expand by allowing firms to set up distribution networks that would otherwise be disrupted by today's volatility in real exchange rates. Finally, adopting procedures to allow for greater labor mobility—particularly in professional services—can help to put in place the fundamentals of regional price stability and deep integration (see Durevall 2011; Newfarmer and Soderbom 2012).

Another reason to work on the deep integration of the region now but to defer establishing a monetary union is that the gains from deep regional integration are much higher than the benefits from a single currency. A common currency is estimated to lead to an increase of GDP in the EAC of only one-tenth of 1 percentage point (0.01 percent). Mayer and Thoenig (2016) note:

> The implementation of a common currency, by alleviating exchange rate risk, would boost intraregional trade. However, the quantitative impact is small, around four times smaller than the impact of a common market. Our interpretation is that those expected economic gains are too low for justifying paying the political, institutional, and legal costs attached to the implementation of a common currency. This is naturally reinforced by the fact that our evaluation of economic gains does not account for the costs of abandoning discretionary monetary policy as a tool for achieving macro-stabilization.

Adopting a currency union requires a full common market as well as common fiscal policies to underpin its success. The steps of liberalizing trade in goods and services as well as harmonizing tax and subsidy policies are worthy in of themselves, even if subsequent steps toward monetary integration are left to the distant future.

Use Standards to Foster Regional Exports

Harmonizing standards across the EAC offers both an opportunity and a potential risk. The EAC has adopted more than 1,500 product standards, with plans for 5,000 more. Although uniformity can improve quality, international product standards also can be prohibitively difficult and expensive for smaller firms, limiting competition. The Rwanda Standards Board (RSB) therefore distinguishes between two standards. Inspection standards are mandatory (with penalties for noncompliance) so as to protect consumer welfare. Certification standards are voluntary and cover higher, international standards (such as the International Organization for Standardization's ISO 9001 for quality management) that firms use for marketing purposes. Currently, some EAC regional standards go far beyond international standards in setting very demanding requirements that have little or no connection with actual food risks or buyer needs. Such requirements can result in additional trade costs and at worst can disconnect poor farmers from poor consumers in regional and domestic markets (Keyser 2014). Formalizing a dual set of standards, tailored to differing needs of firms, will be a key for harmonizing standards in East Africa.

Rwanda has a comparative advantage in the region with regard to product quality. The proliferation of counterfeit products in neighboring countries—in seeds, fertilizer, and pharmaceuticals, to name a few critical products—constitutes an opportunity for the "Made in Rwanda" brand (box 2.2 describes a program to stimulate product upgrading in Chile). Given its comparative advantage in governance, Rwanda is uniquely placed to become a regional leader for product quality and reliability. This potential is undermined by poor regional assessment processes.

Better enforcement of regional standards will help to strengthen Rwanda's exports. Recent examples of neighboring countries certifying domestic products that fail to meet minimum standards undermines the reliability of regional "S-mark" quality brand. The RSB rigorously enforces its standards, which can lead to unfair competition for Rwanda's products within the EAC. A similar challenge lies with "counterfeit" versions of Rwanda's products abroad, which are often indistinguishable to foreign consumers but may be unsafe and hurt the reputation of the "Made in Rwanda" brand. Current "peer assessment" processes to deal with such violations are slow and ineffective and do not address the underlying difference in national enforcement standards. Strengthening the EAC Secretariat to enforce minimum regional assessment procedures would strongly benefit Rwanda.

Rwanda also should use its policy and regulatory environment to build an export capacity in standards applications. Rwanda could choose to become a regional hub for product testing and certification by consolidating all testing units among different government bodies into one agency that would allow testing to be offered faster and at more competitive rates to producers.

BOX 2.2 Stimulating product upgrading through a supplier development program

An important obstacle to raising product quality is that the average low-income consumer is sensitive to prices and may not be willing to pay the higher cost of quality products (Bastos, Silva, and Verhoogen 2016). Although the export market may provide the demand, firms often do not know exactly what is required of them or how best to compete in such a market. Yet countries often have a small number of highly demanding domestic firms, generally large multinational anchor firms. Becoming a supplier for multinational firms thus offers an important training ground for domestic firms, enabling them to learn to meet specific quality and specification requirements.

A supplier development program can help to develop these domestic supply chains. Domestic supply chains are developed by bringing together large anchor firms and potential local suppliers and then providing additional support and incentives to ensure that suppliers receive the appropriate training so that their products meet the specific quality and specification standards of the anchor firm. Arraiz, Henriquez, and Stucchi (2013) evaluated this program in Chile and found that participating suppliers saw a large increase in their sales, employment, and survival rates. Rwanda would benefit from a similar program.

Source: Steenbergen and Sutton 2017.

Establish New Initiatives to Develop Regional Scale Economies, Especially in Energy and Finance

Rwanda should build on recent initiatives to develop regional market opportunities. When Rwanda joined the EAC in 2009, regional integration was shallow and limited mainly to reciprocal market access for partner states. In recent years, this integration has expanded to include several projects to develop regional scale economies. One important avenue has been the Northern Corridor Integrated Projects (NCIP) Initiative between Kenya, Rwanda, and Uganda. The NCIP operates at the highest political level (often driven directly by presidential decrees), together with strong technical and administrative support to align domestic regulatory frameworks. Several important recent projects have come out of the NCIP, including the following (Vanguard Economics 2017):

- *A single customs territory.* To reduce transport time and cost along the Northern Corridor transport network, this project started regional collection and monitoring of data. This effort was followed by the adoption of a wide number of reforms related to customs control and trade facilitation, elimination of nontariff barriers (such as weighbridges), and adoption of technology upgrades to track and monitor container movements. These efforts strongly reduced trade costs (see priority 2).
- *East Africa tourist visa.* This project enabled international visitors to obtain a single tourist visa covering Kenya, Rwanda, and Uganda, encouraging visitors to spend time in multiple countries during a single trip and to increase the overall length of their stay in the region.
- *A single network area.* High regional roaming charges led to high cross-border interference in communication. Creation of the One Network Area, covering Kenya, Rwanda, South Sudan, and Uganda, aimed to increase telecommunications connectivity along the corridor by moving gradually toward a single network area in terms of costs, network coverage, and reliability.
- *Airspace management.* To improve air connectivity and increase competition, this project aimed to establish "open skies" within the EAC. So far, open skies have been achieved for only two routes: Entebbe to Juba (launched in August 2014) and Entebbe to Nairobi (launched in January 2015), but with considerable impact (see priority 2).

The Northern Corridor initiatives have been highly effective. This is best illustrated through the One Network Area project, which offered a one-time regulatory intervention that strongly improved competition and helped to establish a regional telecommunications market. Within the first 10 days of adoption, phone traffic between Kenya and Rwanda increased by almost 200 percent (figure 2.14). Within four months, daily minutes of roaming traffic increased by more than 950 percent. Regulatory reductions encouraged suppliers to compete through lower prices, and volumes expanded sufficiently to allow for greater profitability for telecommunications firms and lower prices for consumers.

FIGURE 2.14 Impact of One Network Area on mobile phone traffic between Rwanda and Kenya

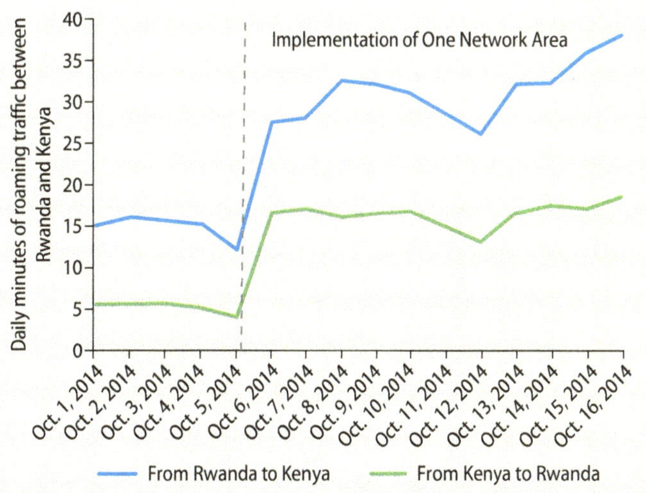

Source: Kelly and Kemei 2016.

This coordinated, competition-inducing approach is worth emulating in other areas, especially for electricity. Unlike other African regional organizations like the Economic Community of West African States and SADC, the EAC does not have specific protocols aimed at promoting regional electricity investments. The region made an initial attempt in 2005 at cooperation through the Eastern Africa Power Pool, which aimed to pool energy resources, promote power exchanges between utility companies, and reduce the costs of power supply. Rwanda is a member of the Nile Basin Initiative and the Eastern Africa Power Pool. However, apart from using its share of two regional hydro plants,[10] Rwanda is not connected to any regional transmission network (AfDB 2013).

Rwanda would strongly benefit from a competitive regional energy market. Interconnection can provide important benefits to sharing a reserve margin with other countries. Rwanda's current 30-megawatt interconnection capacity with Burundi and the Democratic Republic of Congo has served it in critical periods of shortages in recent years (AfDB 2013). It also offers an opportunity for more regular electricity transfer to take advantage of short-term diversity of demand between the two power systems. Rwanda's current energy use and production are limited, with only about 16 percent of Rwanda's households connected to the grid and a total generation of 210 megawatts of installed capacity. However, Rwanda has signed a wide range of new electricity contracts, which are expected to come on board in 2020 and could more than double capacity (512 megawatts). This capacity will likely exceed overall demand in Rwanda. Sharing this energy with neighboring Tanzania and Uganda will provide a way to limit the potential risk of excess energy (EAPP 2014). Establishing regional energy markets may further help to lower costs and drive electricity production costs down to Tanzania's level (table 2.8).

A new presidential initiative could help to establish a regional energy market. Despite initial efforts, little progress has been made in establishing regional energy markets or adopting cross-border electrification projects. Recent attempts to establish a 200-megawatt interconnected transmission line between Uganda (Mbarara) and Rwanda (Birembo) have been halted (Nalule 2016). A presidential initiative would help to provide new momentum and even speed up some of the regional reforms.

TABLE 2.8 Cost of electricity in 2016 in select East African Community countries

Country	Cost (U.S. cents per kilowatt-hour)
Rwanda	17.9
Kenya	17.6
Uganda	22.7
Tanzania	15.1

Source: Calabrese, Papadavid, and Tyson 2017.

Additional efforts also should be made to develop a regional financial market in the EAC. The financial sectors of EAC partner states are small and underdeveloped, which can limit investment, especially for large, lumpy investment projects. Regional financial integration can help to achieve economies of scale, which would deepen domestic financial opportunities, expand the opportunities for financial intermediation, and reduce the overhead costs of maintaining financial infrastructure. However, significant restrictions are preventing the flow of capital across borders. At the same time, there is also a need to remain aware of the risks of increasing cross-border financial links. The path forward should thus combine facilitating capital flows between EAC members with providing more careful oversight of the volumes and consequences of these flows (Wagh, Lovegrove, and Kashangaki 2012).

Strengthen the EAC Secretariat to Shield the Region from National Beggar-Thy-Neighbor Initiatives

The EAC risks moving backward in several areas, because the common market protocol is under threat from various national beggar-thy-neighbor initiatives tabled by partner states. Several recent issues have slowed EAC regional integration and are placing it under threat of moving backward. The Burundi crisis resulted in high-level frictions that ultimately led Burundi to block all trade with Rwanda in 2015. More countries faced with trade deficits have responded by adopting national initiatives aimed at import substitution (such as Uganda's recent "Build Uganda, Buy Uganda" strategy). Diverging positions on regional trade (related to secondhand clothing, for example) and claims of unfair competition in agricultural input subsidies (such as for Tanzanian rice) have exacerbated tensions in the region. Amid all of these challenges, the EAC Secretariat is facing increasing financial hardship given cutbacks in donor contributions.

Rwanda benefits most from a strong, rule-oriented EAC and should thus advocate for a more powerful secretariat. As a smaller member state, Rwanda would significantly benefit from having a stronger EAC Secretariat with the ability to prevent dominance of any individual country. The EAC Secretariat could also improve collective decision making by offering member states a transparent overview of regional economic dynamics and providing lessons from regional best practices (for example, in tax administration, industrial policy, and regulatory harmonization). Encouraging new high-level initiatives that deepen the responsibilities of the EAC while advocating for granting additional powers to the EAC Secretariat to enforce such tasks will be pertinent. Increasing the financial contributions to the EAC Secretariat by all member states is another prerequisite for deepening regional integration.

Priority 2: Improve Trade Connectivity by Lowering Transport Costs within the Region and with the World

The single most important determinant of long-run trade growth is reducing the costs of getting goods to market and getting inputs to local producers. Rwanda is a landlocked country, which means that transport costs typically add some 50 percent to the cost of exporting products and importing inputs. Because more than 90 percent of goods exports are transported by truck (Cameron and Viviers 2017), Rwanda relies heavily on the land transport corridors of other countries for access to the sea. Almost all of Rwanda's trade in global markets goes through two East African trade corridors: the Northern Corridor (Mombasa) and the Central Corridor (Dar es Salaam). Distance remains the single most important source of trade costs worldwide (Rastogi and Arvis 2014).[11] Yet the lack of facilitation at the border, fragmentation of the supply chain, and limited access to affordable air cargo opportunities are equally important factors that contribute to the high cost of trading.

Lower Transport Costs Further through Intensive Collaborations on Rwanda's Two Trade Corridors and Potentially through a Regional Rail Network

Although the Central Corridor has historically had lower costs for Rwandan trade, several initiatives along the Northern Corridor have sharply reduced transport times. These initiatives include the introduction of a single customs declaration (reducing the number of declarations required from three to one), a regional customs transit guarantee (a single regional customs bond recognized in all three territories), and a joint electronic cargo tracking system (allowing containers to be tracked in real-time) (Vanguard Economics 2017). Transport times have fallen 70 percent (from 21 to 6 days; figure 2.15) and could be reduced even further to as little as 1.4 days (NCTTCA 2017). The increased competition between corridors has placed downward pressure on the transport price for a 40-foot container along the Central Corridor (which fell from US$4,200 in 2013 to US$3,700 in 2016), so transport remains marginally less expensive through the Central Corridor than through the Northern Corridor (figure 2.16). Rwanda should continue to identify barriers to intra-EAC transport of goods, agree on detailed reforms, and monitor the outcomes using the two corridor observatories.

FIGURE 2.15 Average transport time, by route

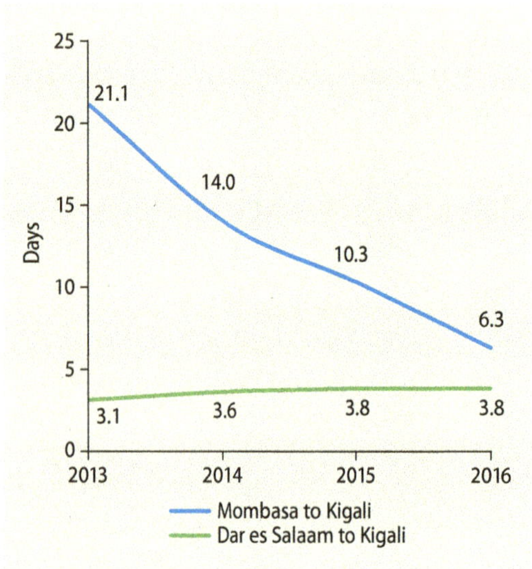

Sources: Calculations based on CCTTFA 2013, 2014, 2015, 2016; NCTTCA 2014, 2015, 2016a, 2016b.
Note: CCTTFA = Central Corridor Transit Transport Facilitation Agency; NCTTCA = Northern Corridor Transit Transport Coordination Authority.

FIGURE 2.16 Transport rates for a 40-foot container, by route

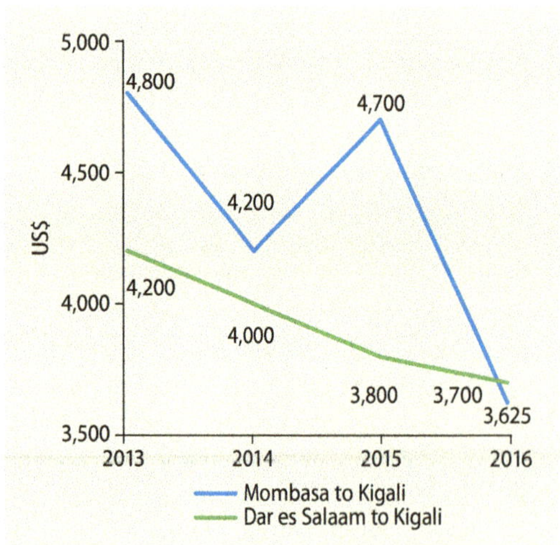

Source: Calculations based on CCTTFA 2013, 2014, 2015, 2016; NCTTCA 2014, 2015, 2016a, 2016b.
Note: CCTTFA = Central Corridor Transit Transport Facilitation Agency; NCTTCA = Northern Corridor Transit Transport Coordination Authority.

For Rwanda, road tolls that discriminate against its truckers dampen services income and reduce competition. Negotiating within the EAC framework for applying the road toll equally across all EAC vehicles[12] and lowering the rate at which it is applied appear to be the best options for Rwanda.[13] As with road tolls, tax policy toward trucking within the EAC also will influence competitiveness. The value added tax (VAT) threshold of FRW 12 million reduces the incentives for creating larger-scale transport firms (which are typically more competitive), because in-house transport services from businesses that pay VAT are better able to recover investment costs. Reviewing tax policy to ensure that truckers from all countries compete on a level playing field is a high priority. In addition, the corporate and personal income tax burden on domestic trucking firms is high because they face informal costs that are not deductible for tax purposes. Because of this fact and the strategic nature of the industry, Rwanda might consider adjusting the accepted deductibles for Rwandan truckers.

A long-standing ambition to build a railway along both transport routes (Northern Corridor and Central Corridor) holds considerable promise. The Kenyan government recently completed the first leg of the Northern Corridor, developing a parallel standard-gauge railway between Mombasa and Nairobi along an old meter-gauge colonial rail line, with plans to extend it all the way to Kigali. Railways can reduce freight costs considerably compared with roads, in part because of the lack of weighbridge stops and police checkpoints, and can bring goods to port more quickly than trucks. Railways also help to reduce the prevalence of truck transport, limiting traffic congestion while lowering the costs to maintain roads and operate weighbridges (Frazer 2016a).

However, rail construction is extremely costly and should only be pursued when financed through special, long-term bonds that offer highly concessionary rates. Most rail construction in Africa is financed through foreign assistance (including the recent Kenyan expansion, which relied on Chinese financing). Faced with a strict debt ceiling, Rwanda should avoid financing a new rail project through direct borrowing, which otherwise would displace public investments with higher short-run returns in favor of investments that take decades to produce positive net social benefits. Instead, Rwanda should use other financial instruments, such as a new "big bond" suggested by Birdsall and Okonjo-Iweala (2017), where donors would offer long-term bonds at subsidized rates (borrowing in the market against future aid flows). Such a long-term, low-interest bond could offer a good source of finance for railways because of its synchronicity with the payoff horizon of a regional railway project.

Develop Rwanda as a Regional Logistics Hub by Attracting Pioneer Foreign Firms in Logistics

Attracting international logistics services may further improve the efficiency of cross-border supply chains and reduce trade costs. Logistics performance depends not only on infrastructure but also on the institutions and processes of trade—such as processing by customs—and the quality of services available for trade, which itself depends on regulation and competition (Rastogi and Arvis 2014). According to the logistics performance indicator, Rwanda and other EAC countries are perceived to outperform their income-group peers (World Bank, various years).

Despite these significant improvements, logistics services are provided mostly by the owners of the goods (first-party logistics providers) or the assets (second-party logistics providers) used to provide these services.[14] Other than freight forwarders, third-party service providers such as Kumwe are limited. The international third-party logistics providers providing services in Rwanda, mostly Bollore (transport and warehousing services) and DHL (courier services or airfreight) operate mainly out of Kenya and, to some extent, Tanzania. As trade between Rwanda and its neighbors and the world expands, the government should actively encourage them to establish operations in Rwanda.

Several projects are ongoing, including the recent award of a 25-year concession by Dubai-based marine terminal operator DP World to develop and operate the Kigali Logistics Center. Five potential components typically make up a logistics hub. The first is a major distribution center for imported consumer goods, machinery and parts, and other goods requiring short delivery times to importers in neighboring countries, most prominently the Democratic Republic of Congo. The second is a group of one or more centers for consolidating agricultural products for export by land and air. The third is one or more distribution centers that supply imported and domestic products to retail outlets throughout the country. The fourth, which may be co-located with the third, is a location near the country's large industrial zones where the service providers for these industries cluster. The fifth is an air transport hub for both passengers and freight linking countries in West Africa with Asia and Europe. Although these five activities have some synergies, they are separate businesses, compete in different markets, use different networks, and offer different value propositions in terms of cost, time, and reliability. The government has already made progress on developing these components, so creating a regional hub now requires finding synergies and ways to market new advantages.

A new international airport at Bugesera is planned in the near future, equipped with modern cargo facilities. These facilities include a cargo village with a packing area, cold chain facilities, and multiple ground-handling companies. A neighboring special economic zone that will be closely integrated with the airport's facilities will also be operational and is expected to increase air freight demand. The airport will further support Rwanda's tourism by offering self-check-in, different (closed) boarding gates, multiple duty-free shops, several restaurants, and a business lounge. Exploring ways to extend the capacity of the current airport in the short term will enable the government to push back the necessary timeline for delivery, which may limit cost overruns to this high-profile public investment project.

Aggressively Pursue Open Skies Arrangements in Air Transport

The best way to expand air transport is to reduce restrictions on competition. Governments everywhere often support their own national carriers by making it difficult for foreign airlines to access certain routes. Yet allowing nondomestic airlines to land and take passengers to a third country ("5th Freedoms")[15] can significantly reduce air fares and increase passenger traffic. Examples of the effectiveness of such open skies agreements can be found in the Nairobi–Johannesburg route, which saw a 69-fold increase in passenger volume when liberalized in 2003. Similarly, when routes for the SADC opened, fares dropped 18 percent (Bofinger 2017).

Air traffic has increased considerably for EAC routes that have been liberalized. Discussing open skies for the EAC started through a Northern Corridors Initiative, first introduced by the heads of state in October 2013. By December 2014, negotiations were finalized for bilateral air service agreements along two routes: Entebbe to Juba and Entebbe to Nairobi. RwandAir has proactively targeted new routes for which bilateral air service agreements have been granted. The total direct benefit to the airline industry on the two routes is estimated at US$40 million (Vanguard Economics 2017). Other flights within Northern Corridor airspace have also grown steadily, in anticipation of new EAC open skies agreements. Between 2013 and 2016, the annual number of passengers on RwandAir routes in this airspace grew by 65 percent, while ticket prices on those routes fell 14 percent.

The potential benefits from airspace liberalization are large and should be pursued with vigor. Many intra-EAC routes are still restricted for third-party operators. This is driven partly by resistance from Kenya Airways, as it attempts to reposition itself in the EAC market (Vanguard Economics 2017). InterVistas Consulting (2016) estimated that liberalization between the five EAC countries could result in 9 percent lower average fares and 41 percent more frequent flights. These changes, in turn, would be expected to increase passenger traffic 29 percent for the five countries and 42 percent for Rwanda. Important indirect effects of open skies would be an additional 45,800 tourism visits for Rwanda and a 2.5 percent increase in Rwandan air cargo trade. Jointly, in the short term, these effects are expected to provide an additional 30,700 jobs (7,300 for Rwanda) and to increase GDP by US$124 million a year (US$24 million for Rwanda). In the medium term, these benefits could grow much larger, because they would provide an important strategic means for Rwanda to lower the cost of its exports in goods and services.

Priority 3: Increase Service Sector Productivity, Both as a Critical Input to Other Priority Sectors and as a Source of Exports

Trading in services provides a double value: exports of services earn foreign exchange and assist diversification, while imports of services can lead to greater competition, lower prices, and better quality, thus enhancing efficiency gains and competitiveness. Backbone service sectors (such as transport, telecommunications, and professional services) serve as critical inputs into manufacturing global value chains, which can help to raise exports and improve sectoral productivity (see priority 1). To realize these benefits, there is a need to lower policy barriers to services competition and to strengthen services trade for EAC professionals. Services trade also offers prominent opportunities for direct exports. To realize these benefits, there is a need to elevate tourism promotion and continue to address persisting skills shortages for professionals by leveraging private sector knowledge and financing.

Lower Policy Barriers to Services Competition and Services Exports

Fostering greater competition among suppliers across borders would lower prices to consumers and producers. While other factors (for example, small scale, high operating costs, inadequate regulation) contribute to inefficient services, the payoff to increased competition and efficiency could be large. Hoekman and Shepherd (2015) argue that competition improves services efficiency and thus benefits downstream users, particularly manufacturing firms. Using cross-country data for the world and East Africa, they found that a 10 percent reduction in a country's Services Trade Restrictiveness Index is associated with a 4.4 percent increase in manufactured exports from a country like Rwanda.

Competition can occur through either cross-border provision of services by foreign companies or the establishment of a commercial presence in the country.[16] To foster competition, EAC member states could negotiate to permit greater cross-border services trade within the EAC itself. At present within the EAC, some key markets are tightly knit oligopolies, typically with a dominant supplier. The absence of competition is one reason why some industries experience high costs. For example, despite the advent of quality Internet service and the spread of mobile telephony, telecommunications in Rwanda still suffer from higher-than-average consumer prices and costly restrictions.[17] Given the government's desire to promote the ICT sector, it may be useful to reexamine why telecommunications prices are high. Other examples relate to energy and finance, the use of airspace, and services trade for EAC professionals.

The imposition of VAT is constraining Rwanda's service exports. VAT is commonly charged only in the destination where the transaction takes place. To avoid double taxation, exporters are exempted from paying VAT after they declare the products to customs. However, in Rwanda most services exports are not exempted from VAT (with the exception of tourism, transport, and finance) because services exports often have no physical border control, making verification more difficult than for goods. As a result, most of Rwanda's services now face a type of export tariff that puts exporters at a competitive disadvantage (because their products are now 18 percent more expensive). Recent improvements in OECD countries show that services exports can be tracked reliably by requiring the exporting firm to present evidence that the customer resides outside the country and has paid for the services (OECD and WTO 2017). Rwanda should follow the OECD guidelines that allow for exemption of VAT for any goods, services, and intangibles (such as digital products) with similar evidence requirements. Following these guidelines would also help Rwanda to collect more reliable data on services exports (which are gathered through national surveys, limiting understanding of firm-level dynamics). Broad exemptions on services exports would move Rwanda ahead of the EAC partner states, but in line with leading African countries such as Mauritius and South Africa.

Elevate Tourism Promotion

Earnings from tourism are the single largest source of exports in Rwanda, almost equaling the value of mineral, tea, and coffee exports combined in 2016. Tourism receipts almost doubled from US$200 million in 2010 to US$390 million by 2016. About half of this revenue comes from a small number of leisure tourists (about 100,000 between 2012 and 2014), 30 percent comes from business tourists (about 400,000 between 2012 and 2014), and 20 percent comes from other sources (for example, visiting family and friends).

The government's MICE (meetings, incentives, conferences, and exhibitions) strategy aims to grow tourism receipts, as gorilla tourism approaches saturation.

Through its investments in the Kigali Convention Center, RwandAir, and hotel construction, the government has put in place a set of facilities that can drive tourism growth for years to come. Moreover, it has established promising contractual relationships with blue-ribbon foreign companies, such as Marriott and Radisson, to aid in bringing tourists and large conferences to Rwanda. Conference tourism (MICE) is doing well, increasing by 24 percent in 2014 and offsetting some of the decline in other business travel.

The biggest rewards will be obtained if the country can expand leisure tourism beyond gorillas and convince tourists—both leisure and MICE—to spend more time in Rwanda. The average visitor spends only about 3.2 days in the country. If visitors were enticed to double the average length of their stays, the sector could generate another US$60 million without increasing the number of tourists (English 2017). Rwanda has two other national parks that offer complementary attractions. Indeed, Akagera now receives more visitors than Volcano National Park and its gorillas because of greater interest from nationals.

To scale up tourism, both the Ministry of Trade and Industry and the RDB should improve their capacities to champion the tourism sector and to develop midrange tourism opportunities (for example, birdwatching and adventure tourism). Rwanda can also improve its targeted "destination management authorities" to help develop specific locations (for example, Lake Kivu) by providing public goods such as infrastructure and sign-posting and by coordinating private sector actors. Offering a website with comprehensive, timely information, which enables visitors to book government permits online and brings together the vacation packages of different private tour operators, is another area for improvement. A well-staffed authority would have greater capacity to engage in all of these planning and support activities. Because the sector accounts for the largest share of export earnings and has some of the best potential for future growth, it also merits greater institutional support.

Working with tour operators to give Rwanda more visibility in regional tours is another promising avenue. Most tour operators market Rwanda as part of a regional package, allowing only a few days in-country for gorilla trekking. Although regional packaging has enabled Rwanda to piggyback on the established East African safari market, this may be an opportune time to distinguish Rwanda as an alternative, offering more variety in a more secure environment with less travel. The government might consider giving priority—or discounts—for gorilla permits to tourists who plan to stay in Rwanda longer than the few days typically necessary to visit the gorillas, at least during the peak season.

Several other initiatives—some easy and some more difficult—might be integrated into a higher-visibility strategy:

- The regional tourist visa, a worthwhile initiative, should be expanded to include Tanzania.
- Training in tourism merits more investment, both to satisfy Rwanda's internal demand but also to position any local training institution as a center for excellence that could become part of Rwanda's educational exports. It might be possible to finance a project that builds the human and institutional capacity to manage the tourism sector, fills infrastructure and skill gaps, and attracts private investors.
- In the long run, if the government were able to establish working tourism agreements with the Democratic Republic of Congo, Rwanda could enhance its own already high-growth tourist industry by becoming a gateway to several remarkable tourist attractions in eastern Democratic Republic of Congo, including, for example, the Mount Nyiragongo lava lake. A regional accord could help to protect Lake Kivu's development from threats of pollution.

- Finally, the government could develop a program to enhance the links of the tourist sector with the rest of the economy through increases in local purchases by hotels and by tourists themselves. Developing the local supply chains to hotels is a priority.

Further Liberalize Services Trade for EAC Professionals

Professional services are critical for improving the productivity of other economic activities, especially for SMEs. Although professional services account for only a small fraction of the service sector (and services exports), they play an important role in shaping economic development. Business services such as accounting, legal support, and engineering offer important intermediate inputs for other agricultural, industrial, and service sectors. Dihel, Fernandes, and Mattoo (2012) show that, for firms in East Africa, there is a strong positive correlation between the use of professional accounting and legal services and average labor productivity. This effect is particularly pronounced for SMEs, which have more than 40 percent higher labor productivity than similar enterprises that do not use professional services.[18] Improving access to affordable, high-quality professional services can thus help to boost productivity for the wider economy.

Harmonizing regional standards for EAC professionals offers an important opportunity to foster professional services. Differences in regulation provide critical nontariff barriers that limit integration in the East African Common Market and prevent the exploitation of economies of scale. An important example for services lies with professional accreditation requirements. Previously, each country in the EAC had its own criteria that either would require extensive retraining to receive the necessary licenses to operate (for example, in accounting) or would prevent some professionals from operating altogether (for example, in Kenya and Tanzania, only nationals can practice domestic law) (Dihel and Goswami 2016). Similar restrictions are also considered important nontariff barriers in the movement of goods within the EAC (EABC 2016). Country-specific costs of regulation can have a serious impact on the entry decisions of SMEs (especially if firms do not expect large sales in the foreign market), which further increases sectoral costs and impairs productivity.

Services trade for professionals would benefit from recognizing additional licenses and standards obtained in other EAC countries and from adopting common qualifications criteria. The EAC has introduced mutual recognition agreements (MRAs) in three professional services: accounting and architectural services have been covered in Rwanda since 2013, and engineering services have been covered since 2016. So far, intra-EAC movement of these professionals remains limited, with about 130 persons registering in another country to work as accountants (1 percent of the total EAC profession), 22 to work as architects, and 9 to work as engineers (Hook 2013). Yet these agreements have already offered important benefits for certifications and learning institutions (box 2.3).

The MRAs should be given formal treaty status as soon as possible, be broadened in their purpose, and be expanded to other professions. The three concluded MRAs were negotiated by professional bodies and subsequently presented to the EAC Council of Ministers. Although this approach contributed to fast recognition, it also gave the MRAs an uncertain legal status that weakened their implementation and created a situation in which conflicts with domestic provisions (such as nationality requirements in competition policy, public procurement, or freedom of establishment) would not hold up in a court of law. The MRAs should thus be given treaty status that formally establishes their legal precedence over such domestic policy issues. They should also address unintended consequences such as when EAC nationals with foreign qualifications are ineligible for MRA benefits (Hook 2013).

BOX 2.3 The benefits of a mutual recognition agreement for Rwanda's engineering professional body

The Institute of Engineers of Rwanda (IER) was established in 2013 through a parliamentary act. Its main responsibility is to regulate, promote, and raise training standards of the engineering profession. It was also Rwanda's key representative to negotiate the mutual recognition agreement (MRA) for engineering with the EAC, which it signed in March 2016. To date, the MRA has had limited impact on intraregional trade in engineers (which has been low). Instead, the main benefit has been to formalize Rwanda's engineering profession and professional body.

Before the MRA could be signed, the EAC came to inspect whether the IER followed the appropriate rules and regulations. Such an "audit" helped the IER to improve its standards and to establish the required procedures and documentation in a very short period of time. This effort was accelerated by extensive support from other EAC countries, including the Ugandan Institute of Engineering, and quickly turned the IER into one of the best-organized professional bodies in Rwanda. This process also improved the quality of accredited engineers. Following the EAC-prescribed process, Rwanda now requires engineers to submit and defend a "technical report" in a forum of professional peers, further raising the reputation for quality of Rwanda's engineers within the EAC.

To extend services trade further, MRAs should be drafted for other professional sectors, including legal, finance, and consulting professionals.

To facilitate short-term assignments, the EAC should further abolish work-permit regimes for all eligible professionals. The MRA still requires eligible professionals from EAC partner states to obtain permits prior to being employed, which is a burdensome and slow process (Basnett 2013). It also requires registration for professional bodies in both the "home" and "visiting" country, each requiring an initial certification process and an annual financial contribution. These administrative burdens prevent professionals from accepting short-term assignments. Instead, any eligible professional certified from any EAC professional body should be automatically exempt from work-permit regimes.

Address Persisting Skills Shortages for Professionals by Leveraging Private Sector Knowledge and Financing

Rwanda is facing a skills deficit that, if not remedied, will constrain potential growth for high-skill services exports. There is a strong relationship between per capita services exports and tertiary gross enrollment rates (figure 2.17) as well as secondary completion rates (figure 2.18). Taking the predicted level of exports to GDP required to achieve upper-middle-income status and assuming that half of it derives from services exports (the current share of services exports in total exports) yields the average level of skills associated with services exports per capita. This calculation suggests that Rwanda trails significantly behind on both tertiary enrollment and secondary completion. Although these figures are only indicative (and some countries have managed to achieve such services exports with less human capital), they illustrate the significant challenge facing Rwanda in the next two decades with regard to increasing its human capital. Part of this constraint may be relieved by greater inflows of professionals from the EAC (see priority 4), but for the most part human capital will have to be increased through significant additional investments in education (discussed in chapter 1 of this report).

Expansion of the private sector in East Africa is opening up opportunities that require specialists with a new set of skills. The growth of the financial sector, for example, has drastically increased the demand for accountancy and legal services. A skills assessment estimated that Rwanda needs 5,000 accountants in the public sector and another 2,325 accountants in the financial sector to meet demand, yet it has only 6 percent of that number (ICPAR 2017). Rwanda is lagging behind the rest of the EAC in the number of professionals and is far behind African leaders in services exports such as Mauritius and South Africa. This lag is particularly noticeable for accountants and lawyers (figure 2.19).

Skills shortages provide both an opportunity and a risk for trade in services within the EAC. The MRAs provide a key means to fill high-paying vacancies in the private sector using regional experts. Yet, if this is seen to be a one-sided movement (for example, from Kenya to Rwanda), the use of regional experts may lead to resentment and result in a backlash to EAC regional integration. For that reason, it is important to increase the number of professionals in Rwanda through a combination of student loan programs, private sponsorships, and in-company mentoring.

Skills mismatches are another serious concern for professionals. The EAC is faced with jobless accountants despite high demand (Dihel, Fernandes, and Mattoo 2012). Similar patterns are found in Rwanda, where low-quality training has resulted in an important distinction between accountancy graduates (often struggling to find employment) and accountants registered with the Institute of Chartered Accountants of Rwanda (having received additional training). Potential explanations for this pattern include poor links between the education system, labor market, and professional associations.

Integrating professional skills within polytechnics can help to address skills shortages. In previous years, formal classes in accounting often covered separate material and did not contribute to a student's certification as a public accountant. Now, the Institute of Certified Public Accountants of Rwanda has started supporting polytechnics to offer accounting modules that can also fast-track a student's accreditation. Such initiatives have increased the total number of students from 165 in 2012 to 1,771 in 2016 (ICPAR 2017). Extending them to other professional skills could help to increase the overall number of professionals in Rwanda quickly.

FIGURE 2.17 Tertiary gross enrollment rate and log services exports per capita, 2000–16

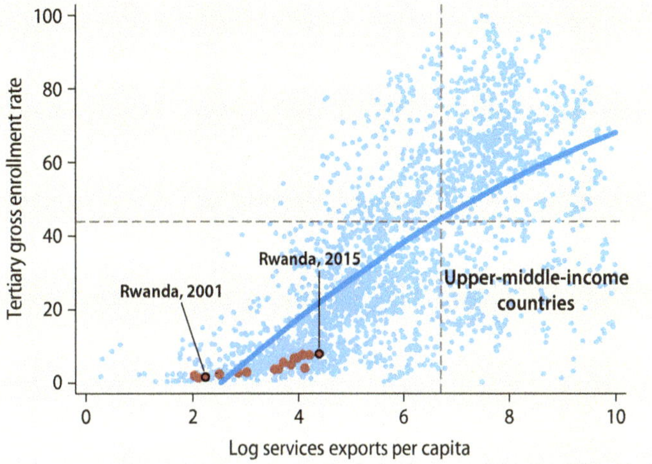

Source: Calculations based on World Development Indicators data (World Bank, various years).

FIGURE 2.18 Upper-secondary completion rate and log services exports per capita, 2000–16

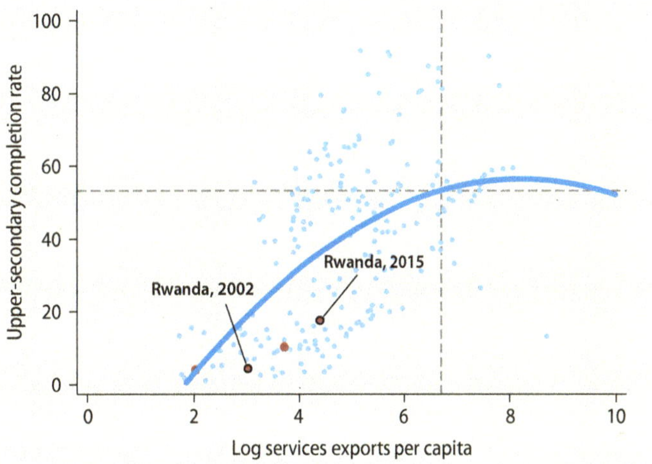

Source: Calculations based on World Development Indicators data (World Bank, various years).

FIGURE 2.19 **Number of professionals per 100,000 inhabitants in select African countries**

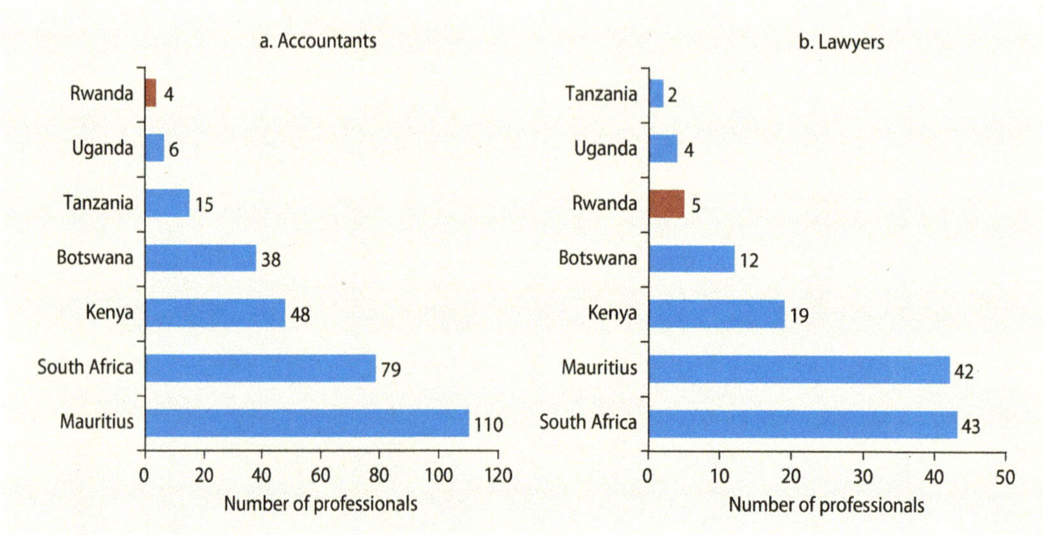

Sources: For accountants, ICPAR 2017; for lawyers, Dihel, Fernandes, and Mattoo 2012.
Note: ICPAR = Institute of Certified Public Accountants of Rwanda.

Setting up private sector–sponsored student loan programs offers another opportunity. At the moment, all student loan programs are on a needs basis. However, for many service sector jobs, students are expected to earn large returns on this investment, so offering commercial loans may make sense. There is considerable interest from the private sector in helping to develop special-purpose financial instruments that can be used for such purposes, but seed funding from government and some broad support are needed to limit the risk in case of defaults.

Government could work more closely with industry to ensure relevant skills training. To avoid skills mismatches, the curricula for professionals in both polytechnics and universities should be aligned more closely with the needs of particular industries. The industrial bodies offer a particularly helpful platform that can negotiate on behalf of dominant firms and the curriculum review board. To enable students to signal their completion of an industry-certified course, industrial bodies should introduce and enforce accreditation schemes (where absent).

Priority 4: Stimulate Foreign and Domestic Investment into Tradable Sectors by Using Selective and Performance-Driven Incentives

More private investment is needed in tradable sectors like tourism and manufacturing. Private finance has experienced strong growth over the last decade, with private credit nearly tripling between 2000 (10 percent of GDP) and 2016 (28 percent of GDP). However, most of this private finance has gone to sectors with little to no trade, such as construction, real estate, and microfinance (households). By contrast, in 2015 only 12 percent of the stock of private finance was in manufacturing, and 18 percent was in tourism. Given the broader aspirations of the government for private sector–led transformation, more needs to be done to attract additional FDI and domestic private capital into tradable sectors.

Rwanda recently has experienced a remarkable increase in FDI as a share of GDP. Whereas FDI inward stock constituted only about 3 percent of GDP in 2000, by 2016 its share had increased to almost 27 percent (figure 2.20). This has been made possible partly through establishment of a strong international reputation and brand, exemplified by Rwanda's rank (second-highest in Africa) on the World Bank Doing Business Indicators, a broad range of special tax incentives to attract investors, and a highly proactive investment promotion agency (Rwanda Development Board) that also offers extensive investor aftercare.

Rwanda's main FDI stock centers on telecommunications and financial service sectors, but it has recently expanded to include more manufacturing, tourism, and mining. Manufacturing now amounts to 15 percent of all FDI (table 2.9), partly due to proactive government partnerships in the garment sector including a designated action plan, targeted investment missions, and designated government support for eligible investors. FDI to other sectors has been more sporadic, driven to a large extent by large individual projects: the top four projects constitute more than 26 percent of all registered investment. Although such large projects can quickly raise overall investment, the number of investments needs to increase to sustain this level and strengthen resilience.

FIGURE 2.20 FDI stock as a share of GDP in select East African countries, 2000–16

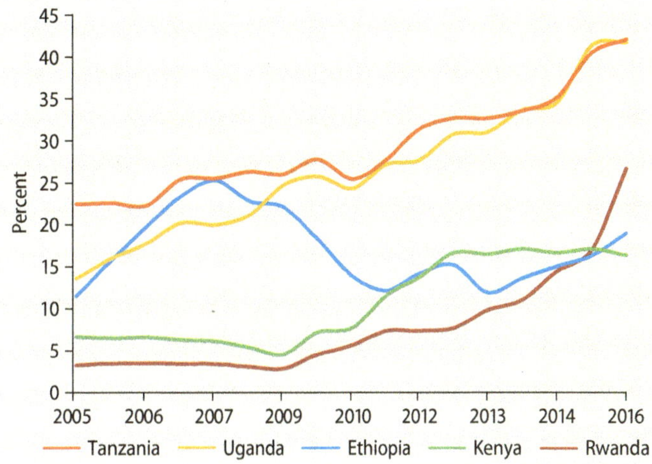

Source: United Nations Conference on Trade and Development (UNCTAD) data.
Note: FDI = foreign direct investment.

TABLE 2.9 Stock of foreign direct investment in Rwanda, by sector, 2015

Sector	US$ (millions)	Share (%)
Information and communication technology	592	28
Financial and insurance activities	477	22
Manufacturing	329	15
Tourism	219	10
Agriculture	104	5
Mining	90	4
Wholesale and retail trade	89	4
Electricity, gas, steam	70	3
Other	61	3
Transport and storage	46	2
Total	**2,139**	**100**

Source: BNR 2017.

Increase Efforts to Attract Additional "Priority" FDI

Comparisons with other Eastern African countries suggest that more can be done to attract FDI. Rwanda's inward stock of FDI as a share of GDP exceeded that of Ethiopia and Kenya for the first time in 2016, yet still trails behind that of Tanzania and Uganda (figure 2.20). Additional efforts in Rwanda might well attract more FDI.

Although Rwanda welcomes all investment, prioritizing sectoral investment would help to assist strategic sectors. FDI has the greatest effectiveness for economic growth when it strengthens the wider sector. Firms often complement each other in a broader value chain, so the introduction of a new anchor firm could help to alleviate specific sectoral challenges (for example, finance, skills, logistics) and generate important spillovers for local buyers and suppliers (Farole and Winkler 2014). Making use of such opportunities, the RDB could package and present high-potential opportunities to investors in strategic sectors through targeted investment missions in key markets (MINEACOM 2017). This effort would mimic the recent successes in garments (box 2.4). Evidence suggests that sectors explicitly targeted by investment promotion agencies (IPAs) are associated with more than

BOX 2.4 The strategy to transform the textiles, apparel, and leather sector

In 2015, the Ministry of Trade and Industry classified the textiles, apparel, and leather sector a key priority industry, with high potential for manufacturing growth, employment, and exports. However, the domestic apparel sector was facing a range of challenges, including lack of investment, limited skills, and fragmented value chains, all of which limited Rwanda's competitiveness and restricted potential exports.

In response, a cross-government strategy was drafted in 2016 to transform the textile, apparel, and leather sector. The Rwanda Development Board took the lead in promoting private direct investment from both foreign and domestic sources through targeted investment missions. The Ministry of Trade and Industry ensured prioritized access to land in a new special economic zone. The Ministry of Finance and Economic Planning, through the Rwanda Revenue Authority, exempted key garment inputs from import tariffs. Finally, all new investors received support for training, technology upgrading, and certification through a coalition of the Rwanda Standards Board, the Workforce Development Authority, and the National Integrated Rural Development Agency.

Initial results of this initiative are impressive, mobilizing significant private investment and foreign direct investment. Sectoral growth accelerated from 3 percent in 2015 to 10 percent in 2016, while exports increased from US$16 million (1.1 percent of all exports) to US$20 million (1.5 percent of all exports). More than 5,000 jobs are expected to be created by 2020. This approach now stands as a wider model for industrial policy and for attracting foreign direct investment in Rwanda.

Source: MINICOM 2017.

twice the FDI inflows as nontargeted sectors (Javorcik 2004).

Investor promotion can be strengthened further through a designated tracking system. Establishing an integrated system that compiles all challenges reported by investors will strongly assist the RDB in identifying which issues have been addressed and in providing better investor aftercare, which can also help to attract additional FDI inflows (Harding and Javorcik 2013).[19] A tracking system also can bring together data from other government sources (for example, tax and customs) to track a firm's key performance indicators, such as total investments, profits, exports, and employment. This data could then be compared with a firm's overall amount of government support, which includes tax incentives, other financial incentives (for example, training support), and nonfinancial benefits received. Such a monitoring system could help to ensure that government support is conditioned on performance and to assess whether a sector's overall incentives are in accordance with its overall potential.

Make Integrated Government Support Selective and Performance Driven

Offering integrated government support can stimulate production for priority sectors. The Rwandan government has been experimenting with different approaches to industrial policy. One key means has been the KSEZ, which has attracted both foreign and domestic investors in nontraditional, tradable sectors. Between 2013 and 2016, the KSEZ accounted for between 4.5 and 10 percent of all national goods exports and provided an important source of new manufacturing and agroprocessing exports. The KSEZ also has three important, nonfiscal benefits over other locations: more reliable infrastructure and utilities, better trade facilitation, and closer ties to government agencies to make firms better aware of relevant incentives, laws, and regulations. This type of integrated government support was found to contribute to large firm-level increases in sales, value added, and employment (Steenbergen and Javorcik 2017).

The aspiration of Rwanda's new Private Sector Development Strategy is to mainstream integrated government support across all priority value chains. Through the new Growth Anchor Firm Initiative, the Private Sector Development Strategy aims to extend the benefits of the KSEZ to all anchor firms in priority value chains (including light manufacturing and agroprocessing). Given the limited resources available, it may be more effective to address specific challenges comprehensively (for example, access to export finance, trade infrastructure) for a select number of priority anchor firms than to offer a cross-cutting focus across the whole private sector. This support is further tied to broad export performance targets between the government and the private company (MINICOM 2017). This system closely mimics the Republic of Korea's supportive approach to large holding companies (*chaebols*), where the government provides broad support and then rewards or penalizes enterprise managers on the basis of their performance outcomes (Khan 2007).

To assist industrialization, an integrated government support project needs to be selective, performance driven, and time bound. Admission needs to be based on a demonstrated high potential for exports, employment, and domestic productivity enhancement. To avoid firm abuse of government benefits, the state should be able to discontinue support for inefficient firms. Firm participation also should be time bound (for example, five years in length) to ensure that participants make optimal use of integrated government support.

Revise Tax Incentives to Align with Export Promotion Objectives

Tax incentives are another key policy that influences price incentives to producers. Under the new 2015 Investment Code, the government provides substantial tax incentives to new investment in selected activities. Although the new code targets incentives better than before, these incentives are expensive. According to Bode, Steenbergen, and Lohmann (2017), they amounted to about 3.3 percent of GDP in 2016, equivalent to almost 10 percent of government expenditure. Three deductions for corporate income tax constitute between 75 and 90 percent of all tax incentive costs: nonoperational expenses, investment allowances, and investment expenditures. With some adjustments and better targeting, there may be scope for increasing the return to tax incentives, while at the same time raising more revenue (discussed in chapter 4 of this report). These incentives merit review to ensure that they are having their desired effect in attracting foreign and domestic investment and that efforts are paying dividends in the form of new exports.

Priority 5: Accelerate Industrialization through Diversification, Value Addition, and Quality Upgrading

Increasing the size of the industrial sector is a critical component of Rwanda's structural transformation, because of its large employment and export potentials. Increasing mineral exports through value addition will be critical to raising exports (chapter 4 of this report). Developing nascent agroprocessing and other manufacturing sectors will be another important avenue. Rwanda has expanded nonmining industrial sectors by exporting new products such as garments, mechanical appliances, and grain milling. Expanding their production further will be key to continuing Rwanda's structural transformation.

Create a Supplier Development Program to Promote Domestic Supply Chains

Another way to increase exports is to deepen the domestic supply chain of value added. To the extent that domestic suppliers can substitute for imports now going into exports, increasing domestic value added contributes to embodied exports—a key objective of the government's "Made in Rwanda" program (MINEACOM 2017). This program requires upgrading quality to improve links between domestic suppliers and large international "anchor" firms. As Sutton (2014) argues, "The most powerful engine of capability building lies in firm-to-firm interactions in supply chains." Firm-to-firm interactions are particularly important because such anchor firms often have detailed technical and quality requirements for their supplies that may differ from generic quality certification. Globally recognizable producers with "brands" to uphold thus often require suppliers to comply with additional "'private standards" for social, environmental, and safety norms that may go beyond national legal requirements (UNIDO 2010).

Chile's Supplier Development Program offers a model of ways to foster domestic supply chains in a market-supportive way. It eschews the mandated rules for domestic value addition that led to failure in some Latin America countries and eventually led the World Trade Organization to enact strict limits on performance requirements. The program aimed to improve commercial links between SMEs and their large foreign customers. It helped buyers to identify potential suppliers and married this help with subsidized credit and market support to create links. Arraiz, Henriquez, and Stucchi (2013) found that this program was significantly effective in increasing sales, employment, and the sustainability of SMEs. Similar programs have been launched in Colombia and El Salvador.

Rwanda is considering the creation of a supplier development unit in the RDB that could facilitate links between anchor firms and local suppliers and identify the training needed for suppliers to meet the technical specifications and quality standards. Steenbergen and Sutton (2017) illuminate how this could be implemented effectively in Rwanda. A supplier development program could also be linked to the Export Development Facility at the Development Bank of Rwanda.

Use Standards to Foster Regional Manufacturing Exports

Upgrading product quality, establishing and satisfying standards for products, and harmonizing regional standards are critical priorities and opportunities to promote Rwandan products. Preparing companies to meet product standards for certification also has long-term export benefits. In Rwanda, TradeMark East Africa and the RSB have been providing hazard analysis and critical control point (HACCP) training since 2011 to help firms to prevent food contamination and prepare them to attain further certifications. HACCP certification is a difficult process, requiring considerable time and investment; with 24 applicants, only 10 enterprises were ultimately expected to be certified to HACCP and one to ISO 22000 (the global food safety management standard). This process has contributed to higher-value domestic contracts and increased exports in the EAC (TradeMark East Africa 2015). However, steering this process through external actors is costly and difficult to scale up.

In-country processes are needed to support standards upgrading and offer cost-effective monitoring. Professional bodies (for example, Rwanda's Chamber of Agriculture and its product-specific members) could play a much larger role in these processes. These bodies could be the first point of contact for producers to learn about product standards and to receive support for quality upgrading. They also could absorb the initial cost for small-scale, routine quality-monitoring exercises in return for producers' membership contributions. Initial support from government (under leadership of the RSB) and development partners to train these private sector bodies could yield long-term rewards.

Conclusion

Rwanda has set for itself a huge but worthy challenge: to become an upper-middle-income country by 2035. Achieving the growth rates necessary to make this goal a reality would be almost unprecedented in the history of development. The difficulties cannot be underestimated. Achieving this goal will require harnessing the full potential of regional and global markets—not only to expand exports at a rapid pace but also to tap into new sources of FDI, opportunities for technological progress, and knowledge, with the objective of speeding structural change through dynamic employment creation. The five priorities laid out in this chapter provide the outlines of a road map—abstract, but indicative of ways in which Rwandans themselves might fill in the details and achieve trade-led growth.

Notes

1. Rwanda's accession to the EAC involved three shifts: a new tariff structure, free trade with Tanzania and Uganda (as Rwanda already had free trade with Burundi and Kenya under the Common Market for Eastern and Southern Africa Free Trade Agreement), and removal of transport costs from tariff calculations, which further reduced Rwanda's effective trade tax rates (Argent 2014).
2. UNIDO Industrial Statistics (INDSTAT) database; UN Comtrade database; and University of Minnesota's Integrated Public Use Microdata Series (IPUMS) International database.
3. Brazil, China, the Arab Republic of Egypt, India, Nigeria, and the Russian Federation.
4. Copper production offers an important international example. Whereas the United States in the early 20th century used its copper mining sector to develop expertise in chemistry and metallurgy that laid the foundations for subsequent diversification and industrialization, Chile focused on mining alone and failed to develop similar industries (Maloney and Valencia Caicedo 2016).
5. Baumol's example is that, to play a string quartet, the same number of musicians is needed today as was needed in the 19th century, so the productivity of classical music performance has not increased. However, the real wages of musicians (as in all other professions) have increased greatly since the 19th century.
6. EAC membership expanded gradually over time, with Kenya, Tanzania, and Uganda joining in 2005, and Burundi and Rwanda joining in 2009. For Burundi and Rwanda, "5 years after" captures their import share 1 year after joining, and "10 years after" reflects 6 years of membership in the EAC.
7. Services exports are underreported because of the use of customs data, which do not register most services trade.
8. Spray (2017a) found that a recent large (broadly exogenous) reduction in transport costs significantly increased the likelihood of firms exporting. He exploits this fact using an instrumental variables approach to identify the impact on productivity for firms that export for the first time as well as for their domestic suppliers.
9. The main way in which Rwanda deals with the misclassification is to make use of the Duty Remission Scheme, which leaves SMEs at a competitive disadvantage. This allows manufacturing firms to avoid tariff duties when they can prove that a good is used as a basic input, thus improving the competitiveness of their finished products. However, the scheme has also created inconsistencies within the EAC and presents serious challenges for customs administration. Larger firms have also been more successful in obtaining import tariff exemptions on their inputs, whereas the effective tax rates facing SMEs are much closer to the official CET rate. The current CET is biased against SMEs.
10. These plants are owned by a private actor and have equal joint participation from Burundi, the Democratic Republic of Congo, and Rwanda. Rwanda purchases 3.5 megawatts of electricity from Rusizi I plant and 12 megawatts from Rusizi II.
11. Trade costs are the price equivalent of the reduction in international trade as compared with the potential implied by domestic production and consumption in the origin and destination markets. Higher bilateral trade costs result in smaller bilateral trade flows (Arvis et al. 2013)
12. With reference to the transit toll, the Kenya Public Road Tolls Act states, "Vehicles bearing Kenyan registration are for the time being exempted," suggesting that lawmakers recognized that the discriminatory practice could require revision.
13. Removing the road toll for vehicles registered in any EAC country altogether would align with the stated long-term vision for the EAC to become a fully functional customs union, with free flow of goods across borders, but it also would have a significant impact on Rwanda's own road toll income (which totaled just under FRW 514 billion

(approximately US$8 million) in fiscal year 2011–12, making up 27 percent of the current road fund revenues and probably close to the current total raised by Kenya and Tanzania collectively).

14. A first-party logistics provider is a firm transporting products from a sender to a receiver. A second-party logistics provider is a carrier that owns the means of transport, such as a shipping line, airline, or trucking company that owns, leases, or charters its vessels. A third-party logistics provider offers outsourced or "third-party" logistics services to companies for parts of their supply chain management function.
15. Schlumberger (2010) describes the nine "freedoms" regulating air transport through the lens of African air service.
16. In World Trade Organization parlance, these reflect mode 1 and mode 3 types of services trade, respectively. Additional modes include consumption abroad (mode 2, for example, tourism) and temporary presence of persons (mode 4, for example, servicing short-term construction contracts).
17. Argent (2014) found that, to protect its market share, the dominant mobile phone supplier charged consumers more to call an out-of-network phone in competing networks than to call London.
18. One example is the use of accounting technicians to provide basic record keeping services, which can help firms to meet economic gains by shifting to a more organized and targeted management style (Bloom et al. 2016).
19. Harding and Javorcik (2013) found that an IPA's ability to attract FDI depends on strongly on quality, which also includes the ability of staff to handle investor inquiries. A 1–10 quality rating of IPAs found that a 1-point rating increase was associated with a 15 percent increase in FDI inflows.

References

AfDB (African Development Bank). 2013. "Rwanda Transport Sector Review and Action Plan." African Development Bank Group, Tunis.

Amiti, M., and J. Konings. 2007. "Trade Liberalization, Intermediate Inputs, and Productivity: Evidence from Indonesia." *American Economic Review* 97 (5): 1611–38.

Andersen, M., B. Kett, and E. von Uexkull. 2017. "Corporate Tax Incentives and FDI in Developing Countries." In *Global Investment Competitiveness Report 2017/2018: Foreign Investor Perspectives and Policy Implications*, ch. 3, 73–99. Washington, DC: World Bank. https://doi.org/10.1596/978-1-4648-1175-3_ch3.

Argent, J. 2014. "Review of EAC Common External Tariff." TradeMark East Africa, Kigali.

Arraiz, I., F. Henriquez, and R. Stucchi. 2013. "Supplier Development Programs and Firm Performance: Evidence from Chile." *Small Business Economics* 41 (1): 277–93.

Arvis, J.-F., B. Shepherd, Y. Duval, and C. Utoktham. 2013. "Trade Costs and Development: A New Data Set." Economic Premise 104, World Bank, Washington, DC.

Baines, T., H. Lightfoot, and P. Smart. 2011. "Servitization within Manufacturing: Exploring the Provision of Advanced Services and Their Impact on Vertical Integration." *Journal of Manufacturing Technology Management* 22 (7): 947–54.

Bamber, P., O. Cattaneo, K. Fernandez-Stark, G. Gereffi, E. van der Marel, and B. Shepherd. 2017. "Diversification through Servicification." Unpublished paper, World Bank, Washington, DC.

Basnett, Y. 2013. "Labour Mobility in East Africa: An Analysis of the East African Community's Common Market and the Free Movement of Workers." *ODI Development Policy Review* 31 (2): 131–48.

Bastos, P., J. Silva, and E. Verhoogen. 2016. "Export Destinations and Input Prices." Policy Research Working Paper 6914, World Bank, Washington, DC.

Baumol, W. J. 1967. "Macroeconomics of Unbalanced Growth: The Anatomy of Urban Crisis." *American Economic Review* 57 (3): 415–26.

Birdsall, N., and N. Okonjo-Iweala. 2017. "A Big Bond for Africa." Project Syndicate, Center for Global Development, Washington, DC, April 17.

Bloom, N., J. Van Reenen, A. Choudhary, and R. Lemos. 2016. "Management in Pakistan: First Evidence from Punjab." International Growth Centre, Islamabad.

BNR (National Bank of Rwanda). 2017. "Monetary Policy and Financial Stability Statement—22nd February 2017." Government of Rwanda, Kigali.

Bode, M., V. Steenbergen, and J. Lohmann. 2017. "Attracting Investments While Raising Tax Revenue: Recommendations for Reviewing Rwanda's Tax Incentives." IGC Policy Note, International Growth Centre, Kigali.

Bofinger, H. C. 2017. "Air Transport in Africa: Opportunities and Issues." Draft prepared for *Industries without Smokestacks: African Industrialization Revisited*, edited by R. Newfarmer, J. Page, and F. Tarp. Oxford: Oxford University Press, forthcoming.

Calabrese, L., and A. Eberhard-Ruiz. 2016. "What Types of Non-Tariff Barriers Affect the East African Community?" Overseas Development Institute, London.

Calabrese, L., P. Papadavid, and J. Tyson. 2017. "Rwanda: Financing for Manufacturing." SET Report, June, Overseas Development Institute, London.

Cameron, M., and W. Viviers. 2017. "Identifying Realistic Export Opportunities for Rwanda Based on the TRADE-DSM Approach." IGC Policy Paper, International Growth Centre, Kigali.

CCTTFA (Central Corridor Transit Transport Facilitation Agency). 2013. *Central Corridor Transport Observatory Annual Report 2013*. Kigali: CCTTFA and TradeMark East Africa. http://observatory.centralcorridor-ttfa.org/media/Annual_Reports/Central_Corridor_Transport_Observatory_Annual_Report_2014.pdf.

———. 2014. *Central Corridor Transport Observatory Annual Report 2014*. Kigali: CCTTFA and TradeMark East Africa.

———. 2015. *Central Corridor Transport Observatory Annual Report 2015*. Kigali: CCTTFA and TradeMark East Africa.

———. 2016. *Central Corridor Transport Observatory Annual Report 2016*. Kigali: CCTTFA and TradeMark East Africa.

Dihel, N., A. M. Fernandes, and A. Mattoo. 2012. "Developing Professional Services in Africa through Regional Integration." In *De-Fragmenting Africa: Deepening Regional Trade Integration in Goods and Services*, edited by P. Brenton and G. Isik. Washington, DC: World Bank.

Dihel, N., and A. G. Goswami. 2016. "The Unexplored Potential of Trade in Services in Africa: From Hair Stylists and Teachers to Accountants and Doctors." World Bank, Washington, DC.

Duarte, M., and D. Restuccia. 2010. "The Role of the Structural Transformation in Aggregate Productivity." *Quarterly Journal of Economics* 125 (1): 129–73.

Durevall, D. 2011. "East African Community: Pre-conditions for an Effective Monetary Union." International Growth Centre, London.

EABC (East African Business Community). 2016. "East African Common Market Scorecard." EABC, Nairobi.

EAPP (Eastern Africa Power Pool). 2014. *EAPP Regional Power System Master Plan 2014*. Addis Ababa: EAPP, February.

Ebling, G., and N. Janz. 1999. "Export and Innovation Activities in the German Service Sector: Empirical Evidence at the Firm Level." ZEW Discussion Paper 99-53, Center for European Economic Research, Mannheim.

Eichengreen, B., and P. Gupta. 2012. "Exports of Services: Indian Experience in Perspective." Working Paper 12/102, National Institute of Public Finance and Policy, New Delhi.

English, P. 2017. "Rwanda: Raising Exports and Attracting Foreign Direct Investment: Some Ideas for Action." International Growth Centre, London.

Farole, T., and D. Winkler, eds. 2014. *Making Foreign Direct Investment Work for Sub-Saharan Africa: Local Spillovers and Competitiveness in Global Value Chains*. Washington, DC: World Bank.

Frazer, G. 2012. "The EAC Common External Tariff (CET) and Rwanda." IGC Policy Paper, International Growth Centre, London.

———. 2016a. "The Boring Infrastructure That Rwanda Needs." International Growth Centre blog, August 6,

———. 2016b. "Imports and Skill Utilization in a Low-Income Country." University of Toronto.

———. 2017. "Examining the Impact of the Common External Tariff of the East African Community in Rwanda." IGC Policy Paper, International Growth Centre, London.

Freund, C., and T. Moran. 2017. "Multinational Investors as Export Superstars: How Emerging Market Governments Can Reshape Comparative Advantage." Working Paper 17-1, Peterson Institute for International Economics, Washington, DC.

Freund, C., and M. Pierola. 2012. "Export Surges." *Journal of Development Economics* 97 (2): 387–95.

Gelb, A., C. J. Meyer, V. Ramachandran, and D. Wadhwa. 2017. "Can Africa Be a Manufacturing Destination? Labor Costs in Comparative Perspective." CGD Working Paper 466, Center for Global Development, Washington, DC.

Ghani, E., and H. Kharas. 2010. "The Service Revolution in South Asia: An Overview." In *The Service Revolution in South Asia,* edited by E. Ghani, 1–32. New York: Oxford University Press.

Hallward-Driemeier, M., and G. Nayyar. 2017. *Trouble in the Making: The Future of Manufacturing-Led Development.* Washington, DC: World Bank.

Harding, T., and B. S. Javorcik. 2013. "Investment Promotion and FDI Inflows: Quality Matters." *CESifo Economic Studies* 59 (2): 337–59.

Herrendorf, B., R. Rogerson, and Á. Valentinyi. 2013. "Growth and Structural Transformation." NBER Working Paper 18996, National Bureau of Economic Research, Cambridge, MA.

Hoekman, B., and B. Shepherd. 2015. "Services, Firm Performance, and Exports: The Case of the East African Community." IGC Paper, International Growth Centre, London, October.

Hook, A. 2013. "Mutual Recognition Agreements in Services Trade in Africa: Lessons from the East African Community." World Bank, Washington, DC.

ICPAR (Institute of Certified Public Accountants of Rwanda). 2017. "ICPAR Five Year Strategy: 2017–2021." ICPAR, Kigali.

InterVistas Consulting. 2016. "Costs and Benefits of 'Open Skies' in the East African Community (EAC): Key Findings." InterVistas Consulting, Washington, DC.

Jaud, M., and C. Freund. 2015. *Champions Wanted: Promoting Exports in the Middle East and North Africa.* Directions in Development. Washington, DC: World Bank. doi: 10.1596/978-1-4648-0460-1.

Javorcik, B. S. 2004. "In Search of Spillovers through Backward Linkages." *American Economic Review* 94 (3): 605–27.

———. 2014. "Does Foreign Direct Investment Increase the Productivity of Domestic Firms? In Search of Spillovers through Backward Linkages." *American Economic Review* 94 (3): 605–27.

Kelly, T., and C. Kemei. 2016. "One Network Area in East Africa." Background paper for the *World Development Report 2016: Digital Dividends,* World Bank, Washington, DC.

Kenya Association of Manufacturers. 2017. "KAM Study on the Review of the East African Community Common External Rates." Kenya Association of Manufacturers, Nairobi.

Keyser, J. 2014. "Avoiding the 'Harm' in Harmonized Standards for Food Staples in Africa." World Bank Trade Post blog, December 1.

Khan, M. 2007. "Governance, Economic Growth, and Development since the 1960s." DESA Working Paper 54, United Nations Department of Economic and Social Affairs, New York, August. ST/ESA/2007/DWP/54.

Lalui, A. 2016. "Analysis of Cross-Border Trade in Services: Issues and Trends with a Focus on Rwanda and DRC." TradeMark East Africa, Kigali.

Loungani, P., and S. Mishra. 2014. "Not Your Father's Service Sector." International Monetary Fund, Washington, DC.

Maloney, W. F., and F. Valencia Caicedo. 2016. "The Persistence of (Subnational) Fortune." *Economic Journal* 126 (598): 2363–401.

Mayer, T., and M. Thoenig. 2016. "Regional Trade Agreements and the Pacification of Eastern Africa." International Growth Centre, London.

McMillan, M., D. Rodrik, and C. Sepulveda. 2017. "Structural Change, Fundamentals, and Growth: A Framework and Country Studies." Policy Research Working Paper 8041, World Bank, Washington, DC.

Melitz, M. 2003. "The Impact of Trade on Intra-Industry Reallocations and Aggregate Industry Productivity." *Econometrica* 71 (6):1695–725.

MINEACOM (Ministry of East African Community). 2017. "Made in Rwanda Policy." Government of Rwanda, Kigali.

MINICOM (Ministry of Trade and Industry), Rwanda. 2015. "Revised National Export Strategy." MINICOM, Kigali.

———. 2016. "Strategy to Transform the Textile, Apparel, and Leather Sectors." MINICOM, Kigali.

———. 2017. "Private Sector Development Strategy 2 (PSDS2) 2018–2024." MINICOM, Kigali.

Morjaria, A., and V. Steenbergen. 2017. "Understanding Constraints to Value Addition in Rwanda's Coffee Sector." IGC Policy Brief, International Growth Centre, London, February.

Nalule, V. 2016. "Energy in the East African Community: The Role of the Energy Charter Treaty." International Energy Charter, East Asian Community.

Nayyar, G. 2017. "The Future of Manufacturing-Led Development in Rwanda." Background note for the "Future Drivers of Growth" project, World Bank, Washington, DC.

NCTTCA (Northern Corridor Transit Transport Coordination Authority). 2014. "The Northern Corridor Transport Observatory Report." Issue 5, NCTTCA, Kigali.

———. 2015. "The Northern Corridor Transport Observatory Report." Issue 6, NCTTCA, Kigali.

———. 2016a. "The Northern Corridor Transport Observatory Report." Issue 7, NCTTCA, Kigali.

———. 2016b. "The Northern Corridor Transport Observatory Report." Issue 8, NCTTCA, Kigali.

———. 2017. "The Northern Corridor Transport Observatory Report." Issue 9, NCTTCA, Kigali.

Newfarmer, R., J. Page, and F. Tarp, eds. Forthcoming. *Industries without Smokestacks: African Industrialization Revisited*. Oxford, U.K.: Oxford University Press.

Newfarmer, R., and M. Soderbom. 2012. "Rwanda and the East Africa Monetary Union." IGC Policy Brief, International Growth Centre, London, March.

Newman, C., J. Page, J. Rand, A. Shimeles, M. Soderbom, and F. Tarp. 2016. *Made in Africa: Learning to Compete in Industry*. Washington, DC: Brookings Institution Press.

OECD (Organisation for Economic Co-operation and Development) and WTO (World Trade Organization). 2017. *Aid for Trade at a Glance 2017: Promoting Trade, Inclusiveness, and Connectivity for Sustainable Development*. Geneva: WTO; Paris: OECD Publishing.

Rastogi, C., and J.-F. Arvis. 2014. *The Eurasian Connection: Supply-Chain Efficiency along the Modern Silk Route through Central Asia*. Directions in Development Series: Trade. Washington, DC: World Bank.

Rodrik, D. 2008. "The Real Exchange Rate and Economic Growth." *Brookings Papers on Economic Activity* 39 (2): 365–439.

Schlumberger, C. E. 2010. *Open Skies for Africa: Implementing the Yamoussoukro Decision*. Directions in Development Series: Infrastructure. Washington, DC: World Bank. https://openknowledge.worldbank.org/handle/10986/2467.

Shepherd, B., J. de Melo, and R. Sen. 2017. "Reform of the EAC Common External Tariff: Evidence from Trade Costs." IGC Policy Paper, International Growth Centre, Kampala.

Spray, J. 2017a. "Assessing the Influence of EAC Trade Costs Reductions in Exports and Export Supply-Chains in Rwanda." International Growth Centre, Kigali.

———. 2017b. "Exports and Promoting Backward Linkages: Ideas and Lessons for the Made in Rwanda Policy." International Growth Centre, Kigali.

Spray, J., and S. Wolf. 2016. "Industries without Smokestacks in Uganda and Rwanda." International Growth Centre, London.

Steenbergen, V., and B. Javorcik. 2017. "Analysing the Impact of the Kigali Special Economic Zone on Firm Behaviour." IGC Working Paper, International Growth Centre, London, August.

Steenbergen, V., with J. Sutton. 2017. "Establishing a Local Content Unit for Rwanda." Policy Note, International Growth Centre, London.

Sutton, J. 2014. "Gains from the Natural Gas: Local Content and Tanzania's Industrial Development." Seventh Gilman Ruthinda Memorial Lecture, Bank of Tanzania, June.

Szirmai, A. 2012. "Industrialisation as an Engine of Growth in Developing Countries, 1950–2005." *Structural Change and Economic Dynamics* 23 (4): 406–20.

TradeMark East Africa. 2015. "Setting Standards in Rwanda's Food Industry." TradeMark East Africa, Nairobi, August 30. https://www.trademarkea.com/impact-stories/setting-standards-in-rwandas-food-industry/.

Tybout, J., J. de Melo, and V. Corbo. 2015. "The Effects of Trade Reforms on Scale and Technical Efficiency: New Evidence from Chile." In *Developing Countries in the World Economy*, edited by J. de Melo, 237–56. Hackensack, NJ: World Scientific Publishing.

United Nations. Various years. UN Commodity Trade Statistics (Comtrade) database. New York: United Nations.

UNIDO (United Nations Industrial Development Organization). 2010. "Making Private Standards Work for You: A Guide to Private Standards in the Garments, Footwear, and Furniture Sectors." UNIDO, Vienna.

University of Minnesota. Various years. Integrated Public Use Microdata Series (IPUMS) International database. University of Minnesota.

Vanguard Economics. 2017. "Measuring the Economic and Social Impact of Northern Corridor Integration Projects (NCIP) in Rwanda." Vanguard Economics, Kigali.

Wagh, S., A. Lovegrove, and J. Kashangaki. 2012. "Scaling up Regional Financial Integration in the EAC." In *De-Fragmenting Africa: Deepening Regional Trade Integration in Goods and Services,* edited by P. Brenton and G. Isik. Washington, DC: World Bank.

World Bank. 1993. *The East Asian Miracle: Economic Growth and Public Policy.* New York: Oxford University Press.

———. 2017. "Rwanda Economic Update: Sustaining Growth by Building on Emerging Export Opportunities." World Bank, Kigali.

———. 2019. *Doing Business 2019: Training for Reform.* Washington, DC: World Bank.

———. Various years. Doing Business database. Washington, DC: World Bank. https://www.doingbusiness.org/en/custom-query.

WTO (World Trade Organization). 2018. World Integrated Trade Solution online database. Geneva: WTO.

3

Faster Urbanization, Greater Agglomeration

"No country has grown to middle income without industrializing and urbanizing. None has grown to high income without vibrant cities. The rush to cities seems chaotic, but it is necessary" (World Bank 2009).

Introduction

Rapid and well-managed urbanization is essential for Rwanda to achieve its aspirations for growth. Urbanization generates enormous economic benefits by increasing *density,* which facilitates the transmission of knowledge and ideas, increases economies of scale and opportunities for specialization by reducing transport costs, and improves firms' access to critical services and a large pool of labor with varied skills. Workers who are closer to a wider range of goods and services benefit from such opportunities to deepen their human capital and strengthen their bargaining power. These *agglomeration economies* mean that the more workers and firms are added to an urban location, the higher their individual productivity becomes.

Rwanda's urban population has more than doubled since 2002, and from 2002–12 Kigali was one of the fastest-growing cities in Africa. Rural workers have migrated to urban areas in droves, where their productivity is double that in rural areas; urban areas have accounted for 48 percent of national labor productivity growth over the past 15 years.

Nevertheless, urban areas in Rwanda, and Kigali in particular, have not generated the kind of productivity gains that rapidly growing cities in successful East Asian economies have achieved. This is largely because the agglomeration economies from urbanization have been limited. To rectify this, Rwanda should focus more on delivering the fundamental drivers that *link* urbanization to robust economic growth and less on setting targets for *levels* of urbanization itself. In essence, Rwanda should focus on reshaping public policy, prioritizing investments, and strengthening institutions along three dimensions—*spatial*, *sectoral*, and *institutional*:

1. *Spatial.* A bullish view is needed to unleash the potential of Kigali to connect Rwanda with the regional and global economy, enabling the city to be built and grow in response to international demand.

2. *Sectoral.* To enhance efficiency of capital investment in infrastructure, housing, and commercial structures, there is urgent need to strengthen land markets.
3. *Institutional.* Stronger intergovernmental coordination of economic and spatial planning processes is needed to overcome coordination challenges in urban development.

Regulatory Policies

For the rapid economic growth targeted until 2050, Rwanda needs an economic engine to deliver dynamic agglomeration economies of the kind seen only in large cities. Only Kigali's economy, which is already seven times the size of the next largest urban area, can perform this role. However, Kigali's urban fabric is fragmented by small-scale, patchy land development, which disconnects firms, labor, and input and product markets, undermining the agglomeration economies and raising the costs of private inputs and public infrastructure.

The main priority is to strengthen land markets so that private developers face the appropriate incentives to increase density. Rwanda's urban planning has been inappropriate within cities, leading to fragmented development, as peripheries are less strictly regulated than the center. This creates perverse incentives to build in peripheries, in exactly the scattered and inefficient way that planners wish to avoid. Bedrock reforms that strengthen land markets and urban planning should be in place first to enhance the efficiency of investment and generate high economic returns. In dynamic, fast-changing cities, the economic vocations of places are transformed regularly as the economy grows in sophistication and land markets facilitate the transformation of structures to meet the economic needs and opportunities of the time.

Rwanda should move from highly prescriptive zoning requirements for structures to a system that allows structures to evolve to serve the changing economy. However, regulations on structures should be used to mitigate *negative externalities* like environmental degradation.

Investments

Another priority is to provide efficient, affordable, and integrated public transport and to boost investment in roads. Public transit routes to Kigali's center are congested and likely to become more so. To limit sprawl, excellent *central* public transport should be combined with quality public transport to a small number of strategic peripheral locations. *Grids* should be provided (in Kigali and in secondary cities) to ensure that rapid peripheral development takes place in a planned way. Greater investment in roads also is necessary to improve the integration of Rwanda's cities with the countryside and with neighboring countries and to strengthen the connections between urban centers.

Kigali's growth needs to be accompanied by a more calibrated approach toward developing a complementary set of secondary cities and small towns. International experience shows that such investments should center on increasing external connectivity and laying urban grids to plan for future expansion. In addition, investments in health and education would raise workers' productivity without tying them to a particular place, so that markets can pick the location and form of private sector development more efficiently. Kigali needs to operate more like an effective, integrated labor and product market, which would increase its potential for the realizing agglomeration economies and reduce the cost of private inputs and public infrastructure.

The government has pursued a policy of grouped villages (*imidugudu*), which, in some cases, has implied large sunk-cost investments that, with effective urbanization, often become redundant. The program facilitates rural-urban links as well as indirectly preparing future urban dwellers for urban life while they are in rural areas. Improving planning and establishing settlements, while minimizing huge infrastructure costs and potential future financial losses, are recommended to ensure that they serve the purpose. Policy also needs to prioritize *rural-urban connectivity* and *anticipate migration* to larger urban areas. This approach can be complemented with "off-grid" rural infrastructure, which delivers key services while placing smaller "bets" in the long-run vocation of more remote locations.

Institutions

These changes will require stronger institutions. Urban planning capabilities at the city and district levels need strengthening. Plans should respond to markets and community needs, while safeguarding against capture by special interests through strong public oversight and engagement.

Urban planning also needs to be rationalized. "Economic" planning is often disconnected from "spatial" planning. As Rwanda works to strengthen the economic dividend of urbanization, economic planners should start to think spatially, and spatial planners should become more aligned with economic planning and goals.

Further, economically connected districts must be encouraged and required to coordinate land use plans, transport and service provision, major infrastructure like special economic zones, tourism infrastructure, and so on, to reduce waste and exploit complementarities.

Finally, stronger institutions are needed to value land and to assign and protect property rights. Rwanda has a strong basis for efficient and transparent valuation, with centralized and digitized landownership and transaction records, a professional valuation body, and credible institutions for oversight. Credible land valuation will also enable urban areas to fiscalize public investments in land through land value capture.

The Promise of Urbanization and Agglomeration

Urbanization, Agglomeration, and Economic Development

Few countries have attained upper-middle-income status without substantial, rapid, and well-managed urbanization. Urbanization is the *spatial* corollary of the process of economic structural transformation that involves the movement of workers from less to more productive sectors—typically from farming to off-farm sectors in the early stages of development. Although high birth rates make the natural increase of the population an important source of urban growth, rural-urban migration is an even more significant force driving the urbanization process. Migration depends on forces that "pull" migrants to their destinations as well as forces that "push" them to leave their origins. Better economic opportunities in urban areas, partly due to agglomeration economies, are a major pull factor, often providing the main motivation for rural-urban migration (Brueckner and Lall 2014). In China's urbanization process, for example, employment in manufacturing and services grew from less than 30 percent of the labor force 30 years ago to more than 60 percent now. The reallocation of labor to manufacturing and services—sectors in urban areas that rapidly increased their productivity—accounted for almost one-fifth of China's gross domestic product (GDP) growth during that period (World Bank and Development Research Center of the State Council, China 2014).

Agglomeration economies strengthen the links between urbanization and economic development. The enormous benefits of urbanization are seen most vividly in East Asia, where growth in the last half century is among the most spectacular episodes of development in recorded human history. Figure 3.1 shows changes in urbanization and GDP per capita from 1985 to 2010, when the processes of urbanization and economic development were intertwined. Countries such as China, the Republic of Korea, Thailand, and Vietnam have supported the development of vibrant cities that allowed frenetic, productive interactions among people and businesses, marked by the transmission of knowledge and ideas. Increasing returns to scale were driven by economic density, triggered primarily by

FIGURE 3.1 Changes in urbanization and income in East Asia and Pacific, 1985–2010

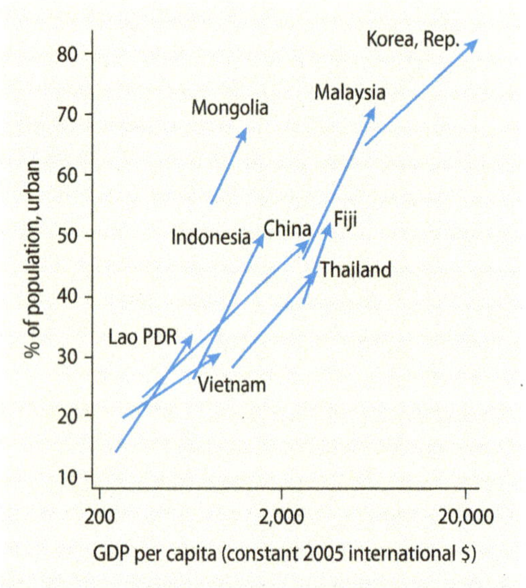

Source: Based on World Development Indicators data (World Bank, various years); *Economist* 2012.
Note: Bottom of arrow = 1985; top of arrow = 2010.

lower transport costs for goods and people. Well-functioning cities also can create markets for specialized services, including logistics, advertising, legal support, and management consulting. These services are critical for entrepreneurs, who can focus on their "big idea" or core competencies without having to worry about developing in-house supporting functions. Cities are also instrumental in matching skilled people with jobs that value those skills. International evidence suggests that a 1 percentage point increase in the urban population is associated with a 3–8 percent increase in a country's per capita income (Rosenthal and Strange 2003). Each doubling of its size raises a city's productivity by 5 percent on average.

Successful urban-led development has often involved intense spatial concentration of economic activity, typically in locations that are well connected to domestic and external markets. A common feature of rapidly growing Asian countries has been the heavy concentration of economic activity in and around coastal metropolitan regions (map 3.1). This pattern is no less striking in high-income economies. Simply put, big cities deliver extremely dense and varied labor and product markets, multiplying the forces of agglomeration, while enabling economies of scale in the provision of infrastructure, public spaces, and services. Seoul provides a powerful example of how a major city in a small country can put in place policies and investments to deliver agglomeration economies (box 3.1).

Faster Urbanization, Greater Agglomeration, and Greater Growth Dividends for Rwanda

Rwanda has started its journey to urbanization, and the government has picked urbanization as one of the key areas for economic transformation and job creation. Rwanda's population has become considerably more urban since 2002. The urban population almost doubled during this time (box 3.2).

Kigali is the largest urban agglomeration (1,133,000 people in 2012) and home to a major share of Rwanda's urban population. With population growth of 6.4 percent a year from 2002 to 2012, Kigali is one of the fastest-growing cities in Africa and the most favored destination for rural migrants. In 2014, 57 percent of Kigali's population had migrated to Kigali at some point in their lives, and 14 percent had migrated from rural areas in the past three years.

Sectors *bordering* Kigali have also seen higher than average population growth.[1] Half of the urban population outside Kigali is found along two urban corridors: the Musanze–Rubavu corridor (one-third)[2] and the Muhanga–Huye corridor (18 percent).[3] Much of Rwanda's remaining urban population is spread between the roads connecting Kigali to Bugesera, Kayonza, the Burundian border, and the more isolated settlements of Nyagatare and Rusizi. Almost a quarter of the urban population resides in small settlements of fewer than approximately 15,000 people (Diao, Randriamamonjy, and Thurlow 2017).

Urbanization in Rwanda has contributed significantly to economic growth and

MAP 3.1 Visualizing economic concentration across five countries

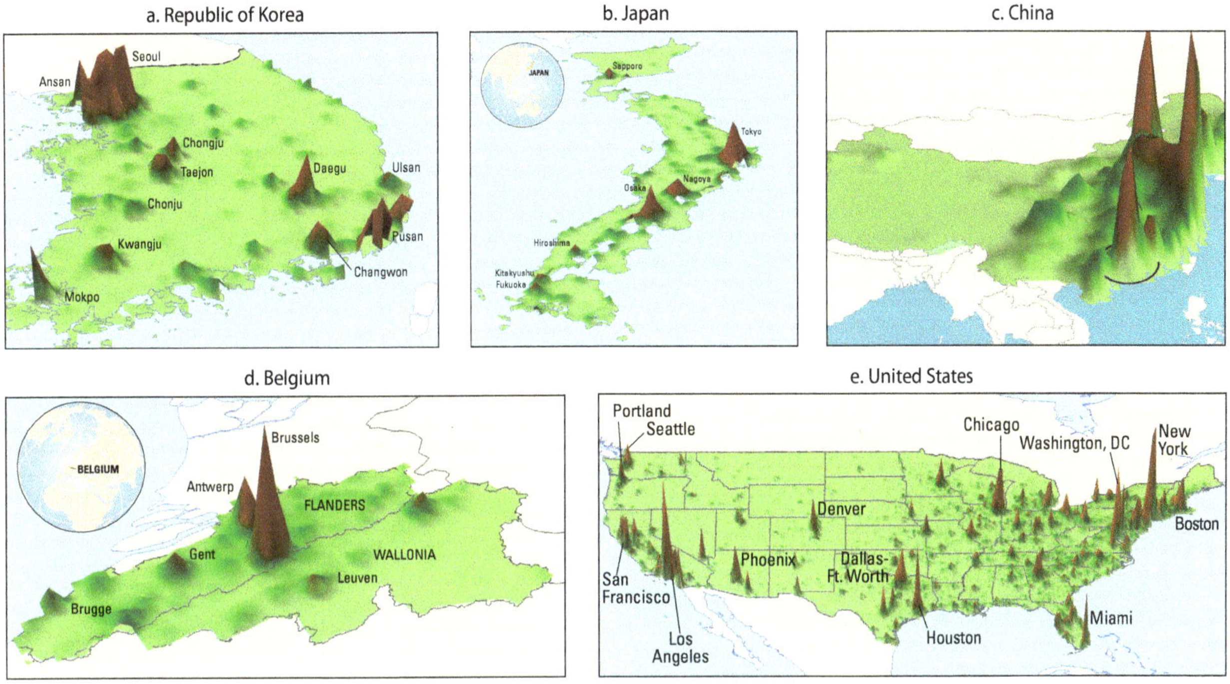

Sources: For panels a and d, WDR 2009 team and World Bank Development Research Group, based on subnational GDP estimates for 2005. See also Nordhaus 2006. For panels b and e, WDR 2009 team. For panel c, World Bank 2015.

BOX 3.1 Seoul becomes a global city

Home to more than 10 million people, producing one-quarter of national GDP on 1 percent of its land area, Seoul is the Republic of Korea's interlocutor with the global economy. The broader Seoul Metropolitan Area (SMA) comprises 29 towns (including Incheon and Seoul) on 12 percent of the country's land; this area contains half of the national population and generates about half of national GDP.

Over the past 70 years, tension has arisen over how best to manage the SMA. Some policy makers, concerned that rapid SMA growth would lead to regional imbalances, argued that such growth should be constrained with strict regulations. Regulations restricted development in certain areas, imposed fines on buildings exceeding given parameters, limited allocations of land to industry, limited the industrial output allowed in the SMA, prohibited various classes of activities, and required national government approval for land development projects exceeding 1 million square meters. In the 1970s a greenbelt strategy was employed to constrain Seoul's growth and promote 14 cities across the country.

These controls were not successful. Investors and citizens led a rapid succession of new projects regardless of policies, including residential complexes, metropolitan highways, new towns, and a new international hub airport—bypassing the objective of limiting growth. However, the controls did hurt efficiency: more than 200,000 factories in the SMA are unregistered, contributing to unmanaged urban development. And urban growth is fragmented, exacerbating congestion and environmental degradation.

As Korea sought to position Seoul as a 21st-century world city, the government relaxed quantity limits that restricted the location of new colleges, firms, industrial estates, and housing sites. It adopted price instruments to regulate urban construction, levying a development charge on new commercial buildings. By recalibrating city management through deregulation and market instruments, Korea is making Seoul's quest to become a global city more likely to succeed.

BOX 3.2 Measuring urbanization in Rwanda

A change in the definition of urban areas has made it difficult to compare urbanization levels in 2002 and 2012 censuses.

The 2002 and 2012 population censuses show an almost stagnant level of urbanization in Rwanda—with the urbanization rate falling slightly from 16.9 to 16.5 percent. This decline is at odds with the urbanization that is observed on the ground.

This counterintuitive result is partly explained by a change in the definition of urban areas between the two censuses. For the 2002 census, 15 cities were delineated and all settlements within these catchment areas were considered urban, even those that previously would have been classified as rural. The 2012 census defines urban-rural status based on the smallest administrative entity: the village. To qualify as urban, a village has to possess an important built-up area and important infrastructure (education facilities, electricity and water, markets, and banks and other financial institutions). As a result of the change in definition, the two census figures cannot be compared directly to evaluate urban population trends.

Classifying settlements on the basis of the presence or absence of infrastructure also risks overlooking true urbanization patterns, such as the emergence of large, densely populated areas on the edges of formally planned areas that are lacking infrastructure but are nonetheless functionally part of the broader urban landscape.

Different definitions of "urban" used in Rwanda. Beyond the change of definition between the two censuses, different institutions and policies have defined "urban" in Rwanda differently.

The National Land Use Master Plan defines "urban" and "built-up" areas from a land use planning perspective, which considers spatial, population, density, administrative, size, and zoning aspects. It defines an urban area as a built-up agglomeration if it exceeds 20 square kilometers and has a population of more than 10,000 inhabitants, resulting in a population density of more than 500 persons per square kilometer.

Law no. 10/2012 of 02/05/2012, "Governing Urban Planning and Building in Rwanda," defines three categories of urban settlements according to population size. It categorizes urban areas into (1) a city with at least 200,000 inhabitants, (2) a municipality with at least 30,000 but less than 200,000 inhabitants, and (3) an agglomeration with at least 10,000 inhabitants but less than 30,000 inhabitants.

An alternative approach to measuring and comparing past and recent urbanization levels in Rwanda. It is possible to study urbanization over time in Rwanda by applying a simple approach to classifying settlements on the basis of population size and density. Settlements are commonly classified as urban if they contain a minimum of 5,000 persons living at a minimum density of 1,000 persons per square kilometer.

Applying this definition to an analysis of geocoded population data indicates that Rwanda's urban population increased from 15.8 percent in 2002 to 26.5 percent in 2015. This reflects growth of the urban population of just under 2 million people, from 1.49 million to 3.46 million between 2002 and 2015, at an average annual rate of 6.7 percent. These estimates are based on an analysis of population data from the WorldPop project and an analysis that classifies settlements by breaking the national territory into grid cells of 1 square kilometer, as opposed to villages or sectors, which have variable areas.

structural change through the reallocation of labor off farm. The contribution of urbanization to growth depends on the productivity gap between similar sectors in rural and urban areas, which occurs because (1) urban workers are generally better educated and higher skilled and (2) capital-labor ratios tend to be higher in urban sectors where capital investments are more likely to be concentrated. A comparison of wages for similarly educated workers provides a broad estimate of the urban-rural productivity gap; urban workers in Rwanda earn, on average, twice the rural wage for similar work in similar sectors of employment. Using these estimates, analysis done for this report shows that urbanization has accounted for 37 percent of national structural change (GDP growth through labor reallocation across sectors), and urban areas have accounted for 48 percent of national labor productivity growth over the past 15 years (Diao, Randriamamonjy, and Thurlow 2017; figure 3.2).

Rwanda's economy could be 20 percent larger by 2050 with faster urbanization. A spatial computable general equilibrium (CGE) model developed for this report examines how alternative urbanization scenarios would affect key economic and welfare outcomes in Rwanda until 2050 (see annex 3A; Diao, Randriamamonjy, and Thurlow 2017 for details). On the basis of past trends in migration and population growth, the urban population's share of total population (using current official definitions) is expected to grow to 41.2 percent in 2050. Simulations of faster urbanization are developed by increasing rural-urban migration above historical rates. In 2050, the urban share of the population is increased to 54.6 percent, up from 41.2 percent in the baseline.[4] This scenario is consistent with the targeted pace of urbanization outlined in Vision 2020. The model shows that, compared with on-trend urbanization, faster urbanization raises the total GDP growth rate by 0.5 percentage point per year over the 2015–50 period. Cumulatively, this means that by 2050 the economy is almost a fifth larger than it would be with slower urbanization (figure 3.3). Almost all of this additional GDP growth is generated in Kigali, where value added increases by 63 percent compared with the baseline. This positive growth effect is due entirely to more people leaving rural areas for urban centers—that is, the total population and workforce remain unchanged from the baseline.

To achieve the rapid economic growth targeted until 2050, Rwanda will need to harness agglomeration economies through well-managed cities. Kigali is undoubtedly the prime economic hub of Rwanda. Its output exceeds that of the six secondary cities plus Bugesera, Gicumbi, and Rwamagana-Kayonza combined. Firms registered in Kigali accounted for 92 percent of all turnover declared to the Rwanda Revenue Authority in 2015, and more than

FIGURE 3.2 Contribution of urbanization to structural transformation and labor productivity in Rwanda, 2002–12

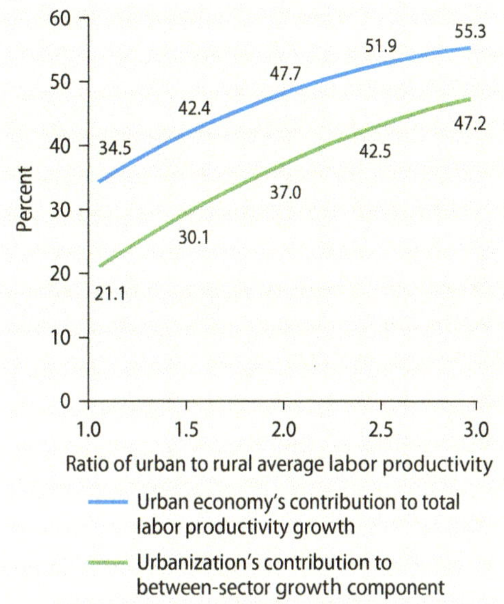

Source: Diao, Randriamamonjy, and Thurlow 2017.
Note: The x axis shows the assumed ratio of urban to rural labor productivity in the same sector. For example, how much more productive is an urban versus a rural construction worker? These assumptions are combined with data on the productivity of different sectors and changes in the sectors in which people are employed in rural and urban areas.

FIGURE 3.3 Simulated changes in growth outcomes with faster urbanization in Rwanda

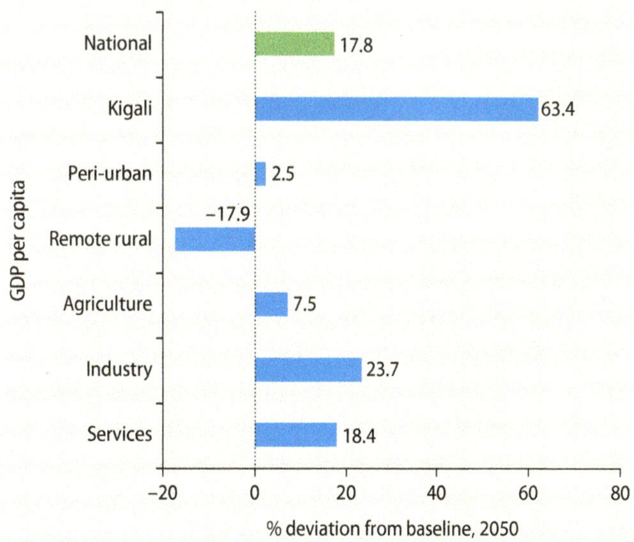

Source: Diao 2017.

half of all formal firms and half of formal employment are located in Kigali. Per capita consumption in Kigali is five times that in rural areas, and, although regional GDP is not calculated, nightlights-based estimations suggest that Kigali accounted for 40 percent of GDP in 2012. Kigali is also the most urbanized economy, with 80 percent of nonagricultural employment even in 2002, compared with just 30 percent in other urban areas. A dynamic Kigali is central to harnessing agglomeration economies in Rwanda. If managed well, Kigali has the potential to become a much larger economy and to provide most of the gains from faster urbanization; it will be home to a much larger population, who will need well-planned neighborhoods, affordable housing, services, physical mobility, and digital connectivity.

A Vision for Rwanda's Urbanization

Faster urbanization and greater agglomeration hold the potential to accelerate economic growth and structural transformation in Rwanda. The movement of workers off farm into urban areas and the spatial concentration of economic activity are central to Rwanda's long-term growth.

The *World Development Report 2009: Reshaping Economic Geography* provides a framework for realizing the potential gains from urbanization (World Bank 2009). Building on research in industrial organization, economic growth, international trade, and economic geography, the framework explicitly incorporates the effects of scale economies in production. The main insight is that rising economic density—concentration of people, investment, and economic activity—is critical for faster economic development. Economic density is supported by shortening economic distance through lower transport and trade costs and increasing incentives to enhance scale and specialization.

Economic density is a major driver of productivity. Large plants that operate in dense environments generate increasing returns to scale. They arise because of fixed costs of production (internal to a firm) and proximity to workers, customers, and people with new ideas (external to a firm and even an industry). However, places do not have to be huge to generate some of these gains. The size of settlements matters less than their function: with reasonable transport costs, towns can be large enough to facilitate internal scale economies. Medium-size cities are often large enough for "localization" economies that come from thick input markets. Nevertheless, "urbanization" economies—especially those involving knowledge spillovers—are generated mainly by large cities. The implication is that policy makers should focus on the functions of different types of cities and support agglomeration though economic density.

The nature of agglomeration economies differs by the function of different settlements. Rwanda's small towns, secondary cities, and Kigali should be performing complementary functions, each differentiated by the type of scale and agglomeration economy they can deliver. It would be counterproductive to slow the growth of Kigali and disperse people and businesses to secondary cities. Businesses locate in Kigali because of the range of diverse financial and related services not available elsewhere in the country (urbanization economies). Indeed, several firms are located in Kigali to enjoy improved trade facilitation and business services and to benefit from strong transport links from Kigali to all of Rwanda's borders. Substitutes for Kigali are not going to be found in Rwanda's secondary cities or smaller towns. Many countries have tried to slow the growth of their large cities to balance development outcomes spatially, but they have had limited success. For example, policy makers in the Arab Republic of Egypt have encouraged the development of secondary cities in order to reduce population pressure in Cairo, which accounts for 50 percent of Egypt's GDP but just 0.5 percent of its land. These towns, meant for 5 million people, have drawn barely 800,000.

From a long-term perspective, policy makers in Rwanda need to take a bullish view toward unleashing the potential of Kigali to nurture agglomeration economies through scale and specialization, intertwining Rwanda's growth engine with the regional and global economy. A differentiated approach is required for each type of settlement, informed by its function, opportunities, and challenges. Market forces—reflected by the location decisions of people and businesses—have chosen Kigali. Durable investments in infrastructure, housing, and other amenities will be needed to ensure that the city is productive and livable. The prospects for growth of different locations are difficult to predict, because they depend on the future of agriculture, peace, and conflict in neighboring countries, the development of mineral deposits, major infrastructure investments, and many other factors. Thus, potential investments in other settlements should be divided into those that can be made at low risk before market demand has emerged versus those that are better suited after it has emerged. Here, choices will need to be made between investments in place-specific durable assets (such as infrastructure, industrial complexes, and housing) and people-focused portable assets (such as health, education, and water and sanitation). Portable assets are important both for improving the welfare of people in situ and for facilitating long-term mobility. Further, broad institutional and governance reforms such as clarification of land and property rights set the foundations for urbanization and urban development.

Reducing the distance between people and economic density can amplify agglomeration economies. While conventional economic analysis implies that people should move to where their skills are scarce, in reality human capital tends to move to where it is abundant: educated migrants seek places where many others have similar skills. Among the 100 largest metropolitan areas in the United States, the 25 cities with the highest share of college graduates in 1990 had, by 2000, attracted graduates at twice the rate of the other 75. The reason is that skilled workers gain from proximity to others. The implication is that policies should not fight the market forces that pull skilled people together; migration is the most effective way to reduce distance and thus to promote economic density.

Investments in mass education across Rwanda can encourage faster rural-to-urban migration and support opportunities for more advanced specialization and knowledge spillovers. Education encourages rural-urban migration: only 1.5 percent of rural residents who did not complete primary school migrated to urban areas, compared with 2.8 percent who completed primary, 7.6 percent who completed secondary, and 16.2 percent who had some higher education (World Bank 2017a). Poor learning outcomes in Rwanda today have implications for the sequencing of urban-led growth; urban areas may gain the most dynamism after only 10–15 years, once higher investments in education today filter through to the labor market. Returns to education are high in urban areas in Rwanda. Incomes are five times higher in Kigali than in rural areas, and 57 percent of this difference is explained by differences in the *returns* to education (33 percent is due to higher *levels* of education).

Finally, overcoming frictions from high transport costs can help to amplify scale economies in Kigali, as well as to provide the potential for other cities to develop their vocations. Falling transport costs tend to increase trade more with neighboring, not distant, regions or countries; trade has become more localized than globalized. Places trade more with regions or countries that are similar, because falling transport costs increase specialization. Thus, the basis of trade increasingly becomes the exploitation of economies of scale rather than the differences in natural endowments. The implication is that falling transport costs change the composition of trade and make it even more sensitive to such costs. Policies to reduce trade and transport costs should be a big part of growth strategies for low- and middle-income economies.

Greater agglomeration supported by faster migration and specialization are the fundamental drivers linking urbanization with faster economic development and structural change. Policies and investment should help firms and workers to benefit from these transformative forces. Institutions and regulations should strengthen land markets and business development, support the spatial mobility of workers and capital (factor markets), and integrate product markets. Infrastructure—for example, transport and information and communication technology—is critical to connect regional product markets and urban labor markets. Finally, spatially targeted interventions may be needed to support the development of untapped resources. But these interventions need to be implemented with great care, because they often do not solve underlying market or coordination failures and sometimes are implemented at the expense of national economic growth.

The next section assesses key constraints, followed by a section outlining priorities for policy and investment.

Constraints to Successful Urbanization in Rwanda

Low Density of Urban Settlement

Development in Rwandan cities is spatially fragmented. Neighborhoods within Kigali are poorly connected with one another: development is common in many, separate parts of the city rather than concentrated in the center and along transport corridors. This translates into scattered peak densities beyond the central business district instead of clustered densities that could enhance scale economies (map 3.2). Kigali scores very low on the Puga Index, a measure of the degree of connectedness of people in a city (Lall, Henderson, and Venables 2017) compared with cities of similar size (figure 3.4). Fewer central areas experienced large population increases from 2002 to 2012 (for example, net migration over this period was equal to 21 percent of the 2012 population in Gasabo), while some more central areas retained similar, or even smaller, populations (net migration was only 3 percent of the 2012 population in Nyarugenge). From 2000 to 2012, more than 40 percent of Kigali's land development was in small patches disconnected from the preexisting urban fabric. Moreover, Kigali's built area expanded greatly from 1990 to 2010, consistent with increasing fragmentation (map 3.3). Rapid physical expansion also has been observed around secondary cities, particularly Musanze, where the urban footprint increased by 6 percent a year from 1999 to 2015, although less so in Huye (map 3.4).

Spatial fragmentation reduces the benefits of urbanization for productivity. The large distances between firms and workers

FIGURE 3.4 Puga Index of connectedness in Kigali and select comparators

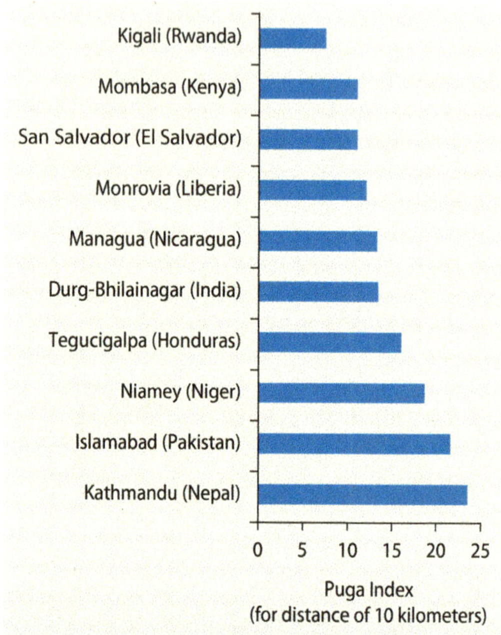

Source: Lall, Henderson, and Venables 2017.
Note: The Puga Index considers the share of city residents accessible within 5 or 10 kilometers of each location in the city. Source locations are weighted according to their share of the urban population.

reduce workers' access to jobs by raising commuting costs, thus limiting firm size; prevent job market pooling and matching; and hinder the transfer of skills and knowledge. A 1 percentage point increase in connectedness as measured by the Puga Index is associated with urban costs that are 12 percentage points lower, controlling for income levels and city population size. To a considerable extent, high urban costs are driven by poor land management practices, as efficient land use requires efficient city and neighborhood grids and appropriate zoning regulations that encourage density, affordability, and formality (Wainer, Ndengeyingoma, and Murray 2016). Such high costs play an important role in reducing the international competitiveness of labor in African cities[5] by putting pressure on firms to pay higher wages; although wages, in absolute terms, are typically lower in Sub-Saharan Africa than in competing destinations, they are higher than expected *considering income and skill levels* (for example, Gelb et al. 2017).

Fragmented urban land development may encourage informality, because the most accessible urban jobs are those pursued at and around the home. For example, in Kigali, the home is the usual headquarters for the 72 percent of firms that are run by a single individual (table 3.1). To be sure, formal jobs are concentrated in central Kigali, just as they are in most cities; other examples include Kampala (Uganda) and Lusaka (Zambia) (map 3.5). But 97 percent of all firms in Kigali are informal. Of those informal sector firms, 90 percent engage in nontradable activities dominated by retail, personal services (such as domestic work) and local construction labor. Such nontradable activities are not concentrated in the center; rather, they are scattered throughout Kigali's urban expanse.

Fragmented development is driven partly by building requirements tied to the use of master plans. This is due to inadequate local urban planning capacity.

MAP 3.2 Fragmentation of densities beyond the central business district of Kigali

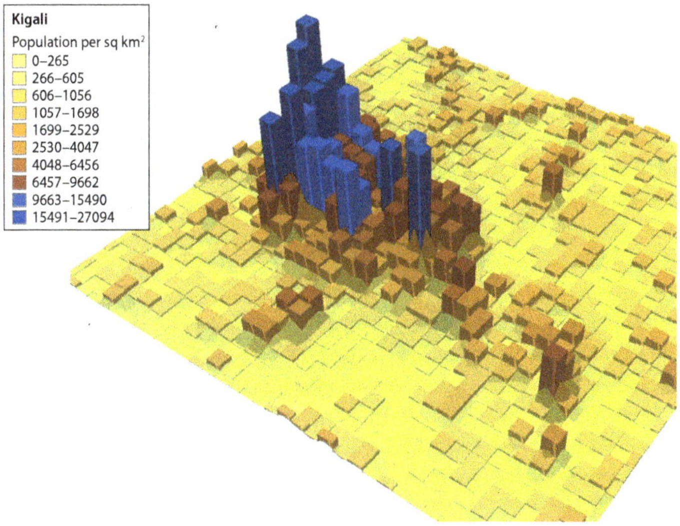

Source: Henderson and Nigmatulina 2016.
Note: The figure represents (through tower heights) the population density across Kigali Province. High densities are found in the central business district, but also are scattered across the city.

With the rising complexity of the urban environment, institutional adaptation is now required to build flexibility into planning. In dynamic, fast-changing cities, the economic vocations of places are transformed regularly as the economy grows in sophistication, and land markets facilitate the transformation of structures on land to meet the economic needs and opportunities of the time. The use and form of structures undergo successive cycles of change and renewal, as structures depreciate and productive opportunities evolve. In other countries, master plans communicate the development vision for locations, coordinate investments, and raise confidence in the future environment, but they also are "living" documents that are updated regularly in response to market signals and citizen feedback and typically are not legally binding.

Regulatory inconsistencies across neighboring jurisdictions and within cities also have contributed to fragmented development. Within the boundaries of master plans, zoning regulations are often far

MAP 3.3 Built land in Kigali, 1990, 2000, and 2010

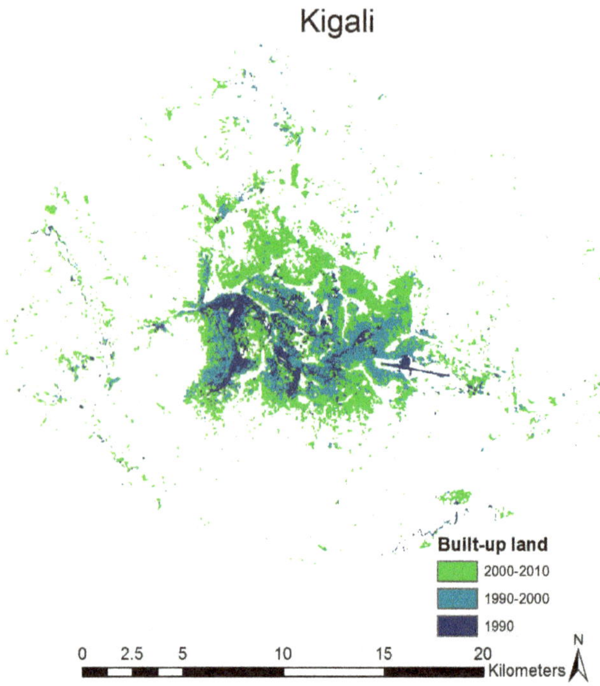

Source: Jones, Murray, and Ferreira 2016.
Note: Data generalized from Landsat images showing built cover in 1990 and newly built-up land in subsequent decades.

less demanding, inspections are less thorough, and master plan implementation is scheduled for later stages the closer to the periphery. Combined with "futuristic" central regulations, this discrepancy creates perverse incentives to build in the peripheries, in exactly the scattered and inefficient way that planners wish to avoid. New construction in Kigali from 2009 to 2015 was strongly concentrated in peripheral areas; even building improvements were more common in the suburbs than in the center (map 3.6). Likewise, areas just outside Kigali's border have less stringent requirements and have seen considerable development. These areas include Kamonyi District, parts of which are just 7.5 kilometers from Kigali's central business district and whose population increased 28 percent annually from 2002 to 2012.

Poor transport infrastructure exacerbates the impact of spatial fragmentation. In Kigali, the connectedness of the local population by public transport is already strained: public transit routes to the center

MAP 3.4 Building footprint in central areas of three secondary cities in Rwanda

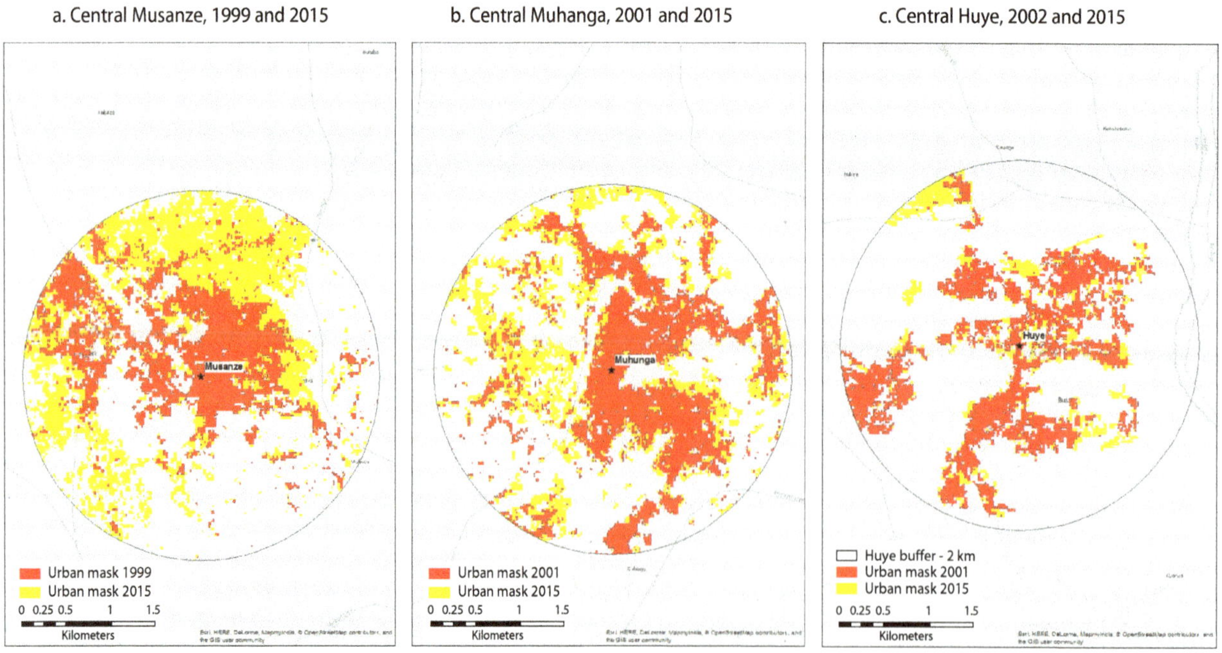

Total expansion 1999–2015: 120%; Average yearly expansion: 6%

Total expansion 2001–15: 81%; Average yearly expansion: 4.4%

Total expansion 2002–16: 34%; Average yearly expansion: 2.2%

Source: World Bank 2017e.
Note: The maps show the footprint of buildings for three secondary cities in 2001 or starting year (red) and 2015 or ending year (yellow).

TABLE 3.1 Share of firms in Kampala, Uganda; Lusaka, Zambia; and Kigali, Rwanda, by size, 2011
% of firms

Size of firm	Kigali	Lusaka	Kampala
Self-employed	72.23	50.65	55.5
Micro (2–4)	22.49	28.36	36.03
Small (5–49)	5.05	18.74	6.25
Medium (50–99)	0.14	1.15	0.13
Large (100+)	0.08	1.09	0.09
Total number of firms	123,364	17,117	184,335

Sources: Jones, Bird, et al. 2016; Jones, del Frari, et al. 2016; Jones, Murray, and Ferreira 2016. Data from Rwanda, Uganda, and Zambia economic censuses (2011).

MAP 3.5 Location of formal jobs in Kampala, Uganda; Lusaka, Zambia; and Kigali, Rwanda

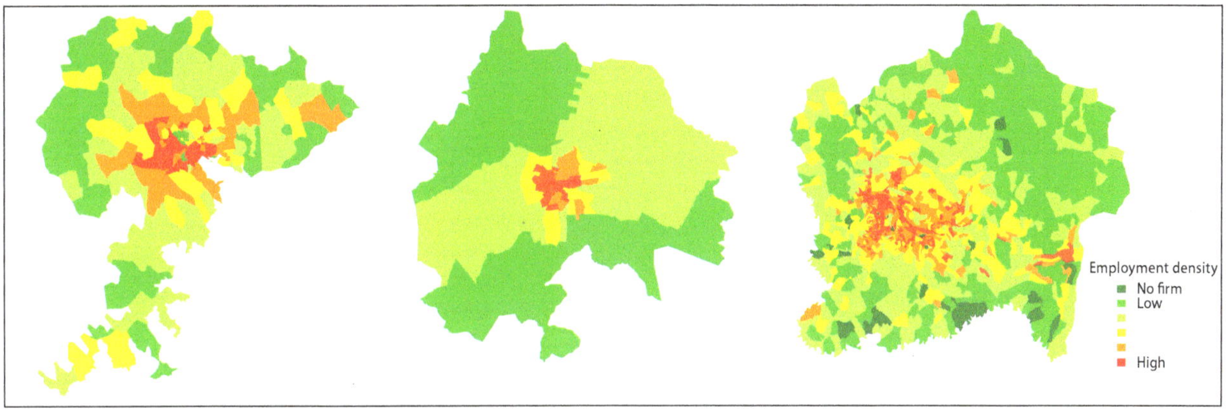

Sources: Jones, Bird, et al. 2016; Jones, del Frari, et al. 2016; Jones, Murray, and Ferreira 2016.

MAP 3.6 Changes in building stock in Kigali, by cell, 2009–15

a. Greenfield construction in peripheral northeast

b. Rebuilt or upgraded buildings in suburbs

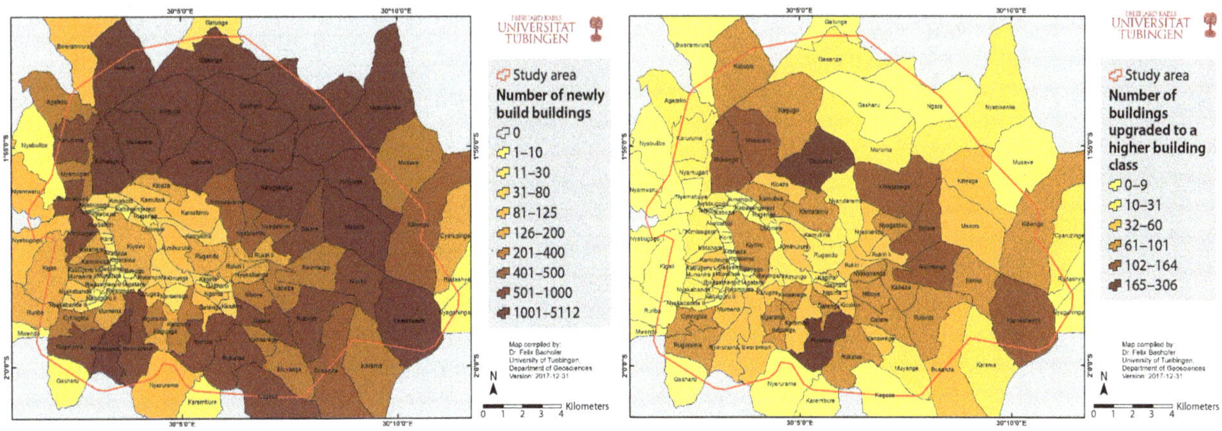

Source: Bachofer and Murray 2018. Analysis conducted through remote sensing of aerial and satellite images, plus manual correction.
Note: These maps show the frequency of key changes in the building stock (new greenfield buildings, panel a, and building upgrades, panel b) by cell in Kigali. In a period of rapid population growth, there has been very little transformation in central Kigali. Construction on previously unbuilt land was strongly concentrated in peripheral areas (cells shaded dark brown, in panel a, saw between 1,000 and 5,000 new buildings on greenfield sites from 2009 to 2015). Even building improvements were more common in suburbs (panel b).

are congested, and significant central areas are unplanned or underdeveloped settlements with few vehicular access routes. Further, models show that transport will become extremely restricted with rising congestion, deeply fragmenting urban labor markets. As in many African cities, Kigali allocates little land to roads. In a sample of 30 cities around the world, 8 African cities rank in the bottom 12 spots for road density, including Kigali (ranked 19), Addis Ababa (24), and Nairobi (27). African cities devote less than 16 percent of their land to roads, compared with more than 20 percent in most cities in high-income countries. The lack of roads, coupled with low affordability of motorized public transport, means that locations across the city are difficult to reach. Low affordability of transport increases the number of people who must walk, while the lack of roads increases congestion and pollution. Quiros, Murray, and Bajpai (2014) found that, when bus speeds drop 50 percent because of congestion (for example, at peak hours), residents in Kigali's periphery (shaded red in map 3.7) lose access to 50–66 percent of jobs in the city (where access is defined as a job that can be reached within an hour by bus and walking).

MAP 3.7 Simulated change in access to employment in Kigali with a 50 percent drop in bus journey speed

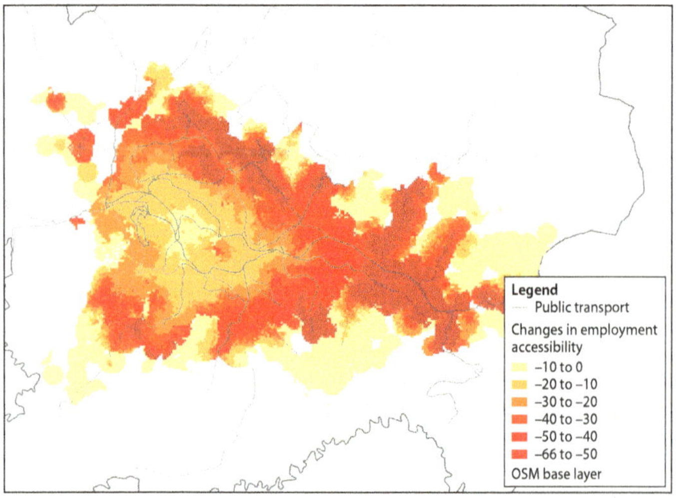

Source: Quiros, Murray, and Bajpai 2014.

Slow Pace of Rural-Urban Migration

Limited rural-to-urban migration constrains urbanization and the resulting benefits from agglomeration. Rural-urban migration has been a key component of urbanization in many countries, especially in East Asia. For example, rural-urban migration accounted for 41 percent of urban residents in China during the 1990s (Cai, Park, and Zhao 2008). By contrast, only 14 percent of Rwanda's urban population were recent migrants from rural areas in 2014.[6] Of all internal migration between 2011 and 2014, only 20 percent went from rural to urban areas (figure 3.5); rural-rural migration was the dominant form of internal population movement.[7] Population movements included both moves toward density, with Kigali attracting 29 percent of recent migrants (including migrants from other urban areas), and parallel moves away from density, with Eastern Province (the least densely populated province in Rwanda) attracting 33 percent of recent migrants. Investing more in education in rural areas could play an important role in increasing rural-urban migration.

Even if growth is spatially unbalanced, growth in Kigali can be expected to improve household incomes throughout the country, through migration, remittances, and demand for rural products, not to mention tax revenue for broad-based public service provision. Data from the Integrated Living Conditions Survey 2013–14 (EICV4) show that Kigali's households send more than twice the value of remittances to rural areas as all other Rwandan towns combined (NISR 2015) (figure 3.6).[8]

Rwanda has pursued a policy of grouped villages (*imidugudu*) (map 3.8), with the goal being to improve access to health and education services as well as broader infrastructure and to preserve agricultural land. The policy also lays a fundamental foundation that reduces land fragmentation, improves land use efficiency, and encourages creation of agglomeration economies that stimulate rural productivity and consequently rural transformation. The investments made have had a positive impact on land consolidation

FIGURE 3.5 Share and scale of rural-urban migration in Rwanda, 2014

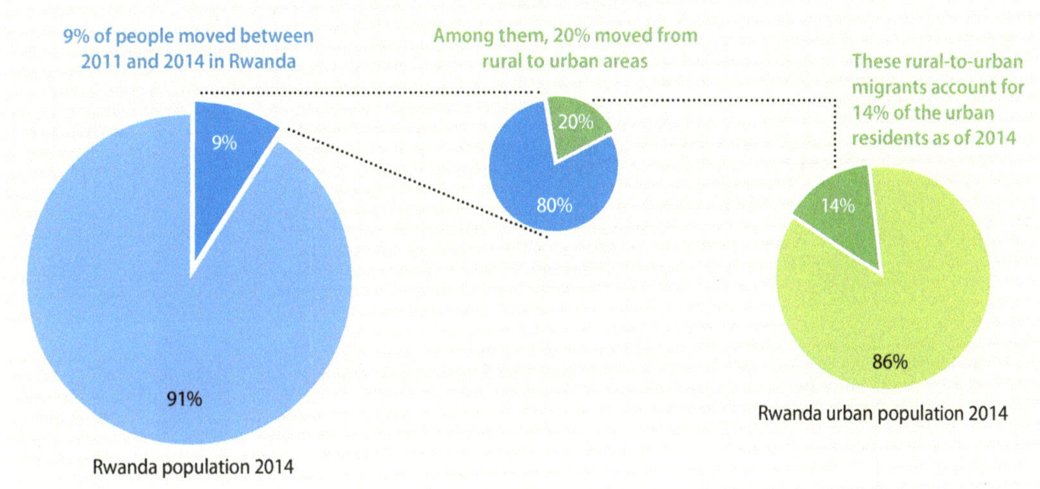

Source: Calculation based on NISR 2015.

FIGURE 3.6 Remittances from Kigali (and other locations) to rural areas of Rwanda, by province

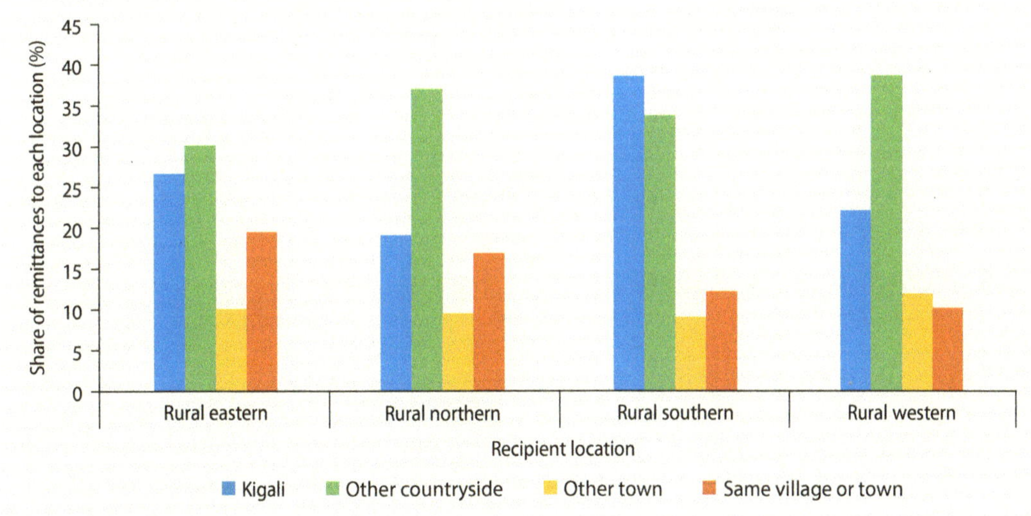

Source: Integrated Living Conditions Survey (EICV4) data (NISR 2015).

and productivity. They have also had an immediate impact on quality of life (decent housing and access to infrastructure and service, among others).

However, there is a need for a clear rural settlement planning and development strategy linked to the national development agenda. This requires large public investments in many highly scattered rural settlements. The government needs to ensure that this investment does not become redundant in the future under a higher-growth strategy characterized by rapid growth in urban areas and driven by investments in higher-demand locations, improvements in rural-urban connectivity, and more rapid rural-urban migration.

MAP 3.8 Location of planned *imidugudu* (grouped villages) in 12 districts of Rwanda, 2016–17

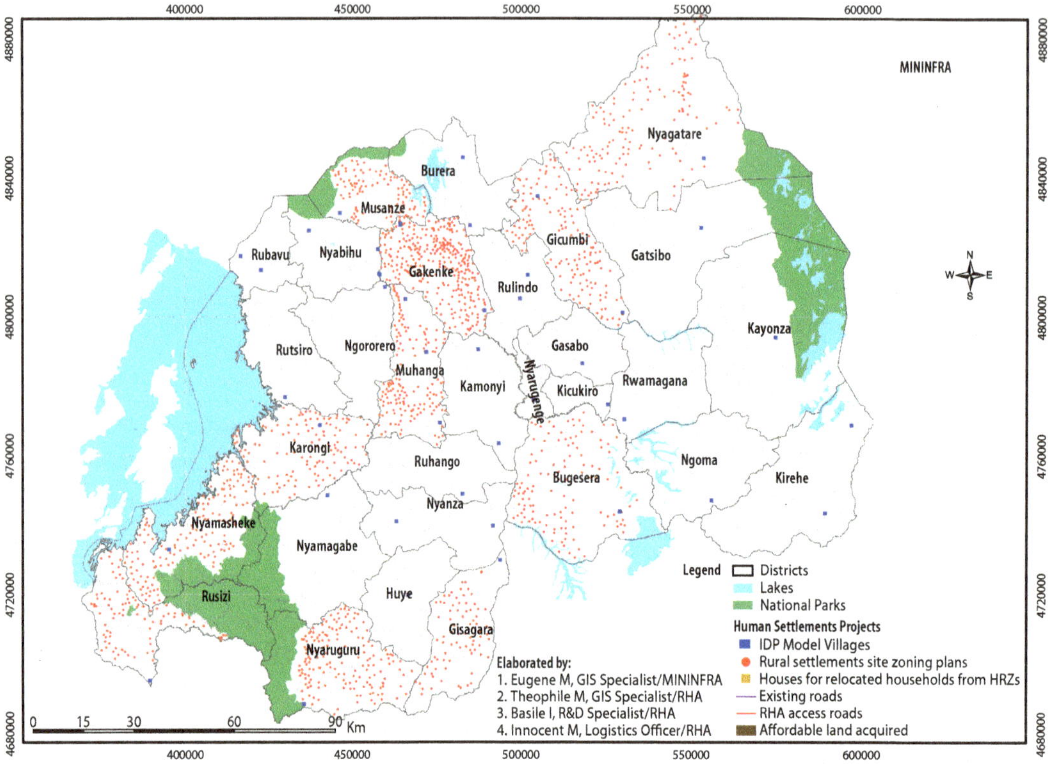

Source: MININFRA 2017.

Note: The map, made available by the Ministry of Infrastructure, shows in red the location of planned *imidugudu* in the 12 districts planned so far. Developing so many *imidugudu* (one is required by law for every 5 kilometers of the countryside) may be extremely costly and consume considerable agricultural land (because of large plot size and high servicing requirements). *Imidugudu* are not located on economically strategic locations, for example, along roads or around secondary cities. HRZ = high-risk zones; IDP = Integrated Development Programme; RHA = Rwanda Housing Authority.

Planning for *imidugudu* should be strategic and reliant on well-studied spatial aspects that will trigger effective rural productivity, while minimizing huge infrastructure investment costs and potential financial losses. As such, settlements could be located in places with higher connectivity to urban areas, which would improve rural residents' access to services, product markets, and employment in small towns, secondary cities, and Kigali and, in turn, raise demand for clustered settlements.

High Transport Costs and Limited Market Access

The poor quality of rural roads impairs the integration of Rwanda's cities with the countryside and with neighboring countries. Half of the rural population lacks access to a road network in good condition within a walking distance of 2 kilometers (World Bank 2017d). The impact of poor-quality rural roads is evident in the wide variation in food prices within and across districts, implying poorly integrated national food markets (for example, map 3.9). The lack of rural-urban links limits the opportunities for rural workers (including off-farm rural workers) to raise their efficiency, specialization, and ultimately productivity, which can slow rural poverty reduction and constrain the supply of inputs to urban areas. Poor quality is due to very low spending on infrastructure repair and maintenance by districts containing secondary cities. The level of spending is an order of magnitude lower

MAP 3.9 Variation in tomato prices in western Rwanda

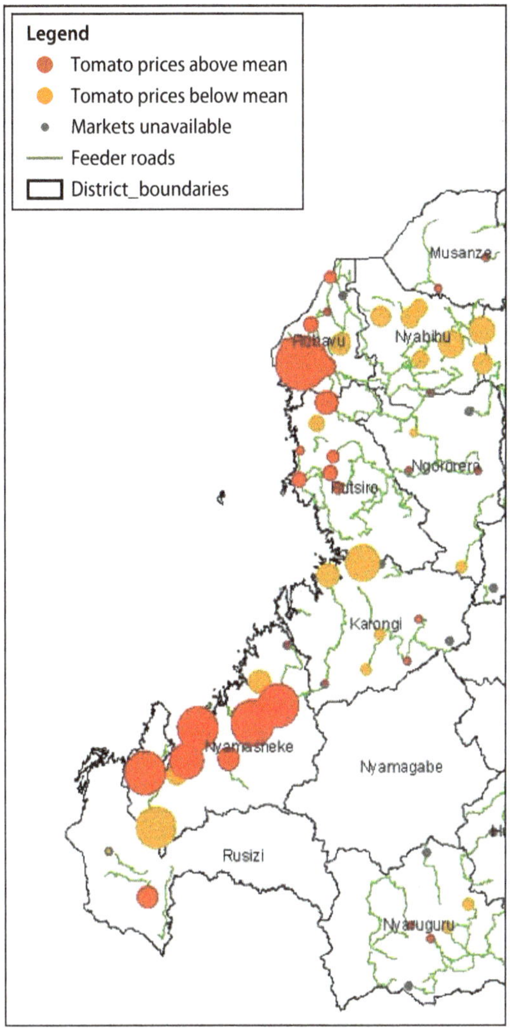

Source: World Bank 2017d.

than it should be, based on international comparisons relevant to Rwanda (World Bank 2015).

A particular missed opportunity lies in the fact that a third of Rwanda's poor live within 20 kilometers of a secondary city, yet the productivity and welfare advantages of these cities are undetectable more than 5 kilometers from their centers (World Bank 2017b). Strengthening rural-urban links around secondary cities could both improve their access to inputs and raise the cities' impact on the surrounding environment.

Connectivity between urban areas is also important for integrating the national economy. Korea used incremental investments to improve connectivity between cities, increasing specialization, reaping economies of scale, and helping major cities to lift the entire population (map 3.10). In Rwanda, a clear trend of urbanization along major transport routes (urban corridors) is also emerging (World Bank 2017c). By strengthening such urban-urban links (for example, through improved conditions for night transport, more efficient routes, and the effective location of industrial parks), Rwanda can leverage its compact geography to deliver an integrated portfolio of urban places. Such connectivity encourages the efficiency-driving specialization of productive activities between locations. However, it does not guarantee the greater development of secondary cities and other towns versus Kigali. Connectivity and specialization could also entail *greater* concentration of activities in Kigali.

Priorities for Faster Urbanization, Greater Agglomeration

Getting on the path to faster urbanization and greater agglomeration will involve determining *where* to prioritize urban development, *what* policies and investments would yield high dividends, and *who* needs to be in charge of implementing solutions. Although the optimal choices on the *where, what,* and *who* of urban development differ across countries, international experience during episodes of high growth and assessment of Rwanda's urbanization highlight the following priorities:

- *Where.* A bullish view is needed to unleash the potential of Kigali, which market forces—reflected in the choices made by people and businesses—have chosen as the main center of production and commerce.

MAP 3.10 Expressways in the Republic of Korea, 1970–2010

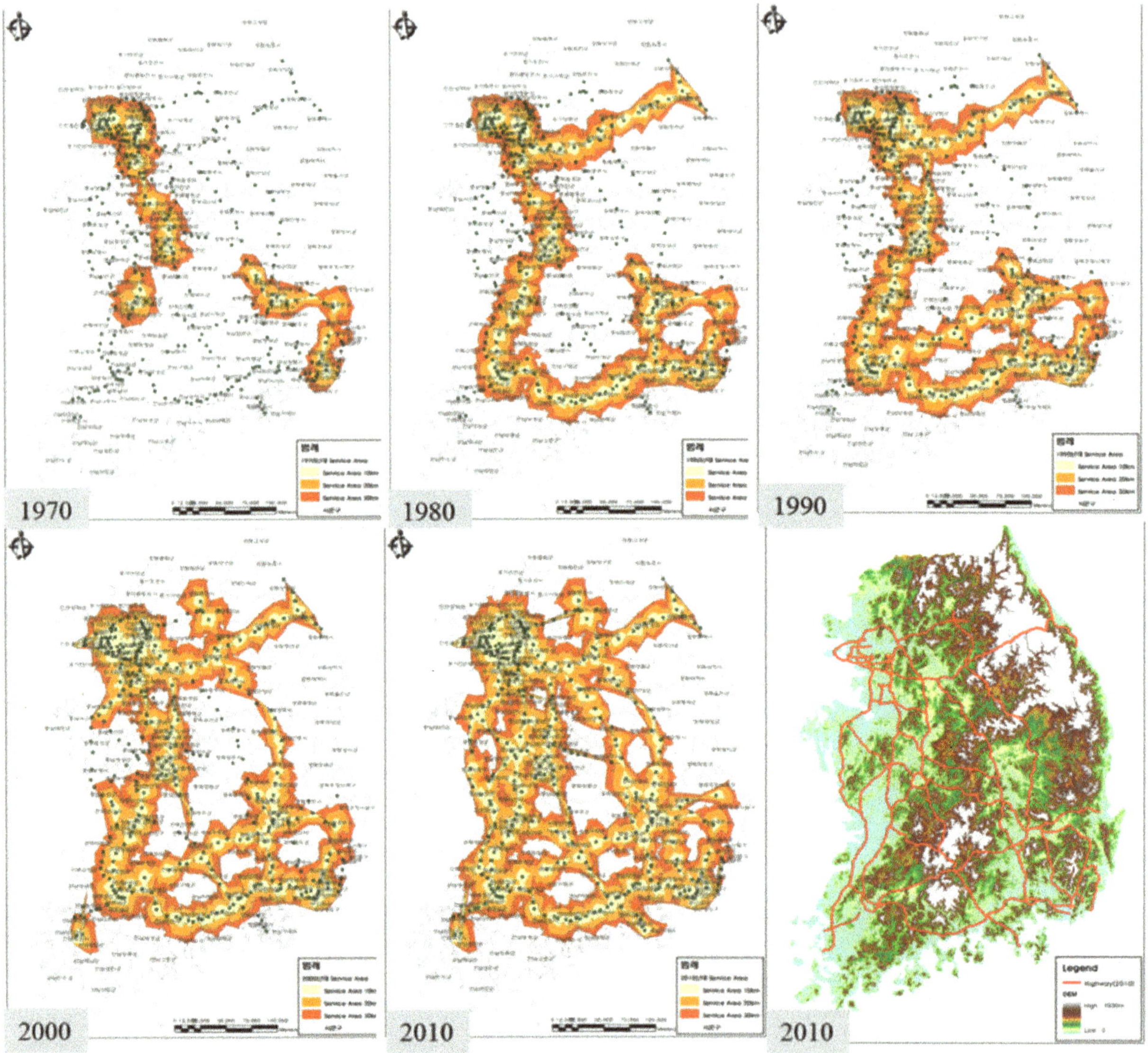

Source: Wang 2011.
Note: The colors represent locations within 10, 20, and 30 minutes of an expressway station for the given year.

For rapid national growth, policies and investment need to follow market signals, accelerate Kigali's development, and intertwine its economy with that of Africa and the world. Kigali is Rwanda's main interface with regional and global economies and needs to be allowed to respond to market demand and fulfill its significant economic potential. These policies would be accompanied by a more calibrated approach toward a complementary (and well-networked) set of secondary cities and small towns.

- *What.* Investment in infrastructure, housing, and commercial structures is needed to manage urbanization; but bedrock reforms that strengthen land markets and urban planning should be in place first to enhance the efficiency of investment and generate high economic returns.

- *Who*. Stronger intergovernmental coordination of economic and spatial planning processes is needed to overcome coordination challenges in urban development.

Supporting Agglomeration Economies in Kigali and Other Cities

Master Planning for Density

Efforts to increase density require a detailed, flexible approach. There is no "optimal" density, but defragmenting the urban fabric allows for density to change in response to the needs of businesses and people. Cities need Goldilocks density—not too high or low, but just right (Guardian 2014). And what is "just right" changes over time and varies by neighborhood.

Density should not overwhelm infrastructure; nor should regulators keep density below what the infrastructure can support. Planners in New York, Seoul, and Singapore have taken the "just right" approach to heart by developing a *fine-grain* pattern of small density zones (map 3.11), guided by infrastructural (particularly transit) capacity. Areas of these cities that are economically dynamic, such as central business districts, can be served efficiently by transit systems to accommodate large daytime populations; these cities and districts are therefore allowed the highest densities. Outlying areas adjacent to transit stations or where highways intersect also have higher density allowances to increase uptake of the transit system and limit the use of cars. Such regulations are intended to ensure that the urban form does not become costly and inefficient to service, rather than to *force* density in locations where market demand does not yet exist.

Such density regulations are developed iteratively, to work with rather than against market demand, nudging rather than overhauling investors' plans. Regulations that fight against market demand, by contrast, inevitably result in informality and sprawl in less regulated areas and underinvestment in high-potential locations. Likewise, an excessively detailed and rigid quantitative regulation of land use (such as zoning for detailed building characteristics and functions) makes inevitable the misallocation of capital, reduces the adaptive capacity of the city, and considerably dampens returns to private investment.

Private investments in urban structures in Rwanda's urban areas in 2017 need not, and should not, be regulated to deliver the spatial form for the 2040 economy. Moving closer to the allocation of structures according to

MAP 3.11 Goldilocks density: Getting density "just right" through fine-grain differentiation and adaptation over time

a. Singapore: FAR values in downtown area

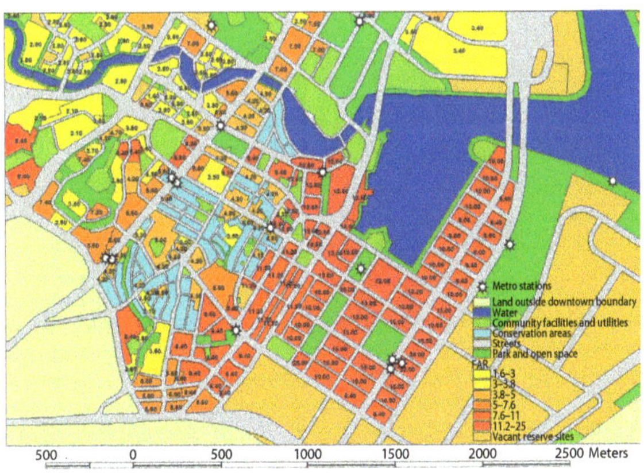

b. Seoul: Variations in FSI are linked to the location of metro stations and to the network of main streets

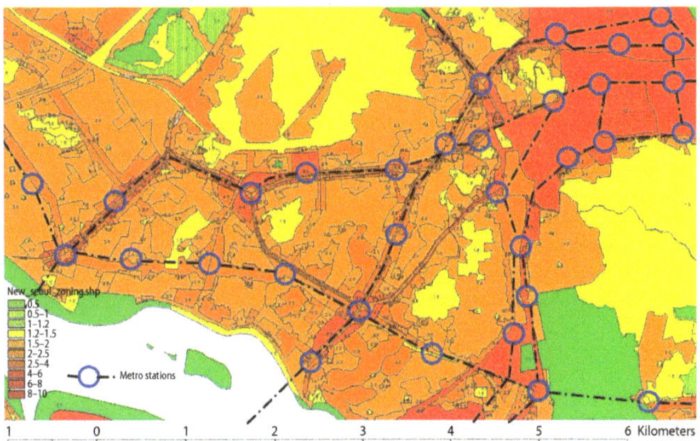

Source: Vishwanath et al. 2013.
Note: FAR = floor area ratio; FSI = floor space index.

market demand (prices) is recommended rather than relying on centrally planned zoning (quantity). Land *prices* reflect the demand for and scarcity of locations; they can efficiently allocate private investments across space and allow structures to serve the evolving economy, delivering the "Goldilocks density" for each neighborhood.

To achieve this vision, investors should be guided to invest in structures with no specific building heights, floor area ratios, and so on that match neither the existing nor the potential market demand. Regulations should focus on mitigating *negative externalities* like environmental degradation, ensuring structural safety, and reserving space for the existing or planned *infrastructure grid*. With a price-based allocation of structures, scattered and sprawling land development can result if no area offers particularly higher amenities or more accessibility. Such development is avoided by *privileging* certain areas for higher density through the strong public provision of transport corridors and public spaces.

Key institutional requirements for the price-based allocation of land include the strong protection of property rights, transparent valuations processes, and oversight.

Within the existing master plan framework, planning standards could be amended to encourage density and affordability by reducing minimum plot sizes and raising maximum ground cover ratios in strategic locations. To achieve high densities in lower-cost structures—such as terraced housing with back yards as opposed to high rises—small plots with high ground cover are necessary. Yet several master plan zones in Kigali promote large minimum plot sizes or a low maximum ground cover, even in central areas.[9] Revising the minimum plot sizes downward and revising the maximum ground cover requirements upward, combined with more regular adjustments of requirements in response to market demand, would go a long way to encouraging densification, affordability, and formality.

Deregulation would not promote informality and poor standards of housing and structures, as some fear; international evidence shows that, with strong *property rights* and *infrastructure provision*, deregulation tends to promote more formalization (see, for example, box 3.3). Stringent regulations raise costs above affordability, leading people to live in informal dwellings. Legalizing structures brings them into the formal market where investments are secure, incentivizing owners to upgrade dwellings over time, while also, typically, mandating government service provision. Together, these are powerful mechanisms to raise living conditions, encourage formality, and mobilize investment.

BOX 3.3 Avoiding slums through property rights and infrastructure

Hanoi, Vietnam. Despite rapid and low-income development, Hanoi has, uniquely, largely avoided the development of large slums. Faced with rapid urban expansion and mass illegal building, its city authorities legalized all past unpermitted construction that met building standards. This effort incentivized owners of previously illegal houses to invest in their buildings and, in turn, committed the government to providing roads, sanitation, and basic services, ensuring an adequate standard of housing.

Bogotá, Colombia. City leaders in Bogotá similarly succeeded by coordinating regulatory reform with infrastructure development. The Programa de Mejoramiento Integral de Barrios targeted 26 of the poorest city areas, called the *unidades*. The *unidades* included 1,440 informal settlements, 300,000 untitled plots, and about 500,000 structurally substandard dwellings. The program legalized homes and neighborhoods and expanded infrastructure (roads, rainwater traps, and sanitary and aqueduct networks) and urban facilities (stairs, parks, and community rooms). Living conditions improved for about 650,000 people (World Bank 2012).

Servicing Land for Density

The market-based allocation of investments across space will not provide the *public space* and *infrastructure* essential to raise the productivity of land. Investments like roads, sanitation, and laying out urban grids require huge coordination and deliver returns over long horizons, so they must be provided by the state. Two priorities are (1) providing dense and good-quality *central infrastructure* to crowd in capital and (2) reserving space for roads in a wide peripheral *urban expansion area* through grid planning.

Kigali could increase the density of central building and investment by providing quality infrastructure services for central areas. Demand for a location is typically related to its level of amenities, accessibility, and security of investing there (particularly low risk of future expropriation). Broad-use infrastructure—particularly, roads and road *grids*—serve these three functions.

While developing central servicing, *grids* should be provided for the wider urban expansion area to ensure that rapid peripheral development takes place in a planned way, reducing future expropriation and adjustment costs and raising the security of new investments. Such investments in the grid would be beneficial not just for Kigali but also for the wide urban expansion areas around secondary and emerging cities, which, as noted, have expanded rapidly and with fragmented and largely unplanned land use. They may require some readjustment of plots, in conjunction with improved infrastructure services, in areas where development has been haphazard. It is critical for Kigali to "get ahead" of its rapid expansion with a more intensive program to protect the grid and regularize plots in fast-developing neighborhoods. A useful example of this process is New York City, where the 1811 grid plan envisioned an infrastructure network for a city 10 times its size at the time. Infrastructure was not laid directly, but the city worked with communities to readjust plots to fit the new plan around dirt roads and stone way-markers. Expansion of the city's buildings responded to market forces and was orderly, with minimal expropriation costs and high formality (box 3.4). Similar practices have been tried in Rwanda, with promising results, but at a fairly low scale (box 3.5).

Enhancing Urban Mobility

Investment in public transport would help to reduce spatial fragmentation in Kigali. Weak public transport around the central

BOX 3.4 The New York grid: Transformation of structures and the economy around a planned grid

The 1811 Plan of Manhattan mapped roads for an area more than 10 times the area of the city at the time (map B3.4.1). This plan became the skeleton around which the city expanded, supporting connectivity, formality, and density and reducing future expropriation costs.

The grid was not imposed on a blank slate: in addition to challenging topography, many landowners lost large parts of their plots or had them totally reshaped to fit the new road grid. However, land values rose dramatically after road openings, creating high demand from landowners for their areas to be readjusted. Property taxes created strong incentives for implementation on the side of the city government: as the roads raised land values, property tax revenue in the city rose fivefold from 1830 to 1837. A large share of road openings was funded through direct benefit charges to adjacent landowners.

The economic vocation of each neighborhood has evolved dramatically since 1811, transforming its structures and their uses. Wall Street has progressed from mostly residential in the mid-1800s,

(Box continues next page)

BOX 3.4 (continued)

MAP B3.4.1 Plan of Manhattan, New York City, 1811

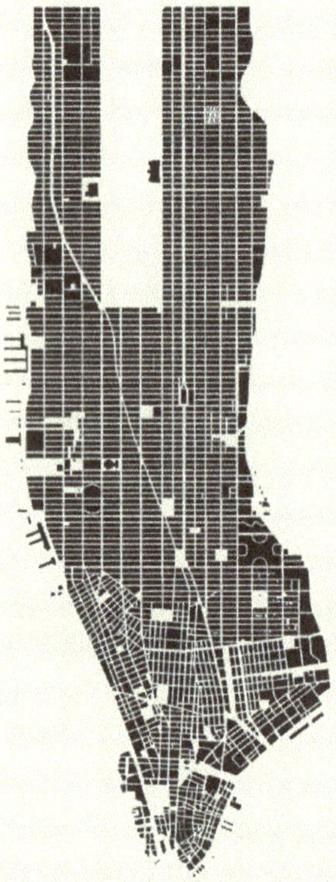

Source: New York City Planning Department.

to industrial (residents gradually moved uptown as the noise and congestion of industry rose), to financial by 1920. The Meatpacking District mixed residential and a range of heavy industries in the mid-1800s, coming to focus specifically on meat factories by 1900. The industry declined with changes in meat cooling and transport technologies, and the district evolved into at first a low-end and then a highly fashionable and gentrified entertainment district. Now it is also home to many of New York's tech companies.

Even the 1811 grid plan was adjusted over time, however. The now iconic Broadway, cutting diagonally across the city, was not in the original plan; neither were Central Park or the superblocks created for larger buildings like Grand Central Terminal. From 1916 to 1961, the city added zoning regulations, limiting the mass of building allowed on each lot. Realizing that these restrictions were holding back investment, productivity, and tax revenues, the revised 1961 Zoning Resolution switched to rewarding property owners with extra height allowances in return for reserving public land on the floor of their plot (such as plazas or mid-block passageways); this resolution allowed density and investment to climb again, while improving streetscapes and pedestrian connectivity.

BOX 3.5 Land readjustment for urban renewal

Land readjustment refers to a process whereby neighboring landowners collectively adjust their parcels to support servicing and regularization (figure B3.5.1). It has been used to manage urban expansion into rural peripheries, upgrade underserviced land in inner cities, or facilitate reconstruction after disasters and conflicts.

Residents typically transfer their land to a government agency or other body (a cooperative or corporation), which invests in the proposed upgrading (road widening, public facilities, parks, or regularization) and may reserve some land for sale to recover costs. On completion of the project, the agency returns to each owner a site of at least equal value in the vicinity of the original parcel. The size of parcels is typically reduced, but their value is typically higher due to formality and servicing, leaving landowners better off (photo B3.5.1).

Land readjustment has been piloted in several sites in Rwanda, including for central redevelopment (*agatare*) and managed expansion on the periphery (*gahanga*) (photo B3.5.2). In *gahanga*, district authorities estimated that most plots were worth FRW 500,000 before readjustment and afterward sold for FRW 3 million–FRW 6 million, with 20 percent of project costs financed by landowners themselves.

(Box continues next page)

BOX 3.5 (continued)

FIGURE B3.5.1 Land readjustment

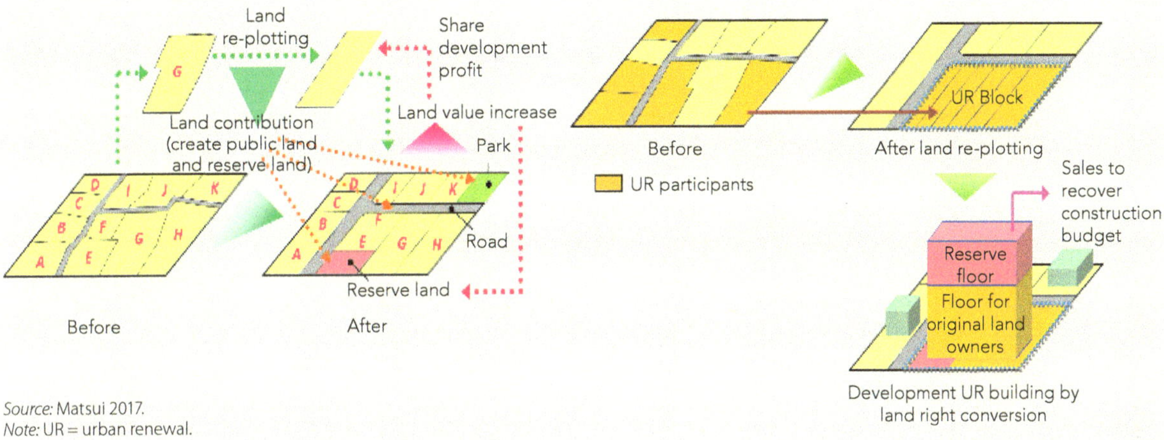

Source: Matsui 2017.
Note: UR = urban renewal.

PHOTO B3.5.1 Way-markers map plot boundaries

Credit: Sally Murray.

PHOTO B3.5.2 Land readjustment sites in Gahanga, Kigali

Credit: Sally Murray.

city reduces the returns to residing or locating firms in and visiting (for example, for job search) central areas. As with road infrastructure, a priority is to bring the quality of transport service up to a high level in central areas and in areas already densely populated to encourage and deliver the benefits of density. An *extensive* public transport network also encourages a degree of sprawl. Successful urbanization has often combined excellent *central* public transport with selected quality public transport to a small number of strategic *peripheral* locations such as satellite towns, as the city has grown.

Providing enough space for roads through the grid (discussed above) is important for avoiding congestion and upholding fluidity, but, if it is done alone, households quickly respond by buying more cars, further congesting roads. In Rwanda, rising incomes will increase the demand for cars. A priority is to reduce people's tendency to drive by privileging public transport.

The right public transport solutions for Kigali will evolve with urban *density* and *institutional capacity*. For example, at present densities, technologies like dedicated bus lanes and safe walkways and cycleways are appropriate. Improving institutional capacity will allow the introduction of more flexible, demand-responsive route and schedule planning. Bus rapid transit requires very high-density catchment areas around stops, and light rail even more so; hence, these approaches become appropriate at much later stages. With strong institutional capacity, more effective mass public transport management and charges to deter the use of cars can also be considered.[10]

Options for mobility will evolve dramatically by 2050. Rwanda needs to invest in mobility that connects today's residents with opportunities, while taking advantage of new technologies in the medium term. Important here is improved management of traffic and travel demand. Ubiquitous data flows will facilitate more effective use of existing transit capacity, through better matching of supply of and demand for mobility across time and space for all types of trips. New technologies provide ways to manage the overall transit network more efficiently in real time and provide on-demand services for mobility needs. Some novel mass transit concepts have emerged, such as on-demand buses developed by the University of Tokyo, which replace fixed-route bus lines by dynamically routing pickups and drop-offs based on user demand. Key urban mobility trends are summarized in box 3.6.

Mobilizing Scale and Specialization in the Informal Sector

In every country in the world, as urban *formal* sector jobs expanded, informality also rose. The *expectation* of securing formal sector jobs pulls far more rural migrants into cities than the formal sector can employ, and the surplus ends up in the informal sector. The informal sector is also a common destination for workers suffering temporary unemployment, which may enable them to hold out longer to find a more suitable job, improving the matching of firms with workers. Thus, more broadly, the informal sector provides an important safety net that facilitates the growth of urban populations and increases the fluidity of their labor markets.

The informal sector also offers important benefits for urban productivity. Low cost and flexible, small firms support the competitiveness of more productive sectors and workers by keeping urban input costs (food, housing, services, and so on) low. For some firms, remaining small and informal can be a rational strategy to uphold efficiency and flexibility; remaining small can occur in response to regulations, but it can also occur in response to rising urban density and changes in technology, which make operating at smaller scale less inefficient than was previously the case. Experiences from other countries show that, if properly harnessed, the informal sector can also breed powerful human capital development through "learning by doing" in the off-farm sector.

Scale and specialization, which are facilitated by dense urban environments, matter just as much in the nontradable, informal sector as in the formal economy. Enabling

BOX 3.6 How will urban mobility change by 2050?

Several emerging trends are expected to help cities to reduce pollution and congestion and to increase urban mobility over the next 35 years:

- *Last-mile solutions.* Electric-powered last-mile solutions will transport people from their home to mass transit stations and from stations to their final destination. They may involve self-stabilizing two-wheel scooters and transporters and public electric bike systems, which will be shared and available on demand. Mass use of these solutions will require barrier-free infrastructure and protection from vehicular traffic. In combination with mass transit, they will offer a green urban mobility option for most city dwellers. Cities will also encourage walking. Singapore is already building covered walkways from homes and offices to mass transit stations to encourage people to walk to stations.
- *Increased use of low-energy and active transportation options.* Cities are likely to reclaim part of the streetscape from cars, reallocating it to walking and biking. Bike sharing will continue to expand, improving both human and environmental health. Bike networks will likely be shared with electric bikes, with some separation to ensure safe travel.
- *Autonomous vehicles.* Autonomous vehicles are likely to be widespread by 2050. Following lobbying by Google, which produces a driverless car, the U.S. states of California, Florida, and Nevada allow such vehicles. The development of autonomous vehicles with car-to-car communication is expected to reduce traffic accidents and eliminate the need to build heavy cars, which will contribute to energy efficiency. Autonomous vehicles will also be able to follow one another closely, improving synchronization with traffic signals and reducing stop and start delays. Some experts claim that driverless technology may reduce traffic flow by as much as 40–50 percent, greatly reducing emissions. Driverless cars will also reduce the need for parking space in cities.
- *Cleaner technologies.* Cleaner technologies will increase fuel economy and greatly reduce emissions. Electric vehicles and new engine technologies will improve both driving and environmental performance. The cost of electric vehicle batteries is expected to decline by about 8 percent a year, making electric vehicles competitive with conventional cars within the next decade.
- *Vehicle sharing and vehicle pooling.* The combination of better data and autonomous vehicles will increase vehicle sharing and pooling. Vehicle sharing allows users to rent vehicles by the hour. It provides users with access to mobility whenever they need it without the burden and expense of car ownership. Car sharing has obvious benefits for cities. Zipcar estimates that every shared vehicle replaces up to 20 private automobiles, reducing both total vehicle miles and the land allocated to parking. Carmakers, including BMW, Daimler, and Ford, are developing their own programs. Data sharing will enable groups of people to pool autonomous vehicles, supporting mobility where density of population may not warrant mass transit systems. The line between the public and private provision of mobility services will become increasingly blurred as capacity in private vehicles is used more effectively.

Source: Lall 2017.

small businesses to develop clusters of economic activity creates the density of demand necessary to facilitate productivity gains through specialization in nontraded goods and services, while scale helps to keep costs down. By specializing and keeping costs low, informal and small-scale businesses can have better options to connect with citywide and broader value chains.

Given that most businesses in Kigali are in the informal and nontraded sector, enhancing productivity in this sector should be a high priority. Cities that successfully harnessed the power of the informal sector to mobilize savings, provide jobs, and raise human capital addressed factors that kept firms and households in informality unnecessarily; they did so through deregulation, technical support, and provision of public goods (such as infrastructure). The government can learn from cities that developed successful relationships with small firms to enhance their role in absorbing rural-urban migrants, raising human capital, and keeping inputs into the formal sector competitive (box 3.7).

Supporting Inclusive Urbanization

In a fast-changing landscape like Rwanda's, making the most of rural-urban links requires anticipating migration to cities. Chengdu in China has pursued coordination of its rural and urban areas (box 3.8), emphasizing support for early rural-urban migrants to succeed in the city through skills training and micro loans and raising agricultural productivity through land exchange platforms to reduce the fragmentation that forces people to cities.

Anticipating Demand: People-Focused, Portable Assets

Investments in human capital can have a particularly large role in facilitating migration and raising earnings in large cities like Kigali. Several studies show that workers in more educated cities typically earn more than workers in less educated cities, even holding their own years of schooling constant. This connection between a city's education level and earnings appears to be even stronger in

BOX 3.7 Examples of successful engagement by large cities with the informal sector

Medellín, Colombia. In Medellín, the local government's policy had been to seek out and punish (usually through fines) businesses that operated illegally. Thus, the small business community saw the state as an added nuisance, rather than as a provider of useful services, and low-income entrepreneurs struggled in the city. Federico Restrepo Posada, the newly appointed secretary of planning in Medellín, chose a strategy to change the government's relationship with the informal sector, raising its productivity, tax contribution, and goodwill. He made the city budgeting process more transparent and began a publicity campaign that explained to citizens where their tax money was being spent. The municipal government also changed the law so that informal microbusinesses were no longer illegal; made visible and effective urban investment in the poorest neighborhoods, demonstrating that tax money supports the community; and created business centers using expertise and staffing from local nongovernmental organizations and the Chamber of Commerce, to provide basic skills in business registration, accounting, marketing, and management.

Durban, South Africa. Durban has taken one of the oldest and most innovative approaches to the informal sector in Africa. The municipality adopted a policy on informal trading to clarify the rules of the game; established a department of street vendor management and provided infrastructure for traders; provided business support, capacity building, and market assistance; and enhanced communication through an Informal Economy Forum.

Singapore. Singapore's Skills Development Fund (SDF) offers lessons for supporting human capital development in informal and small firms. Singapore established the SDF in 1979 to support *employers* in developing a more skilled, adaptable workforce. In international experience, small employers typically do not benefit from such schemes, because releasing employees for training harms production, the small scale of training raises unit costs, and smaller firms are less able to assess training needs to select appropriate programs. Recognizing this, the SDF incorporated special incentives to encourage participation by small firms. The SDF offered vouchers to companies with fewer than 50 workers, which supported 30–50 percent of training costs. This helped small enterprises to ease cash flow problems and reduced administrative procedures. With many smaller firms employing workers without education, the SDF also supported programs providing the equivalent of a sixth-grade (P6) level of functional literacy and numeracy and increasing access to English and mathematics at the secondary education level. The voucher helped the SDF to reach 65 percent of enterprises with 10–49 workers and 14 percent of those with fewer than 10 workers (Arvil 2009; Yaushi 1997).

BOX 3.8 Mobilizing rural-urban links: Chengdu's coordinated development model

Following rapid urban growth, Chengdu, China, has pursued a model of urban-rural coordination since 2003. The model aims to replace previous *impediments* to rural migrants' moving to the city, shifting the emphasis to a combination of support for early rural-urban migrants to succeed in cities and "retention effects" that raise the welfare of rural residents who remain or move to rural towns.

The coordinated development model consists of three main policies:

1. *Helping rural residents to settle in urban areas.* To help rural migrants to find employment in the urban sector, government offered subsidies to urban firms to train rural residents, micro loans to a small set of migrants to encourage self-employment in the city, preferential employment conditions for migrants who gave up their land to become urban residents, and subsidies to firms that provided the same social insurance to rural migrants as to urban workers.
2. *Desegmenting land to realize scale economies.* Improved land exchange has reduced fragmentation of land use and improved land use efficiency. Key mechanisms include farmers voluntarily giving up land for urban settlement packages, rural land-for-land exchanges to reduce fragmentation, and land-use rights for shareholding, whereby farmers exchange their land for shares in a specialized agricultural enterprise (which reorganizes the land to encourage large-scale production).
3. *Agglomerating firms in industrial areas to encourage the creation of nonfarm jobs.* Chengdu's 21+10 Industrial Restructuring Plan reorganized 116 industrial development areas into 21 areas and designated 10 major periphery towns with greater resource endowments for new industrial projects.

Over the course of these policies, income has grown in Greater Chengdu, and the urban-rural disparity has narrowed at a faster rate than in the rest of China. The model has been successful in encouraging rural migrants to move to periphery townships and in creating off-farm jobs in these urban areas.

Sources: Chen and Gao 2011; Yumin and LeGates 2013.

China and India than in the United States, suggesting that big gains in developing and emerging markets may be available. Senator Moynihan once claimed, "If you want to build a world-class city build a great university and wait 200 years." Although cognitive skills—like the ability to draft a complicated legal contract—have long been recognized in the theoretical and empirical literature as an important determinant of productivity and wages, new research also reveals that large cities pay a wage premium to workers with better *social skills,* which is not surprising: urban dividends reflect the benefits of interactions (Fujita and Thisse 2002). In France, human capital has been shown to affect earnings via greater communication at the workplace, an effect larger in bigger and more educated cities (Duranton and Charlot 2006).

Successful urbanizers invested heavily, and from early stages, to raise human capital. They prioritized *basic education* at an early stage, as the necessary foundation for effective urban labor markets, and later invested in higher-level skill development. Perhaps the most important urban dividend came from speeding up the flow of ideas; in the 1980s the new growth theory, led by scholars such as Paul Romer and Robert Lucas, focused on knowledge spillovers as the source of increasing productivity that enabled sustained economic growth. The focus on the flow of knowledge pointed both toward education and toward cities.

Human capital investments are a priority for rural areas and secondary cities. A general principle is to deliver a basic standard of services to all people, while letting markets pick the pace and form of private sector development by location. This principle is exemplified by Korea, which allowed the dense concentration of economic activity in Seoul, while delivering basic services like education, health care, and clean water evenly across the population (map 3.12). Investments in human capital, in particular, are "safe" bets, regardless of location. This is because human capital is a *portable* asset that can have powerful effects on people's welfare and productivity in situ as well as on their ability to succeed in higher-productivity areas.

Step-changes in Kigali's productivity will be possible from 2025 to 2030, as investments made today to raise the quality of mass education across Rwanda begin to filter into Rwanda's labor market, delivering opportunities for more advanced specialization and knowledge spillovers.

Institutional Requirements for High-Growth Urbanization

Emerging and growing cities will benefit from strong and adaptive investments in human resources and institutions. These investments should deepen the decentralization agenda, enabling local leaders to mobilize local knowledge and resources and to act as effective change-managers in an environment in considerable flux.

Fiscalizing Public Investments in Cities

Successful, rapid-growth cities made huge investments in public infrastructure. These investments, in turn, dramatically raised the productivity of urban land, crowding in large private investment and raising land values many fold.

Given its high cost, such investment is only attainable when public investments in land are *fiscalized* through land value capture. A range of tools exist to capture the land value increments accompanying investment—such as land value and property taxes, capital gains taxes, betterment fees for landowners or developers, special assessment districts (with temporary additional taxes applied in return for infrastructure improvements), land purchases by infrastructure agencies (for example, box 3.9), and the direct commissioning and financing of infrastructure by property developers.

Effective land value capture should ensure that tax rates track values in a way that is

MAP 3.12 Concentrated urban development and universal basic services in the Republic of Korea

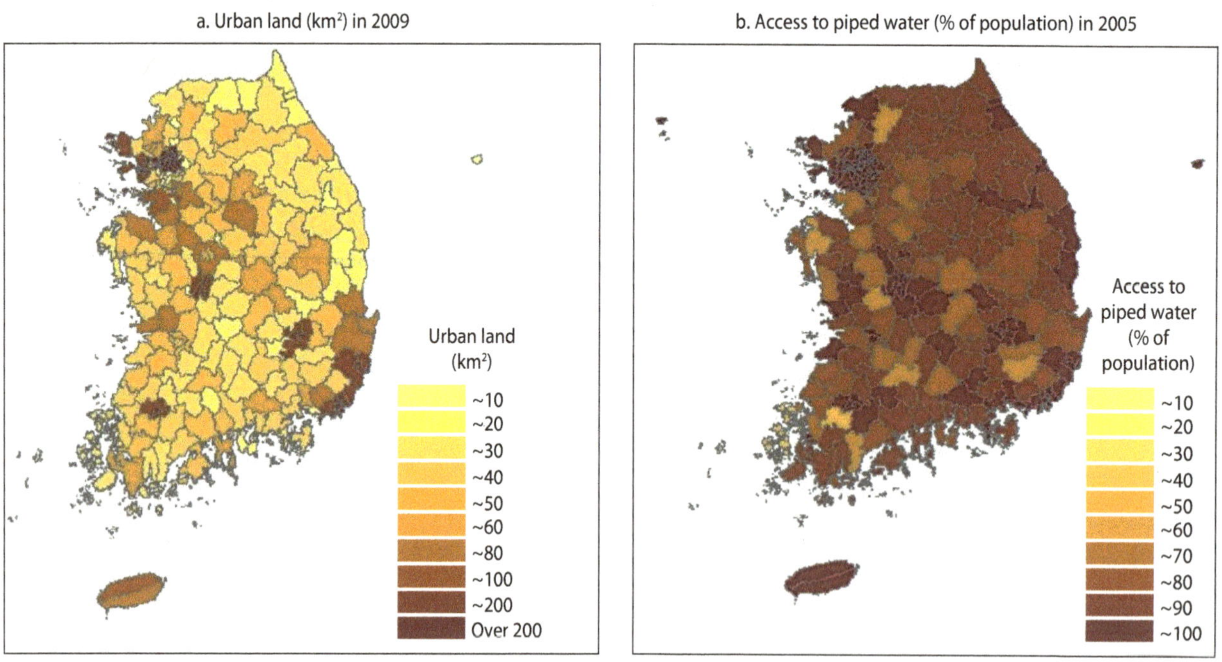

Source: Lall et al. 2013.

BOX 3.9 Land value capture: The rail + property program in Hong Kong SAR, China

Hong Kong, SAR, China, has financed a large portion of its transit system using land value capture. Its metro system—Mass Transit Railway Corporation (MTRC)—operates without government subsidy and is highly profitable, thanks to profits generated by its real estate business. MTRC invests in and shares profits with private developers in real estate sales and property management.

MTRC's property development program uses the following process:

- MTRC, with the city government, assesses the cost of construction and prepares a master plan to identify property development along railway sites.
- MTRC purchases the right to develop property above underground stations and land adjacent to the railway (development rights). This land premium is paid to the government but does not include the increased value resulting from the transport project.
- MTRC then tenders out its development rights to private developers (dividing them into smaller, more manageable lots).
- Private developers bear the construction and commercialization costs of residential and commercial properties.
- Profit-sharing mechanisms are included in the agreements with private developers. For example, for residential units, the MTRC receives an agreed portion of profit generated by the sales if the private partners sell all units before a contractual deadline. Otherwise, MTRC obtains the unsold units either to sell or to lease in the open market.

The transport company is not in charge of construction; instead, it supervises the work and carries out civil works required for integrating the railway and property development.

Sources: Cervero and Murakami 2009; Salon 2014.

both acceptable to taxpayers and able to deliver the revenue required by districts. Governments can soften contestation by communicating the approximate nature of valuations: in certain U.S. states, the valuation for property tax purposes is by law 70 percent of the real assessed property value to soften contestation, whereas in the United Kingdom, properties are assigned to broad value bands to avoid making precise claims liable to contestation. Rwanda has struck a sensible balance with its new decentralized taxes law, avoiding communicating explicit plot valuations that may be contested, but preparing ground for area-based fees that track market values. Some countries in East Asia recognized the importance of appropriate land taxes to generate the revenues required for adequate infrastructure investment (box 3.10).

Land valuation is critical for effective land value capture. District land value capture has the capacity to strengthen decentralization in the future. Outside of Kigali, own-source revenue mobilization is low—estimated at 10 percent of district budgets in 2013–14.[11] Districts therefore rely on central revenues and do not capture many of the gains of their investments, which flow largely to private landlords (many of whom acquire land speculatively to reap the gains of public investment) and the national government (in the form of centralized corporate taxes). This reliance both reduces district *resources* for investment and reduces their *incentives* to identify and prioritize investments where they are most likely to unlock growth.

Rwanda has a strong basis for efficient and transparent valuation, with centralized and digitized landownership and transaction records, a professional valuation body, and credible institutions for oversight like the Ombudsman's Office. However, significant additional investment is needed in human and institutional resources for valuation. Optimal systems combine the analysis of large-scale transaction price (and geo) data with on-the-ground audits and assessments

BOX 3.10 Land value capture in East Asia

Property—especially land—taxes were central to the urban development strategies of East Asian developmental states. In Taiwan, China, by 1975, property-related taxes were 70 percent of local government collections. By 2000 property taxes constituted a higher proportion of tax revenue in the Republic of Korea than in any other high-income country. In Singapore, property taxes constitute 8 percent of national tax revenue.

These states saw that investments in urban infrastructure are expensive, but crowd in private investment, translating directly into higher land and property values. It is not uncommon, internationally, for the combined effects of public infrastructure investment and in-migration from rural areas to appreciate urban land values 10- to 20-fold in less than a decade. For example, in Seoul, Korea, land prices rose 33-fold between 1974 and 1996 (Goodfellow 2017). A tax that captures those elevated land values for reinvestment in broad-use infrastructure unlocks a virtuous cycle of self-financing urbanization.

Taxes on land were also used to align investors' incentives with the manufacturing sector, in the context of high land speculation. Whereas property and land taxes were high, taxes on productive sectors were typically *lower* than those seen today in Rwanda and other African countries; ratios of final tax to GDP were similar to those in contemporary Sub-Saharan Africa.

The fact that revenues flowed back to the cities meant that local governments were not just *financed* to make high and appropriate investments, but also highly *motivated* to do so. Incentives to select the right investments were created by the promise that more effective investments would raise land and property values, and hence city budgets, more.

to derive and publish transparent valuation formulas. Lessons from Bogotá, Colombia may be useful for Rwanda (box 3.11).

Strengthen Urban Planning

A limited local planning capacity explains the problems affecting the use of master plans in Rwandan cities. In all cities, skilled urban planning teams are required to ensure that managed urbanization supports growth, investment, and community aspirations. As urban complexity rises, a particularly skilled, credible, and empowered team is required to carry out adaptive, market-responsive planning. The ongoing restructuring of local government bodies should ensure adequate urban planning capacities in all locations. To this effect, urban planners will be integrated in the district structures.

There is a fear that more flexible and market-responsive land use regulation planning would open the floodgates for special interests, on the one hand, and accusations of complicity by planners, on the other. Other cities have combatted these risks by combining the *high skill* and *credibility* of planning teams with institutions that *forced transparency* about planning revisions both within government and with the public. Making the process more transparent and participatory can ensure that plans respond to markets and community visions, while safeguarding against special interests through strong public oversight and engagement.

Rwanda should begin to experiment with developing institutions that *require* and *facilitate* regular, responsive, and transparent planning adjustments. These adjustments should include agreed and transparent procedures for investors and citizens to apply for changes in regulations and for review of these applications (Huang 2016). Examples from India, Japan, and a sample of global cities are provided in boxes 3.12, 3.13, and 3.14, respectively.

Cross-District Coordination

Many urban areas are developing as cross-district "corridors" (such as the Musanze–Nyabihu–Rubavu corridor, Kigali–Muhanga–Huye–Rusizi,

BOX 3.11 Updating land values in Bogotá, Colombia

A pioneer in land valuation, Bogotá updated its cadastral database over 2008–10 by revaluing its 2.1 million urban properties. The update yielded a 30 percent (US$171 million) increase in property tax revenues, bringing these to 40 percent of own revenues by 2010; the cost of the improvements was US$15 million. The update was achieved by improving human resource management, introducing information technology, enacting policies to soften property tax jumps (to manage political implications), engaging stakeholders and career civil servants, reviewing the project's results in a public and transparent manner, and adopting technical innovations to improve assessments.

Hundreds of temporary workers surveyed plots and buildings, but technological innovations helped. Spatial information from Geographic Information Systems, such as a property's distance from key sites and amenities, was incorporated into the statistical techniques for estimating property values. Going forward, construction permits were to be used to update physical data automatically; another option is to use satellite data with manual identification or remote sensing of buildings. Given a shortage of market information in Bogotá, initial price estimates were collected from expert appraisers who combined sales price, construction cost, and income (rental) valuation approaches. Today valuation data are shared throughout the government to improve planning across agencies and sectors.

Because the cadastral values had long lagged behind actual market values, the property tax base was expected to increase sharply after the update. To prevent excessive resistance by property owners—while nevertheless retaining the assumption that property values are strongly correlated with ability to pay—the city limited property tax increases proportionally to the logarithm of its value (with differentiated ceilings for residential and nonresidential uses).

Sources: Ruiz and Vallejo 2010; Uribe 2010.

BOX 3.12 Institutions for market-responsive urban planning: Yokohama, Japan

A visionary mayor, Ichio Asukata, and his appointed urban planner, Akira Tamura, helped to transform Yokohama, Japan from a declining, dirty port town in the 1960s to a thriving, attractive, modern city. This transformation was achieved through the following:

- *Leadership of an elevated and skilled planning bureau.* A new Bureau of Planning and Coordination was given a "slightly higher" status than other institutions and empowered to adjust plans and coordinate institutions. It was staffed with 15 rising young officials from across institutions, hand-picked by Tamura. Tamura himself had three degrees (law, politics, and architecture) and a strong reputation from experience across government.
- *Transparent implementation and adjustment of plans.* Tamura chaired monthly cross-institutional meetings to resolve blockages and discuss and approve adjustments to plans. The planning bureau also held regular public meetings with residents and businesses to receive feedback. A city official from the time was asked what share of the city's plans were revised; he responded that 80 percent were revised, but that the share should have been even higher, because planners can never get everything right in advance.
- *Urban planning as "community-building."* A serious Citizen Councils initiative was launched, led by a seasoned civil society campaigner and staffed with former student activists, that engaged residents and businesses to contribute to and update district plans. Plans were then presented to citizens through a robust campaign. The citizen ownership this engendered meant that plans were pursued long after Mayor Asukata left office.

Source: Tokyo Development Learning Center 2017.

BOX 3.13 Participatory planning and budgeting: Kerala, India

In 1996, India's Kerala State launched a remarkable experiment in participatory planning. The People's Plan Campaign for the Ninth Plan devolved 35 percent of the state budget to the lowest tier of local government structures and developed a series of local-level planning including seminars, task forces, local council meetings, implementation and monitoring committees, and so on. Local meetings, facilitated by a popular nongovernmental organization, discussed and prioritized the development needs of the community and presented them to the local government council, which consolidated them to produce an annual plan and budget. This plan was presented back to citizens and then sent to district planning committees, which scrutinized it to iron out inconsistencies and fill in gaps.

The plan radically improved the delivery of public infrastructure and services, raised caste and ethnic equality, facilitated the participation of women in public life, and improved state-people relationships. The scheme was so popular and comprehensive that even a change of government in 2001 could not overturn the model.

Source: Franke 2007.

BOX 3.14 Involving stakeholders in city development: Lessons on participatory planning from global cities

More and more cities have shifted their planning practice toward creating a sense of place and engaging communities in the planning process. Recognizing that certain places hold special meaning for particular groups, planners engage local people in transformation.

Hong Kong SAR, China. In Hong Kong SAR, China, for example, people-oriented planning follows a process of "Communicate—Understand—Interpret—Plan," using citizens' views to inform the design. The planning process also pays attention to the scale of the plan, with a sense of place generally identified for small neighborhoods.

London, United Kingdom. In London, the development of King's Cross entailed major engagement based on the publication of proposals and discussions with residents. This process led to 10 design principles for a human city as well as parameters for regeneration based on lessons learned from other projects in London. Design frameworks embedding these parameters guided the individual parcels and mixed-use plans. The procedure entailed four rounds of public consultation with some 30,000 people that allowed a balancing of local benefits against profitability for the developer.

New York City, United States. In Manhattan, a nongovernmental organization called Friends of the High Line used participatory planning methods, such as focus group interviews and community campaigns, to boost the involvement of local communities. Their efforts eventually fostered the transformation of an abandoned elevated urban rail into a vibrant public space. This linear park project upgraded the physical and social landscape of the neighborhood along its route.

Seoul, Republic of Korea. Seoul's 2030 plan was the first to build on wide engagement of local residents. Through onsite discussion and online platforms, citizens helped the planning authorities to shape the vision and identify 5 core issues and 17 specific goals.

Kigali–Rwamagana–Kayonza, and the newer Kivu Belt). Kigali's bordering districts are also increasingly integrated with Kigali's economy. Economically connected districts should be encouraged and required to coordinate land use plans (to avoid sprawl), transport and service provision, major infrastructure like special economic zones, tourism infrastructure, and so on, to reduce waste and exploit complementarities. Box 3.15 shows how Korea's central government supported cross-jurisdiction collaboration through "happy living zones."

BOX 3.15 Cross-district governance: The Republic of Korea's happy living zones

Korea experienced rapid urbanization following the Korean War, with a high number of displaced rural peasants leaving villages for Seoul in search of more economic opportunities. The growth of Seoul and its surrounding capital region has driven the Korean economy, but regional disparities have persisted as a primary concern for Korean policy since the 1980s.

Since 2013, the central government has pursued a new spatial concept, happy living zones, as a basis for regional development policy. These zones are intended to enhance happiness and quality of life outside the capital city region to retain and attract people. The primary goal is to encourage cooperation among local governments that share common features (such as commuting routes, industries, geography, and culture) and to develop policies tailored to broader "places" rather than to specific jurisdictions. Since its inception, 63 zones have been established. Each zone has established an association of local governments, which prepares and implements development projects tailored for the zone, including economic revitalization, education, culture, welfare, and basic infrastructure. Central governments have supported the preparation and implementation of happy living zones by coordinating local governments, funding initiatives through the special account for regional development, consulting and offering technical assistance, and deregulating to support initiatives.

Source: Roberts 2014.

Unite Spatial and Economic Planning

Economic planning, as carried out by the Ministry of Finance and Economic Planning, Ministry of Agriculture and Animal Resources, Ministry of Trade and Industry, Rwanda Development Board, and so on, is sometimes not aligned with "spatial" planning, as conducted by the Ministry of Infrastructure, Ministry of Local Government, and Ministry of Environment.

As Rwanda works to strengthen the economic dividend of urbanization, economic planners should start to think spatially, and spatial planners should become more aligned with economic planning and goals. In Korea, for example, a dedicated spatial development research entity supports higher-level structures to marry spatial and economic planning.

Annex 3A The Rwanda Spatial CGE Model and Scenarios

This study commissioned a CGE model of Rwanda to examine how alternative urbanization policy scenarios would affect key economic and welfare outcomes until 2050. Five urbanization scenarios were considered:

- *Scenario 1.* Business as usual
- *Scenario 2.* Faster rural-urban migration
- *Scenario 3.* Faster migration, with higher public investment in urban areas and lower public investment in rural areas (due to a fixed government budget)
- *Scenario 4.* Faster migration, with higher public investment in urban areas that is financed by urban taxation, meaning that rural investment stays the same
- *Scenario 5.* Scenario 4, with public urban investment that is effective in attracting private urban investment and raises productivity in urban areas

The researchers drew on a spatially disaggregated social accounting matrix (SAM) constructed in 2015. A SAM is a consistent accounting framework that captures all income and expenditure flows in an economy during a given year; it includes all sectors, households, and the government, as well as the economy's interactions with the rest of the world. The SAM for Rwanda was built using national accounts, censuses, and agricultural and economic surveys from the National Institute of Statistics of Rwanda; government revenue and expenditure data from the finance ministry; and balance of payments data from the central bank (see Diao, Randriamamonjy, and Thurlow 2017).

Inputs and results were disaggregated for Kigali, other urban and peri-urban areas, and remote rural areas; and interactions between all three locations also were considered. Trends were also distinguished according to household poverty and education levels.

The model assumes that labor and their dependents move across Rwanda on the basis of wage differentials. It assumes that the migration effect of wage differentials observed in 2015 is equal to that observed in the 2012 population census data. This results in an average net annual outflow from rural areas of 75,700 migrants, with 50,200 moving to Kigali City and 25,500 moving to other urban areas.

Labor productivity and GDP are key variables of interest. Disaggregating these for urban and rural locations is challenging, because government GDP statistics are only published at the national level. To overcome this challenge, the model combines data on national sectoral labor productivity and regional sectoral employment trends with *assumptions* about how labor productivity in each sector differs in rural versus urban areas. Overall, labor productivity gains are constituted by *within-sector* productivity gains (the productivity in each economic sector, weighted by initial labor share in the national economy) and *structural change* (gains caused by workers moving from less to more productive sectors).

The comparative impacts on urban welfare of rural and urban public investments were modeled. This modeling examined how rural outflows of food and migrants both help and hinder urban areas. As households migrate to urban areas, productivity gains from agglomeration economies are assumed, as well as "congestion effects" through pressures on public infrastructure and services. The latter must be offset by public urban investment.

Modeling such outcomes for the five urbanization scenarios considered, the study shed light on how fundamental policy decisions regarding urban migration, public investment, and taxation may affect growth, welfare, and equity across Rwanda over the course of Vision 2050.

Notes

1. A 40 percent increase in Kigali's population from 2002 to 2012, compared with a 30 percent increase in the national population.
2. Musanze, Nyabihu, and Rubavu districts.
3. Huye, Muhanga, Nyanza, and Ruhango districts.
4. The annual flow of migrants leaving rural areas rises from 75,700 in the baseline to 107,900 in the faster urbanization scenario, with 22,300 arriving in (peri-)urban areas and 85,600 arriving in Kigali City.
5. Food, housing, and transport prices are higher in African cities than in competing low- and middle-income countries elsewhere (by around 35, 55, and 42 percent, respectively). "Overall, urban households pay 20 to 31 percent more for goods and services in African countries than in other developing countries" (Lall, Henderson, and Venables 2017).
6. Integrated Household Living Conditions Survey 2013–14 (EICV4) district-level analysis (NISR 2015).
7. Internal migration is defined as moving from one district to another, so changes of residence within districts are not captured as internal migration. That is, neither rural-to-urban migration within districts nor urban-to-rural migration within districts is counted as part of the population movement. For details on methodology and results, see World Bank (2017a).
8. Analysis of EICV4 data, exempting high outliers.
9. Kigali's R1 residential zone, for example, covers many central areas, enforcing a minimum plot size of 600 square meters and requiring that 60 percent of the plot be left unbuilt. The R2 zone (also common in central areas) demands that 40 percent of each plot be left undeveloped. It allows plots of 90 square meters—better, but still high as a minimum; consider that Philadelphia allowed 30 square

meters as it was settled, whereas Singapore's minimum plot size today is 90 square meters.

10. The key requirements for effective congestion charging are not technological, but the *authority* and *capacity* of the implementing institution, for which Rwanda has some advantages.
11. For Kigali, own-source revenues are closer to 50 percent.

References

Arvil, A. 2009. *Skills Development in the Informal Sector of Sub-Saharan Africa.* Washington, DC: World Bank.

Bachofer, F., and S. Murray. 2018. "Remote Sensing for Measuring Housing Supply in Kigali." International Growth Centre, Kigali.

Brueckner, J., and S. V. Lall. 2014. "Cities in Developing Countries: Fueled by Rural-Urban Migration, Lacking in Tenure Security, and Short of Affordable Housing." In *Handbook of Regional and Urban Economics.* Vol. 5, ch. 21. Amsterdam: Elsevier.

Cai, F., A. Park, and Y. Zhao. 2008. "The Chinese Labor Market in the Reform Era in China's Great Economic Transformation." In *The Chinese Labor Market in the Reform Era,* edited by L. Brandt and T. Rawski, 167–214. Cambridge, U.K.: Cambridge University Press.

Cervero, R., and J. Murakami. 2009. "Rail and Property Development in Hong Kong: Experiences nd Extensions." *Urban Studies* 46 (10): 2019–43.

Chen, A., and J. Gao. 2011. "Urbanization in China and the Coordinated Development Model—The Case of Chengdu." *Social Science Journal* 48 (3): 500–13.

Diao, X. 2017. *A Growth Analysis.* Washington, DC: International Food Policy Research Institute.

Diao, X., J. Randriamamonjy, and J. Thurlow. 2017. "Urbanization and the Future of Economic Development in Rwanda." International Food Policy Research Institute, Washington, DC. Background paper for *Future Drivers of Growth in Rwanda.*

Duranton, G., and S. Charlot. 2006. "Cities and Workplace Communication: Some Quantitative French Evidence." *Urban Studies* 43 (8): 1365–94.

Economist. 2012. "Daily Chart: The Urbanization Trap." *Economist* (online), October 2.

Franke, R. W. 2007. "Local Planning: The Kerala Experiment." In *Real Utopia: Participatory Society for the 21st Century,* edited by C. Spannos, 130–35. Oakland, CA: A. K. Press.

Fujita, M., and J.-F. Thisse. 2002. *Economics of Agglomeration: Cities, Industrial Location, and Regional Growth.* Cambridge, U.K.: Cambridge University Press.

Gelb, A., J. Meyer, V. Ramachandran, and D. Wadhwa. 2017. "Can Africa Be a Manufacturing Destination? Labor Costs in Comparative Perspective." CGD Working Paper 466, Center for Global Development, Washington, DC.

Goodfellow, T. 2017. "Taxing Property in a Neo-Developmental State: The Politics of Urban Land Value Capture in Rwanda and Ethiopia." *African Affairs* 116 (465): 549–72.

Guardian. 2014. "Cities Need Goldilocks Housing Density—Not Too High or Low, but Just Right." *Guardian,* April 16.

Henderson, Vernon, and Dzhamilya Nigmatulina. 2016. "The Fabric of African Cities: How to Think about Density and Land Use." Draft, London School of Economics.

Huang, C.-Y. 2016. "Enabling Structure: Role of Public Sector and Institutions." Background paper for *Africa's Cities: Opening Doors to the World,* World Bank, Washington, DC.

Jones, P., J. Bird, C. Beck, and A. Haas. 2016. *Kampala: A Policy Narrative.* Washington, DC: World Bank.

Jones, P., K. del Frari, L. Ferreira, and M. Sladoje. 2016. *Lusaka: A Policy Narrative.* Washington, DC: World Bank.

Jones, P., S. Murray, and L. Ferreira. 2016. *Kigali: A Policy Narrative.* Washington, DC: World Bank.

Lall, S. 2017. "How Will Urban Mobility Change by 2050?" Unpublished paper, World Bank, Washington, DC.

Lall, S., B. Dasgupta, N. Lozano, and H. Wang. 2013. "Cities: A New Habitat for Tigers." Unpublished presentation, World Bank, Washington, DC.

Lall, S., V. Henderson, and A. Venables. 2017. *Africa's Cities: Opening Doors to the World.* Washington, DC: World Bank.

Matsui, Minoru. 2017. "Case Study: Land Readjustment in Japan." Knowledge Product, Tokyo Development Learning Center, Tokyo, and World Bank Group, Washington, DC.

MININFRA (Ministry of Infrastructure and Water and Sanitation Cooperation), Rwanda. 2017. *Site Distribution of Rural Settlement Layout Plans since 2017 to May 2017.* Kigali: MININFRA.

NISR (National Institute of Statistics of Rwanda). 2015. *Rwanda Poverty Profile Report 2013–2014: Results of Integrated Living Conditions Survey (EICV)*. Kigali: Government of Rwanda, September.

Nordhaus, William D. 2006. "Geography and Macroeconomics: New Data and New Findings." *Proceedings of the National Academy of Sciences* 103 (10): 3510–7.

Quiros, T., S. Murray, and J. Bajpai. 2014. *Managing Accessibility for Sustainable Development of Kigali*. Washington, DC: World Bank; London: International Growth Centre.

Roberts, B. 2014. *Managing Systems of Secondary Cities: Policy Responses in International Development*. Brussels: Cities Alliance.

Rosenthal S., and W. Strange. 2003. "Geography, Industrial Organization, and Agglomeration." *Review of Economics and Statistics* 85 (2): 377–93.

Ruiz, F., and G. Vallejo. 2010. *Using Land Registration as a Tool to Generate Municipal Revenue: Lessons from Bogotá*. Washington, DC: World Bank.

Salon, D. 2014. "Location Value Capture Opportunities for Urban Public Transport Finance." White Paper prepared for the 2014 Transit Leadership Summit, Regional Plan Association, London, May.

Tokyo Development Learning Center. 2017. *Yokohama: Reinventing the Future of a City*. Competitive Cities for Jobs and Growth. Washington, DC: World Bank.

Uribe, M. C. 2010. "Land Information Updating, a De Facto Tax Reform Bringing up to Date the Cadastral Database of Bogotá." In *Innovations in Land Rights Recognition, Administration, and Governance,* edited by K. Deininger, C. Augustinas, S. Enemark, and P. Munro-Faure, 180–207. Washington, DC: World Bank.

Vishwanath, T., S. Lall, D. Dowall, N. Lozano-Gracia, S. Sharma, and H. Wanga. 2013. *Urbanization beyond Municipal Boundaries: Nurturing Metropolitan Economies and Connecting Peri-Urban Areas in India*. Directions in Development: Countries and Regions. Washington, DC: World Bank.

Wainer, L. S., B. Ndengeyingoma, and S. Murray. 2016. *Incremental Housing and Other Design Principles for Low-Cost Housing*. Kigli: International Growth Centre.

Wang, H. 2011. "Lessons from Korea's Urbanization Policies to Facilitate Rapid Urban Transition." Unpublished presentation, World Bank, Washington, DC.

World Bank. 2009. *World Development Report 2009: Reshaping Economic Geography*. Washington, DC: World Bank.

———. 2012. *Planning, Connecting, and Financing Cities—Now: Priorities for City Leaders*. Washington, DC: World Bank.

———. 2015. "Background Study for the Rwanda Urban Development Project (RUDP)." World Bank, Kigali.

———. 2017a. "Note 2: Internal Migration in Rwanda." Reshaping Urbanization in Rwanda, World Bank, Washington, DC.

———. 2017b. "Note 3: Urbanization, Job Creation, and Poverty Reduction in Rwanda." Reshaping Urbanization in Rwanda, World Bank, Washington, DC.

———. 2017c. *Reshaping Urbanization in Rwanda: Economic and Spatial Trends and Proposals; Synthesis Report*. Washington, DC: World Bank.

———. 2017d. "Rwanda Feeder Road Development Program: Impact Evaluation." Unpublished paper, Development Impact Evaluation, World Bank, Washington DC.

———. 2017e. "Urbanisation and the Evolution of Rwanda's Urban Landscape." Reshaping Urbanization in Rwanda, World Bank, Washington, DC.

World Bank and Development Research Center of the State Council, China. 2014. *Urban China: Toward Efficient, Inclusive, and Sustainable Urbanization*. Washington, DC: World Bank.

Yaushi, H. 1997. *Skills Development Fund: A Preliminary Assessment of a Financing Alternative for Enterprise-Based Training in the Context of APEC*. Nagoya, Japan: Graduate School of International Developoment, Nagoya University; Asia-Pacific Economic Cooperation.

Yumin, Y., and R. LeGates. 2013. *Coordinating Urban and Rural Development in China: Learning from Chengdu*. London: Edward Elgar Publishing.

4

Competitiveness and Enterprise Development for Innovation-Led Growth

Introduction

In the immediate aftermath of the genocide against the Tutsi, the level of economic activity was extremely low. Private enterprises were almost nonexistent, and even the government was severely constrained in the resources it could mobilize. Over the course of the reconstruction years, the government was able to channel capital into more productive uses and to kick-start entire sectors of the economy through the establishment of state-owned enterprises (SOEs). The government also took steps to enable the development of a vibrant private sector, including by liberalizing some industries previously run as state or quasi-state monopolies. Rwanda's *Vision 2020* states, "The emergence of a viable private sector that can take over as the principal growth engine of the economy is absolutely key."

As Rwanda's economy develops and matures, the need for the private sector to play a leading role in achieving the rapid growth required to reach Rwanda's ambitious income aspirations only increases. The massive rise in investment required to achieve Rwanda's growth aspirations has to come predominantly from the private sector, since public investment is constrained by rising debt and limits on external assistance. Moreover, private sector entrepreneurs can provide the dynamism, innovation, and risk taking required for a modern, sophisticated, and rapidly growing economy.

The government has built a strong track record of reforms to support the development of viable enterprises. This is evidenced, for example, in Rwanda's rapidly improved ranking in the Doing Business Index. The work is by no means finished, however. Many private sector firms are small and informal; they have limited scale economies critical for competitiveness and have limited export presence and capacity for innovation. The number of formal sector firms is expanding gradually, and the pace of job creation in the sector has slowed.

The limited private sector presence reflects two high-level challenges that need to be at the center of policy responses:

1. High economywide costs faced by enterprises in Rwanda relative to costs in other economies at similar stages of their development, most importantly in energy, transport, and finance
2. Productivity that has not grown at a rate capable of sustaining rapid economic growth because of a suboptimal allocation of resources and insufficient technological innovation

To address these constraints, the following are key areas for the government's continued reform agenda:

- Reducing business costs by tackling cross-cutting constraints
- Improving the effectiveness of the government's tax incentives and other industrial policy interventions by shifting from general support to performance-based targeting of successful enterprises
- Defining the future role of SOEs and further strengthening their corporate governance
- Building an effective national innovation system (NIS).

These constraints and reform areas are explored in further detail in the remainder of this chapter, after a general overview of the current state of Rwanda's enterprise sector.

Current State of Rwanda's Enterprise Sector

Rwanda's enterprises, together with its people (chapter 1) and institutions (chapter 6), are key to harnessing the significant opportunities that arise from modern-day technologies, global trade and investment patterns, and urban agglomeration.

The number of nonfarm enterprises, although still low in absolute terms, has grown rapidly, from a state of decimation after the genocide against the Tutsi to about 150,000 firms in 2014. In that year, these firms employed about 360,000 workers, or 6 percent of the overall workforce. A majority of these firms are small, although the size distribution is beginning to shift up gradually: 65 percent of the firms in 2014 were one-person firms, down from 73 percent in 2011 (figure 4.1). The number of large firms (those employing 100 workers or more) more than doubled (to 216) from a small base between 2011 and 2014, and their share of total employment increased to 20 percent (figure 4.2). The number of medium firms (51–99 employees) also increased sharply (by around 60 percent), but their share of enterprise employment (4 percent) remains insignificant. There is strong international evidence that small firms are less productive than large firms (Bartelsman, Haltiwanger, and Scarpetta 2009), so the lack of scale and size is an important impediment to growth that will need to be addressed.

FIGURE 4.1 Share of firms in Rwanda, by firm size, 2011 and 2014

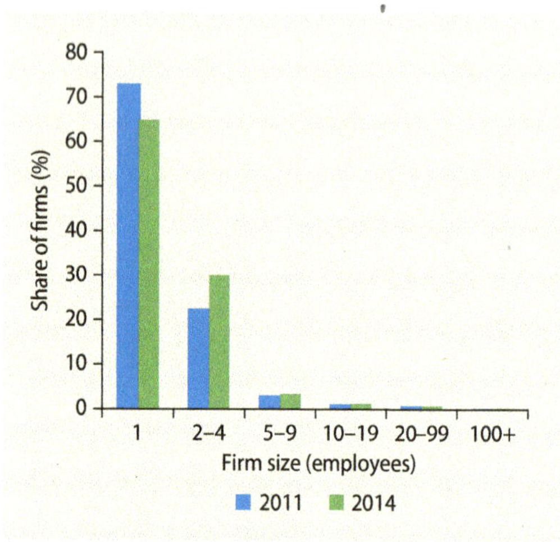

Sources: Calculations based on 2011 and 2014 Rwanda Census of Business Establishments data (NISR 2011, 2015).

FIGURE 4.2 Share of employment in Rwanda, by firm size, 2011 and 2014

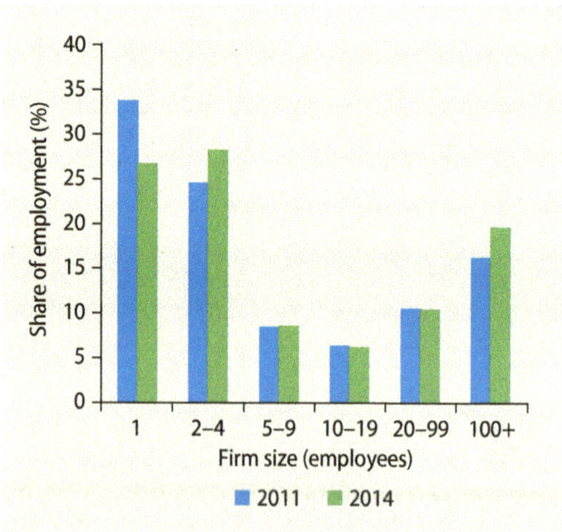

Source: Calculations based on 2011 and 2014 Rwanda Census of Business Establishments data (NISR 2011, 2015).

FIGURE 4.3 Share of firms and employment in Rwanda, by year of establishment

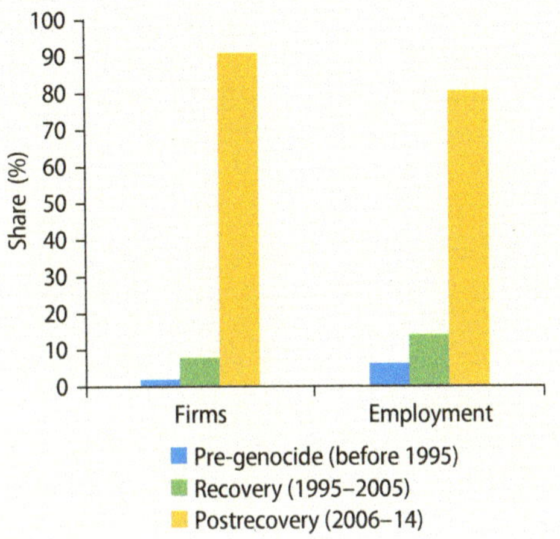

Source: Calculations based on 2014 Rwanda Census of Business Establishment data (NISR 2015).

Rwandan firms, for the most part, are young and concentrated in the nontradable sector. About 90 percent of the enterprises that were operational in 2014, accounting for 80 percent of employment in the enterprise sector, were established after 2006 (figure 4.3). The two main sectors—wholesale and retail trade and accommodation and food services—accounted for 75 percent of all firms and 45 percent of total employment in 2014 (figure 4.4). Although the number of manufacturing firms increased between 2011 and 2014, the sector's share of employment declined.

As in other low-income countries, many firms are informal (figure 4.5). The government has taken a policy stand to promote formalization of enterprises. Informal establishments added less than 24,000 jobs

FIGURE 4.4 Share of firms and employment in Rwanda, by sector, 2011 and 2014

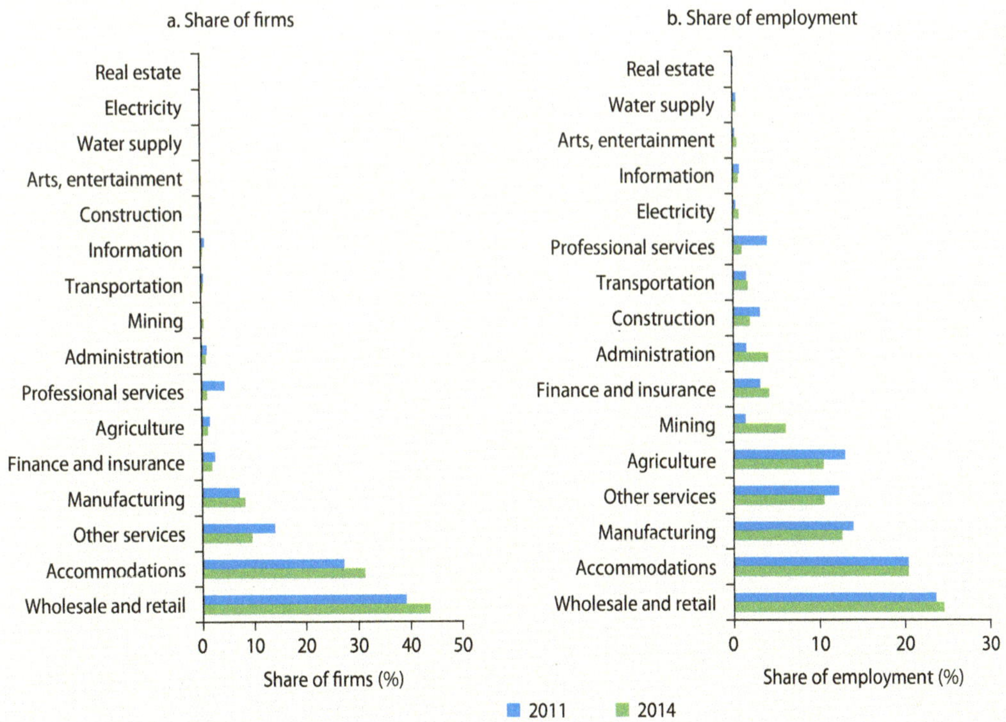

Source: Calculations based on 2011 and 2014 Rwanda Census of Business Establishments data (NISR 2011, 2015).
Note: Excludes health, education, public administration, and defense sectors and one-person formal and informal firms.

FIGURE 4.5 Informality as a share of total firms and employment in Rwanda, 2011 and 2014

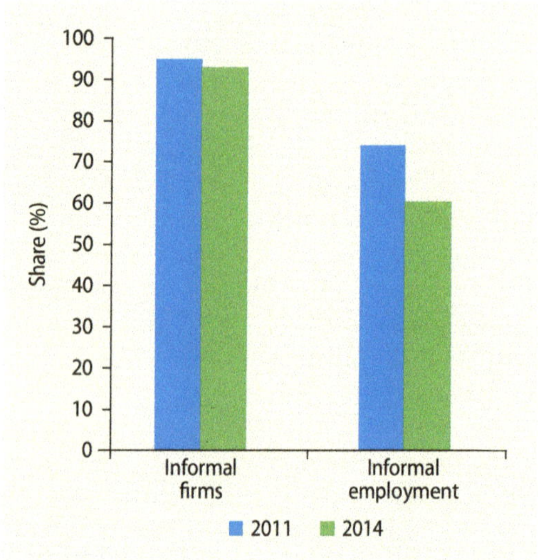

Source: Calculations based on 2011 and 2014 Rwanda Census of Business Establishments data (NISR 2011, 2015).
Note: NISR = National Institute of Statistics of Rwanda.

between 2011 and 2014. Yet job creation in the informal sector can be a major contributor to the country's structural transformation and thus productivity, providing opportunities to close to 70 percent of the workforce still in low-productivity subsistence agriculture. Box 4.1 takes a fresh look at the potential of informality on the basis of international experience.

Between 2013 and 2016, the pace of new firms' entry and job creation in the sector slowed (figure 4.6, panel b). Job creation has been driven mainly by the expansion of incumbent formal firms, not by the entry of new firms. Over the 2011 to 2016 period, only 3 percent of formal firms experienced high employment growth (more than 20 percent a year on average) for three years in a row, but the number of these "high-growth firms" declined.

BOX 4.1 Is informal normal?

In other countries, the informal nonfarm sector has often been a remarkably persistent and important driver of early-stage development, even during periods of high GDP growth. A major contributor to the structural transformation process, the informal nonfarm sector provides a valuable pathway for surplus labor to move out of agriculture, with opportunities that are often more remunerative and productive than in agriculture. Reviewing the experience of certain Latin American and Southeast Asian economies (figure B4.1.1), a 2009 Organisation for Economic Co-operation and Development study concludes, "Informality is increasingly becoming normal, not least in middle- and even high-income countries.... The development in selected countries in Southeast Asia and Latin America is telling in this respect: over the last 30 years, growth in these countries was accompanied by increasing, not falling, informal employment" (Jütting and de Laiglesia 2009).

While *informal is normal* across the low- and middle-income world, government responses have varied considerably. Some countries (Bangladesh, Cambodia, and Ghana) have been more forthcoming in embracing it, while others (including several countries in Sub-Saharan Africa) have been more cautious. Resistance to informality, however forcefully applied, has not succeeded in stemming its rising tide, including in Sub-Saharan Africa. What it has done is to forgo some of the sector's significant economic and job-creating potential in the early stages of development. This loss particularly affects mobility and opportunities for young people who lack the education and skills required for a wage job.

Policy makers need to recognize the informal sector's significant potential and then follow up with supportive policies. To identify the appropriate policies, it is important for the sector to be represented in consultations between the government and the private sector (as in Ghana, for example).

(Box continues next page)

BOX 4.1 (continued)

It is also important for policy makers not to view informal sector enterprises as small and medium enterprises in the making. Both have a role to play in early-stage economic expansion and job creation.

Whatever their specific form, policies targeted at enhancing the productive potential of informal sector firms need to address three key areas.

The first priority is for governments to incorporate the growth of informal sector firms in their planning processes and then provide them with adequate space in key areas of foot traffic in the city. This can avoid overcrowding and congestion, while ensuring good market access for the firms. Informal sector firms (just like those in the formal sector) also need key services (such as security, sanitation, electricity, transport, and water supply) to operate and have proved willing to pay for them through fees and taxes.

The second priority is to provide access to finance, a key requirement for business, whether formal or informal. Finance is needed for household enterprises that otherwise suffer from lack of financial inclusion (Filmer and Fox 2014).

The third priority is to provide skills and training opportunities. Such opportunities can go a long way in supporting youth employment in household enterprises. Trainings can consist of private courses and apprenticeships. Governments should not attempt to deliver training directly; rather, they should focus on market-enhancing programs that disseminate information about training opportunities and enable disadvantaged youth to access training that is already available.

FIGURE B4.1.1 Informal employment as a share of GDP per capita in Latin America and Southeast Asia, various years

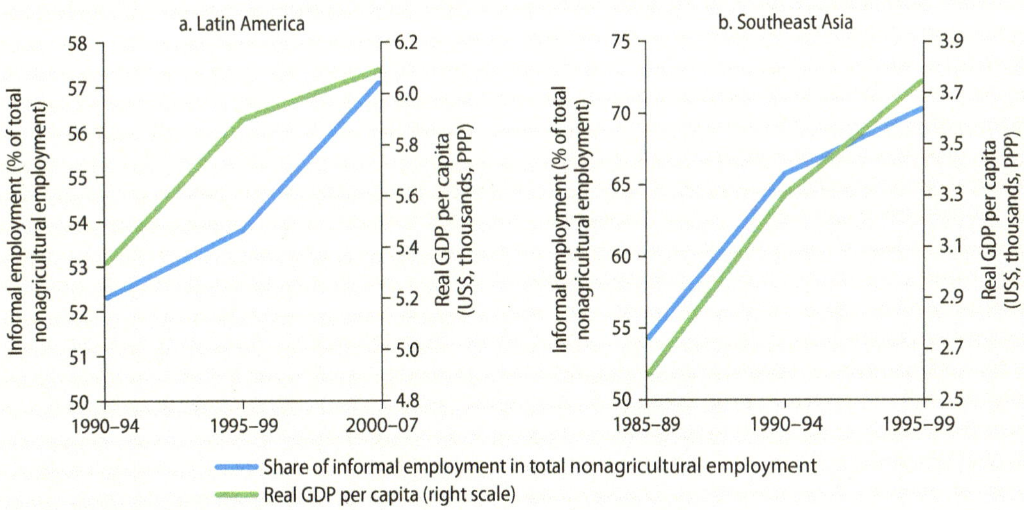

Source: Jütting and de Laiglesia 2009. GDP data from Penn World Tables (Feenstra, Inklaar, and Timmer 2015).
Note: PPP = purchasing power parity.

Rwanda's currently small domestic market makes it necessary for exports to be a driver of growth. There is still quite some room for improvement on this, because the country had only 69 manufacturing exporters (mostly involved in agroprocessing) in 2015 (figure 4.7). From a policy perspective, increasing integration in regional and global markets is an important objective for achieving high growth,

FIGURE 4.6 Number of formal firms and total employment in Rwanda, by type of firm, 2011–16

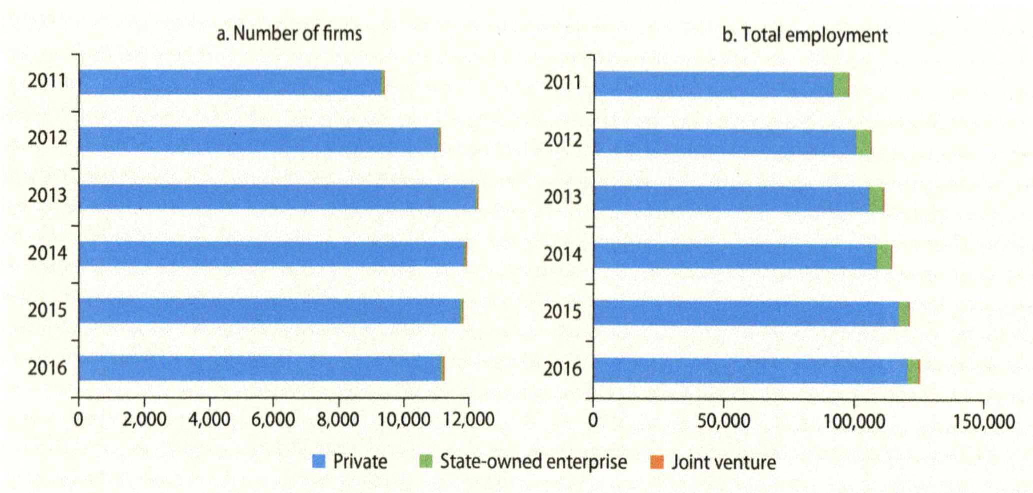

Source: Calculations based on Rwanda Revenue Authority data.

FIGURE 4.7 Number and share of exporters in Rwanda, by sector, 2015

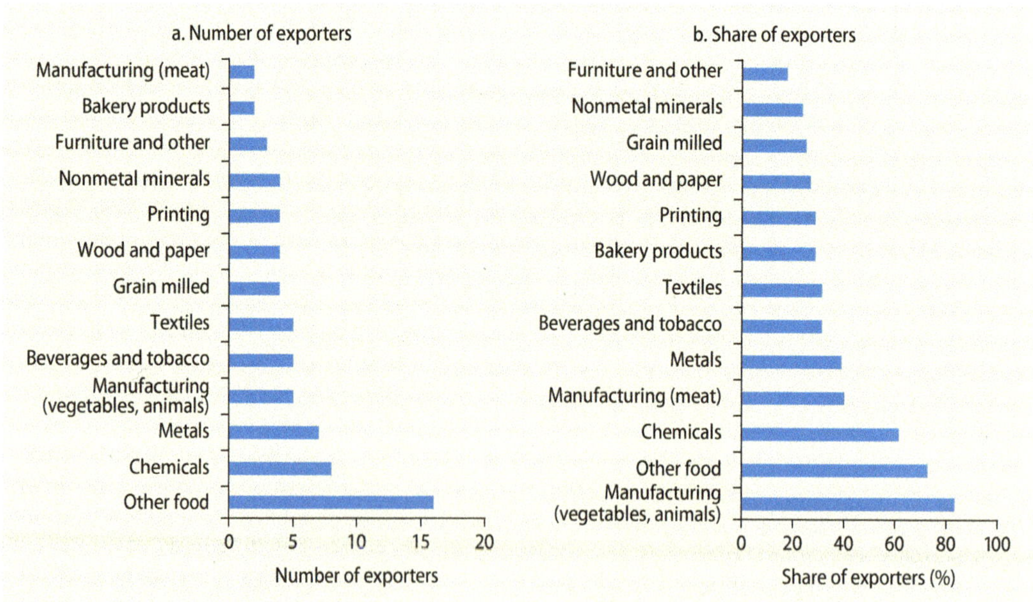

Source: Calculations based on NISR 2017.

a discussion taken up in chapter 2 of this report.

SOEs, either fully or nearly fully owned by the government or held by public-private investment groups in which government has invested along with private investors, are present in many sectors, including in air transport, financial services, agriculture, utilities, real estate, cement, services, metals, dairy, and tea holdings. In the absence of a strong private sector, SOEs have played a significant role in the enterprise sector.

They have been used to de-risk strategic sectors, paving the way for private sector entry. Under well-defined conditions, their presence can remain beneficial for future growth, if the level of competition and competitiveness of SOEs versus private firms is strategically managed. In sectors where the role of SOEs is no longer or will soon cease to be necessary, clear paths need to be drawn for the government's withdrawal, alongside efforts to build up private sector capacity.

Constraints Faced by Rwanda's Enterprise Sector

Rwanda's private sector must play a leading role in the country's drive for high growth. But the sector is generally small-scale, informal, and has a small foothold in external markets, despite the impressive set of business-friendly reforms that Rwanda has implemented. What, then, are the binding constraints faced by the private sector? Several factors, principally high costs, low economic returns, suboptimal allocation of resources, and a low capacity for innovation, impede the competitiveness of Rwanda's private enterprises.

High Costs That Undermine Competitiveness of Rwandan Enterprises

Price levels and thus input costs are high in Rwanda, which constrains the competitiveness of its enterprises. Low- and middle-income countries tend to have lower price levels than high-income economies because of the lower costs of nontradable goods and services (the prices of tradable goods tend to be similar across all countries). This divergence in prices tends to close as countries' income levels rise. Rwanda's relative prices have also followed such patterns, but at more elevated levels compared with other economies at similar stages of development. The contrast is especially stark when compared with the relative price trajectories of the Asian high-growth economies whose long-term performance Rwanda aspires to surpass (figure 4.8). It was only when these economies reached income per capita of more than US$5,000 (2010 U.S. dollars purchasing power parity) that the ratio of their price levels to those of the United States exceeded Rwanda's current ratio.

What drives Rwanda's price levels higher? In the past, high price levels partly reflected overvaluation of the Rwanda franc. That overvaluation has been corrected through depreciation of the franc over 2015–17 (IMF 2017). The high costs now stem from limited access to credit, high cost of energy generation, remaining impediments to competition, and distance to markets (by virtue of being landlocked) exacerbated by weak transport links and costly logistics (see chapter 2). There are also still some areas of improvement for Rwanda's generally well-regarded business regulations, which can lower business transaction costs indirectly.

FIGURE 4.8 Price levels and GDP per capita in Rwanda and comparator countries and economies, 2011

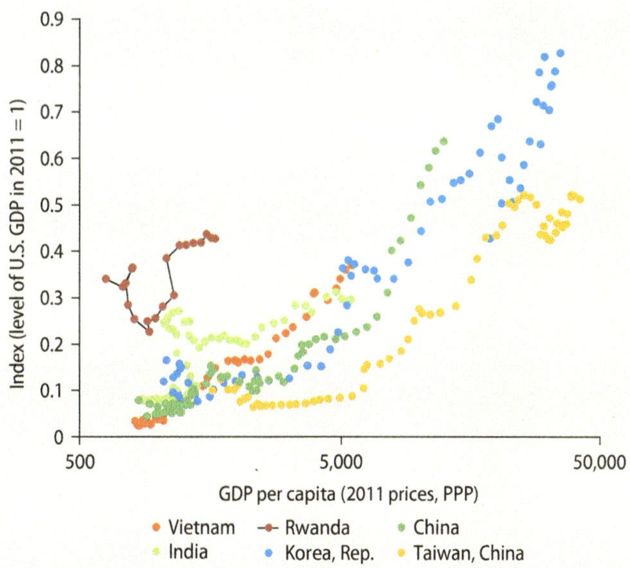

Source: Calculations based on Penn World Tables 9.0 data (Feenstra, Inklaar, and Timmer 2015).
Note: PPP = purchasing power parity.

High Cost of Finance

As in many other low- and middle-income economies, the cost of finance is high in Rwanda. With an average nominal lending rate of about 17 percent (figure 4.9), or 12 percent in real terms, borrowing costs are a constraint for many private enterprises, especially smaller ones. This reflects low domestic savings, the small size of most firms (which makes it harder for banks to recoup the fixed costs of lending), as well as higher operational costs (due to small market size and a comparatively large number of competing banks). This latter challenge becomes evident when the profitability indicators of banks in Rwanda are compared with those in neighboring countries. Because of a larger domestic market, Kenyan banks, for example, are able to reach greater economies of scale, reflected in their lower costs (table 4.1). Similarly, insurance penetration (ratio of gross written premium to GDP), also hampered by high costs and low scale, remains below 2 percent compared with 3.6 percent for the overall African insurance market.

Capital markets, which can be a vehicle for raising medium- and long-term financing, continue to grow rapidly, but they reflect similar scale, cost, and low-base issues. Stock market capitalization was estimated at about 26 percent of GDP as of end-2016, the second lowest in the East African Community (EAC). The stock market is also thinly traded, with just seven listed companies, including four local companies and three cross-listings. The bond market, introduced in 2008, is shallow. The market also lacks intermediaries (primary dealers) and is illiquid, because most investors hold securities to maturity, so there is limited presence of a secondary market. Although the size of the government primary market has increased, corporate sector participation remains limited, with only two issuances in 2016.

FIGURE 4.9 Average lending and deposit rates in Rwanda, 2000–17

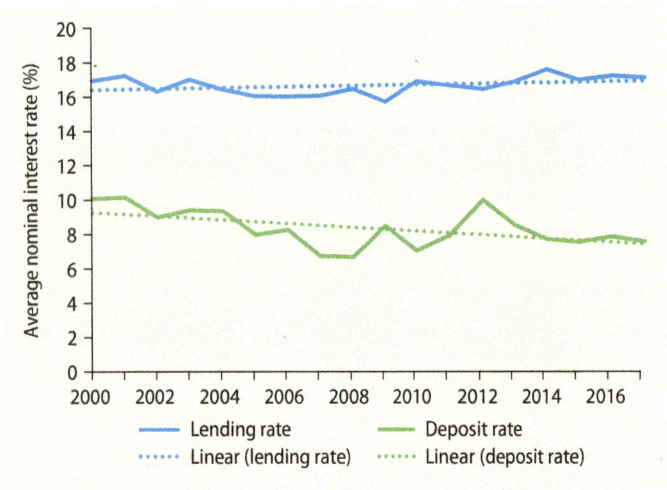

Source: National Bank of Rwanda data.

High Cost of Infrastructure

The cost of electricity in Rwanda remains high because of high unit costs for generation (about US$0.27 per kilowatt-hour in fiscal

TABLE 4.1 Efficiency and profitability of banks in Rwanda and other East African Community countries, 2013
percentages

Country	Return on assets	Return on equity	Ratio of overhead to total assets	Cost-to-income ratio	Net interest margin
Rwanda	1.8	10.5	8.3	67.7	10.3
Burundi	1.3	9.3	6.9	70.2	7.3
Kenya	3.4	21.2	5.2	50.3	8.3
Tanzania	1.6	14.0	5.8	64.1	7.5
Uganda	2.7	16.6	6.8	55.6	10.2
Expected median	1.8	17.5	4.5	58.1	6.0
Low income	1.8	16.7	5.3	62.4	6.3

Source: FinStats and Bankscope data for 2015.
Note: To ensure comparability, Bankscope figures are used for all countries in the peer comparisons. Expected median is the predicted level based on a set of country characteristics, reported by FinStats.

2016–17) (figure 4.10). The government has put in place measures to reduce the impact of high energy costs on enterprises through a subsidized rate for industrial users (US$0.11 per kilowatt-hour on average), which has fiscal implications (Kojima and Trimble 2016). There are also concerns about the access to and reliability of electricity supply. Almost a third (31.5 percent) of firms participating in the Integrated Business Enterprise Survey (IBES) reported access to reliable electricity as a major challenge (NISR 2017). These concerns are also reflected in Rwanda's ranking (68) on the "getting electricity" component of Doing Business indicators (figure 4.11).

The government has embarked on an impressive rollout of telecommunications infrastructure, which now reaches more than 90 percent of the population. It will now be important to improve affordability to ensure widespread use of the infrastructure. Looking at cost relative to gross national income per capita, mobile cellular prices amount to 10 percent, whereas fixed broadband prices amount to 166 percent (ITU 2016).

High Cost of Transport

Rwanda's landlocked geography continues to result in high transport costs. Despite sustained efforts to reduce transport costs through improved logistics and reduced time duration of transport (with a fall of 72 percent since 2013 in the time it takes for a container to reach Kigali from Dar es Salaam, for example), the average cost of moving a container from Mombasa to Kigali is US$3,633.[1]

Trade continues to rely wholly on road and air transport (discussed in more detail in chapter 2 of this report). To address this, two regional railway projects are in the pipeline. Kenya–Uganda–Rwanda (Northern Corridor) and Tanzania–Rwanda (Central Corridor) will connect Rwanda to East Africa's major ports. These projects are very complex and will require consensus on their feasibility and financing framework; in this regard, recent developments regarding the Central Corridor have been encouraging.

FIGURE 4.10 Cost of electricity in Rwanda and other Sub-Saharan African countries, 2016

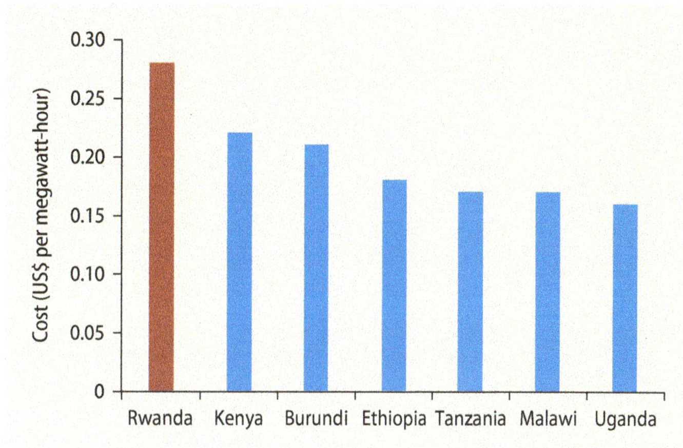

Source: Calculations based on World Bank 2016.

FIGURE 4.11 Rwanda's global rankings on Ease of Doing Business indicators

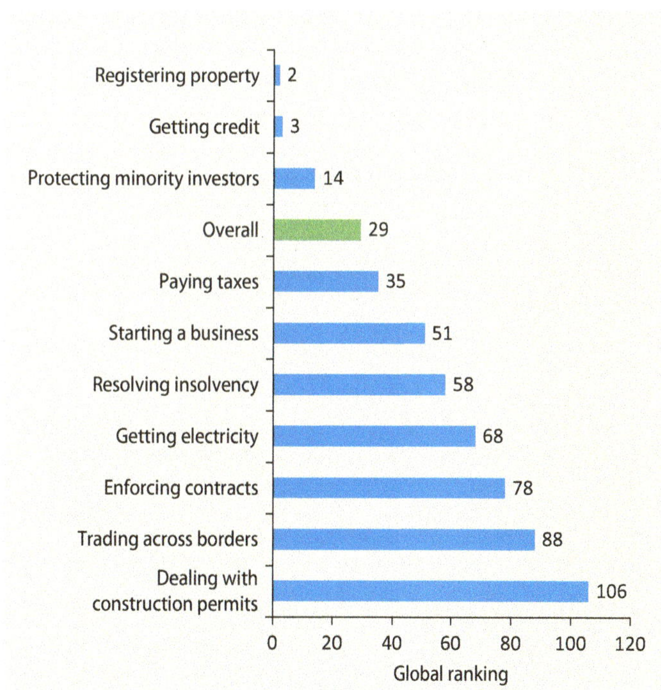

Source: World Bank 2019.

Business Regulations

Despite a high aggregate score on the Doing Business Indicators, Rwanda still has room to decrease the regulatory costs associated with starting a business, resolving insolvency, enforcing contracts, trading across borders, and obtaining construction permits and electricity connections.

Low Productivity Growth

Low returns (real and perceived) contribute to the slow uptake in private sector activity. Trends in productivity are an important indication of economywide returns. Rwanda's labor productivity (output per worker) is still relatively low (figure 4.12), explained by negative or weak growth in within-sector labor productivity across most sectors (figure 4.13). Three factors can explain this outcome:[2] slow accumulation of physical capital, slow accumulation of human capital, and low levels of total factor productivity (TFP). On the first, Rwanda's investment rate, currently at 26 percent, has been relatively healthy for a while (although investment will need to increase sharply to meet Rwanda's aspirations for growth, as discussed in the overview of this report). Therefore, physical capital accumulation does not explain Rwanda's low labor productivity. Challenges with human capital accumulation are discussed in chapter 1. Rwanda's TFP levels are low for its income (figure 4.14), which undercuts its labor productivity. TFP growth has fallen since 2008, widening the gap with other countries.

FIGURE 4.12 Labor productivity and GDP per capita in Rwanda and other countries

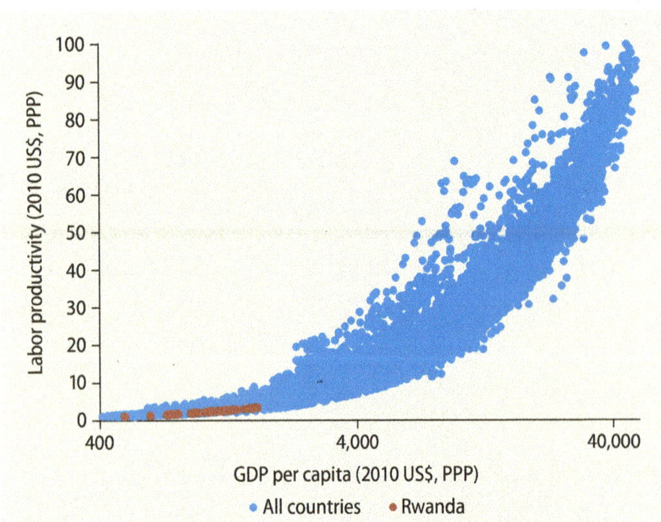

Source: Calculations based on Penn World Tables 9.0 data (Feenstra, Inklaar, and Timmer 2015).
Note: PPP = purchasing power parity.

An additional concern for Rwanda is the perception of low returns (especially among foreign investors) because of its small market size. More than half of the companies responding to a recent Investor Perception Survey cited access to national markets as a key reason to invest in Africa.[3] In a survey of potential investors in Rwanda, 40 percent cited the small market as a weakness of the country as a foreign direct investment (FDI) location—more than double any other response. Rwanda has the potential to overcome this barrier by targeting larger markets and supply chains outside its borders, an agenda discussed in chapter 2.

What explains Rwanda's weak TFP performance? A country's TFP has two key determinants. The first is the allocative efficiency of its resources (land, labor, capital)—that is, the extent to which these public and private resources get channeled to their most productive use. The second is the pace of technological innovation in the economy—that is, the pace at which the frontiers of technology and good business practices expand. The significance of technological innovation will gather pace as the Rwandan economy moves toward middle-income status and beyond, becoming an increasingly pressing subject of reform for future growth.

Resource Misallocation

Resource misallocation refers to inefficient enterprises commanding more resources (land, labor, and capital) than warranted by their productivity levels. Analysis of Rwanda's manufacturing sector suggests that TFP in Rwanda's manufacturing sector could be doubled by reallocating resources to more efficient firms (figure 4.15).[4] The scope for productivity improvements through more efficient resource allocation is likely to be even larger in other sectors: this is because it is typical to witness less dispersion between countries in TFP in the manufacturing sector than in other sectors of the economy, largely because of the sector's tradability (see annex 4A for a technical explanation). Aggregate productivity could be improved further through more efficient allocation of resources across sectors.

Decisions on public investment—accounting for more than half of total investment in the economy—need to be guided by analysis of economic returns. Rwanda has made good progress in this regard, for example in developing a robust public investment management (PIM) system, which can be applied more rigorously across priority projects. Moreover, the government's focus in its industrial policy needs to shift toward differentiating firms and sectors by performance (past or potential). Finally, remaining gaps in market institutions (as discussed in chapter 6) likely contribute to the inefficient allocation of resources.

Role of the State in Resource Allocation. Rwanda has developed a strong PIM system overall, but gaps remain, especially with respect to project selection and ex post evaluation. Moreover, the rigors of PIM are not always applied to investments undertaken by nonbudgetary public agencies (such as special investment vehicles for large infrastructure projects). Often, decisions through off-budget processes target long-term strategic priorities where expected benefits take time to materialize and can therefore be uncertain. At the same time, less than 10 percent of total investments are targeted at agriculture, where the scarcity of infrastructure is more clearly visible.

Rwanda's industrial policy involves active government interventions in many areas. The government offers firms a wide range of industrial policy incentives to develop the enterprise sector. The largest recurrent item consists of tax incentives introduced by the 2015 Investment Code, estimated at 1 percent of GDP (Bode, Lohmann, and Steenbergen 2017). Large resources have also gone into meetings, incentives, conferences, and exhibitions and the "Made in Rwanda" plan, which is in the process of scaling up. Rwanda should monitor and assess the costs

FIGURE 4.13 Average growth of labor productivity in Rwanda, by sector, 2001–16

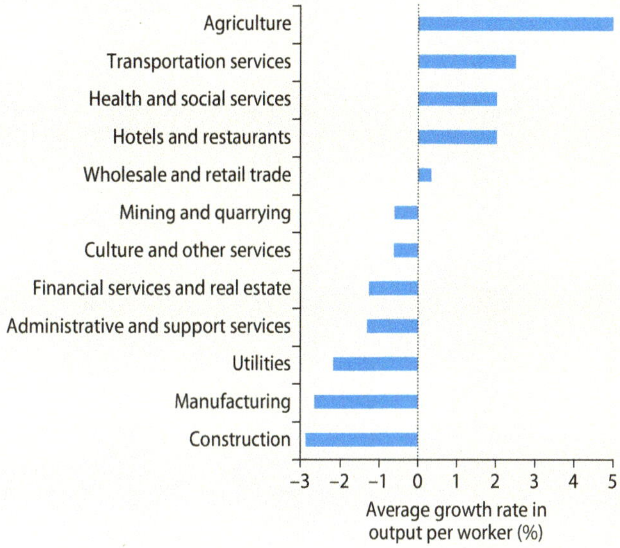

Source: Calculations based on Diao, Randriamamonjy, and Thurlow 2017.

FIGURE 4.14 Total factor productivity and GDP per capita in Rwanda and other countries

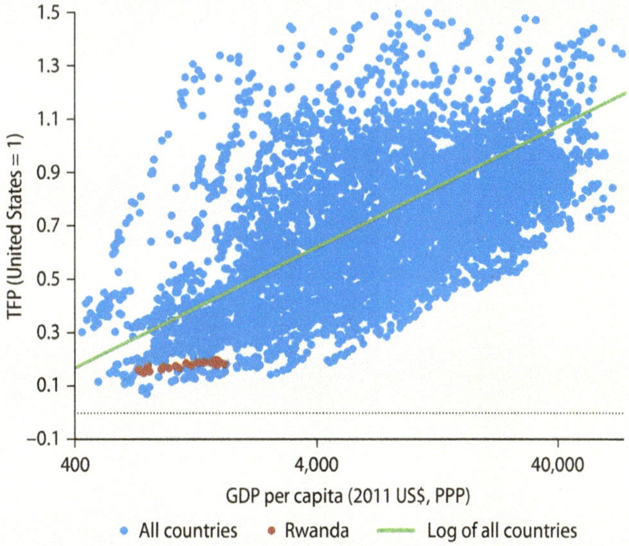

Source: Calculations based on Penn World Tables 9.0 data (Feenstra, Inklaar, and Timmer 2015).
Note: PPP = purchasing power parity; TFP = total factor productivity.

of such incentives and ensure that that these and other incentive regimes are not overlapping and are being directed toward the most efficient firms likely to increase their returns as a result of the incentives.

FIGURE 4.15 Resource misallocation in formal manufacturing in Rwanda and select countries

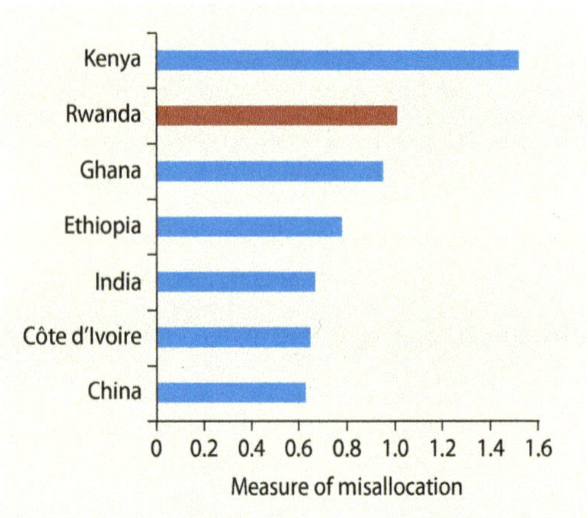

Source: Calculations based on NISR 2017.
Note: Resource misallocation is measured by the dispersion of marginal products of inputs across firms. Large dispersions suggest that frictions in input and output markets prevent the movement of productive resources across firms and that inefficient firms command more resources than warranted by their productivity.

FIGURE 4.16 Probability of receiving tax incentives in Rwanda, by size of firm revenue, 2013–16

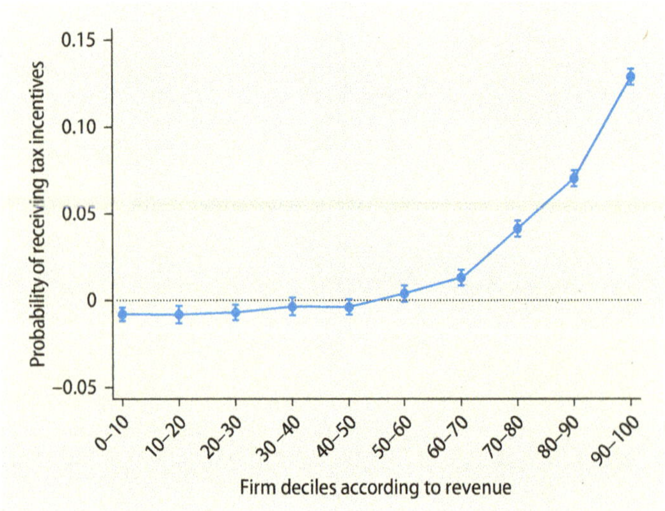

Source: Bode, Lohmann, and Steenbergen 2017.

These incentives can be made more effective in several ways. First, they appear to prioritize export promotion and import substitution activities equally. Past attempts at import substitution, for the most part, have led countries down the path of inefficiency and low growth, with the lost decade of the 1980s for Latin America as a good example. A stronger focus on firm productivity, scale, and export promotion in areas aligned with the country's comparative advantages would be more rewarding for Rwanda, just as it was for the high-growth East Asian economies.

Second, as part of industrial policy, fiscal incentives are granted to a range of sectors rather than built around performance criteria targeting successful firms. For example, all manufacturing firms are uniformly given value added tax exemptions regardless of performance. Accelerated depreciation is similarly available for any substantial capital investment, while electricity subsidies are available to any industrial user.

Tax incentives are expansive. Figure 4.16 shows the probability of receiving tax incentives, broken down by firm size. The larger the firm, the higher the likelihood of receiving tax incentives; firms in the bottom 50 percent of the revenue distribution have a negative likelihood of receiving tax incentives. Figure 4.17 compares the sectoral composite annual growth rate (in revenue) with the amount of tax incentives as a share of revenue between 2010 and 2016. Sectors like information and communication technology (ICT), financial services, construction, and manufacturing receive a disproportionate share of tax incentives; but these sectors have also grown less quickly in terms of overall revenue.

Further, current incentives are not necessarily targeted optimally across firms: only about a third of expenditures go to firms whose investment decisions are likely influenced by the incentives (for current purposes, these are firms whose rate of return on investment without the incentives was between 10 and 20 percent) (table 4.2). At the same time, 28 percent of all incentives are given to firms that would have achieved high rates of return on investment (in excess of 20 percent) even without the incentives. Similarly, 38 percent of the incentives go to firms that achieved low returns (below 10 percent) even after benefitting from the incentives. These failing firms (roughly half of which had negative returns) are unlikely to survive under normal market conditions, with or without the tax incentives.

Resource Misallocation Caused by Shortcomings in Market Institutions. Resource allocation through market signals is efficient only to the extent that the signals are generated in competitive and well-regulated markets. Despite having made major gains in the past 20 years, Rwanda still faces several challenges in this regard. Its factor markets and core market institutions for competition and contract and property rights enforcement are still in an early stage of development and face a significant agenda for further reform (discussed in chapter 6).

Technological Innovation

Rwanda is in the early stages of building its innovation capacity, which is the ability to introduce new products, processes, ideas, technologies, and solutions. It needs to continue strengthening firm capabilities for productivity-led growth to meet its long-term income ambitions. Although structural transformation and improved allocation of resources can stimulate labor productivity growth for another decade or so, sustaining it over a longer period will only be possible through innovation and technology diffusion. The strong positive correlation between a country's innovation capacity and its TFP illustrates this point (figure 4.18). Global technological advancements have raised the stakes even more

FIGURE 4.17 Sectoral revenue growth and tax incentives in Rwanda, 2010–16

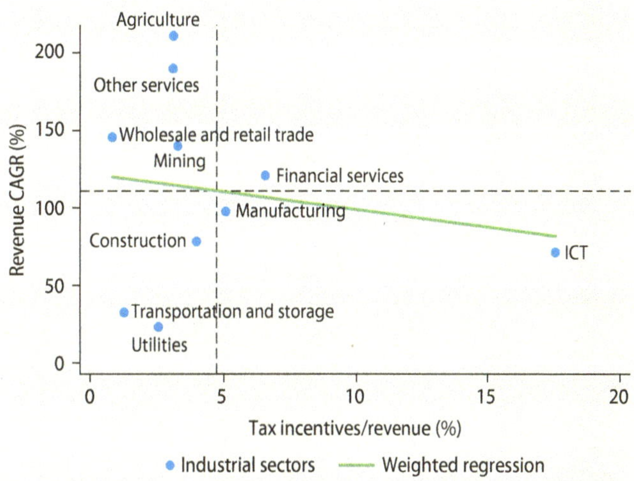

Source: Bode, Lohmann, and Steenbergen 2017.
Note: CAGR = compound annual growth rate; ICT = information and communication technology.

TABLE 4.2 Share of total tax revenue for firms, by return on investment with and without incentives
% of total tax revenue

ROI with incentives (%)	ROI without incentives (%): All firms < 0	All firms 0–10	All firms 10–20	All firms > 20	FDI firms < 0	FDI firms 0–10	FDI firms 10–20	FDI firms > 20	Domestic firms < 0	Domestic firms 0–10	Domestic firms 10–20	Domestic firms > 20
< 0	21.0				14.8				22.5			
0–10	13.8	3.2			0.0	2.8			17.7	2.6		
10–20	0.4	6.8	16.9		0.0	2.7	0.1		8.2	0.2	20.5	
> 20	5.2	0.0	4.8	27.8	0.0	0.0	4.3	75.2	6.4	0.8	4.7	16.2

Source: Steenbergen and von Uexkull 2018.
Note: ROI = return on investment; FDI = foreign direct investment. Yellow: unviable incentives (firm is still not profitable with tax incentives). Green: marginal firms (effective tax incentives). Orange: redundant incentives (firm is profitable even without tax incentives).

for Rwanda (and other low- and middle-income countries), by revolutionizing the world economy and presenting major opportunities and challenges that need to be managed proactively (box 4.2).

FIGURE 4.18 Correlation between innovation capacity and total factor productivity

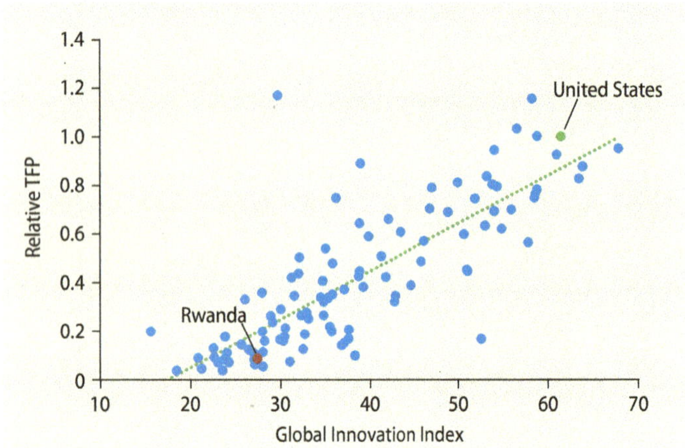

Sources: Cornell University, INSEAD, and WIPO 2017; Jones 2016. Total factor productivity (TFP) is computed for 2010 using Penn World Tables 8.0 data (Feenstra, Inklaar, and Timmer 2015).
Note: TFP is calculated as labor-augmenting. TFP = 1 for the United States.

Developing the capacity to innovate is not an overnight endeavor; it requires an ecosystem that takes decades to develop. It involves sustained investments to cultivate and upgrade a dynamic private sector by building higher-order human capital (chapter 1) and a general societal and institutional openness to new ideas, learning, and risk taking (chapter 6). An effective NIS—an ecosystem for innovation—is needed to ensure strong uptake of learning, innovation, and technology diffusion from both the demand and the supply sides. Countries have found the NIS framework to be a useful conceptual anchor for developing and implementing innovation policies and for building the necessary infrastructure and institutions (box 4.3).

The good news is that the innovation capacity of Rwandan firms has been on an upward trend, as reflected in Rwanda's global rankings. For example, on the Global Innovation Index, Rwanda moved from 112 in 2013 to 99 (out of 126) in 2017 (figure 4.19). That improvement made

BOX 4.2 The global context and technological transformation

The world is undergoing a significant technological transformation. Some are calling it the fourth industrial revolution, or Industry 4.0, while others see it as a continuation of the information and communication technology revolution. This new industrial revolution is characterized by the adoption of cyber-physical systems such as robotics and drones, three-dimensional printing, artificial intelligence, and machine learning across all sectors of the economy, reshaping both the way in which and where production is done.

Industry 4.0 has the potential to make a large impact on employment and income distribution (Autor and Dorn 2013; Frey and Osborne 2016). This impact is already becoming apparent, with robotics and artificial intelligence enabling the reshoring of advanced manufacturing (as well as services) to mature economies, although typically with fewer jobs that require more sophisticated skill sets (Acemoglu and Restrepo 2017; Ford 2015). These technologies also create new complementarities across sectors (for example, manufacturing, agriculture, and services) that open up new areas of comparative advantage for both high-income and low- and middle-income economies. These complementarities create both opportunities and important challenges for Rwanda, as well as other low- and middle-income economies, as traditional labor cost advantages become less relevant with advanced automation and manufacturing (Cirera, Frias, and Hill 2017).

In the low- and middle-income world, benefits thus far have been most visible in East Asia, where countries have accelerated economic growth by harnessing technological advancements to evolving opportunities in global trade. Other parts of the world—Sub-Saharan Africa in particular—would do well to learn from the Asian responses, including by upgrading their technological and innovation capacity.

BOX 4.3 The national innovation system

In its most basic sense, the national innovation system (NIS) encompasses an ecosystem of organizations and policies that allow workers and firms to produce in new and better ways, continuously adding knowledge to products (figure B4.3.1).

On the supply side of NIS are institutions that generate knowledge to feed the innovation process. These institutions include universities, research institutes, technology centers, business development providers, skills providers, small and medium enterprise support services, and domestic and foreign firms that generate knowledge. For low- and middle-income countries, innovation for the most part consists of adopting (localizing) and applying existing knowledge and technology, largely generated in higher-income countries.

On the demand side of NIS are firms that apply new knowledge to business and production activities in order to generate economic and commercial returns. High returns are necessary incentives for firms to continue their quest for the best available knowledge and technology, including by investing in the necessary managerial and human capital capabilities.

But to engage in innovation activity, firms need an enabling environment that includes effective institutions and infrastructure to support the NIS and sound innovation policies. Other necessary complementary factors include availability of skills, access to technology and finance, competition, economies of scale, favorable conditions for business, and good managerial and organizational practices.

FIGURE B4.3.1 The national innovation system as an ecosystem for economywide innovation

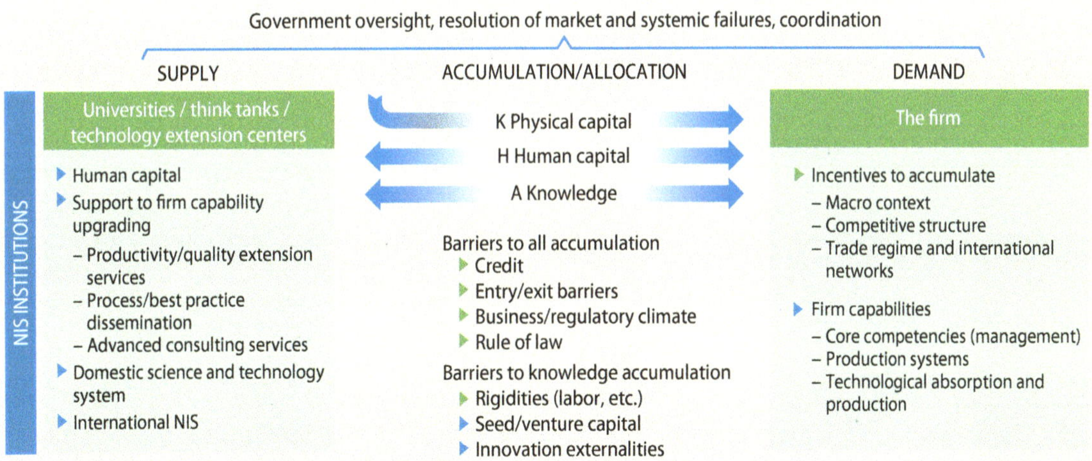

Source: Maloney 2017.
Note: NIS = national innovation system.

Rwanda the best-performing low-income country, with some of the subindicators not far from the top performer in Africa (South Africa), though still some distance from Switzerland (the top performer in the world) (figure 4.20). The 2017–18 Global Competitiveness Index similarly ranked Rwanda 44 (out of 137) on a measure of innovation, ahead of many Asian and Latin American economies. Yet in some areas Rwanda appears to be doing less well, especially in areas related to knowledge and technological readiness (figure 4.20). This ranking can be traced to gaps in human

FIGURE 4.19 Ranking of Rwanda and other East African Community countries on the Global Innovation Index, 2013 and 2017

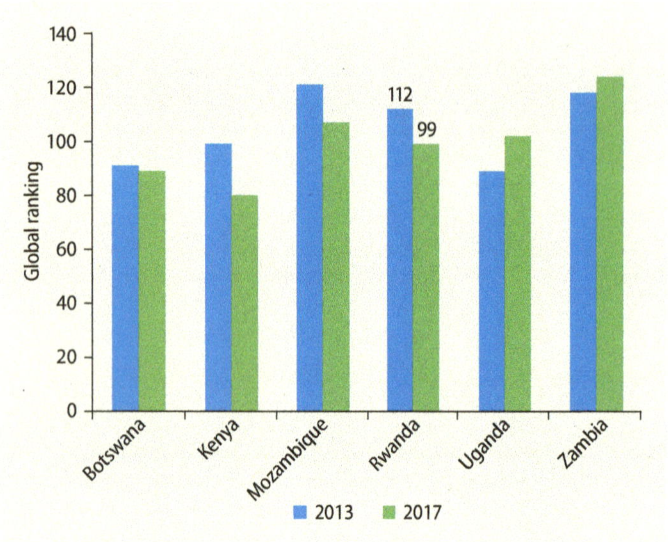

Sources: Cornell University, INSEAD, and WIPO 2013, 2017.
Note: Ranking is out of 140 countries.

FIGURE 4.20 Frontier of innovation capacity in Rwanda, South Africa, and Switzerland

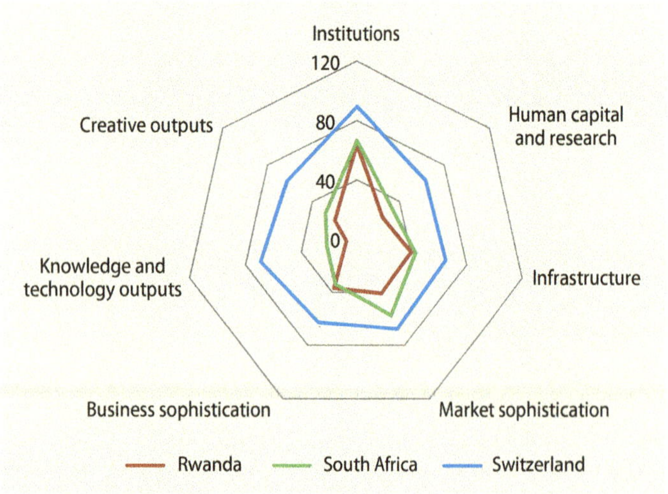

Sources: Cornell University, INSEAD, and WIPO 2013, 2017.
Note: Main components of the Global Innovation Index.

capital and research (chapter 1), as well as to low levels of knowledge creation and technology outputs (for example, number of patents and number of scientific and technical publications per unit of GDP), ICT infrastructure, and creative outputs (for example, industrial designs and online creativity).

Demand for Innovation

The demand side of Rwanda's NIS is composed of a small universe of firms that are mostly informal, small-scale enterprises, as highlighted earlier. As a result, Rwandan firms, for the most part, are not yet strong demanders of innovation. Demand for innovation is hampered by low capabilities for innovation among firms (even larger ones), which generally do not utilize the quality of research being done in the country (figure 4.21, panel a). The capabilities gap relative to other countries also is reflected in the low number of patent applications per capita (figure 4.21, panel b). However, Rwanda has made significant progress in increasing the number of trademarks that originate from the country (figure 4.22).[5] This increase was mostly on account of nonresidents, underscoring the importance of importing external talent. Low firm capabilities stem from skills constraints and shortfalls in management practices (PSF 2013). Almost 20 percent of firms report that access to skills is a constraint to their business (NISR 2017). Large businesses report more constraints regarding access to skills than do small businesses.

Innovation is also hampered by the scarcity of links with foreign firms and export markets (chapter 2). FDI is another important external source of technological catch-up. FDI inflows to Rwanda have risen in recent years, but they are concentrated mostly in the nontradable sectors, where the scope for technology transfers can be limited.

Supply of Innovation

The supply side of Rwanda's innovation system is only beginning to emerge and will have to address two key challenges: (1) a skilled workforce and (2) the quality and relevance of research and advanced training (see chapter 1 for details).

FIGURE 4.21 Quality of research institutions and number of patent applications in Rwanda and other countries

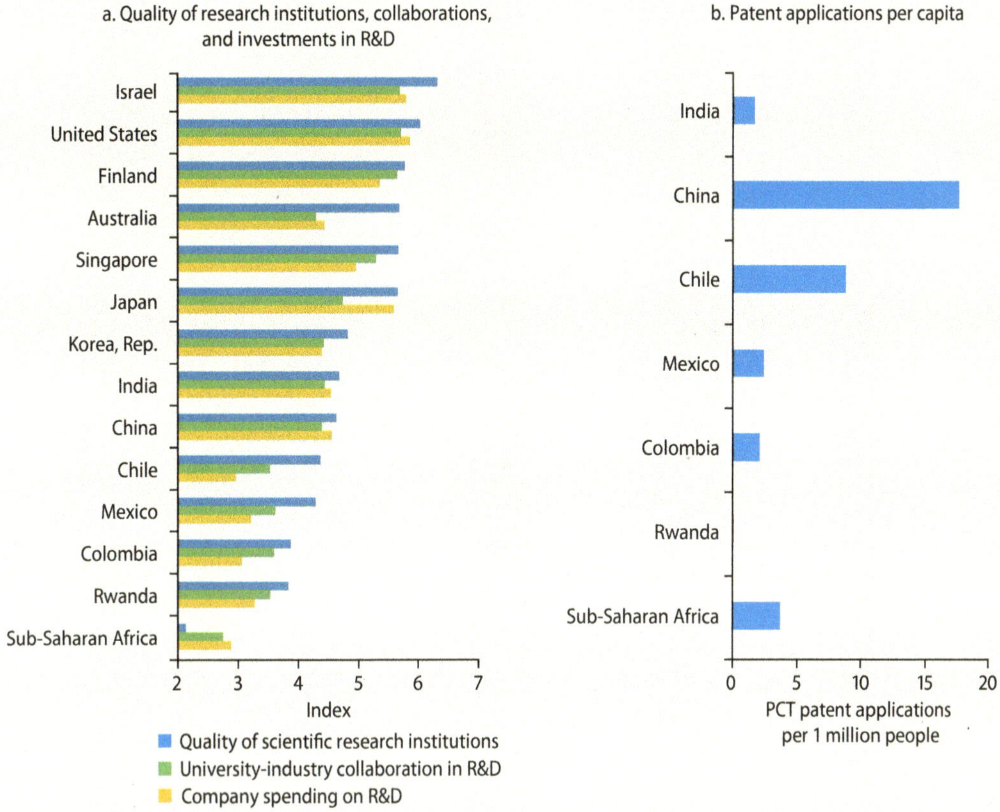

Source: World Economic Forum 2017.

Note: The quality of research institutions assesses the prevalence and standing of private and public research institutions, calculated as the sum of the inverse ranks of all research institutions of a country included in the SCImago Institutions Rankings. Collaboration in R&D is the average score on the World Economic Forum's Executive Opinion Survey (1–7) on the question: In your country, to what extent do business and universities collaborate on R&D (1 = not at all; 7 = to a great extent)? Investments in R&D are the expenditure on research and development as a percentage of GDP. Patent applications are the total number of patent families filed in at least two of the five major offices in the world, from the PATSTAT database (EPO, various years). EPO = European Patent Office; PCT = Patent Cooperation Treaty; R&D = research and development.

The Enabling Environment for Innovation

An effective innovation system also involves an enabling environment that allows the demand and supply sides to interact efficiently. The factors that shape the enabling environment include protection of intellectual property rights, quality ICT and other infrastructure, availability of start-up finance, and the overall business climate. Rwanda's performance on these measures has shown strong improvements. On intellectual property rights, the 2009 law is in line with good practices established by the World Intellectual Property Organization. Tighter implementation is now the key. The Rwanda Standards Board was established in 2013 to provide standardization services. It is a quality institution that is well regarded by investors and consumers at home and abroad, providing a comparative advantage to Rwanda.

FIGURE 4.22 Number of trademark applications and registrations in Rwanda, 2001–15

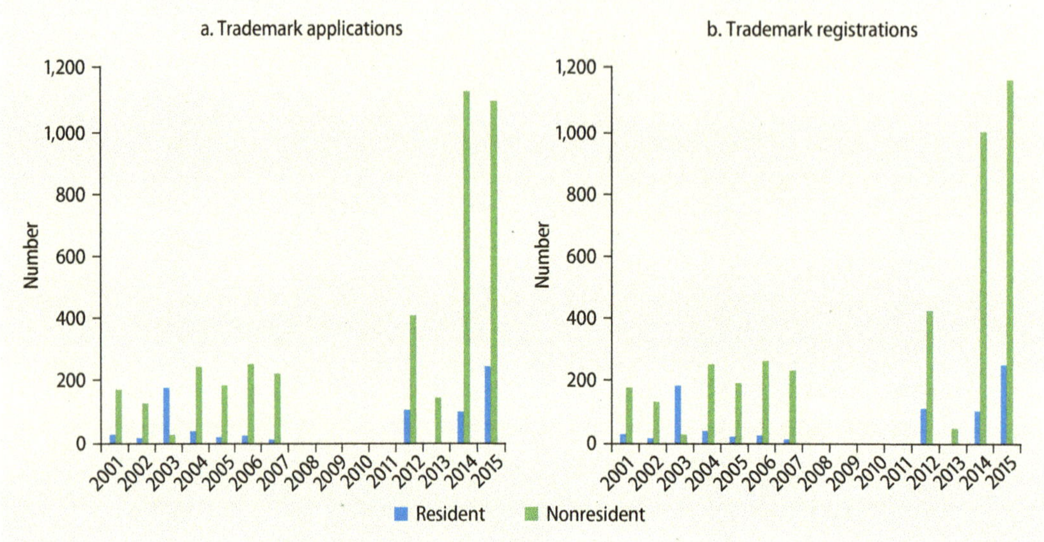

Source: WIPO 2017.
Note: No information is available on patent applications between 2008 and 2011.

Government has made substantial investments in ICT infrastructure, but continued efforts are needed to upgrade the quality (and uptake) of ICT infrastructure. ICT infrastructure needs to be high-speed, reliable, available, and accessible, and continued investments are required to improve bandwidth and infrastructure reliability. The Networked Readiness Index is a comprehensive composite index that assesses a country's "preparedness to reap the benefits of emerging technologies and to capitalize on the opportunities presented by the digital revolution and beyond" (World Economic Forum, INSEAD, and Cornell University 2016). Rwanda performs least well in readiness (115) and is ranked 106 in infrastructure. In terms of digital infrastructure, Rwanda is lagging because of the lack of investment and inadequate metropolitan and last-mile access networks. The high cost of broadband lines, combined with low computer ownership and an erratic supply of electricity, put the service beyond the reach of most private users.

Reform Agenda for Reaching Upper-Middle-Income Levels

Emergence of a vibrant, competitive, and innovation-driven enterprise sector—both private and public firms—that responds with agility to emerging domestic, regional, and global opportunities is essential for future growth. Private enterprises create jobs and generate incomes, drive economic transformation, compete in global export markets, and, ultimately, drive aggregate productivity growth and innovation. Moreover, the private sector will have to provide much of the huge investment needed to support future growth ambitions, because public investment is already at the limits set by financing options. Efforts to boost private investment need to be accompanied by measures to scale up domestic savings. Ongoing efforts to boost long-term savings are crucial in this regard (box 4.4).

The state will have an equally important, but complementary, role to play in correcting various (clearly identified)

BOX 4.4 Rwanda's Long-Term Saving Scheme: Opportunities and challenges

The Long-Term Saving Scheme went into effect in 2018. What its impact on household savings will be is still unclear. Because of the large proportion of Rwandan workers whose income varies significantly throughout the year or who work in the informal sector, participation is not mandatory. Rwandans will need to be sensitized on the benefits of this type of scheme; otherwise savings could be suboptimal.

Using public commitment as an incentive can be useful. When people make a public commitment to how much they will save, they are more likely to save (Gugerty 2005); self-help peer groups increase the number of deposits in a formal savings account 3.5-fold and almost double the average savings balance (Kast, Meier, and Pomeranz 2012). This approach may work for Rwanda because of widespread respect for authority, the importance of reputation, and the informal nature of most people's work. Using *umuganda*—the last Saturday of each month when Rwandans between 18 and 65 come together to do a variety of public works such as infrastructure development and environmental protection—could provide behavioral economic insights to increase the savings rate. The government could recommend a range of savings rates per income group per month. In monthly *umuganda* meetings, people could contribute the money they committed to saving into a savings scheme, which could be attached to the Long-Term Saving Scheme. This type of policy allows people to make an (informed) choice about their actions and nudges them in a positive direction with the understanding that they know their own choices best. Thus, the costs of failing to meet the savings target should simply be the knowledge of falling short. A heavier sanction—for example, some degree of social ostracism—would undermine the policy.

Policy makers also may wish to consider other complementary measures to boost savings. One approach would be to adjust macroprudential regulations for the banking sector to discourage households from overborrowing for consumption. In 2014, more than 70 percent of the population had an outstanding loan or had repaid a loan within the past 12 months. Only one-third of households with loans reported borrowing for investment or education-related expenses, including buying agricultural equipment or inputs or expanding a business, while two-thirds of households reported borrowing for consumption (NISR 2016).

Source: MINECOFIN.

market failures and defining its role in private investment—by implementing well-targeted public investments, strengthening bureaucratic capacity, withdrawing gradually from productive activity while enhancing its regulatory and facilitating functions, and developing capable and accountable market institutions. Public investments will remain important for several years to come, given the vast infrastructural and social needs of the country; that said, with growing financing needs under the First National Strategy of Transformation and tightening limits on public borrowing, the relative share of public investment will decline over time as the share of private investment increases. SOEs will also remain crucial for several years to come, as the private sector needs time to build.

The policy response will have four main elements:

1. Strengthening the overall business environment by continuing to tackle key cross-cutting constraints (such as finance and other backbone services, infrastructure, and market institutions)
2. Improving the effectiveness of the government's tax incentives and other industrial policy interventions by shifting from general support to performance-based targeting of successful enterprises

3. Defining the future role of SOEs, clarifying their objectives, and improving their corporate governance
4. Building an NIS to support effective uptake of innovation from both the demand and supply sides

Reduce Business Costs by Tackling Cross-Cutting Constraints

Rwanda has made substantial progress toward reforms that improve the business environment, and the government has put in place a variety of programs to provide support for firms. Nevertheless, more effort is needed in three key areas: (1) developing the financial sector and other backbone services, (2) building accessible and affordable infrastructure, and (3) strengthening market institutions and fiscal prudence.

Develop the Financial Sector and Other Backbone Services

Development of modern services (including finance) is crucial for competitiveness and long-term growth. A country's service sector typically grows in size (relative to GDP) and complexity as its income level rises. But income is not the only factor at play. Structural characteristics such as the quality of institutions and the urbanization rate of the country also matter. For example, in India services that were the most underdeveloped were also the most heavily regulated (Eichengreen and Gupta 2010). Countries with better institutions have larger and more dynamic service sectors (Amin and Mattoo 2008). Relatively slow urbanization has been identified as a reason why the service sector has developed more slowly in China than in India (Wu 2007).

Rwanda has been actively developing its service sector, an emphasis that will remain important for the foreseeable future. An efficient service sector not only makes direct contributions to a country's GDP and export capabilities but also serves as an important input to manufacturing and agriculture. High-value-added segments of value chains are especially rich in services content—services supply the majority of added value within value chains—which calls for policies that emphasize developing a strong financial sector (discussed below), developing other professional services (chapter 2), and building the skills base (chapter 1).

Rwanda's financial sector has taken important strides toward better serving the economy's growing complexity and needs. Apart from banks and other deposit-taking institutions, insurance companies, pension funds, and other nonbank financial institutions have established a presence and are providing an expanding range of products and services, including for payments, savings, credit, insurance, and retirement products, with different levels of sophistication and innovation.[6] The positive trends are visible in several financial sector indicators. For example, in 2016, 89 percent of adults had an account at a financial institution, compared with 72 percent in 2012 and far higher than comparator countries in the region. Private sector credit equaled 15.7 percent of GDP as of end-2016, a four-point increase over 2009, but the ratio remains on the low side. Strong progress has been made in the use of electronic payments and mobile banking. As of end-2016, more than 9.7 million users had subscribed to mobile payment systems, nearly 1 million users had subscribed to mobile banking services, and the value of total e-payments had risen to more than 30 percent of GDP within five years.

The banking sector's assets have almost tripled in nominal terms since 2008, as existing banks have grown larger and several new ones have entered. The rising presence of foreign-owned commercial banks (which accounted for 46 percent of banking sector assets as of end-2016) reflects the increasing attractiveness of the Rwandan market to foreign investors, particularly from within the EAC. In an especially welcome move, some foreign banks have started to cover underserved market segments (low-income households and small and medium enterprises [SMEs]) using innovative lending techniques (such as cash-flow-based lending and agent banking).[7] The National Bank of Rwanda (BNR) and the government have played an important role in this regard by providing an accommodating legal and regulatory framework and business environment.

Despite these positive developments, several challenges remain, reflecting the low base and small size of financial institutions and the high costs of finance. Rwandan enterprises often cite limited access to and high cost of long-term finance among their key challenges. The lack of adequate long-term financing is a key concern, which may have been exacerbated in recent years by the crowding-out impact of the rise in lending to large-scale infrastructure or hospitality projects (often backed by sovereign guarantees). The rise in large exposures in the banking sector may be an indirect indicator of this phenomenon (table 4.3).

Although Rwanda's banking sector is sound on a systemwide basis, on the basis of typical stability indicators, the sector's liquidity, efficiency, and profitability indicators should be monitored carefully. As of March 2017, capital in the sector was well above regulatory requirements, and balance sheet vulnerabilities from liabilities denominated in foreign currency were low (BNR 2016). But the ratio of nonperforming loans to gross loans has been on the rise, increasing from 6.2 percent in December 2015 to 8.1 percent in March 2017, albeit still lower than that of regional peers.[8] Indicators of banking sector efficiency (cost-to-income ratio, overhead-to-income ratio) and profitability (return on assets, return on equity) have stagnated or declined over the last two years, which may indicate the limitations of efficiency gains in the context of a small economy, increased competition from new market entrants, or a more challenging economic environment.

Sustained reforms in the financial sector will remain important for Rwanda's high-growth ambitions. The backdrop of shrinking external assistance raises the stakes even more, because it requires Rwanda to mobilize more domestic resources and use them more efficiently. Moreover, only long-term finance (defined as maturities of at least five years or stable financing sources with no specific maturity) can effectively substitute for development assistance.

Four key areas are on the reform agenda to alleviate long-term financing constraints.

Preserve and Strengthen the Stability and Performance of the Financial Sector. The success of the financial sector as a catalyst for Rwanda's ambitious growth aspirations is contingent on its ability to sustain and consolidate its role as an efficient and reliable provider of financial services. The rapid growth of the sector has realized demonstrable results, but also revealed vulnerabilities that need to be monitored and mitigated. The need to address these vulnerabilities holds for all parts of the financial sector, from banking to pensions, insurance, and capital market. Investors are attracted to markets that are sound, stable, and efficient, including a stable macroeconomic framework.

The government, through the National Bank of Rwanda, has undertaken major

TABLE 4.3 Large exposures in the banking sector in Rwanda, 2015–17

	2015				2016				2017
Indicator	**March**	**June**	**September**	**December**	**March**	**June**	**September**	**December**	**March**
Insider loans to core capital	2.1	2.8	3.0	4.0	3.1	3.5	3.6	2.3	4.4
Large exposures to core capital	86.0	107.2	98.6	112.6	99.2	122.7	141.0	154.2	166.8
Large exposures to gross loans	20.1	22.5	20.9	23.4	22.6	26.5	29.9	31.7	33.1

Source: National Bank of Rwanda data.

reforms of the legal and regulatory framework for the financial sector, including strengthening the system to deal with a financial crisis, if one were to occur. These reforms will enable Rwanda to become a more attractive destination for local, regional, and international investments. Underpinning these developments is the need for financial education and awareness to build a culture supportive of long-term savings and investment. A sound debt management policy, already in place in Rwanda, is similarly important to proactively identify and mitigate debt risks. Fiscal and industrial policies also have a role; tax breaks and other policy incentives for investments in strategic sectors would need to be balanced better against the objectives of financial stability and fiscal sustainability.

Broaden the Base of Institutional Investors. Institutional investors are an important source of long-term financing, yet the base of institutional investors is quite narrow in Rwanda (as in the rest of the EAC). In 2014, institutional investors had about US$1.05 billion in assets, which was less than the net overseas development assistance received by the country that year. Although some of these funds were invested in long-term projects, a more efficient allocation of the remaining funds could contribute to the investment needs of the country.

Supporting the Rwanda Social Security Board (RSSB), for example, in strengthening its investment policy and fund management is a necessary precursor to establishing a larger base of institutional investors. Rwanda is still at an early stage of reforming its predominantly public pension sector with the establishment of a new regulatory regime and other measures aimed at strengthening the management and governance of the institution. The RSSB's fund management capacity also requires further strengthening. Investments in equity have grown over time, but they need to be more diversified. At the same time, the investments need to be commensurate with the risk profile of the RSSB. Because the RSSB is responsible for managing all public pension funds, it has to ensure that the funds are kept safe and, at the same time, earn a sufficient return.

A modern insurance sector will be able to play its part in strengthening the investor base. The split-up of the composite insurers[9] is increasing the demand for longer-term investments, a trend that will only grow over time. It is also expected that longer-term savings products will become more widely available as new market entrants offer different product menus. The to-be-introduced risk-based approach to regulation and supervision also will encourage insurers to diversify their investments and invest in assets with better credit ratings and liquidity. This approach could increase the demand for government and corporate bonds as well as encourage banks to seek credit ratings, which would help to develop the market further.

Deepen Regional Market Integration. Tapping into regional sources of funding will be a necessary complement to domestic resources, given the limited size of the domestic financial market. Global experience shows that smaller countries tend to benefit more from regional integration by leveraging the position of the largest market in the region to create advantages of greater scale, efficiency, and visibility with institutional investors.

Reducing barriers and costs to attract a wider range of investors will require action at the regional (EAC) level. The 2014 EAC Common Market Scorecard calls for a significant rollback of laws, regulations, and investment codes that impede and limit the benefits from regional investment. There is a need to address several gaps in the legislation and regulations of partner states regarding trading in securities and derivatives and to develop regional market intermediaries. Wagh, Lovegrove, and Kashangaki (2012) mention five other key priorities for regional integration of financial markets:

1. *Harmonizing the legal and regulatory frameworks.* The EAC still faces differential tax regimes and

regulatory discrepancies. Further aligning supervisory frameworks and reporting requirements is also important.

2. *Adopting a single-licensing regime and mutual recognition among regulators.* Single licensing can reduce cross-border transaction costs and barriers to entry and should be made available for banks, brokers, and insurance companies. Single licensing should be accompanied by mutual recognition among regulators, converging around international principles (for example, Basel agreements).
3. *Building up regionally compatible financial infrastructure.* Critical parts of national financial infrastructure need to be compatible at the regional level, including central securities depositories and trading platforms for national exchanges.
4. *Strengthening cross-border supervisory practices.* Consolidated supervision is important to ensure that weaknesses in one financial institution do not put the regional financial system at risk.
5. *Strengthening data gathering.* Information on current volumes of cross-border trade in financial products is often incomplete or inaccurate. Data gaps limit the possibilities for supervision, while also obscuring the extent of cross-border links (thus hiding the potential opportunities from regional integration). These issues are compounded by high volumes of unrecorded informal trade and the widespread use of physical cash. Stronger capacity for data collection and analysis would be beneficial both at the national level and for the EAC Secretariat.

Although the EAC Council of Ministers has set out several key directives that would increase the regional scope of financial laws and regulations, little progress has been made in the last few years (EABC 2016). Using a presidential forum to fast-track these initiatives could help to transform this sector, which is critical for Rwanda's development.

Attract Finance beyond the Region. The success of the International Finance Corporation's (IFC's) *umuganda* bond[10] demonstrated that the Rwandan capital market can facilitate long-term, local-currency financing from beyond the region. The bond helped to attract attention to the Rwandan market and may entice other potential issuers to follow suit. The IFC issue considerably increased the value of nongovernment bonds outstanding and contributed to building the capacity of regulators, market intermediaries, and investors in Rwanda. The regulatory framework for nongovernment bond issuance is considered supportive, but more work is needed to develop a pipeline of credible issuers (including subnational issuers) and build a credit culture and capacity among investors.

Build Accessible and Affordable Infrastructure

Expanding and improving infrastructure are key priorities for Rwanda. Public investments have greatly improved Rwanda's infrastructure and service delivery. To ensure the successful upgrading of the country's infrastructure for meeting the demands of the next phase of sustained growth, effective planning and prioritization of infrastructure and efficient allocation of infrastructure financing resources (public, donor, and private) will be required. Four reform priorities are important in this regard.

Strengthen the Public Investment Framework for Infrastructure. Rwanda's national PIM system establishes the processes and benchmarks to assess trade-offs and prioritizes among public investment opportunities. To improve it further, the first imperative is to continue strengthening the public investment planning process to prioritize public infrastructure spending, select appropriate structures and financing sources, and manage multiyear fiscal commitments and financial implications that can materialize in the medium to long term. This would help to achieve a better balance between long-term strategic priorities and areas where returns are more clearly identified. The second imperative is to broaden the coverage of the PIM framework to include public nonbudgetary investments. Rwanda's strengths in PIM need to be extended to budgetary agencies, to eliminate any potential risks of misallocation. The third imperative is to prioritize ex post evaluation and external audit, while further strengthening the cost management framework. These issues are discussed in more detail in chapter 6.

Leverage Private Finance in Support of Infrastructure Investment. Rwanda has had mixed experience with implementing public-private partnership projects.[11] On the one hand, 39 projects that can be broadly defined as public-private partnerships (PPPs) have already been implemented: 29 in the energy sector, 3 in ICT projects, 1 in manufacturing, and 6 in mining. On the other hand, these transactions were processed on a project-by-project basis, outside of a dedicated PPP law and were procured under sector-specific or project-specific laws that are designed for traditional public procurement processes and lack the detailed multistage, PPP-specific processes that can ensure transparency and competitiveness (box 4.5).

The following recommendations are intended to strengthen the PPP framework:

- Finalize and approve the PPP guidelines to create the enabling framework for PPPs.
- Develop a PPP pipeline via a clearly defined project-screening process.
- Develop a fiscal commitments and contingent liabilities framework and ensure that the long-term sustainability and management of the government's financial commitments to PPPs are integrated into the current medium-term debt management strategy.
- Clarify accounting and budgetary treatment of PPPs to enable the government to deliver long-term financial commitments to PPPs (which is not possible under the current framework).
- Prepare municipal PPP guidelines to facilitate the development of municipal-level PPP projects.
- Design and deliver a communications strategy to demonstrate government commitment to and ownership of the PPP program.
- Develop a framework to deal with unsolicited proposals to ensure value for money, for instance, by allowing the evaluation of alternative proposals.

High-level government support for PPPs is shown by enactment of the PPP Law in 2016. Attention must now focus on building over time a robust PPP pipeline, in parallel to building the required institutional processes and capacity (especially among implementing agencies). Project identification, preparation, procurement, implementation, and overall contract and fiscal oversight methodologies need more work. In Rwanda, the central PPP entity is placed in the Rwanda Development Board, which serves as the chief negotiator for government on strategic investment deals.

BOX 4.5 Institutional framework for PPPs: An international perspective

The institutional framework for public-private partnerships (PPPs) varies across countries that have enacted a PPP law, dependent on each country's specific political and bureaucratic context. However, the most common institutional framework lays out clear roles for three entities, in particular:

- *Line ministries or contracting agencies:* responsible for identifying, preparing, procuring, and implementing PPPs
- *Ministry of Finance:* responsible for assessing and managing the fiscal implications of PPPs
- *Centralized PPP entity:* responsible for promoting and coordinating PPP activities and for supporting line ministries or contracting agencies in the development of PPPs. This entity is most typically located within the Ministry of Finance.

This means that RDB and the Ministry of Finance and Economic Planning need to closely coordinate on the assessment and management of fiscal commitments.

Tackle the High Cost of Electricity. Rwanda has implemented a suite of restructuring measures to improve governance of the electricity utility. The private sector has become a strategic partner for Rwanda's power sector through its investments in power generation and off-grid access. Blackouts have become less frequent. Nevertheless, the high cost of electricity poses a constraint on Rwanda's economic and industrial development, as discussed earlier.

Electricity supply is expensive because Rwanda has limited low-cost energy resources, and it does not have a large enough market to benefit from scale economies. As firms are caught between the high cost of electricity and limited affordability, the government has stepped in with fiscal support, at some risk to the budget. Going forward, the negative impact of high production costs could be exacerbated if generation capacity far exceeds expected demand. If the power plants in the pipeline are completed according to the government's schedule, the supply of electricity will far exceed the expected peak demand by 2025.

Recognizing these challenges, the government is preparing a framework to institutionalize least-cost sector planning and competitive procurement, together with reliable demand forecasts. Finalizing and operationalizing the Least-Cost Power Sector Development Plan will be an important step in this direction. As part of least-cost planning, the government also should consider accelerating its preparations for coordinating energy imports from and exports to neighboring countries, building capacity to procure and implement power-purchasing agreements, strengthening demand forecasting, and better integrating system planning and system operations functions in the utility. If the plans to make the utility holding company (Rwanda Energy Group) financially independent play out and the new PPP law is fully implemented as planned, the governance framework in the power sector could become a model for sector governance in Rwanda more broadly.

Specific actions are needed to ensure a reliable and affordable supply of energy:

- Institutionalize least-cost sector planning through adoption and regular updates of the power sector master plan, based on reliable updated demand forecasts; competitive implementation of the resulting least-cost projects is essential.
- Institute a process to assess, measure, monitor, and manage contingent liabilities from the power sector.
- Conduct a comprehensive assessment of the potential of indigenous energy resources available for electricity generation and options for their optimal exploitation, with a focus on dissolved methane in Lake Kivu.
- Promote regional electricity trade to take advantage of the regional energy potential of lower-cost sources of supply through bilateral contracts (consistent with keeping adequate levels and secure supply), closely coordinate with neighboring countries to ensure that the planned cross-border transmission infrastructure projects are not delayed further, and participate actively in developing the East Africa Power Pool platform to balance regional short-term mismatches between demand and supply.
- Take full advantage of off-grid private sector investment to boost rural electrification in areas where extending the grid is not financially viable, while closely monitoring the private sector's adherence to the International Electrotechnical Commission standards for off-grid solar technology.
- Promote energy efficiency in consumption to take advantage of available energy-efficient technologies (energy-efficient street lighting, energy-efficient appliances) to mitigate the effect of the country's limited energy resources and resulting high costs of service delivery.

- Define and put in place a trajectory toward the permanent application of tariffs that would allow for the recovery of efficient operating costs from all electricity consumers who can afford them, accompanied by a social safety net to protect low-income users, and adopt arrangements to cover the funding gap between sector costs and tariff revenues while the trajectory is completed.

Boost Access to and Reduce the Cost of Broadband Connectivity. Rwanda's telecommunications market is one of the fastest-growing wireless markets in Southern and Eastern Africa. Mobile cellular telephone subscriptions are the rule in Rwanda, with hardly any landline subscriptions. In 2016, close to 70 percent of inhabitants had a mobile cellular subscription; the mobile cellular penetration rate has increased rapidly in Rwanda in recent years.[12]

The 4G LTE network was launched in 2014 with the target of covering 95 percent of the population by 2018. Rwanda has adopted a unique wholesale model for the nationwide deployment of 4G LTE services. In 2013, the government entered a 25-year joint venture arrangement with Korea Telecom to design and deploy a 4G LTE network using the fiber backbone that government had built. Yet most of the country's connectivity is still through 2G and 3G connectivity. The household penetration rate of fixed high-speed Internet subscribers is less than 1 percent, well below the regional average of 6 percent. The high cost of a broadband connection, combined with low computer ownership and an erratic electricity supply, puts the service beyond the reach of most private users.

The development of the telecommunications sector calls for effective competition in key telecommunications markets. Publication of a detailed regulatory framework for managing the single wholesaler of high-speed wireless broadband and its rights on radio frequencies is a priority area. The Rwanda Utilities Regulatory Authority (RURA) should have all of the resources necessary to set the regulatory framework and conditions for wholesale data services regarding nondiscriminatory access at regulated prices that mimic the results of a competitive market and to grant spectrum rights in an efficient way. With respect to mobile telephony and short message services, revised mobile termination fees have encouraged price competition and created a more level playing field among operators. The full implementation of lower termination rates by January 2019 also should improve affordability and access. Monitoring implementation and its impact will showcase the power of pro-competition rules to achieve sector goals. The European Union's state aid control framework for designing government support for broadband deployment provides a useful framework for effective PPPs in telecommunications that would allow the government to refocus its direct participation in the sector toward setting an enabling framework for full private solutions (European Commission 2003). RURA and the Bank of Rwanda should set rules for mobile financial services, particularly regarding essential services by mobile providers, is key to supporting the development of these services.

Strengthen Market Institutions

Accelerated private sector development will require robust market institutions. The evidence is compelling that functioning markets require well-defined rules of the game, enforced transparently and predictably. Rwanda has already made significant advances in building the basic structures of its market economy, as reflected in its strong standing on the 2019 Doing Business Indicators (in which Rwanda ranked 29th in the world overall, above all other low-income countries and second only to Mauritius on the continent). It has made good progress in strengthening its pro-competition regulations, but considerable scope remains for further improvement, as noted earlier and discussed in more detail in chapter 6. Significant progress has also been made in improving the regulatory regime for property rights. The proper enforcement of expropriation procedures, further improvements in the efficiency of the land management system, and provision of more resources to implement the 2008 law on intellectual property would further strengthen property rights. There is also scope to further improve efficiency of the commercial dispute resolution process, including contract enforcement—an important aspect of a functioning market economy—on which Rwanda ranked 78th globally (among 190 economies) on the Doing Business Indicators (World Bank 2019).

Improve Effectiveness of Tax and Industrial Policy Incentives through Better Targeting

Rwanda has already established some of the key preconditions for an effective industrial policy, including strong macroeconomic management, institutional coherence, reasonable implementation capacity, and good dialogue with the private sector. In addition to these, closer monitoring of incentives for results is needed to ensure that any direct government support for specific industries or sectors is effective.

Incentives need to be linked more clearly to the productivity and export performance of beneficiary firms. Direct support should be focused on export promotion rather than on import substitution, given the absolute necessity of expanding nontraditional exports and the checkered record of import substitution in other low- and middle-income countries. The government should encourage those industries in which Rwanda has a clear comparative advantage. It should set clear policy objectives and performance targets for beneficiary firms from the beginning, ensure that policies are closely coordinated across government entities, and include a rigorous system to monitor progress and enforce sanctions and incentives so as to reward success and punish failure—a model that the Republic of Korea followed closely in its early years of development (box 4.6).

What is lacking are tax expenditures targeted at "efficiency-seeking" investors looking for low-cost destinations for labor-intensive export production. Although efficiency-seeking FDI firms are highly demanding on a country's business

BOX 4.6 Targeted interventions in the Republic of Korea

Korea, a notable example of a successful developmental state, emphasized targeted interventions. In 1960, Korea was a poor country with GDP per capita of just US$160 (US$1,103 in 2015 dollars) and a large but noncompetitive private sector. After some initial missteps, Chunghee Park's military government of 1961–79 systematically provided government privileges to private firms that demonstrated success, first in import substitution and later in export promotion or targeted industries (for example, heavy or chemical industries of military relevance). These privileges included directed credits from state-owned banks, government guarantees, tax incentives, customs exemptions, preferential access to foreign exchange, and licenses to enter new business lines. Various kinds of preferences were linked to export performance; firms that did not perform were encouraged to exit the market.

Korea also pursued financial policies that were highly dedicated to exports and allocated credit in a ruthless fashion to achieve export results. Export promotion incentives tended to be general for successful exporters, while incentives for targeted industries were sector specific and sometimes product or project specific (Kim and Vogel 2011, especially ch. 2–4, 7–9; Lim 2016). In Japan as well as other countries, the effects of interventions on exports where larger when domestic sectors where more competitive (less concentrated) (World Bank 2015).

environment and incentives alone are rarely enough to "seal the deal," global evidence suggests that these investors are highly responsive to special incentives (Andersen, Kett, and von Uexkull 2017; IMF, UN, and World Bank 2015; James 2009).

Reforms that enhance the predictability of incentives and reduce up-front costs to obtain information and gain approval for incentives could help to reduce the market-distorting effects. Ideally, these reforms would go hand in hand with (1) implementation of a framework to evaluate the effects on markets and competition of investment incentives and any other government support for specific firms and (2) effective implementation of competition rules to deter anticompetitive practices.

Incentives should also be linked with export performance. Already, the Export Growth Facility provides matching grants for new market entry; a subsidy to narrow the gap between the interest rate on export financing and prime access rates, through an investment catalyst fund; and export guarantee facilities. One example of a performance-based approach stipulated in the export strategy is that the government supports firms with the potential to repeat past successes. In this context, the focus on the so-called "64 million dollar exporters" (64 MDEs) is welcome.[13] The "Made in Rwanda" policy identifies many priority sectors (box 4.7). Mining is an example of a sector that would benefit from a focused strategy for its development (box 4.8).

Such incentives should be time bound and revocable to encourage sustainable gains and avoid dependency. Ten-year incentives could, for example, be phased out during the last five years. For example, an enterprise that engages in irresponsible investment or borrowing or in mismanagement should have its privileges revoked. In Brazil, for example, if a company is found to have infringed competition law (participated in a cartel or abused its dominant position), it can be withdrawn from the list of companies eligible for government subsidies or tax exemptions.

BOX 4.7 "Made in Rwanda" policy

The "Made in Rwanda" policy, launched in 2017, aims to improve competitiveness, enhance demand for Rwandan value-added products, narrow the trade balance, and generate jobs. It brings together existing government interventions under a clear policy framework and addresses supply-side bottlenecks via targeted interventions aimed at improving quality, boosting cost competitiveness, deepening domestic supply chains, and developing action plans for specific high-potential value chains.

The policy has five main pillars: (1) changing mind-sets, (2) improving quality, (3) reducing the cost of production, (4) promoting backward links, and (5) undertaking sector-specific strategies.

The following interventions are key:

- Conduct a national communication campaign about the policy.
- Give local preference in public procurement.
- Upgrade the quality of infrastructure.
- Boost training, certification, and inspection of standards.
- Facilitate small and medium enterprises with high growth potential to access land in special economic zones.
- Establish a local content unit in the Rwanda Development Board.
- Support industrial research and development.
- Boost access to finance through partnership with commercial banks and through creation of the Industrial Development Corporation.
- Improve access to industrial inputs through support for regional value chains, simplified procedures for value added tax, and import duty exemption for and monitoring of the supply of critical raw materials.

BOX 4.8 Developing Rwanda's mining sector

Minerals, represented mostly by tin, tantalum, and tungsten, traditionally have been an important export commodity for Rwanda and, in recent years, have accounted for 15–20 percent of total exports of goods and services. Despite considerable potential, the volume of traditional minerals has increased little recently, with the recent resurgence in mining revenues in the fourth quarter of 2016 and first quarter of 2017 driven mainly by increased exports of other high-value minerals. The general upswing in mineral prices has raised expectations of the sector's prospects (New Times 2017).

Attracting investments in the sector and enabling the government to collect a fair share of the wealth from mineral exports to reinvest in human capital, resilience, and sustainability are important policy objectives for Rwanda. Given the current structure of the sector in Rwanda, these efforts must take into account artisanal miners, larger-scale operators, and the national interest:

- *Artisanal mining (ASM).* Artisanal mining accounts for 80 percent of total minerals production in Rwanda. As much as 30 percent additional value can be obtained from Rwanda's mining sites if mechanized processing is implemented instead of manual methods (Heizman and Libetrau 2017). Production at some sites is reaching limiting depths of "easy to mine" resources using artisanal methods, which highlights the importance of having better tools and methods to maintain and increase production. In addition, miners are not always able to capture a fair share of export receipts because of their weak bargaining power relative to licensed traders, which discourages ASM operators from investing in new tools and learning. Creating incentives that promote investments in new tools and skills, organizing fragmented operations into cooperative operations, creating strong links between ASMs and processors, and providing basic skills training and extension services to ASMs are all important ways the government can support the artisanal mining sector.
- *Larger-scale private investments in production, processing, and value addition.* Developing an industrial mining sector will require foreign capital and knowledge of mineral processing with accurately targeted incentives. To attract investments into Rwanda, the government should provide incentives to conduct and share prospecting surveys through competitive auctioning of potential resource "blocks," perform a detailed value chain analysis of Rwanda's minerals to identify the particular stage of value addition that is economically viable for Rwanda, further adapt the legal and regulatory framework to the geology and mineral potential of Rwanda, and strengthen the capacity of the Rwanda Mining Board to promote, support, and regulate the mining sector properly.
- *Fiscal regime and management of mineral wealth.* Developing an optimal fiscal regime so that the government can capture an efficient and fair share of mineral wealth is a policy priority. Tax administration should be the focus of reforms, especially in the context of greater formalization in the sector. So far, profit tax performance has been weak, in part due to transfer pricing and deficient export pricing that often does not reflect the value of other minerals accompanying the main mineral. To address this, the government needs to develop the capacity of Rwanda Revenue Authority to administer taxation in the sector.

The government is also considering playing a direct role in the mineral sector by having an equity participation in production and processing companies. This is a valid policy option and would strengthen government's capacity to collect taxes on the sector. Minority equity participation can be used to fund geological studies. Larger participation to gain a greater share of mineral revenues should be exercised with caution to avoid undermining private investments and knowledge transfer.

Stabilization is another important function that is needed to achieve improved fiscal management of mineral wealth. As mining exports grow and the government captures its fair share, mechanisms that can insulate the budget from price volatility, such as introducing countercyclical principles in the use of mineral revenues, will be important.

Depending on the scale of new discoveries, Rwanda should make intertemporal choices with respect to the consumption of current and future generations. The government has established a sovereign wealth fund, which can serve the purpose of smoothing intergenerational consumption of mineral resources and stabilizing countercyclical spending of mineral revenues.

Define the Role of SOEs in the Economy and Strengthen Corporate Governance

SOEs played an important role in the early stages of Rwanda's economic development. Investments in them were a response to the massive investments needed in the aftermath of the genocide against the Tutsi, when a viable domestic private sector was absent. Observers have debated the relative merits and development attributes of Rwanda's SOEs. Some have asserted that they contribute to economic development and social stability (Behuria 2012; Booth and Golooba-Mutebi 2012), while noting that, as in Indonesia and Malaysia, rents have been "deployed in ways that assisted national development" (Booth and Golooba-Mutebi 2012; see also Behuria and Goodfellow 2016). Others have concluded that SOEs cause a fiscal drain and use public capital inefficiently, while constraining private sector development (Gokgur 2012).

There was strong justification for state involvement in the economy, given the large reconstruction needs in the aftermath of the genocide against the Tutsi, an incapacitated private sector, and ready availability of foreign assistance. This justification holds in the medium term, and SOEs have a crucial role to play in Rwanda's future development. The practical question is how they can do so in the most effective way, so that public capital is preserved and put to good use while the development of the private sector is not undermined.

Ultimately, Rwanda's First National Strategy of Transformation and Vision 2050 establish a pathway for the private sector, over time, to play a leading role in Rwanda's growth; to achieve this goal, resources have to be allocated through efficient market mechanisms. As Rwanda approaches middle-income levels, the complexities of its market economy will grow almost exponentially. Strong government support will still be needed, but its role will increasingly be to facilitate private investment and build strong market institutions that ensure predictable rules of the game for the private sector. Enterprise development in Rwanda should continue to contribute to alleviating market failures and encouraging private sector development, especially given that investment capacity among Rwanda's private sector remains low. SOEs are also seen as playing a useful role in maintaining social and political stability.

Strengthen Corporate Governance of SOEs

Effective corporate governance achieves a necessary balance between *autonomy* for enterprise "agents" and *oversight* by enterprise owners (principals). Enterprise agents normally include enterprise management and a board of directors, the latter overseeing the former. It is essential to determine the appropriate authority at each level—management, directors, and owners.

The guidelines of the Organisation for Economic Co-operation and Development (OECD) for the corporate governance of SOEs[14] could usefully be adapted—with any necessary modifications—for Rwanda's SOEs, which are already following some of the guidelines. Following international good practices, the government has already implemented most of the corporate governance principles detailed below. First, government should consistently act as an informed *owner.* Proper ownership functions include

- Being represented at shareholder meetings and voting owned shares;
- Establishing merit-based and transparent processes for nominating the board of directors in full- or majority-owned SOEs, actively participating in the nomination of all SOE boards, and contributing to board diversity;
- Setting and monitoring the implementation of broad SOE objectives and mandates (for example, financial targets, capital structure, risk tolerance);
- Setting up reporting systems that allow the owner to monitor, audit, and assess SOE performance regularly and to oversee and monitor SOE compliance with corporate governance standards;

- Developing a disclosure policy for SOEs that identifies what information should be publicly disclosed, appropriate channels for disclosure, and measures to ensure information quality;
- Maintaining appropriate dialogue with external auditors and government control organs; and
- Establishing a clear remuneration policy for SOE boards that reflects the long-term interests of the SOE and can attract and motivate qualified professionals to serve on SOE boards of directors.

If a SOE is listed on the Rwanda Stock Exchange or otherwise includes nongovernment investors among its owners, the relevant laws and regulations should be followed. The participation of minority shareholders in shareholder meetings should be facilitated so that they can take part in key decisions, such as elections to the board of directors. Transactions between the government and SOEs or between SOEs should take place on market terms. If an SOE is required to pursue a public policy objective, information on this requirement should be available to all shareholders (OECD 2015, ch. IV). The government's ownership rights and oversight should be exercised only periodically (for example, at shareholder meetings) and through normal mechanisms (for example, voting of shares). Autonomy for SOEs needs to be maintained while ensuring that SOEs have the necessary competencies and accountability.

All listed SOEs should regularly issue audited financial statements to the public. First, the government needs reliable financial information to guide economic policy, regulation, and investment decisions. Second, leading international private investors who might provide additional equity or debt financing require such information. Third, Rwandan citizens are all SOE stakeholders, and regular and reliable financial reporting would serve to maintain the public's trust. Per current practice, the government requires full International Financial Reporting Standards (IFRS) for all domestic companies whose securities trade in a public market. In addition, "companies with *public accountability* (banks or other financial institutions) must use full IFRS."[15]

In addition to financial reporting, SOEs should publicly disclose other important information. This information includes the following:

- Governance, ownership, and voting structures of the SOE, including the content and implementation of any corporate governance code
- Remuneration of board members and key executives
- Board member qualifications, selection process, roles of other company boards, and whether these other boards are considered as independent by the SOE board
- Any material foreseeable risk factors and risk mitigation measures
- Any financial assistance, including guarantees, received from the government and SOE commitments arising from public-private partnerships
- Any material transactions with the government or government-related entities
- Any material issues relating to SOE employees or other stakeholders (OECD 2015, ch. VI)

Rwandan SOEs already follow many of these corporate governance practices. For example,

- SOEs typically have a seven-person board of directors;
- Separate individuals are appointed to serve as the SOE's chief executive officer and as the board chair;
- The board of directors often maintains specialized board committees, such as for audit and human resources or remuneration;
- The board of directors is generally obliged to meet at least four times a year and may have a predetermined meeting calendar;

- The chief executive officer and board chair often sign performance contracts;
- Many SOEs have an internal audit department that reports to the board or its audit committee;
- An independent external auditor audits SOE annual financial statements;
- Some SOEs require periodic rotation of external auditors;
- Each SOE is expected to have a multiyear strategic plan and a risk management policy (MINECOFIN 2017); and
- At least some SOEs have budget for corporate governance training for new directors.[16]

Clarify the Government's Ownership Policy

The Ministry of Finance and Economic Planning's Government Portfolio Management Unit is tasked with ensuring that the government acts as an informed owner. In its annual *Fiscal Risk Review of Government Investment*, the Government Portfolio Management Unit highlights corporate governance issues for the board's attention, tracks the disposition of issues previously identified, analyzes financial performance and position for each state-owned enterprise, and summarizes key financial risks for the government (MINECOFIN 2017). Overall, the *Financial Risk Review* represents an excellent foundation for further development of an SOE ownership policy, establishing greater clarity for potential private investors. This policy should define, among others, the rationale for ownership, the government's role in the corporate governance of SOEs, how the government will implement ownership, and the respective roles and responsibilities of any ministries or agencies involved in implementation. For SOEs with noncommercial objectives, the economic or social rationale for each "public service mandate" should be stated clearly. In general, SOEs should be reimbursed at least for the costs of any public service mandate. This ownership policy should be subject to appropriate procedures of political accountability, disclosed to the public, and reviewed at regular intervals (OECD 2015, ch. I). Several OECD jurisdictions have recently undertaken state ownership policy initiatives along these lines (table 4.4).

An accompanying strategy for public share offerings in successful SOEs would offer multiple benefits. Even just a minority public share offering facilitates SOE access to follow-on capital market financing. Oversight by public shareowners would strengthen the corporate governance of listed SOEs. A regular program of SOE public share sales and listings would energize the Rwanda Stock Exchange and raise Rwanda's profile among international investors. Other economies have successfully followed similar approaches with their state-owned enterprises.[17]

TABLE 4.4 State-owned enterprise policy initiatives in the OECD since 2006

Country	Policy initiative
Finland	Government Resolution on State Ownership Policy (May 2007), establishing key principles and operating policies for the state's ownership function
Norway	Government Ownership Policy for SOEs, published since 2007
Poland	Draft legislation identifying state companies of "key importance" to the Treasury
Portugal	Council of Ministers 2007 best practices for public companies to increase transparency and improve corporate governance
Spain	2009 Royal Decree on General Rules on the Assets of the Central Government, stating an ownership policy for SOEs, establishing guidelines for commercial and noncommercial objectives, outlining the role of shareholder meetings, and establishing transparency and other good practices for SOEs
Switzerland	Federal Council Corporate Governance Reports since 2006, establishing criteria for outsourcing tasks to SOEs and SOE governance guidelines

Source: OECD 2011.
Note: OECD = Organisation for Economic Co-operation and Development; SOE = state-owned enterprise.

On the basis of these analyses, the government might usefully categorize Rwanda's real economy by four sector types:

1. Sectors in which SOEs will retain a monopoly
2. Sectors in which SOEs will remain present and compete with private firms
3. Sectors from which SOEs will withdraw when efforts to build up private sector capacity prove successful (discussed below)
4. Sectors from which SOEs will withdraw immediately (for example, through a well-planned and well-supported privation program) because the private sector is already sufficiently capable and there is no compelling social rationale for SOEs

For type 2–4 sectors in which private firms are competitive with SOEs, state support for enterprises could be based on common sector goals, such as demonstrated market-based achievements in export promotion; any such privileges should be time bound and revocable. For type 2–4 sectors in which private firms cannot generally compete with SOEs, the government could give private firms some opportunities to catch up. This could involve, for example, time-bound and revocable privileges, for example, lower performance thresholds for certain incentives, some private sector set-asides for government procurement contracts, or partial credit guarantees for private SMEs.[18]

Public-private boundaries can shift as the private sector gains strength. The priority now is to lay strong economic foundations and to design, implement, and enforce a sector-based enterprise strategy that considers short-term competitiveness, long-term economic development goals, and social stability needs.

Develop an Effective NIS

An innovation-driven economy will demand an unambiguous commitment to cultivating and upgrading a dynamic private sector and far-reaching reforms in the education and training systems for generating higher-order human capital. More generally, it will demand a competitive societal climate that values openness to new ideas and stimulates risk taking and technology upgrading. All three were crucial to the rapid growth of Japan, Korea, and Singapore—examples that Rwanda holds up for its own growth and innovation ambitions.

Developing a strong NIS, therefore, is the fourth reform priority for Rwanda in its efforts to build a competitive enterprise sector. NIS development involves developing an ecosystem that ensures strong uptake of learning and innovation from both the demand and the supply sides.

The first requirement of a functioning NIS is a critical mass of dynamic and competitive firms that provide the demand side for innovation. These enterprises also must have the absorptive capacity to adopt and carry out new research and hold longer-term strategic views on firm and product upgrading and human resources necessary for innovation. The lack of such abilities in many low- and middle-income economies reflects limited competition in product markets and the low capabilities of firm managers (Bloom and Van Reenen 2007; Maloney and Sarrias 2014). Addressing management capability gaps was a crucial element of the "East Asian Miracle" (Cirera and Maloney 2017). As discussed earlier, firm capabilities in Rwanda require significant improvement. Management practices also tend to be better in older firms (those that have been in business for more than 20 years; Cirera and Maloney 2017), which is a challenge for Rwanda given that 90 percent of its firms are less than a decade old. Firms that participate in foreign trade or are part of global value chains also tend to have better management practices (Bloom and Van Reenen 2010; Maloney and Sarrias 2017), earn higher returns on innovation, and face lower research and development (R&D) costs (Guadalupe, Kuzmina, and Thomas 2012). Rwandan enterprises are nascent in this area, with about 8 percent of formal manufacturing firms exporting their products and very few embedded in global value chain production networks (chapter 2).[19]

The supply side of the NIS (discussed in chapter 1) also has strong requirements, especially with regard to a skilled workforce and the quality and relevance of research and advanced training in universities and research institutes.

The capabilities escalator provides a useful framework for conceptualizing and building an effective NIS (figure 4.23). A good starting point for economies with incipient innovation systems (stage 1, which is Rwanda's current situation) are policies and investments to strengthen the capabilities of local firms to adopt new technologies, improve their access to technologies, develop human capital (especially in science, technology, engineering, and mathematics), and put in place quality infrastructure. The emphasis on building firms' technological capabilities, improving the quality and relevance of research in the country, and developing effective research collaborations between industry and academia comes next (stage 2), followed by development of cutting-edge R&D and technological programs when the country reaches a mature state of innovation (stage 3).

FIGURE 4.23 The capabilities escalator: A framework to support innovation and entrepreneurial activity

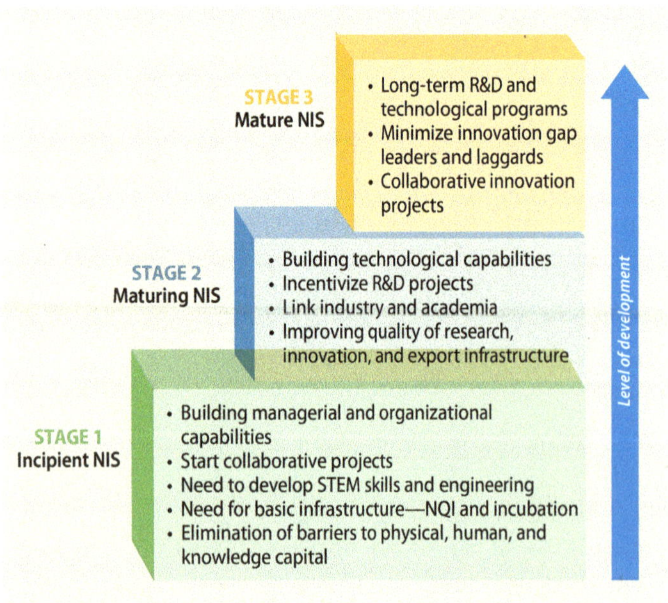

Source: Adapted from Cirera and Maloney 2017.
Note: NIS = National Innovation System; NQI = national quality infrastructure; R&D = research and development; STEM = science, technology, engineering, and mathematics.

The first imperative is to develop a strong, competitive, and innovation-driven enterprise sector. Otherwise, all efforts on the innovation side will be supply-push and, in the worst case, costly and valueless high-tech ventures. But the presence of such firms is not enough. To show greater urgency in pressing for new technologies, firms must also see a strong business case for innovation and believe that they can manage any potential challenges and risks. This can be encouraged by providing (1) technological extension services to build the managerial and organizational capabilities of firms and (2) incentives for technology absorption and diffusion.

Provide Technological Extension Services to Build Managerial and Organizational Capabilities

Innovation cannot develop without adequate sophistication among firms and farmers, beginning with the basics. Throughout the high-income world and in dynamic low- and middle-income economies, governments have employed extension services to facilitate technological transfers to enterprises (box 4.9). Integrated support programs—providing support for companies to improve their management and other internal capabilities—are especially well suited in this regard.

The Rwandan government already has taken important steps to raise the innovation of firms and the bureaucracy—significant among them has been the establishment of the National Industrial Research and Development Agency (NIRDA), the National Commission of Science and Technology (NCST), and a few other organizations.[20] The task at hand now is to consolidate the activities of these institutions to ensure effective coordination of the NIS. This effort is important to identify where to invest scarce resources and who the key stakeholders are and to define clear roles for how these institutions could collaborate to strengthen the system. NIRDA can play a key role in facilitating technology adoption by firms, improving their managerial and organizational capabilities, facilitating their access to innovation and technology adoption funds, and, in close coordination with the

BOX 4.9 The importance of firm capabilities for productivity: Examples from Brazil, India, and Singapore

Brazil. PEIEX (Industrial Extension Project for Exporting) is a program from the Brazilian Export Promotion Agency (Apex-Brasil) that focuses on enhancing the competitiveness of Brazilian small and medium enterprises by providing coaching and consulting on management and production best practices. The initiative was set up as supplementary assistance for firms interested in taking part in export promotion services already provided by the agency (for example, participation in trade fairs and business rounds or meetings with foreign buyers). Once these firms confirm their interest in participating in the program, they receive a standard competitive strength assessment covering different areas of the enterprise (for example, strategic organization, human capital, finance and costs, sales and marketing, international trade, product design, production, and innovation), with a final report identifying their strengths and weaknesses. This assessment is followed by a plan with suggestions focusing on improving firms' competitiveness. The program offers consulting services in partnership with universities and institutes of technology in fields such as marketing, human resources management, finance, product design, and trade. An evaluation found that the PEIEX has been particularly effective in promoting the reorganization of small and medium firms and that changes in firms' organization are positively correlated with export performance (Cruz, Bussolo, and Iacovone 2018).

India. An experiment in India involved evaluating the impact of free consulting on the management practices of large Indian textile firms. Firms that adopted the recommended management practices raised productivity 17 percent in the first year by improving quality and efficiency, reduced inventory, and opened new production plants within three years (Bloom et al. 2013). About 10 years later, the gap in practices between those firms that received support and the others was still large and significant (Bloom et al. 2018).

Singapore. The Singapore Standards, Productivity, and Innovation Board was established in the 1980s with support from the Japanese Productivity Center. It plays a key role in the extensive system of small and medium enterprise support services. Similarly, the Economic Development Board of Singapore introduced the Local Industry Upgrading Program to improve the exchange of knowledge between local firms and foreign multinationals. In addition to providing extended loans to buy machinery and equipment, the Local Enterprise Technical Assistance Scheme run by the Economic Development Board provided grants to hire external experts to upgrade operations and management.

NCST, facilitating the interaction between the demand for and supply of knowledge.[21]

A good starting point for shaping specific policy guidance would be to conduct a survey to measure the management capabilities and practices of Rwandan firms. Several countries have implemented the World Management Survey, including a few countries in Sub-Saharan Africa (Ethiopia, Ghana, Kenya, Mozambique, Nigeria, Tanzania, and Zambia).[22] Findings from management surveys can shape the programs supporting businesses by incorporating components to provide managerial coaching and assistance, such as in the example of PEIEX in Brazil (Cruz, Bussolo, and Iacovone 2018). Interventions to build management capabilities have proved effective and sustained. In Togo, personal initiative training programs to develop behavior associated with a proactive, entrepreneurial mind-set proved to be effective in boosting women-owned small businesses (Campos et al. 2018).

On the basis of this evidence, the following interventions could be adopted in Rwanda: (1) provide training and coaching services to diffuse good business managerial practices; (2) complement business support programs with personal initiative training; (3) expand and improve the quality of graduate-level management courses; (4) provide managerial training to cooperatives that support farmers; and (5) increase interaction between multinational firms and local suppliers. Whereas the first two examples find strong support in previous experiments, such as in India and Togo, the other suggestions adapt these interventions to the constraints and opportunities faced by Rwanda. It would be useful to test these interventions in Rwanda with small-scale experiments before investing large amounts of resources. Such experiments would enable policy makers to learn more about how to adapt them to Rwanda. Similar experiments are in place in other countries, including Argentina, Colombia, and Mozambique.

Strong market demand for their products can be an important motivator for firms to try and upgrade. Interventions that seek to build both firms' capabilities and their access to markets—as opposed to addressing these needs separately—tend to be especially effective. There are various models for Rwanda to consider, ranging from supplier development programs to export competitiveness programs, depending on the specific upgrading needs of the firms and characteristics of their main buyers (Chavhan, Mahajan, and Sarang 2012). The PEIEX is an export competitiveness program providing support for building managerial capabilities. Supplier development programs are usually provided by firms (buyers) with government support. Such programs work by providing funding or getting involved in SME upgrading. Examples of programs include building local value chains, particularly in agribusiness (such as in Haiti), or building international value chains, in some cases tied to investment of multinational corporations, to strengthen the local supplier base (such as electronics in Vietnam) or to strengthen exports (such as special economic zones in Mexico). In this case, the government could facilitate the matching between local providers and exporting firms.

Successful programs of this type have several aspects in common:

- They are always focused on understanding and serving a known market demand.
- They build capabilities that help firms to compete in those markets and meet that demand.
- They usually build firm management capabilities and look to engage in process innovation and new product development.
- They try to expose firms to markets through targeted efforts to connect with potential buyers (for example, trade missions and fairs or "meet the buyer" events).
- They encourage cooperation and group learning between firms and provide a structure to reach out and work with innovation providers.
- They use a variety of innovation policy tools, including advisory services, vouchers, matching grants, and services like national quality infrastructure and intellectual property in an integrated fashion.

These types of programs can become good tools for embedding capability upgrading. By combining support for SMEs to upgrade with a tangible market opportunity, they can be much more effective than supply- or demand-only initiatives, although they are more complex to deliver.

Rwanda already has many initiatives to support incubator or accelerator programs,[23] and further scaling up may be better left to the private sector in many cases. Rather than building new facilities, the government can coordinate these actions and, perhaps more important, support the managerial capabilities of these programs.[24] It also can seek to strengthen the organizational capabilities of the public enterprises involved. For example, Rwanda has recently updated the laws on intellectual property rights and established a standards board.

It will be critical for Rwanda to advance on the coordination, monitoring, and evaluation across policy instruments that support innovation. Any new initiative should be started at a relatively small scale and be evaluated before being scaled up. A good example is in the field of social policy, where Mexico's successful conditional cash transfer programs were designed on the basis of rigorous randomized controlled trials before being scaled up.

Incentivize Technology Adoption and Diffusion

Firms' capabilities alone are not enough. Low innovation can also reflect lack of incentives for firms and other barriers to technology adoption, such as insufficient early-stage financing, weak intellectual property rights protection, and difficult risk management. For example, firms may worry that competitors will copy their innovations, eliminating much of the potential profit of investing in knowledge. Financial incentives from the government, in the form of direct subsidies, tax write-offs, matching grants, or patents, can raise the private return to equal the social return, particularly on the grounds of market failure arising from the appropriability externality.

Business incubator and accelerator programs for the provision of infrastructure and advisory services are increasingly popular instruments for innovation capacity and have already been initiated in Rwanda. Many start-ups have potentially marketable ideas, but they lack the experience to start a company or to scale it up. In addition, new businesses (particularly those that are built around ideas that are new to the country) need to overcome the wariness of traditional financiers and potential buyers. Pre-incubator, incubator, and accelerator programs can be important resources for such start-ups. Many of their interventions are focused on innovative companies or sectors and, in some cases, are linked to public sector research organizations that support the commercialization of knowledge, as in Colombia (box 4.10). Incubators can combine mentoring, business plan preparation, and links to potential finance in an integrated fashion, which encourages networking and mutual learning. Shorter-term accelerator programs may help in the adolescence phase where technical issues are consolidated, but strategic guidance is in demand. Ongoing initiatives in this area in Rwanda include the Incubator Center of the Integrated Polytechnic Regional College and Milicom's "Think" initiative as well as the recently approved Rwanda Innovation Fund, but government also has a role to play, for example, in mapping these initiatives and coordinating among them.

Rwanda's ambitious efforts in developing the Kigali Innovation City are crucial in this regard (box 4.11). It now needs to strengthen the entrepreneurship ecosystem around the innovation city to

BOX 4.10 The experience of Apps.co

Apps.co is a program for start-ups managed by the Ministry of Information Technologies and Communications of Colombia. It comprises activities focusing on a range of start-up development phases (pre-incubator, incubator, and accelerator), including boot camps to increase awareness of business opportunities and activities to accelerate start-ups.

In the pre-incubator phase, Apps.co fosters the creation of businesses in digital content, more specifically creative digital industries, by providing services and methodological training for teams of entrepreneurs to develop a validation process for a product and a sustainable business model.

In the incubator phase, Apps.co provides guidance from mentors and consultants for teams of entrepreneurs on developing sustainable business models with solutions that segment needs in these industries.

In the accelerator phase, Apps.co provides coaching for selected companies in the information and communication technology industry (digital content and web and mobile applications) that require advice regarding how to expand and consolidate their business to reach break-even or investment status. At this stage, companies must have a digital product, a validated business model, and demonstrable traction in a defined segment of real customers.

BOX 4.11 Kigali Innovation City

The Kigali Innovation City (KIC) is Rwanda's flagship initiative for innovation-led economic transformation. This initiative aims to bring together a highly connected ecosystem of growth-stage local and international technology companies, "special innovation centers" nurturing a network of early-stage companies, a community of world-class learning institutions providing an annual supply of high-aptitude pan-African talent, an industry skills academy comprising the global technology academies, a professional services cluster, and the Rwandan Innovation Fund (target fund size of US$250 million) for growth of companies within Rwanda's technology sector.

To attract foreign technology companies, Rwanda offers a package of investment incentives. These incentives include preferential corporate income tax rates, income tax holidays, exemptions from specific customs taxes, accelerated depreciation, and a value added tax refund. The main attraction is the pan-African talent pool accessible to technology companies for "continuous internship" until they eventually join as employees. Carnegie Mellon University-Africa has been operating in Rwanda for the last six years and in early 2018 will occupy its newly finished campus within the KIC site. Other higher learning institutions (African Institute for Mathematical Sciences, African Leadership University, and University of Rwanda's Centre of Excellence for Biomedical Engineering and e-Health), which are operating in Kigali, will commence construction of their KIC campuses in early 2018. The International Centre for Theoretical Physics will continue to reside outside the KIC site, but it will remain a key member of the community.

A key objective of the KIC initiative is to accelerate the growth of human capital. The higher learning institutions will provide an annual supply of "pre-intern" high-aptitude pan-African talent comprising 150 engineers, 150 mathematicians, 150 scientists, and 150 business entrepreneurs. Employers will take advantage of the co-domiciled industry skills academy to turn their talented employees into world-class professionals able to innovate and produce highly competitive products and to provide the professional services required to deploy the products in many economies of Africa. This talent pool will contribute significantly to the creation and commercialization of start-ups. Other projected outcomes of the KIC initiative include the creation of 250 new technology companies by 2022, graduation from the Rwanda Innovation Fund portfolio of at least 10 corporations with a combined market valuation of more than US$500 million, and an increase in export earnings of at least US$180 million by 2025.

ensure its commercial success;[25] to do so, it is important to attract talented and experienced entrepreneurs from across the country and abroad, in addition to the students who come out of the various educational entities within the innovation city. The government should bring in a range of domestic and international players to run start-up, incubator, and accelerator events; investment readiness services; equity investment models; and local and international support and advisory networks from the best ecosystems. It should also regularly map the ecosystem, identify areas of weakness, and coordinate actions for addressing these issues though policy interventions.

Access to finance plays a key role in technology adoption and innovation. Rwanda has several initiatives to provide science, technology, and innovation funds (table 4.5), including NIRDA, RDB, and the Business Development Fund. Finance for innovation should extend beyond just start-up finance; innovation finance also should be made available for established companies that may need to be induced to undertake risky innovation projects for which there is no traditional financial support. It is important to improve coordination, monitoring, and evaluation across these institutions and instruments. A key starting point would be to ensure the functionality of existing support programs to determine whether their

TABLE 4.5 Use of science, technology, and innovation funding initiatives in Rwanda

Fund	Implementing agency	Purpose
Green Fund (National Climate and Environment Fund)	Environment and Climate Change Fund and Ministry of Natural Resources of Rwanda	Fund environment and climate change investment
Rwanda Innovation Endowment Fund	Ministry of Education	Fund R&D for innovation and for priority economic and social areas
Skills Development Facility	Workforce Development Authority	Expand the number of individuals with the relevant skills in critical sectors
Rwanda Innovation Fund	Rwanda Development Board	Fund KIC-related science, technology, and innovation programs
National Research and Innovation Fund	National Commission of Science and Technology	Align research with national priorities
Business Development Fund	Business Development Fund	Provide SME support credit guarantees, credit lines, matching grants, quasi-equity, and advisory services
Fund for African Private Sector Assistance	African Development Bank	Provide untied grants for technical assistance and capacity building
ICT-SME Fund	Ministry of Youth and ICT and Rwanda Development Board	Provide public-private funding for job creation
National Industrial Research and Development Agency	National Industrial Research and Development Agency	Fund R&D for industry needs
Export Growth Facility	Rwanda Development Bank	Catalyze investment through matching grants for market entry costs and export guarantees
Not applicable	Rwanda Development Bank	Provide student loans for graduate programs abroad
Skills, Employability, and Entrepreneurship Program (SEEP III) Fund	Workforce Development Authority and African Development Bank	Fund skills, entrepreneurship development, and job creation program
Student loans for graduate programs	Rwanda Development Bank	Support skills development

Source: UNCTAD 2017.
Note: R&D = research and development; KIC = Kigali Innovation City; SME = small and medium enterprise; ICT = information and communication technology.

objectives are clear, whether they have a sound business model, whether they are efficiently run, and whether they reach the target market. Moreover, it would be important to have a unified database to identify the main beneficiaries, the efficiency, and the effectiveness of these programs, in order to track their impact.

International standards can play an important role in technology adoption. New technologies tend to follow global standards, so firms may find it more challenging to adopt new technologies if they do not already meet global standards. Examples of global standards include internationally recognized safety standards for household products, food testing and labeling, and construction materials, among others. These standards are important for Rwanda (given the role of agricultural exports). They help to make up the national quality infrastructure, which extends firms' market access beyond the national borders to include the availability of and access to decent private labs, testers, and accreditors. Meeting global standards is also important for export firms, because many governments as well as consumers want products to meet certain quality and safety requirements. With all this in mind, Rwanda established a standards board. The availability and affordability of key testing, assessment, and accreditation services are key, as is increasing awareness about standards.

Encouraging collaboration among firms or between firms and knowledge providers is another effective policy to foster innovation. Grants, matching grants, and vouchers are common types of direct support used to increase business innovation activities.

As part of this effort, Rwanda could consider developing voucher schemes. Applicants typically receive vouchers when they meet preset eligibility requirements, which can be used for firm-specific innovation needs, and can take the vouchers to innovation providers on a preapproved list. Voucher schemes have also been used to stimulate innovation in service sectors, where formal R&D may be less common. Global evidence on voucher instruments suggests that the most prominent impacts are follow-up projects for some SMEs and a change in attitude toward collaboration on innovation projects. Collaborative matching grants are another instrument to consider, where the voucher is conditional on collaboration (for example, with a research institute).

Grants are a direct allocation of funding from public agencies to firms to finance all or part of an innovation project or innovation-related firm upgrading. In matching grants, public agencies match a percentage contribution of the project made by the applicant to ensure that the applicant is committed to the activity. The main objective is usually to entice firms to start collaborating with knowledge organizations and providers and to develop innovations. Most of the evidence regarding the impact of these instruments is from OECD countries, including Austria, Ireland, Scotland, and Switzerland, among others, as highlighted by Becker (2015), García-Quevedo (2004), and Zúñiga-Vicente et al. (2014). Vouchers are often valuable in inducing firms to innovate and so have been used to target sectors (for example, in services) that have not traditionally been seen as highly innovative (or at least are not R&D intensive). However, to be effective, a good supply of useful innovation expertise is needed for SMEs to tap into; if this expertise is not available, then the innovation ecosystem should seek to raise capacity on the supply side.

Finally, ensuring intellectual property rights (including their protection and enforcement) will become more important in the medium term. The recent law on intellectual property rights enacted in 2009 is in line with good practices established by the World Intellectual Property Organization.

Annex 4A Measuring Resource Misallocation

Misallocation of resources is measured as the dispersion of the marginal revenue product of factors of production across firms within an industry, following the framework proposed by Hsieh and Klenow (2009). The key assumption underlying this approach is that, in the absence of any distortion, the marginal revenue product of factors should be equalized across firms within an industry. The counterfactual productivity gains of eliminating the misallocation are calculated by equalizing total factor productivity of revenue (TFPR), which is a summary measure of distortions, across the existing set of producers in an industry.

More formally, each firm produces a differentiated product according to the production function

$$Y_i = A_i K_i^{\alpha} L_i^{1-\alpha} \qquad (4A.1)$$

where Y is value added of firm i, and K and L are capital inputs, respectively. A_i is the producer's productivity level (TFP). The economy is endowed with labor and capital stocks, indexed $L = \Sigma_i L_i$ and $K = \Sigma_i K_i$.

A firm maximizes its profit:

$$\pi_i = (1 + \tau_{yi})P_i Y_i - (1 + \tau_{ki})RK_i - w \qquad (4A.2)$$

subject to its demand function

$$Y_i = Y\left(\frac{P}{P_i}\right)^{\sigma}, \qquad (4A.3)$$

where R and w are the common rental cost of capital and the wage rate, respectively. τ_{ki} denotes the firm-specific capital-labor distortion, which increases the cost of capital relative to labor. The capital-labor distortions may reflect government policy such as credit market imperfections or labor regulations that favor particular firms. τ_{yi} denotes the output distortion, which may stem from government restrictions on size, output taxes, or high transport costs.

Profit maximization yields the firm's output price:

$$P_i \propto \frac{\left(1+\tau_{ki}\right)^{\alpha}}{A_i\left(1-\tau_{yi}\right)}, \qquad (4A.4)$$

where the elasticity of price with respect to productivity is –1. The distinction between quantity-based productivity $A_i(TFPQ_i)$ and revenue-based productivity $TFPR_i$ is critical for measuring misallocation, especially in differentiated-product industries. To illustrate, $TFPR_i = P_i \times A_i$, where P_i is the price that a firm charges. Firms with higher productivity charge lower prices, resulting in constant

$$TFPR_i = P_i A_i \propto \frac{\left(1+\tau_{ki}\right)^{\alpha}}{\left(1-\tau_{yi}\right)}. \qquad (4A.5)$$

In a frictionless environment, where all firms face the same level of distortion, that is, $\tau_{ki} = \overline{\tau_k}$ and $\tau_{yi} = \overline{\tau_y}$ TFPR should be equalized across firms. Therefore, TFPR dispersion across firms can be interpreted as a misallocation of resources.

The implicit distortions facing each firm can then be inferred from the firm's profit maximization conditions, including factor (labor and capital) distortions and output distortions. A firm faces a higher capital-labor distortion if the ratio of labor compensation to the stock of capital is larger than what is warranted by the industry elasticity of output with respect to factors of production. A firm faces a higher output distortion if the labor compensation is low compared with what is implied by industry elasticity of output with respect to labor. The output distortion does not distort the optimal combination of factor inputs, because it affects the marginal products of both inputs proportionally.

Notes

1. Rwanda's ranking on the Logistic Performance Index has improved remarkedly, moving from 148 in 2007 to 62 in 2016, driven almost exclusively by public investments.
2. Labor Productivity = TFP * Human Capital * [*a* / (1 – *a*)] * Capital-Labor ratio, where *a* = share of capital in production.
3. Rwanda Investor Perceptions Survey was undertaken by Adam Smith International in late 2017 in conjunction with the World Bank Group (Adam Smith International 2017). The survey identified the perceptions of investors and the constraints of exporting firms in Rwanda's priority economic sectors.
4. Misallocation of resources is measured as the dispersion of the marginal revenue product of factors of production across firms within each sector, following the framework proposed by Hsieh and Klenow (2009). The key assumption in this framework is that, in the absence of any distortion, the marginal revenue product of factors should be equalized across firms within industries. The counterfactual productivity gain is calculated by equalizing TFPR across the existing set of firms in each industry.
5. Trademarks may be viewed as a proxy for innovation in marketing and in services, which is usually not covered by other traditional indicators (Lemarchand and Tash 2015; Millot 2009).
6. Rwanda's financial sector is composed of 504 supervised financial institutions, of which 16 are banks (11 commercial banks, 3 microfinance banks, 1 development bank, and 1 cooperative bank); 472 are microfinance institutions (17 limited liability companies and 455 cooperatives, of which 416 are *umurenge* savings and credit cooperatives and 39 are non-*umurenge* savings and credit cooperatives); 15 are insurers (13 private and 2 public); and 1 is a public pension scheme.
7. Agency banking in that context refers to a bank contracting a retail outlet such as a shop or post office to facilitate client transactions, including payments, deposits, and withdrawals. These agents are not full-fledged banks and therefore offer a smaller range of services, but they are less costly to establish, helping the bank to reach more remote areas. They are common in many

countries across the world, including Brazil, India, and Kenya.

8. Loan loss provisions relative to nonperforming loans stood at 44.5 percent; 80.2 percent of total assets were classified as earning assets in 2017, reflecting strong engagement in lending activities.
9. Composite insurers are companies offering a full range of insurance services, such as life, property, and motor vehicle insurance.
10. The *umuganda* bond is a five-year IFC bond denominated in Rwandan francs, first issued in May 2014. It marked the first placement by a nonresident issuer in Rwanda's domestic capital markets, with the objective of expanding the availability of long-term local-currency finance for local businesses, while strengthening the country's domestic capital markets. See https://ifcext.ifc.org/ifcext/pressroom/IFCPressRoom.nsf/0/9548E38CE030958F85257CDA00424FC1.
11. PPPs are defined as long-term contracts between a public party and a private party for the development or management of a public asset or service, in which the private party bears significant risk and management responsibility through the life of the agreement and remuneration is linked to performance—the demand for or use of the public asset or service.
12. ITU World Telecommunication/ICT Indicators database (ITU, various years).
13. The "64 MDEs" are Rwandan firms that export more than US$64 million per year, many of which grew from being small exporters to being "64 MDEs" within a five-year period. The government of Rwanda looks to support firms with the potential to replicate this success. See MINICOM (2015).
14. OECD first published its *OECD Guidelines on Corporate Governance of State-Owned Enterprises* in 2005. These were revised in 2015 by OECD countries in cooperation with a large and diverse group of partners and stakeholders (OECD 2015). Colombia, Latvia, and the Russian Federation have participated in this review on an equal footing with OECD countries and associate themselves with its outcome. The World Bank participated as an observer. Argentina, Brazil, China, Costa Rica, Kazakhstan, Lithuania, Peru, the Philippines, South Africa, and Ukraine participated directly in discussions of the revision. In addition, comments were received from authorities in the following countries: Cabo Verde, Ecuador, the Arab Republic of Egypt, India, Indonesia, Iraq, the Lao People's Democratic Republic, Malaysia, Mauritania, Morocco, Myanmar, Paraguay, Suriname, Thailand, Uruguay, and Vietnam.
15. See http://www.ifrs.org/-/media/feature/around-the-world/jurisdiction-profiles/rwanda-ifrs-profile.pdf.
16. Based on interviews.
17. For example, Singapore's Temasek state shareholding fund progressively reduced its holdings in government-linked corporations through the sale of shares on the Singapore Stock Exchange and reinvested its cash in new investments (see https://en.wikipedia.org/wiki/Temasek_Holdings). Austria's OIAG state shareholding fund progressively reduced its holdings in strategic state companies to a "blocking minority," in order to maximize access to capital market financing and corporate governance discipline (see http://www.oebib.gv.at/en/mandate/history/). In China, the government undertook about 1,100 public sales of minority shareholdings in state-owned enterprises, which eventually improved their corporate governance and raised China's international investment profile (Mako and Zhang 2008).
18. According to the World Bank, *Doing Business 2018*, Rwanda scores reasonably well with regard to creditors' legal rights and credit information as well as speed of contract enforcement (World Bank 2018). But the credit bureau covers only 20 percent of adults, contract administration costs, on average, 83 percent of claim value, and the creditor can expect to spend 2.5 years on an insolvency case and recover just 19 percent of its loan. Fixing these issues could facilitate SME access to credit. Thus, the government may wish to provide more credit information before establishing a partial credit guarantee facility for SMEs.
19. Calculated using the number of manufacturing firms reporting that they export in the IBES and the total number of formal manufacturing firms in the Census of Enterprises. Census of Enterprises data are used because small firms are underrepresented in the IBES data because of the sampling strategy. Hence, the percentage of export manufacturing firms based solely on the IBES data may lead to an upward bias.

20. These other organizations include the Rwanda Development Board, the National Agricultural Export Development Board, the Rwanda Agriculture Board, the Development Bank of Rwanda, the Business Development Fund, the Rwanda Information Society Authority, the Rwanda Utilities Regulatory Authority, the Capacity Development and Employment Services Board, and the Higher Education Council.
21. The NCST has four key mandates: (1) provide the government with strategic advice on science, technology, innovation, and research policy matters; (2) identify and promote new high-impact areas of technology innovation; (3) support the use of science and technology in sustainable development of national resources and infrastructure; and (4) mobilize funds and manage the National Research and Innovation Fund.
22. See World Management Survey (http://worldmanagementsurvey.org/academic-research/field-experiments/).
23. There are several examples of this kind of initiative. kLab is a start-up incubation center launched and managed in close coordination with the Private Sector Federation's ICT Chamber. The African Entrepreneur Collective (Germany) is a pan-African nonprofit based in Kigali that provides training and resources to local entrepreneurs. 42Kura (Israel) is a commercial development that houses co-working space for ICT start-ups and provides incubation services. FabLab Rwanda (Massachusetts Institute of Technology) boasts of being Africa's first fabrication lab, providing innovators and designers with access to three-dimensional printers and more. The list of programs also includes Impact Hub Kigali, Inkomoko, Spring Rwanda, and Think Rwanda (Kapil and Aridi 2017).
24. Evidence from an evaluation of incubators and accelerators in Kenya shows that lack of managerial capabilities adversely affected the effectiveness of these programs.
25. The entrepreneurship ecosystem is defined as "a set of interconnected entrepreneurial actors (both potential and existing), entrepreneurial organizations (for example, firms, venture capitalists, business angels, banks), institutions (universities, public sector agencies, financial bodies), and entrepreneurial processes (for example, business birth rate, numbers of high growth firms, levels of 'blockbuster entrepreneurship,' number of serial entrepreneurs, degree of sell-out mentality within firms and levels of entrepreneurial ambition) which formally and informally coalesce to connect, mediate, and govern the performance within the local entrepreneurial environment" (Mason and Brown 2014).

References

Acemoglu, D., and P. Restrepo. 2017. "Robots and Jobs: Evidence from US Labor Markets." Working Paper 23285, National Bureau of Economic Analysis, Cambridge, MA.

Adam Smith International. 2017. "Investors' Perceptions and Constraints Faced by Exporting Firms in Rwanda's Priority Economic Sectors." Final Report, Adam Smith International, London.

Amin, M., and A. Mattoo. 2008. "Human Capital and the Changing Structure of the Indian Economy." Policy Research Working Paper 4576, World Bank, Washington, DC.

Andersen, M., B. Kett, and E. von Uexkull. 2017. "Corporate Tax Incentives and FDI in Developing Countries." In *2017–2018 Global Investment Competitiveness Report: Foreign Investor Perspectives and Policy Implications*, ch. 3, 73–99. Washington, DC: World Bank. https://doi.org/10.1596/978-1-4648-1175-3_ch3.

Autor, D., and D. Dorn. 2013. "The Growth of Low-Skill Service Jobs and the Polarization of the US Labor Market." *American Economic Review* 103 (5): 1553–97.

Bartelsman, E., J. Haltiwanger, and S. Scarpetta. 2009. "Cross-Country Differences in Productivity: The Role of Allocation and Selection." NBER Working Paper 15490, National Bureau of Economic Research, Cambridge, MA.

Becker, B. 2015. "Public R&D Policies and Private R&D Investment: A Survey of the Empirical Evidence." *Journal of Economic Surveys* 29 (5): 917–42.

Behuria, P. 2012. "Centralising Rents and Dispersing Power While Pursuing Development? Exploring the Strategic Uses of Military Firms in Rwanda." *Review of African Political Economy* 43 (150): 630–47.

Behuria, P., and T. Goodfellow. 2016. "The Political Settlement and 'Deals Environment' in Rwanda: Unpacking Two Decades of Growth." ESID Working Paper 57, Effective

States and Inclusive Development Research Centre, University of Manchester, Manchester, U.K., April.

Bloom, N., B. Eifert, A. Mahajan, D. McKenzie, and J. Roberts. 2013. "Does Management Matter? Evidence from India." *Quarterly Journal of Economics* 128 (1): 1–51.

Bloom, N., A. Mahajan, D. McKenzie, and J. Roberts. 2018. "Do Management Interventions Last? Evidence from India." NBER Working Paper 24249, National Bureau of Economic Research, Cambridge, MA.

Bloom, N., and J. Van Reenen. 2007. "Measuring and Explaining Management Practices across Firms and Countries." *Quarterly Journal of Economics* 122 (4): 1351–408.

———. 2010. "Why Do Management Practices Differ across Firms and Countries?" *Journal of Economic Perspectives* 24 (1): 203–24.

BNR (National Bank of Rwanda). 2016. *Annual Financial Stability Report: June 2015–June 2016*. Kigali: BNR.

Bode, M., J. Lohmann, and V. Steenbergen. 2017. "Attracting Investments While Raising Tax Revenue: Recommendations for Reviewing Rwanda's Tax Incentives." IGC Policy Note, International Growth Centre, Kigali.

Booth, D., and F. Golooba-Mutebi. 2012. "Developmental Patrimonialism? The Case of Rwanda." *African Affairs* 111 (444): 379–403.

Campos, F., M. Frese, M. Goldstein, L. Iacovone, H. Johnson, D. McKenzie, and M. Mensmann. 2018. "Personal Initiative Training Leads to Remarkable Growth of Women-Owned Small Businesses in Togo." Gender Innovation Lab Policy Brief 22, World Bank, Washington, DC.

Chavhan, R., S. K. Mahajan, and J. Sarang. 2012. "Supplier Development: Theories and Practices." *IOSR Journal of Mechanical and Civil Engineering (IOSR-JMCE)* 3 (3): 37–51.

Cirera, X., J. Frias, and J. Hill. 2017. "Innovation Policy Guide and Technology Adoption in Developing Countries." Unpublished manuscript, World Bank, Washington, DC.

Cirera, X., and W. F. Maloney. 2017. *The Innovation Paradox: Developing-Country Capabilities and the Unrealized Promise of Technological Catch-Up*. Washington, DC: World Bank.

Cornell University, INSEAD, and WIPO (World Intellectual Property Organization). 2013. *Global Innovation Index 2013: The Local Dynamics of Innovation*. Ithaca, Fontainebleau, and Geneva: Cornell University, INSEAD, and WIPO.

———. 2017. *Global Innovation Index 2017: Innovation Feeding the World*. Ithaca, Fontainebleau, and Geneva: Cornell University, INSEAD, and WIPO.

Cruz, M., M. Bussolo, and L. Iacovone. 2018. "Organizing Knowledge to Compete: Impacts of Capacity Building Programs on Firm Organization." *Journal of International Economics* 111 (March): 1–20.

Diao, X., J. Randriamamonjy, and J. Thurlow. 2017. "Urbanization and the Future of Economic Development in Rwanda." International Food Policy Research Institute, Washington, DC. Background paper for *Future Drivers of Growth in Rwanda*.

EABC (East African Business Community). 2016. "East African Common Market Scorecard." EABC, Nairobi.

Eichengreen, B., and P. Gupta. 2010. "The Service Sector as India's Road to Economic Growth?" Working Paper 249, India Council for Research on International Economic Relations (ICRIER), New Delhi.

EPO (European Patent Office). Various years. PATSTAT database. Munich: EPO.

European Commission. 2003. *The Broadband State Aid Rules Explained: An eGuide for Decision Makers*. Brussels: European Commission.

Feenstra, R. C., R. Inklaar, and M. P. Timmer. 2015. "The Next Generation of the Penn World Table." *American Economic Review* 105 (10): 3150–82. www.ggdc.net/pwt.

Filmer, D., and L. Fox. 2014. *Youth Employment in Sub-Saharan Africa*. Africa Development Series. Washington, DC: World Bank. doi:10.1596/978-1-4648-0107-5.

Ford, M. 2015. *Rise of the Robots: Technology and the Threat of a Jobless Future*. New York: Basic Books.

Frey, C. B., and M. Osborne. 2016. "The Future of Employment: How Susceptible Are Jobs to Computerization?" *Technological Forecasting and Social Change* 114 (1): 254–80.

García-Quevedo, J. 2004. "Do Public Subsidies Complement Business R&D? A Meta-Analysis of the Econometric Evidence." *Kyklos* 57 (1): 87–102.

Gokgur, N. 2012. "Rwanda's Ruling Party-Owned Enterprises: Do They Enhance or Impede Development?" Institute of Development Policy and Management, Antwerp.

Guadalupe, M., O. Kuzmina, and C. Thomas. 2012. "Innovation and Foreign Ownership." *American Economic Review* 102 (7): 3594–627.

Gugerty, M. 2005. "You Can't Save Alone: Commitment in Rotating Savings and Credit Associations in Kenya." Daniel J. Evans School of Public Affairs, University of Washington, Seattle.

Heizman, J., and M. Libetrau. 2017. "Efficiency of Mineral Processing in Rwanda's Artisanal and Small-Scale Mining Sector." Federal Institute for Geoscience and Natural Resources, Berlin.

Hsieh, C., and P. J. Klenow. 2009. "Misallocation and Manufacturing TFP in China and India." *Quarterly Journal of Economics* 124 (4): 1403–48.

IMF (International Monetary Fund). 2017. "Article IV for Rwanda." IMF, Washington, DC.

IMF (International Monetary Fund), UN (United Nations), and World Bank. 2015. "Operations for Low-Income Countries' Effective and Efficient Use of Tax Incentives for Investment." In *International Monetary Fund Report to the G-20 Development Working Group.* Washington, DC: IMF.

ITU (International Telecommunications Union). 2016. *Measuring the Information Society.* Geneva: ITU.

———. Various years. ITU World Telecommunication/ICT Indicators database. Geneva: ITU.

James, S. 2009. "Tax and Non-Tax Incentives and Investments: Evidence and Policy Implications." Foreign Investment Advisory Service, World Bank, Washington, DC.

Jones, C. I. 2016. "The Facts of Economic Growth." In *Handbook of Macroeconomics,* vol. 2A, edited by J. Taylor and H. Uhlig, ch. 1. Amsterdam: Elsevier North-Holland.

Jütting, J., and J. de Laiglesia. 2009. "Is Informal Normal? Towards More and Better Jobs in Developing Countries." Development Centre Studies, OECD, Paris.

Kapil, N., and A. Aridi. 2017. "Innovation Agencies: Takeaways from Emerging Innovation Systems." Unpublished paper, World Bank, Washington, DC.

Kast, F., S. Meier, and D. Pomeranz. 2012. "Under-Savers Anonymous: Evidence on Self-Help Groups and Peer Pressure as a Savings Commitment Device." NBER Working Paper 18417, National Bureau of Economic Research, Cambridge, MA.

Kim, B.-K., and E. Vogel, eds. 2011. *The Park Chung Hee Era: The Transformation of South Korea.* Cambridge, MA: Harvard University Press.

Kojima, M. and C. Trimble. 2016. *Making Power Affordable for Africa and Viable for Its Utilities.* Washington, DC: World Bank. https://openknowledge.worldbank.org/handle/10986/2509.

Lemarchand, G. A., and A. Tash, eds. 2015. *Mapping Research and Innovation in the Republic of Rwanda.* GO-SPIN Country Profiles in Science, Technology, and Innovation Policy, vol. 4. Paris: United Nations Educational, Scientific, and Cultural Organization (UNESCO).

Lim, W. 2016. "The Development of Korea's Electronic Industry during Its Formative Years, 1966–1979." Korea Development Institute, School of Public Policy and Management, Seoul.

Mako, W., and C. Zhang. 2008. "Why Is China So Different from Other Transition Economies?" In *Privatization in Transition Economies: The Ongoing Story.* Amsterdam: Elsevier.

Maloney, W. F. 2017. *Revising the National Innovation System in Developing Countries.* Washington, DC: World Bank.

Maloney, W., and M. Sarrias. 2014. "Convergence to the Managerial Frontier." Policy Research Working Paper 6822, World Bank, Washington, DC.

———. 2017. "Convergence to the Managerial Frontier." *Journal of Economic Behavior and Organization* 134 (C): 284–306.

Mason, C., and R. Brown. 2014. "Entrepreneurial Ecosystems and Growth-Oriented Entrepreneurship." Final version of a background paper prepared for "Entrepreneurial Ecosystems and Growth Oriented Entrepreneurship" workshop, OECD LEED Programme and the Dutch Ministry of Economic Affairs, The Hague, Netherlands, November 7, 2013.

Millot, V. 2009. "Trademarks as an Indicator of Product and Marketing Innovations." OECD Science, Technology, and Industry Working Paper 2009/06, OECD, Paris.

MINECOFIN (Ministry of Finance and Economic Planning), Rwanda. 2017. *Fiscal Risk Review of Government Investment.* Kigali: MINECOFIN, Government Portfolio Management Unit, December.

MINICOM (Ministry of Trade and Industry), Rwanda. 2015. "National Export Strategy II." MINICOM, Kigali.

New Times. 2017. "How Smelting Firm Lost Licence to Refine Tin Ore." *New Times*, June 20. http://www.newtimes.co.rw/section/read/214579/.

NISR (National Institute of Statistics of Rwanda). 2011. *Establishment Census 2011*. Kigali: NISR, September.

———. 2015. *Establishment Census 2014*. Kigali: NISR, June.

———. 2016. *Integrated Housing Living Conditions Survey 2013/2014 (EICV4)*. Kigali: NISR.

———. 2017. *Integrated Business Enterprise Survey (IBES) 2015*. Kigali: NISR, July.

OECD (Organisation for Economic Co-operation and Development). 2011. "State-Owned Enterprise Governance Reform: An Inventory of Recent Change." Paris: OECD.

———. 2015. *Guidelines on Corporate Governance of State-Owned Enterprises*. Paris: OECD.

PSF (Private Sector Federation). 2013. "Business Investment Climate Survey." Kigali, Rwanda.

Steenbergen, V., and E. von Uexkull. 2018. "Raising the Cost-Effectiveness of Rwanda's Tax Incentives." Unpublished paper, World Bank, Washington, DC.

UNCTAD (United Nations Conference on Trade and Development). 2017. *Science, Technology, and Innovation Policy Review*. Geneva: UNCTAD.

Wagh, S., A. Lovegrove, and J. Kashangaki. 2012. "Scaling up Regional Financial Integration in the EAC." In *De-Fragmenting Africa: Deepening Regional Trade Integration in Goods and Services*, edited by P. Brenton and G. Isik. Washington, DC: World Bank.

WIPO (World Intellectual Property Organization). 2017. *World Intellectual Property Report 2017: Intangible Capital in Global Value Chains*. Geneva: WIPO.

World Bank. 2015. "Export Competitiveness: Why Domestic Market Competition Matters." *Viewpoint*, June. https://openknowledge.worldbank.org/bitstream/handle/10986/23658/Export0competi00Competition0Matters.pdf?sequence=1&isAllowed=y.

———. 2016. *Making Power Affordable for Africa and Viable for Its Utilities*. Washington, DC: World Bank.

———. 2018. *Doing Business 2018: Reforming to Create Jobs*. Washington, DC: World Bank.

———. 2019. *Doing Business 2019: Training for Reform*. Washington, DC: World Bank.

World Economic Forum. 2017. *The Global Competitiveness Report 2017–2018*. Cologny, Switzerland: World Economic Forum.

World Economic Forum, INSEAD, and Cornell University. 2016. *Global Technology Report 2016*. Geneva: World Economic Forum.

Wu, Y. 2007. "Service Sector Growth in China and India: A Comparison." *China: An International Journal* 5 (1): 137–54.

Zúñiga-Vicente, J. A., C. Alonso-Borrego, F. J. Forcadell, and J. I. Galán. 2014. "Assessing the Effect of Public Subsidies on Firm R&D Investment: A Survey." *Journal of Economic Surveys* 28 (1): 6–67.

5

Transitioning Agriculture and Food as an Engine of Growth

Introduction

Agriculture has been a major source of national income and growth for Rwanda. It accounts for close to 70 percent of employment, more than 30 percent of gross domestic product (GDP), and more than 50 percent of exports of goods. Considerable government effort has been devoted to developing the sector, especially after the food price shocks of 2007–08. Agricultural value added has risen more than 5 percent a year over the past 15 years, and productivity in agriculture has increased strongly. The main question for this chapter is how long and to what extent will agriculture remain an engine of growth in the Rwandan economy? Does Rwanda's highly ambitious economic future continue to have agriculture at its core, or will the sector launch high long-term growth and then gradually take a back seat?

The agriculture sector will remain a major source of comparative advantage for Rwanda, even as it climbs the income ladder over the coming decades. This suggests that the sector should remain a major part of any high-growth strategy. To accomplish this, agriculture will need to continue to modernize, become more responsive to market signals, and integrate more effectively with regional and global markets. Its contribution will need to shift from primarily supplying commodities for domestic use to producing higher-value-added goods as an integral part of food supply chains linked to regional and international markets. This will require a much larger role for the private sector in determining the allocation of agricultural resources. It also will involve a continuing large, but evolving, role for the public sector. The chapter makes the case that Rwanda is well placed to make this happen.

High growth in the future will come from productivity-increasing innovations and technical and allocative efficiency in resource use. Only a few initiatives should receive public financial support, accompanied by a rigorous evaluation to determine whether adequate returns are being achieved. Initiatives with persistently low returns should be reallocated to higher-return activities. Public sector activities in agriculture will nevertheless need to increase, but be targeted more effectively to providing key public goods.

First, Rwanda's effective research and regulatory institutions should continually be adapted to evolving opportunities and threats. The high technical expertise of the agency in charge of agriculture will be increasingly important as improving standards and Rwanda's efforts to increase exports increase the frequency and importance of sanitary and phytosanitary issues. Rwanda's reputation for probity and accountability is one of its most precious assets and is especially important in agriculture, where quality and food safety issues are dominant concerns of consumers.

Second, a more consistent and selective policy needs to be formulated regarding vertical coordination through value chains and horizontal coordination of production across farms. More effective vertical coordination in agriculture would be where private sector partners provide skills, capital, and entrée into international markets and farmers acquire higher incomes and new resources. Rwanda benefits from an active cooperative system, but outcomes from contractual relationships between farmers and private sector aggregators vary widely. The success of such relationships from the point of view of both farmers and aggregators is essential to smallholder inclusion in high-value-growth business models (Delgado 1999).

Third, Rwanda should engage more effectively and opportunistically with neighboring countries on a regional division of labor, both in production based on comparative advantage and in knowledge generation and diffusion. Rwanda has a major stake in increasing the importation of raw materials such as cereals for its food-processing and animal protein industries, while increasing its exports of processed foods and high-value calories—for example, from milk and meat products. Ways should be explored to exploit the huge market potential of neighboring countries by increasing food production. Another initiative might include a more common approach to certification of food safety, sanitary, and phytosanitary conditions. Regional integration also should be pursued through continuing efforts to adopt transparent science-based standards, product registrations, and certification of agricultural inputs.

Fourth, Rwanda needs to profit from the big-data revolution in innovation, making the benefits of big data accessible at reasonable cost to smallholders. Big data approaches are critical to both increasing innovation and private sector investment and dealing with the smallest farms and most densely settled rural areas in Africa. "Smart farming," where just the right amounts of the right inputs are used for each parcel on the basis of information gathered by handheld devices with the right sensors, offers one such opportunity. Big data approaches such as blockchain technology similarly offer the potential to lower the costs of small financial transactions that require secure record keeping and decentralized input, such as land registration and mortgages.

Fifth, public investments in infrastructure—especially rural roads, electricity, and water—should be linked more effectively to agricultural development and higher-value-added products. Irrigation is clearly a constraint. Notably, current yields of rice are insufficient to cover the cost of irrigation investment. Therefore, while emphasizing an increase in rice productivity, other high-value crops like horticulture could also be considered in irrigated areas.

Sixth, to facilitate the transmission of technical knowledge and skills to smallholders, there is a need for more proactive and consistent training of managers and farmers. In particular, a more consistent approach to training managers and technical experts working for aggregators is needed for vertical integration. Companies might be involved in this process through training programs to build up nationally needed skill sets in agribusiness, high-value supply chains, and agricultural technology. The best multinational companies have a track record of making these investments and provide examples of how such investments can be done to mutual advantage.

Seventh, land degradation and global climate change, which threaten the future of Rwandan agriculture, need to be addressed more comprehensively. Although considerable progress has been made in constructing robust "bench" (wide) terraces, much more needs to be done to secure the land asset. Fortunately, the soil and water management interventions central to halting land degradation are also the ones most useful to increase the ability of farmers to adapt to climate change through better water retention and increased soil quality. Landscape restoration and conservation are community-level activities, not individual ones. Local government, producer groups, and national technical expertise and funding all have a role to play in implementation.

Policy Support for Strong Growth in Agriculture

The agriculture sector plays an important role in the Rwandan economy. Agricultural GDP grew 5 percent a year from 1999 to 2016, which is a high rate of growth by global standards. Despite slow growth in sectoral employment over this period (1.1 percent a year), agriculture still accounted for close to 70 percent of total national employment in 2016.[1] Employment in other sectors rose 9.8 percent a year from 1999 to 2016. The rapid movement of workers out of agriculture and into more productive sectors accounted for 3.2 percentage points of the country's 4.4 percent annual rise in labor productivity from 1999 to 2016. Further, growth in agriculture has likely stimulated growth in other sectors through backward links (for example, by encouraging input industries such as fertilizers) or forward links (for example, by increasing food processing), although these links tend to be smaller in agriculture than in other sectors (Hirschman 1958).

Widespread growth in the purchasing power of farm households in remote areas can increase demand for local goods and services, which can mobilize unemployed local resources. Consumption growth links arise from bringing outside spending power into remote areas—whether from the sale of export crops or from unilateral transfers such as remittances.[2] The key is that underemployed resources are mobilized to meet new demand for local consumption items like processed fresh food and drinks and local services; the size of the "growth multiplier" from this effect depends on the extent to which the new income coming into remote areas is spent on locally produced items that have no outlet outside the local area and that can be produced by formerly underused resources (Delgado et al. 1998; World Bank 2007b). The Integrated Household Living Conditions Survey of 2013/14 (EICV4) shows that farmers work, on average, only 20 hours a week in Rwandan agriculture, although this likely reflects periods of both labor slack and labor scarcity (MINAGRI 2017c; NISR 2014). In any event, Diao et al. (2017a) estimate that such multipliers are still evident in more isolated parts of Rwanda. However, this effect, based on demand constraints in rural areas, cannot be expected to last in the longer term as the economy becomes more fully connected.[3]

Supportive policies have helped to boost agricultural production. The National Agricultural Policy of 2004 and its four- to five-year implementation plans (Programs for Support to Agriculture, PSTA1 to PSTA3) emphasized growth in staple food outputs for the domestic market and widespread improvement in the income of smallholders. The emphasis on self-sufficiency in staple food crops was reinforced when the doubling of international food prices in 2008 was accompanied by the shutting off of cereal exports from Tanzania and Uganda. The food price crisis drove a severe compression of welfare (on average, at that time, Rwandan households spent 60 percent of their income on food), especially for the poor.[4]

Government efforts to develop new irrigated land and improve existing land through improved terraces contributed to agricultural growth. From 2008 to 2012, irrigation was introduced in 23,000 hectares of marginally used marshlands and 2,500 hectares of hillsides, and more than 46,000 hectares of "bench" terraces (wider and more level terraces typically requiring substantial labor or other power to construct) were added (MINAGRI 2012; World Bank 2014).

However, the cost of irrigation investments is high, about 7.5 to 10 times the annual earnings (including subsidies and after costs) of rice farmers benefitting from irrigation in the marshlands. Moreover, potato farmers with nonirrigated land in the northern or southern provinces earn some four times, and coffee growers earn more than three times, the amount earned by rice farmers in the irrigated marshlands. Increasing scarcity of land and water suggests that such growth in area cultivated will be difficult to sustain in the longer run and will need to be in higher-value items, especially at the current cost levels for irrigation in Rwanda (US$6,000 to US$8,000 per hectare for irrigation in the marshlands and three to four times that on hillsides).

The government has made significant progress on land consolidation. The average farm size is only 0.6 hectare, with perhaps 0.12 hectare per worker.[5] Production on numerous small plots of land can impose technical inefficiencies related to water control and distribution, crop choice and interactions, and planting materials used, while limiting the potential for mechanized plowing. Land consolidation was launched with the organic land law in 2005,[6] institutionalized through the Land Use Consolidation Program (LUCP) in 2007, and implemented through the Crop Intensification Program (CIP) starting in 2008. Land under consolidated use rose from 28,788 hectares in 2007 to 502,916 hectares in 2012, primarily through the consolidation of production rather than of ownership (World Bank 2014). At this rate of increase, some 39 percent of farm households would have participated by now.[7]

The land consolidation program has been state led, with some room for individual initiative. The government has determined which (food staple) crop varieties and seeds must be planted on adjoining plots, when they are to be planted, and, to a lesser degree, what other inputs will be used. However, consolidation has not involved mandatory consolidation of ownership, and planting, cultivation, and harvesting are still carried out by individual landowners, albeit on a communal schedule (Pritchard 2013). Land consolidation has also facilitated the development of new irrigated agricultural lands in former marshlands and joint soil and water management in other sites to reduce erosion. Thus, consolidation has been a key part of the strategy to increase productivity and expand the area under food production through state leadership (Kathiresan 2012; World Bank 2014).

The government made a major effort to register agricultural land to individual owners from 2009 to 2013. This program, more extensive than similar efforts in most other African countries, has achieved the demarcation, adjudication, and digitization of 10.7 million parcels of agricultural land, resulting in coverage of more than 90 percent of agricultural parcels in the country.[8] Providing secure title has arguably made the job of consolidating production decisions more palatable to farmers (Pritchard 2013). Titling improved land security, especially for women, and led to considerable inceases in farmers' investment in their own soils. However, it also has been associated with a decrease in land sales, suggesting that titling has not promoted land market activity or commercial consolidation, at least not in the short run (Ali, Deininger, and Goldstein 2014).

Cooperative development has been a key component of state-led collective action. Cooperatives are organized along commodity lines corresponding to value chains—for example, rice, maize, potatoes, beans, coffee, tea, horticulture, and dairy. Crop and livestock cooperatives account for roughly half of Rwanda's 8,000 primary cooperatives at the present time (MINICOM 2018). Most of the cooperatives are aggregated into federations along commodity lines, with rice and tea being the most significant in terms of members and value (World Bank 2016). The more organized federations, such as those for rice and tea, offer support services such as finance, aggregation, and marketing. Yet less than 20 percent of farmers belonged to cooperatives in 2016 (NISR 2016b). In part this may be due to the fact that some commodities, such as rice and coffee, more naturally lend themselves to cooperative development in dealing with aggregators. In part it is likely due to resource constraints in government programs such as subsidized seed and fertilizer inputs for maize or wheat cultivation that are distributed through cooperatives.

More than 70 percent of farmers with more than 10 hectares (large farms by Rwandan standards) were members of cooperatives, suggesting that membership was important for obtaining access to government services and other support (World Bank 2016). At the same time, a recent survey conducted for the Ministry of Trade and Industry also indicated dissatisfaction among cooperative members with regard to accountability and transparency in the system (MINICOM 2018).[9] A copious literature on good practice in development of agricultural cooperatives addresses typical sticking points such as transparency, clarity of ownership, and accountability (Zeuli, Cropp, and Schaars 2004). In Rwanda, interviews suggest that linking becoming a member of a specific cooperative, receiving benefits through it, and actually residing in the location concerned will be a particular issue in future discussions regarding cooperative governance.

Government promotion of the use of fertilizer and improved seeds contributed to growth in agriculture. The share of farms applying inorganic mineral fertilizer, associated with substantial improvements in yields, increased from 12 percent in 2008 to 30 percent in 2012 (MINAGRI 2014; World Bank 2014), although use rates have fallen since then, as discussed below. Promotion of fertilizer use has been an important part of the CIP launched in 2007 (MINAGRI 2015b). The government procured fertilizer abroad in bulk and in 2010 created a network of small-scale private dealers for distribution, located throughout the country. Privatization of fertilizer imports was implemented in 2013, rising to eight active importing companies in 2015–16 (MINAGRI 2015b).

Government efforts also contributed to growth in the livestock sector. Livestock value added rose by 5.2 percent per year from 2000 to 2016. Efforts will continue being deployed to increase animal resources products, notably milk, meat, eggs, honey, and fish.

Emerging Policy Challenges

Achieving the government's ambitious growth objectives will require a shift in the sources of growth in agriculture. Periods of rapid growth in agricultural production in Rwanda have largely reflected either expansion of the land devoted to agriculture (1960s and 1970s) or increased use of inputs (2000s) (figure 5.1). However, the scope for further expansion of agricultural land is limited, as is the potential for achieving worthwhile gains from applying ever larger amounts of labor per hectare. There is significant potential for continuing to improve farmer skills, extend

FIGURE 5.1 Decomposition of sources of agricultural growth in Rwanda, 1961–2014

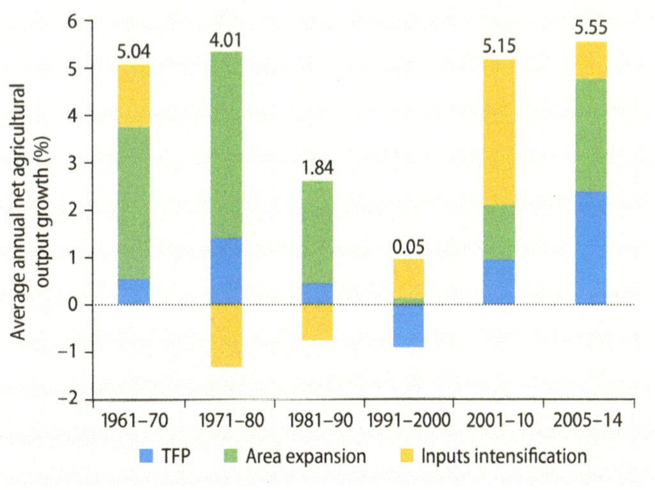

Source: Compiled from U.S. Department of Agriculture 2017 data.
Note: The three sources of growth listed sum to output growth in the period in question. Output growth may be different than column height because of negative contributions to growth in the period in question. Growth not explained by area expansion or increased use per hectare of inputs (including labor) is attributed to total factor productivity (TFP). TFP is a combination of increased allocative and technical efficiency and technological change. Because the numerator of TFP (output growth) is highly affected by weather outcomes in any given year, it makes sense to consider TFP outcomes over at least a 10-year period that includes both good and less good weather. This explains the strategy for handling differences between the early and later parts of the period 2001–14.

irrigated area, stabilize and expand terraces, boost the use of more adapted fertilizers, and increase farmers' use of better seeds. Extending these programs to more farms would likely continue to promote a rate of growth of 5 percent and improve the welfare of large numbers of smallholders for perhaps a few years, as farms yet to be reached adopt more modern practices. However, the impact of such improvements will decline over time as the "low-hanging fruit" are picked and more difficult cases are taken on. Most important, this approach would not generate the agricultural growth necessary to achieve the rapid increases in output envisioned under the government's strategy.

More rapid growth will require a faster increase in total factor productivity (TFP). Total factor productivity growth reflects improvements in technical efficiency, made possibile by the redeployment of inputs, land, and labor to increase physical output; allocative efficiency, which considers the costs of using different inputs and factors in addition to technical issues, in order to maximize profitability; and technological change, which embodies scientific and technical innovation to get more from less (annex 5A). TFP growth in Rwandan agriculture has exceeded 2 percent a year since 2005 (on par with countries in Asia and Latin America), reflecting continuing payoffs from public research and extension to support staple food production.[10] Increases in TFP have been based largely on improved technical efficiency. For Rwanda to become an upper-middle-income country by 2035, further increases in TFP in agriculture will have to be based more on improvements in allocative efficiency and technological change.

More rapid growth in allocative efficiency and technological change, in turn, will require greater reliance on private initiative. Investments will have to be based more on expected economic returns, cutting losses on losing ventures, adding value through processing where it is profitable, specializing in the most profitable opportunities, importing those products that are cheaper in neighboring countries, tapping into larger markets outside the country, actively pursuing scale economies to increase the competitiveness of exports, and benefitting from the experience and networks of successful firms elsewhere in the world. This approach implies creating an institutional, infrastructural, and policy environment led by market signals about where, when, and how agriculture produces and trades and shifting the public role gradually to facilitating the fair implementation of those private sector decisions. Public sector efforts to improve the technical efficiency of smallholders would continue.

The shift in some responsibilities from the state to the private sector will build on recent policy changes in this direction. The first implementation plan for the National Agriculture Policy envisions further boosting the productivity of staple foods while attracting more private sector investment into agriculture (MINAGRI 2017b). At the same time, the National Agricultural Export Development Board has presided over privatization of the tea sector, begun privatizing parts of the coffee sector, and promoted exports by private entities of fruits and vegetables (NAEB 2017).

Rapid increases in productivity will require more mechanization (MINAGRI 2017a). Despite substantial progress in land consolidation, most of Rwandan agriculture is carried out under conditions of abundant—sometimes surplus—labor on small plots, mostly on hillsides (MINAGRI 2017c). As a result, the use of labor-saving machinery, such as tractors and combine harversters, is confined to a few small niches. However, mechanical solutions are needed to expand bench terraces and extend irrigation at lower costs per unit, in both cases involving whole communities. Postharvest mechanization needs—including for smallholdings as much as for large farms—are for transport, processing, and packaging of agricultural commodities along the value chain. In some cases, equipment will need to be owned collectively. It will be critical to match the form of mechanization to actual needs in the system and to ensure that the machines used are serviceable in Rwanda at reasonable cost.

Further efforts are necessary to promote the use of inorganic fertilizer. The share of farms using inorganic fertilizer fell from 30 percent in 2012 to below 20 percent in 2017.[11] This decline may reflect the fall in the level of subsidy from 100 percent in 2007 to between 16 and 50 percent in 2016, depending on the specific formulation (AGRA 2016).[12] Moreover, limited access to financing and extension services may be constraining the growth of fertilizer use (IFDC 2014). Continuing gains could be promoted by expanding the coverage of locations, which there clearly is still scope to do, and improving fertilizer formulations (IFDC 2014). The Rwanda Agriculture Board, for example, is experimenting with fertilizer formulations for Irish potatoes in volcanic soils that are more suitable than the standard 17N-17P-17K fertilizer that Rwanda now imports for use everywhere (MINAGRI 2017c).

The government needs to continue promoting the use of improved seeds and modernizing its seed regulations. The CIP typically purchases improved seeds for cereals in bulk in other countries and distributes them to farmers. Only maize, soybean, and wheat seeds were subsidized at the farm level in 2016; subsidies equaled 75–85 percent of the cost of imported seeds and about 50 percent of the cost of seeds produced locally (AGRA 2016). As part of a move toward a market-oriented seed system, in 2015 Rwanda launched an effort to harmonize Rwanda's seed trade regulations with norms of the Common Market for Southern and Eastern Africa; harmonization was completed in 2017 (COMESA 2017; MINAGRI 2015a). Rwanda is also taking the first steps to legalize agricultural genetically modified organisms. The Rwanda Environment Management Authority drafted a law that will govern genetically modified organisms; the law would implement the Cartagena Protocol, to which Rwanda is a signatory (Ntirenganya 2018).

Important constraints to development of the milk sector have emerged over time. Many beneficiaries of the *Girinka* program lack access to the forage or pasture required to ensure that the cow is well nourished (World Bank 2014). Moreover, payments received by farmers for raw milk appear low, about half to one-third of the level in neighboring countries, even though the price of ultra-high-temperature processed milk in Kigali shops is comparable with that in neighboring countries.[13] Farmers are paid prices jointly set by the Ministry of Agriculture, Ministry of Industry, farmer cooperatives, milk processors, and milk collection centers (MCCs). Interviews suggest that following their own assessments of business prospects, formal milk processors have been reluctant to pay higher prices. The number of MCCs is high, following rapid growth in their numbers driven by policy. Given the difficulty they face in getting higher prices from processors and farmers' reluctance to supply to them, many MCCs are operating at low capacity, in the vicinity of 25 percent on average. Low turnover leads to high unit costs, further compounding the problem of low producer prices (Abdulsamad and Gereffi 2016). Because the roots of the problem seem to be rapid growth in the supply of raw material combined with a limited domestic market, especially at the high end, Rwanda's sales of milk will need to expand into neighboring countries if the sector is to thrive (Abdulsamad and Gereffi 2016).

Lack of agricultural finance remains a major constraint on transformation of the sector. Transforming agriculture requires investment. Rwandan farmers' "financial inclusion" in the formal financial sector is comparable with that of the rest of the population and high compared with farmers' access in the rest of Africa (Access to Finance Rwanda–Finscope 2016). Financial inclusion here is determined by interviews with farmers and other agricultural actors such as small and medium enterprises (SMEs), as well as individuals and SMEs in other sectors. The survey asks questions about ease of physical access, ease of opening an account, convenience, services on offer, access to loans and interest rates charged, and other issues; and a score is computed from the answers. Agricultural entities, including individual farmers, have mean scores similar to participants from other sectors. However, the actual use of formal financial services in the agriculture sector in Rwanda is quite low and occurs mainly through savings and credit cooperatives (SACCOs) and mobile money providers (World Bank 2016). Although the overall ratio of credit to domestic GDP for Rwanda was 20 percent in 2016, the comparable ratio for agricultural credit in relation to agricultural GDP was only 4.6 percent, up from 3.6 percent in 2012 (World Bank 2016).

Agricultural SMEs—critical for agricultural transformation—in particular make less use of formal financial services through banks (as opposed to other loan-making financial institutions such as SACCOs) than other SMEs (World Bank 2016). Reasons identified include low availability and quality of data to decrease lenders' risks; limited financial experience of farmer and producer organizations; limited operational capacity among formal sector banks to serve the agriculture sector; limited availability of medium- to long-term liquidity; and fiscal disincentives to borrowers. With regard to fiscal disincentives, improvements in the land tenure system and collateral registry have resulted in increased use of land as collateral. However, the high costs of registering mortgages for relatively small loans act as a disincentive to financial institutions. These extra costs are typically added to the costs facing borrowers. Furthermore, less than 0.5 percent of farmers surveyed in Rwanda report having access to agricultural insurance (World Bank 2016).[14]

Blockchain technology provides high potential for reducing the cost of registering financially significant transactions. Blockchain is a digital database (or ledger) distributed across a network of computers. The records are protected by cryptography and thus largely protected from human error, editing, and removal.[15] The technology can enable secure transactions, digital authentication, and legally binding signatures. It is widely considered as a way to manage financial transactions, asset transfers, and regulatory obligations. Land registration, where Rwanda has made huge recent progress in clarifying individual data points, is a natural venue for reducing the costs of registration and record keeping through decentralization of updates and safekeeping and transparency of records. Such approaches are now being tried or considered in Georgia, Ghana, the Russian Federation, Ukraine, and the United Kingdom, in addition to some states of India.[16]

The technology offers promise for reducing the costs of registering small mortgages and other loans. In this regard, the Rwandan Blockchain Project was established in 2017 in partnership with the WISeKey's Blockchain Centre of Excellence, a major Swiss information technology company. It aims to position the country as a key player in digital transformation by providing citizens and businesses with access to policy, technical, and business expertise. In October 2017, the government of Rwanda, WISeKey, and Microsoft announced a partnership to adapt Rwanda's land registry specifically to blockchain.[17]

Both the state-owned Development Bank of Rwanda (BRD) and private banks are increasingly investing in agribusiness as opposed to agricultural production. BRD is the largest formal provider of credit to agriculture, primarily for tea production and agroprocessing. Overall, nonperforming loans equaled 18 percent of lending for agricultural production in 2016, compared with 8 percent of total agribusiness lending. Further, 57 percent of the formal banking sector's agricultural loan portfolio in 2016 (FRW 70 billion or US$86 million) supported agroprocessing and agrotrading as opposed to production (World Bank 2016). The implication is that any policies designed to increase formal sector bank finance for agricultural production will need to consider how to reduce the risk of default, but the default risk may be less of a concern for lending to agroprocessing and trading.

Targeting Larger Markets for Growth

Achieving and sustaining higher agricultural growth will require identifying crops, livestock, and food products where Rwanda has a comparative advantage. Farmers should not direct their production just to satisfying rising demand from domestic consumers as urbanization and incomes rise. High growth comes from scale economies and specialization, which can only be achieved through regional and international trade in a small economy such as Rwanda. As incomes rise, consumers will demand greater diversity in product lines; for example, the average traditional food-oriented U.S. supermarket carries roughly 40,000 products originating from around the world, and large megastores that sell food carry far more products.[18] Eventually, diversity in product lines at the consumer level and specialization at the producer level will be the norm everywhere. It will be important for Rwanda to enter the game as early as possible to capture desirable market shares for its specialty products. Producers will have to evaluate shifting patterns of demand and the country's core advantages carefully and then assess how to deploy them to maximize income gains.

Competing in global food markets requires achieving high levels of food quality and safety and receiving credit for product quality and safety through credible certification, traceability, and harmonization of standards. Certification is important to reducing transaction costs in marketing and reaping market recognition for quality (FAO 2010; Jaffee, Henson, and Diaz Rios 2011). The Rwanda Standards Board's global recognition of integrity and competence is a key part of Rwanda's comparative advantage going forward. For example, five private companies presently sell value-added Rwandan tea, benefitting from high quality (single estate brands), Fair Trade certification, and certification as pesticide free by the Rwanda Standards Board. Food safety certification (such as the International Organization for Standardization's ISO 22000:2005) is also practiced. Revenues from tea have risen in recent years, a large share of Rwandan tea traded at the Mombasa tea auctions captures premium prices, and Rwandan tea has won competitions for quality there (NAEB 2017). Tea is a plantation crop, with production managed and bulked by cooperatives that sell to private tea factories. The tea industry currently comprises 14 operational factories, all of which were privatized between 2004 and 2012.

Success in boosting agricultural exports through multiple layers of value chains (for example, cooperatives, federations, factories, and exporters) also requires ensuring that farmers get a decent share of the final wholesale export price. In the case of tea, concern emerged in 2011 that farmers were not getting a high enough share of the "made-tea" price earned by the factory; the system in place was a form of "cost-plus" pricing by factories in which producer prices were delinked from world markets. In 2012, Rwanda's Cabinet mandated a producer price share of 30 percent of the "made-tea" auction price received by the factories. This share was raised to 40 percent in early 2016, despite opposition from the factories. Evaluations by the World Bank found that, after the last price increase, farmer (and not just cooperative) revenues per kilogram increased 40 percent relative to the pre-2011 level. The evaluation did not find any impact on quality, but increased farm investment did lead to higher quantity. Finally, the evaluation found that the 40 percent producer price share had no significant impact on tea factory bought-leaf costs as a share of total costs.[19] Box 5.1, relating to the upgrading of both quality and brand in a Chinese case, illustrates the high potential for adding value to tea.

Unlike tea, coffee is truly a smallholder crop grown on 400,000 diversified individual farms throughout the country and sold through cooperatives (NAEB 2017). Since 2002, Rwanda policy has been to improve the quality as well as the quantity of coffee for export. International coffee prices have fluctuated by a factor of 7 in nominal terms in the last two decades.[20] The decline

BOX 5.1 High-value tea development in Yunnan Province, China

Yunnan Province in China is a mountainous, fertile region that falls within the South China–Vietnam subtropical evergreen forest belt. It is one of China's largest tea-producing regions, with 70 percent of production sold outside the province. Significant environmental challenges have come from erosion on hillsides and overuse of pesticides, leading to soil and water pollution. A large share of production comes from small farms averaging 0.3 hectare each. The very best tea from small tea gardens typically is marketed directly to wealthy urban consumers via specialized middlemen. However, commercially branded teas form the large majority of high-end commercial supplies to cities and virtually all exports; quality and food safety are checked rigorously. Low-end tea is sold in bulk for domestic use and encounters consumer concerns for food safety as well as quality.

Government has been trying to reduce the environmental impacts of tea production and helping small farm communities to shift a larger share of their bulk tea production to higher-value commercial outlets. Reforestation of the most degraded land is actively promoted through cash incentives. Testing and certification of tea for food safety has been pursued vigorously, especially after Yunnan tea exports were rejected in Europe and Japan in 2011. Labeling programs for specific geographic origin, dating, and "greenness" are also being implemented to add value.

At the extreme, raw tea from Pu'er (one of Yunnan's subregions) commanded up to US$20,000 per pound in 2013, although this price could not be sustained. More usually, certified and branded quality teas from Yunnan achieve a 300 to 400 percent markup over bulk tea from the same subregions of Yunnan. Although tea from bulk operations is grown at higher density per hectare, value per hectare is still higher for the branded and certified operations in the same locations.

Source: Havemann 2015, which includes a comprehensive survey of the literature.

in revenues from coffee, shown in table 5.1, in large part reflects steep declines in global coffee prices since the 2011 peak. As a relatively small producer in East African terms, Rwanda sells mainly to traders who bulk up coffees from different sources and are poorly placed to pass on quality premiums to only one supplier. Instead, Rwanda needs to increase the share sold directly to roasters, particularly those that sell to specialty markets willing to pay a premium for certain characteristics.[21] Rwanda produces some of the best Arabica coffees in the world, major players such as Starbucks are involved, and Fair Trade certification has been achieved. Under active promotion from the National Agricultural Export Development Board, the number of coffee-washing stations—full washing is key to improving the quality of coffee—has grown significantly, reaching 300 and adding a final export price premium of US$0.45 per pound (NAEB 2017).[22]

The path that vertical coordination continues to take in coffee is likely key to its future. Much has been achieved through focusing on enforcing zoning to improve traceability of coffee, an element of branding embraced by the private sector and critical for firms to benefit from their investments in farmers (FAO, MAFAP 2017; NAEB 2017). Further quality improvements will result from the transfer of more specialized knowledge and inputs from export customers (such as international roasters) to cooperatives, farmers, and washing stations. This transfer of knowledge and inputs also should encourage companies to pay higher price premiums to cooperatives and encourage farmers to comply with quality standards. Fair Trade certification opens the door to higher retail prices in final markets, but certification requires a minimum level of production to overcome the costs of certification and monitoring at the producer level.[23] These costs are likely too high for most washing stations in

TABLE 5.1 Rwanda's main agricultural exports, 2012/13 to 2015/16
current US$ realized, millions, free on board

Product	2012/13	2015/16	Three-year change (%)
Tea	63.9	73.0	+14
Coffee	69.4	52.3	−25
Livestock and products	54.7	73.9	+35
Fruits and vegetables	5.9	5.7	−3
Cassava and products	1.1	8.2	+720

Sources: NISR 2016a; NAEB website (http://www.naeb.gov.rw).
Note: Coffee and tea volumes from the National Institute of Statistics of Rwanda are converted at net average prices reported by the National Agricultural Export Development Board. "Livestock and products" includes meat, milk, hides, and skins. "Cassava and products" includes flour.

isolation; it is difficult to foresee certification being extended without vertical coordination with multinational firms.

Trends in global demand for higher-value, certifiably organic, green, and high-quality branded agricultural products, such as essential oils, herbs, spices, medicinals, and natural insecticides, also offer considerable potential for value addition. In smallholder systems in Rwanda that face long, wide, and anonymous value chains, vertical integration with value chain actors and collective action will be necessary to gain the international market recognition necessary for success.

Horticulture and floriculture products offer significant opportunities for value addition through diversification of exports. Rwanda has already made substantial public investments in horticulture and floriculture incubators, but exports remain modest—while growing rapidly year-on-year (2015–17). African countries' experiences with horticulture and floriculture exports to European markets highlight several elements critical for success (box 5.2). Their experience offers some lessons for Rwanda's potential to develop horticulture and floriculture exports:

- Rwanda is under pressure to establish a globally competitive industry immediately. Alternative markets that are growing rapidly—Asia and the Far East—may provide some opportunities to gain experience before competing directly with Ethiopia and Kenya in highly competitive European markets. But fundamentally Rwanda will need to board a moving train.
- High-end floriculture destined for Europe is necessarily very capital and knowledge intensive. It is highly competitive, because it is largely a saturated market at this point. It is quite dependent on being able to keep air transport costs as low as possible, when countries such as Kenya have already achieved major economies of scale in this regard. Vegetable enterprises can target less-demanding and less-contested growing markets in low- and middle-income countries, including in the region. However, food safety certification and its credibility become issues if higher-value markets for prepared vegetables, such as prepared foods for hotels and supermarket supply chains, are targeted.
- The government should retain its credible and supportive orientation toward private sector investment to reduce the risks involved in new investments. Focusing on securing additional investment in existing brownfield developments is more likely to succeed than undertaking new greenfield investments. Yet supportive government interventions need to be balanced with allowing an entrepreneurial private sector to determine its own investment opportunities. This includes facilitating the import of skilled labor and key inputs. Given the limited support services present in Rwanda, operators will initially depend on expertise and inputs from elsewhere in the region. Rwanda will need to facilitate this technology transfer, especially the smooth and efficient importation of planting material and the application of

BOX 5.2 Horticulture and floriculture exports from East Africa

The experience of horticulture and floriculture exports from East Africa provides useful lessons concerning the prerequisites for the success of this industry in Rwanda (table B5.2.1 provides summary data on these examples). Microclimates need to permit year-round production in order to distribute fixed costs across a longer production period.[a] This augurs well for Rwanda.

Large-scale production is essential to achieve competitive production costs,[b] gain access to the necessary expertise,[c] and negotiate prices for supporting services (for example, associations may be able to negotiate discounts for bulk purchases, especially airfreight costs). Securing adequate land for large-scale production can be a challenge; even where governments have sought to facilitate "land banks," investors often have sought to secure their own land.

Most successful horticultural-floriculture industries developed with significant foreign investment to secure economies of scale and to gain access to well-established and efficient destination supply chains (marketing costs within the destination country are typically more than half of retail prices).

Reasonably priced airfreight services (accounting for about 20 percent of the U.K. retail price) are essential and can be offered through scheduled passenger flights for limited volumes or through cargo flights for larger volumes.[d]

Required off-farm infrastructure includes quality roads, reliable power (essential for factories and refrigerated storage facilities), water distribution, and port and airport facilities.[e] Absent this, the costs of operator provisioning can raise overall investment costs substantially and strain cash flow, because these are essential up-front services.

Standards and traceability are essential to success, particularly in more remunerative markets, for

TABLE B5.2.1 Exports to Europe of flowers, vegetables, and fruits from select African countries, 2017

Indicator	Kenya	Ethiopia	Tanzania	Uganda	Zambia	Ghana	Senegal
Total value of exports (US$, millions)	1,050	250	63	98	19	180	130
Floriculture	750	248	26	57	17	—	—
Vegetables	150	2	12	25	2	40	95
Fruit	50	—	7	16	—	140	25
Total tonnage							
By air	248,000	90,000	3,200	17,000	8,000	5,000	—
By sea	52,000	—	—	—	—	140,000	125,000
Main products	Cut roses, green beans	Cut roses	Cut roses	Cut roses	Cut roses	Bananas, pineapples	Cherry tomatoes, bobby beans
Unit value (US$ per kilogram)							
Floriculture	3.95	2.76	8.13	3.80	2.36	—	—
Vegetables	2.59	—	0.80	1.25	2.50	1.14	0.92
Fruit	0.96	—	0.78	2.00	—	1.27	0.92
Land area (hectares)	4,000 (roses); 12,000 (vegetables)	1,600 (roses), 250 (summer flowers)	—	75 (cut roses)	—	—	—
On-farm employment	150,200	55,000	2,750	10,450	2,250	17,200	24,400

Source: Accord Associates 2017.
Note: — = not available.

(Box continues next page)

BOX 5.2 (continued)

example, supermarkets in high-income countries. The many competing standards regimes, including industry standards such as GlobalGAP, ethical standards appealing directly to consumer preferences (for example, Fair Trade), and the standards of individual retailers (for example, Sainsbury and Waitrose in the United Kingdom), can present a barrier for new entrants. Not surprising, a large share of investment in African horticulture and floriculture is backward integration of European Union growers, importers, and distributors who are fully aware of these standards and how to achieve them. Traceability is necessary to avoid penalizing entire industries for the violation of phytosanitary conditions by one or two exporters (as recently happened in Ghana).

Government has typically played a supporting role by providing political stability and an efficient regulatory environment.[f] Investors are typically wary of greenfield schemes, so government's ability to offer turnaround opportunities can be important. Given the long gestation for investments, tax holidays rarely matter as an investment incentive.

Finally, because initial, high-value horticulture and floriculture investments often fail—a trend consistent with the outcomes of commercial agribusiness investments more generally—the ability to recycle sunk investments rapidly to new investments is critical.

a. Ethiopia, Ghana, and Kenya benefit from stable weather conditions, whereas Zambia and Zimbabwe face greater seasonal variability and have trouble reducing unit costs.
b. A competitive rose production unit requires 40–50 hectares initially, rising to 100 hectares. An open-field flower or vegetable farm requires 500–1,000 hectares.
c. Larger companies can afford separate specialist positions in enterprise and agronomic management, but smaller operations need to combine the two with some loss of expertise. Established industries like Kenya have a strong pool of talent that can be hired by new entrants; Zambia established a research and training farm that provides a regular flow of well-trained supervisors and operatives.
d. Tanzania (especially from Kilimanjaro, the closest airport to the production areas), Uganda, and Zambia struggled because of a limited number of passenger flights. Uganda reached critical volume for dedicated cargo flights once its fresh fish export industry developed. Ethiopia directed its national airline to carry all cut flower exports to Europe, possibly at subsidized rates (with rates at about US$1.80 per kilogram currently). Opportunities for back-loading can help to keep costs low. Kenya continues to cut costs and improve competitiveness as scale increases and unit air transport costs decline; Kenya now exports 0.25 million tons of high-value perishable products annually by air.
e. On-farm infrastructure is best managed by individual operators. Kenya has well-maintained infrastructure around the Lake Naivasha region. Ethiopia invested heavily in four horticulture hubs, although private sector uptake has been skewed with slower uptake of the more heavily promoted Bahr Dar zone. Successful government-sponsored cold storage facilities include airport storage in Lusaka and Nairobi and the multipurpose refrigerated cold storage facility in Tema port in Ghana.
f. For example, stable political institutions encouraged Kenyan horticulture and floriculture, whereas instability plagued Ethiopian and Ugandan industries. Ethiopia has been an unusual case in state-led development of its floriculture sector, whereas other countries have had equally supportive but less interventionist public policy.

agrochemicals purchased elsewhere in East Africa for use in Rwanda.

- RwandAir's direct flights from Kigali to London are helpful if freight rates remain comparable to those paid by Kenyan exporters to Air Kenya—reported to be US$1.80–US$2.50 per kilogram, which already imposes a cost disadvantage for competitors who pay higher rates. Costs need to fall without undermining the financial sustainability of the airline.

Issues involving regional market competitiveness are, in some respects, different from global issues, in that the consumers, products, and markets in question are closer in nature to those in Rwanda. In addition, institutional factors such as regional integration agreements, the existence of regional transboundary business networks, and possible concerns about overdependence on a small number of neighbors for strategic food supplies come into play. Furthermore, food safety, sanitary, and phytosanitary issues that are so complex in exporting to the Organisation for Economic Co-operation and Development countries are typically less evident in regional exports. However, this situation will change over time, especially for products sold through supermarkets to higher-income consumers in regional capitals. Rwanda already has a regional comparative advantage given the credibility of its certification procedures and institutions. It has every interest in maintaining this advantage and extending it to increasingly complex and valuable food products.

Rwanda's growth ambitions are contingent on expanding its reach in trade, as discussed in chapter 2, particularly in agroprocessing. Ultimately, the goal of pursuing regional trade opportunities, like global ones, is to be able to specialize and profit from economies of scale. Thus, Rwanda would like to export high-value processed items like certified-safe baby food, horticulture, and packaged perishable animal products using the credibility of its certifying procedures and to import lower-value commodities, such as maize, that benefit from large consolidated land areas and mechanized commercial farming.

Regional agricultural trade is likely to include trade in starchy food staples as well as higher-value items like processed foods, horticulture, and animal products. Rwanda is likely to continue to have a strong comparative advantage (domestic resource cost ratios well below unity) in several products, such as Irish potatoes, horticulture, tea, coffee, essential oils, dairy products, and meat (table 5.2). For example, milk sold by Rwandan farmers at FRW 100 per liter in Rwanda is sold by Kenyan farmers in the Nairobi milkshed at the equivalent of FRW 350 per liter. Demand for these products is growing rapidly in Rwanda and is likely to increase rapidly in neighboring countries if their incomes rise at similar rates. Table 5.3 shows that Rwandan exports of Irish potatoes and green beans rose dramatically from 2003 to 2013. By contrast, Rwanda would do better importing lower-value cereal crops and bulk starches (for example, cassava) from neighbors and exporting higher-value items in return.

Livestock products face constraints in both regional and international trade, linked to the cross-border transmission of animal diseases such as foot-and-mouth disease and to the transmission of potentially serious pathogens with transmissibility to humans (zoonoses), such as avian influenza. Traceability is key both to controlling these diseases and to creating confidence in purchasers. As in the provision of extension services and banking, electronic solutions also have high potential for improving monitoring and surveillance to prevent animal disease and facilitate certification of disease-free status. Rwanda's export revenues from meat reached US$23 million in the year ending June 2017 (NAEB 2017). Botswana provides an example of how radio monitoring technologies that are both feasible for small-scale producers and cost-effective overcame the natural constraints keeping a major African beef exporter out of the European market (Moreki et al. 2012).

TABLE 5.2 Indicators of comparative advantage for select crops in Rwanda, 2016

Crop	Best-performing province[a]	DRC ratio	Rank among 8 selected crops
Irish potatoes	Northern	0.19	1
Coffee	Western	0.30	2
Beans (runner)	Western	0.31	3
Soybeans	Eastern	0.40	4
Maize	Southern	0.45	5
Cassava	Eastern	0.50	6
Wheat	Northern	0.85	7
Rice	Eastern	1.00	8

Source: Cambridge Resources International 2017.

Note: DRC = domestic resource cost ratio. DRC < 1 indicates likely comparative advantage. DRCs here are the ratio of the shadow value of domestic resources used to produce one unit of the commodity divided by the shadow value of tradable outputs from one unit. DRCs less than 1 are normally thought to indicate comparative advantage. Values shown are for the best-performing province.

a. These are the best cases across provinces for each crop; a comparable value is 1.23 for maize in Northern Province; 1.24 for wheat in Southern Province; and 1.13 for rice in Western Province. Given higher numerical findings for cereals, regional variations in results, and inevitable questions about the myriad assumptions used to produce these kinds of indicators, caution should be exercised in attributing a favorable comparative advantage for any DRC > 0.75. The main value is in the ranking.

TABLE 5.3 Exports of Irish potatoes and green beans by Rwanda and select African competitors, 2003 and 2013
tons

Country	Product	2003	2013	Change (times)
Ethiopia	Irish potatoes	5,539	118,019	21.3
	Green beans	1,712	5,879	3.4
South Africa	Irish potatoes	28,107	117,891	4.2
	Green beans	216	5,474	25.3
Rwanda	Irish potatoes	84	8,066	96
	Green beans	0	11,715	n.a.
Kenya	Irish potatoes	490	2,981	6.1
	Green beans	27,193	32,081	1.2
Tanzania	Irish potatoes	2,306	827	0.36
	Green beans	82	4,912	59.9

Source: Data from FAOStat, courtesy of International Finance Corporation colleagues.
Note: n.a. = not applicable.

Understanding major structural changes in nearby trade partners provides some insight into Rwanda's prospects in regional markets. Farm sizes in countries in Eastern and Southern Africa outside of Rwanda rose following the cereal price increase in 2008. For example, surveys show that the total land area in Tanzania operated by farms of less than 5 hectares fell by 6.1 percent between 2008 and 2012, but land operated in farms greater than 5 hectares rose by the same amount.[24] Even more striking, 43 percent of all farmland in Tanzania was formally purchased or rented in 2014 (Tanzania National Panel Survey 2014/15),[25] suggesting that markets were active in allocating agricultural land. Similarly, the percentage of cultivated land in farms larger than 5 hectares in Zambia was 52 percent higher in 2012 than in 2001.[26] Early results in both cases suggest that this primarily reflected increased investment by urban elites in farming, which if sustained could lead to increased capital investment and faster technological change.[27] These results have direct implications for Rwanda's ability to compete in the production of field crops like cereals, for which there are economies of scale in production.

An analysis of producers' opportunities in the domestic market can provide some insight into the prospects for Rwanda's regional exports. Rapid changes in demand associated with income growth and urbanization are already having major impacts on the quantity and quality of food items demanded. For example, the demand for high-value items like animal proteins, fruits, vegetables, and dining out increases sharply as incomes rise, whereas in Kigali, income elasticities for unprocessed starches other than Irish potatoes have already turned (faintly) negative (table 5.4). Results are broadly as expected from work in other countries with income levels similar to Rwanda's: research using household data by Michigan State University in five countries of East and Southern Africa estimates that demand for processed foods in urban areas will increase by a factor of 8 over the next three decades.[28] Thus, demand for Rwandan agriculture and food products has strong prospects in Rwanda and in the region. This augurs well for value addition strategies based both on diversifying production patterns into higher-value commodities such as animal and horticultural products and on processing cereals and other starches into products more convenient to use and of more consistent quality.

Income growth and urbanization are also driving changes in the quality of products required and in wholesale and retail market structures. Kigali has already begun to experience the "Supermarket Revolution." Events in neighboring countries such as Kenya, Tanzania, and Uganda suggest that

TABLE 5.4 Response of demand to a 1 percent increase in household income in Rwanda, by degree of urbanization
demand response (%)

	Rural		Urban	
Product	**Remote rural**	**Peri-urban**	**Small towns**	**Kigali**
Unprocessed cereals	0.71	0.61	−0.09	−0.03
Processed cereals and products	1.18	1.16	0.88	0.77
Irish potatoes	0.71	0.36	0.50	0.39
Other roots and tubers and plantains	0.41	0.52	0.09	−0.04
Legumes	0.54	0.61	0.31	0.31
Vegetables	0.73	0.75	0.76	0.67
Fruits	1.23	1.24	0.84	0.73
Meat, poultry, and eggs	1.71	1.36	1.46	1.13
Fish	0.90	1.32	1.72	0.78
Dairy products	1.94	1.41	1.38	1.35
Vegetable oil	1.00	1.07	0.92	0.66
Sugar products	1.46	1.36	0.91	0.57
Dining out	1.16	1.15	0.89	1.00
Other manufactured foods	1.24	0.21	1.80	0.81
Nonfood	1.25	1.24	1.08	1.11

Sources: International Food Policy Research Institute estimates using Integrated Household Living Conditions Survey household-level data for 2013–14 and the approach developed by King and Byerlee (1978). See Diao et al. (2017b).
Note: Own-produced food is included in expenditures with purchased food, at market prices. Plantains (cooking bananas) are included with roots and tubers, rather than with mangos, sweet bananas, and other fruits.

this revolution will take off in Rwanda in the next decade and spread widely to secondary and even tertiary towns, even as it continues to spread throughout East and Southern Africa. Supermarket procurement systems involve the consolidation of purchases, a shift to specialized wholesalers, and tough quality and safety standards. To meet these requirements, producers need to invest and adopt new practices. This is hardest for small producers, who risk exclusion from dynamic urban markets increasingly dominated by supermarkets. Smallholders will need to address these difficulties through collective action (Jaffee, Henson, and Diaz Rios 2011; Weatherspoon and Reardon 2003). The rise of supermarket procurement in Rwanda is likely to spur specialization and regional trade, as supermarket chains source products in least-cost countries.

The following are the key takeaways regarding regional competitive advantage in exports of food-related products for Rwanda:

- Given a small domestic market, Rwanda has every interest in developing regional trade in higher-value, processed, and certified commodities in which it has a comparative advantage.
- Rwanda also has considerable comparative advantage in a few higher-value staples suitable for industrial processing, such as potatoes and dairy. It should be able to develop these products to capture much larger and fast-growing regional markets.
- With the explosion in agricultural trade in the last 15 years in the region, there are grounds for broader recognition of the value of free markets and the need for reliable export markets for staple foods in the face of volatile international prices.
- For those commodities and processed products in which Rwanda has a comparative advantage, capturing regional markets will involve addressing logistics, quantity and quality management, joint ventures to smooth cross-border trade, and regional agreements.

These issues are relevant to most sectors in Rwanda and are covered extensively in chapter 2 of this report.

Securing the Natural Resource Base for Innovation

Agriculture is the most natural resource–dependent of all economic sectors. It is thus very susceptible to fluctuations in rainfall and temperature and is dependent on the quality of soils (structure, mineral content, and health) and on the management of water that reaches those soils. Agricultural outcomes are particularly vulnerable to climate change and to soil degradation, both multiyear conditions that can limit production in the medium and long term. Adapting to the first and halting the second are critical long-term priorities.

At the best of times, Rwanda experiences high year-to-year differences in rainfall and is affected by El Niño–Southern Oscillation events (El Niño and La Niña). Consequently, the country experiences periodic floods and droughts. Rwanda has two annual rainy seasons (seasons A and B for reporting purposes, with a drier season between), and average annual rainfall is 1,250 millimeters, a relatively high amount. However, there are large differences across the country. Average temperatures differ significantly between the cooler, mountainous northern regions and the warmer, low-lying southwestern valleys and drier eastern flatlands. Average rainfall declines significantly as one moves from the western to the eastern part of the country.

Since 1970, Rwanda has experienced a mean temperature rise of 1.4°C, higher than the global average, with projections of a further 1°C to 2.5°C increase by 2050 (Agri-TAF 2016; Future Climate for Africa 2014; MINIRENA 2012). Higher temperatures have led to the spread of pests and diseases, impairing the health of livestock and humans, lowering crop yields, harming food security, and decreasing export earnings. It is likely that gradual shifts in agroclimatic zones will affect some crops as well as husbandry practices for livestock, cumulating to significant changes by 2050 in addition to any other influences that may be felt (Agri-TAF 2016).

Rainfall patterns have become more variable, with projections of a 20 percent increase in variability by the 2050s (REMA 2011). The prevalence of small-scale, rain-fed farming that relies on traditional technologies and practices renders the sector especially vulnerable to rainfall variability. Heavier rains increase floods and landslides, resulting in crop losses, health risks, and damage to infrastructure, particularly in the north and west of the country. Poor smallholders in Rwanda typically have little access to the wealth, liquid assets, credit, knowledge support, and infrastructure that wealthier farmers elsewhere rely on when adapting to climate or other shocks. In seasons A and B in 2015 in Rwanda, between 1.1 and 1.5 percent of all agriculture operators practiced irrigation, compared with between 24 and 28 percent of large-scale operators.[29] Moreover, the combination of rain-fed, small-scale agriculture, high rainfall levels, and steep hillsides also leads to very high rates of soil erosion. A higher variability of rainfall implies more frequent droughts, which limits the availability of water and feed for livestock, particularly in the east and parts of the south, and increases vulnerability to diseases. Production losses to the dairy value chain are most significant in major drought years. Although subsistence farmers are most affected, climate variability affects all agriculture sectors and lowers annual production and exports. Increasing the resilience of Rwanda's productive system, including to climatic risks, is essential for sustainable production and higher productivity as well as for greater food and nutrition security.

The development and use of agricultural technologies adapted to abiotic and biotic stresses would help to cope with these difficulties.[30] Such technologies include the development of early-yielding crop varieties and of crops that are more tolerant to extremes of heat and water availability; the promotion of higher nutritive quality fodder; the use of expanded rotation and multicropping for more sustainable and integrated pest and disease management and sustainable yield; the use of early warning systems for pest and disease management and the development of seasonal schedules for sowing based on weather forecasts (for example, promotion of earlier sowing for specific crops); and the promotion of climate-smart agricultural technologies to increase crop and livestock productivity while maintaining the natural resource base.

Agriculture accounted for an estimated 46 percent of Rwanda's total annual greenhouse gas (GHG) emissions in 2010 (CIAT 2015). That same year, roughly 84 percent of the agriculture sector's GHG emissions were from livestock, split evenly between enteric fermentation in ruminants such as cattle and manure management or manure left on pastures (CIAT 2015). Not surprising, agriculture featured prominently in Rwanda's "national determined contribution" to global GHG mitigation at the December 2015 Conference of Parties in Paris (REMA 2015).

Technical approaches would mitigate agricultural GHG emissions in Rwanda, but it is hard to see how they would be implemented when farmers have no way of capturing a return for the extra effort. These techniques include

- Increased efficiency of manure management through the promotion of collective cattle keeping;
- Reduction of the livestock population and progressive replacement of local breeds with more productive breeds to maintain and increase productivity per unit of GHG emission;
- Expansion of less-emission-intensive types of animal-source foods (for example, fisheries and poultry);
- More judicious use of fertilizer based on crop nutrient requirements (such as microdosing and burying pellets);
- Large-scale tree planting for reforestation to invest in a future carbon sink to cover 30 percent of land with planted trees; and
- Promotion of energy for cooking stoves other than firewood in urban and peri-urban areas (REMA 2015).

Considerable progress will need to occur in global carbon offset markets and certification procedures before they can become a viable source of future finance for mitigating agricultural GHGs in Rwanda. Fortunately, innovation is starting to provide ways to improve productivity while also reducing GHG emissions; two examples follow.

Big data technologies are quickly coming on stream to link large numbers of individual sample points providing a wide variety of data with huge databases and analytical capacity to provide data-based recommendations on remedial action. In climate-smart agriculture, the precise analysis of needed soil nutrients and the ability to measure sequestration of carbon in soil down to 30 or 40 centimeters provide a promising example. A cost-effective technology would save on inputs for climate smartness, increase productivity and profit, and create the ability to monitor soil carbon sequestration on smallholders' fields. A new generation of handheld soil scanners provides an easy-to-use way to diagnose soil fertility in the root zone and needed additives, based on cellular transmission of scanned data to a large central database and a 10-minute automated report back.[31] In the smallholder context, ownership of the equipment and training would likely best be done through existing cooperatives.

Addressing land degradation, a major environmental problem for agricultural productivity in Rwanda, also offers considerable hope for mitigation of GHG emissions.[32] Land degradation affects all types of land use systems in Rwanda and is an explosive and largely neglected problem for long-term development in most of Sub-Saharan Africa, where more than 65 percent of arable land, 30 percent of grazing land, and 20 percent of forests regionwide are degraded (FAO 2017). It is especially difficult to ignore this danger given Rwanda's erosion-prone steep slopes and strong seasonal rains.

Fortunately, the government of Rwanda has made tremendous efforts to address these challenges comprehensively. During PSTA2 (2008–12), for example, the land area protected by trenches and "progressive" terraces (essentially narrow, traditional, sloped terraces) increased by nearly 300,000 hectares, a 60 percent increase (World Bank 2017). Other core programs implemented to control land degradation included control of erosion through bench terraces, reforestation of the tops of slopes, irrigation, mechanization, and fertilizer subsidies.

Although initial progress was made on the construction of bench terraces under PSTA2 and beyond, these terraces are costly to build and underexploited. Using these terraces to maximum advantage involves complexities of management for which many farmers may not be ready. Further, involvement of the private sector may not be profitable under current mandates to produce food staples. Ultimately, the return on investment for these terraces, whether public or private, will depend on the choice of crops or livestock products and the inclusion of output in higher-value markets. Increased allocative efficiency will be needed in the sense of targeting resources to their highest-value returns. Irrigated bench terraces, in particular, will need to have much higher returns than cereals such as maize can provide.

In the future, more sustainable farming systems in Rwanda will likely be characterized by expanded areas of wide, flat terraces stabilized by "multipurpose" trees and grasses, nutrient replenishment based on crop needs, reduction of nutrient leaching off farms, and rainwater harvesting and expanded tree and forest planting. China is a successful example of how to handle major changes in degraded agricultural land on densely populated steep slopes, as exemplified by the Loess Plateau projects profiled in box 5.3.

Key elements of interest for Rwanda include the halting of activities that led to degradation; the construction of wide terraces, an expensive undertaking that required the planting of high-value crops to generate adequate returns; a shift from grazing

BOX 5.3 Successful restoration of the productive landscape on China's Loess Plateau

Deforestation, degradation of grasslands, overgrazing, and cultivation of marginal land led to huge soil erosion problems in China, reducing grain production by an estimated 5.7 million metric tons a year in the late 1980s and increasing the risks of floods and landslides. One of the most degraded areas was the Loess Plateau, a region of about 640,000 square kilometers covering four of China's poorest interior provinces and parts of Inner Mongolia (photo B5.3.1).

The Chinese Ministry of Water Resources and the World Bank worked together to produce two watershed rehabilitation projects spanning 1994 to 2005, mobilizing US$491 million between them. The key goals were to halt the activities that led to land degradation—in particular, planting on steep slopes, cutting of trees, and free-range grazing of goats—and to encourage biomass regeneration. Land tenure responsibilities and benefits were clarified. Earth-moving equipment was brought in to replace the farmers' hand-dug terraces, which crumbled each year, with more stable terraces three or four times as wide (6–12 meters). Land that was unsuitable for grain production was planted with trees or shrubs instead or was allowed to grow wild again, resulting in large-scale reforestation and grasslands regeneration. All livestock were confined to pens.

To ensure local buy-in and sustainability of the projects, farmer groups and county-level government entities were fully engaged in decision making and implementation. At the request of

(Box continues next page)

BOX 5.3 (continued)

farm groups, loans and advice were mobilized to introduce smallholder dairy and Kashmiri sheep, new to the region. The World Bank estimates that the projects lifted more than 2.5 million people out of poverty and boosted incomes from about US$70 to about US$200 per person per year through higher farm productivity and diversification. Per capita grain output rose from 365 to 591 kilograms per year, and the employment rate increased from 70 to 87 percent. Water retention increased, making farms more resilient to drought. Soil erosion was curbed on 920,000 hectares, and soil losses were reduced by 60 million–100 million tons per year. Soil carbon storage also increased, mostly because of the restoration of forests and grasslands. The overall economic rate of return of the two projects was estimated at 20 percent, but the livestock components had an economic rate of return of 27, which is very high for this measure. Moreover, the approaches developed through the project have been applied more broadly across the Loess Plateau—where, as of 2008, more than half the degraded area had been restored—and in the Yangtze and Pearl River basins.

PHOTO B5.3.1 China's Loess Plateau, 1990 and 2012

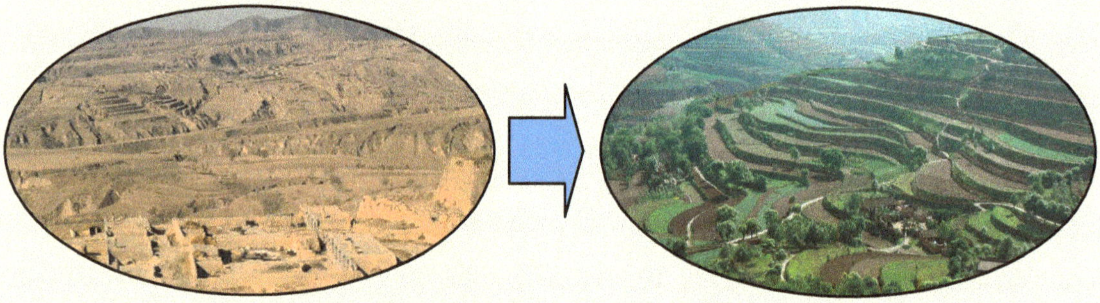

Credits: Left: Till Niermann, GNU free documentation license v1.2 (1990); *right:* Erick Fernandes (2012).

Sources: Dang et al. 2014; Global Commission on the Economy and Climate 2014; Huang, Gallichand, and Zhang 2003; Xie et al. 2010. See also World Bank 2007a.

for ruminants to cut-and-carry and fodder production systems; and the importance of active involvement by farmer groups and local government.[33]

Rwanda should consider improvements in the allocation of scarce water supplies to agriculture. User fees should not be off the table, especially for larger ventures; it will become harder, but even more important, to tackle this issue as time passes. Israeli experience illustrates how the allocative efficiency of agricultural water under very difficult conditions can be addressed sustainably through a combination of public leadership, transparency, technology, and market allocation procedures (box 5.4).

Policies to Achieve Rapid and Sustainable Growth in Agriculture

Over the next 20 years, Rwanda's agriculture sector will aim to increase productivity while adapting to the future. State-led efforts to increase agricultural productivity and maximize the sector's potential in Rwanda will continue in the medium term, serving a complementary role to more market-oriented agriculture over time. State efforts involve extending the approach to consolidation of production decisions and staple food crop–oriented intensification that has already reached at least 20 percent

BOX 5.4 Israeli success at being more efficient with agricultural water

Israel is a diversified, small country with a highly productive export agriculture sector under irrigation, despite being one of the most water-stressed countries in the world and facing steadily increasing demands for water withdrawals outside agriculture. Although many of the structural water issues faced by Israel are quite different than those faced by Rwanda, Israel's experience offers lessons of direct relevance for Rwanda:

- Water needs to be recognized and treated as the scarce resource it is. In Israel, large public awareness campaigns were carried out to emphasize the value of water, accompanied by the pricing of water at its actual cost.
- Effective enforcement of a data-based and transparent system of water allocation immune from political intervention is critical.
- Investing massively in new water infrastructure needs to be done in ways that promote fiscal neutrality in the water sector. These ways include both public-private partnerships and a clear separation of roles among policy setting, regulation, planning, and operation of infrastructure.
- Wastewater recycling is very expensive and requires high ongoing subsidies for treatment and storage; it is likely only viable in very high-return cases.
- Water use efficiency can be promoted most cost-effectively in the case of high-value crops, such as fruits and vegetables, including on slopes, through drip irrigation technology.

Source: Marin et al. 2017.

(level of cooperative membership) and at most 40 percent (extent of contact with the CIP and LUCP) of farms. Public support should continue to improve the efficiency of small farms that are still not using fertilizer in appreciable amounts, lack access to adequate agricultural water, are situated on unprotected hillside slopes, or use inferior seeds, so that such farms can achieve the technical efficiency of Rwanda's better farmers.

To produce the transformative growth rates sought by Rwanda, both public and private sector expertise in agriculture must be leveraged. It is estimated that continued state-led efforts would extend the 5 percent annual agricultural growth experienced in recent years. Moreover, these efforts soon will approach various limits, including the mounting fiscal burden, rising unit costs as less accessible agricultural land is exploited, competition from neighboring countries in crops promoted by the CIP, and shifting internal and external demand for animal proteins, fruits, vegetables, and highly processed foods. Higher agricultural growth can only be achieved by reaping the benefits of scale economies and specialization through exports and the production of higher-value-added goods. Such efforts will require a rapid response to market signals, ready access to investment resources, technical expertise, and ability to organize production and provide appropriate incentives for workers, generated by the private sector. The state needs to retain a lead role as umpire, generator of public knowledge, and provider of public goods such as infrastructure and basic research. Many key innovation public goods for smallholders and for basic food staples will likely need to be provided by public actors for the foreseeable future.

Achieving higher growth rates in the future will require responding to major changes in demand (locally, regionally, and globally); gains from specialization, economies of scale, and a larger division of labor through trade; changes in industrial organization (how farmers are linked with markets and with each other and who decides what) in order to take advantage of opportunities; and changes in the contact that farmers have with infrastructure, information, and technology and the sophistication of those technologies, leading to higher productivity and sustainability.

The demands faced by Rwandan farmers are changing rapidly, as demand grows for higher-value products, food safety, convenience, and qualities such as Fair Trade and organic certification (in global markets). Major shifts in demand are occurring in domestic markets, but even more so in regional markets, including all of Africa, as urbanizing and increasingly richer people are eating more animal products, more fruits and vegetables, and especially more highly processed food items that better fit urban lifestyles. The large cities of Africa are the contested markets of rapid growth in demand for high-value items for which agricultural interests all over the world are competing.

Rwanda should ramp up its efforts to promote trust in regional trade in Rwandan food products, including through continued engagement in the East African Community and Common Market for Eastern and Southern Africa agricultural processes. Rwanda has a major stake in increasing its imports of raw materials such as cereals for its food-processing and animal protein industries, while increasing its exports of processed foods and high-value calories—for example, from milk and meat products. Ways should be explored to exploit the huge market potential of neighboring countries by increasing food production, for example, through the provision of financial guarantees under a regional process. Another initiative might include a more common approach to certification of food safety, sanitary, and phytosanitary conditions. Regional integration also should be pursued through continuing efforts to adopt transparent science-based standards, registration of products, and certification of agricultural inputs. Rwandan manufacturing has interests here and should be engaged.

Government could support vertical coordination arrangements by expanding participation in cooperatives and encouraging private sector aggregators. Beyond the tea and coffee cases discussed earlier, aggregators have shown interest in partnering with producers and government in animal feed, avocados, bananas, beans, dairy, eggs, essential oils, fish, flowers, various forms of fruit and vegetable processing, meat processing, cereal milling, and sugar.[34] These firms often bring managerial skills, capital, extension of knowledge to farmers, and entree into commercial networks outside Rwanda. They have the expertise to achieve global certifications in desirable traits. Government could play a role in ensuring the enforcement of agreements—especially regarding recouping input credits that companies give to farmers, securing adequate supplies from zones where extension investments have been made, and ensuring the traceability of supplies of raw materials, allowing farmers to garner premiums for quality. In many cases, multinationals seek the active financial involvement of the government, which can be highly beneficial for the promotion of high-value specialized crops. Government should clarify goals and define satisfactory performance as well as provide an institutional structure to follow up transparently at regular intervals and redeploy public resources where performance has fallen short. In the Republic of Korea, for example, this system is highly developed for public-private partnerships for infrastructure.[35] Government financial participation should likely be limited to a very small number of activities that have a compelling need for public participation.

Support for aggregator activities should reflect different requirements for different commodities.[36] In milk, for example, food safety is paramount, asymmetries of information are large (especially when dilution with unclean water is easy and many small batches are mixed together), and market power changes radically from producer to buyer depending on the season. For these reasons, dairy cooperatives work well, despite being high cost. Coffee requires a different form of industrial organization to ensure quality and reliability and to achieve a verifiable process of production (such as organic or Fair Trade). Typically, best results are achieved when roasters can assist small farms or cooperatives directly with inputs and expertise under contract farming agreements and can be sure of getting the resulting produce for their own operations, which may require state zoning of washing and marketing. In horticulture, prices achieved will depend not only on the right sorting of produce for retail delivery of a perishable at the right time, but also on the absence of residue on items coming from many farms, and so forth. Outgrower schemes—where a large farm or agribusiness that is producing a commodity according to international norms provides management, expertise, inputs, and marketing services to small farmers in the same locality to produce the same commodity on their own land—tend to work well here, particularly to control and store chemicals that are toxic or give rise to residue.

Government should seek to develop a knowledge platform regarding which forms of industrial organization work best for addressing specific industrial organization problems in Rwanda's smallholder context. The platform could provide reliable data on vertical coordination, finance, prices, costs, and weather; this information will be critical to reducing uncertainties and risks for investors and should encourage competition. Documenting and publicizing the impact of different private, public, and public-private experiences with vertical coordination can help to share experiences across commodities. Doing so also will facilitate a key policy role of government: to promote a level playing field of knowledge and regulation that encourages formal sector private investment while advancing the interests of the farming population.

Government policy should encourage skills development by private firms to complement public sector extension activities. Vertical integration with aggregators is a key private sector method of transmitting skills to smallholders for specialty crops destined for export; these firms in Rwanda generally have brought in regional and non-African managers and technical experts to fill gaps. Government should consider developing programs to increase the prevalence of these skills domestically. Companies might be involved through instituting training programs to build up nationally needed skill sets in agribusiness, high-value supply chains, and agricultural technology. Cargill and Nestlé have been pioneers in Africa and beyond, providing technical training for small farm suppliers, business training for cooperative leaders, and managerial and higher technical training for their own national staff (Cargill 2014; Nestlé 2016). Where government financial participation is sought in a joint venture, such training might be a reasonable point to consider.

One aspect of promoting increased reliance on markets postharvest involves the development of more efficient wholesale markets. Wholesale markets are curiously scarce in Rwanda, perhaps because of the small size of the urban population. The bulking, grading, and transport functions of value chains appear to be carried out either at the source (a cooperative or large enterprise) or by the retail firm (a supermarket, dairy store, or exporter). As specialization, scale, and trade grow, the need for independent intermediaries will likely grow as well. How this function develops and is supported by regulators will be important to success. A first step was the establishment in 2016 of a new wholesale potato market in Kigali,[37] and this trend is expected to accelerate. South African experience yields two important insights: first, wholesale markets tend to develop first for items like potatoes, onions, fruits, and vegetables, as urban demand spikes. They facilitate reliable supplies for urban retailers and financing, quality control, and price predictability for smallholder suppliers. Second, over time with the growth of supermarket and chain store retail outlets and growth in the size of farm suppliers, direct retail-farmer vertical coordination becomes more common (Seidler 2001; Vermeulen, Kirsten, and Sartorius 2008).

Improving SMEs' access to finance is important for the formal private sector to play a bigger role in agricultural decision making. Four areas of action could serve to foster this process, while strengthening the role of SMEs in agriculture:[38]

- First, strengthen the enabling environment for agricultural finance by improving the quality, granularity, and accessibility of relevant data, including data on firms, agricultural finance, and weather. Also needed are efforts to reduce the high cost of registering mortgages on land for small loans.
- Second, increase the financial inclusion of agricultural SMEs and commercial farmers by increasing the business transparency of cooperatives and commodity federations, by promoting electronic payments for settlements and government transfers, and by creating a public (electronic) directory of enterprises.[39]
- Third, deepen the agricultural financing market by strengthening the operational capacity of banks, microfinance institutions, and SACCOs in agricultural finance to provide financing packages that meet the needs of small-scale and commercial farmers. In particular, the credits and matching grants of the BRD play a big role in shaping the formal allocation of capital to the agriculture sector. BRD's agricultural capacity can be strengthened. BRD loans might also transit from retail to wholesale—for example, funding SACCOs that would then fund the retail end.
- Fourth, scale up formal agricultural insurance. While a public-private partnership model will likely be needed, a formal assessment of options is necessary to target funding effectively for capacity building.

Rwanda's agrarian structure based on smallholders reinforces the critical importance for agriculture of innovations in finance such as blockchain technology. Rwanda's public-private partnership in applying blockchain technology to its land registry represents a major advance for both efficiency and good governance under smallholder conditions. Land registration is just a beginning, however, and similar partnerships will be vital to increasing financial inclusion and investment into relatively small farms and cooperatives of small farms. Possible applications might involve cutting the costs of registering small mortgages on land and leveling the playing field a bit for smallholders.

Public investment in infrastructure such as roads, electricity, and water is critical to encourage private sector entry into agribusiness. Reliable electricity is key for cold storage and processing, which are vital for the safe handling of horticulture, floriculture, and animal products. It is striking that agroprocessing, primarily of horticulture, accounted for 55 percent of all manufacturing value added in Tanzania in 2015—horticulture used raw material from 450,000 farms from all over the country and sold products all over the country—yet the 287 firms involved were almost all located in Dar-es-Salaam (Kumar and Agarwal 2016). As shown in other chapters of this report, Rwanda has made tremendous progress in extending the reach of the electrical grid and providing piped water to secondary and tertiary towns. However, unit costs in this regard will remain key parameters in achieving competitiveness relative to other countries in the region, and agricultural development based on high-value perishables, as opposed to starchy staples, will require infrastructure that permits rapid processing and refrigeration after harvest. It hardly seems plausible that the least-cost option for fast processing will always be truck transport to the capital city. Yet decentralization of infrastructure into agroparks that combine reliable electricity, water, and various agricultural service industries is not without dangers. A key lesson from experience with agroparks oriented to high-value agribusiness in Latin America is that the choice of locations needs to be based solely on commercial reasons (FAO 2010).

Irrigation is clearly a constraint, especially in the drier eastern regions of the country

(Malesu et al. 2010). Less than 5 percent of all land used for production and less than 3 percent of cropped land (that is, agricultural land not including pasture or forest) is irrigated at the present time, estimated to be equivalent to 7.5 percent of irrigable potential (MINAGRI 2017c). But more than half of the land deemed irrigable is on hillsides, where irrigation costs can run very high (World Bank 2014). A more useful estimate might be that 16 percent of potentially irrigable marshlands have been developed for irrigation.[40] In any event, there is potential for much greater investment in the irrigation of marshlands at US$6,000–US$8,000 per hectare (World Bank 2014). Current yields of rice are not sufficient to cover the investment cost. Therefore, while emphasizing the increase in rice productivity, other high-value crops like horticulture also should be considered in irrigated areas. Horticulture for export would likely be able to cover these cost levels more easily, including exports to the rapidly growing market in the Democratic Republic of Congo and possibly farther west by air.[41] The take-away lesson is that linking irrigation expansion plans with market development is necessary for higher-value products like horticulture and dairy, which, especially the market for horticulture products, are most likely to be regional markets.

Rwanda's strong public institutions and high level of governance provide important advantages in supporting rapid growth in agriculture. The ability to provide credible product certification in the organic, Fair Trade, and ISO 22000 areas needs to be protected, particularly as the demand for certification escalates. The Rwanda Agricultural Board and its staff should be encouraged to reach out to public and private colleagues in neighboring countries and elsewhere in the world to build technical links for resolving common problems through research, analysis, and extension.

Government support for agricultural research and extension is essential to boost productivity growth in the sector. The Rwanda Agricultural Board already invests heavily in providing extension services for staple food crops under the CIP. However, only 0.7 percent of public expenditures on agriculture were allocated to research and innovation in fiscal 2014/15–2015/16, whereas 64 percent were allocated to crop intensification, including input subsidies (Policy Associates 2017). Strategic training of scientists and development and maintenance of research infrastructure to target high-technology research are needed. Given an increasing international shift to private (and proprietary) funding of agricultural research and likely continued budgetary pressures in Rwanda, the share of privately funded research will need to increase in order to have an overall increase in funding and to ensure that Rwanda remains engaged in the premier international research consortiums. Private research will likely be focused on high-value crops or other items that provide major private sector opportunities for profitability. Public research should also become more demand driven. This can be accomplished by establishing innovation platforms with the private sector as a major player and demander or sponsor and interacting with leading research centers to develop necessary expertise.

The big-data revolution can also cost-effectively promote collective action with advice tailored to the individual conditions of small operations at low unit costs. The application of "climate-smart" agricultural practices to a large number of small farms on steep hillsides will be greatly facilitated by fast-moving developments that allow even small farms to interact with major regional and global databases in order to access knowledge to solve their particular problems. This is likely to be one of the fastest and most promising areas of innovation in the sector, delivering very high-tech solutions to users with only modest information technology skills. It will require active participation and expertise from researchers and extension agents at public organizations such as the Rwanda Agriculture Board and can benefit from the existing cooperative organizations. It also has great potential to lower the costs of private investors to work with large numbers of dispersed small farms.

Another promising reform related to big data is the introduction of electronic delivery of extension services (e-extension) to create an electronic and interactive bridge network where farmers and other stakeholders meet and transact. The use of high-tech solutions for delivering more efficient extension messages (such as the use of drones in crop surveys for assessing crop growth, pests, and disease management) needs to be encouraged. In an upper-middle-income Rwanda, the traditional extension and advisory services will need to focus on farmer-promoter knowledge development. A continuous training program and e-feedback system will also be needed to deliver extension messages on existing challenges, seed availability and sowing dates, rain forecasts, fertilizer rates, and so forth.

A strong and well-organized public extension system will be needed to contribute to messages and adapt as needed, especially in food staples of lesser interest to the private sector. This system could be achieved through delivering farmer-promoter knowledge (exemplary farmers elected by the community to facilitate the delivery of extension messages at the village level); increasing access to training and advisory services delivered by the private sector; and enabling access to improved extension service delivery by expanding feeder roads, in both peri-urban and rural areas. The Farmer Field School approach, which involves farmers meeting in local field settings with a trained facilitator to discuss common problems, should be expanded.

Adapting to climate change, stopping land degradation, and managing groundwater remain a public priority. Most agriculture in Rwanda is practiced on steep slopes prone to erosion during the rainy season. While considerable progress has been made in constructing robust "bench" (wide) terraces, much more needs to be done to secure the land asset. In conjunction with the private sector, investments will be required in infrastructure, other public services, and processing to support the restoration and conservation of productive landscapes. Whole-landscape approaches emphasizing soil, water, and biomass management are critical to achieving the triple wins of productive growth in agriculture, increased adaptation to climate shocks, and mitigation of GHG emissions through carbon sequestration. How livestock is handled in hillside development is key to success. Confinement of stock with cut-and-carry fodder systems will likely be needed. Implementation of landscape approaches requires associating high agricultural science expertise with farmer consultation and follow-up activities. Local government capacity is key.

Annex 5A A Graphic Presentation of the TFP Story in Rwandan Agriculture

Rwanda has been highly successful at maintaining an impressive rate of agricultural growth, on the order of 4–5 percent or more per year since the early 1960s, with the exception of the "lost decade" of the 1980s (in common with many other African countries) and the 1990s. However, success in boosting agricultural growth in earlier years was attributable largely to land expansion, as seen in figure 5.1. Success in the 2000s was largely due to increased use of inputs, especially from 2007 onward, and some expansion of area. This was also the time of the beginnings of TFP growth. Actions undertaken by the government under the CIP had major impacts on the growth of output in staples through improved seeds and fertilizer subsidies. Land development and improvement under the LUCP implemented through CIP also contributed, including bench terraces and development of new irrigated lands in marshlands. Heavy emphasis on extension throughout undoubtedly promoted increased technical efficiency and thus TFP. Measured TFP growth took off in the second half of the 2000s and continued through at least 2014.

TFP is the gain in output that results from some combination of at least one of three improvements. The first is improved technical efficiency, which comes from redeploying existing inputs, land, and labor regardless of prices in a way that leads to net physical gains using existing technologies. The second is allocative efficiency, which considers the costs of using different inputs and factors in addition to technical issues, in order to maximize profitability. The third is technological change, which embodies scientific and technical innovation to get more from less.

In economic parlance, technical efficiency is moving production to the production possibility frontier (PPF), allocative efficiency is moving along the frontier to the most profitable point given relative prices of different inputs and outputs, and technological change is pushing the frontier outward. In smallholder farming systems such as those in Rwanda, boosting technical efficiency is largely a matter of extension services, typically public; raising allocative effciency is often a combination of policy, private sector involvement, and functioning markets; and technological change is largely the product of successful agricultural research and innovation systems, in partnership with other research bodies inside and outside the country and sometimes with the private sector, in the case of high-value specialty items.

This complex set of relationships in TFP relevant to Rwandan agriculture can be illustrated simply in the heuristic diagram in figure 5A.1. Consider a starting point from a base of low agricultural productivity following the events of 1994 (point a). Agricultural productivity in the late 1990s was lower in Rwanda than in regional comparators, whose situation is summed up in a theoretical PPF. PPF is the maximum level of productivity for a given state of technology; as drawn, it symbolizes the trade-off in resource use between producing staple food crops and nonstaples. Concerted efforts by the government of Rwanda—not least the CIP and the LUCP—successfully increased *technical efficiency,*

FIGURE 5A.1 Heuristic diagram of the production possibility frontier

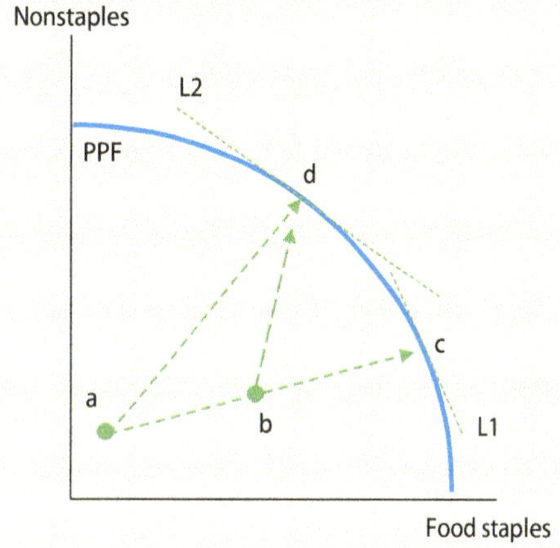

Note: The production possibility frontier (PPF) represents the maximum level of productivity for a given state of technology. a, b, c, and d show Rwanda's different possible positions with "a" as the starting point. L1 and L2 show different scenarios of relative prices of staples versus nonstaples.

shown as moving from point a to point b closer to the frontier defined by good agricultural practice. Here Rwanda is producing both more staples and more nonstaples with the same set of resources, largely because of improved extension and input supply systems. Continuing in this vein leads to point c on the frontier, in effect catching up with the most technically efficient neighbors and favoring staple foods.

However, although point c is technically efficient, it is only *economically efficient* if the relative prices of staples and nonstaples in Rwanda are portrayed adequately by the slope of line L1. If instead nonstaples become more valuable relative to staples than implied by L1 (that is, you get more staples for a given amount of nonstaples), the price ratio may now be portrayed by line L2. In that case, policies that keep the price ratio artificially at L1 will succeed in producing more staples than otherwise but will have a cost in terms of lost economic (or *allocative*) efficiency. In theory, producing at point d in a market system would allow a trading country to have more of both staples and nonstaples under price regime L2 than producing at point c. Under a true free-market system, aggregate production would move from point c to point d, which would maximize the value of agricultural output at price ratio L2. Allocative efficiency is largely the result of improved policies and better-functioning markets.

The best solution is for true technological change to occur. This implies that farmers literally produce more with less than they could on the old PPF. Technological change would be represented by a movement of the PPF outward and away from the origin. Technological change is made possible by successful agricultural research and innovation systems. Unlike efficiency, which is limited in scope once basic changes are made, technological change can power productivity growth indefinitely. The sum of growth in technical efficiency, allocative efficiency, and technological change is *total factor productivity*. The technical efficiency component is where Rwanda has become quite successful since 2005, but where the components of allocative efficiency and technological change will increasingly need to lead longer term.

Most of these forms of agricultural productivity growth since 1999, which stressed expanding cropped area, improving land, using more purchased inputs, and more recently improving technical efficiency, have worked well, but may have decreasing replicability in the future as more land is brought under existing programs. Longer-term strategies for addressing continued agricultural productivity growth under Rwandan conditions will require continual processes for boosting TFP in agriculture. Past success in moving a large share (20–40 percent) of the smallholder population closer to the PPF defined by existing technologies and resources has done the country great good and demonstrably boosted national growth overall. However, expanding agricultural output at the rate required to achieve upper-middle-income status by 2035 will require the more rapid growth in TFP that can only be achieved by moving the PPF outward, which is where innovation systems, institutional development, infrastructure, and the private sector will need to come in.

Notes

1. The growth rates and subsectoral decomposition are from Diao et al. (2017a), using MINECOFIN data.
2. This effect can produce growth multipliers in many parts of Africa on the order of 2 or more (meaning that every unit of agricultural growth induces at least an extra unit of nonagricultural growth) (Delgado et al. 1998; Diao et al. 2017a; World Bank 2007b). Such growth in farm incomes needs to originate from outside the local area if it is to have a true effect inside the local area (and not just redistribute purely local income); an example is income from export crops or even from crops and livestock sold elsewhere in Rwanda.
3. As local economies become more integrated with larger economic spaces, any additional local consumption from new income sources tends to be met either by increases in imports from outside the locality in question or by decreases in exports from the locality in question, leading to no net gain in local production. See Delgado et al. (1998) for a fuller description.
4. This point was made on several occasions by Rwandan government officials interviewed in September and December 2017; it is consistent with experience in several other African countries at the time and with the evolution of Rwandan policy interventions after 2008. The figure of 60 percent is from EICV2, which pertains to 2005/06 (NISR, various years). EICV4, which pertains to 2013/14, yields an average of 50 percent (Diao et al. 2017b; NISR, various years).
5. Only one-quarter of Rwandan farms are larger than 0.7 hectare in total, and in the 10 most densely settled rural districts, 40–50 percent of farms are 0.2 hectare or less (MINAGRI 2017a).
6. More formally the Organic Law no. 08/2005 of 14/7/2005, "Determining the Use and Management of Land in Rwanda." See Pritchard (2013).
7. Just under 30 percent of farm households participated in land consolidation according to the most recent household survey (EICV 2013/14); if progress has continued at the same rate since then (7 percent a year since the 2010/11 survey), some 39 percent of farm households would have been affected by 2017/18 (NISR, various years).

8. Through the highly successful Land Tenure Regularization Program prepared starting in 2005 (DfID 2015).
9. The new cooperative strategy of the government is built around addressing these and other issues that have arisen during the meteoric expansion of primary cooperatives in Rwanda, which have grown from less than 1,000 in 2005 to more than 8,000 presently (MINICOM 2018).
10. It is likely that the rise in food staple prices in Africa in 2008, which endured at least through 2012–13, helped to improve allocative efficiency in staples production and boosted the value of output growth independent of increased use of inputs or land expansion.
11. Nineteen percent in season A and 15 percent in season B (NISR 2017).
12. In 2016, subsidized fertilizers were available to smallholder producers of maize, wheat, soybean, rice, beans, cassava, Irish potatoes, and vegetables.
13. The reasons for these low payments are not clear. The prices reported here were observed informally from a small sample during a field trip in September 2017. More research in this area is warranted.
14. The fiscal treatment of insurance discourages financial institutions and borrowers from seeking to expand agricultural insurance. Although agricultural insurance premiums have been exempted specifically from the value added tax of 18 percent, a 15 percent reinsurance withholding tax remains. This makes insurance expensive for farmers and limits the revenue generated by insurance companies, without making a substantial contribution to the government's tax revenues (World Bank 2016).
15. For example, see https://www.lexology.com/library/detail.aspx?g=a57dec69-283d-4bb0-a684-61a798fbd6c4.
16. See http://www.osborneclarke.com/insights/blockchain-and-land-registries-records-of-the-future/.
17. See https://www.wisekey.com/press/wisekey-and-microsoft-collaborate-to-support-rwandan-government-make-secure-transactions-using-blockchain-technology/.
18. See the U.S. Food Marketing Institute, a trade group, at https://www.fmi.org/our-research/supermarket-facts.
19. World Bank (2015) is the baseline evaluation report. Two subreports focusing, respectively, on farmers and factories were completed in 2017 and are forthcoming. Although the farmers' share of bought-leaf costs rose, bought-leaf costs remained a constant share of overall costs.
20. With a low of US$0.40 per pound in fall 2001, a high of US$2.80 per pound in spring 2011, and a price of US$1.25 per pound in January 2018. See http://www.macrotrends.net/2535/coffee-prices-historical-chart-data.
21. Professor Ameet Morjaria (Kellogg School of Management, Northwestern University), personal communication.
22. Professor Ameet Morjaria (Kellogg School of Management, Northwestern University), personal communication.
23. For details of many certification experiences, see https://www.fairtradecertified.org/why-fair-trade/our-impact.
24. Professor Thomas Jayne (Michigan State University), personal communication, using Living Standards Measurement Survey data.
25. See http://microdata.worldbank.org/index.php/catalog/2862.
26. See http://microdata.worldbank.org/index.php/catalog/2862, but using Zambian Ministry of Agriculture and Livestock Crop Forecast Surveys.
27. See http://microdata.worldbank.org/index.php/catalog/2862.
28. Professor David Tschirley (Michigan State University), personal communication. Also see Tschirley et al. (2015) for background.
29. Season A starts in September and ends in February of the following year, season B starts in March and ends in June of the same year, and season C starts in July and ends in September of the same year. The source is the 2015 Seasonal Agricultural Surveys (NISR 2016b).
30. Biotic stresses include disturbances from living organisms such as pests, bacteria, and fungi. Abiotic stress arises from factors such as heat, sunlight, and wind.
31. For a current example in the field, see http://www.soilcares.com/en/products/scanner/.
32. Addressing agricultural land (that is, soil) and forest degradation (loss of biomass) jointly through conservation and restoration of productive landscapes is now seen as central to agricultural adaptation to and mitigation of climate change in the tropics and indeed globally. This argument is laid out more fully in the Global Commission on the Economy and Climate Change (2014),

which went on to have a seminal impact on the December 2015 United Nations Committee of Parties Summit in Paris. It can also be seen in the work on agriculture and climate change of the Consultative Group on International Agricultural Research (https://ccafs.cgiar.org).

33. The source and original documentation for this paragraph are from Global Commission on the Economy and Climate (2014).
34. All proposals for government participation in agribusiness ventures go through the Investment Promotion Coordination Committee chaired by the Rwanda Development Board. The commodities listed all have had projects submitted at one time or another, and this is substantiated by the background material, by commodity or commodity group, prepared for the committee. See RDB (2017).
35. See, for example, http://blogs.worldbank.org/ppps/how-national-ppp-units-can-influence-regional-performance-korea-s-experience.
36. This argument is set out in detail in Delgado (1999).
37. See http://www.minagri.gov.rw/index.php?id=469&tx_ttnews%5Btt_news%5D=1175&cHash=0caddb1dfa0a480df74016a3d6872b23.
38. The source for the recommendations that follow in this area is the World Bank's "Agriculture Finance Diagnostic for Rwanda," which provides details (World Bank 2016).
39. A comprehensive electronic business directory is a simple tool that is easily updated. It helps to keep track of a rapidly changing business environment, lowers search costs for foreign firms seeking partners in Rwanda, and helps to encourage increased communications within the national business community. Government participation would lower the costs of keeping the directory current through current information on registrations.
40. Dividing estimated irrigated marshland of 46,000 hectares (reducing the figure of 48,511 hectares of total irrigation in 2016–17 in MINAGRI [2017c] by the figure of 2,500 hectares on hillsides from World Bank [2014] and dividing by an estimate of 277,164 hectares of potentially irrigable marshland in MINAGRI [2017c]).
41. Producing for regional horticulture markets like the Democratic Republic of Congo will have a revenue advantage over producing staples for the domestic market and provide more experience and time for Rwanda to work its way into highly competitive international markets for horticulture. Including subsidies and after costs are paid, rice farmers might earn US$800 per hectare in high-cost irrigation projects in the marshlands and maize farmers might earn US$250 per hectare on hillsides, compared with US$3,000 to US$3,500 per hectare by farmers with potato lands in the northern or southern provinces and US$2,000 for coffee farmers (Cambridge Resources International 2017). Returns to smallholder horticulture farmers producing for the domestic market or the Democratic Republic of Congo have not been estimated comprehensively, but they are thought to be at least on a par with the returns to potato farmers or four times as high as the returns to rice farmers.

References

Abdulsamad, A., and G. Gereffi. 2016. *East Africa Dairy Value Chains: Firm Capabilities to Expand Regional Trade.* IGC Report F-38202-RWA-1. London: International Growth Centre; Durham, NC: Center on Globalization, Governance, and Competitiveness, Duke University, October.

Access to Finance Rwanda–Finscope. 2016. *Financial Inclusion in Rwanda 2016.* Kigali: Access to Finance Rwanda.

Accord Associates. 2017. "Future Sources of Growth in Rwanda Export Horticulture." Draft report prepared for the World Bank, Washington, DC, November.

AGRA (Alliance for a Green Revolution in Africa). 2016. "Towards a Third Generation Subsidy Model, Rwanda Country Report." Draft report, AGRA, Nairobi.

Agri-TAF (Agriculture Technical Assistance Facility). 2016. "Climate Risk Assessment of Agriculture in Rwanda." International Fund for Agricultural Development, Rome, November 26.

Ali, D. A., K. Deininger, and M. Goldstein. 2014. "Environmental and Gender Impact of Land Tenure Regularization in Africa: Pilot Evidence from Rwanda." *Journal of Development Economics* 110 (September): 262–75.

Cambridge Resources International. 2017. "Study on Comparative Economic Advantage of Crop Production in Rwanda." Cambridge Resources International, Cambridge, MA, March 31.

Cargill. 2014. "Cargill and IFC Invest $2.5 Million to Expand Cocoa Farmer Coop." SCOPEinsight, Côte d'Ivoire, October. http://www.scopeinsight.com/news/cargill-and-ifc-invest-2-5-million-to-expand-cocoa-farmer-coop/.

CIAT (International Center for Tropical Agriculture). 2015. "Climate Smart Agriculture in Rwanda." CIAT, Calí.

COMESA (Common Market for Eastern and Southern Africa). 2017. "Country Harmonized COMESA Seed Regulations Have Been Launched." COMESA, June 13. http://www.comesa.int/country-harmonized-comesa-seed-regulations-have-been-launched.

Dang, Y., W. Ren, B. Tao, G. Chen, C. Lu, J. Yang, S. Pan, G. Wang, S. Li, and H. Tian. 2014. "Climate and Land Use Controls on Soil Organic Carbon in the Loess Plateau Region of China." *PLOS ONE* 9 (5): e95548. doi:10.1371/journal.pone.0095548.

Delgado, C. 1999. "Sources of Growth in Smallholder Agriculture in Sub-Saharan Africa: The Role of Vertical Integration with Processors of High Value Items." *Agrekon* 38 (Special Issue, May): 165–89.

Delgado, C., J. Hopkins, V. Kelly, P. B. R. Hazell, A. A. McKenna, P. Gruhn, B. Johhati, J. Sil, and C. Courbois. 1998. *Agricultural Growth Linkages in Sub-Saharan Africa*. IFPRI Research Report 107. Washington, DC: International Food Policy Research Institute.

DfID (Department for International Development). 2015. "Rwanda Inclusive Growth Diagnostic." DfID, Kigali, June 19.

Diao, X., P. Fang, J. Randriamamonjy, and J. Thurlow. 2017a. "A Growth Analysis—Drivers of Growth in Rwanda." International Food Policy Research Institute, Washington, DC. November 21.

———. 2017b. "Patterns of Food Consumption in Rwanda: An Analysis of EICV4 Data." International Food Policy Research Institute, Washington, DC, November 13.

FAO (Food and Agriculture Organization). 2010. *Agro-Based Clusters in Developing Countries: Staying Competitive in a Global Economy*. Agricultural Management, Marketing, and Finance Occasional Paper 25. Rome: FAO.

———. 2017. *Agroforestry for Landscape Restoration*. Forest Landscape Restoration Mechanism. Rome: FAO.

FAO, MAFAP (Monitoring and Analysing Food and Agricultural Policies Programme). 2017. "MAFAP Commodity Dashboard Template: Rwanda, Monitoring Price Incentives for Coffee." Draft, FAO, MAFAP, Rome.

Future Climate for Africa. 2014. *Report Rwanda*. Cape Town: Future Climate for Africa.

Global Commission on the Economy and Climate. 2014. "Land Use." In *Better Growth, Better Climate: The New Climate Economy Report 2014*, ch. 3. Washington, DC: Global Commission on the Economy and Climate. http://newclimateeconomy.report/2014/land-use/.

Havemann, T. 2015. "Tea Landscapes in Yunnan, China." In *Steps toward Green: Greening Export Agriculture in East and Southeast Asia; Policy Responses to the Environmental Footprint of Commodity Agriculture in East and Southeast Asia*, edited by S. Scherr, K. Mankad, S. Jaffee, and C. Negra, 143–66. Washington, DC: EcoAgriculture Partners.

Hirschman, A. 1958. *The Strategy of Economic Development*. New Haven: Yale University Press.

Huang, M., J. Gallichand, and P. Zhang. 2003. "Runoff and Sediment Responses to Conservation Practices: Loess Plateau of China." *Journal of the American Water Resources Association* 39 (5): 1197–207. doi:10.1111/j.1752-1688.2003.tb03702.x.

IFDC (International Fertilizer Development Center). 2014. *Rwanda Fertilizer Assessment*. Muscle Shoals, AL: IFDC, August.

Jaffee, S., S. Henson, and L. Diaz Rios. 2011. *Making the Grade: Smallholder Farmers, Emerging Standards, and Development Assistance Programs in Africa: A Research Program Synthesis*. Report 62324-AFR. Washington, DC: World Bank, June. https://hubs.worldbank.org/docs/ImageBank/Pages/DocProfile.aspx?nodeid=442392.

Kathiresan, A. 2012. "Farm Land Use Consolidation in Rwanda: Assessment from the Perspectives of Agricultural Sector." MINAGRI, Kigali, June 29.

King, R., and D. Byerlee. 1978. "Factor Intensities and Locational Linkages of Rural Consumption Patterns in Sierra Leone." *American Journal of Agricultural Economics* 60 (2): 197–206. https://doi.org/10.2307/1240048.

Kumar, R., and A. Agarwal. 2016. "Promoting More, Better, and Inclusive Jobs: Using a 'Jobs Lens' for the Tanzanian Horticulture Sector." Jobs Group, World Bank, Washington, DC, January.

Malesu, M. M., A. R. Oduor, K. Chrogony, D. Nyolei, D. K. K. Gachene, E. K. Biamah, M. O'Neil, M. Lyama, and J. Mogoi. 2010. *Rwanda Irrigation Master Plan*. Kigali: Ministry of Agriculture and Animal Resources, Ebony Company, and World Agroforestry Centre.

Marin, P., S. Tal, J. Yeres, and K. B. Ringskog. 2017. "Water Management in Israel: Key Innovations and Lessons Learned for Water-Scarce Countries." Water Global Practice Working Paper, World Bank, Washington, DC.

MINAGRI (Ministry of Agriculture and Animal Resources), Rwanda. 2012. "Strategic Plan for the Transformation of Agriculture in Rwanda, Phase 3 ('PSTA3')." MINAGRI, Kigali.

———. 2014. "National Fertilizer Policy." MINAGRI, Kigali, June.

———. 2015a. "COMESA Seed Trade Harmonisation Regulations Launched in Rwanda." Government of Rwanda, Kigali, February 25. http://www.gov.rw/news_detail/?tx_ttnews%5Btt_news%5D=1082&cHash=46ceb55f78e.

———. 2015b. "Privatized Fertilizer Importation and Distribution System in Rwanda: Contribution to Boosting Productivity." *New Times*, June 18. www.newtimes.co.rw/files/promo/1435924746Minagri-July-3.pdf.

———. 2017a. "Rwanda Comprehensive Mechanization Policy." MINAGRI, Kigali, June 15.

———. 2017b. "Rwanda National Agricultural Policy: A Productive, Green, and Market-Led Agricultural Sector towards 2030." MINAGRI, Kigali, October.

———. 2017c. "Strategic Plan for Agricultural Transformation 2018–24 ('PSTA4')." MINAGRI, Kigali, November.

MINICOM (Ministry of Trade and Industry), Rwanda. 2018. "National Policy on Cooperatives in Rwanda: Toward Private Cooperative Enterprises and Business Entities for Socio-Economic Transformation." MINICOM, Kigali, January.

MINIRENA (Ministry of the Environment), Rwanda. 2012. "Second National Communication." MINIRENA, Kigali.

Moreki, J. C., N. S. Ndubo, T. Ditshupo, and J. B. Ntesang. 2012. "Cattle Identification and Traceability in Botswana." *Journal of Animal Science Advances* 2 (12): 925–33.

NAEB (National Agricultural Export Development Board). 2017. "Coffee." NAEB, Kigali. http://www.naeb.gov.rw/index.php?id=48.

Nestlé. 2016. *Nestlé in Society: Creating Shared Value and Meeting Our Commitments 2016*. Lausanne: Nestlé. https://www.nestle.com/asset-library/documents/library/documents/corporate_social_responsibility/nestle-in-society-summary-report-2016-en.pdf.

NISR (National Institute of Statistics of Rwanda). 2014. *Fourth Population and Housing Census 2012: Thematic Report; Population Projections*. Kigali: NISR, January.

———. 2016a. *Rwanda Statistical Yearbook 2016*. Kigali: NISR.

———. 2016b. "Seasonal Agricultural Surveys—Season A (May)." NISR, Kigali.

———. 2017. "Seasonal Agricultural Surveys—Season A (May) and Season B (September)." NISR, Kigali.

———. Various years. *Integrated Household Living Survey (EICV)*. Kigali: NISR.

Ntirenganya, E. 2018. "Rwanda Takes Early Steps towards Legalising GMOs." *New Times*, January 16. http://www.newtimes.co.rw/section/Printer/227457/.

Policy Associates. 2017. *Rwanda Agriculture Public Expenditure Review 2016*, 2 vols. Kigali: World Bank Group and UKAid.

Pritchard, M. 2013. "Land, Power, and Peace: Tenure Formalization, Agricultural Reform, and Livelihood Insecurity in Rural Rwanda." *Land Use Policy* 30 (1): 186–96.

RDB (Rwanda Development Board). 2017. "Investment Opportunities in the Irrigation and Mechanization Sectors." RDB, Kigali. http://www.rdb.rw/fileadmin/user_upload/Documents/Agriculture/Irrigation%20and%20Mechanization%20projects.pdf.

REMA (Rwanda Environment Management Authority). 2011. "Green Growth and Climate Resilience National Strategy for Climate Change and Low Carbon Development." REMA, Kigali.

———. 2015. *Rwanda: State of Environment and Outlook Report 2015*. Kigali: REMA.

Seidler, E. 2001. "Wholesale Market Development: FAO's Experience." Paper prepared for the 22nd Congress of the World Union of Wholesale Markets, Food and Agriculture Organization, Durban, South Africa, September.

Tschirley, D., T. Reardon, M. Dolislager, and J. Snyder. 2015. "The Rise of a Middle Class in East and Southern Africa: Implications for Food System Transformation." *Journal of International Development* 27 (5): 628–46.

U.S. Department of Agriculture. 2017. International Agricultural Productivity database. Washington, DC: Economic Research Service. https://www.ers.usda.gov/data-products/international-agricultural-productivity/.

Vermeulen, H., J. Kirsten, and K. Sartorius. 2008. "Contracting Arrangements in Agribusiness Procurement Practices in South Africa." *Agrekon* 47 (2, June): 198–221.

Weatherspoon, D., and T. Reardon. 2003. "The Rise of Supermarkets in Africa: Implications for Agrifood Systems and the Rural Poor." *Development Policy Review* 21 (3): 333–55.

World Bank. 2007a. "Restoring China's Loess Plateau." Feature Story, World Bank, March 15. http://www.worldbank.org/en/news/feature/2007/03/15/restoring-chinas-loess-plateau.

———. 2007b. *World Development Report 2008: Agriculture for Development*. Washington, DC: World Bank.

———. 2014. "Promoting Agricultural Growth in Rwanda: Recent Performance, Challenges, and Opportunities." Policy Note ACS9719, World Bank, Washington DC, June 7. http://documents.worldbank.org/curated/en/883411468305660877/pdf/ACS97190WP0P1400Box385238B00PUBLIC0.pdf.

———. 2015. "Rwanda Green Leaf Price Reform Impact Evaluation Baseline Report." Investment Climate Impact Program, World Bank, Washington, DC. http://pubdocs.worldbank.org/en/858581473702690438/COMPEL-rwanda-baselinereport.pdf.

———. 2016. "Agricultural Finance Diagnostic." Rwanda Country Support Program, Financial Inclusion Support Framework, World Bank, Washington, DC.

———. 2017. World Development Indicators database. Washington, DC: World Bank. https://data.worldbank.org/products/wdi.

Xie, M., J. Li, N. Asquith, J. Tyson, A. Kleine, and Y. Huan. 2010. "Rehabilitating a Degraded Watershed: A Case Study from China's Loess Plateau." World Bank Institute, Climate Change Unit, Washington, DC.

Zeuli, K., R. Cropp, and M. Schaars. 2004. *Cooperatives: Principles and Practices in the 21st Century*. University of Wisconsin Extension A1457, Madison. August.

6

Capable and Accountable State Institutions

> "*We never stopped learning because the situation kept on changing and we had to adjust our own policies.*" (Lee 2000, 686)

> "*We are moving ahead, learning from what works and what doesn't work and adjusting without losing sight of our goals.*" (Kagame 2015)

Introduction

Starting from very difficult initial conditions after the 1994 genocide against the Tutsi, Rwanda has made remarkable progress in strengthening governance. International rankings place Rwanda at the average level of upper-middle-income countries, with particularly strong performance on indicators of *government effectiveness, control of corruption, rule of law,* and *regulatory quality.*[1] The formerly bloated civil service has been downsized, and the skills of government officials have improved markedly. Reliance on homegrown approaches to performance management has instilled a strong culture of results at all levels of government, greatly increasing government effectiveness. Rwanda's strong governance is a driving force behind its rapid growth and provides a key comparative advantage over most other countries in the region.

Nevertheless, achieving middle-income status will require further improvements in institutions to encourage greater creativity and initiative by central and local government officials. As the economy gets bigger and more complex, it will require far deeper *coordination* between institutions (for managing urbanization, industrialization, export promotion, and decentralization, for example) and *cooperation* between the state and the private sector (for public investments, for example), on the one hand, and between the state and the society (to support innovation at the local level and generate strong feedback loops), on the other. Achieving all of this will require greater social capital of *trust* between citizens, between civil society and the government, and among local officials, civil servants, and national political leadership to promote the innovation (in the bureaucracy, in the society) required for rapid economic growth.

This chapter addresses the following question: How should Rwanda strengthen its state efficiency and accountability to best support successful transition to becoming a modern, competitive, and globally connected middle-income economy?

The chapter applies the analytical framework of the *World Development Report 2017* (World Bank 2017) to discuss institutional adaptation to induce the behavior changes needed—in government, firms, and citizens—to promote higher levels of development. It describes Rwanda's performance on core measures of institutional development and highlights three pillars, or broad policy objectives, to strengthen trust and improve government effectiveness.

Pillar 1: Enabling Innovative, Coordinated, Capable Bureaucracy, and Local Governments

Key challenges relate to incentives for innovation among bureaucrats and local governments and to shortfalls of some core competencies in the civil service. *Imihigo* (performance contracts) have made a strong contribution to instilling a culture of results, but these contracts can be improved to foster coordination between institutions, bottom-up initiatives, and innovation. To enhance innovation, Rwanda could consider adopting multiyear targets in *imihigo* with annual benchmarks, making greater use of qualitative surveys, and focusing more on outcomes rather than processes. Another step forward could be to increase the importance of the joint *imihigo* to at least 50 percent and to take bold measures to improve interagency coordination on key cross-cutting issues. Further increases in training by the Rwanda Management Institute (RMI) should be supported by skills audits and functional reviews to identify the missing skills in the public sector. Regular compensation reviews, higher compensation for individuals with scarce skills, and the development of nonfinancial incentives will become increasingly important to retain and attract highly skilled staff.

Pillar 2: Strengthening Market Institutions and Building the State's Financial Capacity

Despite Rwanda's impressive improvements in governance, private sector investment and the entry of new firms remain low, reflecting gaps in market institutions. Creating special courts and fast-track procedures to adjudicate small claims; further promoting alternative means of resolving commercial disputes (such as arbitration, mediation, and conciliation); boosting reliance on technology; increasing training and specialization of judges, prosecutors, and investigators; and improving case management techniques would enhance the effectiveness of the judiciary system for contract enforcement. Further improvements in the efficiency of the land management system and implementation of the intellectual property law would strengthen property rights. Reviewing the performance of fiscal incentives with a view to reducing Rwanda's tax expenditures, increasing local government revenue collection, ensuring that the state captures an appropriate share of the expected rise in mineral revenues, and raising Rwanda's strong public financial management to international standards would strengthen the state's financial capacity. A better balance needs to be achieved between public investments that are expected to generate high returns over the long term and investments in areas with potential high short-term returns based on market signals of scarcity.

Pillar 3: Enhancing the State's Accountability to Citizens

Strengthening key watchdog agencies (the Public Accounts Committee, the Office of the Auditor General, the Ombudsman's Office, and the Rwanda Governance Board) with more operational capabilities and strengthening the media sector would further strengthen government accountability. Increasing own revenue raising by local government and providing greater fiscal decentralization would be a bold step toward making local officials and service providers more accountable. Deepening the initiatives that have sought to involve citizens in local decision making (for example, in setting *imihigo* objectives) and to provide greater local flexibility and reliance on more qualitative information in monitoring performance would strengthen support for local government and improve the quality of services.

Rwanda's Record in Governance and Government Effectiveness

Institutional quality in Rwanda has improved significantly. Public sector reforms have led to an effective state with relatively low corruption and capable institutions. An almost across-the-board upward trajectory in institutional quality is seen in the governance assessment conducted by the Rwanda Governance Board (RGB) since 2010 (table 6.1).[2] This assessment is backed up by several cross-country measures of governance, where Rwanda emerges at par with middle-income countries, with particularly strong performance on indicators of *government effectiveness, control of corruption, rule of law,* and *regulatory quality* (figures 6.1 and 6.2). According to the 2017 Ibrahim Index of African Governance, Rwanda is the only country to have made consistent year-on-year improvement on *overall governance* since the index was started.

Considering the grim conditions following the genocide against the Tutsi, Rwanda has achieved high levels of stability and security. According to the 2016 World Internal Security and Police Index, which measures the ability of a country's security apparatus to respond to internal security challenges, Rwanda (together with Botswana) performs the best in the Sub-Saharan Africa region and is ranked 50 globally. This positive assessment reflects Rwanda's strong performance in *process* (low corruption, high efficiency) and *compliance*.

The Rwandan government has maintained high-profile anticorruption efforts.

FIGURE 6.1 Relationship between government effectiveness and level of development

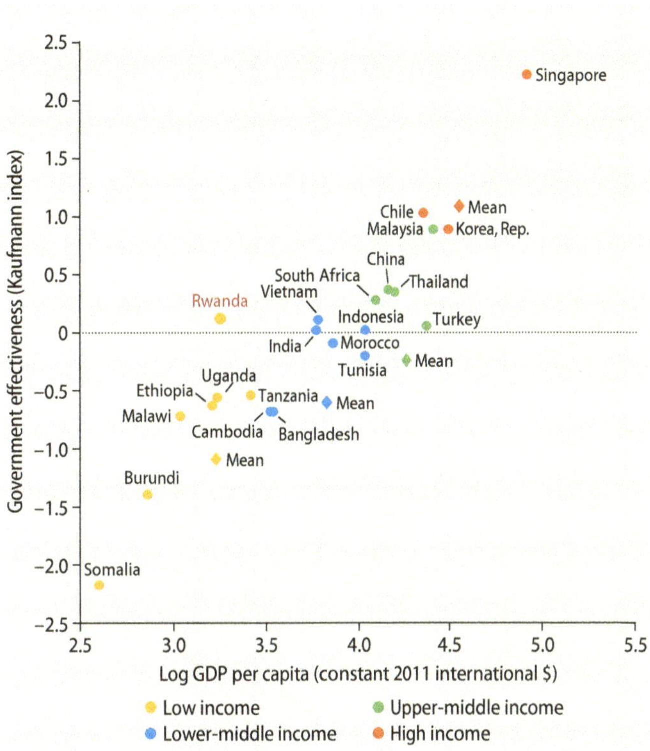

Sources: Kaufmann, Kraay, and Mastruzzi 2010; World Development Indicators data from World Bank, various years.

TABLE 6.1 The Rwanda Governance Scorecard: Scores for 2016 compared with previous scores

Indicator	First edition	Second edition	Third edition	Fourth edition	Change over five years	Trend
Rule of law	67.71	73.37	81.68	79.68	+11.97	↑
Political rights and civil liberties	71.43	73.62	77.05	81.83	+10.4	↑
Participation and inclusiveness	74.23	75.26	75.36	77.01	+2.87	↑
Safety and security	87.26	91.35	91.96	92.62	+5.36	↑
Investing in human and social development	82.41	78.8	81.54	74.88	−7.53	↓
Control of corruption transparency and accountability	76.22	77.1	79.04	86.56	+10.34	↑
Quality of service delivery	66.21	70.44	72.00	72.93	+6.72	↑
Economic and corporate governance	—	74.93	72.20	76.82	+1.89	↑

Source: RGB 2016b.
Note: — = not available. The Rwanda Governance Scorecard is composed of eight indicators based on the guidelines of international context, recognized international indexes, and Rwandan homegrown indicators (RGB 2016a, 3).

Institutions such as the Ombudsman's Office have sought to root out corruption, and the courts have prosecuted cases at all levels of government. Consistent with this, in 2017 Rwanda was ranked 48 (out of 180 countries) for control of corruption in Transparency International's Corruption Perception Index, a vast improvement over its 2006 ranking of 121, placing it 3 (alongside Mauritius) on the continent.

The 2003 Constitution called for politicians and civil servants to declare their assets, which has been followed by various enforcement measures (Freedom House 2007), including prosecution of prominent government officials. The 2016 Bertelsmann Stiftung's Transformation Index, which assesses whether public servants and politicians are held accountable,[3] found Rwanda to be at the level of upper-middle-income countries (figure 6.3).

The country has also built relatively strong fiscal institutions that have supported rapid growth. Prudent fiscal management has contributed to macroeconomic stability, while good-quality public financial management has improved service delivery. An important measure in this regard is revenue generation. Government revenues (excluding grants) equal almost 17 percent of gross domestic product (GDP) and in 2015 were above the average ratio for lower-middle-income countries (figure 6.4).

The expenditure side of the budget is defined by a high ratio of public investment to GDP. At its peak in 2013–15, public investments reached 13 percent of GDP; quite high by international standards. They have declined since then, stabilizing at about 10 percent of GDP.[4] However, this number does not capture the full extent of public investment, because it does not include net lending (on average, 2 percent of GDP in recent years).[5] Transport, energy, and health have been the important priority sectors for public investment. The other large item is governance and decentralization, which includes capital transfers to the communities

FIGURE 6.2 Benchmarking of Rwanda along the various dimensions of governance

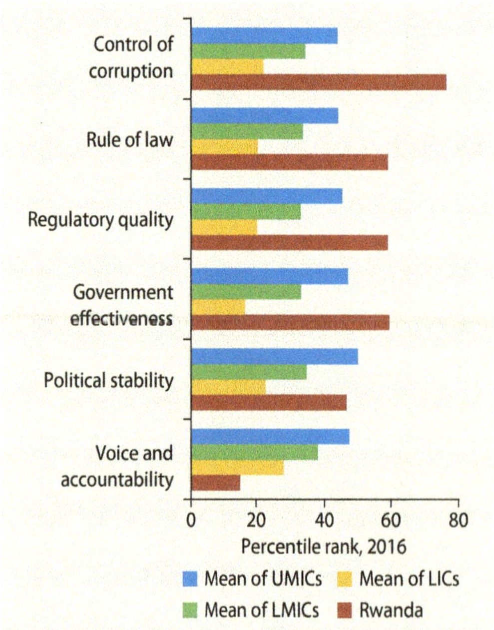

Source: 2016 Worldwide Governance Indicators from Kaufmann, Kraay, and Mastruzzi 2010.
Note: LIC = low-income country; LMIC = lower-middle-income country; UMIC = upper-middle-income country.

FIGURE 6.3 Correlation between prosecution of office abuse and GDP per capita

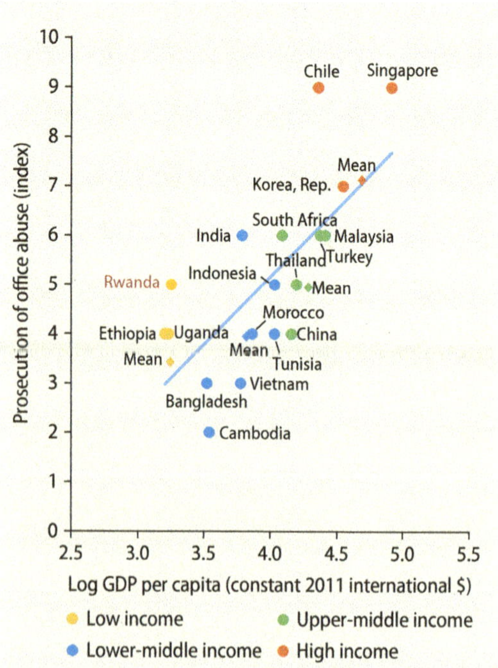

Sources: 2016 Bertelsmann Stiftung's Transformation Index, Q3.3: Prosecution of office abuse; World Development Indicators 2016 data (World Bank, various years).

for various infrastructure needs. On balance, public investment has been managed well, and project implementation has been particularly strong.[6] Rwanda scored high among low-income countries and came in ahead of 19 middle-income countries in a 2012 International Monetary Fund assessment (Dabla-Norris et al. 2012).[7] The 2016 public expenditure and financial accountability assessment (PEFA Secretariat 2017) also shows strength in project selection and costing (table 6.2).

These achievements are due in large part to a strong developmental vision driven by the urgent need for recovery in the aftermath of the genocide against the Tutsi. Rwanda has been characterized as a "developmental state" (Booth and Golooba-Mutebi 2012; Crisafulli and Redmond 2012), with the top leadership playing a central role and showing the capacity to commit credibly to coherent reform policies and to ensure that the bureaucracy and other relevant actors carry through on implementation. Strengthening administrative capacity, instituting a decentralized system, and building effective civil service monitoring were seen early on as being crucial for political legitimacy.[8] These aspects were complemented by a series of homegrown initiatives that sought to instill "Rwandan values" and mobilize collective action.

Strong gains have been made in building a capable civil service (box 6.1). An international assessment noted favorably, "Despite the limited technical capacity in some fields, Rwandan public administration is relatively efficient, recruitment

FIGURE 6.4 Revenue (tax and nontax) excluding grants

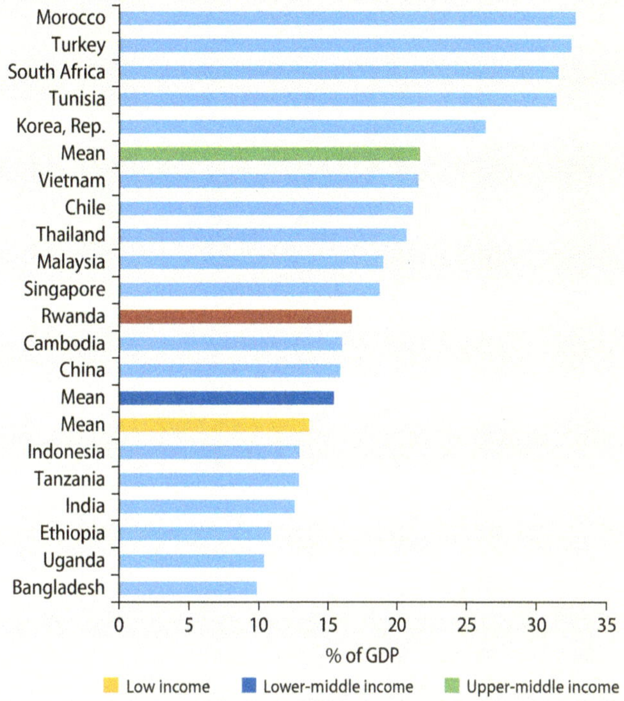

Source: World Development Indicators (World Bank, various years); available years: 2011 for Ethiopia, Morocco, and the mean of low-income countries; 2012 for Tunisia; 2013 for India, Vietnam, and the mean of low- and middle-income countries; 2014 for China and the mean of upper-middle-income countries; 2015 for all the others.

TABLE 6.2 Components and ratings of public investment management framework

P1–11	Dimension	Score	Justification
Public investment management		B+	Scoring method M2
11.1	Economic analysis of investment proposals	B	Ministries, departments, and agencies as well as district councils submit all proposed capital investment projects to the Public Investment Committee for economic appraisal before approval in accordance with the public investment guidelines issued by National Development Planning and Research. Some results are published.
11.2	Investment project selection	A	All major investment projects are prioritized on the basis of the public investment guidelines before they are included in the budget.
11.2	Investment project monitoring	A	Public investment guidelines outline a comprehensive costing framework for both investment cost and forward-linked recurrent costs. The information is included in the budget documentation.
11.4	Investment project monitoring	C	The Project Management and Monitoring Unit of the Ministry of Finance and Economic Planning undertakes at least quarterly physical inspection of all approved government projects. It also prepares quarterly and annual project progress and financial reports, but these are not published.

Source: PEFA Secretariat 2017.

practices have improved over time, and most technical positions, as well as most low- to middle-ranking officials, seem to be indeed recruited based on candidate merit" (Hertie School of Governance 2014). A strong civil service, together with a strong system of vertical accountability, explains Rwanda's strong reputation for implementation, control of corruption, and public financial management and its success in building basic infrastructure and improving outcomes.

Given the historical legacy of conflict, strengthening subnational institutions was considered a national priority. The country embarked on a transformative process of decentralization to improve the efficiency of the public sector, strengthen social cohesion, improve local governance, and promote access to basic infrastructure and service delivery. In 2000, a comprehensive National Decentralization Policy[9] was adopted to "enhance the participation of citizens in planning and [to] strengthen,

BOX 6.1 A major turnaround in the Rwandan civil service

The state inherited a heavily depleted civil service after the genocide. In the absence of a well-organized state apparatus, public sector organizations began hiring at their own discretion.[a] Overstaffing soon became common, sometimes with several employees holding the same position. Moreover, many of the new recruits lacked the necessary skills. By the end of 1997, there were about 40,600 civil servants, and Rwanda was facing problems that afflict many other countries in Sub-Saharan Africa: lack of uniform procedures for recruitment, promotion, or performance that contributed to an unsustainable wage bill (given the government's limited resources), even though the salaries offered were not competitive.[b] The Rwandan civil service had become too large, inefficient, and not sufficiently deconcentrated or decentralized for service delivery (Hausman 2011).

The first plan to reform the civil service, adopted in 1998, included downsizing, decentralization of personnel, uniform recruitment policy and procedures, and stronger selection of candidates. Downsizing and voluntary departure programs were implemented in 1999, 2004, 2006, and 2009. As a result, the size of the civil service and, more important, the profile of civil servants changed dramatically: the share of civil servants with university degrees rose from just 6 percent in 1998 to 79 percent in 2005 (Hausman 2011). Today, Rwanda's civil service is dominated by young, well-educated graduates, with a mean age below 35 years, making it one of the youngest among comparators. Based on New Public Management approaches, reorganizations since the early 2000s have sought to streamline the number of institutions while separating the policy-making function (left to ministries) from the implementation function (assigned to boards, agencies, and districts).

Transparent and merit-based recruitment, an area where many countries fail, was considered central to reconstruction of the country. Under the *urugwiro* dialogue (in 1998–99),[c] transparent and merit-based recruitment was increasingly emphasized, becoming a principle enshrined in the 2003 Constitution (Chemouni 2017),[d] replacing the practice of favoritism that dominated the pre-genocide era and contributed to social tensions (Hausman 2011). The Public Service Commission, set up in 2007,[e] was made responsible for the recruitment of central government employees.[f] The law provided both the commission and the ombudsman (who organized annual visits to different state organizations to detect cases of nepotism) with administrative autonomy, requiring them to report directly to Parliament and the president.

a. According to the interviews organized with the former head of the National Tender Board on February 18, 2015, some state organizations, such as the Ministry of Civil Service, were informally administering written exams and interviews when hiring for top positions (Chemouni 2017).
b. In 1995 salaries accounted for 73.6 percent of total expenditures (Ministry of Public Service, Skills Development, and Labor 2005).
c. Meetings at the Office of the President between politicians and civil society representatives to debate on the reconstruction of Rwanda (May 1998–March 1999).
d. Articles 45 and 126.
e. Article 181 of the 2003 Constitution.
f. A series of measures have been introduced to improve transparency in the recruitment process, such as guidelines on timing and the modalities for publishing vacancies and job interviews, but also the provision that a candidate who feels that he or she has been treated unfairly can report the case to the Ombudsman's Office or the Public Service Commission. The publication of the decisions taken at each stage of the recruitment process and the involvement of private companies to organize and evaluate recruitment tests also have supported transparent and merit-based recruitment.

through various means, the 'voice' of citizens in influencing service delivery providers." In the September 2005 National Conference on Decentralization, Accountability, and Service Delivery, the "Rwanda model" of decentralization was laid out further, inspired by the latest international knowledge in the fields of citizens-centered governance and public service delivery, including the *World Development Report 2004* (World Bank 2003b). The government confirmed this approach and further defined tools and mechanisms to incorporate the decentralization framework in subsequent policies, legislation,[10] guidelines, and sectoral reforms (figure 6.5).[11]

FIGURE 6.5 Rwanda's decentralization framework for service delivery

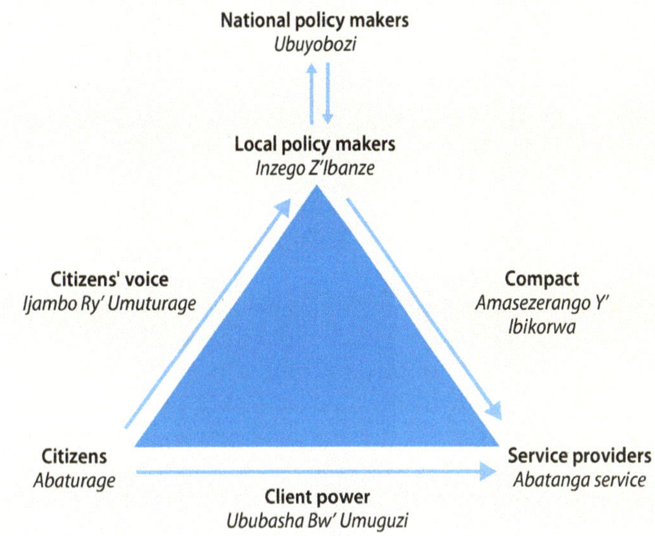

Source: MINALOC 2006.
Note: MINALOC = (Rwanda) Ministry of Local Government.

Traditional Rwandan concepts and practices have been strengthened and new initiatives have been put in place to improve government accountability and enhance the voice and power of beneficiaries. Multiple platforms for citizen-state interaction have been institutionalized at central and local levels, such as *Umushyikirano* (National Dialogue Council), a forum that brings together the president of the republic and citizens' representatives to debate national issues; the Joint Action Development Forum, a key participatory planning mechanism to improve alignment between citizens' and districts' priorities and the Accountability Day (*Inteko' z'abaturage*); the district budget hearings and Budget Day to present and discuss the district budget; and the post *umuganda*[12] meetings. Furthermore, a bottom-up planning approach has been outlined in improved versions of the local planning and budgeting guidelines issued by the Ministry of Local Government and the Ministry of Finance (see MINECOFIN 2007, 2009, 2013).

Concrete measures have sought to deepen the public sector's accountability further. A law to strengthen access to information came into effect on March 11, 2013. Overseen by the Ombudsman's Office, the law has clear provisions on proactive disclosure of information and is especially valuable in its broad scope, covering not only public bodies but also private bodies that provide public services.[13] Nevertheless, the number of access-to-information requests seems low.[14] In the health sector, after an encouraging pilot program, the government adopted performance-based financing at the national level. This approach allows the government to contract both private and public health facilities for the delivery of a package of services. Health facilities are then paid according to verifiable measures of quantity, quality, and equity of services.[15]

Imihigo (performance contracts), a genuine Rwandan management tool, have been adopted for boosting vertical accountability of civil servants and local governments toward central ministries and the presidency. The first *imihigo* were signed between the president of the republic and district mayors in 2006. The *imihigo* have since become an annual undertaking (box 6.2). The original goal was to enable local governments to articulate their own objectives, which reflect priorities of the local citizenry, and to set strategies to achieve the objectives. According to the Ministry of Local Government's decentralization assessment, *imihigo* became the most engaging and credible planning instrument at the subnational level, with better-funded activities and the most effectively evaluated targets (MINALOC 2017). *Imihigo* have made a strong contribution to instilling a culture of results in Rwanda, thereby increasing government effectiveness.

The justice sector, too, has carried out several important reforms. In 2005, the government reestablished the traditional community court system called *Gacaca* to mete out justice, achieve reconciliation, and heal some of the festering wounds from the time of the genocide. Under the *Gacaca*, a fully homegrown system, local communities selected citizens as judges to hear trials of suspects accused of all crimes (except their planning) during the genocide. By the time the *Gacaca* courts officially closed down on May 4, 2012, they had handled officially at that time a total of 1,237,356 cases. In 2006, also with the purpose of promoting reconciliation and the rule of law and tackling the huge court backlogs (this time for common-law offenses), the government created the *abunzi* (mediation committees) to provide free mediation services to resolve small conflicts. *Abunzi* have been effective, handling more than 50,000 cases in 2017 and earning high levels of citizen satisfaction (RGB 2016a).

Remaining Governance Challenges

Rapid improvements in governance and institutional structures have served Rwanda well, contributing to its impressive broader development outcomes. But the requirements of a middle-income Rwanda will be different—more demanding—from those that have sufficed in the low-income period. The ambitious aspirations being adopted are bound to rub against emerging institutional limitations. One of the most robust results of the development literature is that no non-resource-rich country has reached high income levels without highly capable and accountable institutions. And building effective institutions is a long-term endeavor. The improvements are necessarily incremental, building on global and local lessons and factoring in the specific context of the country. The process is also not linear. Rwanda's work in this regard will be critical.

To assess remaining challenges and guide the way forward, this chapter adopts an analytical framework that considers societal trust as a core underpinning of state effectiveness and long-term development. A high level of societal trust is necessary for the state to establish its legitimacy and to ensure cooperative relationships between itself, the business sector, and citizens. Although necessary for economic development in any

BOX 6.2 *Imihigo:* A Rwandan management tool of accountability

Performance contracts have played a major role in creating a strong vertical chain of accountability in the civil service. *Imihigo* is the plural in Kinyarwanda of *umuhigo*, which means a "vow to deliver." It also includes the concept of *guhiganwa*, which means "to compete among one another." It describes a practice in which a set of targets or goals must be achieved by an official within a specific period, following certain guiding principles and overcoming all hurdles (RGB 2016b), short of which the official may be sanctioned or even fired. A fully homegrown initiative, it was introduced in 2006 and has since become an invaluable tool for planning and implementation of development policies (RGB 2014). Derived from the traditional practice where individuals voluntarily set their own targets and publicly commit to achieve them within time-bound periods, the revived concept was intended to strengthen participatory priority setting, bottom-up planning, and accelerated implementation while focusing on time-bound results.[a]

a. The *imihigo* are set yearly, but they are evaluated every six months. Citizens Report Cards, produced by the Rwanda Governance Board, are now part of the evaluation of *imihigo* (with a weight of 10 percent).

BOX 6.3 Relationship between trust and long-term development

Above all, strong growth requires building a deeper level of trust. A vast literature demonstrates how trust (between the people and the government and among the people) plays a major role in growth and economic development (Fukuyama 1995; Knack and Keefer 1997, for example). Trust lowers transaction costs (Fukuyama 1995); encourages the establishment of long-term arrangements—for example, in the form of financial and employment contracts—and fixed investments; shapes the relationship between voters and politicians, which can lead to improved public policy, institutional reform, and stability; and strengthens the social compact (Knack and Keefer 1997).

Comparative experiences and a wealth of literature point to the importance of deepened trust and state legitimacy in resolving collective action problems that impede economic growth (La Porta et al. 1997; Putnam 1993). Low- and middle-income countries that fail to overcome vested interests through rules-based and transparent decision making, efforts to improve inclusion, and strong accountability mechanisms often stagnate (for many countries, referred to as the "middle-income trap"), because they are unable to induce the behavioral changes needed to promote investment and innovation (World Bank 2017, spotlight 6). Trust also facilitates adaptation to change without excessive disruption. Low- and middle-income countries experience violent transitions every eight years on average (Cox, North, and Weingast 2015), underlining the difficulties involved in adapting institutions to the management of emerging social tensions.

FIGURE 6.6 A framework for assessing effectiveness of state institutions in Rwanda

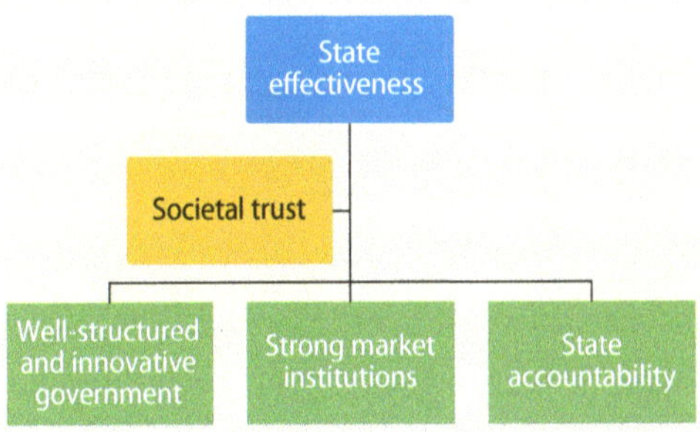

situation (box 6.3), trust is especially meaningful in a postconflict situation.

State effectiveness and societal trust both depend on three institutional pillars (figure 6.6):

1. The level and quality of the state's capacity, which are shaped by governance structures and the level of meritocracy, coordination, and rules-based authority in the country
2. The presence of a well-functioning market-based economic system, which ensures that resource allocation is guided by efficient price signals, rests on a strong partnership between the private and public sectors, and is complemented by fiscal discipline to match policies with the state's financial capacity
3. The extent to which the state is accountable to its citizens, which ensures that policies and programs are aligned with the needs and aspirations of the people

Building Trust

Building trust and cooperation is an ongoing challenge in Rwanda. Interpersonal trust was understandably very low in the immediate aftermath of the genocide against the Tutsi. Impressive progress has been made since then in the way of reconciliation, promoting economic and social development, and strengthening the structures of governance; such progress has helped to close the trust gap. But more work is needed in this regard.

Structure and Capacity of Government

Despite the substantial progress that has been made, important challenges remain for building a well-structured, high-capacity government. The main ones emerge from the following: a centralized decision-making approach and lack of foresight and innovation mind-set in local governments, ineffective coordination mechanisms across different government entities, limited capacity, and insufficient training.

A key challenge is the issue of weak innovation among bureaucrats and local governments. The identification and encouragement of local innovations in the current *imihigo* evaluation framework are good examples to emulate in order to mitigate the possible negative effects of centralized evaluation and control. Strong performance monitoring can also create a culture of internal competition or a "hyper performance orientation" (MacArthur 2012).[16] This culture can discourage information sharing and coordination among public officials. The *imihigo* coordination unit should continue to monitor *imihigo* planning and implementation closely.

Moreover, even though transfers to local governments have increased in the last decade, they, too, can be overly prescriptive. For example, 80 percent of transfers are earmarked funds, which involve compulsory spending by local governments, and 14 percent are discretionary block grants. Worldwide, establishing an enabling and less restrictive environment has proved to be more effective in encouraging local innovation than strengthening the technical capacity of the local governments in question (Campbell and Fuhr 2004). Rwanda's current strategy of granting more flexibility to districts over their own generated revenues provides a good opportunity to spur creativity and efficiency in wealth creation at the local level, which directly affects local and national economic development. The experience of the World Bank Municipal Innovations project in Indonesia (World Bank 2003a) confirms that successful innovations are more likely if central and local governments share a political commitment to create a supportive enabling environment.

Coordination between ministries and public sector agencies is still a challenge. With the development of several semiautonomous agencies, some institutions (and staff) may have competing mandates, which increases the coordination costs for businesses and citizens. An example may be the Rwanda Revenue Authority (RRA), which is mandated to collect tax revenues, and the Rwanda Development Board, which is mandated to attract and develop investment. Streamlining coordination between these two institutions is essential to avoid any possible confusion to investors.

Coordination challenges also may arise from some of the poorly perceived overlapping responsibilities of central and local authorities. Attempts to clarify the assignment of expenditure responsibilities have been successful to implement because of coordination efficiencies between local governments and sectoral ministries. Taking sectoral decentralization to the next level will help to address these challenges.

In order to improve coordination between public institutions (such as between line ministries and local governments), in 2015 the government adopted the joint *imihigo*, which means that both institutions have to perform tasks to achieve the joint performance contract. A weight is assigned to an individual institution's *imihigo* and the joint *imihigo*. Final lessons on the joint *imihigo* will have to be drawn later, taking into account, among other things, the relationship between cooperation and competition during the implementation of *imihigo* and the impact of each on delivery.

Rwanda's public administration needs to improve some core competencies. For example, public institutions in the agriculture and energy sectors suffer from inadequate staff levels in central ministries and districts compared with agencies and boards and from a lack of long-term skills development plans, including in the public sector (a 2009 skills audit found that 60 percent of skills were in short supply in both sectors) (MacArthur 2012). Staffing requirements in some units also need to be evaluated more closely. For example, some small units (with only two to three staff) are in charge of several megaprojects and are subject to exceptionally heavy workloads and possible efficiency problems.[17] Gaps are also emerging in public sector training. In the last five years, the RMI only reached 9 percent of all civil servants (World Bank 2016).

Market Institutions and Fiscal Management

Rwanda's future ambitions will require the government to strengthen key market institutions, while backing them up with financial capacity generated by a prudent fiscal stance. The evidence is compelling that well-functioning markets require well-defined rules of the game that are enforced transparently and predictably. The counterfactual yields an entrepreneurial landscape that is not conducive to private-sector-led growth. As described by North (1991), "With insecure property rights, poorly enforced laws, barriers to entry, and monopolistic restrictions, the profit-maximizing firms will tend to have short time horizons and little fixed capital and will tend to be small. The most profitable businesses may be in trade, redistributive activity, or the black market. Large firms with substantial fixed capital will exist only under the umbrella of government protection with substantial subsidies, tariff protection, and payoff to the polity—a mixture hardly conducive to productive efficiency." This caution is pertinent to Rwanda, where the private sector is small and informal for the most part (chapter 4 of this report).

Rwanda has made good progress in improving regulations that support competition, but considerable scope remains for further improvement. This is borne out by the country's performance on cross-country comparisons. The *Global Competitiveness Report 2016–2017* ranks Rwanda 77 among 138 countries and 10 among 29 Sub-Saharan African countries on the intensity of local competition, while giving it high rankings on the extent of market dominance (34) and effectiveness of antimonopoly policy (26) (World Economic Forum 2016). According to the Bertelsmann Stiftung's Transformation Index 2018, Rwanda scores 6 points out of 10 on the existence and implementation of antitrust rules. The World Bank/Organisation for Economic Co-operation and Development product market regulation indicators similarly show Rwanda's mixed performance on various underpinnings of competition (figure 6.7).[18] The regulatory framework protects incumbents in key input sectors, with especially high barriers to entry in network industries such as telecommunications and electricity.

Major progress has been made in strengthening private ownership rights, which are enshrined in the 2003 Constitution (revised in 2015) and backed by several laws (for example, the 2013 land law and the 2007 expropriation law), other legal instruments, and land registration efforts. Article 34 of the Constitution notes, "Private property, whether individually or collectively owned, is inviolable," while allowing for exception to the inviolability for "public interest" purposes. Delays in compensation and their low levels relative to market value remain a challenge.

There is considerable scope to improve efficiency of the commercial dispute resolution process further, including contract enforcement—an important aspect of a functioning market economy that is essential to economic development and sustained growth (Esposito, Lanau, and Pompe 2014). Globally, Rwanda ranks 78 on the ease of enforcing contracts (among 190 economies), which shows both the extent of progress made to date and the scope for further improvement that remains. According to the Rwanda Governance Scorecard 2016 (RGB 2016b), with regard to the performance of the judiciary, "Citizens are less satisfied by the level of backlog of courts cases, the independence of courts, and implementation of courts resolution." There is widespread consensus among stakeholders that justice sector staff need continuous training in several categories important for commercial matters, such as intellectual property, insurance disputes, receivership cases, banking and finance, corporate governance, and arbitration.[19] A backlog of commercial cases, limited

FIGURE 6.7 Rwanda's performance on product market regulations

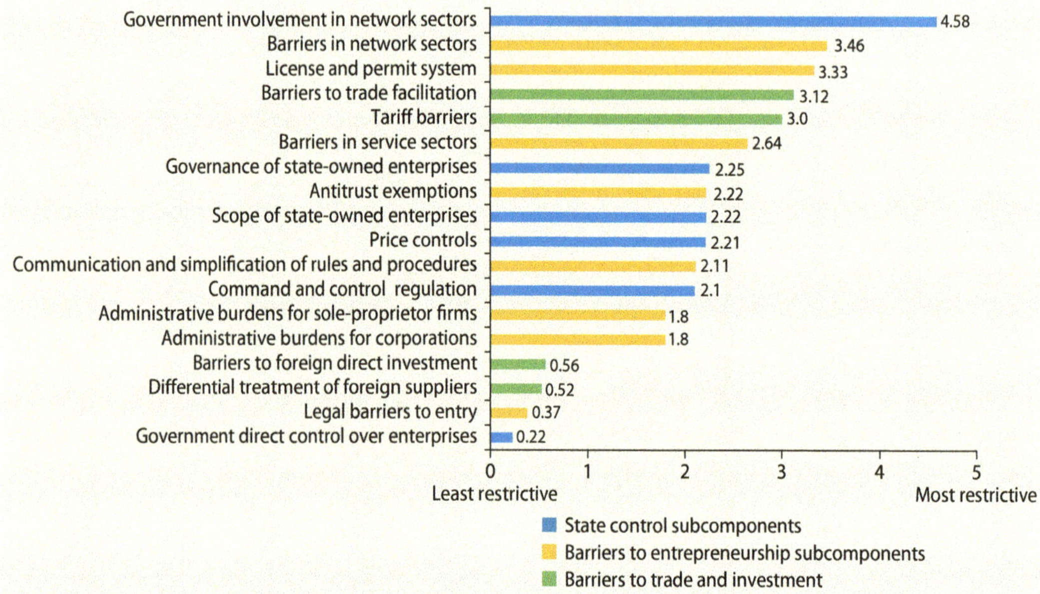

Sources: For OECD (Organisation for Economic Co-operation and Development) countries, OECD Product Market Regulation database (http://www.oecd.org/eco/growth/indicatorsofproductmarketregulationhomepage.htm); for non-OECD countries, product market regulation data from the World Bank Group's Markets and Competition Policy database.
Note: Based on a scale from 0 to 6, from least to most restrictive for competition.

presence of commercial courts, and underdeveloped case management techniques within the judiciary are other important issues in need of redress. The recent creation of the Court of Appeals within the Supreme Court could possibly help to reduce the backlogs.

With regard to maintaining a prudent and supportive fiscal policy, one challenge will be responding to the financing needs of the economy while keeping a sustainable level of public and publicly guaranteed debt, which now equals about 48 percent of GDP (figure 6.8). The upward debt trajectory has been driven by a public investment push that has coincided with declining external grant financing. Fiscal space has shrunk considerably as a result, which may affect Rwanda's ability to implement countercyclical macro management in the future. Grant financing is likely to continue declining as Rwanda approaches middle-income status. This decline will result in higher public debt if the government offsets it with commercial borrowing. Rebuilding fiscal buffers by rationalizing spending and strengthening revenue mobilization has become an important medium-term priority. A comprehensive assessment of contingent fiscal liabilities and close monitoring of emerging fiscal risks will also be important to having realistic assessments of available fiscal space and maintaining fiscal sustainability. The fiscal challenges extend to public investment management, especially to weaknesses in ex post evaluation arrangements and monitoring mechanisms for midcourse adjustments and the lack of a well-developed and clear cost management system over the course of the project life cycle.

Public Sector Accountability

A final set of governance challenges has to do with strengthening accountability mechanisms between the local government and citizens. Representation of the most vulnerable and poor has increased in the councils. The list of remaining challenges runs along several dimensions. District councils, often constrained by limited budget and staff, are not always effective in listening to citizens' needs. In addition, district councils need capacity building for effective delivery of their mandate (GIZ 2013; MINALOC 2017). The role of civil society organizations (CSOs) in public policy remains limited as a result of various capacity gaps. Citizens themselves could be better empowered and better informed to ensure that their views are heard by district authorities.

Even though participation in *ubudehe*[20] and *umuganda* meetings and forums as well as citizens' engagement in finding solutions are high, their capacity in influencing decisions is limited. Citizens' participation and district-level accountability have been found to be limited (Ndahiro 2015). Consequently, citizens' participation in the *imihigo* process also needs to be improved.

In recent years, CSOs' capacity to enhance public accountability has increased but needs to grow further. Their capacity to mainstream citizens' input in policy planning has improved. Although CSOs engage in government programs, organizational and institutional capacity gaps continue to hamper the growth and role of CSOs in public policy. The government and some development partners have jointly put in place the CSO empowerment program that enhances CSOs capacity to spur accountability and service delivery to citizens. In 2016, the government of Rwanda adopted a joint program with CSOs in order to improve the implementation of social protection programs within communities. The interim evaluation of this program in pilot districts found that CSOs have an important role to play in improving delivery and enhancing accountability in pro-poor programs. It also revealed that openness on the part of districts to work with and receive inputs from CSOs can be improved.

In principle, associations and interest groups can mobilize citizens to find local solutions (Boix and Posner 1998; Edwards and Foley 1998; Ehrenberg 1999). Rwanda has already had some early success in this regard, which needs to be broadened. The neighborhood security (*irondo*) and hygiene (*isuku*) initiatives,[21] which help to improve security and sanitation in many localities, are interesting examples of citizens' mobilization for the provision of public goods. In this regard, China's experience of solidarity groups for informal accountability and local provision of public goods (Heilmann 2008; Tsai 2007) shows how associations and interest groups could help citizens to voice their needs more effectively and contribute to improved service delivery in Rwanda.

FIGURE 6.8 Public and publicly guaranteed debt as a percentage of GDP in Rwanda, 2010–17

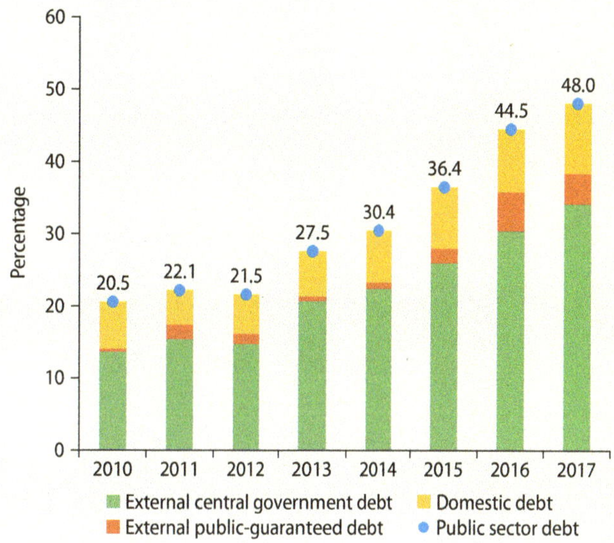

Source: IMF and World Bank 2017.
Note: IMF = International Monetary Fund.

Citizens' limited information about, and power over, service providers (schools and health facilities) impairs service delivery. Parents' involvement in school management through parent-teacher committees or as members of parent-teacher associations is, in most of cases, still limited. According to a study conducted in Gasabo District in 2013, parents are interested in the education of their children, but large families and parents' high illiteracy rates, among other factors, limit parental involvement in schools (Kabarere et al. 2013). A 2014 Transparency

International assessment reveals that parents rarely attend general meetings to discuss issues related to school management or their children's education. As global experience shows, this is a missed opportunity. For example, the provision of information to parents had a strong positive impact on learning by teachers and students in Chile (Bruns and Luque 2015) and Mexico (Gertler, Patrinos, and Rubio-Codina 2012).

Remaining gaps in the provision of health care highlight some of the limitations of existing accountability mechanisms. For example, performance-based financing has had impressive results in health outcomes, but clients' influence over health service providers has largely failed to improve. The performance culture outstrips the verification of quality of services and does not always rely on citizen monitoring and feedback. In the 2016 Citizens Report Card, citizens said that they highly appreciate health infrastructure, such as buildings and facilities, but their appreciation is substantially lower with regard to services provided at hospitals, health centers, and health posts (RGB 2016a). Inadequacy of health staff (doctors and nurses) and scarcity of medicines are the critical pitfalls in the health sector (RGB 2016a). The Rwandan experience is similar to that of many low-income countries with performance-based funding.

An Agenda for Reforms

An upper-middle-income economy (which Rwanda aspires to have by 2035) will necessarily be more complex, innovative, and sophisticated, requiring more adaptive institutions. It will also be more inclusive, with strong emphasis on providing equality of opportunity for all citizens. With income inequality already at elevated levels (the Gini coefficient for income equals 0.45), Rwanda will need to be keenly mindful of its future trends. Building a strong system of social protection to provide basic safety nets to the most vulnerable and expanding access to quality public services (education, health care, and basic infrastructure such as sanitation, potable water, electricity, and road and telecommunications connectivity, for example) would give everyone a fair chance to enjoy the fruits of growth.

The governance structures will have to become adept at encouraging local solutions, taking informed risks, ensuring effective coordination within the government, engendering the commitment and trust of nonstate actors (including the private sector), and instituting highly developed feedback loops. Past ingredients of success, such as strong implementation capacity and vertical accountability, will need to be complemented with elements that enable economic institutions to be more innovative, receptive to feedback, and solution driven. Vertical accountability can contain corruption in the short to medium term, but, as soon as the pressure from the top diminishes or gets diffused in a more complex setting, corruption and other forms of institutional malaise can reemerge (Khan 2017).

Strong and inclusive growth over the next decades will entail specific institutional requirements, closely aligned with the framework described in figure 6.6. It starts with continuing to build trust between the executive, the bureaucracy, the private sector, and the society more broadly. Otherwise, transaction costs will be higher, long-term investments will be lower, and innovation (in the bureaucracy, in the economy, and in the society) will not happen. Trust, above all, is about building social capital within local communities by generating more voice and improving the quality of citizen participation in decision making.

The task of continuing to build trust and enhance state effectiveness will, therefore, have three core institutional pillars: (1) innovative, coordinated, capable, and empowered bureaucracy and local governments; (2) efficient market signals to allocate resources and enable strong cooperation between the state and the business sector, backed by fiscal discipline to match policies with the state's financial capacity; and (3) popular participation to ensure that policies and programs are aligned with the needs of citizens.

The chapter argues that all four components (trust and the three institutional pillars) are essential for an effective state, which, in turn, is necessary for sustained high growth: the absence of any of the four components (and, therefore, of state effectiveness itself) will yield unsatisfactory outcomes.

Pillar 1: Enabling Innovative, Coordinated, Capable Bureaucracy and Local Governments

Strong growth over the next decades will require well-structured, capable, and empowered civil service and local governments, with resources and other incentives to be innovative (even entrepreneurial). Such institutions are needed to inform decision makers and challenge them with evidence and analysis when needed; share information and coordinate actions within and outside the administration; and take informed risks, experiment, scale up successes, and learn from failures. Creating this type of institutions will require increasing the autonomy of civil servants and local government, strengthening capacity and coordination within the government, and making progress on decentralization to encourage local initiatives and enable local transformation, both in relation to human security and accountability challenges, as well as boosting local economic development.

Continually Adjust Imihigo *to Promote More Flexible Approaches*

On the basis of worldwide experiences of performance contracting, *imihigo* will need to be adjusted continually and enforced with a view to enhancing innovation within the government. The following main challenges need to be considered:

- Improve interagency coordination and consider increasing the importance of the joint *imihigo*.
- Improve outcome-based monitoring of *imihigo* and adopt "multiyear targets, with annual benchmarking as opposed to the current practice of setting only annual targets" (Shyaka et al. 2016), particularly in joint *imihigo*.
- Emphasize qualitative surveys and a stronger focus on outcomes as well as processes.

Strengthen Coordination within Government

Coordination within government could possibly be improved through the strengthening of the delivery unit,[22] based on agencies in high-performing East Asia economies—for example, Malaysia's Performance Management and Delivery Unit. This unit would have the authority to coordinate public policy setting and implementation for some key cross-cutting issues, such as industrial policy or local development.[23] Delivery units focus on producing better results more quickly through a combination of change-management techniques and approaches to public service improvement. Having a delivery unit near the nexus of political power is a mechanism for government leadership to signal its focus on results and improve the unit's management capacity. The approach seems to work best when it is embedded in a robust organizational performance management framework (which is already present in Rwanda); focuses on establishing high-profile, well-publicized priorities; and uses high-frequency data to support improvement processes (Shostak et al. 2014). In Rwanda, it will be important to look into the existing institutional setup and how it could be adjusted to play that role fully and to facilitate coordination and greater delivery.

Strengthen Civil Service Capacity

Further progress is necessary to attract, retain, and motivate public servants to deliver high-quality services. The foundations of an effective civil service cover several critical dimensions, including merit-based recruitment, the right incentives and compensation for staff, right training at entry and on the job, career progression and performance monitoring, efficient human resource information

FIGURE 6.9 The main elements for an efficient and capable civil service

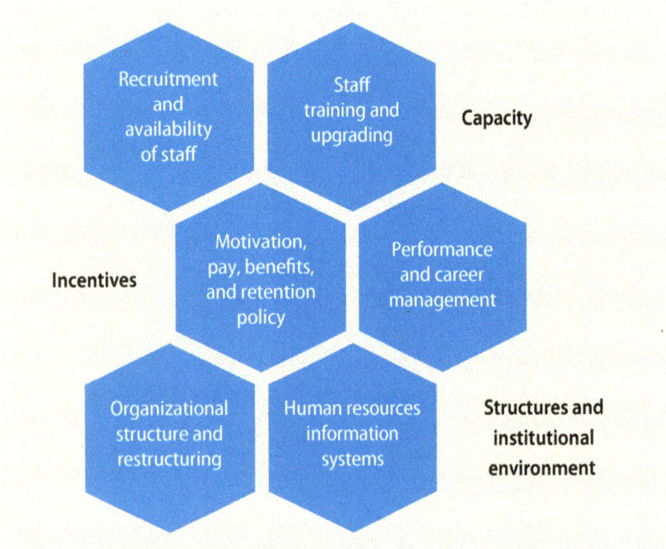

Source: Based on MacArthur 2012.

systems, and organizational structures that encourage high performance (figure 6.9).

Rwanda has to find its own way to build a modernized public administration, but it could learn from the experience of successful East Asian economies (box 6.4).

RMI could be expanded further to meet current constraints and future training needs of the civil service. Although not all civil servants need to be trained, creating a critical mass requires a significant scale of training (MacArthur 2012). RMI is planning to train as many as 2,000 civil servants a year. Skills audits and functional reviews should be carried out to identify the missing skills in the public sector, and a new approach is needed to financing RMI. A successful example is the use of both public and private funding by the Singapore Civil Service College. The government of Singapore provides a minimum level of funding, while requiring

BOX 6.4 Lessons from East Asia on strengthening public administration

The East Asia experience offers several lessons that would be useful for Rwanda. First, public administration can be modernized through a variety of means. For example, civil service recruitment in Japan and the Republic of Korea is through a unified civil service exam, which has never been the case in Singapore or in Taiwan, China. Nevertheless, all of these economies have achieved a certain level of meritocratic recruitment, "complemented by a career structure that produces rewards commensurate with those that capable individuals could attain in the private sector" (Evans 1998).

Second, civil servants should keep learning, adapting, and innovating. For example, management of state-owned enterprises and institutional organization of the state have evolved considerably over the years in Taiwan, China. Public administrators need to feel empowered to disrupt and try new options (even if they ultimately fail).

Third, political authorities need to delegate some powers to bureaucrats and trust that they will make the best technical decisions. Even though political power was concentrated in the executive for several decades, some independent decision-making authority was delegated to relatively insulated technocratic agencies (Cheng, Haggard, and Kang 1998). Political leadership strived to insulate some key parts of the economic bureaucracy from other branches of government and from interest group pressures.

Finally, successful East Asian countries have adopted two main approaches to implementing industrial policies and coordinating public interventions: either by leaving line ministries in charge, as in Japan or Korea, or by creating "pilot agencies" or "task forces," as in Taiwan, China, or "statutory boards," as in Singapore. Despite these different approaches, coherence was achieved by strong continuity in the economic technocrats, who shifted positions but maintained a vision of the overall development goals (Evans 1998). Moreover, in order to improve public policy coordination, Taiwan, China, has emphasized promoting within the civil service rather than hiring managers from outside. This has enabled top bureaucrats to establish relationships across various structures and administrations and contributed to esprit de corps and loyalty in the civil service. Over the years, several task forces and agencies have been incorporated gradually back into the bureaucracy, but some small-scale units outside ministerial structures have remained (Cheng, Haggard, and Kang 1998).

ministries or departments and state-owned enterprises (SOEs) to devote at least a share of their budget to the trainings offered. The college has developed joint programs and is funded partly by its development cooperation or technical assistance budget. However, to adopt this model, RMI will have to demonstrate that it remains up-to-date, has methods for systematically collecting data on training needs and tailoring its programs to meet those needs, and is delivering top-quality training and capacity building, including "after-sales service." If successful, the government could encourage donors to use RMI in their support for capacity building.

Career development instruments and regular compensation reviews will become increasingly important to establish adequate incentives for civil servants, particularly as private companies increasingly compete for scarce skills.[24] Although intrinsic motivation seems to be important in the Rwandan public sector, compensation for some groups of civil servants, such as teachers in primary schools, is low. Better career development instruments and nonfinancial incentives could be developed, especially in sectors where retention of scarce skills is crucial (technical line ministries and the judicial system, for example). A specific issue concerns the health sector, where success has depended on community health workers. It will be important to design and implement a package of targeted interventions to improve the recruitment, retention, performance, and motivation of health workers, particularly given the possibility of an increase in the rate of attrition and a consequent "generational change" in the pool of prospective candidates (LSTM, RBC, and UNICEF 2016).[25]

Pillar 2: Strengthening Market Institutions and Maintaining Fiscal Prudence

The evidence is compelling that functioning markets require well-defined rules of the game, enforced transparently and predictably. Advanced economies (almost as a rule) have a system of highly evolved economic institutions that convey prices, define property rights, enforce contracts and competition policies, and close informational gaps between buyers and sellers (Commission on Growth and Development 2008). As part of its long-term development, Rwanda also has to develop these key market institutions, backed by the strong financial capacity of the state.

Strengthen the Policy Framework for Free and Fair Competition

Competitive markets enhance private sector dynamism through cost reductions, innovation, and productivity growth. As noted in World Bank (2014), "Firms operating in a competitive environment are more likely to innovate and to increase their productivity. Competition boosts investment, generates employment, speeds up economic growth, and improves overall welfare. Competition in input markets is a key driver of efficiency and productivity growth in sectors that use these inputs. Empirical evidence strongly supports the positive effects of well-enforced competition policy on productivity growth. Tough enforcement against the practices of cartels is an effective tool in reducing the negative impact of anticompetitive behavior, benefitting consumers with lower prices, direct savings, and improvements in the variety and quality of goods and services."

An effective competition framework addresses four broad areas: agency effectiveness, effective enforcement, probity of investigations, and effective advocacy. First, the effectiveness of the competition authority in encouraging compliance with the law depends on the institutional design, degree of independence of technical decisions, strategic planning, and technical capacity of its staff. Second, characteristics of the legal framework, including the enforcement powers granted and provisions that regulate how the agency will assess restrictive trade practices and mergers, help to determine the effectiveness of enforcement. Third, the reputation of the agency, which is based on confidence in the probity of its investigations, is essential for effectiveness. Finally, advocacy for pro-competition regulations and elimination of anticompetitive practices is important to generate a competition culture that can create demand for enforcement actions and regulations that improve market functioning.

Recognizing the importance of competitive markets, Rwandan authorities have several initiatives to strengthen the competition policy framework. Parliament enacted the competition and consumer law in 2012 and a law creating a competition authority in 2013, which was replaced in August 2017 by Law no. 31/2017 creating the Rwanda Inspectorate and Competition Authority (RICA). Law no. 36/2012 tackles practices that undermine, prevent, or restrict competition (such as abuse of dominance and cartels) and mergers that are likely to prevent or lessen competition significantly. However, RICA is not operational, and the competition law has not yet been fully enforced. In addition, the government reformed the investment code to level the playing field generated by firm-specific incentives, but investment incentives still need to be made more efficient and less distortive of competition (see chapter 4 of this report). Effective implementation of these important regulatory measures remains important to achieve desired outcomes.

The competition policy framework needs to be expanded to incorporate competitive neutrality—the principle that government activities should not be accorded an advantage over competing private sector activities—and it would be useful to expand the mandate of RICA to monitor SOEs and assess competitive neutrality issues. Similarly, rules that designate joint ventures and select private sector partners for SOEs would benefit from provisions to enhance transparency and equal treatment of potential partners.

There is also a strong need to support RICA to develop its operational framework, enforce the competition law, and strengthen a culture of competition in Rwanda. Despite a strong legal mandate, RICA is not fully operational, making the allocation of budget and staff with sufficient expertise a high priority. In Korea, the Korea Fair Trade Commission plays a major role relative to the nation's largest business conglomerates (*chaebols*), including the monitoring of limits on cross shareholdings and cross-debt guarantees (box 6.5).

Finally, ongoing initiatives to eliminate distortions generated by differential incentives for competitors in the same sector are important and need to be scaled up.

BOX 6.5 The role of competition policy in regulatory reform in the Republic of Korea

Competition policy in Korea was developed and enforced alongside an overall program of reforms in the 1980s and 1990s. These reforms prompted greater reliance on markets than on central government direction to drive growth and achieve greater openness and transparency in public institutions and major private enterprises. The basic competition law, the Monopoly Regulation and Fair Trade Act, covers all of the principal problems with competition policy: collusion, monopoly, mergers, unfair practices, contract fairness, and consumer protection.

The Korea Fair Trade Commission, Korea's independent competition agency, plays a central role in major reform efforts as well as enforcement. It has multiple purposes, including the promotion of balanced development and fairness as well as free competition and efficiency. It prevents and punishes anticompetitive practices, protects consumers and small and medium enterprises, and is a key member of the Regulatory Reform Committee in charge of eliminating regulations that restrict competition and affect the business environment. An important policy issue in Korea was establishing an environment in which the *chaebols* could compete on equal terms with other market actors; the act also gave the Korea Fair Trade Commission the power to regulate the *chaebols*' corporate and investment structure, establishing new units to specialize in those subjects.

Source: OECD 2000.

In the telecommunications and electricity sectors, regulatory barriers could be mitigated through vertical separation rules and regulations ensuring third-party access to essential facilities. In other sectors (air transport and professional services, for example), regulations that result in differential treatment of foreign suppliers or providers can discourage competition and their impact needs to be monitored constantly and reviewed in the future. The Bar Association's practice of setting binding minimum and maximum legal fees needs to be reviewed with time because it may restrain competition on pricing and goes against antitrust principles.

Strengthen Enforcement of Contracts

When U.S. businesses were asked, "How likely would you say it is that the litigation environment in a state could affect an important business decision at your company such as where to locate or do business?" two-thirds of respondents stated "very likely" or "somewhat likely" (U.S. Chamber Institute for Legal Reform 2010). Efficient contract enforcement is essential to economic development and sustained growth (Ball and Kesan 2010; Dakolias 1999; Dam 2006; Esposito, Lanau, and Pompe 2014; Rosales-López 2008). Economic and social progress cannot be achieved without respect for the rule of law and effective protection of rights, both of which require a well-functioning judiciary that resolves cases in a reasonable time frame and is predictable and accessible to the public (Dakolias 1999; Sherwood, Shepherd, and de Souza 1994). Economies with a more efficient judiciary, in which courts can effectively enforce contractual obligations, have more developed credit markets and a higher level of development overall (Dam 2006). A stronger judiciary is also associated with more rapid growth of small firms (Islam 2003). Overall, enhancing the efficiency of the judicial system can improve the business climate, foster innovation, attract foreign direct investment, and secure tax revenues (Esposito, Lanau, and Pompe 2014).

A study examining the efficiency of courts in different provinces of Argentina and Brazil found that firms located in provinces with more effective courts have greater access to credit (World Bank 2004). A study focusing on Mexico found that states with better court systems have larger and more efficient firms (World Bank 2004). Effective courts reduce the risks faced by firms and increase their willingness to invest. Firms in Brazil, Peru, and the Philippines report that they would be willing to invest more if they had greater confidence in the courts (World Bank 2004).

Specific recommendations for Rwanda follow from these challenges and are motivated by the impact of contract enforcement on long-term growth. These recommendations include (1) creating small-claims courts or a fast-track procedure for handling small claims (short term), (2) establishing strong cooperation between different actors in the commercial process (short term), (3) determining clear rules for adjournments and case-flow management (short term), (4) promoting the use of alternative means to resolve commercial disputes, including arbitration (medium to long term), and (5) continuing to develop and implement the e-court system (medium to long term).

Small-claims courts are specialized courts with specific duties and powers to adjudicate and resolve small-value disputes through a special, more relaxed proceeding.[26] Fast-track procedures represent another option, where small claims are processed by the first-instance courts applying a different set of or simplified procedural rules. Small-claims courts or fast-track procedures play a special part in building public trust and confidence in the judicial system (Ramsay 1996). They help to meet the objectives of efficiency and cost-effectiveness by providing a mechanism for resolving legal disputes involving small sums of money quickly and inexpensively (Axworthy 1976; Ramsay 1998). In addition, they tend to reduce backlogs and caseloads in higher or specialized courts. Faster and less costly dispute resolution is extremely important to small and medium enterprises, which may not have the resources for long, costly litigation.

Recognizing these benefits, Rwanda is already considering establishing a fast-track procedure for handling small claims at the primary courts level. Once the procedure is instituted, regular reviews of the small-claims caseload and an assessment of the effectiveness of this special proceeding should be undertaken to ensure that it is meeting the needs of court users as well as to identify areas for improvement. In addition, the following good-practice elements need to be woven in (Gramckow et al. 2016):

- *Coverage and monetary caps.* Applicability to all civil cases is important so as not to leave room for interpretation and confusion. Capping the case at limited monetary value is also important,[27] with scope to review the monetary thresholds regularly to account for different types of cases, inflation, economic growth, and local factors.
- *Affordability.* Affordability is key for small-claims courts or fast-track proceedings to work. The costs should be kept significantly lower in such courts than in regular first-instance courts.[28] Various forms of legal aid also should be available to provide greater accessibility and affordability, including free legal help, representation, and advice; fee waivers and exemption schemes; and the acceptance of self-representation.
- *Simplified rules and informality.* Small-claims courts or proceedings are based on the use of straightforward specific procedures, which are separate from the rules of regular civil procedures, are easier for litigants to understand and follow, and do not require the parties to rely on the assistance of lawyers. In Norway, the rules allow unrepresented parties to file a case and submit their defense verbally. In Sweden, the entire process, from filing to issuance of a judgment, is informal. According to World Bank (2018), only 12 of the 133 economies in which a small-claims court or fast-track procedure is in place mandate that parties be represented by a lawyer during such disputes.
- *Speedy resolution of disputes.* Small-claims courts or fast-track proceedings generally apply short time limitations for the completion of action by the court and litigants. For example, in Korea (ranked number 1 on enforcing contracts in the Doing Business 2018 rankings), a judge may take steps to expedite the process, such as having the party concerned file an application for evidence even before the legal date for pleading. Similarly, in Norway, once the case is filed and not resolved through mediation, the judgment must be issued no later than three months from filing.[29]

To improve predictability for decision making in the courts, a systematic approach to training judges and court staff should be considered, along with increased specialization. Specialized judges who have experience in the subject matter of their case can be expected to feel greater confidence in their judgment than their generalist counterparts (Baum 2009). Further, building cooperation between different actors in the commercial process could be considered an interim step, as judges get trained and experienced. Commercial dispute resolution is constantly changing, requiring regular dialogue between politicians, members of the judiciary, civil society, and the private sector to stay abreast of the changes. This initiative could result, for example, in the organization of regular workshops on the issues that might require special substantive legal or procedural knowledge. Regular cooperation on such issues will help judges to educate themselves using the feedback and experience of the private sector and other involved entities, whereas the private sector can obtain practical information on the procedures from judges in order to avoid common mistakes that might result in unnecessary adjournments and delays. Constructive cooperation would also generate ideas to improve the procedural and substantive issues on the legislative level.

To tackle the challenge of underdeveloped case management techniques within the judiciary, the following actions should be targeted: (1) limit adjournments to unforeseen and exceptional circumstances and (2) maintain realistic calendars of event hearings and trials. Well-performing courts manage cases according to clear rules that establish meaningful hearing schedules and limit adjournment options (Gramckow et al. 2016).

To verify that a court is meeting legal and organizational performance standards, practical and meaningful measurement systems need to be in place (Gramckow et al. 2016). Rwanda maintains certain internal statistics—for example, to track the number of cases resolved versus the number of incoming cases. Currently, such statistics are available to the public only on an annual basis.[30] Rwanda may consider making them publicly available on a quarterly basis in order to enhance transparency of the judiciary's performance, while providing a solid basis—and broadening support—for any other reform.

Alternative dispute resolution (arbitration, mediation, conciliation) has proved a valuable pillar in enhancing access to justice, bringing rapid, consent-based dispute resolution to businesses in many economies. Effective systems of domestic commercial arbitration and mediation or conciliation matter to private investors. Especially in smaller cases, having a neutral mediator or arbitrator saves businesses time and money in resolving commercial disputes and provides greater control over outcomes and confidentiality (Love 2011; Pouget 2013; Stipanowich 2004). Rwanda scores a credible 2.5 points out of 3 on the Alternative Dispute Resolution Index of Enforcing Contracts regarding the quality of judicial processes.[31] However, further improvement, particularly with regard to enhancing trust in the enforceability of conciliation agreements, would be another good step forward.

As a first step for increasing trust and confidence in the conciliation process, the legislation could establish a clearer rule regarding enforceable settlement agreements or any other agreement that is reached out of a conciliation or mediation process. Provision of financial incentives for parties to attempt mediation or conciliation could also be considered. Nonetheless, such measures should not seek to make mediation a mandatory process (at least not for all cases) before a case is filed at the court. Alternative dispute resolution should be seen not as a replacement for traditional litigation but as a tool for resolving disputes in a timely, cost-effective, and transparent way. Rwanda has been commended for digitalizing access to justice, through the Integrated Electronic Case Management System, and further consolidation of efforts can only yield positive outcomes.

Strengthen Enforcement of Property Rights

Strong property rights underpin investment in market-based societies, leading to economic growth and new and better jobs. In low- and middle-income countries, many people depend on land for their livelihoods: land is an important natural resource for the survival and development of people and ecosystems globally and, therefore, plays a critical role in the economy of every nation.

Rwanda has done well by focusing attention on securing property rights, particularly land property rights. Its strong efforts in this space have contributed to the strong reputation for governance and its leadership in Africa in the areas of land demarcation, registration, and transfer. Consolidating, strengthening, and deepening the institutions that support property rights is an important long-term priority in Rwanda. The following measures are priorities for attention: (1) ensure proper enforcement of legislation on land expropriation for public purposes, (2) maintain a robust system of land rights management, (3) maintain a comprehensive and accurate land register, (4) provide public information on land transaction values, and (5) strengthen implementation of the law on intellectual property.

Irregular implementation of expropriation procedures risks undermining recently confirmed land rights. Rwanda's formal legislation governing the expropriation process is generally considered appropriate, but there are growing concerns over cases where the legal process has not been adhered to during implementation. Expropriation complaints are among the top land-related challenges expressed by citizens in governance assessments conducted by RGB.

Expropriation in the national interest is often used to support new land uses mandated by the master plans, with land being expropriated at its current use value (agricultural, residential), before seeing considerable appreciation as it gets developed for commercial or industrial purposes. The profits accrue to the government or are used as a financial inducement for developers. This practice can lead to perceptions that land is being expropriated from poor landowners at low values to transfer to well-connected developers. The perceived inequality is exacerbated when landowners are paid out at low values that do not enable them to purchase similar property on the open market and where the procedures set out in the expropriation law are not followed. Going forward, Rwanda may look at peer lessons in rapidly growing cities in the global South for alternative innovative approaches to spur people-centered urbanization.

The issue can be best addressed by reviewing ministerial orders on expropriation and otherwise ensuring fair and timely compensation for land; ensuring consistent application of current laws and regulations; creating extensive public awareness, together with clarity and public consultations (as provided for by the law) as to what constitutes "national interest" for land expropriation; establishing rapid intervention to ensure that expropriation procedures are respected and to advocate for people whose property has been expropriated without following the established procedures; and building better public awareness and consultation on expropriation matters. Rwanda has made remarkable strides toward establishing a strong land rights management system—by far the best in Africa and on many measures among the best in the world. On the Doing Business 2018 ranking for registration of property, Rwanda ranks second only to New Zealand, which it surpasses on some submeasures of the ranking (World Bank 2018). Maintaining a robust system is necessary to secure these remarkable achievements. Skilled personnel are needed in three areas related to managing the land register effectively: database and software development, business and strategy development, and cybersecurity. Benchmarking Rwanda's resourcing against other leading small economies (that is, Denmark, Estonia, Latvia, and New Zealand) would highlight the key issues that require closer attention. Maintaining the transparency and accountability of land administration institutions is also important. In many countries, citizens lose trust in such institutions owing to rent-seeking activities.

Keeping the land register comprehensive, accurate, and current is critical. With land registration completed, it is now important to ensure that all secondary land transactions are captured in the land register. There have been recent reports (for example, GCC Ltd. 2016) of informal secondary land transactions. The underlying reasons—including a flat transaction fee of FRW 27,000 (irrespective of size, location, and value), restrictions on the subdivision of agricultural land smaller than 1 hectare, costs to subdivide land, and lack of awareness of procedures—should be looked at systematically and addressed. A system of cross-subsidy could be considered—for example, to replace the current flat fee—so as not to deter the less well-off from registering land transactions. Sustained emphasis is needed to build greater awareness of the importance and benefits of recording land transactions, given that land historically has been transacted informally. Further, as new types of land rights (such as multilevel urban residential buildings) take shape, more awareness will be needed on how these buildings are owned and managed, using, for example, the new condominium law in Rwanda as a reference point. If restrictions on the subdivision of agricultural land are to remain, alternative approaches such as co-ownership and land use consolidation may be needed to prevent transactions from happening informally.

Use of e-titles (pdf format) could be offered to reduce paperwork and cost. This option could be instituted incrementally, starting with urban areas where access to the Internet is relatively high. Government could also consider partnering with the private sector in the provision of some land-related services, including certification of land transactions (private notary services).

With a comprehensive land disputes database in place, it will be important to record and expedite the resolution of outstanding land disputes. A web service currently being developed to link the land register with the e-court system is an important step, although the register does not yet provide a clear categorization of disputes.

As Rwanda rapidly urbanizes and undertakes structural reform in agriculture, better information on market values of all categories of land will support the transition and enable people to understand, value, and preserve their rights and lay stronger foundations for a growing property industry. Rwanda has a world-class land management system and has gathered information on the sales price of private land transactions for nearly five years. However, the price of land has been recorded in a database in only about half of 112,000 land transactions. Gathering the residual information should be relatively simple, because it is recorded on the pdf files attached to each transaction. This information will be invaluable, because it will enable the establishment of market-based valuation rolls to underpin property valuations. Following the example of other countries with developed land markets, this information should be made public. Rwanda can again make use of the new technologies to leapfrog legacy printing technologies and disclose this information online.

The land valuation industry needs accurate transaction values. The valuation profession in Rwanda is relatively new: the law establishing and organizing the real property valuation profession was enacted in 2010.[32] Although this legislation has gone a long way toward establishing a strong industry, limited information still results in a wide range of valuations. The establishment of "reference prices" to be used predominantly for land acquisition by the state offers some guidance, but the wide range of published prices limits their utility. The banking sector would also benefit from better information, because it needs better price discovery to underpin its mortgage business. Financial institutions complain that insufficient hard information makes it difficult to assess land values accurately, leading to a reluctance to extend further credit to this sector and restricting the growth of an asset-backed wholesale lending industry, which would inject further capital into the sector.

The law on intellectual property draws heavily on model legislation. Although the legislation is considered good practice, the institutions supporting it are not yet well developed and awareness of the legislation is low. At present, financial and human resources to implement the law are limited. The government needs to review the current legal framework to support implementation and to increase awareness of the value of intellectual property among developing businesses. It also needs to enhance the capacity to carry out due diligence required for trademark or brand registration to prevent avoidable disputes.

Tighten Fiscal Management for Stronger State Financial Capacity

Maintaining fiscal prudence over the long term requires careful planning. Grant financing is likely to continue to decline, even as public investment remains a priority to achieve the government's ambitious development targets. Therefore, eliminating inefficient expenditures and increasing revenues are necessary to limit borrowing and to create some fiscal cushion for withstanding possible shocks. A comprehensive assessment of contingent liabilities as a result of the government's proactive interventions and close monitoring of emerging fiscal risks also are important to assess available fiscal space realistically.

Improving the allocation of resources and operational efficiency of budget institutions is critical. The government should focus on adjusting the composition of spending to enhance the allocative efficiency of public finance. Finding a better balance between spending priorities is key for ensuring the optimal use of scarce public resources, especially given the expected decline in grant financing. A better balance needs to be achieved between public investments that are expected to generate high returns over the long term and those that have potential high economic or social returns in the short term according to market signals regarding scarcity.

Even though revenue targets are usually exceeded, revenue collection remains below potential. This may be due in part to the major role played by the informal sector in the economy. However, according to the Tax Administration Diagnostic Assessment Tool (IMF 2015), revenue collection is impaired by unreliable tax records, questionable on-time tax-filing data, inadequate generation and archiving of internal documentation, difficulty in obtaining data on tax arrears, and lack of an independent survey of the public's confidence in the RRA. When Rwanda reaches a much higher level of development, RRA management will have to improve its documentation and archival practices and to expand the taxpayer database. The low ratio of local government revenue to GDP indicates that there is still scope for improvement in local government revenue collection in Rwanda (see chapter 3 of this report for a discussion of increasing local revenues from improved land use).

Rwanda's public financial management is reasonably strong and improving, but more can be done to strengthen the operational efficiency of fiscal institutions. The fiscal accounting system needs to be made compliant with international standards. The government has rolled out the Integrated Financial Management Information System, which is fully integrated with procurement and payroll systems. However, the system could be used more effectively in monitoring the allocation of funds to the service delivery units and in tracking analyses. Last, independent performance evaluations of the efficiency and effectiveness of service delivery programs by RGB will have to be strengthened to ensure greater coverage and more impact on national transformation.

Various aspects of debt management also need to improve further. Producing statistical bulletins and annual reports on government debt operations could help to improve transparency in debt management.

The final issue has to do with the management of mineral revenues, which are expected to pick up sharply in the coming years. Volatility in commodity prices has had only a limited impact on fiscal policy so far because of the artisanal nature of the sector and the relatively low revenues that the government collects from mineral exports. However, recent discoveries are expected to raise mineral exports, so establishing an optimal fiscal regime to capture an efficient and fair share of mineral wealth is a policy priority. Government may envisage capturing a larger share of mineral revenues through the involvement of SOEs in the sector. A portion of mineral revenues could be deposited in a sovereign wealth fund to limit short-term volatility in revenues due to swings in mineral prices.

Pillar 3: Strengthening the State's Accountability to Citizens

There is a risk of disconnect between citizens and government if citizens' views are not reflected adequately in local government services. A feedback loop is needed between civil society and local governments and service providers. A lack of participation may ultimately have a negative impact on the political settlement and in the short term may undermine the effectiveness of investments, for example, in the education sector.

The Rwandan state has opted for a citizen-centered governance strategy. Different programs have been put in place to ensure that this approach is effective, although some of them may need further consolidation. The government of Rwanda can become more effective in the use of public resources, while containing any future conflict through greater public involvement and feedback in decision making. The capacity and motivation of citizens to aggregate and voice their concerns and to participate with state actors in assessing the performance of service delivery are critical (Brinkerhoff and Wetterberg 2016; World Bank 2003b).[33] However, participation does not lead to more accountability without local political support for such involvement and discipline imposed by higher levels of government (Brinkerhoff and Wetterberg 2016). These two factors are essential to ensure that decentralization can foster social accountability.

Improve Accountability over the Executive

Reform measures can seek to strengthen checks and balances further to improve accountability over the executive. Several institutions created in recent years have made progress in strengthening oversight over the executive branch, but their independence and capacity need to be strengthened. Parliamentary oversight of the executive is increasingly effective. For example, the Public Accounts Committee was created in 2011 to scrutinize external audit reports and enforce audit recommendations. The committee has conducted in-depth hearings on audit findings, covered by radio and national television and with attendance by senior officials, ministers, and the like (PEFA Secretariat 2017). The Office of the Auditor General (OAG) has built its own credibility as Rwanda's supreme audit institution by contributing to improved public financial management in line with standards of the International Organization of Supreme Audit Institutions. More than 80 percent of government expenditures were audited (in fiscal 2013/14), and 60 percent of the recommendations in the OAG report were implemented (PEFA Secretariat 2017). The legally independent Ombudsman's Office and RGB have an important mandate (among others) to carry out the fight against corruption and monitor service delivery. Strengthening checks and balances among the branches of government would help to increase accountability.

Strengthening the operational and outreach capacity of the media will be key to monitoring public policy decisions and implementation on behalf of the population. In 2013, the media sector was moved from statutory to self-regulation. "Media self-regulation is a joint endeavor by media professionals to set up voluntary editorial guidelines and abide by them in a learning process open to the public. By doing so, the independent media accept their share of responsibility for the quality of public discourse in the nation, while fully preserving their editorial autonomy in shaping it" (OSCE 2008).

The Rwanda media self-regulatory body was set up to regulate the daily functioning of the media and the conduct of journalists (2013 media law, art. 4). The Rwanda Media Barometer indicates that, overall, the level of media development in the country stood at 69.6 percent in 2016 (up from 60.7 percent in 2013 when the first Media Barometer was published), reflecting the positive impact of the reforms (RGB 2016c). Complaints to the Rwanda Media Commission have gradually increased over the last years, along with the number of media houses.

Access to information is also essential to create more space and opportunity for the public to participate meaningfully in the affairs of state. Limited use of the access-to-information law shows that further outreach is necessary; even more important, it may reflect loopholes in the law. The biggest weaknesses are in the areas of appeals and promotional measures. Therefore, the current law likely still has a limited impact. Rwanda is ranked 56 out of 111 in the global right-to-information rating.[34]

Strengthen Accountability of Local Officials and Service Providers

Decentralization should be deepened to generate adaptive and innovative local governance, to increase accountability, and to overcome inefficiencies in coordination and in the use of public resources. One of the most important steps, in order to increase accountability, is to overcome inefficiencies in the coordination and allocation of public resources. With this end in view, a comprehensive package should be defined. A new framework to strengthen sectoral decentralization should go hand in hand with corresponding fiscal decentralization adjustments. Local government should use free programmable resources to satisfy citizens' needs and preferences and to invest in local economic development on the basis of the locality's comparative advantages, while ensuring overall alignment with national priorities and goals.

In the short term, it will be desirable to restructure the system of conditional or earmarked grants (see also the discussion under pillar 1). The conditional grant program should be conceived as supporting major thrusts in central government policies. Performance-based grants also should be explored to drive central government policies while ensuring performance.

The revenue-raising powers of subnational governments should also be increased. This would allow districts to have a greater level of control regarding their own revenues, which would allow them satisfy citizens' needs and preferences.

Strengthening citizens' participation in decision making at the local level will balance government power and spur ownership and localization of centrally driven development. An essential step is to continue to adapt the *imihigo* system. It will be crucial to ensure that associations of citizens participate in determining *imihigo* objectives, setting targets, and selecting investment projects; to provide more flexibility in monitoring performance; and to use more qualitative information in performance evaluations. In addition, it will be important to enhance the role and capacity of the district councils to channel input from citizens into decision making and feedback to local government and to articulate citizens' needs effectively in local development policies.

Improvements in the enabling environment for citizens organizations, for deep community initiatives such as post-*umuganda,* and for student-parent committees should be considered, and efforts should be expanded to include feedback loops. These community initiatives also can be used for quality assurance. Indeed, community initiatives can work to uphold standards of service and inform the government of inconsistencies in the regulations or enforcement.

Annex 6A Rwanda's Territorial Organization

Rwanda is divided into two levels of administration: the central level and the local self-governments. Local self-government in Rwanda is formed at the district level. The provinces and the City of Kigali are deconcentrated administrative units of the central government. Sectors, cells, and villages are integrated into districts, but these entities do not have administrative and financial autonomy (figure 6A.1). The 2005 Law on Territorial Organization consolidated 12 provinces into 4 and 106 districts into 30. In addition, the City of Kigali serves as a special city-province.

FIGURE 6A.1 Territorial organization in Rwanda

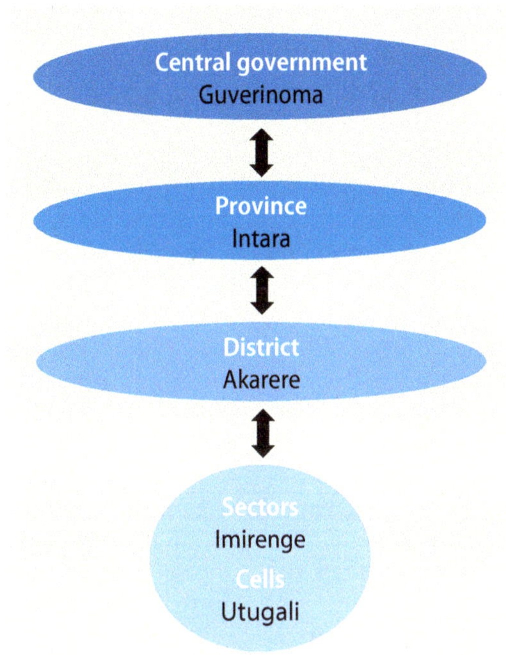

Source: 2015 Law on Territorial Organization.

Annex 6B Investment as a Share of GDP

FIGURE 6B.1 Gross fixed capital formation as a share of GDP in Rwanda, 1965–2015

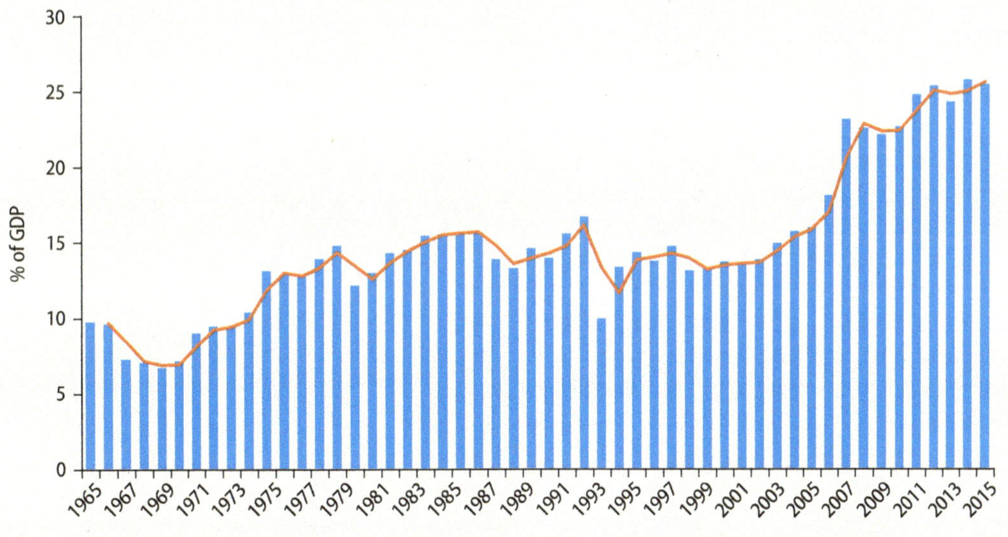

Source: World Development Indicators data (World Bank, various years).

Note: Gross fixed capital formation (formerly gross domestic fixed investment) includes land improvements (fences, ditches, drains, and so on); plant, machinery, and equipment purchases; and the construction of roads, railways, and the like, including schools, offices, hospitals, private residential dwellings, and commercial and industrial buildings. According to the 1993 System of National Accounts, net acquisitions of valuables are also considered capital formation.

Annex 6C Overview of the Public Investment Management Assessment Questionnaire

Rwanda has a well-publicized strategic guidance for preparing public investment project proposals at central and subnational levels, including long-term national development strategies (Vision 2020 and the Economic Development and Poverty Reduction Strategy, 2013–18) as well as sector strategy papers and district development strategies. The overall public investment management is guided by the National Investment Policy. All projects are submitted to the Public Investment Committee for approval to be considered in the budgeting process. This screening includes a multistage process, ranking, and prioritization and planning consultations. On the basis of recent data, about 60 percent of project proposals are rejected at this stage.

In project appraisal, the Ministry of Finance and Economic Planning (MINECOFIN) plays the main role. This process is governed by the National Investment Policy and the Guidance on National Feasibility Study, which provides guidance on investment planning process and procedures. For projects above a threshold of FRW 750 million (less than US$1 million), a cost-effectiveness and benefit analysis is required. There are no mechanisms for independent project appraisal, however.

In project selection, MINECOFIN leads the planning and budget consultations with all institutions. Project selection is based on three criteria: desirability, achievability, and viability. Projects not approved at an earlier stage by the Public Investment Committee cannot be considered for selection by MINECOFIN. Financing of the projects is usually adjusted downward in this process, with an average approved budget at 60–65 percent of initial requests.

In project implementation, no specific guidance specifies institutional arrangement, roles, responsibilities, and requirements for efficiency and accountability. All ministries and other budget agencies, however, are required to prepare and publish their procurement plans and follow the procurement guidelines in their implementation based on e-procurement. Costs have escalated in a few cases, mostly as a result of unforeseen events.

In project adjustment and monitoring, implementing agencies are required to prepare progress reports, which are compiled by MINECOFIN for a quarterly reporting to the Council of Ministers on project performance. In rare cases, projects may be canceled because of changes in situation, but no clear guidance is available for this process.

In project evaluation, there is no practice of ex post evaluation, including formal institutional arrangements. However, the new National Investment Policy provides for ex post evaluation. Guidelines on their conduct still need to be developed.

Notes

1. However, according to World Governance Indicators, Rwanda's ranking on *voice and accountability* remains low.
2. The Rwanda Governance Scorecard is composed of eight governance indicators developed based on international guidelines, recognized international indexes, and Rwandan homegrown indicators (RGB 2016a, 3). Apart from measuring performance over time, the scorecard also serves as an advisory tool, with each edition concluding with key recommendations for improving the worst-performing indicators.
3. It also includes conflicts of interest and ethical misconduct.
4. The Rwanda Social Security Board also has invested in real estate as part of portfolio diversification. Taking this investment into account, it is possible that public investments through public agencies reached 16 percent of GDP in 2013–15. This figure does not include investments made by state-owned enterprises, which have a prominent role in the economy. Public investments play an important role in Rwanda, where overall investments are about 25 percent of GDP. For the total trend of capital formation, see figure 6B.1 in annex 6B.

5. Most of net lending has gone to SOEs, such as Kigali Convention Center and Rwanda Air, for investment. The government also used a special investment vehicle for Kigali Convention Center, which, in addition to receiving net lending from the budget, also borrowed from commercial banks with a government guarantee.
6. For the results of a recent public investment management assessment, see annex 6C.
7. Aspects such as open competition for award of contracts and complaints mechanisms relating to procurement, funding flows during budget execution, effective internal controls (including commitment controls), and internal audit were the main strengths cited in the International Monetary Fund's assessment (Dabla-Norris et al. 2012). The assessment found relatively weak performance in ex post evaluations and external audits, the integration of recurrent and investment expenditures in the budget, and public access to key fiscal information.
8. The first plan to reform the civil service, adopted in 1998, included, among others, downsizing, decentralization of personnel, uniform recruitment policy, and stronger selection of candidates.
9. The National Decentralization Policy was revised in 2013.
10. The Laws Determining the Organization and the Functioning of the Provinces, Districts, Sectors, Cells, and Villages (adopted in 2006), defining the composition, organic structure, and competencies of these entities and regulating entities' operations in a comprehensive manner; the Law on the Organisation and Functioning of the Different Layers of the Government and the Law Establishing the Source of Revenue for Districts and Its Management (2002), defining the financial sources at the disposal of the districts; the Minister of Finance decrees; the Law 59/2011 of 31/12/2011, establishing the sources of revenue and property of decentralized entities and governing their management; Ministerial Order no. 005/12/10/TC of 22/06/2012, determining the modalities for implementation of Law no. 59/2011 of 31/12/2011, establishing the source of revenue and property of decentralized entities and governing their management; and Presidential Order no. 59/01 of 15/09/2009 modifying and complementing Presidential Order no. 02/01 of 31/03/2008, establishing the list of fees charged by districts and determining their limits.
11. These guidelines include the 2006 revised Fiscal Decentralization Strategy, 2007 Rwanda Decentralization Strategic Framework, and performance-based financing in the health sector.
12. *Umuganda* refers to the tradition, prevalent in the Great Lakes region, of obligatory communal labor on public projects. In Rwanda, *umuganda* takes place on the last Saturday morning of every month. Following the physical work, a meeting is held where, in theory, the communal work carried out that day is evaluated and plans for further works are discussed and agreed, together with community issues and plans more broadly.
13. A website was created in January 2015 to facilitate requests for information (www.sobanukirwa.rw). Since introduction of the law, 21 appeals have been lodged with the Ombudsman's Office for having been refused access to information (15 of these were in 2015–16). The RGB carries out information campaigns regarding this legislation through radio shows and meetings with citizens.
14. According to the access-to-information website, only 162 requests were made in the last two years (www.sobanukirwa.rw).
15. Health facilities submit invoices containing service delivery data on each of the performance indicators to the District Steering Committee in charge of verification. Additional layers of verification also exist at the hospital and national level.
16. Bevan and Hood (2006) explain how the former Soviet Union achieved dramatic increases in production from the 1930s to the 1960s based mainly on increases in quantity but not in quality, which became increasingly problematic. They further explain, "In the Soviet system, as all bodies responsible for supervising enterprises were interested in the same success indicators, the supervisors ... connived at, or even encouraged, gaming."
17. This statement is based on interviews.
18. Of the 20 low- and middle-income countries in the product market regulation database with updated information as of 2013 or 2014, Rwanda ranks 11 (and 46 in the full sample of 58 countries).
19. This statement is based on interviews.

20. "*Ubudehe* provides a mechanism for the mapping of poverty levels through a participative categorization of households in each village by the community members themselves. It also allows community participation in selecting the most critical poverty challenges and to agree on appropriate practices to meet these needs both at community and household level. [It] is a traditional Rwandan practice of mutual help or mutual assistance among people in order to solve their problems" (RGB 2014).
21. Other similar initiatives include community mediators (*abunzi*) and community agricultural advisers (*abajyanama*).
22. Numerous countries have established such structures in the last two decades, one of the first being the delivery unit in the United Kingdom.
23. For more details on the prerequisites for a delivery unit to be successful, see Shostak et al. (2014).
24. The total public wage bill in Rwanda (measured as percentage of GDP) is still low (less than 5 percent of GDP and less than 20 percent of total public expenditures) when benchmarked internationally, whereas some professions may be paid at a low level compared with regional benchmarks.
25. A long-term strategy is needed for the future role of community health workers, including efforts to increase their integration into the public service.
26. Small-claims courts usually use informal hearings, simplified rules of evidence, and more streamlined rules of civil procedure and typically allow the parties to represent themselves.
27. For example, in the Small-Claims Court in Washington, DC in the United States, the limit is currently set at US$5,000, while the Small-Claims Tribunal in Singapore has a cap of S$10,000, which can be increased to S$20,000 with the consent of both parties. However, establishing a cap on small-value cases should not be final.
28. For example, the rules of the Small-Claims Court in Washington, DC stipulate that, for claims of US$500 or less, the cost for filing a new claim is US$5; for claims of US$500 or more and up to US$2,500, the fee is US$10; and for claims over US$2,500 and up to US$10,000, the fee is US$45.
29. See Article 7 of the Trial of Small Claims Act of the Republic of Korea.
30. Annual reports are published at the website of the Judiciary of Rwanda (http://judiciary.gov.rw/media_house/reports/judicial_reports.html). The website provides a combined overview of the whole judiciary, and information on specific courts is limited to the clearance rate reports, which are not easily accessible (the annual report is lengthy and difficult to navigate).
31. See more at http://www.doingbusiness.org/data/exploreeconomies/rwanda#enforcing-contracts.
32. Law no. 17/2010 of 12/05/2010.
33. The capacity and motivation of citizens to participate and engage are called the "short route of accountability" in the *World Development Report 2004* (World Bank 2003b).
34. See http://www.rti-rating.org/country-data/.

References

Axworthy, C. S. 1976. "Controlling the Abuse of Small Claims Courts." *McGill Law Journal* 22: 480–95.

Ball, G. G., and J. P. Kesan. 2010. "Judges, Courts, and Economic Development: The Impact of Judicial Human Capital on the Efficiency and Accuracy of the Court System." Paper presented at the 15th "Annual Conference of the International Society for New Institutional Economics," Stanford University, Stanford, CA, June 16–18, 2011.

Baum, L. 2009. "Probing the Effects of Judicial Specialization." Ohio State University.

Bevan, G., and C. Hood. 2006. "What's Measured Is What Matters: Targets and Gaming in the English Public Health Care System." *Public Administration* 84 (3): 517–38.

Boix, C., and D. N. Posner. 1998. "Social Capital: Explaining Its Origins and Effects on Government Performance." *British Journal of Political Science* 28 (4): 686–93.

Booth, D., and F. Golooba-Mutebi. 2012. "Developmental Patrimonialism: The Case of Rwanda." *African Affairs* 111 (444): 379–403.

Brinkerhoff, D., and A. Wetterberg. 2016. "Gauging the Effects of Social Accountability on Services, Governance, and Citizen Empowerment." *Public Administration Review* 76 (2): 274–86.

Bruns, B., and J. Luque. 2015. *Great Teachers.* Washington, DC: World Bank.

Campbell, T., and H. Fuhr. 2004. *Leadership and Innovation in Subnational Government: Case Studies from Latin America.* WBI Development Studies. Washington, DC: World Bank. http://openknowledge.worldbank.org/handle/10986/15023.

Chemouni, B. 2017. "The Politics of Core Public Sector Reform in Rwanda." ESID Working Paper 88, University of Manchester, Manchester, U.K. www.effective-states.org.

Cheng, T.- J., S. Haggard, and D. Kang. 1998. "Institutions and Growth in Korea and Taiwan: The Bureaucracy." *Journal of Development Studies* 34 (6): 87–111.

Commission on Growth and Development. 2008. *The Growth Report: Strategies for Sustained Growth and Inclusive Development.* Washington, DC: World Bank.

Cox, G. W., D. C. North, and B. R. Weingast. 2015. "The Violence Trap: A Political-Economic Approach to the Problems of Development." Hoover Institution Working Paper, Stanford University, Stanford, CA.

Crisafulli, P., and A. L. Redmond. 2012. *Rwanda, Inc.: How a Devastated Nation Became an Economic Model for the Developing World.* New York: St. Martin's Press.

Dabla-Norris, E., J. Brumby, A. Kyobe, Z. Mills, and C. Papageorgiou. 2012. "Investing in Public Investment: An Index of Public Investment Efficiency." *Journal of Economic Growth* 17 (3): 235–66.

Dakolias, M. 1999. "Court Performance around the World: A Comparative Perspective." Technical Paper 430, World Bank, Washington, DC.

Dam, K. W. 2006. "The Judiciary and Economic Development." John M. Olin Law and Economics Working Paper 287 (Second Series), University of Chicago Law School, Chicago.

Edwards, B., and M. W. Foley. 1998. "Civil Society and Social Capital beyond Putnam." *American Behavioral Scientist* 42 (1): 124–39. https://doi.org/10.1177/0002764298042001010.

Ehrenberg, J. 1999. *Civil Society: The Critical History of an Idea.* New York: NYU Press.

Esposito, G., S. Lanau, and S. Pompe. 2014. "Judicial System Reform in Italy: A Key to Growth." IMF Working Paper 14/32, International Monetary Fund, Washington, DC.

Evans, P. 1998. "Transferable Lessons? Re-Examining the Institutional Prerequisites of East Asian Economic Policies." *Journal of Development Studies* 34 (6): 66–86.

Freedom House. 2007. *Countries at the Crossroads.* Washington, DC: Freedom House. https://freedomhouse.org/report/countries-crossroads/countries-crossroads-2007?page=140&edition=8.

Fukuyama, F. 1995. *Trust: The Social Virtues and the Creation of Prosperity.* New York: Free Press.

GCC (Growth Consultants for Change) Ltd. 2016. "An Investigation into Informal Transactions under the LTR Programme in Rwanda." Report sponsored by Rwanda Natural Resources Authority and Department for International Development.

Gertler, P. J., H. Patrinos, and M. Rubio-Codina. 2012. "Empowering Parents to Improve Education: Evidence from Rural Mexico." *Journal of Development Economics* 99 (1): 68–79.

GIZ (German Agency for International Cooperation). 2013. *Analysis of the Involvement of the District Councils in Ensuring Effective Financial Management of District Resources.* Bonn: GIZ.

Gramckow, H., O. Ebeid, E. Bosio, and J. L. Silva Mendez. 2016. *Good Practices for Courts: Helpful Elements for Good Court Performance and the World Bank's Quality of Judicial Process Indicators; Key Elements, Lessons Learned, and Good Practice Examples.* Washington, DC: World Bank Group.

Hausman, D. 2011. "Rebuilding the Civil Service after War: Rwanda after the Genocide: 1998–2009." Innovations for Successful Societies, Princeton University, Princeton, NJ. https://successfulsocieties.princeton.edu/sites/successfulsocieties/files/Policy_Note_ID163.pdf.

Heilmann, S. 2008. "Policy Experimentation in China's Economic Rise." *Studies in Comparative International Development* 43 (1): 1–26.

Hertie School of Governance. 2014. Background paper on Rwanda for ANTICORR. Hertie School of Governance, Berlin.

IMF (International Monetary Fund). 2015. "TADAT Rwanda—Report Assessment." IMF, Washington, DC.

IMF and World Bank. 2017. "Staff Report for the 2017 Article Iv Consultation, Seventh Review under the Policy Support Instrument, and Second Review under the Standby Credit Facility—Debt Sustainability Analysis Update." IMF and World Bank, Washington, DC.

Islam, R. 2003. "Do More Transparent Governments Govern Better?" Policy Research Working Paper 3077, World Bank, Washington, DC.

Kabarere, V., L. N. Makewa, T. Muchee, and E. Role. 2013. "Parental Involvement in High- and Low-Performing Schools in Gasabo District, Rwanda." *International Journal about Parents in Education* 7 (1): 30–42.

Kagame. P. 2015. "Homegrown Solutions Were Born out of High Ambitions and Scarce Resources." Speech before a delegation from St. Andrews University, Kigali, March 24. http://paulkagame.com/?p=4019.

Kaufmann, D., A. Kraay, and M. Mastruzzi. 2010. *The Worldwide Governance Indicators: Methodology and Analytical Issues*. Washington, DC: Brookings Institution Press.

Khan, M. 2017. "A New Approach to Tackle Corruption: Lessons from a Decade of Anti-Corruption Programmes." Presentation at a high-level conference on anti-corruption, Dar es Salaam, June.

Knack, S., and P. Keefer. 1997. "Does Social Capital Have an Economy Payoff? A Cross-Country Investigation." *Quarterly Journal of Economics* 112 (4): 1251–88.

La Porta, R., F. Lopez-de-Silanes, A. Shleifer, and R. W. Vishny. 1997. "Trust in Large Organizations." *American Economic Review* 87 (2): 333–38.

Lee, K. Y. 2000. *From Third World to First: The Singapore Story, 1965–2000*. New York: Harper.

Love, I. 2011. "Settling out of Court." Financial and Private Sector Development Vice Presidency, World Bank, Washington, DC.

LSTM (Centre for Maternal and Newborn Health), RBC (Rwanda Biomedical Centre), and UNICEF (United Nations Children's Fund). 2016. *Comprehensive Evaluation of the Community Health Program in Rwanda*. Kigali: Ministry of Health.

MacArthur, T. 2012. *Developing Sustainable Public Sector Capacity for Rwanda's Vision 2020: Enhancing Human Resource Management*. Washington, DC: World Bank. http://documents.worldbank.org/curated/en/960861468307137641/Developing-sustainable-public-sector-capacity-for-Rwandas-vision-2020-enhancing-human-resource-management.

MINALOC (Ministry of Local Government), Rwanda. 2006. *Making Decentralized Service Delivery Work in Rwanda: Putting the People at the Center of Service Provision*. Kigali: MINALOC.

———. 2017. *Assessment of the Impact of Decentralization Policy Implementation in Rwanda (2001–2017)*. Kigali: MINALOC.

MINECOFIN (Ministry of Finance and Economic Planning), Rwanda. 2007. "Guide to the District Development Planning and Budgeting Process." MINECOFIN, Kigali.

———. 2009. "Planning and Budgeting Guidelines for Local Government Consolidated." MINECOFIN, Kigali.

———. 2013. "Planning and Budgeting Guidelines for Decentralized Development Projects." MINECOFIN, Kigali.

Ministry of Public Service, Skills Development, and Labor, Rwanda. 2005. "Reform Paper: Salary Structure in the Public Sector." Ministry of Public Service, Skills Development, and Labor, Kigali, September 5.

Ndahiro, I. 2015. "Explaining Imigiho Performance in Gicumbi District, Rwanda: The Role of Citizens Participation and Accountability (2009–2014)." Master's thesis, Erasmus University, The Hague. https://thesis.eur.nl/pub/32926/.

North, D. C. 1991. "Institutions." *Journal of Economic Perspectives* 5 (1): 97–112.

OECD (Organisation for Economic Co-operation and Development). 2000. "Korea—The Role of Competition Policy in Regulatory Reform." Country Studies, OECD, Paris.

OSCE (Organization for Security and Cooperation in Europe). 2008. *The Media Self-Regulation Guidebook*. Vienna: OSCE.

PEFA (Public Expenditure and Financial Accountability) Secretariat. 2017. *Public Expenditure and Financial Accountability Assessment 2016: Final Report (February 2016 Framework)*. London: AECOM International Development Europe for the Government of Rwanda.

Pouget, S. 2013. "Arbitrating and Mediating Disputes: Benchmarking Arbitration and Mediation Regimes for Commercial Disputes Related to Foreign Direct Investment." Policy Research Working Paper 6632, World Bank, Washington, DC.

Putnam, R. D. 1993. "What Makes Democracy Work?" *National Civic Review* 82 (2): 101–07.

Ramsay, I. 1996. "Small Claims Courts: A Review." In *Rethinking Civil Justice: Research Studies for the Civil Justice Review,* 491–541. Toronto: Ontario Law Reform Commission.

———. 1998. "Review: Lowered Horizons and Broadened Vistas: The Small-Claims Court and Access to Justice." *Justice of Law and Society* 25 (3): 438–42.

RGB (Rwanda Governance Board). 2014. *The Assessment of the Impact of Homegrown Initiatives.* Kigali: RGB.

———. 2016a. *Rwanda Citizens Report Card.* Kigali: RGB.

———. 2016b. *Rwanda Governance Scorecard Report.* Kigali: RGB.

———. 2016c. *Rwanda Media Barometer.* Kigali: RGB.

Rosales-López, V. 2008. "Economics of Court Performance: An Empirical Analysis." *European Journal of Law and Economics* 25 (3): 231–51.

Sherwood, R. M., G. Shepherd, and C. M. de Souza. 1994. "Judicial Systems and Economic Performance." *Quarterly Review of Economics and Finance* 34 (Suppl. 1): 101–16.

Shostak, R., J. Watkins, A. Bellver, and I. John-Abraham. 2014. "When Might the Introduction of a Delivery Unit Be the Right Intervention?" Governance Practice Note, World Bank, Washington DC. http://siteresources.worldbank.org/PUBLICSECTORANDGOVERNANCE/Resources/285741-1368636830774/When_Might_the_Intro_of_a_DU_Be_the_Right_Intervention_FINAL.pdf.

Shyaka, A., S. Kamikazi, J. Murwanashyaka, and A. Mulindwa. 2016. "National Umushyikirano Council." RGB, Kigali.

Stipanowich, T. 2004. "ADR and the 'Vanishing Trial': The Growth and Impact of Alternative Dispute Resolution." *Journal of Empirical Legal Studies* 1 (3): 843–912.

Tsai, L. 2007. "Solidarity Groups, Informal Accountability, and Local Public Goods Provision in Rural China." *American Political Science Review* 101 (2): 355–71.

U.S. Chamber Institute for Legal Reform. 2010. *Lawsuit Climate 2010: Ranking the States.* Washington, DC: U.S. Chamber Institute for Legal Reform.

World Bank. 2003a. "Indonesia Municipal Innovations Project." World Bank, Washington, DC.

———. 2003b. *World Development Report 2004: Making Services Work for the Poor People.* Washington, DC: World Bank.

———. 2004. *World Development Report 2005: A Better Investment Climate for Everyone.* Washington, DC: World Bank.

———. 2016. *What Works for Strengthening Public Service Training in Postconflict Environments?* Washington, DC: World Bank.

———. 2017. *World Development Report 2017: Governance and the Law.* Washington, DC: World Bank.

———. 2018. *Doing Business 2018: Reforming to Create Jobs.* World Bank Group Flagship Report. Washington, DC: World Bank.

———. Various years. World Development Indicators database. Washington, DC: World Bank.

World Economic Forum. 2016. *Global Competitiveness Report 2016–2017.* Geneva: World Economic Forum.

ECO-AUDIT

Environmental Benefits Statement

The World Bank Group is committed to reducing its environmental footprint. In support of this commitment, we leverage electronic publishing options and print-on-demand technology, which is located in regional hubs worldwide. Together, these initiatives enable print runs to be lowered and shipping distances decreased, resulting in reduced paper consumption, chemical use, greenhouse gas emissions, and waste.

We follow the recommended standards for paper use set by the Green Press Initiative. The majority of our books are printed on Forest Stewardship Council (FSC)–certified paper, with nearly all containing 50–100 percent recycled content. The recycled fiber in our book paper is either unbleached or bleached using totally chlorine-free (TCF), processed chlorine–free (PCF), or enhanced elemental chlorine–free (EECF) processes.

More information about the Bank's environmental philosophy can be found at http://www.worldbank.org/corporateresponsibility.

green press INITIATIVE